Transitions II: Reading and Writing for College English 095

CUSTOM EDITION CREATED FOR OCEAN COUNTY COLLEGE

Taken from:
Bridging the Gap: College Reading, Ninth Edition
by Brenda D. Smith

Wordsmith: A Guide to College Writing, Fourth Edition
by Pamela Arlov

Wordsmith: A Guide to Paragraphs and Short Essays, Third Edition
by Pamela Arlov

D1401801

Custom Publishing

New York   Boston   San Francisco
London   Toronto   Sydney   Tokyo   Singapore   Madrid
Mexico City   Munich   Paris   Cape Town   Hong Kong   Montreal

Cover Art: Courtesy of Photodisc, Stockbyte/Getty Images.

Taken from:

Bridging the Gap: College Reading, Ninth Edition
by Brenda D. Smith
Copyright © 2008 by Pearson Education, Inc.
Published by Longman
New York, New York 10036

Wordsmith: A Guide to College Writing, Fourth Edition
by Pamela Arlov
Copyright © 2010 by Pearson Education, Inc.
Published by Prentice Hall
Upper Saddle River, New Jersey 07458

Wordsmith: A Guide to Paragraphs and Short Essays, Third Edition
by Pamela Arlov
Copyright © 2007, 2004, 2000 by Pearson Education, Inc.
Published by Prentice Hall

This special edition published in cooperation with Pearson Custom Publishing.

Printed in the United States of America

12 13 14 15 V092 16 15 14 13

2009240474

JK/JR

Pearson
Custom Publishing
is a division of

www.pearsonhighered.com

ISBN 10: 0-558-33960-3
ISBN 13: 978-0-558-33960-9

Where reading and writing come together!

Access to MySkillsLab comes complimentary with your purchase of a new text. Throughout your text you will find references to both MyReadingLab and MyWritingLab - MySkillsLab encompasses the resources from both of these sites.

What Is MySkillsLab?

MySkillsLab is an easy-to-use multimedia resource that helps students strengthen their basic skills — reading, writing, and study skills — that are critical to college success. MySkillsLab offers the best online resources for developing readers and writers, all in one easy-to-use application.

Resources for Reading

PRACTICE

- Four levels of reading skill practice are available.
- A new Reading Level practice engine, powered by MetaMetrics' Lexile Framework for Reading (www.lexile.com), measures students' readability and enables them to practice holistic reading.
- Based on the student's diagnostic results, an individualized Study Plan is formed to prioritize the areas in need of help.
- Improved question delivery: questions are now delivered one at-a-time and provide instant feedback.
- Open-ended questions are available for instructors who would like to emphasize critical thinking and writing about a reading.

ASSESSMENT

- The new mastery-based format yields a more accurate assessment of students' skill abilities.
- Constant re-diagnosis via the Lexile measurement enables instructors and students to track readability progress.
- An improved at-a-glance grade book view for instructors makes pinpointing class/student averages and problem areas much more efficient.

Resources for Writing

PRACTICE

- Progressive exercise sets that move students from literal comprehension to critical application to demonstrating their ability to write correctly and help students transfer their skills into their writing.
- Based on the student's diagnostic results, an individualized Study Plan is formed to prioritize the areas in need of help.
- Improved question delivery: questions are delivered one at-a-time and provide instant feedback.
- Animated tutorials are available for students who desire a visual refresher.

ASSESSMENT

- The new mastery-based format yields a more accurate assessment of students' skill abilities.
- An improved at-a-glance grade book view for instructors makes pinpointing class/student averages and problem areas much more efficient.

Resources for Study Skills

- **Study Skills:** Students review strategies for college success, learn time management and stress management skills, learn study strategies, and more.
- **Vocabulary:** Practice with hundreds of exercises in ten topics to strengthen and increase vocabulary knowledge.

Where reading and writing come together!

STUDENT REGISTRATION & LOGIN
MySkillsLab

BEFORE YOU BEGIN

To register for MySkillsLab you will need:

☑ **Your school's zip code:** _____
☑ **A MySkillsLab "Course ID" from your instructor:** _____
   "Course ID" is not required, but it helps you quickly locate your instructor.
☑ **A MySkillsLab student access code** (packaged with your new text or available for
   purchase at http://www.myskillslab.com)

HOW TO REGISTER A STUDENT ACCESS CODE:

- Go to http://www.myskillslab.com
- Click on *Students* in the "Register or Buy Access" box
- Click *I already have an access code*
- Click *I accept* after reading the Pearson License Agreement and Privacy Policy
- Do you have a Pearson Education account?
  - If *Yes* – Fill in your username and password (TIP! Choosing *Yes* will allow you to
    use the same username and password used for your other Pearson products)
  - If *No* – Follow the onscreen steps to create a username and password.
  - If *Not Sure* – Enter your email address and click *Search*.
- Check and enter required information in the appropriate fields on the next page
- Review and print your **Confirmation and Summary** page (a confirmation will also be
  sent to your email address)

  TIP! Be sure to take note of your username and password—write them down or save
  them on your computer in a place you will not forget

HOW TO LOGIN:

- Go to http://www.myskillslab.com
- Click on *Login* in the "Returning Users" box
- Enter your **Login** name and **Password** in the fields provided
- Click *Login*

We wish you success in your course!

Brief Contents

Detailed Contents

Chapter 3   Strategic Reading and Study   73

Chapter 4   Main Idea   109

Chapter 5   Patterns of Organization   167

Chapter 6 Organizing Textbook Information   215

Chapter 7   Inference   249

Chapter 8 Point of View 283

Chapter 21 taken from:
Wordsmith: A Guide to College Writing, Fourth Edition by Pamela Arlov
Wordsmith: A Guide to Paragraphs and Short Essays, Third Edition by Pamela Arlov

Chapters 22–32 taken from:
Wordsmith: A Guide to College Writing, Fourth Edition by Pamela Arlov

Chapter 22   Verbs and Subjects   571

Chapter 23   Subject-Verb Agreement   587

1 Active Learning

- What is active learning?
- How does the brain "pay attention"?
- Can you do two things at once?
- How can you improve your concentration?
- What are common internal and external distractors and cures?
- Why is your syllabus important?

Fernand Leger (1881–1955), *The Reading*, 1924. Oil on canvas. Photo Bertrand Prevos.

What Is Active Learning?

Active learning is not just a single task; it is a *project with multiple components*. You, your instructor, your textbook, and your classmates are all parts of the project. Learn to use all four effectively, and you are on the road to success.

As a starting point, active learning requires concentration and attention to details beyond academics. You must manage yourself, manage the assignment or learning task, and manage others who can contribute to or detract from your success. In this chapter, we discuss many factors that contribute to your ability to become an effective active learner. First, however, let's consider what psychologists have to say about focusing your attention, thinking, and learning. Understanding these cognitive aspects is a part of managing yourself.

What Is Concentration?

Regardless of your intelligences and the way you learn, knowing how to concentrate is critical to college success. Concentration is a skill that is developed through self-discipline and practice. It is a **habit** that requires time and effort to develop for consistent success. Athletes have it, surgeons have it, and successful college students must have it. *Concentration is essential for active learning.*

Concentration can be defined as the process of *paying attention*—that is, focusing full attention on the task at hand. Someone once said that the mark of a genius is the ability to concentrate completely on one thing at a time. This is easy if the task is fun and exciting, but it becomes more difficult when you are required to read something that is not very interesting to you. In such cases, you may find yourself looking from word to word and spacing out.

Poor Concentration: Causes and Cures

The type of intense concentration that forces the RAS and cortex to close out the rest of the world is the state we would all like to achieve each time we sit down with a textbook. Most of the time, however, lots of thoughts compete for attention.

Students frequently ask, *How can I keep my mind on what I'm doing?* or they say, *I finished the assignment, but I don't understand a thing I read.* The best way to increase concentration is not by using some simple mental trick to fool the brain; rather, it involves a series of practical short- and long-range planning strategies targeted at reducing external and internal distractions.

External Distractions.

External distractions are the temptations of the physical world that divert your attention away from your work. They are the people in the room, the noise in the background, the time of day, or your place for studying. To control these external distractions, you must create an environment that says, "Now this is the place and the time for me to get my work done."

Create a Place for Studying. Start by establishing your own private study cubicle; it may be in the library, on the dining room table, or in your bedroom. Wherever your study place is, choose a straight chair and face the wall. Get rid of gadgets, magazines, and other temptations that trigger the mind to think of *play*. Stay away from your bed because it triggers *sleep*. Spread out your papers, books, and other symbols of studying, and create an atmosphere in which the visual stimuli signal *work*. Be consistent by trying to study in the same place at the same time.

Use a Pocket Calendar, Assignment Book, or Personal Digital Assistant. At the beginning of the quarter or semester, record dates for tests, term papers, and special projects on some kind of planner, such as a calendar or personal digital assistant (PDA). Use your planner to organize all course assignments. The mere sight of your planner will remind you of the need for both short- and long-term planning. Assigned tests, papers, and projects will be due whether you are ready or not. Your first job is to devise a plan for being ready.

Schedule Weekly Activities. Successful people do not let their time slip away; they manage time, rather than letting time manage them. Plan realistically and then follow your plan.

Use the weekly activity chart shown on page 4. First, write your fixed activities—including class hours, work time, mealtime, and bedtime. Next, estimate how much time you plan to spend on studying and how much on recreation. Plug those estimates into the chart. For studying, indicate the specific subject and exact place involved.

Make a fresh chart at the beginning of each week because responsibilities and assignments vary. Learn to estimate the time you usually need for typical assignments. Always include time for a regular review of lecture notes.

Examinations require special planning. Many students do not realize how much time it takes to study for a major exam. Spread out your studying over several days, and avoid last-minute cramming sessions late at night. Plan additional time for special projects and term papers to avoid deadline crises.

Take Short Breaks. Even though it is not necessary to write this on the chart, remember that you need short breaks. Few students can study uninterrupted for two hours without becoming fatigued and losing concentration. In fact, research shows that studying in chunks rather than long spans is most efficient.[1] Try the *50:10 ratio*—study hard for fifty minutes, take a ten-minute break, and then promptly go back to the books for another fifty minutes.

Internal Distractions.

Internal distractions are the concerns that come repeatedly into your mind as you try to keep your attention focused on an assignment. You have to run errands, do laundry, make telephone calls, and pay bills. How do you stop worrying about

---

[1]H. P. Bahrick, L. E. Bahrick, A. S. Bahrick, and P. E. Bahrick, "Maintenance of Foreign Language Vocabulary and the Spacing Effect," *Psychological Science 4*, no. 5 (September 1993): 316–21.

getting an inspection sticker for the car or about picking up tickets for Saturday's ball game when you need to be concentrating completely on your class assignment?

Make a List. To gain control over mental disruptions, make a list of what is on your mind and keeping you from concentrating on your studies. Jot down on paper your mental distractions, and then analyze each to determine if immediate action is possible. If you decide you can do something right away, get up and do it. Make that phone call, write that e-mail, or finish that chore. Maybe it will take a few minutes or maybe half an hour, but the investment will have been worthwhile if the quality of your study time—your concentration power—has improved. Taking action is the first step in getting something off your mind.

For a big problem that you can't tackle immediately, ask yourself, "Is it worth the amount of brain time I'm dedicating to it?" Take a few minutes to think and

WEEKLY ACTIVITY CHART

Time	Monday	Tuesday	Wednesday	Thursday	Friday	Saturday	Sunday
7:00–8:00							
8:00–9:00							
9:00–10:00							
10:00–11:00							
11:00–12:00							
12:00–1:00							
1:00–2:00							
2:00–3:00							
3:00–4:00							
4:00–5:00							
5:00–6:00							
6:00–7:00							
7:00–8:00							
8:00–9:00							
9:00–10:00							
10:00–11:00							
11:00–12:00							

make notes on possible solutions. Jotting down necessary future action and forming a plan of attack will help relieve the worry and clear your mind for studying.

Right now, list five things that are on your mind that you need to remember to do. Alan Lakein, a pioneer specialist in time management, calls this a **to do list.** In his book, *How to Get Control of Your Time and Your Life,* Lakein claims that successful business executives start each day with such a list.[2] Rank the activities on your list in order of priority, and then do the most important things first. Some people even make a list before they go to sleep at night.

To Do List	Sample
1. _____	1. Get hair cut
2. _____	2. Do my book report
3. _____	3. Buy stamps
4. _____	4. Call power co.
5. _____	5. Pay phone bill

Increase Your Self-Confidence. Saying "I'll never pass this course" or "I can't get in the mood to study" is the first step to failure. Concentration requires self-confidence. Getting a college degree is not a short-term goal. Your enrollment indicates that you have made a commitment to a long-term goal. Ask yourself, "Who do I want to be in five years?" In the following space, describe how you view yourself, both professionally and personally, five years from now:

Five years from now I hope to be _____

_____

_____

_____

Sometimes, identifying the traits you admire in others can give you insight into your own values and desires. Think about the traits you respect in others and your own definition of success. Answer the two questions that follow, and consider how your responses mirror your own aspirations and goals:

Who is the person that you admire the most? _____

Why do you admire this person? _____

_____

_____

[2]A. Lakein, *How to Get Control of Your Time and Your Life* (New York: Signet,1974).

Improve Your Self-Concept. Have faith in yourself and in your ability to be what you want to be. How many people do you know who have passed the particular course that is worrying you? Are they smarter than you? Probably not. Can you do as well as they did? Turn your negative feeling into a positive attitude. What are some of your positive traits? Are you a hard worker, an honest person, a loyal friend? Take a few minutes to pat yourself on the back. Think about your good points, and in the following spaces, list five positive traits that you believe you possess:

Positive Traits

1. _____

2. _____

3. _____

4. _____

5. _____

What have you already accomplished? Did you participate in athletics in high school, win any contests, or master any difficult skills? Recall your previous achievements, and in the following spaces, list three accomplishments that you view with pride:

Accomplishments

1. _____

2. _____

3. _____

Reduce Anxiety. Have you ever heard people say, "I work better under pressure"? This statement contains a degree of truth. A small amount of tension can help you direct your full attention on an immediate task. For example, concentrated study for an exam is usually more intense two nights before, rather than two weeks before, the test.

Yet too much anxiety can cause nervous tension and discomfort, which interfere with the ability to concentrate. Students operating under excessive tension sometimes "freeze up" mentally and experience nervous physical reactions. The causes of high anxiety can range from fear of failure to lack of organization and preparation; the problem is not easily solved. Some people like to go for a run or a brisk walk when they feel overly stressed. Sustained physical activity can change the blood chemistry and improve mood, increasing the odds of focusing successfully on what needs to be done.

Another immediate, short-term fix for tension is muscle relaxation exercises and visualization. For example, if you are reading a particularly difficult section in a chemistry book and are becoming frustrated to the point that you can no longer concentrate, stop your reading and take several deep breaths. Use your imagination to visualize a peaceful setting in which you are calm and relaxed. Imagine yourself rocking back and forth in a hammock or lying on a beach listening to the surf; then focus on this image as you breathe deeply to help relax your muscles and regain control. Take several deep breaths, and allow your body to release the tension so you can resume reading and concentrate on your work. Try that right now.

As a long-term solution to tension, nothing works better than success. Just as failure fuels tension, success tends to weaken it. Each successful experience helps to diminish feelings of inadequacy. Early success in a course—passing the first exam, for instance—can make a big psychological difference and replace anxiety with confidence.

Spark an Interest. Make a conscious effort to stimulate your curiosity before reading, even if it feels contrived. Make yourself want to learn something. First, look over the assigned reading for words or phrases that attract your attention, glance at the pictures, check the number of pages, and then ask yourself the following questions: "What do I already know about this topic?" and "What do I want to learn about it?"

With practice, this method of thinking before reading can create a spark of enthusiasm that will make the actual reading more purposeful and make concentration more direct and intense. We will cover this in greater depth in Chapter 3.

Set a Time Goal. An additional trick to spark your enthusiasm is to set a time goal. Study time is not infinite; and short-term goals create a self-imposed pressure to pay attention, speed up, and get the job done. After looking over the material, predict the amount of time you will need to finish it. Estimate a reasonable completion time, and then push yourself to meet the goal. The purpose of a time goal is not to "speed read" the assignment but to be realistic about the amount of time to spend on a task and to learn how to estimate future study time. The Reader's Tip summarizes how you can raise your level of concentration while studying.

Reader's *Tip* ── Improving Concentration

- Create an environment that says, "Study."
- Use a calendar, assignment book, or PDA for short- and long-term planning.
- Keep a daily to do list.
- Take short breaks.
- Visualize yourself as a successful college graduate.
- Reduce anxiety by passing the first test.
- Spark an interest.
- Set time goals for completing daily assignments.

Successful Academic Behaviors

Good concentration geared toward college success involves more than the ability to comprehend reading assignments. College success demands concentrated study, self-discipline, and the demonstration of learning. If the "focused athlete" can be successful, so can the "focused student." Begin to evaluate and eliminate behaviors that waste your time and divert you from your goals. Direct your energy toward activities that will enhance your chances for success. Adopt the following behaviors of successful students.

Attend Class. At the beginning of the course, college professors distribute an outline of what they plan to cover during each class period. Although they may not always check class attendance, the organization of the daily course work assumes perfect attendance. College professors *expect* students to attend class; and they usually do not repeat lecture notes or give makeup lessons for those who are absent, although some post lecture notes on a course Web site. Be responsible and set yourself up for success by coming to class. You paid for it!

Be on Time. Professors usually present an overview of the day's work at the beginning of each class, as well as answer questions and clarify assignments. Arriving late puts you at an immediate disadvantage. You are likely to miss important "class business" information. In addition, tardy students distract both the professor and other students. Put on a watch and get yourself moving.

Recognize Essential Class Sessions. Every class session is important, but the last class before a major test is the most critical of all. Usually, students will ask questions about the exam that will stimulate your thinking. In reviewing, answering questions, and rushing to finish uncovered material, the professor will often drop important clues to exam items. Unless you are critically ill, take tests on time because makeups are usually more difficult. In addition, be in class when the exams are returned to hear the professor's description of an excellent answer.

Read Assignments Before Class. Activate your knowledge on the subject before class by reading homework assignments. Look at the illustrations and read the captions. Jot down several questions that you would like to ask the professor about the reading. Then the lecture and class discussion can enhance your newly created knowledge network.

Review Lecture Notes Before Class. Always, always, always review your lecture notes before the next class period, preferably within twenty-four hours after the class. Review them with a classmate during a break or on the phone. Fill in gaps and make notations to ask questions to resolve confusion.

Consider Using a Tape Recorder. If you are having difficulty concentrating or are a strong audio or linguistic learner, with the professor's permission, tape-record the lecture. Take notes as you record, and you can later review your notes while listening to the recording.

Predict the Exam Questions. Never go to an exam without first predicting test items. Turn chapter titles, subheadings, and boldface print into questions, and then brainstorm the answers. Outline possible answers on paper. Preparation boosts self-confidence.

Pass the First Test. Stress interferes with concentration. Do yourself a favor and overstudy for the first exam. Passing the first exam will help you avoid a lot of tension while studying for the second one.

Network with Other Students. You are not in this alone; you have lots of potential buddies who can offer support. Collect the names, phone numbers, and e-mail addresses of two classmates who are willing to help you if you do not understand the homework, miss a day of class, or need help on an assignment. Be prepared to help your classmates in return for their support.

Classmate _____   Phone _____   E-mail _____

Classmate _____   Phone _____   E-mail _____

Form a Study Group. Research involving college students has shown that study groups can be very effective. Studying with others is not cheating; it is making a wise use of available resources. Many professors assist networking efforts by posting the class roll with e-mail addresses. A junior on the dean's list explained, "I e-mail my study buddy when I have a problem. One time I asked about an English paper because I couldn't think of my thesis. She asked what it was about. I told her and she wrote back, 'That's your thesis.' I just couldn't see it as clearly as she did." Use the Internet to create an academic support group to lighten your workload and boost your grades. Manage e-mail efficiently, as indicated in this Reader's Tip.

Learn from Other Students' Papers. Talking about an excellent paper is one thing, but actually reading one is another. In each discipline, we need models of excellence. Find an A paper to read. Don't be shy. Ask the A students (who should be proud and flattered to share their brilliance) or ask the professor. Don't miss this important step in becoming a successful student.

Collaborate. When participating in group learning activities, set expectations for group study so that each member contributes, and try to keep the studying on target. As a group activity, ask several classmates to join you in discovering some campus resources by answering the questions in Exercise 1.1. First, brainstorm with the group to record answers that are known to be true. Next, divide responsibilities among group members to seek information to answer unknown items. Finally, reconvene the group in person or on the Internet to share responses.

Reader's *Tip* — Managing E-mail Efficiently

- Always fill in an appropriate subject header to guide your reader.
- Don't recycle the same subject header over and over. Unless it is important to see the thread of e-mail exchanges, write a new one to get your reader's attention.
- Keep your message short and to the point. People are busy.
- Use correct grammar, spelling, and punctuation. Your message represents you.
- Use consecutive uppercase letters sparingly. They YELL, which is called "flaming."
- In formal messages, avoid emoticons—combinations of keyboard characters that represent emotions, such as smileys :-).
- Use an autoreply if you are away for a week or longer.
- If appropriate, save time by using the same message for several individual replies.
- Don't feel you have to reply to everything.
- If pressed for time, save your message as "new" and reply later.
- Delete unwanted advertisements without reading them after reporting them as spam.
- Do not reply to an entire group when an individual reply is more appropriate.
- Know your group before sending humor.
- If you are unsure about a group member, seek permission before forwarding a message. If sending humor, cut and paste as a new message rather than forwarding with many group member names.
- When sending a single message to many people, mail the message to yourself and list other recipients as blind copies (bcc) to protect their e-mail address privacy.
- Monitor how much time you spend on e-mail.

exercise 1.1   Campus Facts

Form a collaborative study group to answer the following questions.

1. What does a student need in order to obtain a library card? Is there a fee?

   _____

   _____

2. If your instructor is an adjunct faculty member, how can you reach him or her? Is there a part-time faculty office? Where is it located, and what are the hours? _____

   _____

   _____

3. Does your school have an academic support center? Where is it located? What must you do to schedule an appointment?_____

_____

_____

4. If you accidentally leave your materials in your car, are there convenient places on campus at which you can purchase pens, pencils, or paper? Where are they located? _____

_____

5. Suppose you begin to feel unwell during class. Is there a nurse or health aide available? Where is the health services office? What are the staff able to provide students? Do they offer evening and weekend hours?_____

_____

_____

6. After the term begins, you realize that money is tight. Is there a career services office that helps students find jobs? Where must you go to find out about student employment?_____

_____

7. You were able to afford your tuition, but the cost of books is another story. Does your financial aid office provide textbook scholarships? What must you do to apply? What other types of scholarships or grants are available through this department?_____

_____

8. In a rush to get to class, you inadvertently lock your keys in your car. Where can you go to get help?_____

_____

9. You realize that you left some of your books underneath the seat in a previous class. However, when you return to collect them, the books are not there. Where would you go to locate missing items or to report them as missing?

_____

_____

10. Your car is on its last legs. You need to find another way to get to campus while the mechanic takes a look. Is there public transportation to campus? Where are the stops? Where can you go to find out about a possible ride share?_____

_____

Use the Syllabus. A syllabus is a general outline of the goals, objectives, and assignments for the entire course. Typically, a syllabus includes examination dates, course requirements, and an explanation of the grading system. Most professors distribute and explain the syllabus on the first day of class.

Ask questions to help you understand the "rules and regulations" in the syllabus. Keep it handy as a ready reference, and use it as a plan for learning. Three-hole-punch it for your binder or staple it to your lecture notes; tape a second copy to your wall or door. Devise your own daily calendar for completing weekly reading and writing assignments.

The following is a syllabus for Psychology 101. Study the course syllabus and answer the questions that follow.

INTRODUCTION TO PSYCHOLOGY

Class: 9:00–10:00 a.m. daily   Dr. Julie Wakefield
10-week quarter   Office: 718 Park Place
Office hours: 10:00–12:00 daily   Telephone: 555–651–3361
                                       E-mail: JuWakeABC.edu

Required Texts

Psychology: An Introduction, by Josh R. Gerow
Paperback: Select one book from the attached list for a report.

Course Content

The purpose of Psychology 101 is to overview the general areas of study in the field of psychology. An understanding of psychology gives valuable insights into your choices and behaviors and those of others. The course will also give you a foundation for later psychology courses.

Methods of Teaching

Thematic lectures will follow the topics listed in the textbook assignments. You are expected to read and master the factual material in the text as well as take careful notes in class. Tests will cover both class lectures and textbook readings.

Research Participation

All students are required to participate in one psychological experiment. Details and dates are listed on a separate handout.

Grading

Grades will be determined in the following manner:

Tests (4 tests at 15% each)	60%
Final exam	25%
Written report	10%
Research participation	5%

Tests

Tests will consist of both multiple-choice and identification items as well as two essay questions.

(continued)

Important Dates
Test 1: 1/13
Test 2: 1/29
Test 3: 2/10
Test 4: 2/24
Written report: 3/5
Final exam: 3/16

Written Report
Your written report should answer one of three designated questions and reflect your reading of a book from the list. Each book is approximately 200 pages long. Your report should be at least eight typed pages. More information to follow.

Assignments
Week 1: Ch. 1 (pp. 1–37), Ch. 2 (pp. 41–75)
Week 2: Ch. 3 (pp. 79–116)
  TEST 1: Chapters 1–3
Week 3: Ch. 4 (pp. 121–162), Ch. 5 (pp. 165–181)
Week 4: Ch. 5 (pp. 184–207), Ch. 6 (pp. 211–246)
  TEST 2: Chapters 4–6
Week 5: Ch. 7 (pp. 253–288), Ch. 8 (pp. 293–339)
Week 6: Ch. 9 (pp. 345–393)
  TEST 3: Chapters 7–9
Week 7: Ch. 10 (pp. 339–441), Ch. 11 (pp. 447–471)
Week 8: Ch. 11 (pp. 476–491), Ch. 12 (pp. 497–533)
  TEST 4: Chapters 10–12
Week 9: Ch. 13 (pp. 539–577), Ch. 14 (pp. 581–598)
  WRITTEN REPORT
Week 10: Ch. 14 (pp. 602–618), Ch. 15 (pp. 621–658)
  FINAL EXAM: Chapters 1–15

exercise 1.2   **Review the Syllabus**

Refer to the syllabus to answer the following items with *T* (true), *F* (false), or *CT* (can't tell).

_____ 1. This professor is available for student conferences in the afternoon.

_____ 2. Tests will be based on both classroom lectures and assigned readings.

_____ 3. The written report counts for the same percent of a student's final grade as one test.

_____ 4. The final counts for more points than the midterm exam.

_____ 5. The syllabus does not provide a due date for the research participation project.

exercise 1.3   **Review Your Own Course Syllabus**

Examine your syllabus for this college reading course, and answer the following questions.

1. Will you have weekly or daily quizzes or tests in this course? _____

   _____

   _____

2. Does the instructor penalize students for poor attendance? _____

   _____

   _____

3. What is your instructor's policy regarding late work? _____

   _____

   _____

4. Does your instructor allow makeup tests, quizzes, or assignments? _____

   _____

   _____

5. Are tardies penalized?_____

   _____

6. Will you be having both a midterm and a final exam in this class? _____

   _____

   _____

7. Does your instructor require any special projects or reports? Are due dates

   given for these?_____

   _____

8. Are any other materials required for this class, aside from your reading text-

   book?_____

   _____

9. Does your instructor require any outside reading, such as a novel, during the

   term?_____

   _____

10. Do you have any questions that do not appear to be addressed within the syl-

    labus? Write them on the following lines._____

    _____

    _____

Summary *Points*

➤ **What is active learning?**
Active learning is your own intellectual involvement with the teacher, the textbook, and fellow learners in the process of aggressively accumulating, interpreting, assimilating, and retaining new information.

➤ **How does the brain "pay attention"?**
Research indicates that the brain has two cooperating systems, the RAS and the cortex, that allow it to selectively attend to certain inputs and to block out others.

➤ **Can you do two things at once?**
The ability to do several tasks at once depends on the amount of cognitive resources required for each.

➤ **What are multiple intelligences?**
Gardner's theory of multiple intelligences changed the way many people view intelligence. According to his theory, there are eight types of abilities or intelligences for problem solving and understanding complex materials.

➤ **What are common internal and external distractors?**
External distractions are physical temptations that divert your attention. Internal distractions are mental wanderings that vie for your attention.

➤ **How can you improve your concentration?**
Concentration requires self-confidence, self-discipline, persistence, and focus. You can manipulate your study area to remove external distractions. You can learn to control internal distractions by organizing your daily activities, planning for academic success, and striving to meet your goals for the completion of assignments.

➤ **What academic behaviors can lead to college success?**
Adopt successful academic behaviors, including networking with other students and collaborating on assignments, to focus your energy and enhance your chances for success. Use your syllabus as a guide for learning.

➤ **Why is your syllabus important?**
Your syllabus is the learning guide designed by the instructor to document the goals and requirements of the course.

selection 1 Psychology

Contemporary *Focus*

An unfortunate new trend—bringing home adorable little puppies at earlier than eight weeks of age—robs the animals of critical time needed to imprint. During the first eight to sixteen weeks of life, a puppy learns socialization skills from its parents and siblings. If separated from them before eight weeks, the puppy is more likely to be fearful, run away, bite, and bark.

Early Pup Separation Leads to Aggression

By Joan Klucha
North Shore News (British Columbia), October 23, 2005

New dog owners may see nothing wrong with this, but the reality of the situation is a puppy brought home before eight weeks of age is almost doomed to develop behavioral problems regarding aggression and self-control.

Acclaimed animal behaviorist Roger Abrantes says that the first signs of aggression are shown at around four to five weeks of age, and this is a normal stage of development at this time as the puppies seek and engage in conflicts and begin to become more assertive. These conflicts with their litter mates and parents are necessary for them to become social animals by developing methods of compromise. They may challenge one another, and that challenge is either met with success or failure. In either case, they still remain a part of the social group, so they understand that failure doesn't have a negative consequence. As a result, they develop confidence. Thus, you can imagine what happens when puppies are then removed during this period to be on their own or are born into litters without siblings. They never learn how to initiate conflict without aggression or to end conflict with compromise instead of aggression. As a result they have little or no ability to resolve issues and harbor aggression long after a conflict is over.

Not only do pups have less confidence when removed from the litter earlier than eight weeks, they also have less or no bite inhibition. Bite inhibition is a skill a pup learns from its parents and siblings (how much or little to bite is necessary to resolve an issue). This means that young pups never learn that it is okay to walk away from conflict instead of biting to get their way. Even at eight weeks bite inhibition is limited. They often have issues with being selfish and have a higher than normal level of resource guarding—threatening behavior such as growling, snapping and biting to prevent a valuable item from being taken away.

COLLABORATE Collaborate on responses to the following questions:

➤ Why are puppies being separated from their litters before eight weeks of age?

➤ How would you try to socialize a four-week-old abandoned puppy?

➤ Is it just a stereotype, or do you think only children are more selfish than children raised with siblings? Why or why not?

Skill Development: Active Learning

Before reading the following selection, take a few minutes to analyze your active learning potential and answer the following questions.

1. **Physical Environment**   Where are you and what time is it? _____

_____

What are your external distractions? _____

_____

2. **Internal Distractions**   What is popping into your mind and interfering with your concentration?_____

3. **Spark Interest**   Glance at the selection and predict what it will cover. What do you already know about the topic? What about the selection will be of interest to you? _____

4. **Set Time Goals**   How long will it take you to read the selection? _____ minutes. To answer the questions? _____ minutes.

Increase Word Knowledge

What do you know about these words?

hypothesis	incubator	genetic	instinctive	sustain
restrained	inseminate	disrupted	irreversible	coax

Your instructor may give a true-false vocabulary review before or after reading.

Time Goal

Record your starting time for reading. ____:____

CRITICAL-PERIOD HYPOTHESIS

There is some evidence that the best time for a child to learn a given skill is at the time the child's body is just mature enough to allow mastery of the behavior in question. This belief is often called the *critical-period hypothesis*—that is, the belief that an organism must have certain experiences at a *particular time* in its develop-
5 mental sequence if it is to reach its mature state.

There are many studies from animal literature supporting the critical-period hypothesis. For instance, German scientist Konrad Lorenz discovered many years ago that birds, such as ducks and geese, will follow the first moving object they see after they are hatched. Usually the first thing they see is their mother, of course,
10 who has been sitting on the eggs when they are hatched. However, Lorenz showed that if he took goose eggs away from the mother and hatched them in an incubator, the fresh-hatched *goslings* would follow him around instead.

Nina Leen/Time Life Pictures/Getty Images

Lorenz swims with the goslings who have imprinted on him.

After the goslings had waddled along behind Lorenz for a few hours, they acted as if they thought he was their mother and that they were humans, not geese. When
15 Lorenz returned the goslings to their real mother, they ignored her. Whenever Lorenz appeared, however, they became very excited and flocked to him for protection and affection. It was as if the visual image of the first object they saw moving had become so strongly *imprinted* on their consciousness that, forever after, that object was "mother."

During the past 20 years or so, scientists have spent a great deal of time study-
20 ing *imprinting* as it now is called. The effect occurs in many but not in all types of birds, and it also seems to occur in mammals such as sheep and seals. Whether it occurs in humans is a matter for debate. Imprinting is very strong in ducks and geese, however, and they have most often been the subjects for study.

The urge to imprint typically reaches its strongest peak 16 to 24 hours after the
25 baby goose is hatched. During this period, the baby bird has an innate tendency to follow anything that moves, and will chase after its mother (if she is around), or a human, a bouncing football or a brightly painted tin can that the experimenter dangles in front of the gosling. The more the baby bird struggles to follow after this moving object, the more strongly the young animal becomes imprinted to the
30 object. Once the goose has been imprinted, this very special form of learning cannot easily be reversed. For example, the geese that first followed Lorenz could not readily be trained to follow their mother instead; indeed, when these geese were grown and sexually mature, they showed no romantic interest in other geese. Instead, they attempted to court and mate with humans.

35 If a goose is hatched in a dark incubator and is not allowed to see the world until two or three days later, imprinting often does not occur. At first it was thought that the "critical period" had passed and hence the bird could never become imprinted to anything. Now we know differently. The innate urge to follow moving objects does appear to reach a peak in geese 24 hours after they are hatched, but it
40 does not decline thereafter. Rather, a second innate urge—that of fearing and avoiding new objects—begins to develop, and within 48 hours after hatching typically overwhelms the prior tendency the bird had to follow after anything that moves. To use a human term, the goose's *attitude* toward strange things is controlled by its genetic blueprint—at first it is attracted to, then it becomes afraid of, new objects in
45 its environment. As we will see in a moment, these conflicting "attitudes" may explain much of the data on "critical periods" in both animals and humans.

How might these two apparently conflicting behavioral tendencies help a baby goose survive in its usual or natural environment?

50 In other experiments, baby chickens have been hatched and raised in the dark for the first several days of their lives. Chicks have an innate tendency to peck at small objects soon after they are hatched—an instinctive behavior pattern that helps them get food as soon as they are born. In the dark, of course, they cannot see grain lying on the ground and hence do not peck (they must be hand-fed in the dark during this period of time). Once brought into the light, these chicks do begin to peck, but they
55 do so clumsily and ineffectively, as if their "critical period" for learning the pecking skill had passed. Birds such as robins and blue jays learn to fly at about the time their wings are mature enough to sustain flight (their parents often push them from the nest as a means of encouraging them to take off on their own). If these young birds are restrained and not allowed to fly until much later, their flight patterns are often
60 clumsy, and they do not usually gain the necessary skills to become good fliers.

THE "MATERNAL INSTINCT" IN RATS

Suppose we take a baby female rat from its mother at the moment of its birth and raise the rat pup "by bottle" until it is sexually mature. Since it has never seen other rats during its entire life (its eyes do not open until several days after birth), any sexual or maternal behavior that it shows will presumably be due to the natural un-
65 folding of its genetic blueprint—and not due to learning or imitation. Now, suppose we inseminate this hand-raised female rat artificially—to make certain that she continues to have no contact with other rats. Will she build a nest for her babies before they are born, following the usual pattern of female rats, and will she clean and take care of them during and after the birth itself?

70 The answer to that question is yes—*if.* If, when the young female rat was growing up, there were objects such as sticks and sawdust and string and small blocks of wood in her cage, and which she played with. Then, when inseminated, the pregnant rat will use these "toys" to build a nest. If the rat grows up in a bare cage, she won't build a nest *even though we give her the materials to do so once she is impreg-*
75 *nated.* If this same rat is forced to wear a stiff rubber collar around her neck when she is growing up—so that she cannot clean her sex organs, as rats normally do—she will not usually lick her newborn babies clean *even though we take off the rubber collar a day or so before she gives birth.* The genetic blueprint always operates best within a particular environmental setting. If an organism's early environment is
80 abnormal or particularly unusual, later "innate" behavior patterns may be disrupted.

OVERCOMING THE "CRITICAL PERIOD"

All of these examples may appear to support the "critical-period" hypothesis—that there is one time in an organism's life when it is best suited to learn a particular skill. These studies might also seem to violate the general rule that an organism can "catch up" if its development has been delayed. However, the truth is more compli-
85 cated (as always) than it might seem from the experiments we have cited so far.

Baby geese will normally not imprint if we restrict their visual experiences for the first 48 hours of their lives—their fear of strange objects is by then too great. However, if we give the geese tranquilizing drugs to help overcome their fear, they can be imprinted a week or more after hatching. Once imprinting has taken place, it
90 may seem to be irreversible. But we can occasionally get a bird imprinted on a human to accept a goose as its mother, if we coax it enough and give it massive rewards for

approaching or following its natural mother. Chicks raised in darkness become clumsy eaters—but what do you think would happen if we gave them special training in how to peck, rather than simply leaving the matter to chance? Birds restrained in the nest
95 too long apparently learn other ways of getting along and soon come to fear heights; what do you think would happen if we gave these birds tranquilizers and rewarded each tiny approximation to flapping their wings properly?

There is not much scientific evidence that human infants have the same types of "critical periods" that birds and rats do. By being born without strong innate be-
100 havior patterns (such as imprinting), we seem to be better able to adjust and survive in the wide variety of social environments human babies are born into. Like many other organisms, however, children do appear to have an inborn tendency to imitate the behavior of other organisms around them. A young rat will learn to press a lever in a Skinner box much faster if it is first allowed to watch an adult rat
105 get food by pressing the lever. This learning is even quicker if the adult rat happens to be the young animal's mother. Different species of birds have characteristic songs or calls. A European thrush, for example, has a song pattern fairly similar to a thrush in the United States, but both sound quite different from blue jays. There are *local dialects* among songbirds, however, and these are learned through imitation. If a
110 baby thrush is isolated from its parents and exposed to blue jay calls when it is very young, the thrush will sound a little like a blue jay but a lot like other thrushes when it grows up. And parrots, of course, pick up very human-sounding speech patterns if they are raised with humans rather than with other parrots.

(1,631 words)

—by James V. McConnell, *Understanding Human Behavior*, Copyright © 1974.
Reprinted with permission of Wadsworth, a division of Thomson Learning.

Time Goals

Record your finishing time: _____:_____

Calculate your total reading time: _____

Rate your concentration as high _____ medium _____ or low _____.

Recall what you have read, and review what you have learned.

Your instructor may choose to give you a true-false comprehension review.

Write About the Selection

Provide proof that a critical period exists during which an organism must have certain experiences to reach its normal mature state.

Response Suggestion: Review the selection and number the experiments that provide proof of the hypothesis. Define the hypothesis and describe three to five suporting examples from the text.

Contemporary *Link*

Using the studies on the critical period for the development of instinctive behaviors in chicks, rats, and birds, explain why you think there should or should not be a law forbidding professional dog breeders from selling puppies prior to eight weeks of age.

Check Your Comprehension

After reading the selection, answer the following questions with *a, b, c,* or *d.* In order to help you analyze your strengths and weaknesses, the question types are indicated.

Main Idea   _____   1. Which is the best statement of the main idea of this selection?

    a. Studies show that goslings can imprint on humans.
    b. A particular few days of an animal's life can be a crucial time for developing long-lasting "natural" behavior.
    c. Imprinting seems to occur in mammals but is very strong in ducks and geese.
    d. The "crucial period" of imprinting is important but can be overcome with drugs.

Detail   _____   2. The critical-period hypothesis is the belief that

    a. there is a "prime time" to develop certain skills.
    b. most learning occurs during the first few days of life.
    c. fear can inhibit early learning.
    d. the "maternal instinct" is not innate but is learned.

Detail   _____   3. In Lorenz's studies, after the goslings imprinted on him, they would do all of the following *except*

    a. follow him around.
    b. flock to him for protection.
    c. return to their real mother for affection.
    d. become excited when Lorenz appeared.

Detail   _____   4. The author points out that in Lorenz's studies, the early imprinting of geese with humans

    a. was easily reversed with training.
    b. caused the geese to be poor mothers.
    c. later produced sexually abnormal behavior in the geese.
    d. made it difficult for the goslings to learn to feed themselves.

Inference   _____   5. The author suggests that by 48 hours, the innate urge to imprint in geese is

    a. decreased significantly.
    b. increased.
    c. overwhelmed by the avoidance urge.
    d. none of the above.

Inference   _____   6. In a small gosling's natural environment, the purpose of the avoidance urge that develops within 48 hours of hatching might primarily be to help it

    a. learn only the behavior of its species.
    b. follow only one mother.
    c. escape its genetic blueprint.
    d. stay away from predators.

Inference   _____   7. The author suggests that there is a critical period for developing all the following *except*

    a. the desire to eat.
    b. pecking.
    c. flying.
    d. cleaning the young.

Inference   _____   8. The studies with rats suggest that nest-building and cleaning behaviors are

    a. totally innate behaviors.
    b. totally learned behaviors.
    c. a combination of innate and learned behaviors.
    d. neither innate nor learned behaviors.

Detail   _____   9. Abnormal imprinting during the critical period can later be overcome by using all of the following *except*

    a. tranquilizing drugs.
    b. natural tendencies.
    c. special training.
    d. massive reward.

Inference   _____   10. Because humans do not seem to have strong innate behavior patterns, the author suggests that humans

    a. are better able to adapt to changing environments.
    b. have more difficulty learning early motor skills.
    c. find adjustment to change more difficult than animals do.
    d. need more mothering than animals.

Answer the following with *T* (true) or *F* (false).

Detail   _____   11. The author states that whether imprinting occurs in humans is a matter of debate.

Inference   _____   12. The author implies that a goose can be imprinted on a painted tin can.

Inference   _____   13. In the author's opinion, studies show that organisms can catch up adequately without special training when skill development has been delayed past the critical period.

Inference   _____   14. If an abandoned bird egg is hatched and raised solely by a human, the author suggests that the bird will be abnormal.

Inference   _____   15. The author suggests that the urge to imitate is innate in both humans and animals.

Build Your Vocabulary

According to the way the italicized word was used in the selection, select *a, b, c,* or *d* for the word or phrase that gives the best definition. The number in parentheses indicates the line of the passage in which the word is located.

_____ 1. "The critical-period *hypothesis*" (3)
a. association
b. tentative assumption
c. law
d. dilemma

_____ 2. "in an *incubator*" (11)
a. cage
b. electric enlarger
c. nest
d. artificial hatching apparatus

_____ 3. "its *genetic* blueprint" (44)
a. sexual
b. emotional
c. hereditary
d. earned

_____ 4. "an *instinctive* behavior pattern" (51)
a. desirable
b. innate
c. early
d. newly acquired

_____ 5. "to *sustain* flight" (57)
a. support
b. imitate
c. begin
d. imagine

_____ 6. "birds are *restrained*" (59)
a. pressured
b. pushed
c. held back
d. attacked

_____ 7. "suppose we *inseminate*" (66)
a. imprison
b. artificially impregnate
c. injure
d. frighten

_____ 8. "may be *disrupted*" (80)
a. thrown into disorder
b. repeated
c. lost
d. destroyed

_____ 9. "seem to be *irreversible*" (90)
a. temporary
b. changeable
c. frequent
d. permanent

_____ 10. "*coax* it enough" (91)
a. encourage fondly
b. punish
c. feed
d. drill

Time Goal

Record your time for answering the questions: _____:_____

Calculate your total time for reading and answering the questions: _____

What changes would you make to enhance your concentration on the new selection?

_____

_____

Search the Net

Use a search engine such as Google, AltaVista, Excite, Infoseek, Dogpile, or Lycos to find autobiographical information on Konrad Lorenz. Describe the experiences that led to his interest in imprinting. For suggested Web sites and other research activities, go to http://www.ablongman.com/smith/.

Concept Prep for Psychology

What does psychology cover?

Psychology is the scientific study of behavior and the mind. Behavior is observed, studied, and measured with the ultimate objective of explaining why people act and think as they do. Special areas that you will study in psychology include the following:

Biological psychology: How do your genes, brain, and hormones affect your behavior?

Behavioral psychology: What stimulus in the environment triggers your response?

Cognitive psychology: How do you think and remember?

Humanistic psychology: Can you be anything you want to be? Do you control your destiny?

Life span psychology: How do thoughts, desires, and actions differ in infancy, childhood, adolescence, adulthood, and old age?

Cross-cultural psychology: How do cultural differences affect your behavior and sense of self?

Why is Freud so important?

Sigmund Freud was a physician in Vienna, Austria, who formulated a theory of personality and a form of psychotherapy called **psychoanalysis.** Freud emerged as a leader in modern psychology and wrote twenty-four books popularizing his theories. After Freud's death in 1939, psychologists questioned many of his ideas and criticized him because of his focus on sexual desires. Still, Freud has contributed many ideas to our culture and words to our vocabulary.

Freud's theories evolved from observing and treating patients who suffered ailments without any visible physical basis but who responded favorably to hypnosis. He believed in treating their problems by tracing difficulties back to childhood experiences. Freud also believed in **dream interpretation,** a process in which the unconscious mind provides clues to psychological problems.

akg-images

Sigmund Freud theorized that mundane behavior has underlying psychological causes.

Freud's basic theories suggest that people are driven from early childhood by three principal unconscious forces: the **id** (an animal instinct and desire for pleasure), the **ego** (the sense of self that fights the id for reasonable compromises), and the **superego** (the social feeling of right and wrong and community values). Other terms that Freud established include **pleasure principle,** which refers to an instinctive need to satisfy the id regardless of the consequences; **libido,** which refers to sexual drive; and **egotism,** which refers to a sense of self-importance and conceit.

Other words we use today emerge from Freud's five stages of personality development: *oral, anal, phallic, latency,* and *genital.* An **oral personality** is fixated in the first stage of sucking and is satisfied by the pleasures of the mouth—for example, talking, smoking, eating, and chewing gum excessively. An **anal personality** is associated with the childhood period that involves bowel control and toilet training and as an adult is excessively focused on details and orderliness. Another term Freud popularized is *Oedipus complex,* which suggests that a young boy has a sexual desire for his mother. Finally, Freud was the originator of the

25

Freudian slip, which is a misspoken word—such as *sex* for *six*—that reveals unconscious thoughts.

Who was Carl Jung?

Carl Jung was a Swiss psychologist who classified people as **introverts** (shy) or **extroverts** (outgoing). Jung was one of the original followers of Freud but later broke with him. Adding to Freud's theory of repressed personal experiences, Jung believed that we also inherit the memories and symbols of ancestors in an **inherited collective unconscious.** He believed this was exhibited in an inborn fear of snakes or spiders. Jung also developed theories about concrete and abstract learning stages. Many of his theories are used as a basis for the Myers-Briggs Type Indicator.

Review *Questions*

After studying the material, answer the following questions:

1. Using visual images on note cards to improve memory of vocabulary words suggests what area of psychology? _____

2. Desiring a rocky road ice cream cone after passing a Baskin-Robbins store suggests what area of psychology? _____

3. Mapping physical activity in different areas of the brain as people read or listen to music suggests what area of psychology? _____

4. Attending a motivational seminar to become salesperson of the year suggests what area of psychology? _____

5. What is psychoanalysis? _____
_____

6. What are the goals of the id, ego, and superego? _____
_____
_____

7 How does Freud relate dreams to reality? _____
_____

8. Why did some psychologists break with Freud? _____
_____

9. How do the theories of Jung and Freud differ? _____
_____

10. What is Jung's inherited collective unconscious? _____
_____

Your instructor may choose to give a true-false review of these psychology concepts.

selection 2   Health

Contemporary *Focus*

One high school in South Carolina reported that 7 percent of the boys were using anabolic steroids. This figure is twice the national average. What factors in the environment foster steroid use? What personal dangers does a young athlete risk by taking steroids?

Keeping Kids Off the Juice

By Anne M. Peterson
Associated Press State & Local Wire, April 23, 2006.
Used with permission of the *Associated Press*; copyright © 2006. All rights reserved.

The police officer investigating Taylor Hooton's suicide emerged from the bedroom where the 17-year-old baseball player hanged himself and pointedly asked the teen's father if he knew anything about steroids.

Sure. Taylor had experimented with steroids, but his flirtation had passed, Donald Hooton thought, up until that moment.

Suddenly, the insidiousness of the drug became clear.

"I needed to understand, what happened to this kid? We're a good family. Taylor had everything he needed," Donald Hooton said. "I needed to know what in the heck happened here."

Taylor Hooton wanted to be a baseball player like Mark McGwire and Sammy Sosa. But along the way a misguided coach told him that to reach the next level, he needed to get bigger. So he turned to the juice.

COLLABORATE   Collaborate on responses to the following questions:

➤ At $50 to $150 a test, should high school athletes be randomly tested for steroid use? Why or why not?

➤ How do professional athletes manipulate the thinking of teen wannabees?

➤ What is the responsibility of a gifted athlete to be a role model?

➤ What is the responsibility of a coach regarding steroid use among team players?

Skill Development: Active Learning

Before reading the following selection, take a few minutes to analyze your active learning potential and answer the following questions.

1. **Physical Environment**   Where are you, and what time is it? _____

_____

What are your external distractions? _____

_____

_____

2. **Internal Distractions**   What is popping into your mind and interfering with your concentration? _____

_____

3. **Spark Interest**   Glance at the selection, and predict what it will cover. What do you already know about the topic? What about the selection will be of interest to you? _____

_____

4. **Set Time Goals**   How long will it take you to read the selection? _____ minutes. To answer the questions? _____ minutes.

Increase Word Knowledge

What do you know about these words?

heightened	promote	extent	euphoria	adverse
atrophy	alternatives	alleged	OTC	disclose

Your instructor may give a true-false vocabulary review before or after reading.

Time Goal

Record your starting time for reading. _____:_____

STEROIDS

Public awareness of anabolic steroids recently has been heightened by media stories about their use by amateur and professional athletes, including Arnold Schwarzenegger during his competitive bodybuilding days. Anabolic steroids are artificial forms of the male hormone testosterone that promote muscle growth
5 and strength. These ergogenic drugs are used primarily by young men who believe the drugs will increase their strength, power, bulk (weight), speed, and athletic performance.

EXTENT OF ABUSE

Most steroids are obtained through the black market. It once was estimated that approximately 17 to 20 percent of college athletes used them. Now that stricter
10 drug-testing policies have been instituted by the National College Athletic Association (NCAA), reported use of anabolic steroids among intercollegiate athletics has dropped to 1.1 percent. However, a recent survey among high school students found a significant increase in the use of anabolic steroids since 1991. Little data exist on the extent of steroid abuse by adults. It has been esti-
15 mated that hundreds of thousands of people age 18 and older abuse anabolic steroids at least once a year. Among both adolescents and adults, steroid abuse is

Roy Madhur/Reuters/Landov

The use of anabolic steroids has increased in recent years.

higher among males than among females. However, steroid abuse is growing most rapidly among young women.

TWO AVAILABLE FORMS

Steroids are available in two forms: injectable solution and pills. Anabolic steroids
20 produce a state of euphoria, diminished fatigue, and increased bulk and power in both sexes. These qualities give steroids an addictive quality. When users stop, they can experience psychological withdrawal and sometimes severe depression that in some cases leads to suicide attempts. If untreated, such depression associated with steroid withdrawal has been known to last for a year or more after steroid use stops.

EFFECTS

25 Adverse effects occur in both men and women who use steroids. These drugs cause mood swings (aggression and violence) sometimes known as "roid rage," acne, liver tumors, elevated cholesterol levels, hypertension, kidney disease, and immune system disturbances. There is also a danger of transmitting AIDS through shared needles. In women, large doses of anabolic steroids may trigger the development of
30 masculine attributes such as lowered voice, increased facial and body hair, and male pattern baldness; they also may result in an enlarged clitoris, smaller breasts, and changes in or absence of menstruation. When taken by healthy males, anabolic steroids shut down the body's production of testosterone, which causes men's breasts to grow and testicles to atrophy.

PENALTIES

35 To combat the growing problem of steroid use, Congress passed the Anabolic Steroids Control Act of 1990. This law makes it a crime to possess, prescribe, or dis-

tribute anabolic steroids for any use other than the treatment of specific diseases. Anabolic steroids are now classified as a Schedule III drug. Penalties for their illegal use include up to five years' imprisonment and a $250,000 fine for the first offense, 40 and up to ten years' imprisonment and a $500,000 fine for subsequent offenses.

TRENDS

A new and alarming trend is the use of other drugs to achieve the supposed performance-enhancing effects of steroids. The two most common steroid alternatives are gamma hydroxybutyrate (GHB) and clenbuterol. GHB is a deadly, illegal drug that is a primary ingredient in many performance-enhancing formulas. GHB does not 45 produce a high. However, it does cause headaches, nausea, vomiting, diarrhea, seizures and other central nervous system disorders, and possibly death. Clenbuterol is used in some countries for veterinary treatments, but it is not approved for any use—in animals or humans—in the United States.

New attention was drawn to the issue of steroids and related substances when 50 St. Louis Cardinals slugger Mark McGwire admitted to using a supplement containing androstenedione (andro), an adrenal hormone that is produced naturally in both men and women. Andro raises levels of the male hormone testosterone, which helps build lean muscle mass and promotes quicker recovery after injury. McGwire had done nothing illegal, since the supplement can be purchased OTC (with esti- 55 mated sales of up to $800 million a year). Also, its use is legal in baseball, although it is banned by the National Football League, the NCAA, and the International Olympic Committee. A recent study found that when men take 100 mg of andro three times daily, it increases estrogen levels up to 80 percent, enlarges the prostate gland, and increases heart disease risk by 10 to 15 percent. This finding may or may 60 not affect its use in major league baseball—no decision has yet been made.

Although andro has been banned by many sports organizations, visits to the locker rooms of many teams belonging to these organizations would disclose large containers of other alleged muscle-building supplements, such as creatine. Although they are legal, questions remain whether enough research has been done 65 concerning the safety of these supplements. Some people worry that they may bring consequences similar to those of steroids, such as liver damage and heart problems.

(805 words)

—by Rebecca J. Donatelle,
Health: The Basics,
4th edition

Time Goals

Record your finishing time: _____:_____

Calculate your total reading time: _____

Rate your concentration as high _____ medium _____ or low _____.

Recall what you have read, and review what you have learned.

Your instructor may choose to give you a true-false comprehension review.

Write About the Selection

Describe the effects and danger of steroids and the newer performance-enhancing alternatives.

Response Suggestion: Describe the available forms with their effects and dangers, and then do the same for GHB, clenbuterol, and andro.

Contemporary *Link*

What mentality accepts steroid use? Why do some competitive athletes believe that steroid use is not a sign of poor sportsmanship? Why do they endanger their bodies for enhanced short-term performance?

selection **2**

Check Your Comprehension

After reading the selection, answer the following questions with *a, b, c,* or *d.* In order to help you analyze your strengths and weaknesses, the question types are indicated.

Main Idea _____ 1. Which is the best statement of the main idea of this selection?

    a. Readers should push for harsher legal penalties for the use of steroids and related drugs.

    b. Those contemplating the use of steroids and related drugs should be careful to learn the laws concerning their use.

    c. Although steroids and related drugs offer short-term advantages to athletes, serious medical risks are associated with their use.

    d. Although some medical dangers exist, media coverage of celebrities' use of steroids and other drugs has greatly exaggerated these dangers.

Detail _____ 2. Anabolic steroids can be defined as

    a. having no ergogenic characteristics.

    b. artificial forms of the male hormone testosterone.

    c. drugs that contain high levels of GHB.

    d. drugs that contain estrogen, which stimulates breast development.

Detail _____ 3. According to the passage, the use of steroids has been most effectively decreased in college athletes by

    a. stricter policies of drug testing by college athletic associations.

    b. the increased availability of other less dangerous drugs.

    c. increased public awareness of health dangers of steroid use.

    d. reluctance on the part of college athletes to use a drug popular with high school students.

Inference _____ 4. The author suggests that **AIDS** can be contracted by steroid users who

    a. use the drug for a prolonged period of time.

    b. experience psychological withdrawal symptoms.

    c. share needles with other users.

    d. have already experienced hypertension or kidney disease.

Detail _____ 5. According to the passage, the Anabolic Steroids Control Act of 1990 does all of the following *except*

    a. criminalize prescribing steroids to enhance athletic performance.

    b. increase the penalty for repeat offenses.

    c. remove steroids from the Schedule III drug category.

    d. allow steroids to be used for the treatment of specific diseases.

Inference _____ 6. U.S. policy regarding the use of clenbuterol might best be defined as

    a. more stringent than that of some other countries.

    b. acceptable for treatment of animals but not for treatment of humans.

    c. likely to permit legalization for most uses in the near future.

    d. allowing its use by athletes as long as they have been warned of the possible dangers.

Detail   _____ 7. Androstenedione (andro) can most accurately be defined as

a. a drug that decreases testosterone.
b. a hormone that strengthens bones.
c. a drug that can be obtained only by prescription.
d. an adrenal hormone produced by men and women.

Inference   _____ 8. The reader can conclude that if Mark McGwire had been a football player at the time he used andro

a. his use of the drug would have been considered legal.
b. his use of the drug would have been considered illegal.
c. the supplements would have been provided free by the OTC.
d. the legality of his drug use would have been determined by the St. Louis Cardinals.

Inference   _____ 9. The passage implies that steroid use may cause

a. a decrease in breast size for both men and women.
b. an increase in breast size for both men and women.
c. no changes in sexual characteristics for men or for women.
d. the growth of some male sex characteristics in women and the growth of some female sexual characteristics in men.

Detail   _____ 10. Of the drugs mentioned in the passage, the only one explicitly cited as promoting faster recovery after injury is

a. creatine.
b. andro.
c. GHB.
d. clenbuterol.

Answer the following with *T* (true) or *F* (false).

Detail   _____ 11. The slang term "roid rage" refers to the enhanced sense of athletic competitiveness caused by the use of steroids.

Inference   _____ 12. Steroids produce euphoria (a high) among users, but GHB does not.

Detail   _____ 13. According to the passage, the rate of increase in abuse of steroids is highest among young women.

Inference   _____ 14. The reader can conclude that creatine is also a steroid.

Detail   _____ 15. The most dangerous symptom associated with steroid withdrawal is physical exhaustion.

Build Your Vocabulary

According to the way the italicized word was used in the selection, select *a, b, c,* or *d* for the word or phrase that gives the best definition. The number in the parentheses indicates the line of the passage in which the word is located.

_____ 1. "Has been *heightened*" (1)
    a. intensified
    b. examined
    c. rubbed
    d. lessened

_____ 2. "*promote* muscle growth" (4)
    a. graduate
    b. discredit
    c. encourage
    d. idealize

_____ 3. "*extent* of steroid abuse" (14)
    a. exit
    b. discussion
    c. amount
    d. decline

_____ 4. "state of *euphoria*" (20)
    a. gloom
    b. depression
    c. sleepiness
    d. bliss

_____ 5. "*adverse* effects" (25)
    a. reverse
    b. wonderful
    c. negative
    d. positive

_____ 6. "to *atrophy*" (34)
    a. shrink
    b. enlarge
    c. hurt
    d. change

_____ 7. "steroid *alternatives*" (42)
    a. difficulties
    b. choices
    c. medications
    d. disorders

_____ 8. "purchased *OTC*" (54)
    a. or through contracts
    b. only the cheapest
    c. openly through countries
    d. over the counter

_____ 9. "would *disclose*" (62)
    a. negate
    b. withhold
    c. cover
    d. expose

_____ 10. "*alleged* muscle building supplements" (63)
    a. supposed
    b. illegal
    c. dangerous
    d. hidden

Time Goal

Record your time for answering the questions: _____:_____

Calculate your total time for reading and answering the questions: _____

What changes would you make to enhance your concentration on the new selection?

_____

_____

$\mathcal{S}earch$ the Net

Use a search engine such as Google, AltaVista, Excite, Infoseek, Dogpile, Yahoo, or Lycos to find information about substances banned by professional sports. List the substances banned by football, baseball, basketball, and hockey organizations, and determine if there are differences among their steroid policies. For suggested Web sites and other research activities, go to http://www.ablongman.com/smith/.

2 Vocabulary

- How do you remember new words?
- What are context clues?
- Why learn prefixes, roots, and suffixes?
- What will you find in a dictionary?
- What is a glossary?
- What is a thesaurus?
- What are analogies?
- What are acronyms?
- How are transitional words used?

Stuart Davis (1894–1964) *International Surface No. 1*. 1960. oil on canvas. Gift of S.C. Johnson & Son. Inc. Courtesy of VAGA, New York.

Remembering New Words

Have you ever made lists of unknown words that you wanted to remember? Did you dutifully write down the word, a colon, and a definition, and promise to review the list at night before going to bed? Did it work? Probably not! Memorization can be an effective cramming strategy, but it does not seem to produce long-term results. Recording only the word and definition does not establish the associations necessary for long-term memory.

Instead, use clever memory techniques to expand your vocabulary. With these tricks, or **mnemonic devices,** you visualize and organize units into new relationships. You can also use rhymes to tie words together. For example, to remember the word *mnemonics*, think of Nem-on-ic as in remembering by putting a name on it. To remember that *suppression* means to force out bad thoughts, visualize SUPerman PRESSing evil thoughts away. A noted speaker, John Berthoud, usually begins a speech by explaining how to pronounce his last name, which is French. He tells audiences to think, "Not one *bear*, but *two*," or "You are naked, and I am *bare, too*." The following suggestions can help you associate and organize.

Associate Words in Phrases

Never record a word in isolation. Rather, think of the word and record it in a phrase that suggests its meaning. The phrase may be part of the sentence in which you first encountered the word or one you imagine yourself. Such a phrase provides a setting for the word and enriches the links to your long-term memory link.

For example, the word *caravel* means a small sailing ship. Record the word in a phrase that creates a memorable setting, such as "a caravan of gliding caravels on the horizon of the sea."

Associate Words with Rhymes or Sounds

Link the sound of a new word with a rhyming word or phrase. The brain appreciates connections and patterns. For example, the word *hoard*, which means to accumulate or stockpile, can be linked with *stored*, as in "He stored his hoard of Halloween candy in the closet."

Associate Words with Images

Expand the phrase chosen for learning the word into a vivid mental image. Create a situation or an episode for the word. Further, enrich your memory link by drawing a picture of your mental image.

For example, the word *candid* means frank and truthful. Imagine a friend asking your opinion on an unattractive outfit. A suggestive phrase for learning the word might be "My candid reply might have hurt her feelings."

Associate Words in Families

Words, like people, have families that share the same names. In the case of words, the names are called *prefixes*, *roots*, and *suffixes*. A basic knowledge of word parts can help you unlock the meaning to thousands of associated family members.

For example, the prefix *ambi-* means both, as in the word *ambivert*, which means "being both introverted and extroverted." You can apply your knowledge of *ambi-* to new words such as *ambidextrous, ambiguous,* and *ambivalence* to help determine and remember their meanings.

Seek Reinforcement

Look and listen for your new words. You will probably discover that they are used more frequently than you thought. Notice them, welcome them, and congratulate yourself on your newfound word knowledge.

Create Concept Cards

Many students use index cards to record information on new words. As illustrated below, one good system is to write the word in a phrase on the front of the card, also noting where the word was encountered. On the back of the card, write an appropriate definition, use the word in a new sentence, and draw an image illustrating the word. Review the cards, quiz yourself, and watch your vocabulary grow.

Front   Back

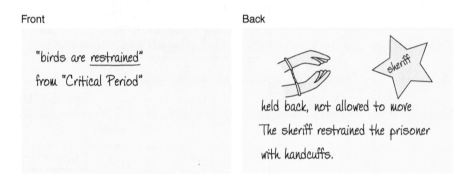

The concept card is elevated to a new level in *Vocabulary Cartoons*, a series of inventive books by a father-son team in which humor is skillfully combined with the techniques of association.[1] The idea for the books came from the son's inability to remember the definition of *aloof*. His father asked him for a rhyming word, and they envisioned the family cat being "so aloof that she hid on the roof." To illustrate, the father drew a cartoon with an accompanying word link and playful sentence, and his son never forgot the definition. The rhyme, the image, and the humor all became mnemonics. When the authors tested their cartoons on 500 Florida students, they found that students who had been given definitions and cartoons learned 72 percent more words than those who had been given definitions only.

Try adding rhyme and other sound associations to your own concept cards. The illustration on page 40 shows how cleverly the authors use sound and images to form memory links for the words *irascible* and *curtail*.

---

[1]S. Burchers, M. Burchers, and B. Burchers, *Vocabulary Cartoons I* and *Vocabulary Cartoons II* (Punta Gorda, FL: New Monic Books, 1997 and 2000).

IRASCIBLE
(i RAS uh bul)
easily angered, irritable
Link: **WRESTLE BULLS**

"When he became IRASCIBLE, the Masked Marvel would WRESTLE BULLS."

CURTAIL
(ker TALE)
to truncate or abridge; to lessen,
usually by cutting away from
Link: **CAT TAIL**

"Rex readies himself to CURTAIL the CAT'S TAIL."

Courtesy of New Monic Books, publisher of *Vocabulary Cartoons SAT Word Power*.

exercise 2.1   **Creating Mnemonics to Associate Meaning**

Pair up with a classmate to create your own mnemonics for the following words. For each item, use rhyme and imagery to create a word link, a playful sentence, and a cartoon.

1. *scrutinize:* to look very carefully; to examine

2. *dormant:* asleep or inactive

3. *entreat:* to ask earnestly; to implore, plead, beg

4. Make up a mnemonic to help people remember your name.

Using Context Clues

What strategies can you use to figure out the meaning of a new word? Using **context clues** is the most common method of unlocking the meanings of unknown words. The *context* of a word refers to the sentence or paragraph in which it appears. Readers use several types of context clues. In some cases, words are defined directly in the sentences in which they apear; in other instances, the sentence offers clues or hints that enable the reader to arrive indirectly at the meaning of the word. The following examples show how each type of clue can be used to figure out word meanings in textbooks.

Definition or Synonym

Complex material, particularly scientific material, has a heavy load of specialized vocabulary. Fortunately, new words are often directly defined as they are introduced in the text. Often, **synonyms**—words with the same or a similar meaning as the unknown word—are given. Do you know the meaning of *erythrocytes* and *oxyhemoglobin?* Read the following textbook sentence in which these two words appear, and then select the correct definition for each word.

EXAMPLE   When oxygen diffuses into the blood in external respiration, most of it enters the red blood cells, or erythrocytes, and unites with the hemoglobin in these cells, forming a compound called oxyhemoglobin.

—Willis H. Johnson et al.,
Essentials of Biology

_____ *Erythrocytes* means

a. diffused oxygen.
b. red blood cells.
c. the respiration process.

_____ *Oxyhemoglobin* means

    a. hemoglobin without oxygen.
    b. dominant oxygen cells.
    c. a combination of oxygen and hemoglobin.

EXPLANATION The answers are *b* and *c*. Notice that the first word, *erythrocytes*, is used as a synonym. Sometimes a signal word for a synonym is *or*. Other signal words that will help you discover meaning through the use of definition are *is, that is, in other words, for example,* and *is defined as*. The second word, *oxyhemoglobin*, is part of the explanation of the sentence.

Elaborating Details

Terms are not always directly defined in the text. Instead, an author may give descriptive details that illustrate meaning. In political science texts, for example, you may come across the term *confederation*. Keep reading and see if you can figure out the meaning from the hints in the following paragraph.

EXAMPLE

There is a third form of governmental structure, a *confederation*. The United States began as such, under the Articles of Confederation. In a confederation, the national government is weak and most or all the power is in the hands of its components, for example, the individual states. Today, confederations are rare except in international organizations such as the United Nations.

—Robert Lineberry,
Government in America

_____ A *confederation* is a governmental structure with

    a. strong federal power.
    b. weak federal power.
    c. weak state power.
    d. equal federal and state power.

EXPLANATION The answer is *b* and can be figured out from the details in the third sentence.

Examples

At other times, examples will be given to clarify meaning. In psychology courses, for example, you will frequently encounter a complicated word describing something you have often thought about but not named. Read the following paragraph to find out what *psychokinesis* means.

EXAMPLE

Another psychic phenomenon is psychokinesis, the ability to affect physical events without physical intervention. You can test your powers of psychokinesis by trying to influence the fall of dice from a mechanical shaker. Are you able to have the dice come up a certain number with a greater frequency than would occur by chance?

—Douglas W. Matheson,
Introductory Psychology: The Modern View

_____ *Psychokinesis* means

    a. extrasensory perception.
    b. an influence on happenings without physical tampering.
    c. physical intervention affecting physical change.

EXPLANATION   The answer is *b*. Here the word is first directly defined in a complicated manner, and then the definition is clarified by a simple example.

Comparison

In certain cases, complex concepts are best understood when compared with something else. Economics texts, for example, include many concepts that are difficult to understand. The use of a familiar term in a comparison can help the reader relate to a new idea. Can you explain a *trade deficit*? The following comparison will help.

EXAMPLE

When the United States imports more than it exports, we have a *trade deficit* rather than a trade balance or surplus. Similarly, a store manager who buys more than she sells will create a financial deficit for the company.

_____ A *trade deficit* means that a nation

    a. sells more than it buys.
    b. buys more than it sells.
    c. sells what it buys.

EXPLANATION   The answer is *b*. The comparison explains the definition by creating a more understandable situation.

Contrast

In other cases, a contrast is made to help you read between the lines and infer word meaning. Can you explain what *transsexuals* are and how they differ from *homosexuals?* The following paragraph gives some clues.

EXAMPLE

Transsexuals are people (usually males) who feel that they were born into the wrong body. They are not homosexuals in the usual sense. Most homosexuals are satisfied with their anatomy and think of themselves as appropriately male or female; they simply prefer members of their own sex. Transsexuals, in contrast, think of themselves as members of the opposite sex (often from early childhood) and may be so desperately unhappy with their physical appearance that they request hormonal and surgical treatment to change their genitals and secondary sex characteristics.

—Rita Atkinson et al.,
Introduction to Psychology

_____ A *transsexual* is a person who thinks of himself or herself as a

  a. homosexual.
  b. heterosexual.
  c. member of the opposite sex.
  d. person without sex drive.

EXPLANATION The answer is *c*. By contrasting homosexuals and transsexuals, the reader is better able to infer the difference between the two. Signal words that indicate contrast are *but, yet, however*, and *in contrast*.

Antonyms

Finally, the context clue may be an **antonym,** or a word that means the opposite of the unknown word. Antonyms are signaled by words and phrases such as *however, but, yet, in contrast*, or *on the other hand*. Using the following context, is *nonconfrontational* behavior violent?

EXAMPLE

Some passive belief systems call for *nonconfrontational* behavior; yet others call for rebellion.

—Adapted from Daniel G. Bates and Elliot M. Franklin,
Cultural Anthropology, 3rd ed.

_____ A *nonconfrontational* behavior is

  a. violent.
  b. rebellious.
  c. not openly rebellious.
  d. sympathetic.

EXPLANATION The signal word *yet* suggests that *nonconfrontational* is the opposite of violent and rebellious, so *c* is correct. The word *passive* is also a clue to the meaning.

Limitations of Context Clues

Although the clues in the sentence in which an unknown word appears are certainly helpful in deriving the meaning of the word, these clues will not always give a complete and accurate definition. To understand totally the meaning of a word, take some time after completing your reading to look up the word in a glossary or dictionary. Context clues operate just as the name suggests: they are hints, not necessarily definitions.

exercise 2.2   **The Power of Context Clues**

How can context clues assist you in unlocking the meaning of unknown words? For each of the following items, make two responses. First, without reading the sentence containing the unknown word, select *a, b, c,* or *d* for the definition that you feel best fits each italicized word. Then read the material in which the word is used in context and answer again.

Compare your answers. Did reading the word in context help? Were you initially uncertain of any word but then able to figure out the meaning after reading it in a sentence?

_____ 1. *usurped*

      a. shortened
      b. acknowledged
      c. aggravated
      d. seized

      _____ Henry, to the end of his life, thought of himself as a pious and orthodox Catholic who had restored the independent authority of the Church of England *usurped* centuries before by the Bishop of Rome.

—Shepard B. Clough et al.,
A History of the Western World

_____ 2. *assimilationist*

      a. one who adopts the habits of a larger cultural group
      b. a machinist
      c. a typist
      d. one who files correspondence

      _____ When members of a minority group wish to give up what is distinctive about them and become just like the majority, they take an *assimilationist* position. An example is the Urban League.

—Reece McGee et al.,
Sociology: An Introduction

_____ 3. *dyad*

      a. star
      b. two-member group
      c. opposing factor
      d. leader

      _____ George Simmel was one of the first sociologists to suggest that the number of members in a group radically transforms its properties. He began with an analysis of what happens when a *dyad*, a two-member group, becomes a triad, a three-member group.

—Ibid.

_____ 4. *hyperthermophiles*

a. animals
b. heat lovers
c. birds
d. winter plants

_____ Another group of archaea, the *hyperthermophiles,* thrive in very hot waters; some even live near deep-ocean vents where temperatures are above 100°C, the boiling point of water at sea level.

—Neil Campbell et al.,
Biology: Concepts & Connections, 3rd ed.

_____ 5. *expropriated*

a. took from its owners
b. industrialized
c. approximated
d. increased in size

_____ Under a decree of September 1952, the government *expropriated* several hundred thousand acres from large landholders and redistributed this land among the peasants.

—Jesse H. Wheeler, Jr., et al.,
Regional Geography of the World

_____ 6. *adherents*

a. children
b. followers
c. instigators
d. detractors

_____ One of the fundamental features of Hinduism has been the division of its *adherents* into the most elaborate caste system ever known.

—Ibid.

_____ 7. *stimulus*

a. writing implement
b. distinguishing mark
c. something that incites action
d. result

_____ While we are sleeping, for example, we are hardly aware of what is happening around us, but we are aware to some degree. Any loud noise or other abrupt *stimulus* will almost certainly awaken us.

—Gardner Lindzey et al.,
Psychology

_____ 8. *debilitating*

    a. weakening
    b. reinforcing
    c. exciting
    d. enjoyable

    _____ However, anyone who has passed through several time zones while flying east or west knows how difficult it can be to change from one sleep schedule to another. This "jet lag" can be so *debilitating* that many corporations will not allow their executives to enter negotiations for at least two days after such a trip.

    —Ibid.

_____ 9. *autocratic*

    a. automatic
    b. democratic
    c. self-starting
    d. dictatorial

    _____ Autocratic leadership can be extremely effective if the people wielding it have enough power to enforce their decisions and if their followers know that they have it. It is especially useful in military situations where speed of decision is critical. Among its disadvantages are the lack of objectivity and the disregard for opinions of subordinates.

    —David J. Rachman and Michael Mescon,
    Business Today

_____ 10. *ice page*

    a. Web page that wiggles to center itself
    b. Web page anchored to the right of the screen
    c. Web page anchored to the left of the screen
    d. Web page that flows to fit any size screen

    _____ Ice, jello, and liquid are related terms describing three approaches to controlling content placement on a Web page. An ice page is one in which the primary content has a fixed width and is "frozen" to the left margin.

    —H. L. Capron,
    Computers: Tools for an Information Age, 6th ed.

exercise 2.3 **Context Clues in Academic Reading**

Use the context clues of the sentence to write the meaning of each of the following italicized words.

1. Some psychologists suspect that negative emotions—especially depression and anxiety—may be the most *infectious* of all. "Stress and depression are like emotional germs—they jump from one person to the next," notes psychologist Ellen McGrath.

   —Adapted from Stacy Colino,
   "Happiness Is Catching: Why Emotions Are Contagious,"
   Family Circle, March 12, 1996

   Infectious means _____

   _____.

2. Robbery, which should not be confused with burglary, is a personal crime and involves a face-to-face confrontation between victim and *perpetrator*.

   —Frank Schmalleger,
   Criminal Justice Today, 8th ed.

   A *perpetrator* is _____

   _____.

3. In 1727 Sir Isaac Newton became seriously ill, and on March 20 one of the greatest physicists of all time died. He was *accorded* a state funeral and interred in Westminster Abbey—a high and rare honor for a commoner.

   —Adapted from Larry D. Kirkpatrick and Gregory E. Francis,
   Physics: A World View, 5th ed.

   Accorded means _____

   _____.

4. At times, two sides cannot—or will not—agree. The speed and ease with which such an *impasse* is resolved depend in part on the nature of the contract issues.

   —Adapted from Ricky W. Griffin and Ronald J. Ebert,
   Business, 8th ed.

   An *impasse* means _____

   _____.

5. Social psychologist Robert Zajonc found that people like previously seen things better than unfamiliar ones; research shows that familiarity breeds not contempt but *affinity*.

> —Adapted from Stephen M. Kosslyn and Robin S. Rosenberg,
> *Psychology: The Brain, the Person, the World*, 2nd ed.

Affinity means _____

_____.

exercise 2.4   ## Context Clues in Short Passages

Use context clues from each passage that follows to write the meaning of the italicized words.

Passage A

Blocked by her family and publicly *maligned*, Florence Nightingale struggled against *prevailing norms* to carve out her occupation. She was the daughter of a wealthy *gentry* family, and from her father she received a man's classical education. Women of her *milieu* were expected to be educated only in domestic arts.

> —Adapted from Mark Kishlansky et al.,
> *Civilization in the West*, 6th ed.

1. maligned _____

_____

2. prevailing _____

_____

3. norms _____

_____

4. gentry _____

_____

5. milieu _____

_____

Passage B

The Clean Air Act, as *amended* in 1990, directed the U.S. Environmental Protection Agency (EPA) to issue regulations that require the gasoline used in pollution-*prone* areas to be "*reformulated*" in order to burn cleaner (that is, to reduce ozone-forming and toxic air pollutants) and not evaporate as easily. The Reformulated Gasoline Program was *implemented* in 1995. Reformulated gasoline is blended with chemicals commonly called "oxygenates," which raise the oxygen content of gasoline. Oxygen helps gasoline burn more completely, reducing harmful tailpipe emissions.

According to the EPA, reformulated gasoline produces 15 to 17 percent less pollution than *conventional* gasoline, and further improvements are expected as new formulas are developed.

—Frederick K. Lutgens and Edward J. Tarbuck,
The Atmosphere: An Introduction to Meteorology, 9th ed.

1. amended _____

_____

2. prone _____

_____

3. reformulated _____

_____

4. implemented _____

_____

5. conventional _____

_____

exercise 2.5   **Context Clues in a Short Essay**

Use the context clues in the sentences to write the meaning of each word or phrase listed after the selection.

E. B.'S VIEW FROM THE COW PASTURE: HE'S BEEN SLEEPING IN MY BED

The Carolina Cattle Connection, *June 2003.*

E.B. Harris, a well-known North Carolina auctioneer of farm equipment, raises cattle and goats on his farm.

The other day I ran into a friend of mine who dates all the way back to my childhood. Her name is Brenda Davis Smith. Brenda's family and my family go back a long way. Brenda's daddy was sheriff of Warren County for many years.

Brenda had two brothers, Ashley and John Hugh. Ashley was the same age as me, and John Hugh was two years younger. Every Sunday afternoon after church they were at my house or I was at theirs, or we were in the woods playing. As a matter of fact, Ashley, John Hugh, and I are blood brothers. When we were about ten years old we did that cowboy and Indian trick. We got a little blood from each other by cutting with a dull knife from each one and rolling it in the cut of the next one. Back in those days, no one had heard of all the blood diseases that are going on now.

This incident I am going to tell you about with Brenda dates back to about 1969. At that time I was doing some custom disking about a mile from the Davis home in the community of Marmaduke for a man named Clifford Robertson. It was early to midspring and Clifford was fixing to put in some milo and had hired me to disk the land. That day I went on up there and finished his job. I was then planning to go to Warrenton to do some work for Hal Connell on the Bar C farm. Mr. Connell was a Charolais breeder and was going to put in some summer grazing.

After I finished the work at Clifford's I really did not feel that well. By the time I reached the Davis home, it was probably about 10:30 to 11:00 A.M. and I was really feeling bad. It was getting so warm, I pulled the tractor into the Davis yard and cut it off.

Rachel, their mom, wasn't there, but I made myself at home because Rachel had always called me one of her boys. The house was unlocked so I went in, lay down in the hallway where it was cool, and went to sleep. Rachel came in about 1:30 to 2:00 P.M. and woke me up. She asked if I was all right, and I told her that I really did not feel that well. She wanted to know if she could get me anything, and I told her no thank you. She then told me to lie in Brenda's bed until I felt better.

I got up out of the hall and lay down in Brenda's bed. Brenda was away at college. By around 3:00 P.M. I was feeling even worse. Rachel called my mama, and Mama and Daddy came and got me and carried me to the doctor's office.

I was running a high fever and they immediately put me in the hospital. About three days later and after a bunch of tests, I thought I was feeling better. I had started to turn yellow and they found out I had hepatitis. Mama came over and told me that I was going to be put in quarantine with no visitors for a week.

They immediately started calling all the folks that I had had close contact with to come and get vaccinated against hepatitis. Brenda had come home the next day after I had been at her house, so she was one of the ones who came to get a shot. Brenda told the nurse she had been in close contact with me. The nurse filling out the paperwork asked what kind of contact she had had with me.

Now Brenda is one of those people who say exactly what is on their mind. Brenda told her that I had been sleeping in her bed. You can imagine how that sounded. The rumor got started that Brenda and I had something going, which was the furthest thing from the truth. Brenda had to come back and clarify her statement.

I guess you have to be careful about what you say and who you say it to because the right thing can be taken the wrong way.

—By E. B. Harris
From *The Carolina Cattle Connection*, June 2003

1. go back a long way _____

   _____

2. blood brothers _____

   _____

3. blood diseases _____

   _____

4. custom disking _____

   _____

5. fixing to put in _____

   _____

6. early to midspring _____

   _____

7. milo _____

   _____

8. Charolais breeder _____

   _____

9. hepatitis _____

   _____

10. in quarantine _____

    _____

Multiple Meanings of a Word

Even when word meaning seems clear, many words—particularly short ones—can be confusing because they have more than one meaning. The word *bank*, for example, can be used as a noun to refer to a financial institution, the ground rising from a river, or a mass of clouds. As a verb, *bank* can mean to laterally incline an airplane, to accumulate, or to drive a billiard ball into a cushion. Thus, the meaning of the word depends on the sentence and paragraph in which the word is used. Be alert to context clues that indicate an unfamiliar use of a seemingly familiar word.

exercise 2.6   **Multiple Meanings**

The boldface words in the following sentences have multiple meanings. Write the definition of each boldface word as it is used in the sentence.

1. Despite a broken leg, the toddler was still amazingly **mobile.** _____

   _____

2. Learning of its exclusive membership policy, she decided not to become a member of the **association.** _____

_____

3. The overcooked cauliflower emitted a **foul,** lingering odor. _____

_____

4. With April 15 looming, the woman began to **comb** the den for her missing W2 forms. _____

_____

5. What she enjoyed most about early morning was that the world seemed so **still.** _____

_____

6. Having misplaced the overdue text, the library patron now owed a **fine** nearly equal to the cost of the book. _____

_____

Understanding the Structure of Words

What is the longest word in the English language and what does it mean? Maxwell Nurnberg and Morris Rosenblum, in *How to Build a Better Vocabulary* (Prentice-Hall, 1989), say that at one time the longest word in *Webster's New International Dictionary* was

pneumonoultramicroscopicsilicovolcanokoniosis

Look at the word again, and notice the smaller and more familiar word parts. Do you know enough of the smaller parts to figure out the meaning of the word? Nurnberg and Rosenblum unlock the meaning as follows:

pneumono: pertaining to the lungs, as in *pneumon*ia

ultra: beyond, as in *ultra*violet rays

micro: small, as in *micro*scope

scopic: from the root of Greek verb *skopein,* to view or look at

silico: from the element *silicon,* found in quartz, flint, and sand

volcano: the meaning of this is obvious

koni: the principal root, from a Greek word for dust

osis: a suffix indicating illness, such as trichinosis

Now putting the parts together again, we deduce that *pneumonoultramicroscopicsilicovolcanokoniosis* is a disease of the lungs caused by extremely small particles of volcanic ash and dust.

This dramatic example demonstrates how an extremely long and technical word can become more manageable by breaking it into smaller parts. The same is true for many of the smaller words that we use every day. A knowledge of word parts will help you unlock the meaning of literally thousands of words. One vocabulary expert identified a list of thirty prefixes, roots, and suffixes and claims that knowing these 30 word parts will help unlock the meaning of 14,000 words.

Like people, words have families and, in some cases, an abundance of close relations. Clusters, or what might be called *word families*, are composed of words with the same base or **root**. For example, *bio* is a root meaning life. If you know that *biology* means the study of life, it becomes easy to figure out the definition of a word like *biochemistry*. Word parts form new words as follows:

prefix + base word or root   base word or root + suffix
prefix + base word or root + suffix

Prefixes and suffixes are added to root words to change the meaning. A **prefix** is added to the beginning of a word and a **suffix** is added to the end. For example, the prefix *il* means not. When added to the word *legal*, the resulting word, *illegal*, becomes the opposite of the original. Suffixes can change the meaning or change the way the word can be used in a sentence. The suffix *cide* means to kill. When added to *frater*, which means brother, the resulting word, *fratricide*, means to kill one's brother. Adding *ity* or *ize* to *frater* changes both the meaning and the way the word can be used grammatically in a sentence.

EXAMPLE To demonstrate how prefixes, roots, and suffixes overlap and make families, start with the root *gamy*, meaning marriage, and ask some questions.

1. What is the state of having only one wife called? _____
   (*mono* means one)

2. What is a man who has two wives called? _____
   (*bi-* means two and *ist* means one who)

3. What is a man who has many wives called? _____
   (*poly-* means many)

4. What is a woman who has many husbands called? _____
   (*andro-* means man)

5. What is someone who hates marriage called? _____
   (*miso-* means hater of)

EXPLANATION The answers are (1) monogamy, (2) bigamist, (3) polygamist, (4) polyandrist, and (5) misogamist. Notice that in several of the *gamy* examples, the letters change slightly to accommodate language sounds. Such variations of a letter or two are typical when you work with word parts. Often you have to drop or add letters to maintain the rhythm of the language, but the meaning of the word part remains the same regardless of the change in spelling. For example, the prefix *con* means with or together, as in *conduct*. This same prefix is used with variations in many other words:

| *cooperate* | *collection* | *correlate* | *communicate* | *connect* |

Thus, *con-*, *co-*, *col-*, *cor-*, and *com-* are all forms of the prefix that means with or together.

exercise 2.7 **Word Families**

Create your own word families from the word parts that are supplied. For each of the following definitions, supply a prefix, root, or suffix to make the appropriate word.

The prefix *bi-* means "two."

1. able to speak two languages: bi_____
2. having two feet, like humans: bi_____
3. representing two political parties: bi_____
4. occurring at two-year intervals: bi_____
5. having two lenses on one glass: bi_____
6. cut into two parts: bi_____
7. mathematics expression with two terms: bi_____
8. instrument with two eyes: bi_____
9. tooth with two points: bi_____
10. coming twice a year: bi_____

The root *vert* means "to turn."

1. to change one's beliefs: _____vert
2. to go back to old ways again: _____vert
3. a car with a removable top: _____vert_____
4. to change the direction of a stream: _____vert
5. activities intended to undermine or destroy: _____vers_____
6. an outgoing, gregarious person: _____vert
7. a quiet, introspective, shy person _____vert
8. conditions that are turned against you; misfortune

   _____vers_____

9. one who deviates from normal behavior, especially sexual: _____vert

10. one who is sometimes introspective and sometimes gregarious:

_____vert

The suffix -*ism* means "doctrine, condition, **or** characteristic."

1. addiction to alcoholic drink: _____ism

2. a brave and courageous manner of acting: _____ism

3. prejudice against a particular gender or sex: _____ism

4. doctrine concerned only with fact and reality: _____ism

5. system using terror to intimidate: _____ism

6. writing someone else's words as your own: _____ism

7. driving out an evil spirit: _____ism

8. purification to join the church: _____ism

9. informal style of speech using slang: _____ism

10. being obsessive or fanatical about something: _____ism

exercise 2.8   **Prefixes, Roots, and Suffixes**

Using the prefix, root, or suffix provided, write the words that best fit the following definitions:

1. *con-* means "with"
   infectious or catching: con_____

2. *sub-* means "under"
   under the conscious level of the mind: sub_____

3. *post-* means "after"
   to delay or set back: post_____

4. *vita* means "life"
   a pill to provide essential nutrients: vita_____

5. *pel* means "drive or push"
   to push out of school: _____pel

6. *thermo* means "heat"
   device for regulating furnace heat: thermo_____

7. *ven* means "come"
   a meeting for people to come together: _____ven_____

8. *rupt* means "break or burst"
   a volcanic explosion: _____rupt_____

9. *meter* means "measure"
   instrument to measure heat: _____meter

10. *naut* means "voyager"
    voyager in space: _____naut

Using a Dictionary

Do you have an excellent collegiate dictionary, such as *Merriam-Webster's Collegiate Dictionary?* Every college student needs two dictionaries: a small one for class and a large one to keep at home. In class, you may use a small paperback dictionary for quick spelling or word-meaning checks. The paperback is easy to carry but does not provide the depth of information needed for college study that is found in the larger collegiate editions.

Several online dictionaries offer easy and free access for limited use but require a yearly subscription fee for premium services. At http://www.Merriam-Webster.com/, for example, you can type your word into the Search window and receive the definition, word origin, pronunciation, and links to Top 10 Search Results (the word in use) for free. The site also provides an encyclopedia link, "Word of the Day" services, word games, an online thesaurus, a dictionary for kids, and an online store for purchases. Another easy-to-use free site, http://www.dictionary.com, includes definitions, foreign dictionaries, translations into foreign languages, a thesaurus, games, a word of the day, and a bookstore. Try these sites and see how they compare with your collegiate dictionary. In evaluating the sites, consider that good dictionaries not only contain the definitions of words but also provide the following additional information for each word.

Guide Words. The two words at the top of each dictionary page are the first and last entries on the page. They help guide your search for a particular entry by indicating what is covered on that page.

In the sample that follows, *flagrante delicto* is the first entry on the page of the dictionary on which *flamingo* appears, and *flappy* is the last entry. Note that the pronunciation of the word *flamingo* is followed by part of speech *(n)*, plural spellings, and the origin of the word.

flagránte delicto • flappy

fla·min·go \flə-'miŋ-(ˌ)gō\ *n, pl* **-gos** *also* **-goes** [obs. Sp *flamengo* (now *flamenco*), lit., Fleming, German (conventionally thought of as ruddy-complexioned)] (1565) : any of several large aquatic birds (family Phoenicopteridae) with long legs and neck, webbed feet, a broad lamellate bill resembling that of a duck but abruptly bent downward, and usu. rosy-white plumage with scarlet wing coverts and black wing quills

\ə\ **abut** \ᵊ\ **kitten,** F **table** \ər\ **further** \a\ **ash** \ā\ **ace** \ä\ **mop, mar**
\au̇\ **out** \ch\ **chin** \e\ **bet** \ē\ **easy** \g\ **go** \i\ **hit** \ī\ **ice** \j\ **job**
\ŋ\ **sing** \ō\ **go** \ȯ\ **law** \ȯi\ **boy** \th\ **thin** \t͟h\ **the** \ü\ **loot** \u̇\ **foot**
\y\ **yet** \zh\ **vision** \k̲, ⁿ, œ, ɶ ʸ\ *see* Guide to Pronunciation

By permission. From *Merriam-Webster's Collegiate® Dictionary*, Eleventh Edition; © 2006 by Merriam-Webster, Incorporated. (http://www.merriam-webster.com)

Pronunciation. The boldface main entry divides the word into sounds, using a dot between each syllable. After the entry, letters and symbols show the pronunciation. A diacritical mark (′) at the end of a syllable indicates stress on that syllable. A heavy mark means major stress; a lighter one indicates minor stress.

As shown in the illustration on page 57, a key explaining the symbols and letters appears at the bottom of the dictionary page. For example, a word like *ragweed* (rag′-wēd) would be pronounced with a short *a* as in *ash* and a long *e* as in *easy*.

The *a* in *flamingo* sounds like the *a* in *abut*, and the final *o* has a long sound as in *go*. The stress is on the first syllable.

Part of Speech. The part of speech is indicated in an abbreviation for each meaning of a word. A single word, for example, may be a noun with one definition and a verb with another. The noun *flamingo* can be used as only one part of speech, but *sideline* can be both a noun and a verb (see the following entry).

> **¹side·line** \-ˌlīn\ *n* (ca. 1862)   **1** : a line at right angles to a goal line or end line and marking a side of a court or field of play for athletic games   **2 a** : a line of goods sold in addition to one's principal line   **b** : a business or activity pursued in addition to one's regular occupation   **3 a** : the space immediately outside the lines along either side of an athletic field or court   **b** : a sphere of little or no participation or activity — usu. used in pl.
> **²sideline** *vt* (1943) : to put out of action : put on the sidelines

By permission. From *Merriam-Webster's Collegiate® Dictionary*, Eleventh Edition; © 2006 by Merriam-Webster, Incorporated. (http://www.merriam-webster.com)

Spellings. Spellings are given for the plural of the word and for special forms. This is particularly useful in determining whether letters are added or dropped to form the new words. The plural of *flamingo* can be spelled correctly in two different ways. Both *flamingos* and *flamingoes* are acceptable.

Origin. For many entries, the foreign word and language from which the word was derived will appear after the pronunciation. For example, *L* stands for a Latin origin and *G* for Greek. A key for the many dictionary abbreviations usually appears at the beginning of the book.

The word *flamingo* has a rich history. It comes from the Spanish *(Sp)* word *flamenco*, which derived from the older, now obsolete *(obs. Sp)* word *flamengo*. It relates to the ruddy complexion once thought typical of German or Fleming (that is, Flemish, from a part of Belgium) people. That's a lot of information packed into an entry on a single pink bird!

Multiple Meanings. A single word can have many shades of meaning or several completely different meanings. The various meanings are numbered.

The word *flamingo* on page 57 has only one meaning. The word *sideline*, however, has several, as shown in the previous entry.

A sideline can be a business, a product, or a designated area. In addition, it can mean to move something out of the action. To select the appropriate meaning, consider the context or the way the word is used in the sentence. For example, consider the intended meaning in "As a sideline to being a full-time student, I also play in a band on the weekends."

exercise 2.9   **Using the Dictionary**

Answer the following questions, using the page from *Merriam-Webster's Collegiate Dictionary* reproduced on page 60. Write *T* (true) or *F* (false).

_____ 1. *Ammonia* is a white compound that is water soluble.

_____ 2. If something is *amiss*, it is out of place.

_____ 3. An *amoral* act could still be legal.

_____ 4. Couples in love are not *amorous*.

_____ 5. *Amnesia* and *amnesty* originate from the same Greek word.

_____ 6. *Ammo* is an abbreviation for *ammonia*.

_____ 7. *Ammonite* can refer to an ancient shell or to an ancient people.

_____ 8. The term *amoeba* is derived from older words meaning "to become."

_____ 9. *Among* and *amongst* are synonyms.

_____ 10. Geometric shapes are also *amorphous*.

Word Origins

The study of word origins is called **etymology.** Not only is it fascinating to trace a word back to its earliest recorded appearance, but your knowledge of the word's origin can strengthen your memory for the word. For example, the word *narcissistic* means egotistically in love with yourself. Its origin is a Greek myth in which a beautiful youth named Narcissus falls in love with his own reflection; he is punished for his vanity by being turned into a flower. Thus, the myth creates an intriguing image that can enhance your memory link for the word.

The amount of information on word origins varies with the type of dictionary. Because of its size, a small paperback dictionary such as the *American Heritage Dictionary* usually contains very little information on word origins, whereas a textbook-size edition of *Merriam-Webster's Collegiate Dictionary* offers more. For the most information on word origins, visit the reference room in your college library, and use an unabridged dictionary such as *Webster's Third New International Dictionary*, the *Random House Dictionary of the English Language*, or the *American Heritage Dictionary of the English Language*.

exercise 2.10   **Word Origins**

Read the following dictionary entries and answer the questions about the words and their origins.

*Amen fl*1693 Swiss Mennonite bishop] (1844) : of or relating to a strict sect of Mennonites who were followers of Amman and settled in America chiefly in the 18th century — **Amish** *n*

[1]**amiss** \ə-ˈmis\ *adv* (13c) **1 a :** in a mistaken way : WRONGLY ⟨if you think he is guilty, you judge ~⟩ **b :** ASTRAY ⟨something had gone ~⟩ **2 :** in a faulty way : IMPERFECTLY

[2]**amiss** *adj* (14c) **1 :** not being in accordance with right order **2 :** FAULTY, IMPERFECT **3 :** out of place in given circumstances — usu. used with a negative ⟨a few remarks may not be ~ here⟩

ami·to·sis \ˌā-mī-ˈtō-səs\ *n* [NL, fr. [2]*a-* + *mitosis*] (1894) : cell division by simple cleavage of the nucleus and division of the cytoplasm without spindle formation or appearance of chromosomes — **ami·tot·ic** \-ˈtä-tik\ *adj* — **ami·tot·i·cal·ly** \-ti-k(ə-)lē\ *adv*

am·i·trip·ty·line \ˌa-mə-ˈtrip-tə-ˌlēn\ *n* [*amino* + *tryptophan* + *-yl* + [2]*-ine*] (1961) : a tricyclic aromatic antidepressant drug $C_{20}H_{23}N$ used in the form of its hydrochloride salt

am·i·trole \ˈa-mə-ˌtrōl\ *n* [*amino* + *triazole*] (ca. 1960) : a systemic herbicide $C_2H_4N_4$ used in areas other than food croplands

am·i·ty \ˈa-mə-tē\ *n, pl* **-ties** [ME *amite*, fr. AF *amyté*, fr. ML *amicitas*, fr. L *amicus* friend — more at AMIABLE] (15c) : FRIENDSHIP; *esp* : friendly relations between nations

am·me·ter \ˈa-ˌmē-tər\ *n* [*ampere* + *-meter*] (1882) : an instrument for measuring electric current esp. in amperes

am·mine \ˈa-ˌmēn, a-ˈmēn\ *n* [ISV *ammonia* + [2]*-ine*] (1897) **1 :** a molecule of ammonia as it exists in a coordination complex ⟨hex-*ammine*-cobalt chloride $Co(NH_3)_6Cl_3$⟩ **2 :** a compound that contains an ammine

am·mo \ˈa-(ˌ)mō\ *n* [by shortening & alter.] (1911) : AMMUNITION

am·mo·nia \ə-ˈmō-nyə\ *n* [NL, fr. L *sal ammoniacus* sal ammoniac, lit., salt of Ammon, fr. Gk *ammōniakos* of Ammon, fr. *Ammōn* Ammon, Amun, an Egyptian god near whose temple at the Siwa oasis it was extracted] (1789) **1 :** a pungent colorless gaseous alkaline compound of nitrogen and hydrogen NH_3 that is very soluble in water and can easily be condensed to a liquid by cold and pressure **2 :** AMMONIA WATER

am·mo·ni·ac \ə-ˈmō-nē-ˌak\ *n* [ME & L; ME, fr. L *ammoniacum*, fr. Gk *ammōniakon*, fr. neut. of *ammōniakos* of Ammon] (15c) : the aromatic gum resin of a southwest Asian herb (*Dorema ammoniacum*) of the carrot family used as an expectorant and stimulant and in plasters

am·mo·ni·a·cal \ˌa-mə-ˈnī-ə-kəl\ *also* **am·mo·ni·ac** \ə-ˈmō-nē-ˌak\ *adj* (1646) : of, relating to, containing, or resembling ammonia

am·mo·ni·ate \ə-ˈmō-nē-ˌāt\ *vt* **-at·ed; -at·ing** (ca. 1928) **1 :** to combine or impregnate with ammonia or an ammonium compound **2 :** to subject to ammonification — **am·mo·ni·a·tion** \-ˌmō-nē-ˈā-shən\ *n*

ammonia water *n* (1852) : a water solution of ammonia

am·mo·ni·fi·ca·tion \ə-ˌmä-nə-fə-ˈkā-shən, -ˌmō-nə-\ *n* (1886) **1 :** the act or process of ammoniating **2 :** decomposition with production of ammonia or ammonium compounds esp. by the action of bacteria on nitrogenous organic matter — **am·mo·ni·fy** \-ˌfī\ *vb*

am·mo·nite \ˈa-mə-ˌnīt\ *n* [NL *ammonites*, fr. L *cornu Ammonis*, lit., horn of Ammon] (1758) : any of a subclass (Ammonoidea) of extinct cephalopods esp. abundant in the Mesozoic age that had flat spiral shells with the interior divided by septa into chambers — **am·mo·nit·ic** \ˌa-mə-ˈni-tik\ *adj*

Am·mon·ite \ˈa-mə-ˌnīt\ *n* [LL *Ammonites*, fr. Heb *ʽAmmōn* Ammon (son of Lot), descendant of Ammon] (1530) : a member of a Semitic people who in Old Testament times lived east of the Jordan between the Jabbok and the Arnon — **Ammonite** *adj*

am·mo·ni·um \ə-ˈmō-nē-əm\ *n* [NL, fr. *ammonia*] (1808) : an ion NH_4^+ derived from ammonia by combination with a hydrogen ion and known in compounds (as salts) that resemble in properties the compounds of the alkali metals

ammonium carbonate *n* (ca. 1829) : a carbonate of ammonium; *specif* : the commercial mixture of the bicarbonate and carbamate used esp. in smelling salts

ammonium chloride *n* (1869) : a white crystalline volatile salt NH_4Cl that is used in dry cells and as an expectorant — called also *sal ammoniac*

ammonium cyanate *n* (ca. 1881) : an inorganic white crystalline salt NH_4CNO that can be converted into organic urea

ammonium hydroxide *n* (1899) : a weakly basic compound NH_4OH that is formed when ammonia dissolves in water and that exists only in solution

ammonium nitrate *n* (1869) : a colorless crystalline salt NH_4NO_3 used in explosives and fertilizers and in veterinary medicine

ammonium phosphate *n* (1880) : a phosphate of ammonium; *esp* : DIAMMONIUM PHOSPHATE

ammonium sulfate *n* (1869) : a colorless crystalline salt $(NH_4)_2SO_4$ used chiefly as a fertilizer

am·mo·noid \ˈa-mə-ˌnȯid\ *n* (1884) : AMMONITE ⟨Mesozoic ~*s*⟩

am·mu·ni·tion \ˌam-yə-ˈni-shən\ *n* [obs. F *amunition*, fr. MF, alter. of *munition*] (1607) **1 a :** the projectiles with their fuses, propelling charges, or primers fired from guns **b :** CARTRIDGES **c :** explosive military items (as grenades or bombs) **2 :** material for use in attacking or defending a position ⟨~ for the defense lawyers⟩

Amn *abbr* airman

am·ne·sia \am-ˈnē-zhə\ *n* [NL, fr. Gk *amnēsia* forgetfulness, alter. of *amnēstia*] (1618) **1 :** loss of memory due usu. to brain injury, shock, fatigue, repression, or illness **2 :** a gap in one's memory **3 :** the selective overlooking or ignoring of events or acts that are not favorable or useful to one's purpose or position — **am·ne·si·ac** \-zhē-ˌak, -zē-\ *or* **am·ne·sic** \-zik, -sik\ *adj or n*

am·nes·ty \ˈam-nə-stē\ *n, pl* **-ties** [Gk *amnēstia* forgetfulness, fr. *amnēstos* forgotten, fr. *a-* + *mnasthai* to remember — more at MIND] (1580) : the act of an authority (as a government) by which pardon is granted to a large group of individuals — **amnesty** *vt*

am·nio \ˈam-nē-ō\ *n, pl* **am·ni·os** (1983) : AMNIOCENTESIS

am·nio·cen·te·sis \ˌam-nē-ō-(ˌ)sen-ˈtē-səs\ *n, pl* **-te·ses** \-ˌsēz\ [NL, fr. *amnion* + *centesis* puncture, fr. Gk *kentesis*, fr. *kentein* to prick — more at CENTER] (1957) : the surgical insertion of a hollow needle through the abdominal wall and into the uterus to obtain amniotic fluid esp. for the determination of fetal sex or chromosomal abnormality

am·ni·on \ˈam-nē-ˌän, -ən\ *n, pl* **amnions** *or* **am·nia** \-nē-ə\ [NL, fr. Gk, caul, fr. *amnos* lamb — more at YEAN] (1667) **1 :** a thin membrane forming a closed sac about the embryos or fetuses of reptiles, birds, and mammals and containing the amniotic fluid **2 :** a membrane analogous to the amnion and occurring in various invertebrates — **am·ni·ot·ic** \ˌam-nē-ˈä-tik\ *adj*

am·ni·ote \ˈam-nē-ˌōt\ *n* [NL *Amniota*, fr. *amnion*] (1887) : any of a group (Amniota) of vertebrates that undergo embryonic or fetal development within an amnion and include the birds, reptiles, and mammals — **amniote** *adj*

amniotic fluid *n* (ca. 1855) : the serous fluid in which the embryo or fetus is suspended within the amnion

amniotic sac *n* (ca. 1881) : AMNION

amn't \ˈänt, ˈant, ˈa-mənt\ (1618) *chiefly Scot & Irish* : am not

amo·bar·bi·tal \ˌa-mō-ˈbär-bə-ˌtȯl\ *n* [*amyl* + *-o-* + *barbital*] (1949) : a barbiturate $C_{11}H_{18}N_2O_3$ used as a hypnotic and sedative; *also* : its sodium salt

amoe·ba *also* **ame·ba** \ə-ˈmē-bə\ *n, pl* **-bas** *or* **-bae** \-(ˌ)bē\ [NL, genus name, fr. Gk *amoibē* change, fr. *ameibein* to change — more at MIGRATE] (1855) : any of a large genus (*Amoeba*) of naked rhizopod protozoans with lobed and never anastomosing pseudopodia, without permanent organelles or supporting structures, and of wide distribution in fresh and salt water and moist terrestrial environments; *broadly* : a naked rhizopod or other amoeboid protozoan — **amoe·bic** \-bik\ *adj*

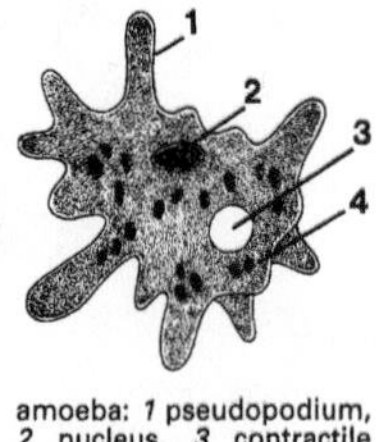

amoeba: *1* pseudopodium, *2* nucleus, *3* contractile vacuole, *4* food vacuole

amoebiasis *var of* AMEBIASIS

amoe·bo·cyte *also* **ame·bo·cyte** \ə-ˈmē-bə-ˌsīt\ *n* (1892) : a cell (as a phagocyte) having amoeboid form or movements

amoe·boid *also* **ame·boid** \ə-ˈmē-ˌbȯid\ *adj* (1856) : resembling an amoeba specif. in moving or changing in shape by means of protoplasmic flow

[1]**amok** \ə-ˈmək, -ˈmäk\ *or* **amuck** \ə-ˈmək\ *n* [Malay *amok*] (1665) : a murderous frenzy that has traditionally been regarded as occurring esp. in Malaysian culture

[2]**amok** *or* **amuck** *adv* (1672) **1 :** in a murderously frenzied state **2 a :** in a violently raging manner ⟨a virus that had run ~⟩ **b :** in an undisciplined, uncontrolled, or faulty manner ⟨films . . . about computers run ~ —*People*⟩

[3]**amok** *or* **amuck** *adj* (1944) : possessed with or motivated by a murderous or violently uncontrollable frenzy

amo·le \ə-ˈmō-lē\ *n* [AmerSp, fr. Nahuatl *ahmōlli* soap] (1831) : a plant part (as a root) possessing detergent properties and serving as a substitute for soap; *also* : a plant (as a yucca or agave) so used

among \ə-ˈməŋ\ *also* **amongst** \-ˈməŋ(k)st\ *prep* [*among* fr. ME, fr. OE *on gemonge*, fr. *on* + *gemonge*, dat. of *gemong* crowd, fr. *ge-* (associative prefix) + *-mong* (akin to OE *mengan* to mix); *amongst* fr. ME *amonges*, fr. *among* + *-es* -s — more at CO-, MINGLE] (bef. 12c) **1 :** in or through the midst of : surrounded by ⟨hidden ~ the trees⟩ **2 :** in company or association with ⟨living ~ artists⟩ **3 :** by or through the aggregate of ⟨discontent ~ the poor⟩ **4 :** in the number or class of ⟨wittiest ~ poets⟩ ⟨~ other things she was president of her college class⟩ **5 :** in shares to each of ⟨divided ~ the heirs⟩ **6 a :** through the reciprocal acts of ⟨quarrel ~ themselves⟩ **b :** through the joint action of ⟨made a fortune ~ themselves⟩ ***usage*** see BETWEEN

amon·til·la·do \ə-ˌmän-tə-ˈlä-(ˌ)dō, -ti(l)-ˈyä-(ˌ)t͟hō\ *n, pl* **-dos** [Sp, lit., done in the manner of *Montilla*, town in Andalusia] (1825) : a medium dry sherry

amor·al \(ˌ)ā-ˈmȯr-əl, (ˌ)a-, -ˈmär-\ *adj* (1779) **1 a :** being neither moral nor immoral; *specif* : lying outside the sphere to which moral judgments apply ⟨science as such is completely ~ —W. S. Thompson⟩ **b :** lacking moral sensibility ⟨infants are ~⟩ **2 :** being outside or beyond the moral order or a particular code of morals ⟨~ customs⟩ — **amor·al·ism** \-ə-ˌli-zəm\ *n* — **amo·ral·i·ty** \ˌā-mə-ˈra-lə-tē, ˌa-, -(ˌ)mȯ-\ *n* — **amor·al·ly** \ˌā-ˈmȯr-ə-lē, (ˌ)a-, -ˈmär-\ *adv*

amo·ret·to \ˌa-mə-ˈre-(ˌ)tō, ˌä-\ *n, pl* **-ti** \-(ˌ)tē\ *or* **-tos** [It, dim. of *amore* love, cupid, fr. L *amor*] (1622) : CUPID, CHERUB 2

am·or·ist \ˈa-mə-rist\ *n* (1581) **1 :** a devotee of love and esp. sexual love : GALLANT **2 :** one who writes about romantic love — **am·or·is·tic** \ˌa-mə-ˈris-tik\ *adj*

Am·o·rite \ˈa-mə-ˌrīt\ *n* [Heb *Ĕmōrī*] (1535) : a member of one of various Semitic peoples living in Mesopotamia, Syria, and Palestine during the third and second millennia B.C. — **Amorite** *adj*

am·o·rous \ˈa-mə-rəs, ˈam-rəs\ *adj* [ME, fr. AF, fr. ML *amorosus*, fr. L *amor* love, fr. *amare* to love] (14c) **1 :** strongly moved by love and esp. sexual love ⟨~ couples⟩ **2 :** being in love : ENAMORED — usu. used with *of* ⟨~ of the girl⟩ **3 a :** indicative of love ⟨received ~ glances from her partner⟩ **b :** of or relating to love ⟨an ~ novel⟩ — **am·o·rous·ly** *adv* — **am·o·rous·ness** *n*

amor·phous \ə-ˈmȯr-fəs\ *adj* [Gk *amorphos*, fr. *a-* + *morphē* form] (ca. 1731) **1 a :** having no definite form : SHAPELESS ⟨an ~ cloud mass⟩ **b :** being without definite character or nature : UNCLASSIFIABLE ⟨an ~ segment of society⟩ **c :** lacking organization or unity ⟨an ~ style of writing⟩ **2 :** having no real or apparent crystalline form ⟨an ~ mineral⟩ — **amor·phous·ly** *adv* — **amor·phous·ness** *n*

amort \ə-ˈmȯrt\ *adj* [short for *all-a-mort*, by folk etymology fr. MF *a la mort* to the death] (1546) *archaic* : being at the point of death

am·or·ti·za·tion \ˌa-mər-tə-ˈzā-shən *also* ə-ˌmȯr-\ *n* (1851) **1 :** the act or process of amortizing **2 :** the result of amortizing

am·or·tize \ˈa-mər-ˌtīz *also* ə-ˈmȯr-\ *vt* **-tized; -tiz·ing** [ME *amortisen* to kill, alienate in mortmain, fr. AF *amorteser*, alter. of *amortir*, fr. VL **admortire* to kill, fr. L *ad-* + *mort-*, *mors* death — more at MURDER] (1867) **1 :** to pay off (as a mortgage) gradually usu. by periodic payments of principal and interest or by payments to a sinking fund **2 :** to gradually reduce or write off the cost or value of (as an asset) ⟨~ goodwill⟩ ⟨~ machinery⟩ — **am·or·tiz·able** \-ˌtī-zə-bəl\ *adj*

\ə\ **abut** \ᵊ\ kitten, F table \ər\ **further** \a\ **ash** \ā\ **ace** \ä\ **mop, mar** \au̇\ **out** \ch\ **chin** \e\ **bet** \ē\ **easy** \g\ **go** \i\ **hit** \ī\ **ice** \j\ **job** \ŋ\ **sing** \ō\ **go** \ȯ\ **law** \ȯi\ **boy** \th\ **thin** \t͟h\ **the** \ü\ **loot** \u̇\ **foot** \y\ **yet** \zh\ **vision, beige** \k͟, ⁿ, œ, ue, ʸ\ *see* Guide to Pronunciation

¹**bribe** \'brīb\ *n* [ME, morsel given to a beggar, bribe, fr. AF, morsel]
(15c) **1** : money or favor given or promised in order to influence the
judgment or conduct of a person in a position of trust **2** : something
that serves to induce or influence
²**bribe** *vb* **bribed; brib·ing** *vt* (1528) : to induce or influence by or as if
by bribery ∼ *vi* : to practice bribery — **brib·able** \'brī-bə-bəl\ *adj* —

By permission. From *Merriam-Webster's Collegiate® Dictionary*, Eleventh Edition;
© 2006 by Merriam-Webster, Incorporated. (http://www.merriam-webster.com)

1. *Bribe* means _____

_____ .

2. Explain the origin: _____

_____

_____ .

¹**scape·goat** \'skāp-ˌgōt\ *n* [¹*scape;* intended as trans. of Heb *'azāzēl*
(prob. name of a demon), as if *'ēz 'ŏzēl* goat that departs—Lev 16:8
(AV)] (1530) **1** : a goat upon whose head are symbolically placed the
sins of the people after which he is sent into the wilderness in the biblical ceremony for Yom Kippur **2 a :** one that bears the blame for
others **b :** one that is the object of irrational hostility
²**scapegoat** *vt* (1943) : to make a scapegoat of — **scape·goat·ism**
\-ˌgō-ˌti-zəm\ *n*

By permission. From *Merriam-Webster's Collegiate® Dictionary*, Eleventh Edition;
© 2006 by Merriam-Webster, Incorporated. (http://www.merriam-webster.com)

3. *Scapegoat* means _____

_____ .

4. Explain the origin: _____

_____

_____ .

mar·a·thon \'mer-ə-ˌthän, 'ma-rə-\ *n, often attrib* [*Marathon,* Greece,
site of a victory of Greeks over Persians in 490 B.C., the news of which
was carried to Athens by a long-distance runner] (1896) **1** : a long-
distance race: **a :** a footrace run on an open course usu. of 26 miles
385 yards (42.2 kilometers) **b :** a race other than a footrace marked
esp. by great length **2 a :** an endurance contest **b :** something (as an
event, activity, or session) characterized by great length or concentrated effort

By permission. From *Merriam-Webster's Collegiate® Dictionary*, Eleventh Edition;
© 2006 by Merriam-Webster, Incorporated. (http://www.merriam-webster.com)

5. *Marathon* means _____

_____ .

6. Explain the origin: _____

_____

_____

om·buds·man \\'äm-,bủdz-mən, 'ȯm-, -bədz-, -,man; äm-'bủdz-, ȯm-\ *n*,
pl **-men** \-mən\ [Sw, lit., representative, fr. ON *umbothsmathr*, fr. *um-
both* commission + *mathr* man] (1959) **1 :** a government official (as in
Sweden or New Zealand) appointed to receive and investigate complaints made by individuals against abuses or capricious acts of public
officials   **2 :** one that investigates reported complaints (as from students or consumers), reports findings, and helps to achieve equitable
settlements — **om·buds·man·ship** \-,ship\ *n*

By permission. From *Merriam-Webster's Collegiate® Dictionary*, Eleventh Edition;
© 2006 by Merriam-Webster, Incorporated. (http://www.merriam-webster.com)

7. *Ombudsman* means _____

_____ .

8. Explain the origin: _____

_____

_____

_____

van·dal \\'van-dᵊl\ *n* [L *Vandalii* (pl.), of Gmc origin] (1530)   **1** *cap* **:** a
member of a Germanic people who lived in the area south of the Baltic
Sea between the Vistula and the Oder rivers, overran Gaul, Spain, and
northern Africa in the fourth and fifth centuries A.D., and in 455
sacked Rome   **2 :** one who willfully or ignorantly destroys, damages,
or defaces property belonging to another or to the public — **vandal**
adj, often cap

By permission. From *Merriam-Webster's Collegiate® Dictionary*, Eleventh Edition;
© 2006 by Merriam-Webster, Incorporated. (http://www.merriam-webster.com)

9. *Vandal* means _____

_____ .

10. Explain the origin: _____

_____

_____

_____

Using a Glossary

Each college subject seems to have a language, or jargon, of its own. For example, words like *sociocultural* or *socioeconomic* crop up in sociology. In truth,
these words are somewhat unique to the subject-matter area—they are *invented*
words. The best definitions of such words can usually be found in the textbook itself rather than in a dictionary. The definitions may be displayed in the *margins*
of a page, or more frequently, in a glossary of terms at the end of the book or each
chapter. The glossary defines the words as they are used in the textbook. At the
end of most textbooks is an index, which helps you find pages on which topics
are discussed. In some large texts, the glossary and index are combined.

Consider the following examples from the glossary of a psychology textbook. These terms are part of the jargon of psychology and would probably not be found in the dictionary.

latent learning   Hidden learning that is not demonstrated in performance until that performance is reinforced.

learning set   An acquired strategy for learning or problem solving; learning to learn.

exercise 2.11   **Using Your Dictionary**

Turn to your dictionary for help defining these words. Write a definition for each in your own words.

1. annotating: _____

   _____

   _____

2. contrast: _____

   _____

   _____

3. mnemonic: _____

   _____

   _____

4. analogy: _____

   _____

   _____

5. denotation: _____

   _____

   _____

Using a Thesaurus

A thesaurus is a writer's tool. It provides synonyms, that is, words similar in meaning, for the word you look up. It is not a dictionary, and it does not include all words. The first thesaurus was compiled in 1852 by Dr. Peter Mark Roget, an English physician, who collected lists of synonyms as a hobby. This book suggested synonyms for commonly used words, but it also included antonyms. A thesaurus entitled *Roget's Thesaurus* is organized according to Roget's format. There are other types of thesauruses available too.

Use a thesaurus to add variety to your writing and avoid repetitious wording. For example, if you find yourself repeating the word *guilt* in a research paper, consult a thesaurus for substitutes. *Roget's 21st Century Thesaurus* suggests synonyms such as *delinquency, fault, misconduct, shame,* and *transgression.*

guilt [*n*] *blame; bad conscience over responsibility*
answerability, blameworthiness, contrition, crime, criminality, culpability, delinquency, dereliction, disgrace, dishonor, error, failing, fault, indiscretion, infamy, iniquity, lapse, liability, malefaction, malfeasance, malpractice, misbehavior, misconduct, misstep, offense, onus, peccability, penitence, regret, remorse, responsibility, self-condemnation, self-reproach, shame, sin, sinfulness, slip, solecism, stigma, transgression, wickedness, wrong; SEE CONCEPTS *101,532, 645,690*

From *Roget's 21st Century Thesaurus.* Published by Dell Publishing, a Division of Random House. Copyright 1992, 1993, 1999 by the Philip Lief Group, Inc. Reprinted by permission.

At the end of the entry, the words SEE CONCEPTS (printed in capitals and followed by numbers) indicate that you can find additional synonyms under these numbers at the end of the book.

Most word-processing programs have an electronic thesaurus. Usually, it is found with the spelling checker or in the Tools pull-down menu. Use your cursor to highlight (select) the word for which you want alternatives, and then click on the thesaurus. Consider the context of your sentence as you choose from the array of words that appear. Be aware, though, that a thesaurus in book form will offer more choices.

exercise 2.12 **Using a Thesaurus**

Use the entries for *carry* in *The Oxford American Desk Dictionary and Thesaurus* to select an alternative word that fits the meaning of *carry* in the following sentences.

1. Pilates and yoga instructors encourage participants to *carry* themselves with good posture. _____

2. The infamous Typhoid Mary was able to *carry* her infectious disease to others through her employment as a cook. _____

3. When one of the wheels on my luggage broke, I was forced to *carry* my belongings in an expandable briefcase. _____

4. Since he was running unopposed, the city councilor was able to easily *carry* the election. _____

5. Positions of power also *carry* great responsibility. _____

carry /káree/ • v. (**-ries, -ried**) **1** tr. support or hold up, esp. while moving. **2** tr. convey with one or have on one's person. **3** tr. conduct or transmit (*pipe carries water*). **4** tr. take (a process, etc.) to a specified point; continue (*carry into effect, carry a joke too far*). **5** tr. involve; imply; entail as a feature or consequence (*principles carry consequences*). **6** tr. (in reckoning) transfer (a figure) to a column of higher value. **7** tr. hold in a specified way (*carry oneself erect*). **8** tr. publish or broadcast esp. regularly. **9** tr. keep a regular stock of. **10** intr. be audible at a distance. **11** tr. **a** win victory or acceptance for (a proposal, etc.). **b** gain (a state or district) in an election. **c** *Golf* cause the ball to pass beyond (a bunker, etc.). **12** tr. endure the weight of; support. **13** tr. be pregnant with. • n. (pl. **-ries**) **1** act of carrying. **2** *Golf* distance a ball travels in the air. □ **carry away 1** remove. **2** inspire; affect emotionally or spiritually. **3** deprive of self-control (*got carried away*). **carry the day** be victorious or successful. **carry off 1** take away, esp. by force. **2** win (a prize). **3** (esp. of a disease) kill. **4** render acceptable or passable. **carry on 1** continue. **2** engage in (a conversation or a business). **3** *colloq.* behave strangely or excitedly. **4** advance (a process) by a stage. **carry out** put (ideas, instructions, etc.) into practice. **carry weight** be influential or important.

■ v. **1, 2** transport, bear, deliver, bring, haul, lug, cart, ship, move, *colloq.* schlep, tote; drive, take; hold. **3** convey, take, transport, transfer, bear. **7** bear, deport, hold up, maintain, keep. **8** put out; air, screen; disseminate, communicate, present, announce, offer, give, release. **9** stock, keep, have in stock, sell, offer, trade in, deal in, have. **11 b** win, take, sweep, capture, pick up. **12** see SUPPORT v. 1, 2. □ **carry away 1** see REMOVE v. 2. **2** see INSPIRE 1, 2. **carry the day** see TRIUMPH v. 1. **carry off 1** abscond with, make away *or* off with, run off with, spirit off *or* away, whisk away *or* off, cart off, drag away, kidnap, abduct. **2** gain, capture, pick up, take, *colloq.* walk away *or* off with. **3** be *or* cause the death of, cause to die, *colloq.* finish off. **4** accomplish, achieve, perform, effect, effectuate, do, execute, succeed in *or* with, handle, manage, work, bring off, carry out *or* through, pull off. **carry on 1** go on, keep on; keep (on) going, last, remain; persist, persevere, push *or* press on. **2** be involved *or* busy, occupy oneself with; follow, pursue, prosecute; manage, conduct, operate, run, administer. **carry out** perform, continue, implement, administer, transact, see through, execute, discharge, prosecute, effect. complete. accomplish, conclude

From *The Oxford American Desk Dictionary and Thesaurus* (2003). By permission of Oxford University Press.

Using Analogies

Analogies are comparisons that call upon not only your word knowledge but also your ability to see relationships. They can be difficult, frustrating, and challenging. Use logical thinking and problem-solving skills to pinpoint the initial relationship, and then establish a similar relationship with two other words.

Reader's *Tip* ———— Categories of Analogy Relationships
—————————————————————————————————————

- **Synonyms:** Similar in meaning
  Find is to *locate* as *hope* is to *wish.*
- **Antonyms:** Opposite in meaning
  Accept is to *reject* as *rude* is to *polite.*
- **Function, use, or purpose:** Identifies what something does; watch
  for the object (noun) and then the action (verb)
  Pool is to *swim* as *blanket* is to *warm.*
- **Classification:** Identifies the larger group association
  Sandal is to *shoe* as *sourdough* is to *bread.*
- **Characteristics and descriptions:** Shows qualities or traits
  Nocturnal is to *raccoon* as *humid* is to *rainforest.*
- **Degree:** Shows variations of intensity
  Fear is to *terror* as *dislike* is to *hate.*
- **Part to whole:** Shows the larger group
  Page is to *book* as *caboose* is to *train.*
- **Cause and effect:** Shows the reason (cause) and result (effect)
  Study is to *graduation* as *caffeine* is to *insomnia.*

exercise 2.13 **Identifying Types of Analogies**

Study the analogies that follow to establish the relationship of the first two words.
Record that relationship, using the categories outlined in the Reader's Tip. Then
choose the word that duplicates that relationship to finish the analogy.

1. *Trash* is to *refuse* as *soil* is to _____.

   Relationship _____

   a. earthworms
   b. dirt
   c. minerals
   d. growing

2. *Burdened* is to *overwhelmed* as *tired* is to _____.

   Relationship _____

   a. sleepy
   b. exhausted
   c. energetic
   d. rested

3. *Cappuccino* is to *coffee* as *jazz* is to _____.

   Relationship _____

   a. singer
   b. opera
   c. rock
   d. music

4. *Excited* is to *dull* as *fancy* is to _____.

   Relationship _____

   a. rich
   b. fortunate
   c. plain
   d. colorful

5. *Fork* is to *eat* as *television* is to _____.

   Relationship _____

   a. video
   b. actor
   c. entertain
   d. produce

6. *Sleeve* is *shirt* to as *lens* is to _____.

   Relationship _____

   a. book
   b. motor
   c. movement
   d. camera

7. *Smart* is to *genius* as *rigid* is to _____.

   Relationship _____

   a. steel
   b. comedy
   c. angle
   d. focus

8. *Recklessness* is to *accident* as *laziness* is to _____.

   Relationship _____

   a. work
   b. money
   c. failure
   d. ability

Easily Confused Words

Pairs or groups of words may cause confusion because they sound exactly alike, or almost alike, but are spelled and used differently. *Stationary* and *stationery* are examples of such words. You ride a stationary bike to work out and you write a business letter on your office stationery. For a memory link, associate the *e* in *letter* with the *e* in *stationery*. Students frequently confuse *your* and *you're*: *your* shows possession, and *you're* is a contraction for *you are*. To differentiate confusing words, create associations to aid memory. **Homonyms,** words with different meanings that are spelled and sound alike, are not as confusing. They tend to be simple words such as *bear* in "bear the burden" or "kill the bear."

exercise 2.14   **Distinguishing Confusing Words**

Study each set of easily confused words, and then circle the one that correctly fits in each sentence.

loose: unconfined; relaxed; not tight

lose: misplace

1. She enjoyed the comfort of long, **(loose, lose)** clothing during the warm

   summer months. _____

hole: opening

whole: entire object

2. His **(hole, whole)** check was insufficient to cover his monthly car payments.

   _____

there: a place

their: belonging to them

they're: they are

3. Over **(there, their, they're)** is the community shelter for the homeless.

   _____

who's: who is

whose: belonging to whom

4. **(Whose, who's)** idea was it to attend that boring concert last weekend?

   _____

heal: mend; cure

heel: part of foot; follow closely (dog)

5. A well-known saying about doctors is *"Physician, (**heal, heel**) thyself."*

   _____

Recognizing Acronyms

An **acronym** is an abbreviation that is pronounced as a word. Acronyms can thus be considered invented words that are often thoughtfully contrived to simplify a lengthy name and gain quick recognition for an organization or agency. For example, *UNICEF* is the abbreviation for the United Nations International Children's Emergency Fund. The arrangement of consonants and vowels formed by the first letter of each word in the title creates an invented term that we can easily pronounce and quickly recognize. When names are created for new organizations, clever organizers thoughtfully consider the choice and sequence of words in order to engineer a catchy acronym. In some cases, acronyms have become so ingrained in our language that the abbreviations have become accepted as words with lowercase letters. An example of this is the word *radar*, which is a combination of the initial letters of the phrase *radio detecting and ranging*.

exercise 2.15   **Recognizing Acronyms**

The following letters are abbreviations made from the initial letters of words (and sometimes other letters as well). Write what each one stands for. Then place an A beside those that are pronounced as words and thus are considered acronyms.

_____ 1. ATV

_____

_____ 2. SCUBA

_____

_____ 3. NPR

_____

_____ 4. GPS

_____

_____ 5. SONAR

_____

_____ 6. DVR

_____

_____ 7. MRI

_____

_____ 8. AMTRAK

_____

_____ 9. NASCAR

_____

_____10. CAT SCAN

_____

Recognizing Transitional Words

Transitional words connect ideas and signal the direction of the writer's thought. These single words or short phrases lead the reader to anticipate a continuation or a change in thought. For example, the phrase *in addition* signals a continuation, whereas *but* or *however* signals a change.

Reader's *Tip* ————— Types of Transitional Words
———

- **To signal addition:** in addition, furthermore, moreover
- **To signal an example:** for example, for instance, to illustrate, such as
- **To signal time sequence:** first, second, finally, last, afterward
- **To signal comparison:** similarly, likewise, in the same manner
- **To signal contrast:** however, but, nevertheless, whereas, on the contrary, conversely, in contrast
- **To signal cause and effect:** thus, consequently, therefore, as a result, furthermore, similarly, consequently, however, for example

---

exercise 2.16   **Anticipating Transitions**

Read each sentence. Then choose a transitional word or phrase from the boxed list to complete each sentence.

in addition	first	likewise	whereas	therefore

1. Rather than immediately train to run in a marathon, you might

   _____ consider entering a 5K or 10K race.

2. Couples do not always share personality traits; Tom is introverted

   _____ his wife could be considered outgoing.

3. Since you already drank two cups of coffee _____ to a glass of iced

   tea, it might be wise to switch to decaffeinated beverages for the rest of the

   night.

4. Cell phones must be turned off and put away before class; _____,

   your instructor expects you do to the same with all other electronic devices,

   except for laptops.

5. Rain seems to develop at the most inopportune moments; _____, it is

   wise to keep an umbrella handy.

Summary Points

➤ **How do you remember new words?**
To remember new words, use mnemonic devices to associate words in phrases, in families, and in images. Use concept cards to record a new word's definition with a phrase and an image that suggest the meaning.

➤ **What are context clues?**
The context clues in a sentence or paragraph can help unlock the meaning of unknown words. These can be definitions or synonyms, details, examples, and comparisons, contrasts, or antonyms.

➤ **Why learn prefixes, word roots, and suffixes?**
A knowledge of prefixes, roots, and suffixes can reveal smaller, more familiar word parts in unknown words.

➤ **What will you find in a dictionary?**
A collegiate dictionary contains definitions, word origins, pronunciations, and spellings.

➤ **What is a glossary?**
A glossary defines words that are unique to a subject matter area.

➤ **What is a thesaurus?**
A thesaurus is a reference book that contains synonyms for frequently used words to add variety to writing.

➤ **What are analogies?**
Analogies are comparisons that fall into different categories of relationships.

➤ **What are acronyms?**
Acronyms are abbreviations that are pronounced as words.

➤ **How are transitional words used?**
Transitional words connect ideas and signal the writer's train of thought.

 **Search the Net**

Use a search engine such as Google, AltaVista, Excite, Infoseek, Dogpile, Yahoo, or Lycos to find exercises on analogies. Select, print, and bring to class five sample analogies that your classmates would enjoy solving. For suggested Web sites and other research activities, go to http://www.ablongman.com/smith/.

3 Strategic Reading and Study

- What is strategic reading?
- What is a study strategy?
- What are the three stages of reading?
- What are the strategies for previewing?
- Why should you activate your schemata?
- What are the strategies for integrating knowledge during reading?
- Why recall or self-test what you have read?

Jacob Lawrence (1917–2000), *The Library*, 1960. Tempera on fiberboard, 24 × 29⅞ inches (60.9 × 75.8 cm). Courtesy of Artist Rights Society, New York.

What Is Strategic Reading?

In college you can expect a demanding course load and, most likely, a greater volume of difficult material than you have been assigned in the past. How can you meet the challenge and become a more effective reader? The answer is to have an arsenal of techniques, or strategies, to help you navigate through the required reading in your courses. For example, mastering the decoding, or sounding out, of words is one strategy. It is an initial and essential one, but college readers must go far beyond this level into the realm of associating and remembering.

Reading strategically means using specific techniques for understanding, studying, and learning. Research studies find that students who systematically learn such techniques score higher on reading comprehension tests. These strategies—previewing, questioning, connecting, recalling, determining the main idea, recognizing significant supporting details, drawing inferences, and others—will be presented throughout the various chapters in this text. Keep in mind, though, that for greatest success, you must do more than understand the strategies. You must also know when, why, and how to use them.

Four Types of Readers

Just as not all types of reading are the same, not all readers are the same. To understand how readers differ, read the following description of the four levels of reading and learning:[1]

- **Tacit learners/readers.** These readers lack awareness of how they think when reading.
- **Aware learners/readers.** These readers realize when meaning has broken down or confusion has set in but may not have sufficient strategies for fixing the problem.
- **Strategic learners/readers.** These readers use the thinking and comprehension strategies described in this text to enhance understanding and acquire knowledge. They are able to monitor and repair meaning when it is disrupted.
- **Reflective learners/readers.** These readers are strategic about their thinking and apply strategies flexibly depending on their goals or purposes for reading. In addition, they "reflect on their thinking and ponder and revise their future use of strategies."[2]

Which type describes your reading now? With this textbook, you are on your way to becoming a strategic and reflective learner and reader! The dynamic process of reading and learning can be broken into manageable pieces. Master the parts and see how they contribute to the whole. We begin by breaking reading into three stages and explaining strategies to use for each.

---

[1]S. Harvey and A. Goudvis, *Strategies That Work* (Portland, ME: Stenhouse Publishers, 2000), p. 17.

[2]D. Perkins, *Smart Schools: Better Thinking and Learning for Every Child* (New York: Free Press, 1992).

The Stages of Reading

In 1946, after years of working with college students at Ohio State University, Francis P. Robinson developed a textbook study system designed to help students efficiently read and learn from textbooks and effectively recall information for exams. The system was called SQ3R, with the letters standing for the following five steps: Survey, Question, Read, Recite, and Review.

Numerous variations have been developed since SQ3R was introduced. One researcher, Norman Stahl, analyzed sixty-five textbook reading/learning systems and concluded that they have more similarities than differences.[3] The common elements in the systems include a previewing stage, a reading stage, and a final self-testing stage.

In the *previewing* stage, which occurs before reading, students make predictions, ask questions, activate schemata (past knowledge), and establish a purpose for reading. In the *knowledge integration* stage, which occurs during reading, students make predictions, picture images, answer questions, continually relate and integrate old and new knowledge, monitor understanding to clarify confusing points, and use correction strategies. The *recall* stage, which occurs after reading, involves reviewing to self-test and improve recall, making connections to blend new information with existing knowledge networks, and reacting and reflecting to evaluate and accept or reject ideas.

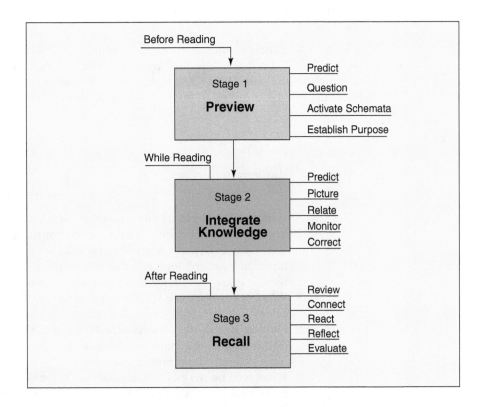

---

[3]N. A. Stahl, "Historical Analysis of Textbook Study Systems" (Ph.D. dissertation, University of Pittsburgh, 1983).

Stage 1: Strategies for Previewing

Previewing is a method of personally connecting with the material before you start to read. When you preview, you look over the material, predict what the material is probably about, ask yourself what you already know about the topic, decide what you will probably know after you read, and make a plan for reading. See the Reader's Tip for useful questions to ask before reading.

To preview, look over the material, think, and ask questions. The focus is "What do I already know, what do I need to know, and how do I go about finding it out?"

Signposts for Previewing

Like public speakers, textbook authors follow the rule "Tell them what you are going to tell them, tell them, and then tell them what you told them." Typically, a chapter begins with a brief overview of the topic, an outline, or questions. The ideas are then developed in clearly marked sections. Concluding statements at the end summarize the important points. Although this pattern does not apply in every case, use it when available as a guide in determining what to read when previewing textbook material.

Because of differences in writing styles, no one set of rules for previewing will work for all materials. Consider the following signposts when previewing.

Title. A title attracts attention, suggests content, and is the first and most obvious clue. Think about the title and turn it into a question. For an article entitled "Acupuncture," ask "What is acupuncture?" For other questions, use the "five-*W* technique" of journalists to find out *who, what, when, where,* and *why*.

Reader's *Tip* —— Asking Questions Before Reading

- **What is the topic of the material?** What does the title suggest? What do the subheadings, italics, and summaries suggest?
- **What do I already know?** What do I already know about this topic or a related topic? Is this new topic a small part of a larger idea or issue that I have thought about before?
- **What is my purpose for reading?** What will I need to know when I finish?
- **How is the material organized?** What is the general outline or framework of the material? Is the author listing reasons, explaining a process, or comparing a trend?
- **What will be my plan of attack?** What parts of the textbook seem most important? Do I need to read everything with equal care? Can I skim some parts? Can I skip some sections completely?

Introductory Material. To get an overview of an entire book, refer to the table of contents and preface. Sophisticated students use the table of contents as a study guide, turning the chapter headings into possible exam items. Many textbook chapters open with an outline, preview questions, or an interesting anecdote that sets the stage for learning. Italicized inserts, decorative symbols, and colored type are also used to highlight key concepts. The first paragraph frequently sets expectations.

Subheadings. Subheadings are titles for sections within chapters. The subheadings, usually appearing in **boldface print** or *italics*, outline the main points of the author's message and thus give the reader an overview of the organization and the content. Turn these subheadings into questions to answer as you read.

Italics, Boldface Print, and Numbers. Italics and boldface print highlight words that merit special attention. These are usually new words or key words that you should be prepared to define and remember. For example, an explanation of sterilization in a biology text might emphasize the words *vasectomy* and *tubal ligation* in italics or boldface print. Numbers can also be used to signal a list of important details. The biology book might emphasize the two forms of sterilization with enumeration: (1) vasectomy and (2) tubal ligation.

Visual Aids. Photographs with their captions, charts, graphs, and maps emphasize important points and sometimes condense text. Reviewing visuals provides clues to what information will be significant.

Concluding Summary. Many textbooks include a summary at the end of each chapter to highlight the important points. The summary can serve not only as a review to follow reading but also as an overview of the chapter prior to reading.

exercise 3.1   **Previewing This Textbook for the Big Picture**

To get an overview of the scope of this textbook and its sequence of topics, look over the table of contents and preface. Think about how the chapter topics fit the goals of college reading. Glance at the chapters to get a sense of the organization, and then answer the following questions.

1. Who is the author? Was the author a professor? _____

    _____

    _____

2. What seems to be the purpose of the Reader's Tip boxes throughout the text?

    _____

    _____

3. Does the book have specific exercises to help build vocabulary? Where are they located? _____

_____

_____

4. Which chapter provides information about increasing reading rate? _____

_____

5. Where might a student record scores received on the reading selections found throughout the text, in order to keep track of progress? _____

_____

6. Is there test-taking assistance provided within the book? _____

_____

_____

7. What seems to be the intent of the Search the Net activities following the longer textbook reading selections? _____

_____

_____

exercise 3.2 **Previewing This Chapter**

To get an overview of this chapter, first look at the table of contents at the beginning of the book, and then read the list of questions at the beginning of the chapter. Flip to the chapter summary points and read them. Use your previewing to answer the following questions.

1. What is strategic reading? _____

_____

_____

2. What is a schema? _____

_____

_____

3. What is metacognition? _____

_____

_____

4. What is the purpose of a recall diagram? _____

_____

_____

5. Which reading selection do you think will be most interesting? _____

_____

_____

6. What are the five thinking strategies used by good readers? _____

_____

_____

Use your answers to these questions to help establish a purpose or a learning strategy goal for reading the chapter. Why is this chapter important, and what do you hope to gain from reading it?

Preview to Activate Schemata

What do you bring to the printed page? As a reader, you are thinking and interacting before, during, and after reading. Your previewing of material first helps you predict the topic. Then, as a further part of the prereading stage, you need to activate your schema for what you perceive the topic to be.

A **schema** (plural, *schemata*) is like a computer file in your brain that holds all you know on a subject. Each time you learn something new, you pull out the computer file on that subject, add the new information, and return the file to storage. The depth of the schema or the amount of information contained in the file varies according to previous experience. For example, a scientist would have a larger, more detailed file for DNA than would most freshman biology students.

The richness of your background determines the amount you can activate. In general, the more schemata you are able to activate, the more meaningful your reading will be. In fact, most experts agree that the single best predictor of your reading comprehension is what you already know. In other words, the rich get richer. Why is that good for you?

Once you have struggled with and learned about a subject, the next time you meet the subject, reading and learning will be easier. You will have greatly expanded your schema for the subject. Does this help explain why some say that the freshman year is the hardest? Some students who barely make C's in introductory courses end up making A's and B's in their junior and senior years. They profited from previous hard work to establish the frameworks of knowledge in building schemata. Comfort yourself during the early struggles by saying, "The smart get smarter, and I'm getting smart!"

Stage 2: Strategies for Integrating Knowledge While Reading

What are you thinking about when you read? Do you visualize? Do you make comparisons? If you don't understand, do you *notice* that you don't understand?

EXAMPLE   Read the following passage to answer the question "What are echinoderms?" Are your thoughts similar to the inserted thoughts of the reader?

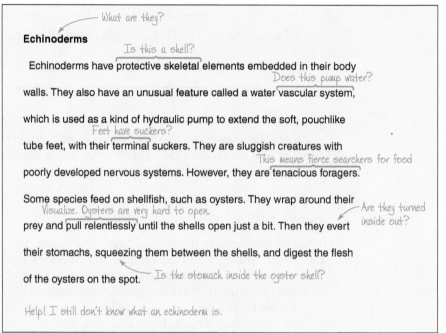

Were you able to follow the reader's inserted thoughts? Do you know what an echinoderm is? Can you guess? If you had known before reading that starfish are echinoderms, the passage would have been more entertaining and less challenging. If you have opened an oyster, you know the tenacity needed to open its shell. Reread the passage with this knowledge, and visualize the gruesome drama. Later in this chapter, be ready to pull out your now enlarged schema on echinoderms and network knowledge on a new passage.

Integrating Ideas: How Do Good Readers Think?

Understanding and remembering complex material requires as much thinking as reading. As illustrated in the previous passage, the good reader is always predicting, visualizing, and drawing comparisons to assimilate new knowledge. Beth Davey, a reading researcher, broke these thoughts down into five manageable and teachable strategies. The Reader's Tip lists the five thinking strategies of good readers.[4] Study them and visualize how you use each.

The first three thinking strategies used by good readers are perhaps the easiest to understand and the quickest to develop. From short stories as a young reader, you quickly learned to predict actions and outcomes. You would see the

---

[4]B. Davey, "Think Aloud—Modeling for Cognitive Processes of Reading Comprehension," *Journal of Reading* 27 (October 1983): 44–47.

Reader's *Tip* — Using Thinking Strategies While Reading

- **Make predictions.** Develop hypotheses.
  "From the title, I predict that this section will give another example of a critical time for rats to learn a behavior."
  "In this next part, I think we'll find out why the ancient Greeks used mnemonic devices."
  "I think this is a description of an acupuncture treatment."
- **Describe the picture you're forming in your head from the information.** Develop images during reading.
  "I have a picture of this scene in my mind. My pet is lying on the table with acupuncture needles sticking out of its fur."
- **Share an analogy.** Link prior knowledge with new information in text. We call this the *"like-a" step*.
  "This is like my remembering, 'In 1492 Columbus sailed the ocean blue.'"
- **Monitor your ongoing comprehension.** Clarify confusing points.
  "This is confusing."
  "This just doesn't make sense. How can redwoods and cypress trees both be part of the same family?"
  "This is different from what I had expected."
- **Correct gaps in comprehension.** Use fix-up correction strategies.
  "I'd better reread."
  "Maybe I'll read ahead to see if it gets clearer."
  "I'd better change my picture of the story."
  "This is a new word to me. I'd better check the context to figure it out."

characters and scenes in your head. Such visualizing increased your level of involvement and enjoyment. You compared the character's reactions and adventures to your own.

When ideas get more complicated and reading becomes more difficult, however, the last two thinking strategies become essential elements in the pursuit of meaning. College textbooks are tough, requiring constant use of the monitoring strategy and frequent use of the correction strategy.

The final strategies involve a higher level of thinking than just picturing an oyster or a starfish. They reflect a deeper understanding of the process of getting meaning, and they require a reader who both understands the thinking process and controls that process. This ability to know and control is called *metacognition* (knowing about knowing).[5]

---

[5]A. L. Brown, "The Development of Memory: Knowing, Knowing About Knowing, and Knowing How to Know," in H. W. Reese, ed., *Advances in Child Development and Behavior*, vol. 10 (New York: Academic Press, 1975), pp. 104–46.

Stage 3: Strategies for Recalling

To recall, you tell yourself what you have learned, relate it to what you already know, react, and evaluate. Actually, you do all this before and during reading, but a deliberate recall is necessary when you finish reading to assimilate knowledge and improve learning. Call it a short conversation with yourself to debrief and digest. You need to be sure you know the content, make connections, and update your schemata, or computer files.

Recalling Through Writing

Answering multiple-choice questions after reading requires one type of mental processing, but writing about the reading requires another type of processing. Experts define writing as a "mode of learning," which means that writing is a process that helps students blend, reconcile, and gain personal ownership of new knowledge. When you write about a subject, you not only discover how much you know and don't know, but you begin to unfold meaningful personal connections.

A humorous adage about the power of writing says, "How do I know what I think until I see what I say?" Writing can be hard work, but it helps you clarify and crystallize what you have learned. You discover your own thinking as you write. Use the power of this valuable tool to take your recall to a higher level. For the longer chapter reading selections in this text, both multiple-choice and writing questions are offered to help you learn.

The Three Steps of Recalling

Recall can be broken down into three manageable steps: self-test, make connections, and react and reflect.

Self-Test. First, test yourself to be sure you understand the content. To have confidence in your opinions, make sure that you clearly understand the facts. You can do this simply by taking a few minutes after reading to recap what you have learned. Do it either in your head or on paper. For practice, use a recall diagram as a learning tool to visualize the main points. On a straight line across the top of a piece of paper, briefly state the topic, or what the passage seems to be mainly about. Indent underneath the topic and state the most significant supporting details.

Make Connections. In the next step of recall, create bridges between what is new to you and what you already know. Ask yourself, "What do I already know that relates to this information?" Your answer will be unique because you are connecting the material to your own knowledge networks. Returning to the recall diagram you started in the previous step, draw a dotted line—your thought line—and write down a related idea, issue, or concern. Connect the text with your personal life experiences, with other things you have read, and with larger global issues. Researchers Harvey and Goudvis categorize these connections in the following way:[6]

---

[6]S. Harvey and A. Goudvis, *Strategies That Work* (Portland, ME: Stenhouse Publishers, 2000), p. 21.

- **Text-to-self.** Readers connect with their own personal experiences and background knowledge.
- **Text-to-text.** Readers connect new text with other written material.
- **Text-to-world.** Readers connect to bigger issues, events, or societal concerns.

How can you translate this theory into practice? Certainly, you can easily relate new reading to yourself. Relating to other written material may seem difficult initially but will be less challenging if you make everyday reading a part of your life. To help you with these connections, the longer reading selections in this text are preceded by a Contemporary Focus feature. These excerpts from recent publications introduce the selection, and later you are asked to answer a question that connects the two. Finally, your ability to make societal or global connections depends on your own interests and knowledge. Your awareness of these kinds of connections will encourage you to dig deeper to relate meaning.

React and Reflect. The final step in recalling is to react to the material. Formulate an opinion about the author and evaluate the message. Returning to your recall diagram, do you agree or disagree with the facts, opinions, and conclusions? How do you feel about the topic? Is this information significant to you? Did the author do a good job? Is this quality work? Your answers will be unique, and there are no right or wrong responses. You are thinking, and you are in control. In all three steps in recalling, you are strengthening your ties to new material. You must link it to own it.

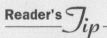 **Reader's Tip** ———— Recalling After Reading ————————————

- **Pinpoint the topic.** Get focused on the subject. Use the title and the subheadings to help you recognize and narrow down the topic.
- **Select the most important points.** Poor readers want to remember everything, thinking all facts have equal importance. Good readers pull out the important issues and identify significant supporting information.
- **Relate the information.** Facts are difficult to learn in isolation. In history, events should not be seen as isolated happenings but rather as results of previous occurrences. Network your new knowledge to enhance memory. Relate new knowledge to yourself, to other written material, and to global issues.
- **React.** Form opinions and evaluate the material and the author. Decide what you wish to accept and what you will reject. Blend old and new knowledge, and write about what you have read.

EXAMPLE   **AUTOPSIES**

Today, many dead people receive some form of autopsy or postmortem examination. At least two main reasons for this are (1) the desire of the family to know the exact cause of death, and (2) the fact that increased medical knowledge results. Because of the important moral and legal restrictions on human experimentation, much of our knowledge of pathology comes from autopsies. This fact prompts many people to donate their bodies to medical schools and/or donate certain organs for possible transplantation.

—John Cunningham,
Human Biology, 2nd ed.

EXPLANATION Remember that the recall diagram is a temporary and artificial format. The diagram below graphically demonstrates a process that you will learn to do in your head. Using the diagram will help you learn to organize and visualize your reading.

(Topic)	Why autopsies are done
(Significant details— examples, facts, or phrases)	To know exact cause of death
	To increase medical knowledge
	— thus donations
(Relate)	Do I want medical students studying my body?
(React)	I would donate my organs but not my body to medical school.

exercise 3.3 **Using Recall Diagrams**

After reading each of the following passages, stop to recall what the passage contained. Use recall diagrams to record what the passage seems to be mainly about. List significant supporting details; identify a related idea, issue, or concern to which you feel the information is connected; and react.

PASSAGE A: ELEPHANTS IN ANCIENT WARFARE

Elephants were the most spectacular, extravagant, and unpredictable element in ancient warfare. Since the time of Alexander the Great, Hellenistic kings and commanders had tried to use the great strength, size, and relative invulnerability of the animals to throw opposing infantry into confusion and flight. Elephants' unusual smell and loud trumpeting also panicked horses not accustomed to the strange beasts, wreaking havoc with cavalry units. Mahouts, or drivers, who were usually Indians, controlled and directed the animal from a seat on the elephant's neck. Normally each elephant carried a small, towerlike structure from which archers could shoot down on the massed infantry. However, as with modern tanks, the primary importance of the beasts was the enormous shock effect created by a charge of massed war elephants.

—Mark Kishlansky et al.,
Civilization in the West, 6th ed.

(Topic) _____

(Significant
details) _____

_____

_____

_____

(Relate) -

(React) _____

PASSAGE B: UNDERSTANDING DROUGHT

Drought is different from other natural hazards in several ways. First, it occurs in a gradual, "creeping" way, making its onset and end difficult to determine. The effects of drought accumulate slowly over an extended time span and sometimes linger for years after the drought has ended. Second, there is not a precise and universally accepted definition of drought. This adds to the confusion about whether or not a drought is actually occurring and, if it is, its severity. Third, drought seldom produces structural damages, so its social and economic effects are less obvious than damages from other natural disasters.

—Frederick K. Lutgens and Edward J. Tarbuck,
The Atmosphere: An Introduction to Meteorology, 9th ed.

(Topic) _____

(Significant
details) _____

_____

_____

(Relate) -

(React) _____

Summary Points

➤ **What is strategic reading?**
Strategic reading is knowing and using techniques for understanding, studying, and learning.

➤ **What is a study strategy?**
All study systems include a previewing stage to ask questions and establish a purpose for reading, a reading stage to answer questions and integrate knowledge, and a final stage of self-testing and reviewing to improve recall.

➤ **What are the three stages of reading?**
Reading is an active rather than a passive process. Good readers preview before reading, integrate knowledge while reading, and recall after reading.

➤ **What are strategies for previewing?**
Previewing is a way to assess your needs before you start to read by deciding what the material is about, what needs to be done, and how to go about doing it.

➤ **Why should you activate your schema?**
If you brainstorm to make a connection with your reading topic before you begin to read, the information will be more meaningful and memorable.

➤ **What is metacognition?**
Good readers control and direct their thinking strategies as they read. They know about knowing.

➤ **What are the strategies for integrating knowledge during reading?**
Students make predictions, picture images, answer questions, continually relate and integrate old and new knowledge, monitor understanding to clarify confusing points, and use correction strategies.

➤ **Why recall or self-test what you have read?**
Recalling what you have read immediately after reading forces you to select the most important points, to relate the supporting details, to integrate new information into existing networks of knowledge, and to react.

selection 1 History

Contemporary *Focus*

Madame C. J. Walker not only created wealth for herself, but she offered opportunities for success to others. In the late 1800s, the hair care needs of African American women were not being addressed. How are those needs being met today? Do new opportunities still exist in the hair care and beauty industry?

Entrepreneur Draws Inspiration from Cosmetics Industry Pioneer

By Maureen Milford
The News Journal (Wilmington, Delaware), October 7, 2005

Crystal Baynard-Norman, 49, of Wilmington, knows the juggling act performed by entrepreneurs who build businesses in their homes while holding down outside jobs.

"I would be sitting at work and thinking, 'Ooh, my gosh, I have to go home and make 20 hair ointments. I have to make 30 body lotions.' Then I'm staying up to 2 or 3 o'clock in the morning. But I love it," she said. Baynard-Norman founded her own hair and body products company, All God's Children Natural Hair & Body Care Products, in 2001.

But Baynard-Norman, who recruits family and friends to her manufacturing operation in her spacious, light-filled kitchen, has an inspiration: Madame C. J. Walker.

"I figured, if she could do it back then with no computers and no information, I could do it with all the information available," Baynard-Norman said.

Manufacturers' sales of ethnic hair-care products totaled $294 million in 2004, according to market research by Kline & Co. in Little Falls, New Jersey. The overall market for makeup and skin care products reached $13.5 billion last year, according Anna Wang, a consultant with Kline.

Last month, Baynard-Norman, a mother of three sons, introduced a line of cosmetics for children called Kidz Only. In addition, she makes more than a half-dozen products for adults, including hair ointment, body wash, body polish, scrubs, and massage oils. Products range in price from $2 to $20 for a gift set. Custom baskets run $40 and up.

COLLABORATE Collaborate on responses to the following questions:

➤ How much do you spend per month on your hair?

➤ Why do people choose expensive hair care and beauty items over cheaper drug store brands?

➤ How much does a busy hair stylist make in a year?

selection

1

Skill Development: Preview

Preview the next selection to predict its purpose and organization and to formulate your learning plan.

Activate Schema

What business opportunities were available for women in the late 1800s?
Why is hard work an important key to success? What else does it take?

Establish a Purpose for Reading

As a widowed mother with a child, she was working as a washerwoman and seemed destined to poverty. Read to find out how Madame C. J. Walker overcame obstacles, achieved success, and offered opportunities to others.

Increase Word Knowledge

What do you know about these words?

acumen	stimulate	lavish	philanthropic	patent
concoctions	implementing	burgeoning	consolidated	prosperous

Your instructor may give a true-false vocabulary review before reading.

Integrate Knowledge While Reading

Questions have been inserted in the margins to stimulate your thinking while reading. Remember to

Predict	Picture	Relate	Monitor	Correct

MADAME C. J. WALKER

What were her chances of success?

"I am a woman who came from the cotton fields of the South. I was promoted from there to the washtub. Then I was promoted to the cook kitchen, and from there I promoted myself into the business of manufacturing hair goods and preparations." With these words, Madame C. J. Walker introduced herself to the National Negro
5 Business League's 1912 convention and summed up her life to that time. Five years later, through her hard work and business acumen, this daughter of former slaves owned and ran the largest black-owned company in the United States.

The Madame C. J. Walker Manufacturing Company produced and distributed a line of hair and beauty preparations for black women, including conditioners to ease
10 styling, stimulate hair growth, and cure common scalp ailments, as well as an improved metal comb for straightening curly hair. So successful was she at marketing her products that Madame Walker became the first female African American millionaire. Her

self-made fortune allowed for a lavish personal lifestyle and extensive public philanthropic commitments, particularly to black educational institutions.

15   Walker was born Sarah Breedlove in 1867. Her parents, Owen and Minerva
Breedlove, were former slaves who had chosen to remain as sharecroppers on the
Burney family plantation near Delta, Louisiana. The family was poor, and both parents died by the time Sarah was seven. She was taken in by her old sister, Louvenia,
and a few years later they moved to Vicksburg, Mississippi.

20   Sarah's education was extremely limited, and she was subjected to the cruelty of
Louvenia's husband. To get away, she married a man named McWilliams when she was
14. In 1885 her daughter, Lelia, was born; two years later, McWilliams was killed, and
the young widow moved to St. Louis, Missouri, where she worked as a washerwoman
and domestic. Through hard work, she managed to see Lelia graduate from the St.

25 Louis public schools and attend Knoxville College, a black private college in Tennessee.

Shortly after her arrival in St. Louis, Sarah began losing her hair. Like many
black women of her era, she would often divide her hair into sections, tightly wrap
string around these sections, and twist them in order to make her hair straighter
when it was combed out. Unfortunately, this hair-care ritual created such a strain

30 that it caused many women to lose their hair.

To keep her hair, Sarah tried every product she could find, but none worked.
Desperate, she prayed to God to save her hair. "He answered my prayer," she later told a
reporter for the *Kansas City Star* in a story recounted in *Ms.* magazine. "One night I had
a dream, and in that dream a big black man appeared to me and told me what to mix

35 up for my hair. Some of the remedy was grown in Africa, but I sent for it, mixed it, put
it on my scalp, and in a few weeks my hair was coming in faster than it had ever fallen
out. I tried it on my friends; it helped them. I made up my mind to begin to sell it."

Would this approach work today? →

Walker experimented with patent medicines and hair products already on the
market, developing different formulas and products in her wash tubs for testing on

40 herself, her family members, and friends. Realizing the commercial possibilities in
the underserved market for black beauty products, she began selling her concoctions door-to-door in the local black community.

Madame C. J. walker sits proudly in the driver's seat of her own electric car.

Was she also an inventor?

After perfecting her "Wonderful Hair Grower" in 1905, she moved to Denver, Colorado, to join her recently widowed sister-in-law and nieces. Other products fol-
45 lowed, including "Glossine" hair oil, "Temple Grower," and a "Tetter Salve" for psori-asis of the scalp. These products, used along with her redesigned steel hot comb with teeth spaced far apart for thick hair, allowed black women to straighten, press, and style their hair more easily.

Soon she had enough customers to quit working as a laundress and devote all
50 her energy to her growing business. In 1906 she married Charles Joseph Walker, a Denver newspaperman. His journalistic background proved helpful in implement-ing advertising and promotional schemes for her products in various black publica-tions, as well as through mail-order procedures. Though the marriage only lasted a few years, it provided a new professional name for herself and her company—the
55 Madame C. J. Walker Manufacturing Company.

Leaving Lelia in charge of her burgeoning mail-order operations in Denver, Walker traveled throughout the South and East, selling her products and teaching her hair care method. In 1908 she established a branch office and a school called Lelia College in Pittsburgh to train black hair stylists and beauticians in the Walker
60 System of hair care and beauty culture. While Lelia managed the school and office, Walker logged thousands of miles on the road, introducing her preparations to black women everywhere she went.

Does her success remind you of other women's achievements?

Stopping in Indianapolis in 1910, she was so impressed by the city's central lo-cation and transportation facilities that she decided to make it her headquarters.
65 That year she consolidated her operations by moving the Denver and Pittsburgh of-fices there and building a new factory to manufacture her hair solutions, facial creams, and related cosmetics. She also established a training center for her sales force, research and production laboratories, and another beauty school to train her "hair culturists."

70 On one of her many trips Walker met a train porter, Freeman B. Ransom, who was a Columbia University law student working during his summer vacation. After he graduated, she hired him to run her Indianapolis operations, freeing Lelia to move to New York in 1913 to expand activities on the East Coast and open another Lelia College. Walker herself continued to travel and promote her beauty program.

75 By 1917 the Madame C. J. Walker Manufacturing Company was the largest black-owned business in the country with annual revenues of approximately $500,000. Much of its success was built around the sales force—thousands of black women known as Walker agents. Dressed in white blouses and long black skirts, they became familiar sights in black communities throughout the United States and
80 the Caribbean. Walking door-to-door to demonstrate and sell Walker products, they easily outpaced their competitors in the newfound black beauty field.

Being a Walker agent or hair culturist was a rare career opportunity for black women in the rigidly segregated pre–World War I era. It enabled many to become financially independent, buy their own homes, and support their childrens' educa-
85 tions. Walker herself considered it one of her greatest accomplishments, telling dele-gates to the National Negro Business League, as recounted in *American History Illustrated:* "I have made it possible for many colored women to abandon the wash-tub for a more pleasant and profitable occupation…. The girls and women of our race must not be afraid to take hold of business enterprise."

90 Once her agents were making money, Walker encouraged them to donate to charitable causes in their own communities. Walker set a good example to her sales-women by becoming the leading black philanthropist of her day.

Even with her generosity, Walker was able to lead a lavish lifestyle. Shrewd real estate investments complemented her self-made business fortune. A striking woman nearly six feet tall, big boned, with brown skin and a broad face, she made heads turn by her presence whenever she entered a room. And her extravagant tastes only enhanced her public image. She dressed in the latest fashions, wore expensive jewelry, rode around in an electric car, was seen in the finer restaurants, owned townhouses in New York and Indianapolis and, befitting the first black female millionaire in the country, built a $250,000, 20-room, elegant Georgian mansion, Villa Lewaro—complete with gold piano and $60,000 pipe organ—in Irvington-on-Hudson.

By 1918 Walker's nonstop pace and lifetime of hard work had begun to take their toll. Despite orders from doctors to slow down to ease her high blood pressure, she continued to travel. During a business trip to St. Louis she collapsed and was transported back to her villa in a private railroad car. She died quietly of kidney failure resulting from hypertension in May of 1919 at the age of 52, leaving behind a prosperous company, extensive property, and a personal fortune in excess of $1 million. Summing up her life, the author of an editorial in *Crisis* said that Madame Walker "revolutionized the personal habits and appearance of millions of human beings."

In her will, Walker bequeathed two-thirds of her estate to charitable and educational institutions, many of which she had supported during her lifetime. The remaining third was left to her daughter, now called A'Lelia, who succeeded her as company president. True to her beliefs, a provision in the will directed that the Madame C. J. Walker Manufacturing Company always have a woman president. In 1927 the Walker Building, planned by Madame Walker, was completed in Indianapolis to serve as company headquarters.

(1,471 words)

Were hypertension drugs available in 1919?

From *Contemporary Black Biography* by Gale Research,
© 1994, Gale Research. Reprinted by permission of The Gale Group.

Recall

Stop to self-test, relate, and react.

Your instructor may choose to give you a true-false comprehension review.

Write About the Selection

What aspects of Walker's business show that she was a clever business strategist as well as an energetic and ambitious entrepreneur?

Response Suggestion: List the unique features of Walker's business plan, and explain how they contributed to her success.

Contemporary *Link*

Why and how does the salon business present such a lucrative opportunity for women? In what new areas might Madame C. J. Walker expand her business today?

Check Your Comprehension

After reading the selection, answer the following questions with *a, b, c,* or *d.* To help you analyze your strengths and weaknesses, the question types are indicated.

Main Idea _____ 1. Which is the best statement of the main idea of this selection?

    a. Despite a discouraging early life, Walker became a very successful businesswoman.

    b. Despite living a life of luxury, Walker gave a lot of money to charities.

    c. The manufacturing of hair goods and preparations experienced a business boom in the early 1900s.

    d. Walker carefully saved her money in order to become a successful millionaire.

Inference _____ 2. The quotation that opens the selection is most likely intended by the author to emphasize

    a. the kinds of jobs women typically had in the early twentieth century.

    b. the importance of receiving job promotions.

    c. the importance of gaining experience in different lines of work.

    d. Walker's decision to take charge of her own life.

Detail _____ 3. Each of the following is mentioned in the selection as one of the products manufactured and distributed by Walker *except*

    a. hair conditioners.

    b. facial creams.

    c. hair coloring products.

    d. a special hair comb.

Inference _____ 4. The selection suggests that Walker's development of various hair products was very much due to

    a. reading insightful books on science and technology.

    b. the guidance of a stranger who worked with her.

    c. do-it-yourself trial and error.

    d. assistance she received from her parents.

Detail _____ 5. Many African American women living in the early twentieth century lost their hair because they

    a. had poor nutrition and thus lacked necessary vitamins.

    b. used poor-quality hair shampoos.

    c. used a harmful hair-straightening technique.

    d. developed psoriasis of the scalp.

Detail _____ 6. Walker decided to establish her headquarters in Indianapolis because of the city's

    a. location.

    b. history.

    c. laboratories.

    d. factories.

Detail _____ 7. Lelia College was established to

    a. train women to be Walker System specialists.

    b. teach ladies to be sales agents.

    c. provide a business education for men and women.

    d. provide a liberal arts education to African American women.

Inference _____ 8. The reader can conclude that Walker spent most of her time

    a. decorating her mansion.

    b. taking business trips.

    c. teaching in her college.

    d. managing her head office on-site.

Inference _____ 9. The sales agents for Walker's company were easily identified because they

    a. were the only female sales agents in the field.

    b. were the only sales agents in the Caribbean market.

    c. gave away free samples.

    d. wore the same uniform.

Inference _____10. The author suggests that one of the most important benefits of being a Walker agent was

    a. the travel opportunities.

    b. the income.

    c. the free beauty products.

    d. the chance to meet people.

Answer the following with *T* (true) or *F* (false).

Detail _____11. Walker was at one time married to Freeman B. Ransom.

Inference _____12. Walker's products sold mostly through mail order.

Inference _____13. Walker's daughter, Lelia, worked in Denver and was not entrusted with major operational responsibilities in the Madame C. J. Walker Manufacturing Company.

Detail _____14. Walker gave generously to charities and schools but did not leave money in her will to her family.

Detail _____15. The director of the Madame C. J. Walker Manufacturing Company has always been a woman because of a stipulation in Walker's will.

Build Your Vocabulary

According to the way the italicized word was used in the selection, select *a, b, c,* or *d* for the word or phrase that gives the best definition. The number in parentheses indicates the line of the passage in which the word is located.

_____ 1. "business *acumen*" (6)
   a. negotiations
   b. wisdom
   c. appeal
   d. training

_____ 2. "*stimulate* hair growth" (10)
   a. slow
   b. cure
   c. increase
   d. manage

_____ 3. "*lavish* personal lifestyle" (13)
   a. interesting
   b. luxurious
   c. entertaining
   d. busy

_____ 4. "*philanthropic* commitments" (13)
   a. institutional
   b. religious
   c. governmental
   d. charitable

_____ 5. "*patent* medicines" (38)
   a. brands
   b. well known
   c. unreliable
   d. chemical

_____ 6. "selling her *concoctions*" (41)
   a. mixtures
   b. concepts
   c. ideas
   d. favorites

_____ 7. "*implementing* advertising" (51)
   a. imagining
   b. selling
   c. searching out
   d. accomplishing

_____ 8. "*burgeoning* mail-order operations" (56)
   a. growing
   b. convenient
   c. new
   d. simple

_____ 9. "*consolidated* her operations" (65)
   a. combined
   b. separated
   c. localized
   d. improved

_____ 10. "*prosperous* company" (107)
   a. large
   b. diverse
   c. wealthy
   d. cosmetic

Search the Net

Use a search engine such as Google, Yahoo, Ask.com, Excite, Dogpile, or Lycos to find information on other self-made American business women. Find the history of two other women and share their stories with your class.

Concept Prep for History

What events led up to World War II?

After Germany was defeated in World War I, supposedly the "war to end all wars," the **Allies** (United States, Britain, France, and Russia) expected Germany to pay for the war they helped start. The Allies also changed the world map by taking away much of the German empire. The German people were stunned at their defeat, angry over the demands of the victors, and eventually unable to meet their debt payments. **Adolf Hitler,** a skillful and charismatic leader, seized this opportunity and tapped into the country's anger. He promised to restore national pride, and consequently many Germans were drawn to him. He became the leader of the **Nazi** party, adopted the **swastika** as its symbol, and eventually became dictator of Germany.

Hitler strengthened the military, forged an alliance with Japan and Italy, and attacked and conquered much of continental Europe. When Britain, under the leadership of Prime Minister **Winston Churchill,** refused to bargain with Germany, Hitler ordered the **Luftwaffe,** the German air force, to destroy Britain from the air. The air raids, known as the **blitz,** failed in their purpose when the Royal Air Force (RAF) won the Battle of Britain. Hitler then attacked Russia.

What was the U.S. role in the war?

The United States, under **Franklin D. Roosevelt,** remained neutral. **Isolationists** opposed foreign involvement. That changed, however, on December 7, 1941, at 7:02 A.M., when the Japanese bombed **Pearl Harbor,** an American naval base in Hawaii. America declared war on that day. **General Douglas MacArthur** and **Admiral Chester Nimitz** were put in charge of forces in the Pacific, and **General Dwight D. Eisenhower** led the Allied soldiers in Europe.

What was D-Day?

Allied forces planned the liberation of Europe, and on June 6, 1944—on what came to be known as **D-Day**—thousands of brave soldiers secretly left England and stormed the beaches of Normandy,

Prime Minister Winston Churchill, President Franklin Roosevelt, and Soviet leader Joseph Stalin pose for pictures at the Yalta Conference in 1945.

France. After two weeks of desperate fighting, the troops moved inland and liberated Paris by August. The Allied armies drove toward **Berlin,** the capital of Germany, and on April 30, Hitler committed suicide to avoid capture. The Germans surrendered one week later, and the European part of the war was over. Hitler, with his anti-Semitic hatred, had killed more than 6 million innocent Jews. Many were taken by trains to concentration camps for extermination in gas chambers. This horrible carnage was called the **Holocaust.**

How did the war with Japan end?

The American forces in the Pacific were moving from island to island against fierce Japanese resistance. Victories were won with great loss of life. Harry Truman had become president and was told of the **Manhattan Project,** a top-secret plan to develop an atomic bomb. On August 6, 1945, the **Enola Gay** flew over **Hiroshima, Japan,** and dropped an atomic bomb that obliterated the city. Three days later, a second bomb was dropped over **Nagasaki.** Within a few days, the Japanese asked for peace, and a month later they officially surrendered to General MacArthur aboard the battleship **U.S.S. *Missouri*** in Tokyo Bay. World War II had come to an end.

95

Review *Questions*

After studying the material, answer the following questions:

1. How did the end of World War I affect the beginning of World War II? _____
   _____
   _____

2. Why were the Germans drawn to Hitler's message? _____
   _____
   _____

3. Who were Germany's allies in World War II? _____
   _____

4. Why did the Luftwaffe strike England? _____
   _____
   _____

5. Who were the isolationists? _____
   _____
   _____

6. What prompted the United States to enter the war? _____
   _____
   _____

7. What was the Holocaust? _____
   _____
   _____

8. What was D-Day? _____
   _____
   _____

9. What ended the war in Europe? _____
   _____
   _____

10. What ended the war in Japan? _____
   _____
   _____

Your instructor may choose to give a true-false review of these history concepts.

selection 2 Sociology

Contemporary *Focus*

Experts say that oral communication is 7 percent actual spoken words, 35 percent tone of voice, and 55 percent body language. In a growing global economy, conducting business across cultures can be tricky. Extra care must be taken to avoid unintentionally offending other people.

Culture Clash: Closing Gaps between Different Worlds Is Crucial to Building Team Trust

By Mary Brandel

Computerworld, February 16, 2006. Reprinted with permission. Copyright © 2006 by Computerworld, Inc., Framington, MA 01701. All rights reserved.

An Indian firm recently sent a greeting card to coworkers worldwide with the image of a swastika, an ancient and sacred symbol in that country. "Many people went ballistic," says Gopal Kapur, founder of the Center for Project Management in San Ramon, California. In fact, it took five managers hours of telephone conversations and many e-mails to calm the waters. The work of 14 international team members came to a halt for more than 11 days, delaying the project and costing thousands of dollars.

With so much room for misinterpretation, it's important to play it straight with both speech and body language. Keep your vocabulary basic, and avoid jokes, Rosen cautions, as they never translate. Don't use a lot of hand gestures—a thumb's up and the OK sign are obscene in places like Brazil, Australia, Spain and the Middle East.

"Since gestures have different meanings in different parts of the world, they can cause confusion," says Terri Morrison, president of Getting Through Customs, which provides books and seminars for international travelers. This is particularly true in "high context" cultures such as Japan, France and many Arab countries.

"While Americans have no problem jumping into a business discussion as soon as a meeting begins, it's considered insulting in places like the Far East to begin negotiations before socializing and forming a relationship, even if that takes days," says Norbert Kubilus of Sunterra Corporation, a resort company in Las Vegas.

COLLABORATE Collaborate on responses to the following questions:

➤ When business is conducted in the United States, how is silence regarded?

➤ How would you react if a same-gender Russian businessperson kissed you on the mouth?

➤ Among Americans, what do words such as *issues* and *challenge* really mean in business conversations?

Skill Development: Preview

Preview the next selection to predict its purpose and organization and to formulate your learning plan.

Activate Schema

Is it wrong for primitive tribal people to wear no clothes?
Does social status exist in primitive cultures?
Would you eat insects if doing so meant survival?

Establish a Purpose for Reading

The phrase "unity in diversity" is a paradox. What does the author mean by this, and what do you expect to learn from this selection?

As you read, notice the author's use of examples to help you fully absorb the concepts of cultural universals, adaptation, relativity, ethnocentrism, norms, and values. Read with the intention of discovering that there are behavior patterns and institutions essential to all known societies, despite wide cultural variations in their expression.

Increase Word Knowledge

What do you know about these words?

curb	naïveté	adornments	articulate	bizarre
smirk	abstained	postpartum	agile	consign

Your instructor may give a true-false vocabulary review before or after reading.

Integrate Knowledge While Reading

Questions have been inserted in the margins to stimulate your thinking while reading. Remember to

Predict	Picture	Relate	Monitor	Correct

UNITY IN DIVERSITY

Does this title make sense, or are these words opposites?

What is more basic, more "natural" than love between a man and woman? Eskimo men offer their wives to guests and friends as a gesture of hospitality; both husband and wife feel extremely offended if the guest declines. The Banaro of New Guinea believe it would be disastrous for a woman to conceive her first child by her hus-
5   band and not by one of her father's close friends, as is their custom.

The real father is a close friend of the bride's father. . . . Nevertheless the first-born child inherits the name and possessions of the husband. An American would deem such a custom immoral, but the Banaro tribesmen would be equally shocked to discover that the first-born child of an Amer-
10   ican couple is the offspring of the husband.

The Yanomamö of Northern Brazil, whom anthropologist Napoleon A. Chagnon named "the fierce people," encourage what we would consider extreme disrespect. Small boys are applauded for striking their mothers and fathers in the face. Yanomamö parents would laugh at our efforts to curb aggression in children, much as they laughed at Chagnon's naïveté when he first came to live with them.

The variations among cultures are startling, yet all peoples have customs and beliefs about marriage, the bearing and raising of children, sex, and hospitality—to name just a few of the universals anthropologists have discovered in their cross-cultural explorations. But the *details* of cultures do indeed vary: in this country, not so many years ago, when a girl was serious about a boy and he about her, she wore his fraternity pin over her heart; in the Fiji Islands, girls put hibiscus flowers behind their ears when they are in love. The specific gestures are different but the impulse to symbolize feelings, to dress courtship in ceremonies, is the same. How do we explain this unity in diversity?

CULTURAL UNIVERSALS

Cultural universals are all of the behavior patterns and institutions that have been found in all known cultures. Anthropologist George Peter Murdock identified over sixty cultural universals, including a system of social status, marriage, body adornments, dancing, myths and legends, cooking, incest taboos, inheritance rules, puberty customs, and religious rituals.

The universals of culture may derive from the fact that all societies must perform the same essential functions if they are to survive—including organization, motivation, communication, protection, the socialization of new members, and the replacement of those who die. In meeting these prerequisites for group life, people inevitably design similar—though not identical—patterns for living. As Clyde Kluckhohn wrote, "All cultures constitute somewhat distinct answers to essentially the same questions posed by human biology and by the generalities of the human situation."

The way in which a people articulates cultural universals depends in large part on their physical and social environment—that is, on the climate in which they live, the materials they have at hand, and the peoples with whom they establish contact.

What would your parents do if you slapped either of them in the face?

Why would incest have to be a taboo for a surviving culture?

In a traditional Indian wedding ceremony, the bride and groom pray at the altar.

Omni Photo Communications Inc./Index Stock Imagery, Inc.

For example, the wheel has long been considered one of humankind's greatest inventions, and anthropologists were baffled for a long time by the fact that the great civi-
lizations of South America never discovered it. Then researchers uncovered a number of toys with wheels. Apparently the Aztecs and their neighbors did know about
wheels; they simply didn't find them useful in their mountainous environment.

What is your mental picture?

ADAPTATION, RELATIVITY, AND ETHNOCENTRISM

Taken out of context, almost any custom will seem bizarre, perhaps cruel, or just
plain ridiculous. To understand why the Yanomamö encourage aggressive behavior in
their sons, for example, you have to try to see things through their eyes. The
Yanomamö live in a state of chronic warfare; they spend much of their time planning
for and defending against raids with neighboring tribes. If Yanomamö parents did not
encourage aggression in a boy, he would be ill-equipped for life in their society.
Socializing boys to be aggressive is adaptive for the Yanomamö because it enhances
their capacity for survival. "In general, culture is . . . adaptive because it often provides
people with a means of adjusting to the physiological needs of their own bodies, to
their physical-geographical environment and to their social environments as well."

In many tropical societies, there are strong taboos against a mother having sexual intercourse with a man until her child is at least two years old. As a Hausa
woman explains,

> A mother should not go to her husband while she has a child who is suck-
> ing . . . if she only sleeps with her husband and does not become pregnant,
> it will not hurt her child, it will not spoil her milk. But if another child en-
> ters in, her milk will make the first one ill.

Undoubtedly, people would smirk at a woman who nursed a two-year-old child
in our society and abstained from having sex with her husband. Why do Hausa
women behave in a way that seems so overprotective and overindulgent to us? In
tropical climates protein is scarce. If a mother were to nurse more than one child at
a time, or if she were to wean a child before it reached the age of two, the youngster
would be prone to *kwashiorkor*, an often fatal disease resulting from protein defi-
ciency. Thus, long postpartum sex taboos are adaptive. In a tropical environment a
postpartum sex taboo and a long period of breast-feeding solve a serious problem.

No custom is good or bad, right or wrong in itself; each one must be examined
in light of the culture as a whole and evaluated in terms of how it works in the context of the entire culture. Anthropologists and sociologists call this *cultural relativity*. Although this way of thinking about culture may seem self-evident today, it is a
lesson that anthropologists and the missionaries who often preceded them to remote areas learned the hard way, by observing the effects their best intentions had
on peoples whose way of life was quite different from their own. In an article on
the pitfalls of trying to "uplift" peoples whose ways seem backward and inefficient,
Don Adams quotes an old Oriental story:

Why did missionaries want to clothe the islanders?

> Once upon a time there was a great flood, and involved in this flood were
> two creatures, a monkey and a fish. The monkey, being agile and experi-
> enced, was lucky enough to scramble up a tree and escape the raging wa-
> ters. As he looked down from his safe perch, he saw the poor fish struggling
> against the swift current. With the very best intentions, he reached down
> and lifted the fish from the water. The result was inevitable.

What is the difference between adaptation and relativity?

85   *Ethnocentrism* is the tendency to see one's own way of life, including behaviors, beliefs, values, and norms as the only right way of living. Robin Fox points out that "any human group is ever ready to consign another recognizably different human group to the other side of the boundary. It is not enough to possess culture to be fully human, you have to possess *our* culture."

VALUES AND NORMS

90   The Tangu, who live in a remote part of New Guinea, play a game called *taketak*, which in many ways resembles bowling. The game is played with a top that has been fashioned from a dried fruit and with two groups of coconut stakes that are driven into the ground (more or less like bowling pins). The players divide into two teams. Members of the first team take turns throwing the top into the batch of
95   stakes; every stake the top hits is removed. Then the second team steps to the line and tosses the top into their batch of stakes. The object of the game, surprisingly, is not to knock over as many stakes as possible. Rather, the game continues until both teams have removed the *same* number of stakes. Winning is completely irrelevant.

What will be covered in this next part?

In a sense games are practice for "real life"; they reflect the values of the cul-
100   ture in which they are played. *Values* are the criteria people use in assessing their daily lives, arranging their priorities, measuring their pleasures and pains, choosing between alternative courses of action. The Tangu value equivalence: the idea of one individual or group winning and another losing bothers them, for they believe winning generates ill-will. In fact, when Europeans brought soccer to the Tangu,
105   they altered the rules so that the object of the game was for two teams to score the same number of goals. Sometimes their soccer games went on for days! American games, in contrast, are highly competitive; there are *always* winners and losers. Many rule books include provisions for overtime and "sudden death" to prevent ties, which leave Americans dissatisfied. World Series, Superbowls, cham-
110   pionships in basketball and hockey, Olympic Gold Medals are front-page news in this country. In the words of the late football coach Vince Lombardi, "Winning isn't everything, it's the only thing."

How do you know appropriate dress for a place of worship? Are rules written on the door?

Norms, the rules that guide behavior in everyday situations, are derived from values, but norms and values can conflict. You may recall a news item that appeared
115   in American newspapers in December 1972, describing the discovery of survivors of a plane crash 12,000 feet in the Andes. The crash had occurred on October 13; sixteen of the passengers (a rugby team and their supporters) managed to survive for sixty-nine days in near-zero temperatures. The story made headlines because, to stay alive, the survivors had eaten parts of their dead companions. Officials, speak-
120   ing for the group, stressed how valiantly the survivors had tried to save the lives of the injured people and how they had held religious services regularly. The survivors' explanations are quite interesting, for they reveal how important it is to people to justify their actions, to resolve conflicts in norms and values (here, the positive value of survival vs. the taboo against cannibalism). Some of the survivors compared their
125   action to a heart transplant, using parts of a dead person's body to save another person's life. Others equated their act with the sacrament of communion. In the words of one religious survivor, "If we would have died, it would have been suicide, which is condemned by the Roman Catholic faith."

(1,679 words)

—By Donald Light, Jr., and Suzanne Keller, *Sociology*, 5th ed.
Copyright © 1989 by The McGraw-Hill Companies, Inc.
Reproduced with permission of The McGraw-Hill Companies.

Recall

Stop to self-test, relate, and react. Use the subheadings in the recall diagram shown here to guide your thinking. For each subheading, jot down a key idea that you feel is important to remember.

```
┌─────────────────────────────────────────────────────────┐
│  (Topic) _____ │
│  (Significant  _____ │
│   details)     _____ │
│                _____ │
│                _____ │
│                _____ │
│                _____ │
│                _____ │
│                                                           │
│  (Relate)    ------------------------------------------   │
│                                                           │
│  (React)     _____  │
└─────────────────────────────────────────────────────────┘
```

Your instructor may choose to give you a true-false comprehension review.

Write About the Selection

Define the following terms and describe two examples for each that are not mentioned in the selection:

cultural	universals	adaptation	relativity
ethnocentrism	norms	values	

Response Suggestion: Define the cultural concepts in your own words and relate examples from contemporary society.

Contemporary *Link*

Why might business meals be considered "minefields of opportunity" for embarrassment in foreign cultures? From a cultural relativity perspective, discuss how certain gestures can be acceptable in one culture but unacceptable in another.

Check Your Comprehension

After reading the selection, answer the following questions with *a, b, c,* or *d*. To help you analyze your strengths and weaknesses, the question types are indicated.

Main Idea _____ 1. Which is the best statement of the main idea of this selection?

   a. Practices and customs in society show few threads of cultural unity.
   b. The unusual variations in societies gain acceptability because of the cultural universals in all known societies.
   c. A variety of cultural universals provides adaptive choices for specific societies.
   d. Cultural universals are found in all known societies, even though the details of the cultures may vary widely.

Inference _____ 2. The author believes that the primary cultural universal addressed in the Eskimo custom of offering wives to guests is

   a. bearing and raising of children.
   b. social status.
   c. hospitality.
   d. incest taboos.

Detail _____ 3. The custom of striking practiced by the Yanomamö serves the adaptive function of

   a. developing fierce warriors.
   b. binding parent and child closer together.
   c. developing physical respect for parents.
   d. encouraging early independence from parental care.

Detail _____ 4. *Cultural universals* might be defined as

   a. each culture in the universe.
   b. similar basic living patterns.
   c. the ability for cultures to live together in harmony.
   d. the differences among cultures.

Inference _____ 5. The author implies that cultural universals exist because of

   a. a social desire to be more alike.
   b. the differences in cultural behavior patterns.
   c. the competition among societies.
   d. survival needs in group life.

Inference _____ 6. The author suggests that the wheel was not a part of the ancient Aztec civilization because the Aztecs

   a. did not find wheels useful in their mountainous environment.
   b. were not intelligent enough to invent wheels.
   c. were baffled by inventions.
   d. did not have the materials to develop them.

selection 2

Inference _____ 7. The underlying reason for the postpartum sexual taboo of the Hausa is

a. sexual.
b. nutritional.
c. moral.
d. religious.

Inference _____ 8. The term *cultural relativity* explains why a custom can be considered

a. right or wrong regardless of culture.
b. right or wrong according to the number of people practicing it.
c. right in one culture and wrong in another.
d. wrong if in conflict with cultural universals.

Inference _____ 9. The author relates Don Adams's Asian story to show that missionaries working in other cultures

a. should be sent back home.
b. can do more harm than good.
c. purposely harm the culture to seek selfish ends.
d. usually do not have a genuine concern for the people.

Inference _____ 10. The tendency of ethnocentrism would lead most Americans to view the Eskimo practice of wife sharing as

a. right.
b. wrong.
c. right for Eskimos but wrong for most Americans.
d. a custom about which an outsider should have no opinion.

Answer the following questions with *T* (true) or *F* (false):

Inference _____ 11. An American's acceptance of the Banaro tribal custom of fathering the firstborn is an example of an understanding by cultural relativity.

Inference _____ 12. The author feels that the need to symbolize feelings in courtship is a cultural universal.

Inference _____ 13. The author feels that culture is not affected by climate.

Detail _____ 14. The author states that all societies must have a form of organization if they are to survive.

Inference _____ 15. The author implies that the rugby team that crashed in the Andes could have survived without eating human flesh.

Build Your Vocabulary

According to the way the italicized word is used in the selection, select *a*, *b*, *c*, or *d* for the word or phrase that gives the best definition. The number in parentheses indicates the line of the passage in which the word is located.

_____ 1. "efforts to *curb* aggression" (14)
   a. stabilize
   b. release
   c. promote
   d. restrain

_____ 2. "To *symbolize* feelings" (23)
   a. represent
   b. hide
   c. ignore
   d. simplify

_____ 3. "body *adornments*" (27)
   a. ailments
   b. treatments
   c. scars
   d. decorations

_____ 4. "*articulates* cultural universals" (37)
   a. remembers
   b. designs
   c. expresses clearly
   d. substitutes

_____ 5. "will seem *bizarre*" (45)
   a. phony
   b. unjust
   c. very strange
   d. unnecessary

_____ 6. "*smirk* at a woman" (62)
   a. refuse to tolerate
   b. smile conceitedly
   c. lash out
   d. acknowledge approvingly

_____ 7. "*abstained* from having sex" (63)
   a. matured
   b. regained
   c. refrained
   d. reluctantly returned

_____ 8. "long *postpartum* sex taboos" (68)
   a. after childbirth
   b. awaited
   c. subcultural
   d. complicated

_____ 9. "being *agile* and experienced" (80)
   a. eager
   b. nimble
   c. young
   d. knowledgeable

_____ 10. "ready to *consign*" (87)
   a. assign
   b. transfer
   c. reorganize
   d. overlook

Search the Net

Use a search engine such as Google, AltaVista, Excite, Infoseek, Dogpile, Yahoo, or Lycos to find information on Latin American business and cultural etiquette, and highlight the differences. Pretend your company wishes to expand into Latin America, and write a memo to the company president summarizing your research. For suggested Web sites and other research activities, go to http://www.ablongman.com/smith/.

Although the "Unity in Diversity" selection is from a sociology textbook, the passage deals with concepts in anthropology. Thus, this section will also explore anthropology.

What is anthropology?

Anthropology is the study of humankind. It focuses on the origins and development of humans and their diverse cultures. By seeking to understand, respect, and applaud human diversity, anthropology might be considered the first multicultural course on college campuses. Special areas that you can study in anthropology include the following:

- **Physical anthropology:** How did humans evolve? What does genetic and fossil evidence reveal about our place in the animal kingdom?
- **Cultural anthropology:** What was the purpose of primitive customs and behaviors, and what do they reveal about contemporary social problems?
- **Archaeology:** What can we reconstruct about extinct societies and their cultures from artifacts such as ancient bones, pieces of pottery, and excavated ruins?

Who are famous anthropologists?

- In search of our human origins, **Louis and Mary Leakey** sifted through the dirt of **Olduvai Gorge** in Tanzania, East Africa, for more than 25 years. Finally, in 1959 they unearthed a humanlike upper jaw with teeth and a skull. This discovery of a hominid 1.75 million years old revealed that the first humans originated in Africa.
- Cultural anthropology was popularized by **Margaret Mead** with the publication of her book *Coming of Age in Samoa*, published in 1928. Mead observed children moving into adolescence and described the transition as happy. She argued that the stress of adolescence is cultural, but others later disagreed. Mead also studied male and female roles in

Husband and wife Louis and Mary Leakey study fossilized skull fragments that might belong to the "missing link" between ape and man.

different societies and argued that gender roles are cultural rather than inborn.

Who were our early ancestors?

- **Lucy,** one of the greatest archaeological treasures, is the nickname for the most complete human skeleton of early ancestors ever found. Lucy is more than 3 million years old and was unearthed in Ethiopia.
- The **Cro-Magnons** were the earliest form of modern humans, who lived about 35,000 years ago. Their cave paintings in Europe are the first known human art.
- The earliest societies were **hunting and gathering societies.** People roamed widely to hunt wild animals and fish and to gather fruits and nuts. Usually, this **nomadic** wandering was seasonal and calculated to create the best opportunities for finding available food. Not until 10,000 years ago did humans begin to domesticate plants and animals and thus remain in one area.

Review *Questions*

After studying the material, answer the following questions:

1. Digging in New Mexico for prehistoric artifacts suggests what area of anthropology? _____

   _____

2. Living with tribal people in the Amazon to study their ways suggests what area of anthropology? _____

   _____

3. Analyzing DNA to link Asian and African people suggests what area of anthropology? _____

   _____

4. What did Mary and Louis Leakey discover? _____

   _____

   _____

5. Why was the Leakey discovery especially significant? _____

   _____

   _____

6. What did Margaret Mead investigate in Samoa? _____

   _____

   _____

7. Why was Mead's work especially significant? _____

   _____

   _____

8. Why is Lucy significant? _____

   _____

   _____

9. What was the artistic contribution of Cro-Magnons? _____

   _____

10. What phenomenon usually ends hunting and gathering societies? _____

   _____

   _____

Your instructor may choose to give a true-false review of these anthropology concepts.

4 Main Idea

- What is the difference between a topic and a main idea?
- What are the strategies for finding stated and unstated main ideas?
- What are the functions of major and minor supporting details?
- What is a summary?

Ford Smith, *Warm Embrace*, 2006. An original painting in acrylics on canvas, 30 × 30 inches.

What Is a Topic?

In this chapter we will discuss and practice what many experts believe is the most important reading skill and the key to comprehension: recognizing the main idea of a paragraph, passage, or selection. As you read—and regardless of what you are reading, whether it is a chapter from your history text or an article in the Sunday paper—it is important to answer the question "What's the point?" However, before attempting to discover the central point of a piece of writing, you must have a good sense of its topic.

A **topic** is like the title of a book or song. It is a word, name, or phrase that labels the subject but does not reveal the specific contents of the passage. Take a moment and flip back to the Table of Contents of this text. As you can see, the title of each chapter reflects its general topic. What's more, boldface heads within a chapter reflect subordinate topics, or subtopics. Similarly, individual passages beneath those heads have their own topics.

Think of the topic of a passage as a big umbrella under which specific ideas or details can be grouped. For example, consider the words *carrots, lettuce, onions,* and *potatoes*. What general term would pull together and unify these items?

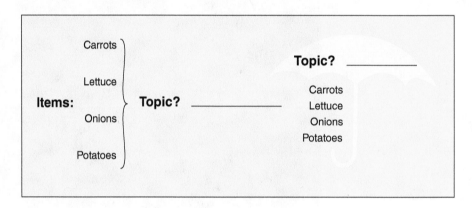

Topic: _____

exercise 4.1   **Identifying Topics**

Each of the following lists includes three specific items or ideas that could relate to a single topic. At the top of each list, write a general topic under which the specific ideas can be grouped.

1. _____
french fried
au gratin
scalloped

2. _____
tulip
rose
daisy

3. _____
Poodle
Schnauzer
terrier

4. _____
snow
rain
sleet

5. _____
triathlon
5K
marathon

What Is a Main Idea?

Using the topic as an initial indicator, the **main idea** of a passage becomes more focused and is the central message that the author is trying to convey about the material. It is a sentence that condenses thoughts and details into a general, all-inclusive statement of the author's point.

Reading specialists use various terms when referring to the main idea. In classroom discussions, a variety of words are used to help students understand its meaning. How many of these have you heard?

Main point

Central focus

Gist

Controlling idea

Central thought

Thesis

The last word on the list, *thesis*, is a familiar word in English composition classes. You have probably had practice in stating a thesis sentence for English essays, but you may not have had as much practice in stating the main idea of a reading selection. Can you see the similarity between a thesis and a main idea statement?

How important is it to be able to find and comprehend the main idea? Experts say that it is *crucial to your comprehension of any text*. In fact, if all reading comprehension techniques were combined and reduced to one essential question, that question might be "What is the main idea the author is trying to get across to the reader?" Whether you read a single paragraph, a chapter, or an entire book, your most important single task is to understand the main idea of what you read.

What Are Supporting Details?

Details are statements that support, develop, and explain a main idea. Specific details can include reasons, incidents, facts, examples, steps, and definitions.

There are important differences between *major details*, which are critical to the support of the main idea and your understanding of a passage, and *minor details*, which amplify the major details. One way to distinguish the two is to pay attention to signal words, which link thoughts and help you anticipate the kind of detail that is coming next. Key signal words for major supporting details are *one, first, another, furthermore, also,* and *finally*. Key signal words for minor details are *for example, to be specific, that is,* and *this means*. We will deepen our discussion of major and minor details later in this chapter.

Distinguishing Topics, Main Ideas, and Details: A Closer Look

We have seen that a topic is a general category, and that a main idea is the author's central message about the topic. Let's explore the difference between them—and the importance of supporting details—a little more closely.

Caffeine is a general term or topic that unifies the items *coffee, tea, cola,* and *chocolate*. If those items were used as details in a paragraph, the main idea could not be expressed by simply saying "caffeine." The word *caffeine* would answer the question, "What is the passage about?" However, only your evaluation of the supporting details in the paragraph would answer the question, "What is the author's main idea?"

Think of some of the very different paragraphs about caffeine that a writer could devise using the same four details as support. If you were that writer, what would be the main idea or thesis—using the four items as details—of your paragraph?

Topic: Caffeine

Main idea or thesis: _____

_____

EXAMPLE   Read the following examples of different main ideas that could be developed in a paragraph about the topic of caffeine. Explanations appear in italicized type.

1. Consumption of caffeine is not good for your health. (*Details would enumerate health hazards associated with each item.*)
2. Americans annually consume astonishing amounts of caffeine. (*Details would describe amounts of each consumed annually.*)
3. Caffeine makes money as the Starbucks star rises. (*Details would show the profits and expansion of the coffee giant.*)
4. Reduce caffeine consumption with the decaffeinated version of popular caffeine-containing beverages. (*Details would promote the decaffeinated version of each item.*)

EXAMPLE   Following are examples of a topic, main idea, and supporting detail.

Topic   **EARLY COGNITIVE DEVELOPMENT**

Main Idea   Cognitive psychologists sometimes study young children to observe the very beginnings of cognitive activity. For example, when children first begin to utter words and

Detail   sentences, they overgeneralize what they know and make language more consistent than it actually is.

—Christopher Peterson,
Introduction to Psychology

EXPLANATION   The topic pulls your attention to a general area, and the main idea provides the focus. The detail offers elaboration and support.

exercise 4.2   **Differentiating Topic, Main Idea, and Supporting Details**

This exercise is designed to check your ability to differentiate statements of the main idea from the topic and supporting details. Compare the items within each group, and indicate whether each one is a statement of the main idea *(MI)*, a topic *(T)*, or a specific supporting detail *(SD)*.

Group 1

_____ a. For poor farm families, life on the plains meant a sod house or a dugout carved out of the hillside for protection from the winds.

_____ b. One door and usually no more than a single window provided light and air.

_____ c. Sod Houses on the Plains

—James W. Davidson et al.,
Nation of Nations

Group 2

_____ a. She was the daughter of English poet Lord Byron and of a mother who was a gifted mathematician.

_____ b. Babbage and the Programming Countess

_____ c. Ada, the Countess of Lovelace, helped develop the instructions for doing computer programming computations on Babbage's analytical engine.

_____ d. In addition, she published a series of notes that eventually led others to accomplish what Babbage himself had been unable to do.

—Adapted from H. L. Capron,
Computers: Tools for an Information Age, 6th ed.

Group 3

_____ a. Fabiola Garcia worked at a 7-Eleven evenings and swing shifts, learning all aspects of the business as part of the screening and training process for prospective 7-Eleven franchise owners.

_____ b. Evaluating a Franchising Opportunity

_____ c. One of the best ways to evaluate a prospective franchisor is to spend a few months working for someone who already owns a franchise you're interested in.

_____ d. Fabiola also worked at headquarters to learn the franchisor's paperwork procedures.

—Adapted from Michael Mescon et al.,
Business Today, 10th ed.

Group 4

_____ a. Mexican American Political Gains

_____ b. During the 1960s, four Mexican Americans—Senator Joseph Montoya of New Mexico and Representatives Eligio de la Garza and Henry B. Gonzales of Texas and Edward R. Roybal of California— were elected to Congress.

_____ c. In 1974, two Chicanos were elected governors—Jerry Apodaca in New Mexico and Raul Castro in Arizona—becoming the first Mexican American governors since early in this century.

_____ d. Since 1960, Mexican Americans have made important political gains.

—James Kirby Martin et al.,
America and Its Peoples, vol. 2, 4th ed.

Group 5

_____ a. Increased contact does reduce prejudice, particularly under certain conditions such as when working toward a shared goal.

_____ b. For example, politically influential members of Israeli and Palestinian groups met informally for intense problem solving.

_____ c. Reducing Prejudice Through Contact

_____ d. The meetings, although not designed to reduce prejudice, nonetheless fulfilled one of the steps in that direction.

—Adapted from Stephen Kosslyn and Robin Rosenberg,
Psychology, 2nd ed.

Prior Knowledge and Constructing the Main Idea

How exactly do you figure out the main idea of a paragraph or passage? Researchers have investigated the processes readers use to construct main ideas. One researcher, Peter Afflerbach, asked graduate students and university professors to "think aloud" as they read passages on both familiar and unfamiliar topics.[1] These expert readers spoke their thoughts to the researcher before, during, and after reading. From these investigations, Afflerbach concluded that expert readers use different strategies for familiar and unfamiliar materials.

Here is the important finding: This research showed that *already knowing something about the topic is the key* to easy reading. When readers are familiar with the subject, constructing the main idea is effortless and, in many cases, automatic. These readers quickly assimilate the unfolding text into already well developed knowledge networks. They seem to organize text into chunks for comprehension and later retrieval. These "informed" readers do not have to struggle with information overload. Again, this shows that the rich get richer, and the initial struggle to build knowledge has many benefits.

By contrast, expert readers with little prior knowledge of the subject are absorbed in trying to make meaning out of unfamiliar words and confusing sentences. Because they are struggling to recognize ideas, few mental resources remain

_____

[1]P. Afflerbach, "How Are Main Idea Statements Constructed? Watch the Experts!," *Journal of Reading* 30 (1987): 512–18; and "The Influence of Prior Knowledge on Expert Readers' Main Idea Construction Strategies," *Reading Research Quarterly* 25 (1990): 31–46.

for constructing a main idea. These "uninformed" experts are reluctant to guess at a main idea and to predict a topic. Instead, they prefer to read all the information before trying to make sense of it. Constructing the main idea is a difficult and deliberate task for these expert but uninformed readers. Even a proven expert reader in history, for example, might struggle to read chemistry books until enough knowledge is built for main idea construction to be automatic.

Strategies for Finding the Main Idea

The following strategies for getting the main idea were reported by Afflerbach's expert readers. Can you see the differences in the thinking processes of the informed and uninformed experts?

"Informed" Expert Readers

Strategy 1. The informed expert readers skimmed the passage before reading and took a guess at the main idea. Then they read for corroboration.

Strategy 2. The informed experts automatically paused while reading to summarize or condense information. They stopped at natural breaks in the material to let ideas fall into place.

"Uninformed" Expert Readers

Strategy 1. Expert readers who did not know about the subject were unwilling to take a guess at the main idea. Instead, they read the material, determined the topic, and then looked back to pull together a main idea statement.

Strategy 2. The uninformed experts read the material and reviewed it to find key terms and concepts. They tried to bring the key terms and concepts together into a main idea statement.

Strategy 3. The uninformed experts read the material and then proposed a main idea statement. They double-checked the passage to clarify or revise the main idea statement.

What differences do you see between these approaches? Since introductory college textbooks address many topics that are new and unfamiliar, freshmen readers will frequently need to use the strategies of uninformed expert readers to comprehend the main ideas of their college texts. Until you build up your reserves of prior knowledge through the college courses you take, constructing main ideas for course textbooks is likely to be a *conscious effort* rather than an automatic phenomenon.

Main Ideas in Sentences

Before identifying main ideas in paragraphs, practice with a simple list of sentences. Read the sentences in the following group. They are related to a single topic, with one sentence expressing a main idea and two other sentences expressing detailed support. Circle the number of the sentence that best expresses the main idea, and write the general topic for the group.

EXAMPLE

1. The 1960 debate between John Kennedy and Richard Nixon boosted Kennedy's campaign and elevated the role of television in national politics.
2. Televised presidential debates are a major feature of presidential elections.
3. Ronald Reagan's performance in 1980 and 1984 debates confirmed the public view of him as decent, warm, and dignified.

Topic: _____

_____

—Adapted from James MacGregor Burns et al., *Government by the People*, 20th ed.

EXPLANATION The second sentence best expresses the main idea, declaring the importance of televised presidential debates. The other two sentences are details offering specific facts in support of the topic, which is the importance of televised presidential debates.

exercise 4.3 **Discovering Topics and Main Ideas in Sentence Groups**

Circle the number of the sentence that best expresses the general main idea, and write the general topic.

Group 1

1. Dentists are trying virtual reality headsets for their patients to help reduce anxiety about dental care.

2. Gradual exposure to takeoff and landing in a virtual environment allows would-be travelers to face their phobias and prepare to take the next step, a real flight.

3. Overcoming fear is a fast-growing application of virtual reality.

4. Topic: _____

_____

—Alan Evans et al., *Technology in Action*, 2nd ed.

Group 2

1. Men hunted, fished, and cleared land, but women controlled the cultivation, harvest, and distribution of crops, supplying probably three-quarters of their family's nutritional needs.

2. The role of women in the tribal economy reinforced the sharing of power between male and female.

3. When the men were away hunting, the women directed village life.

4. Topic: _____

_____

—Gary B. Nash et al., *The American People: Creating a Nation and a Society*, 6th ed., vol. 1: To 1877

Group 3

1. At present, the meaning of correlations between brain size and intelligence is not clear.

2. For example, females have about the same average intelligence as males, but generally have smaller brains.

3. The Neanderthals had larger brains than we do, but there is no evidence that they were smarter.

4. Topic: _____

_____

—Adapted from Stephen M. Kosslyn and Robin S. Rosenberg,
Psychology: The Brain, the Person, the World, 2nd ed.

Group 4

1. Relying on his extensive industry experience, JetBlue founder and CEO David Neeleman focused most of his energy on a few key factors that he felt would make or break his company.

2. JetBlue fills planes to capacity, gets more flying hours out of each aircraft, and saves on maintenance costs because its fleet is brand new.

3. By hiring younger, more productive workers and giving them stock options in lieu of high wages, JetBlue keeps labor expenses down to 25 percent of revenues (compared to Southwest's 33 percent and Delta's 44 percent).

4. Topic: _____

_____

—Adapted from Ricky W. Griffin and Ronald J. Ebert,
Business, 8th ed.

Group 5

1. Despite its rapid growth, the company has no public relations department, no human resources department, and no recruiting apparatus.

2. The founders of Outback Steakhouse have proved that unconventional methods can lead to profitable results.

3. Methods include opening solely for dinner, sacrificing dining-room seats for back-of-the-house efficiency, limiting servers to three tables each, and handing 10 percent of the cash flow to the restaurants' general managers.

4. Topic: _____

_____

—Adapted from John R. Walker,
Introduction to Hospitality, 4th ed.

Questioning for the Main Idea

To determine the main idea of a paragraph, article, or book, follow the three basic steps shown in the box below, and ask the questions posed in the Reader's Tip on page 119. The order of the steps may vary depending on your prior knowledge of the material. If you are familiar with the material, you might find that constructing the main idea is automatic and you can select significant supporting details afterward. If you are unfamiliar with the material, as may often be the case in textbook reading, you would need to identify the details through key terms and concepts first, and from them you would form a topic and a main idea statement.

> **Routes to the Main Idea**
>
> **For Familiar Material**
>
> Determine topic ► ► ► Identify key terms ► ► ► Find main idea
>
> **For Unfamiliar Material**
>
> Identify key terms ► ► ► Determine topic ► ► ► Find main idea

Stated Main Ideas

Like paragraphs, visual images also suggest main ideas. Photographers and artists compose and select images to communicate a message. Look at the picture shown below and then answer the questions that follow.

First and nine.

Milk's number one in my playbook. It has the nine essential nutrients I need to go all the way. So ask somebody to pass the milk. It's your best call.

PLAYERS

got milk?

National Fluid Milk Processor Promotion Board

What is the general topic of the photograph? _____

_____

What details seem important? _____

_____

What is the main idea the photographer is trying to convey about the topic? ____

_____

_____

_____

The topic of the picture is drinking milk. The details show football player Donovan McNabb holding a glass of it. From the white moustache on his upper lip, the viewer assumes that he has just had a sip of the beverage. Though the details are sparse, the viewer can spot references to McNabb's profession in the words on the poster, not to mention the padding he is wearing. The viewer can reason that McNabb is likely to drink milk to stay healthy, thus leading to peak performance in his sport. The main idea, "Drink milk to perform your best," is indirectly stated in the words under the photograph. The message is persuasive: We should imitate this noted athlete and take some time to drink a glass of milk.

Reader's Tip — Using Questions to Find the Main Idea

1. **Determine the topic.** *Who or what is this reading about?*
   Find a general word or phrase that names the subject. The topic should be broad enough to include all the ideas, yet restrictive enough to focus on the direction of the details. For example, the topic of an article might be correctly identified as Politics, Federal Politics, or Corruption in Federal Politics, but the last might be the most descriptive of the actual contents.
2. **Identify details.** *What are the major supporting details?*
   Look at the details and key terms that seem to be significant to see if they point in a particular direction. What aspect of the topic do they address? What seems to be the common message? Details such as kickbacks to senators, overspending on congressional junkets, and lying to the voters could support the idea of corruption in federal politics.
3. **Find the main idea.** *What is the message the author is trying to convey about the topic?*
   The statement of the main idea should be
   A complete sentence
   Broad enough to include the important details
   Focused enough to describe the author's slant
   The author's main idea about corruption in federal politics might be that voters need to ask for an investigation of seemingly corrupt practices by federal politicians.

The Topic Sentence

As in the photo, an author's main point can be directly stated in the material. When the main idea is stated in a sentence, the statement is called a **topic sentence** or **thesis statement**. Such a general statement is helpful to the reader because it provides an overview of the material.

Read the following examples and answer the questions for determining the main idea using the three-question technique.

EXAMPLE

Managers can regain control over their time in several ways. One is by meeting whenever possible in someone else's office, so that they can leave as soon as their business is finished. Another is to start meetings on time without waiting for late-comers. The idea is to let late-comers adjust their schedules rather than everyone else adjusting theirs. A third is to set aside a block of time to work on an important project without interruption. This may require ignoring the telephone, being protected by an aggressive secretary, or hiding out. Whatever it takes is worth it.

—Joseph Reitz and Linda Jewell,
Managing

1. Who or what is this passage about? _____

   _____

2. What are the major details? _____

   _____

   _____

3. What is the main idea the authors are trying to convey about the topic? _____

   _____

   _____

   _____

EXPLANATION   The passage is about managers controlling their time. The major details are *meet in another office, start meetings on time,* and *block out time to work.* The main idea, stated in the beginning as a topic sentence, is that managers can do things to control their time.

EXAMPLE

New high-speed machines also brought danger to the workplace. If a worker succumbed to boredom, fatigue, or simple miscalculation, disaster could strike. Each year of the late nineteenth century some 35,000 wage earners were killed by industrial accidents. In Pittsburgh iron and steel mills alone, in one year 195 men died from hot metal explosions, asphyxiation, and falls, some into pits of molten metal. Men and women working in textile mills were poisoned by the thick dust and fibers in the air; similar toxic atmospheres injured those working in anything from twine-making plants to embroidery factories. Railways, with their heavy equipment and unaccustomed speed, were especially dangerous. In Philadelphia over half the railroad workers who died between 1886 and 1890 were killed by accidents. For injury or death, workers and their families could expect no payment from employers, since the idea of worker's compensation was unknown.

—James W. Davidson et al.,
Nation of Nations

1. Who or what is this passage about? _____

   _____

2. What are the major details? _____

   _____

   _____

3. What is the main idea the author is trying to convey about the topic? _____

   _____

   _____

   _____

EXPLANATION The passage is about injuries from machines. The major details are *35,000 killed, 195 died from explosions and other accidents in iron and steel mills, poisoned dust killed workers in textile mills, and half of the rail workers who died were killed in accidents.* The main idea is that new high-speed machines brought danger to the workplace.

How Common Are Stated Main Ideas?

Research shows that students find passages easier to comprehend when the main idea is directly stated within the passage. How often do stated main ideas appear in college textbooks? Should the reader expect to find that most paragraphs have stated main ideas?

For psychology texts, the answer seems to be about half and half. One research study found that stated main ideas appeared in *only 58 percent* of the sampled paragraphs in introductory psychology textbooks.[2] In one of the books, the main idea was directly stated in 81 percent of the sampled paragraphs, and the researchers noted that the text was particularly easy to read.

Given these findings, we should recognize the importance of being skilled in locating and, especially, in constructing main ideas. In pulling ideas together to construct a main idea, you will be looking at the big picture and not left searching for a single suggestive sentence.

[2]B. Smith and N. Chase, "The Frequency and Placement of Main Idea Topic Sentences in College Psychology Textbooks," *Journal of College Reading and Learning* 24 (1991): 46–54.

What Are Major and Minor Details?

Textbooks are packed full of details, but fortunately all details are not of equal importance. Major details tend to support, explain, and describe main ideas—they are essential. Minor details, by contrast, tend to support, explain, and describe the major details. Ask the following questions to determine which details are major in importance and which are not:

1. Which details logically develop the main idea?
2. Which details help you understand the main idea?
3. Which details make you think the main idea you have chosen is correct?

Key signal words, like those listed in the Reader's Tip, form transitional links among ideas and can sometimes help you distinguish between major and minor details.

Reader's *Tip* — Signals for Significance

- Key words for major details:
  one   first   another   furthermore   also   finally

- Key words for minor details:
  for example   to be specific   that is   this means

EXAMPLE

Selena was the undisputed queen of Tejano, the music of the Texas-Mexico border. Her music epitomized the complexity of the border culture. Tejano music originated in the nineteenth century, when European immigrants introduced the accordion to the Texas-Mexico border. A fast-paced blend of Latin pop, German polka, and country rhythms, Tejano music combined the oompah music of Europeans with Mexican ballads known as *cumbias* and *rancheras*. Unlike many earlier Latina personalities, like Rita Hayworth and Raquel Welch, who gained their fame only after changing their names and projecting an exotic and sexy image, Selena never abandoned her Mexican American identity. Selena, who was 23 years old when she was slain, nevertheless achieved extraordinary popularity.

—Adapted from James Kirby Martin et al.,
America and Its Peoples, vol. 2, 5th ed.

1. The topic of the passage is
   a. Selena was slain.
   b. Tejano Music.
   c. Queen of Tejano Music.
   d. Mexican Ballads.

2. Indicate whether each of the following details is major or minor in support of the author's topic:

   a. Selena was true to her Mexican American identity.
   b. Raquel Welch changed her name.
   c. Selena was popular when she was slain at 23.

3. Underline the sentence that best states the main idea of this passage.

EXPLANATION   For the first response, the topic of the passage is *c*. Both *b* and *d* are too broad and *a* is an unfortunate detail. For the second item, *a* is a major detail because her music is Tejano, *b* is a minor detail not directly related to Selena, and *c* is a major detail because she is no longer living. The first sentence states the main idea.

exercise 4.4   **Identifying Topics, Stated Main Ideas, and Details in Passages**

Read the following passages and apply the three-question system. Select the letter of the author's topic, identify major and minor details, and underline the main idea. For each passage in this exercise, the answer to the third question will be stated somewhere within the paragraph.

Passage A

Experts agree that the crux of Brazil's disastrous prison situation is rooted in overcrowding. Many prisons have two to five times the number of inmates they were designed to hold. A Human Rights Watch/Americas inspection team discovered that single-person cells contained eight to ten prisoners, with some inmates tied to windows to reduce demand for floor space. While some slept in hammocks suspended from the ceiling, others were forced to lie on top of hole-in-the floor toilets.

—Adapted from Steven Barkan and George Bryjak,
Fundamentals of Criminal Justice

_____ 1. The topic of the passage is

   a. Human Rights Watch in Brazil
   b. Brazil's Prisons Overcrowded
   c. More Inspections Needed in Brazil
   d. Sleeping in Hammocks in Brazil

2. Indicate whether each of the following details is major or minor in support of the author's topic:

_____ a. Many prisons operate at two to five times capacity.

_____ b. A Human Rights Watch team inspected prisons in Brazil.

_____ c. Single-person cells contained eight to ten prisoners.

3. Underline the sentence that best states the main idea of this passage.

Passage B

The term *vegetarian* means different things to different people. Strict vegetarians, or *vegans,* avoid all foods of animal origins, including dairy products and eggs. Far more common are *lacto-vegetarians,* who eat dairy products but avoid flesh foods. Their diets can be low in cholesterol, but only if they consume skim milk and other low- or nonfat products. **Ovo-vegetarians** add eggs to their diet, while *lacto-ovo-vegetarians* eat both dairy products and eggs. *Pesco-vegetarians* eat fish, dairy products, and eggs. Some people in the semivegetarian category prefer to call themselves "non–red meat eaters."

—Rebecca J. Donatelle,
Health: The Basics, 4th ed.

_____ 1. The topic of the passage is

        a. Vegetarians Without Dairy Products.
        b. Becoming a Vegetarian.
        c. Different Vegetarian Categories.
        d. Health Issues for Vegetarians.

    2. Indicate whether each of the following details is major or minor in support of the author's topic:

       _____ a. Pesco-vegetarians eat fish.

       _____ b. Lacto-vegetarians have low-cholesterol diets if they consume skim milk.

       _____ c. Ovo-vegetarians add eggs to their diet.

    3. Underline the sentence that best states the main idea of this passage.

Passage C

Building and equipping the pyramids focused and transformed Egypt's material and human resources. Artisans had to be trained, engineering and transportation problems solved, quarrying and stone-working techniques perfected, and laborers recruited. In the Old Kingdom, whose population has been estimated at perhaps 1.5 million, more than 70,000 workers at a time were employed in building the great temple-tombs. No smaller work force could have built such a massive structure as the Great Pyramid of Khufu.

—Mark Kishlansky et al.,
Civilization in the West, 4th ed.

_____ 1. The topic of the passage is

        a. Training Laborers for the Pyramids.
        b. Resources Needed for Building Pyramids.
        c. Pyramid Building Problems.
        d. The Pyramids.

2. Indicate whether each of the following details is major or minor in support of the author's topic:

_____ a. The Old Kingdom had an estimated population of 1.5 million.

_____ b. More than 70,000 workers at a time were employed in building the great temple-tombs.

_____ c. Artisans had to be trained.

3. Underline the sentence that best states the main idea of this passage.

Passage D

If you're upset or tired, you're at risk for an emotion-charged confrontation. If you ambush someone with an angry attack, don't expect her or him to be in a productive frame of mind. Instead, give yourself time to cool off before you try to resolve a conflict. In the case of the group project, you could call a meeting for later in the week. By that time, you could gain control of your feelings and think things through. Of course, sometimes issues need to be discussed on the spot; you may not have the luxury to wait. But whenever it's practical, make sure your conflict partner is ready to receive you and your message. Select a mutually acceptable time and place to discuss a conflict.

—Adapted from Steven A. Beebe, Susan J. Beebe, and Diana K. Ivy, *Communication*

_____ 1. The topic of the passage is

a. Planning for Conflict Resolution.
b. Confrontation.
c. Being Productive.
d. Solving Problems.

2. Indicate whether each of the following details is major or minor in support of the author's topic:

_____ a. Give yourself time to cool off before you try to resolve a conflict.

_____ b. If you are upset, you are at risk for a confrontation.

_____ c. Call a meeting a week later for a group project.

3. Underline the sentence that best states the main idea of this passage.

Passage E

In a Utah case, the defendant fell asleep in his car on the shoulder of the highway. Police stopped, smelled alcohol on his breath, and arrested him for driving while intoxicated. His conviction was reversed by the Utah Supreme Court because the defendant was not in physical control of the vehicle at the time, as required by the law. In freeing the defendant, the Supreme Court judged that the legal definition of sufficiency was not established in this case because the act observed by the police was not *sufficient* to confirm the existence of a guilty mind. In other words, the case against him failed because he was not violating the law at the time of the arrest and because it was also possible that he could have driven while sober, then pulled over, drank, and fell asleep.

—Adapted from Jay S. Albanese,
Criminal Justice, Brief Edition

_____ 1. The topic of the passage is

a. Driving Drunk.
b. The Utah Supreme Court.
c. Sleeping Behind the Wheel.
d. Establishing Sufficiency for Drunken Driving.

2. Indicate whether each of the following details is major or minor in support of the author's topic:

_____ a. Police arrested the defendant for driving while intoxicated.

_____ b. The defendant was not violating a law at the time of the arrest.

_____ c. The case was tried in Utah.

3. Underline the sentence that best states the main idea of this passage.

Unstated Main Ideas

Unfortunately, even if details are obvious, you cannot always depend on the author to provide a direct statement of a main idea. To add drama and suspense to a description or narrative, the main idea may be hinted at or implied rather than directly stated. Main ideas are often unstated in other media as well, such as movies and photographs.

Look at the details in the photo on page 127 to decide what message the photographer is trying to communicate. Determine the topic of the picture, propose a main idea using your prior knowledge, and then list some of the significant details that support this point.

AP Photo

What is the topic? _____

_____

_____

What are the significant supporting details? _____

_____

_____

What is the point the photograph is trying to convey about the topic? _____

_____

_____

The topic of the photo is an emergency rescue. The scene is dominated by a helicopter hovering over people stranded by flood waters that have nearly reached the roof of the home. The viewer can assume that these people were the occupants of the house. Some of their belongings are visible on the roof. Different areas of the roof appear to have had shingles ripped away, possibly from a storm and/or from the victims trying to crawl to the top of the building to save themselves. The main idea the photographer is trying to convey is that the family on the roof has been through a disastrous hurricane and could easily lose their lives without the rescue attempt. This main idea is suggested by the details but is not directly stated in the picture.

Unstated Main Ideas in Sentences

Before identifying unstated main ideas in paragraphs, practice with a simple list of sentences. First, read the related sentences in the following group. Next, create a sentence that states a general main idea for the three related thoughts.

EXAMPLE

1. A landmark 1990 study found that 30 percent of Americans under 35 had read a newspaper the day before—a much lower percentage than their parents.

2. Attempts to win a younger audience have included *USA Today*'s color and glitz, originally aimed at younger readers.

3. By 2000, daily newspaper circulation was down to 52.8 million from a 62.8 million high in 1988.

—John Vivian,
The Media of Mass Communication

Main idea: _____

_____

EXPLANATION   The first sentence states that young readership is low. The second states an attempt to lure young readers, and the third states that circulation has declined by 10 million. The general main idea that reflects these sentences is that daily newspapers are not winning young readers and circulation is down.

exercise 4.5   **Determining Unstated Main Ideas**

Read the following related sentences and state the main idea:

Group 1

1. For over 200 years, *Encyclopedia Britannica* was considered the ultimate reference source.
2. *Britannica* looked the other way as competitors took advantage of new technologies and produced cheaper encyclopedias on CD-ROM.
3. *Britannica*'s sales slumped as consumers snapped up *Encarta* for $50 to $70 or enjoyed the free version installed on new computers.

—Michael Mescon et al.,
Business Today, 10th ed.

Main idea: _____

_____

Group 2

1. The middle class seldom uses the double negative ("I can't get no satisfaction"), whereas the working class often does.
2. The middle class rarely drops the letter "g" in present participles ("doin'" for "doing," "singin'" for "singing"), perhaps because they are conscious of being correct.
3. The middle class also tends to say "lay" instead of "lie," as in "Let's lay on the beach," without suggesting a desire for sex.

—Alex Thio,
Sociology, 5th ed.

Main idea: _____

_____

Group 3

1. The AIDS virus (HIV), which seemed to arise abruptly in the early 1980s, and the new varieties of flu virus that frequently appear, are not the only examples of newly dangerous viruses.
2. A deadly virus called the Ebola virus menaces central African nations periodically, and many biologists fear its emergence as a global threat.
3. In 2003, a deadly new disease called SARS (severe acute respiratory syndrome) appeared in China and soon spread throughout the world.

—Neil Campbell et al.,
Essential Biology

Main idea: _____

_____

Group 4

1. President George Washington converted the paper thoughts outlined in the Constitution into an enduring, practical governing process, setting precedents that balance self-government and leadership.
2. Thomas Jefferson, a skilled organizer and a resourceful party leader and chief executive, adapted the presidency to the new realities of his day with territorial expansions and sponsorship of the Lewis and Clark expedition westward.
3. President Lincoln is remembered for saving the Union and is revered as the nation's foremost symbol of democracy and tenacious leadership in the nation's ultimate crisis.

—James MacGregor Burns,
Government by the People, 20th ed.

Main idea: _____

_____

Group 5

1. Sales prospects are much more inclined to buy from people who make them feel good and with whom they have developed a personal bond, so begin by building a rapport.
2. Ask questions to find out the prospect's real needs, and describe the product or service accordingly to focus on the buyer's benefits.
3. Go for the final close and remember to ask for the order and stop talking so the customer can make the purchase.

—Michael Mescon et al.,
Business Today, 8th ed.

Main idea: _____

_____

Unstated Main Ideas in Paragraphs

Determining the main idea of a paragraph will be easier if you use the three-step questioning stategy on pages 118–119. The questions used to find an unstated main idea have a subtle difference, though. As you approach a passage with an implied or unstated main idea, begin by asking, "What is this about?" Reading carefully to identify key terms and major supporting details, draw a conclusion about the topic. Once you have determined the general topic of the paragraph, then ask yourself, "What do all or most of the key terms or major details suggest?" It is now up to you to figure out the author's point. Think as you read. Create an umbrella statement that brings these concepts together into a main idea statement.

EXAMPLE

Michael Harner proposes an ecological interpretation of Aztec sacrifice and cannibalism. He holds that human sacrifice was a response to certain diet deficiencies in the population. In the Aztec environment, wild game was getting scarce, and the population was growing. Although the maize-beans combination of food that was the basis of the diet was usually adequate, these crops were subject to seasonal failure. Famine was frequent in the absence of edible domesticated animals. To meet essential protein requirements, cannibalism was the only solution. Although only the upper classes were allowed to consume human flesh, a commoner who distinguished himself in a war could also have the privilege of giving a cannibalistic feast. Thus, although it was the upper strata who benefited most from ritual cannibalism, members of the commoner class could also benefit. Furthermore, as Harner explains, the social mobility and cannibalistic privileges available to the commoners through warfare provided a strong motivation for the "aggressive war machine" that was such a prominent feature of the Aztec state.

—Serena Nanda,
Cultural Anthropology, 4th ed.

1. Who or what is this about? _____

_____

_____

2. What are the major details? _____

_____

_____

3. What is the main idea the author is trying to convey about the topic?

_____

_____

EXPLANATION The passage is about Aztec sacrifice and cannibalism. The major details are: diet deficiencies occurred, animals were not available, and members of the upper class and commoners who were war heroes could eat human flesh. The main idea is that Aztec sacrifice and cannibalism met protein needs of the diet and motivated warriors to achieve.

exercise 4.6   **Identifying Unstated Main Ideas**

Read the following passages and apply the three-question system. Select the letter of the author's topic, identify major and minor details, and choose the letter of the sentence that best states the main idea.

Passage A

Until recently, the U.S. census, which is taken every ten years, offered only the following categories: Caucasian, Negro, Indian, and Oriental. After years of complaints from the public the list was expanded. In the year of the 2000 census, everyone had to declare that they were or were not "Spanish/Hispanic/Latino." They had to mark "one or more races" that they "considered themselves to be." Finally, if these didn't do it, you could check a box called "Some Other Race" and then write whatever you wanted. For example, Tiger Woods, one of the top golfers of all time, calls himself Cablinasian. Woods invented this term as a boy to try to explain to himself just who he was—a combination of Caucasian, Black, Indian, and Asian. Woods wants to embrace both sides of his family.

—Adapted from James M. Henslin,
Sociology, 5th ed.

_____ 1. The topic of the passage is

   a. Tiger Woods Speaks Out.
   b. The U.S. Census.
   c. Identify Your Race.
   d. The Emerging Multiracial Identity.

2. Indicate whether each of the following details is major or minor in support of the author's topic:

   _____ a. Tiger Woods is one of the top golfers of all time.

   _____ b. Tiger Woods wants to embrace both sides of his family.

   _____ c. Until recently, the U.S. census offered only four racial categories.

_____ 3. The sentence that best states the main idea of this passage is

   a. Citizens complained about the four categories of the previous census.
   b. The 2000 census took a new approach and allowed citizens to identify themselves as being of more than one race.
   c. Tiger Woods considers himself a combination of Caucasian, Black, Indian, and Asian.
   d. Information from the 2000 census will be more useful than data gathered from the previous census.

Passage B

The rate of incarceration of women in prison increased from 27 per 100,000 women in 1985 to 57 per 100,000 in 1998. Men still outnumber women in the inmate population by a factor of about 14 to 1, but the gap is narrowing—from 17 to 1 a decade ago. Women constituted only 4 percent of the total prison and jail population in the United States in 1980 but more than 6 percent in 1998.

—Adapted from Jay S. Albanese,
Criminal Justice, Brief Edition

_____ 1. The topic of the passage is

   a. Men Versus Women in Jail.
   b. Incarceration in America.
   c. The Increasing Number of Women in Jail.
   d. Overcrowded Prisons.

2. Indicate whether each of the following details is major or minor in support of the author's topic:

   _____ a. The rate of incarceration of women in prison in 1985 was 27 per 100,000.

   _____ b. The rate of incarceration of women in prison in 1998 was 57 per 100,000.

   _____ c. A decade ago men outnumbered women 17 to 1.

_____ 3. Which sentence best states the main idea of this passage?

   a. Men continue to outnumber women in the prison and jail population.
   b. The rate of incarceration is increasing for both men and women.
   c. In the last decade, the rate of women incarcerated has doubled.
   d. The role of women in society has changed in the last decade.

Interpreting the Main Idea of Longer Selections

Understanding the main idea of longer selections requires a little more thinking than does finding the main idea of a single paragraph. Since longer selections, such as articles or chapters, contain more material, tying the ideas together can be a challenge. Each paragraph of a longer selection usually represents a new aspect of a supporting detail. In addition, several major ideas may contribute to developing the overall main idea. Your job is to group the many pieces under one central theme.

For longer selections, add an extra step between the two questions "What is the topic?" and "What is the main idea the author is trying to convey?" The step involves organizing the material into manageable subunits and then relating those to the whole. Ask the following two additional questions: "Under what subsections can these ideas be grouped?" and "How do these subsections contribute to the whole?"

Use the suggestions in the Reader's Tip to determine the main idea of longer selections. The techniques are similar to those used in previewing and skimming, two skills that also focus on the overall central theme.

Reader's *Tip* — Getting the Main Idea of Longer Selections

- **Think about the title.** What does the title suggest about the topic?
- **Read the first paragraph or two to find a statement of the topic or thesis.** What does the selection seem to be about?
- **Read the subheadings** and, if necessary, glance at the first sentences of some of the paragraphs. Based on these clues, what does the article seem to be about?
- **Look for clues that indicate how the material is organized.** Is the purpose to define a term, to prove an opinion or explain a concept, to describe a situation, or to persuade the reader toward a particular point of view? Is the material organized into a list of examples, a time order or sequence, a comparison or contrast, or a cause-and-effect relationship?
- **As you read, organize the paragraphs into subsections.** Give each subsection a title. Think of it as a significant supporting detail.
- **Determine how the overall organization and subsections relate to the whole.** What is the main idea the author is trying to convey in this selection?

---

exercise 4.7   **Getting the Main Idea of Longer Selections**

Read each passage, and use the strategies in the Reader's Tip to determine the author's main idea.

Passage A: The Benefits of a Good Night's Sleep
College students are well known for "all nighters," during which they stay up through the night to study for an exam or to finish—or even to start—a paper due in the morning. Lack of sleep is nothing to brag or laugh about. Sleep is vital to your life and can help you function at optimal levels both physically and mentally.

On the physical side, sleep helps regulate your metabolism and your body's state of equilibrium. On the mental side, it helps restore your ability to be optimistic and to have a high level of energy and self-confidence. To keep your body in balance, more sleep is needed when you are under stress, experiencing emotional fatigue, or undertaking an intense intellectual activity such as learning.

During sleep, most people experience periods of what is called rapid eye movement (REM). These movements can be observed beneath closed eyelids. In REM sleep, the body is quiet but the mind is active, even hyperactive. Some researchers believe that REM sleep helps you form permanent memories; others believe that this period of active brain waves serves to rid your brain of overstimulation and useless information acquired during the day. REM sleep is the time not only for dreams but also for acceleration of the heart rate and blood flow to the brain.

During non-REM sleep, in contrast, the body may be active—some people sleepwalk during this period—but the mind is not. In spite of this activity, non-REM sleep is the time when the body does its repair and maintenance work, including cell regeneration.

Although much still needs to be learned about sleep and its functions, few would disagree that sleep plays a role in the maintenance of good mental health.

—B. E. Pruitt and Jane J. Stein,
Decisions for Healthy Living

1. What does the title suggest about the topic? _____

_____

_____

2. What sentence in the first paragraph suggests the main idea? _____

_____

_____

3. What subtitles would you give the second, third, and fourth paragraphs? _____

_____

_____

4. What is the main idea of the selection? _____

_____

_____

Passage B: Clothing as Communication

Besides protecting us from the elements, clothing is a means of nonverbal communication, providing a relatively straightforward (if sometimes expensive) method of impression management. Clothing can be used to convey economic status, educational level, social status, moral standards, athletic ability and/or interests, belief system (political, philosophical, religious), and level of sophistication.

Research shows that we do make assumptions about people based on their clothing. Communicators who wear special clothing often gain persuasiveness. For example, experimenters dressed in uniforms resembling police officers were more successful than those dressed in civilian clothing in requesting pedestrians to pick up litter and in persuading them to lend a dime to an overparked motorist. Likewise, solicitors wearing sheriff's and nurse's uniforms increased the level of contributions to law enforcement and healthcare campaigns.

Uniforms aren't the only kind of clothing that carries influence. In one study, a male and female were stationed in a hallway so that anyone who wished to go by had to avoid them or pass between them. In one condition, the conversationalists wore "formal daytime dress"; in the other, they wore "casual attire." Passersby behaved differently toward the couple depending on the style of clothing: They responded positively with the well-dressed couple and negatively when the same people were casually dressed.

Similar results in other situations show the influence of clothing. We are more likely to obey people dressed in a high-status manner. Pedestrians were more likely to return lost coins to well-dressed people than to those dressed in low-status clothing. We are also more likely to follow the lead of high-status dressers even when it comes to violating social rules. Eighty-three percent of the pedestrians in one study followed a well-dressed jaywalker who violated a "wait" crossing signal, whereas only 48 percent followed a person dressed in lower-status clothing. Women who are wearing a jacket are rated as being more powerful than those wearing only a dress or skirt and blouse.

As we get to know others better, the importance of clothing shrinks. This fact suggests that clothing is especially important in the early stages of a relationship, when making a positive first impression is necessary in order to encourage others to get to know us better. This advice is equally important in personal situations and in employment interviews. In both cases, your style of dress (and personal grooming) can make all the difference between the chance to progress further and outright rejection.

—Ronald B. Adler and George Rodman,
Understanding Human Communication, 8th ed.

1. What does the title suggest about the topic? _____

   _____

   _____

2. What sentence in the first paragraph suggests the main idea? _____

   _____

   _____

3. What subtitles would you give the second, third, fourth, and fifth paragraphs?

   _____

   _____

   _____

   _____

4. What is the main idea of the selection? _____

   _____

   _____

Passage C: Immigration in the 1800s

What had been a trickle in the 1820s—some 128,502 foreigners came to U.S. shores during that decade—became a torrent in the 1850s, with more than 2.8 million migrants to the United States. Although families and single women emigrated, the majority of the newcomers were young European men of working age.

This vast movement of people, which began in the 1840s and continued throughout the nineteenth century, resulted from Europe's population explosion and the new farming and industrial practices that undermined or ended traditional means of livelihood. Poverty and the lack of opportunity heightened the appeal of leaving home. As one Scottish woman wrote to an American friend in 1847, "We cannot make it better here. All that we can do is if you can give us any encouragement is to immigrate to your country."

Famine uprooted the largest group of immigrants: the Irish. In 1845, a terrible blight attacked and destroyed the potato crop, the staple of the Irish diet. Years of devastating hunger followed. One million Irish starved to death between 1841 and 1851; another million and a half emigrated. Although not all came to the United States, those who did arrived almost penniless in eastern port cities without the skills needed for good jobs. With only their raw labor to sell, employers, as one observer noted, "will engage Paddy as they would a dray horse." Yet, limited as their opportunities were, immigrants saved money to send home to help their families or to pay for their passage to the United States.

German immigrants, the second largest group of newcomers during this period (1,361,506 arrived between 1840 and 1859), were not facing such drastic conditions. But as Henry Brokmeyer observed, "Hunger brought me . . . here, and hunger is the cause of European immigration to this country."

—Gary B. Nash et al.,
The American People, 6th ed., vol. 1

1. What does the title suggest about the topic? _____
   _____
   _____

2. What subtitles could you give paragraphs one through four? _____
   _____
   _____
   _____

3. Is there one sentence that sums up the main idea in the passage? _____
   _____
   _____

4. What is the main idea of the selection? _____
   _____
   _____

Summary Writing: A Main Idea Skill

A **summary** is a series of brief, concise statements, in your own words, of the main idea and the significant supporting details. The first sentence should state the main idea or thesis; subsequent sentences should incorporate the significant details. Minor details and material irrelevant to the learner's purpose should be omitted. The summary should be written in paragraph form and should always be shorter than the material being summarized.

Why Summarize?

Summaries can be used for textbook study and are particularly useful in anticipating answers for essay exam questions. For writing research papers, summarizing is an essential skill. Using your own words to put the essence of an article into concise sentences requires a thorough understanding of the material. As one researcher noted, "Since so much summarizing is necessary for writing papers, students should have the skill before starting work on research papers. How much plagiarism is the result of inadequate summarizing skills?"[3]

Writing a research paper may mean that you will have to read as many as 30 articles and four books over a period of a month or two. After each reading, you want to take enough notes so you can write your paper without returning to the library for another look at the original reference. Since you will be using so many different references, do your note taking carefully. The complete sentences of a summary are more explicit than underscored text or the highlighted topic-phrase format of an outline. Your summary should demonstrate a synthesis of the information. The Reader's Tip outlines how to write an effective summary.

Reader's *Tip* —— How to Summarize

- **Keep in mind the purpose of your summary.** Your task or assignment will determine which details are important and how many should be included.
- **Decide on the main idea the author is trying to convey.** Make this main idea the first sentence in your summary.
- **Decide on the major ideas and details that support the author's point.** Mark the key terms and phrases. Include in your summary the major ideas and as many of the significant supporting details as your purpose demands.
- **Do not include irrelevant or repeated information.** A summary stays very focused and concise.
- **Use appropriate transitional words and phrases.** They'll show the relationship between ideas.
- **Use paragraph form.** Don't use a list or write in incomplete sentences.
- **Do not add your personal opinion.** Stick to the content of the material you are summarizing.

[3]K. Taylor, "Can College Students Summarize?" *Journal of Reading* 26 (March 1983): 540–44.

Read the following excerpt on political authority as if you were doing research for a term paper and writing a summary on a note card. Mark key terms that you would include. Before reading the example provided, anticipate what you would include in your own summary.

EXAMPLE

Types of Authority

Where is the source of the state's authority? Weber described three possible sources of the right to command, which produced what he called traditional authority, charismatic authority, and legal authority.

Traditional Authority

In many societies, people have obeyed those in power because, in essence, "that is the way it has always been." Thus, kings, queens, feudal lords, and tribal chiefs did not need written rules in order to govern. Their authority was based on tradition, on long-standing customs, and it was handed down from parent to child, maintaining traditional authority from one generation to the next. Often, traditional authority has been justified by religious tradition. For example, medieval European kings were said to rule by divine right, and Japanese emperors were considered the embodiment of heaven.

Charismatic Authority

People may also submit to authority, not because of tradition, but because of the extraordinary attraction of an individual. Napoleon, Gandhi, Mao Tse-tung, and Ayatollah Khomeini all illustrate authority that derives its legitimacy from *charisma*—an exceptional personal quality popularly attributed to certain individuals. Their followers perceive charismatic leaders as persons of destiny endowed with remarkable vision, the power of a savior, or God's grace. Charismatic authority is inherently unstable. It cannot be transferred to another person.

Legal Authority

The political systems of industrial states are based largely on a third type of authority: legal authority, which Weber also called *rational authority*. These systems derive legitimacy from a set of explicit rules and procedures that spell out the ruler's rights and duties. Typically, the rules and procedures are put in writing. The people grant their obedience to "the law." It specifies procedures by which certain individuals hold offices of power, such as governor or president or prime minister. But the authority is vested in those offices, not in the individuals who temporarily hold the offices. Thus, a political system based on legal authority is often called a "government of laws, not of men." Individuals come and go, as American presidents have come and gone, but the office, "the presidency," remains. If individual officeholders overstep their authority, they may be forced out of office and replaced.

—Alex Thio,
Sociology, 3rd ed.

1. To begin your summary, what is the main point? _____

_____

_____

_____

2. What are the major areas of support? _____

_____

_____

3. Should you include an example for each area? _____

_____

_____

Begin your summary with the main point, which is that Weber describes the three sources of authority as traditional, charismatic, and legal. Then define each of the three sources, but do not include examples.

Read the following summary and notice how closely it fits your own ideas.

Political Authority

Weber describes the three command sources as traditional, charismatic, and legal authority. Traditional authority is not written but based on long-standing custom such as the power of queens or tribal chiefs. Charismatic authority is based on the charm and vision of a leader such as Gandhi. Legal authority, such as that of American presidents, comes from written laws and is vested in the office rather than the person.

---

exercise 4.8   **Summarizing Passages**

Read the following passages, and mark the key terms and phrases. Begin your summary with a statement of the main point, and add the appropriate supporting details. Use your markings to help you write the summary. Be brief, but include the essential elements.

Passage A: Prosecutors

The task of prosecutors is to represent the community in bringing charges against an accused person. The job of the prosecutor is constrained by political factors, caseloads, and relationships with other actors in the adjudication process.

First, most prosecutors are elected (although some are appointed by the governor), so it is in their interests to make make "popular" prosecution decisions—and in some cases these may run counter to the ideals of justice. For example, prosecution "to the full extent of the law" of a college student caught possessing a small amount of marijuana may be unwarranted, but failure to prosecute may be used by political opponents as evidence that the prosecutor is "soft on crime."

A second constraint is caseload pressures, which often force prosecutors to make decisions based on expediency rather than justice. A prosecutor in a jurisdiction where many serious crimes occur may have to choose which to prosecute to the full extent of the law and which ones to plea-bargain.

Third, prosecutors must maintain good relationships with the other participants in the adjudication process: police, judges, juries, defense attorneys, victims, and

witnesses. Cases typically are brought to prosecutors by the police, and police officers usually serve as witnesses.

—Jay S. Albanese,
Criminal Justice

Use your marked text to write a summary.

Passage B: Suicide Among College Students

Compared to nonstudents of the same age, the suicide rate among college students
is somewhat higher. Why is this so? For one thing, among the younger college students who commit suicide (ages 18–22), a common thread is the inability to separate
themselves from their family and to solve problems on their own. College presents
many of these younger students with the challenge of having to be independent in
many ways while remaining dependent on family in other ways, such as financially
and emotionally.

Several other characteristics of the college experience may relate to suicide. A
great emphasis is put on attaining high grades, and the significance of grades may be
blown out of proportion. A student may come to perceive grades as a measurement of
his or her total worth as a person, rather than just one of many ways a person can be
evaluated. If a student is unable to achieve expected grades, there may be a total loss
of self-esteem and loss of hope for any success in life.

In the college setting, where self-esteem can be tenuous, the end of a relationship can also be devastating. A student who has recently lost a close friend or lover
can become so deeply depressed that suicide becomes an attractive alternative. The
problem can be compounded when depression interferes with coursework and
grades slip.

—Curtis O. Byer and Louis W. Shainberg,
Living Well: Health in Your Hands, 2nd ed.

Use your marked text to write a summary.

Passage C: Alcohol Advertising and College Students

The alcohol industry knows a receptive market when it sees it. Each year, college students spend a reported $5.5 billion ($446 per student) on alcohol, consuming some 4
billion cans' worth of alcohol and accounting for 10 percent of total beer sales. For
brewers, student beer drinking spells not just current sales, but future profits as well,
because most people develop loyalty to a specific beer between the ages of 18 and
24. To secure this lucrative market, brewers and other alcohol producers spend millions of dollars each year promoting their products to college students. One conservative estimate places annual expenditures for college marketing between $15 million
and $20 million. According to one survey, alcohol advertising of local specials in many
college newspapers has increased by more than half over the past decade, stymying
college and community efforts to reduce binge drinking.

—Rebecca J. Donatelle,
Health: The Basics, 4th ed.

Use your marked text to write a summary.

Passage D: Using Tree Rings to Study Past Climates

If you examine the top of a tree stump or the end of a log, you will see that it is composed of a series of concentric rings. Each of these tree rings becomes larger in diameter outward from the center. Every year in temperate regions trees add a layer of new wood under the bark. Characteristics of each tree ring, such as size and density, reflect the environmental conditions (especially climate) that prevailed during the year the ring formed. Favorable growth conditions produce a wide ring; unfavorable ones produce a narrow ring. Trees growing at the same time in the same region show similar tree-ring patterns.

Because a single growth ring is usually added each year, the age of the tree when it was cut can be determined by counting the rings. If the year of cutting is known, the age of the tree and the year in which each ring formed can be determined by counting back from the outside ring. This procedure can be used to determine the dates of recent environmental events such as the maximum number of years since a new land surface was created by a landslide or a flood. The dating and study of annual rings in trees is called dendrochronology.

—Frederick K. Lutgens and Edward J. Tarbuck,
The Atmosphere, 9th ed.

Use your marked text to write a summary.

Passage E: Advantages of Community Colleges

Community colleges provide a number of specific benefits. First, their low tuition cost places college courses and degrees within the reach of millions of families that could not otherwise afford them. Today, it is at community colleges that we find many students who are the first generation of their families to pursue a postsecondary degree. Compared to students who attend four-year colleges, a larger share of community college students are also paying their own way. The low cost of community colleges is especially important during periods of economic recession. Typically, when the economy slumps (and people lose their jobs), college enrollments—especially at community colleges—soar.

Second, community colleges have special importance to minorities. Currently, one-half of all African American and Hispanic undergraduates in the United States attend community colleges.

Third, although it is true that community colleges serve local populations, many two-year colleges also attract students from around the world. Many community colleges recruit students from abroad, and more than one-third of all foreign students enrolled on a U.S. campus are studying at community colleges.

Finally, while the highest priority of faculty who work at large universities typically is research, the most important job for community college faculty is teaching. Thus, although teaching loads are high (typically four or five classes each semester), community colleges appeal to faculty who find their greatest pleasure in the classroom. Community college students often get more attention from faculty than their counterparts at large universities.

—John J. Macionis,
Sociology, 10th ed.

Use your marked text to write a summary.

Summary *Points*

➤ **What is the difference between a topic and a main idea?**
The topic of a passage is the general term that forms an umbrella for the specific ideas presented, whereas the main idea is the message the author is trying to convey about the topic.

➤ **What are the strategies for finding stated and unstated main ideas?**
In some passages the main idea is stated in a sentence, and in others it is unstated. For both, ask, "Who or what is this about?" to establish the topic. Then look for the key supporting details that seem to suggest a common message. Finally, focus on the message of the topic by asking, "What is the main idea the author is trying to convey about the topic?"

➤ **What are the functions of major and minor supporting details?**
Major details support, develop, and explain the main idea, whereas minor details develop the major details.

➤ **What is a summary?**
Summaries condense material and include the main ideas and major details.

selection 1 Psychology

Contemporary *Focus*

What is the bond between a mother and infant, and why is it important? What is the long-term strength of that bond? Researchers have sought to define this special relationship and to test its lasting significance to the infant's development.

Mother's Love Works Like Opiate

By Benedict Carey
From "Addicted to Mother's Love: It's Biology, Stupid," *New York Times*, June 29, 2004.
Copyright © 2004 by The New York Times Co. Reprinted with permission.

A mother's love is like a drug, psychologists say, a potent substance that cements the parent-infant bond and has a profound impact on later development.

Warm, attentive parenting can, in fact, help baby animals overcome some genetic differences. In a series of experiments, scientists at McGill University in Montreal have shown that baby rats repeatedly groomed, cuddled and licked by their mothers grow up to be less anxious than those who received less coddling. In a study appearing in *Nature Neuroscience*, they report that this physical mothering early in life prompts long-lasting changes in the rats' genes that help the animals manage stress throughout their lives.

Researchers at the U.S. National Institutes of Health have demonstrated a similar effect in monkeys: Having parents that are warm and attentive protects young animals from a specific genetic variation that would—in the absence of such comfort and support—put them at high risk for aggressive, disruptive behavior. These well-nurtured monkeys tend to become attentive parents themselves. Their attachment to their mothers provides a model for the relationships they will form much later with their own children.

"The important part of all this is that we're showing that an attentive caregiver can actually alter the baby's genes, for the better," says Dr. Allan Schore, who studies attachment at the School of Medicine at the University of California, Los Angeles.

COLLABORATE Collaborate on responses to the following questions:

➤ How could early nurturing promote a lasting defense against stress?

➤ How is mothering learned by the next generation?

➤ Why do people think that being a good parent is an instinctive behavior?

Preview

Preview the next selection to predict its purpose and organization and to formulate your learning plan.

Activate Schema

Do parents who were not nurtured as children later abuse their own children?
As a child, what brought you the most emotional comfort?

Establish a Purpose for Reading

What does monkey love have to do with human behavior? In this selection, discover how scientists explain the importance of contact comfort and trust in an infant-mother relationship. Notice how the Harlows came to understand the psychological needs of an infant monkey and the effects that deprivation of those needs can have on the whole pattern of psychological development. As you read, predict what the implications of the Harlows' animal research might be for our understanding of human development.

Increase Word Knowledge

What do you know about these words?

surrogate	functional	anatomy	tentatively	novel
desensitized	ingenious	deprived	persisted	deficient

Your instructor may give a true-false vocabulary review before or after reading.

Integrate Knowledge While Reading

Questions have been inserted in the margins to stimulate your thinking while reading. Remember to

Predict	Picture	Relate	Monitor	Correct

MONKEY LOVE

The scientist who has conducted the best long-term laboratory experiments on love is surely Harry Harlow, a psychologist at the University of Wisconsin. Professor Harlow did not set out to study love—it happened by accident. Like many other psychologists, he was at first primarily interested in how organisms learn. Rather
5 than working with rats, Harlow chose to work with monkeys.

Since he needed a place to house and raise the monkeys, he built the Primate Laboratory at the University of Wisconsin. Then he began to study the effects of brain lesions on monkey learning. But he soon found that young animals reacted somewhat differently to brain damage than did older monkeys, so he and his wife
10 Margaret devised a breeding program and tried various ways of raising monkeys in the laboratory. They rapidly discovered that monkey infants raised by their mothers often caught diseases from their parents, so the Harlows began taking the infants away from their mothers at birth and tried raising them by hand. The

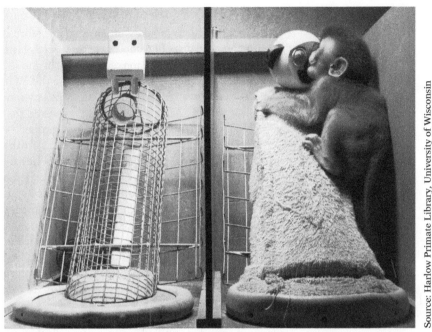

Although the monkey receives milk from Harlow's wire mother, it spends most of its time with the terry cloth version and clings to the terry-cloth mother when frightened.

Did you have a "security blanket" as a child?

15 baby monkeys had been given cheesecloth diapers to serve as baby blankets. Almost from the start, it became obvious to the Harlows that their little animals developed such strong attachments to the blankets that, in the Harlows' own terms, it was often hard to tell where the diaper ended and the baby began. Not only this, but if the Harlows removed the "security" blanket in order to clean it, the infant monkey often became greatly disturbed—just as if its own mother had 20 deserted it.

THE SURROGATE MOTHER

What the baby monkeys obviously needed was an artificial or *surrogate* mother— something they could cling to as tightly as they typically clung to their own mother's chest. The Harlows sketched out many different designs, but none really appealed to them. Then, in 1957, while enjoying a champagne flight high over the 25 city of Detroit, Harry Harlow glanced out of the airplane window and "saw" an image of an artificial monkey mother. It was a hollow wire cylinder, wrapped with a terry-cloth bath towel, with a silly wooden head at the top. The tiny monkey could cling to this "model mother" as closely as to its real mother's body hair. This surrogate mother could be provided with a functional breast simply by placing a milk bottle so 30 that the nipple stuck through the cloth at an appropriate place on the surrogate's anatomy. The cloth mother could be heated or cooled; it could be rocked mechanically or made to stand still; and, most important, it could be removed at will.

While still sipping his champagne, Harlow mentally outlined much of the research that kept him, his wife, and their associates occupied for many years to 35 come. And without realizing it, Harlow had shifted from studying monkey learning to monkey love.

INFANT-MOTHER LOVE

The chimpanzee or monkey infant is much more developed at birth than the human infant, and apes develop or mature much faster than we do. Almost from the moment it is born, the monkey infant can move around and hold tightly to its
40 mother. During the first few days of its life the infant will approach and cling to almost any large, warm, and soft object in its environment, particularly if that object also gives it milk. After a week or so, however, the monkey infant begins to avoid newcomers and focuses its attentions on "mother"—real or surrogate.

During the first two weeks of its life warmth is perhaps the most important
45 psychological thing that a monkey mother has to give to its baby. The Harlows discovered this fact by offering infant monkeys a choice of two types of mother-substitutes—one wrapped in terry cloth and one that was made of bare wire. If the two artificial mothers were both the same temperature, the little monkeys always preferred the cloth mother. However, if the wire model was heated, while the cloth
50 model was cool, for the first two weeks after birth the baby primates picked the warm wire mother-substitutes as their favorites. Thereafter they switched and spent most of their time on the more comfortable cloth mother.

Why is cloth preferable to bare wire? Something that the Harlows called *contact comfort* seems to be the answer, and a most powerful influence it is. Infant
55 monkeys (and chimps too) spend much of their time rubbing against their mothers' skins, putting themselves in as close contact with the parent as they can. Whenever the young animal is frightened, disturbed, or annoyed, it typically rushes to its mother and rubs itself against her body. Wire doesn't "rub" as well as does soft cloth. Prolonged "contact comfort" with a surrogate cloth mother appears to instill confi-
60 dence in baby monkeys and is much more rewarding to them than is either warmth or milk. Infant monkeys also prefer a "rocking" surrogate to one that is stationary.

According to the Harlows, the basic quality of an infant's love for its mother is *trust*. If the infant is put into an unfamiliar playroom without its mother, the infant ignores the toys no matter how interesting they might be. It *screeches* in terror and
65 curls up into a furry little ball. If its cloth mother is now introduced into the playroom, the infant rushes to the surrogate and clings to it for dear life. After a few minutes of contact comfort, it apparently begins to feel more secure. It then climbs down from the mother-substitute and begins tentatively to explore the toys, but often rushes back for a deep embrace as if to reassure itself that its mother is still
70 there and that all is well. Bit by bit its fears of the novel environment are "desensitized," and it spends more and more time playing with the toys and less and less time clinging to its "mother."

> How do toddlers explore and seek security?

GOOD MOTHERS AND BAD

The Harlows found that, once a baby monkey has come to accept its mother (real or surrogate), the mother can do almost no wrong. In one of their studies, the
75 Harlows tried to create "monster mothers" whose behavior would be so abnormal that the infants would desert the mothers. Their purpose was to determine whether maternal rejection might cause abnormal behavior patterns in the infant monkeys similar to those responses found in human babies whose mothers ignore or punish their children severely. The problem was—how can you get a terry-cloth mother to
80 reject or punish its baby? Their solutions were ingenious—but most of them failed in their main purpose. Four types of "monster mothers" were tried, but none of them was apparently "evil" enough to impart fear or loathing to the infant monkeys.

One such "monster" occasionally blasted its babies with compressed air; a second shook so violently that the baby often fell off; a third contained a catapult that fre-
85 quently flung the infant away from it. The most evil-appearing of all had a set of metal spikes buried beneath the terry cloth; from time to time the spikes would poke through the cloth making it impossible for the infant to cling to the surrogate.

The baby monkeys brought up on the "monster mothers" did show a brief pe-riod of emotional disturbance when the "wicked" temperament of the surrogates
90 first showed up. The infants would cry for a time when displaced from their moth-ers, but as soon as the surrogates returned to normal, the infant would return to the surrogate and continue clinging, as if all were forgiven. As the Harlows tell the story, the only prolonged distress created by the experiment seemed to be that felt by the experimenters!

95 There was, however, one type of surrogate that uniformly "turned off" the in-fant monkeys. S. J. Suomi, working with the Harlows, built a terry-cloth mother with ice water in its veins. Newborn monkeys would attach themselves to this "cool momma" for a brief period of time, but then retreated to a corner of the cage and rejected her forever.

100 From their many brilliant studies, the Harlows conclude that the love of an in-fant for its mother is *primarily a response to certain stimuli the mother offers*. Warmth is the most important stimulus for the first two weeks of the monkey's life, then contact comfort becomes paramount. Contact comfort is determined by the soft-ness and "rub-ability" of the surface of the mother's body—terry cloth is better than
105 are satin and silk, but all such materials are more effective in creating love and trust than bare metal is. Food and mild "shaking" or "rocking" are important too, but less so than warmth and contact comfort. These needs—and the rather primitive re-sponses the infant makes in order to obtain their satisfaction—are programmed into the monkey's genetic blueprint. The growing infant's requirement for social and in-
110 tellectual stimulation becomes critical only later in a monkey's life. And yet, if the baby primate is deprived of contact with other young of its own species, its whole pattern of development can be profoundly disturbed.

MOTHER-INFANT LOVE

The Harlows were eventually able to find ways of getting female isolates pregnant, usually by confining them in a small cage for long periods of time with a patient and
115 highly experienced normal male. At times, however, the Harlows were forced to help matters along by strapping the female to a piece of apparatus. When these iso-lated females gave birth to their first monkey baby, they turned out to be the "mon-ster mothers" the Harlows had tried to create with mechanical surrogates. Having had no contact with other animals as they grew up, they simply did not know what
120 to do with the furry little strangers that suddenly appeared on the scene. These motherless mothers at first totally ignored their children, although if the infant per-sisted, the mothers occasionally gave in and provided the baby with some of the contact and comfort it demanded.

Surprisingly enough, once these mothers learned how to handle a baby, they
125 did reasonably well. Then, when they were again impregnated and gave birth to a second infant, they took care of this next baby fairly adequately.

Maternal affection was totally lacking in a few of the motherless monkeys, however. To them the newborn monkey was little more than an object to be abused the way a human child might abuse a doll or a toy train. These motherless mothers

Do abused children return to cruel mothers?

Is mothering an instinctive or learned behavior?

130   stepped on their babies, crushed the infant's face into the floor of the cage, and once or twice chewed off their baby's feet and fingers before they could be stopped. The most terrible mother of all popped her infant's head into her mouth and crunched it like a potato chip.

We tend to think of most mothers—no matter what their species—as having
135   some kind of almost divine "maternal instinct" that makes them love their children and take care of them no matter what the cost or circumstance. While it is true that most females have built into their genetic blueprint the tendency to be interested in (and to care for) their offspring, this inborn tendency is always expressed in a given environment. The "maternal instinct" is strongly influenced by the mother's past
140   experiences. Humans seem to have weaker instincts of all kinds than do other animals—since our behavior patterns are more affected by learning than by our genes, we have greater flexibility in what we do and become. But we pay a sometimes severe price for this freedom from genetic control.

Normal monkey and chimpanzee mothers seldom appear to inflict real phys-
145   ical harm on their children; human mothers and fathers often do. Serapio R. Zalba, writing in a journal called *Trans-action*, estimated in 1971 that in the United States alone, perhaps 250,000 children suffer physical abuse by their parents each year. Of these "battered babies," almost 40,000 may be very badly injured. The number of young boys and girls killed by their parents annually is not
150   known, but Zalba suggests that the figure may run into the thousands. Parents have locked their children in tiny cages, raised them in dark closets, burned them, boiled them, slashed them with knives, shot them, and broken almost every bone in their bodies. How can we reconcile these facts with the much-discussed maternal and paternal "instincts"?

155   The research by the Harlows on the "motherless mothers" perhaps gives us a clue. Mother monkeys who were themselves socially deprived or isolated when young seemed singularly lacking in affection for their infants. Zalba states that most

How can the cycle of abuse be broken?

of the abusive human parents that were studied turned out to have been abused and neglected *themselves* as children. Like the isolated monkeys who seemed unable
160   to control their aggressive impulses when put in contact with normal animals, the abusive parents seem to be greatly deficient in what psychologists call "impulse control." Most of these parents also were described as being socially isolated, as having troubles adjusting to marriage, often deeply in debt, and as being unable to build up warm and loving relationships with other people—including their own children.
165   Since they did not learn how to love from their own parents, these mothers and fathers simply did not acquire the social skills necessary for bringing up their own infants in a healthy fashion.

(2,192 words)

—From James V. McConnell,
Understanding Human Behavior. Copyright © 1974.
Reprinted with permission of Wadsworth, a division of Thomson Learning.

Recall

Stop to self-test, relate, and react.

Your instructor may choose to give you a true-false comprehension review.

Write About the Selection

Explain and give examples of findings from the Harlows' experiments that you believe are applicable to human infants.

Response Suggestion: Describe the experimental finding and use examples to relate it to the psychological needs of human infants.

Contemporary *Link*

Research shows that the nurturing hand of a mother can release endorphins in the body to give feelings of relief and comfort, as well as positive messenger chemicals in the brain, such as dopamine. Accepting this, why are some people drawn into abuse? Why is this a generational cycle that is so difficult to break? What suggestions would you have for breaking the cycle for both the victims and the abuser?

Summarize

Using this selection as a source, summarize on index cards the information that you might want to include in a research paper entitled "Animal Rights: Do Scientists Go Too Far?"

Skill Development: Find the Main Idea

Answer the following with *T* (true) or *F* (false):

_____ 1. The main point of the first four paragraphs is that the Harlows' shift to studying monkey love occurred by accident.

_____ 2. In the second section titled "Infant-Mother Love," the main point is that an infant monkey needs the "contact comfort" of the mother to give it a feeling of security while interacting with the environment.

_____ 3. In the beginning of the section titled "Good Mothers and Bad," the main point is that baby monkeys will reject monster mothers.

_____ 4. In the beginning of the section titled "Mother-Infant Love," the main point is that the maternal instinct is not influenced by the mother's past experiences.

Check Your Comprehension

After reading the selection, write the topic and main idea to answer item 1. Answer items 2–10 with *a*, *b*, *c*, or *d*. To help you analyze your strengths and weaknesses, the question types are marked.

Main Idea   1. Who or what is the topic? _____

_____

What is the main idea the author is trying to convey about the topic?

_____

_____

Inference   _____   2. When Harry Harlow originally started his experiments with monkeys, his purpose was to study

a. love.
b. breeding.
c. learning.
d. disease.

Inference   _____   3. The reason that the author mentions Harry Harlow's revelations on the airplane is to show

a. that he had extrasensory perception.
b. that he liked to travel.
c. that he was always thinking of his work.
d. in what an unexpected way brilliant work often starts.

Detail   _____   4. In their experiments, the Harlows used all the following in designing his surrogate mothers *except*

a. a terry-cloth bath towel.
b. real body hair.
c. a rocking movement.
d. temperature controls.

Detail   _____   5. The Harlows manipulated their experiments to show the early significance of warmth by

a. heating wire.
b. changing from satin to terry cloth.
c. equalizing temperature.
d. creating "monster mothers."

Inference   _____   6. The Harlows found that for contact comfort, the cloth mother was preferable to the wire mother for all the following reasons *except*

a. the cloth mother instilled confidence.
b. the wire mother didn't "rub" as well.
c. the wire mother was stationary.
d. with the cloth mother, the infant felt a greater sense of security when upset.

Detail _____ 7. The Harlows' studies show that when abused by its mother, the infant will

    a. leave the mother.
    b. seek a new mother.
    c. return to the mother.
    d. fight with the mother.

Detail _____ 8. The Harlows' studies show that for an infant to love its mother, in the first two weeks the most important element is

    a. milk.
    b. warmth.
    c. contact comfort.
    d. love expressed by the mother.

Inference _____ 9. The Harlows' studies with motherless monkeys show that the techniques of mothering are

    a. instinctive.
    b. learned.
    c. inborn.
    d. natural.

Inference _____ 10. The Harlows feel that child abuse is caused by all the following problems *except*

    a. parents who were abused as children.
    b. socially isolated parents.
    c. parents who cannot control their impulses.
    d. parents who are instinctively evil.

Answer the following with *T* (true) or *F* (false):

Inference _____ 11. The author feels that love in infant monkeys has a great deal of similarity to love in human children.

Inference _____ 12. The author implies that isolated monkeys have difficulty engaging in normal peer relationships.

Detail _____ 13. After learning how to handle the first baby, many motherless mothers became better parents with the second infant.

Inference _____ 14. Zalba's studies support many of the findings of the Harlow studies.

Detail _____ 15. Harlow had initially planned to perform drug experiments on the monkeys.

Build Your Vocabulary

According to the way the italicized word was used in the selection, indicate *a, b, c,* or *d* for the word or phrase that gives the best definition. The number in parentheses indicates the line number of the passage in which the word is located.

_____ 1. "*surrogate* mother"(21)
    a. mean
    b. thoughtless
    c. loving
    d. substitute

_____ 2. "a *functional* breast"(30)
    a. mechanical
    b. operational
    c. wholesome
    d. imitation

_____ 3. "on the surrogate's *anatomy*" (32)
    a. body
    b. head
    c. offspring
    d. personality

_____ 4. "begins *tentatively* to explore" (68)
    a. rapidly
    b. hesitantly
    c. aggressively
    d. readily

_____ 5. "fears of the *novel* environment" (70)
    a. hostile
    b. literary
    c. dangerous
    d. new

_____ 6. "fears . . . are '*desensitized*'" (70)
    a. made less sensitive
    b. made more sensitive
    c. electrified
    d. communicated

_____ 7. "solutions were *ingenious*" (80)
    a. incorrect
    b. noble
    c. clever
    d. honest

_____ 8. "*deprived* of contact"(111)
    a. encouraged
    b. denied
    c. assured
    d. ordered into

_____ 9. "if the infant *persisted*" (121)
    a. stopped
    b. continued
    c. fought
    d. relaxed

_____ 10. "to be greatly *deficient*" (161)
    a. lacking
    b. supplied
    c. overwhelmed
    d. secretive

Search the Net

Use a search engine such as Google, Yahoo, AltaVista, Ask.com, Excite, Dogpile, or Lycos to find information on the signs of child abuse. List five indicators that a child may be suffering from abuse or neglect. For suggested Web sites and other research activities, go to http://www.ablongman.com/smith/.

Concept Prep for Psychology

What is classical conditioning?

Classical conditioning is the learning that takes place when a subject is taught, or conditioned, to make a new response to a neutral stimulus. This is illustrated by the research of **Ivan Pavlov,** a Russian scientist in the late nineteenth century. Pavlov was studying the basic processes of digestion, focusing on salivation in dogs. Because salivation is a **reflex,** it is an unlearned, automatic response in dogs. When presented with food, dogs will automatically salivate. As his research progressed, Pavlov noticed that the dogs would salivate at the sight of the assistant who delivered the food. At this point, Pavlov decided to investigate learning.

Pavlov reasoned that no learning was involved in the dog's automatic salivation (the **unconditioned response**) when presented with food (the **unconditioned stimulus**). He wondered, however, if he could teach the dogs to salivate at the sound of a bell. To investigate this, Pavlov decided to pair the sound of a bell with the presentation of the food—sound first, food second. The bell alone was a **neutral stimulus** that had never before caused salivation. After a number of **trials** (presenting sound and food together), the dogs became conditioned to associate the sound of the bell with the food. The dogs soon would salivate at the sound, even when the food was withheld. Learning had taken place; Pavlov had taught the dogs to react to a neutral stimulus. Once learning or conditioning had taken place, the sound became a **conditioned stimulus** and the salivation became a **conditioned response.** To take this experiment a step further, if the sound is consistently presented without food, the salivation response will gradually weaken until the dogs completely stop salivating at the sound of the bell (**extinction**). Pavlov's work on animals and learning laid the groundwork for the American behaviorists of the twentieth century.

What is behaviorism?

At the beginning of the twentieth century, many American psychologists disagreed with Freud's

Two pigeons seek food in a box developed by psychologist B.F. Skinner as part of his operant conditioning research.

psychoanalytical approach (see page 25). They wanted to measure behavior in the laboratory and explain personality in terms of learning theories and observable behaviors. **B. F. Skinner** was a leader in this new movement. He borrowed from Pavlov's work and conducted research on operant conditioning.

Skinner posed questions such as, What are your beliefs about rewards and punishments? Do consequences affect your behaviors? Are you a reflection of your positive and negative experiences? Skinner believed that consequences shape behavior and that your personality is merely a reflection of your many learned behaviors.

Skinner demonstrated **operant conditioning** (behaviors used to operate something) by putting a rat inside a small box that came to be known as a **"Skinner box."** The rat explored the box until eventually it found that it could make food appear by pressing a lever. The rat enjoyed the food and dramatically increased the lever pressings. The food was a **positive reinforcer** for the lever pressing. In other words, the food reinforced the behavior and increased it. To stop the lever-pressing behavior (**extinction**), the rat was given a shock each time the lever was touched. The shock was a **negative reinforcer.** Rewards are positive reinforcers, and punishments are negative reinforcers.

Behavior modification, a type of **behavior therapy,** uses the principles of classical and operant conditioning to increase desired behaviors and decrease problem behaviors. You can use these principles to train a pet, stop a smoking habit, or overcome a fear of flying. Does the desire to make a good grade (reward) affect your studying behavior? Skinner would say yes.

Review *Questions*

After studying the material, answer the following questions:

1. Who was Ivan Pavlov? _____

   _____

2. What is a reflex? _____

   _____

3. What is a neutral stimulus? _____

   _____

4. Why is the response to the food called unconditioned? _____

   _____

5. What is a conditioned stimulus? _____

   _____

6. What is extinction? _____

   _____

7. How did B. F. Skinner differ from Freud? _____

   _____

8. How does operant conditioning differ from classical conditioning? _____

   _____

9. What is the role of a positive reinforcer? _____

   _____

10. In behavior modification, what makes you want to change behaviors?

   _____

   _____

Your instructor may choose to give a true-false review of these psychology concepts.

selection 2   Criminal Justice

Contemporary *Focus*

Would you prefer that your 911 call be answered by a male or a female police officer? Studies show that female police officers are making progress toward equality, but biases do exist with public perception and within police departments. How do women actually perform on the job, and what changes are offering new opportunities?

Arresting Development

By Anna Morrell
Western Mail, February 25, 2006

Chief Superintendent Michele Williams of North Wales Police says, "With almost 30 years as an operational police officer I have personally witnessed a sea of change in attitudes towards women officers by both colleagues and members of the public and am encouraged by the opportunities now available to women in the service.

"I started my career in 1976 and was posted to Caernarfon where I was invariably detailed to station duty on a Friday and Saturday night, effectively preventing me from gaining experience in dealing with public order. These were the days when the specialist departments tended to have one token female who dealt, in the main, with issues surrounding women and children, and if you found yourself pregnant, then resignation was your only option (unless you could afford a full-time nanny). Your uniform was comprised of a pencil skirt, fitted tunic, and air

hostess style hat with a complimentary handbag in which you placed your 8-inch wooden baton for protection when you were let out on your own! Opportunities were limited, and there were male and female supervisors who were distinctly suspicious and unnerved by any woman who challenged the status quo."

"On reflection, I did that a number of times, not always in the most tactful of ways, but experience is a great teacher, and I look back with some pride at the changes that I have brought about personally and with the support of my male and female colleagues. Over the next ten to fifteen years I believe that women can be equally represented across all specialists and ranks. This may have to be achieved through government-imposed targets but will be possible. It is encouraging that there is a will at the highest level for this to be achieved."

COLLABORATE   Collaborate on responses to the following questions:

➤ How are you biased against policewomen?

➤ What roles do you view as best for policewomen?

➤ What do you think about government-imposed targets to achieve equity for women in police ranks?

Preview

Preview the next selection to predict its purpose and organization and to formulate your learning plan.

Activate Schema

Think about the female police officers within your community. How effective are they in conducting police business? Are there some aspects of the job in which they might excel because of their gender?

Establish a Purpose for Learning

Police work is a job that attracts and needs both men and women. What are the realities of the job for women? In the following selection, learn the challenges faced by policewomen. As you read, ask yourself about the biases, the performance realities, and the progress being made.

Increase Word Knowledge

What do you know about these words?

criteria	eliminated	restricted	conviction	debunked
peers	aggressive	dominated	perceptions	affront

Your instructor may give a true-false vocabulary review before or after reading.

Integrate Knowledge While Reading

Questions have been inserted in the margins to stimulate your thinking while reading. Remember to

Predict	Picture	Relate	Monitor	Correct

FEMALE POLICE OFFICERS

In 1910 Alice Stebbins Wells became the first woman to hold the title of police officer (in Los Angeles) and to have arrest powers. For more than half a century, female officers endured separate criteria for selection. They were given menial tasks, and were denied the opportunity for advancement. Some relief was gained with the
5 passage of the Civil Rights Act of 1964 and its amendments. Courts have supported the addition of women to police forces by striking down entrance requirements that eliminated almost all female candidates but could not be proven to predict job performance (such as height and upper body strength). Women do not do as well as men on strength tests and are much more likely to fail the entrance physical than

10 male recruits. Critics contend that many of these tests do not reflect the actual tasks that police do on the job. Nonetheless, the role of women in police work is still restricted by barriers that have been difficult to remove. Today, about 6 percent of all sworn officers are women.

Women continue to be underrepresented in the senior administrative ranks.
15 Many believe they are assigned duties that underutilize their skills and training. If they aspire to rise in the police force, policewomen become frustrated when they begin to recognize that few women get promoted to command positions. Female recruits often lack successful female role models on which to shape their career plans. It may not be surprising, then, that female officers report higher levels of job-
20 related stress than male officers.

Is the same true at the upper levels of other professions?

WORK PERFORMANCE

Gender bias is not supported by existing research, which indicates that women are highly successful police officers. In an important study of recruits in Washington, D.C., policewomen were found to display extremely satisfactory work performances. Compared with male officers, women were found to respond to similar
25 types of calls. The arrests they made were as likely to result in conviction. Women were more likely than their male colleagues to receive support from the community and were less likely to be charged with improper conduct. Policewomen seem to be more understanding and sympathetic to crime victims than male officers and are more likely to offer them treatment.

Are criminals less likely to become violent with female officers?

30 Research has also debunked another myth about female officers. Because they are less capable of subduing a suspect physically, they will be more likely to use their firearms. Actually, the opposite is true. Policewomen are less likely to use their firearms in violent confrontations than their male partners. Policewomen are more emotionally stable and are less likely to seriously injure a citizen. They are no more
35 likely to suffer injuries than their male partners. These generally positive results are similar to findings in other studies conducted in major U.S. cities.

Jeff Greenberg/Alamy

The female police officer photographed here works the crowd as a member of the City of Miami Police Department.

GENDER CONFLICTS

Despite the overwhelming evidence supporting their performance, policewomen have not always been fully accepted by their male peers or the general public. Male officers complain that female officers lack the emotional and physical strength to
40 perform well in situations involving violence. Some officers' wives resent their husbands' having a female partner because they consider the policewoman not only a sexual threat but poor support in a violent encounter.

Studies of policewomen indicate that they are still struggling for acceptance. They believe that they do not receive equal credit for their job performance. They
45 report that it is common for them to be sexually harassed by their co-workers. Female officers may also be targeted for more disciplinary actions by administrators. If cited, they are more likely to receive harsher punishment than male officers.

Surveys of male officers show that only one-third actually accept a woman on patrol. More than one-half do not think that women can handle the physical re-
50 quirements of the job as well as men.

DEFINING THE FEMALE POLICE ROLE

Those female officers who fail to catch on to the unwritten police subculture are often written off as "bad police material." Women who prove themselves tough enough to gain respect as police officers are then labeled as "lesbians" or "bitches" to neutralize their threat to male dominance, a process referred to as **defeminization.**
55 Male officers also generally assume that female offices who adopt an aggressive style of policing will be quicker to use deadly force than their male counterparts. Women working in this male-dominated culture may experience stress and anxiety. It is not surprising, then, that significantly more female than male officers report being the victim of discrimination on the job. Male officers who claim to have experienced
60 gender-based discrimination suggest that it comes at the hands of female officers who use their "sexuality" for job-related benefits.

Is strength essential? What about older and/or out-of-shape male officers?

These perceptions of female officers are often based on gender stereotypes and are incorrect. Nonetheless, policewomen are frequently caught in the classic "catch 22" dilemma. If they are physically weak, male partners view them as a risk in street
65 confrontations. If they are actually more powerful and aggressive than their male partners, they are regarded as an affront to the policeman's manhood.

(821 words)

—From Joseph J. Senna and Larry J. Siegel,
Introduction to Criminal Justice, 9th ed. Copyright © 2002.
Reprinted with permission of Wadsworth, a division of Thomson Learning.

Skill Development: Recall

Stop to self-test, relate, and react.

Your instructor may choose to give you a true-false comprehension review.

Write About the Selection

What are the challenges and drawbacks of being a policewoman? Consider both public perception and the police subculture in answering the question.

Response Suggestion: List challenges that are real and those that are not based on fact but exist in the minds of the public and male police coworkers.

Contemporary

Women are meeting with increasing success in police work. Even on television, women are given starring roles in crime investigations. What special skills do women add to police work? Beyond their individual skills, how can women add strength to the mix?

Skill Development: Find the Main Idea

Answer the following with *T* (true) or *F* (false):

_____ 1. The main idea of the third paragraph (Work Performance heading) is that research studies show that the work performance of female police officers is only slightly below that of male officers.

_____ 2. A major detail in the passage is that male officers complain that female officers lack qualities to perform well in violent situations.

_____ 3. A minor detail in the passage is that women continue to be under-represented in senior administrative offices.

Check Your Comprehension

After reading the selection, answer the following questions with *a*, *b*, *c*, or *d*. To help you analyze your strengths and weaknesses, the question types are indicated.

Main Idea _____ 1. Which of the following best states the main idea of the selection?

    a. Female police officers are subject to unjustified gender bias.
    b. Female police officers are better than male police officers.
    c. Women should not become police officers.
    d. The gender discrimination experienced by those in the police force is worse than that of other occupations.

Detail _____ 2. When women first became police officers,

    a. they did not have the power to arrest people.
    b. they did not have to take any physical tests.
    c. they were given unimportant tasks to do.
    d. they were given many opportunities to advance.

Detail _____ 3. Physical tests required by applicants to the police force have been criticized

    a. for being too easy.
    b. for being too hard.
    c. for not being relevant to actual police work.
    d. for not taking height and weight into consideration.

Detail _____ 4. Few women hold senior administrative and command positions in the police force because few women

    a. apply for such positions.
    b. get promoted to such positions.
    c. have the skills and training required for such positions.
    d. want the stress related to such positions.

Detail _____ 5. Compared to male police officers, female police officers

    a. respond to calls more often.
    b. receive more satisfactory work performance reports.
    c. are more likely to be accused of improper conduct.
    d. are more likely to offer help to crime victims.

Detail _____ 6. Because female officers, as compared to male officers, are less capable of subduing a suspect, it is wrongly believed that

    a. they will be seriously injured more often.
    b. they will be more likely to use firearms.
    c. they will make fewer arrests.
    d. they will not respond to the more dangerous calls.

Detail _____ 7. Both male police officers and their wives voice concerns about the behavior of female police officers

    a. when in violent situations.
    b. when off the job.
    c. when they hold supervisory positions.
    d. when they use firearms.

Inference _____ 8. The author implies that one of the unwritten rules of the subculture is that

    a. men make better police officers than women do.
    b. suspects should be treated as if they are always guilty.
    c. there is no such thing as discrimination.
    d. the chain of command must always be followed.

Inference _____ 9. In the police subculture, the process of "defeminization" as described in the passage implies that

    a. women who use their sexuality for job-related advancements are not "real" women.
    b. women are most threatened by not being considered feminine.
    c. women express aggression more directly than men do.
    d. women are most threatening to men when they are both feminine and successful.

Inference _____ 10. By using the term "catch 22," the author suggests that female police officers are often

    a. in a "no need for action" situation.
    b. in a "no win" situation.
    c. in a position to win praise.
    d. in a position to use power over men.

Answer the following with *T* (true) or *F* (false):

Detail _____ 11. Women have been police officers for over two hundred years in the United States.

Detail _____ 12. Arrests made by female police officers are less likely to result in conviction.

Inference _____ 13. The reader can conclude that a citizen fearing injury at the hands of police officers should be more concerned about female police officers than male police officers.

Detail _____ 14. Most male police officers would rather partner with another male police officer.

Inference _____ 15. The reader can conclude that most female police officers are lesbians.

Build Your Vocabulary

According to the way the italicized word was used in the selection, select *a, b, c,* or *d* for the word or phrase that gives the best definition. The number in the parentheses indicates the line of the passage in which the word is located.

_____ 1. "separate *criteria*" (3)
    a. heights
    b. standards
    c. powers
    d. opportunities

_____ 2. "*eliminated* almost all" (7)
    a. added
    b. heightened
    c. removed
    d. required

_____ 3. "still *restricted*" (11)
    a. released
    b. required
    c. underrepresented
    d. limited

_____ 4. "result in *conviction*" (25)
    a. proof of innocence
    b. proof of guilt
    c. proof of support
    d. proof of sympathy

_____ 5. "also *debunked*" (30)
    a. proved
    b. theorized
    c. discredited
    d. liked

_____ 6. "male *peers*" (38)
    a. strangers
    b. opponents
    c. equals
    d. relatives

_____ 7. "*aggressive* style" (56)
    a. happy
    b. masculine
    c. combative
    d. deadly

_____ 8. "male-*dominated* culture" (57)
    a. ruled
    b. subordinate
    c. insignificant
    d. referred

_____ 9. "These *perceptions*" (63)
    a. prejudices
    b. lies
    c. viewpoints
    d. gossiping

_____ 10. "an *affront*" (67)
    a. endorsement
    b. insult
    c. offer
    d. recognition

Search the Net

Use a search engine such as Google, Yahoo, Ask.com, Excite, Dogpile, or Lycos to find information about female police officers in other countries. Do they experience discrimination, and is it different or similar to the bias encountered by female officers in the United States? For suggested Web sites and other research activities, go to http://www. ablongman.com/smith/.

Who's Who in Medicine?

Suffixes	-ist, -ician: "one who"	-ologist: "one who studies"

- ***dermatologist:*** skin doctor (*derma*: skin)

  Dermatologists remove skin cancers.

- ***internist:*** medical doctor for internal organs (*internus:* inside)

  The *internist* will administer a series of tests to determine the cause of Ben's mysterious pain.

- ***intern:*** a medical school graduate serving an apprenticeship at a hospital

  The *interns* work under the close supervision of doctors on the staff.

- ***gynecologist:*** doctor for reproductive systems of women (*gyne:* women)

  The *gynecologist* recommended a Pap smear to check for cervical cancer.

- ***obstetrician:*** doctor who delivers babies (*obstetrix:* midwife)

  Many *obstetricians* are also gynecologists.

- ***pediatrician:*** doctor for children (*paidos:* children)

  Pediatricians use antibiotics to treat infections.

- ***ophthalmologist*** or ***oculist:*** doctor who performs eye surgery

  The *ophthalmologist* performed cataract surgery on the woman.

- ***optometrist:*** specialist for measuring vision

  An *optometrist* tests eyesight and fits glasses and contact lenses.

- ***optician:*** specialist who makes visual correction lenses for eyeglasses and contact lenses

  Opticians usually work behind the scene, often at an optometrist's office.

- ***orthopedist:*** doctor who corrects abnormalities in bones and joints (*orthos:* straight or correct)

  The *orthopedist* set up his practice near a ski area.

- ***orthodontist:*** dentist for straightening teeth

  Her braces had to be adjusted every six weeks by the *orthodontist.*

- ***cardiologist:*** heart doctor (*cardio:* heart)

  Cardiologists treat patients who have had heart attacks.

- ***psychiatrist:*** doctor for treating mental disorders (*psycho:* mind)

  The *psychiatrist* prescribed drugs for the treatment of depression.

- **psychologist:** counselor for treating mental disorders

  The *psychologist* administered tests to determine the cause of the child's behavior.

- **neurologist:** doctor for disorders of the brain, spinal cord, and nervous system (*neuron:* nerve)

  Neurologists are searching for new treatments for patients who have suffered spinal cord injuries.

- **oncologist:** doctor for treating cancer and tumors (*onkos:* mass)

  The *oncologist* recommended various methods for dealing with the cancerous tumor.

- **urologist:** doctor specializing in the urinary tract (*ouro:* urine)

  The urologist was treating several patients for impotence.

- **podiatrist:** specialist in the care and treatment of the foot (*pod:* foot)

  The *podiatrist* knew the best way to deal with blisters, corns, and bunions.

- **anesthesiologist:** doctor who administers anesthesia to patients undergoing surgery (*anesthesia:* insensibility)

  Usually a patient will meet the *anesthesiologist* just before surgery.

- **hematologist:** doctor who studies the blood and blood-forming organs (*hemat:* blood)

  A hematoma is treated by a *hematologist*.

- **radiologist:** doctor using radiant energy for diagnostic and therapeutic purposes (*radio:* radiant waves)

  After the removal of a cancerous tumor, further treatment by a *radiologist* is usually recommended.

REVIEW

Part I

Indicate whether the following sentences are true (*T*) or false (*F*):

_____ 1. *Radiologists* are physicians who evaluate x-rays.

_____ 2. A *psychologist* is unable to prescribe medications for patients.

_____ 3. If a mental illness is suspected, a patient may be referred to a *psychiatrist*.

_____ 4. An *internist* is a medical school graduate serving an apprenticeship at a hospital.

_____ 5. *Dermatologists* recommend the daily use of sunscreen.

_____ 6. A *neurologist* specializes in the treatment of heart attacks.

_____ 7. Medical school is required in order to become an *optician*.

_____ 8. *Pediatricians* examine babies.

_____ 9. *Oncologists* specialize in eye treatment.

_____10. A *hematologist* might help a patient whose blood fails to clot properly.

Part II
Choose the doctor from the boxed list that best fits the job description.

anesthesiologist	podiatrist	urologist	cardiologist	orthodontist
orthopedist	optometrist	obstetrician	intern	ophthalmologist

11. Performs eye surgery _____

12. Treats diseases of the foot _____

13. Delivers babies _____

14. Works with bones and joints _____

15. Treats disorders of the urinary tract _____

16. Administers anesthesia _____

17. Dispenses contact lenses _____

18. Treats heart problems _____

19. Corrects problems with teeth _____

20. Apprentice to physician or surgeon _____

Your instructor may choose to give a multiple-choice review.

5 Patterns of Organization

- How do transitional words signal organizational patterns?
- What organizational patterns are used in textbooks?
- Why are several organizational patterns sometimes combined to develop a main idea?

Jane Wooster Scott (b.1939/American), *Heroes on Wheels*, 1985. Oil on canvas.

Textbook Organization: The Big Picture

The **pattern of organization** in a textbook is the presentation plan, format, or structure for the message. Why is it important to identify organizational patterns in textbooks and other pieces of writing? Basically, such patterns serve as the book's blueprint, showing the reader how the book was built. They signal how facts and ideas are presented. The number of details in a textbook can be overwhelming. Identifying the pattern of organization of a section or chapter can help you master the complexities of the material. If you know the pattern of organization, you can predict the format of upcoming information.

Although key transitional words can signal a particular pattern, the most important clue to the pattern is the main idea itself because it usually dictates the organizational pattern. Your aim as a reader is to identify the main idea, be alert to the signal words, anticipate the overall pattern of organization, and place the major supporting details into the outline or pattern used by the author.

What Do Transitional Words Do?

Small words can carry a big load. A single word can signal the level of importance, a connection, or a direction of thought. For example, if a friend begins a sentence by saying "I owe you $100," would you prefer that the next word be *and* or that it be *but*? The word *and* signals addition and would give you high hopes for the return of your money. However, the word *but* signals a change of thought which, in this case, would be in a negative direction. If the next word were *first*, you would anticipate a sequence of events before repayment. If it were *consequently*, you would hope the positive result would be your $100.

Such words are **transitional words**—sometimes called *signal words*—that connect parts of sentences or whole sentences and lead you to anticipate either a continuation of or a change in thought. Transitions show the relationships of ideas within sentences, between sentences, and between paragraphs. Writers use transitions to keep their readers' comprehension on track and to guide them through the logic of the message. To avoid repetition, authors choose from a variety of signal words to indicate the transition of thought. These signal words or transitions can be categorized as shown in the following examples and in the Reader's Tip on page 170.

Words That Signal Addition

in addition	moreover	furthermore	and	also	another

EXAMPLE José was given a raise after six months at his job. *In addition*, he became eligible for health insurance benefits.

After causing a disturbance in the movie theater, Brian and his friends were asked to leave. *Furthermore*, they were barred from attending that theater ever again.

Words That Signal Examples or Illustrations

for example	for instance	to illustrate	such as	including

EXAMPLE Traffic seems to be getting heavier. *For instance*, last year it took only twenty minutes to get to school, and now it takes thirty.

Some experts believe that a fetus in the womb can be affected by sounds *such as* classical music or the mother's voice.

Words That Signal Time or Sequence

first	second	finally	last	afterward	after	during
while	before	then	previously	until	now	next

EXAMPLE Apply sunscreen while walking on the beach and *before* swimming in the surf. *Afterward*, reapply the sunscreen even if it is waterproof.

To build a good financial foundation, *first* pay yourself in the form of savings, and *then* pay your bills.

Words That Signal Comparison

similarly	likewise	in the same manner	like	as	just as	as well

EXAMPLE If you treat someone with kindness, he or she will probably treat you in kind. *Likewise*, if you treat someone with disrespect, you will probably be disrespected.

Portland is a port city in Oregon; *similarly*, it is a seaport in Maine.

Words That Signal Contrast

however	but	nevertheless	whereas
on the contrary	conversely	yet	in contrast
even though	on the other hand	although	instead

EXAMPLE Using a knife to cut a bagel can be dangerous to the fingers. *On the other hand*, using a bagel holder keeps fingers safe from the falling blade.

Today many families eat dinner separately and on the run, *whereas* in the past the family dinner hour was a time for bonding and an opportunity to instill values or share dreams.

Words That Signal Cause and Effect

thus	consequently	therefore	as a result	because
accordingly	since	so	because of	

EXAMPLE   *Because of* his work to end apartheid in South Africa, Nelson Mandela spent twenty-seven years in prison. Upon his release, Mandela treated his oppressors with respect and worked to unite the country. *Consequently*, he shared a Nobel Peace Prize with then-president de Klerk.

There has been a severe shortage of rainfall this year. *Therefore*, we have instituted a ban on outdoor watering.

Reader's *Tip* ── Signal Words for Transition

> **Addition:** in addition • furthermore • moreover
> **Examples:** for example • for instance • to illustrate • such as
> **Time:** first • second • finally • last • afterward
> **Comparison:** similarly • likewise • in the same manner
> **Contrast:** however • but • nevertheless • whereas • on the contrary • conversely • in contrast
> **Cause and Effect:** thus • consequently • therefore • as a result

---

exercise 5.1   **Signal Words**

Choose a signal word from the boxed lists to complete the sentences that follow.

however	for example	in addition	consequently	in the meantime

1. Forget the boring tourist narrative and turn walking around a city into a hip audio tour experience with Soundwalk CDs. In New York, _____, you can pop in a fifty-minute audio CD to explore Chinatown, the meat-packing district, or Wall Street.

2. The United States has an ever-increasing demand for oil. _____, we are researching alternative sources of energy, such as solar energy, to reduce our dependence on oil.

3. _____ to alternative energy research, we may begin drilling for oil on a small portion of our public lands to lessen our dependence on foreign sources of oil.

4. Drilling on public lands, _____, is not popular with environ-

    mentalists who believe the drilling cannot be done without spoiling the land.

5. _____, we can strive to be more fuel efficient to help reduce

    our demand for energy.

therefore	on the contrary	for instance
in the same manner	furthermore	

6. One way to conserve energy is to drive a fuel-efficient car. _____,

    some hybrid cars that run on both gas and electricity are currently available.

    _____, these cars get up to sixty-eight miles per gallon.

7. The ancient Chinese practice of acupuncture is based on a belief that chi, a

    life force, flows along meridians throughout the body. _____,

    Feng Shui practitioners believe that the same chi flows throughout the earth,

    and that by harnessing the chi of our surroundings, we can improve the flow

    of energy in our bodies.

8. Coretta Scott King felt strongly that her husband's legacy should be celebrated

    nationally. _____, she worked successfully with others to have

    Martin Luther King Jr.'s birthday recognized as a federal holiday beginning in

    1983.

9. The U.S. Postal Service works to raise social awareness of important issues.

    _____, the USPS has issued commemorative stamps for

    causes that include diabetes awareness, breast cancer awareness, and hospice

    care.

10. The popular Harry Potter books are not only for children. _____,

    many adults enjoy reading about Harry's magical adventures at Hogwarts.

furthermore	for example	nevertheless	finally	in contrast

11. African American music in twentieth-century America evolved from ragtime,

    to jazz, to rhythm and blues, to soul, and _____, to rap.

12. The concert tickets were outrageously priced. _____, this was

    a once-in-a-lifetime opportunity, and other luxuries would have to be sacri-

    ficed to compensate for the expense.

13. Mardi Gras as celebrated in New Orleans is similar to Carnaval as celebrated throughout Latin America. Carnaval lasts for five days; _____, Mardi Gras lasts only one day.

14. Internet car sales, rather than hurting auto dealerships, have actually helped them. _____, most customers conduct research on the Net but still visit a dealer to actually buy automobiles. A well-informed consumer who is ready to purchase makes the salesperson's job easier.

15. Since Melissa failed to notify her parents that she had backed into another vehicle in the college parking lot, they were outraged to learn of the accident through a third party. _____, due to her lack of honesty, Melissa's parents decided that she would no longer be covered under their auto insurance policy.

moreover	but	simultaneously	as a result	similarly

16. Nutritionists note that a diet for good health includes five or more servings of fruits and vegetables daily. _____, nutritional studies indicate that an increase in the consumption of these healthful foods can reduce rates of heart disease and cancer.

17. Is chocolate a food or a drug? Chocolate contains antioxidants and minerals like many foods, _____ it also contains a neurotransmitter naturally found in the brain that, like many drugs, makes us feel good.

18. The 2000 U.S. Census shows a dramatic increase in the Hispanic population in the South. This influx was due to a recession in California occurring _____ with a robust economy in the South during the 1990s.

19. Musicians protested the swapping of their songs on the Napster Web site without royalties being paid. _____, journalists have protested their past works being electronically reproduced without royalty payments.

20. Gamblers with an illusion of control delude themselves into thinking that they can control outcomes in games of chance. _____, they lose substantial sums at casinos, racetracks, lotteries, and Internet gaming sites.

Patterns of Organization in Textbooks

As transitional words signal connections and relationships of ideas within and among sentences, they also help signal the overall organizational pattern of the message. When you write, you choose a pattern for organizing your thoughts. That organizational pattern is probably dictated by the main idea of your message. Before beginning to write, you must ask, "If this is what I want to say, what is the best logical pattern to organize my message?"

The next exercise contains examples of the patterns of organization you will encounter in textbooks. Some are used much more frequently than others, and some are typical of particular disciplines. For example, history textbooks often use the patterns of time order and cause and effect. Management textbooks frequently use the simple listing pattern, whereas psychology textbooks make heavy use of the definition-and-example pattern. *The Reader's Tip* following the exercise (see page 181) lists each type of pattern of organization along with some related signal words.

exercise 5.2   **Patterns of Organization**

Notice the outline that accompanies each pattern of organization described in the following paragraphs. After reading each example, enter the key points into the blank outline display to show that you understand the pattern.

Simple Listing

With **simple listing,** items are randomly listed in a series of supporting facts or details. These supporting elements are of equal value, and the order in which they are presented is of no importance. Changing the order of the items does not change the meaning of the paragraph.

Signal words, often used as transitional words to link ideas in a paragraph with a pattern of simple listing, include *in addition, also, another, several, for example, a number of.*

EXAMPLE   **WORK-RELATED STRESS**

Work-related stress has increased significantly in the last few years. People are spending more hours at work and bringing more work home with them. Job security has decreased in almost every industry. Pay, for many, has failed to keep up with the cost of living. Women are subject to exceptionally high stress levels as they try to live up to all the expectations placed on them. Finally, many people feel that they are trapped in jobs they hate but can't escape.

—Curtis O. Byer and
Louis W. Shainberg,
Living Well: Health in Your Hands,
2nd ed.

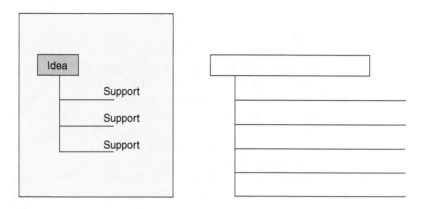

Definition

Frequently in a textbook, an entire paragraph is devoted to defining a complex term or idea. With **definition,** the concept is defined initially and then expanded with examples and restatements. In a textbook, a defined term is usually signaled by *italic* or **bold** type.

EXAMPLE ULTRASOUND

Ultrasound is a technique that uses sound waves to produce an image that enables a physician to detect structural abnormalities. Useful pictures can be obtained as early as five or six weeks into pregnancy. Ultrasound is frequently used in conjunction with other techniques such as amniocentesis and fetoscopy.

—John Dacey and John Travers,
Human Development, 2nd ed.

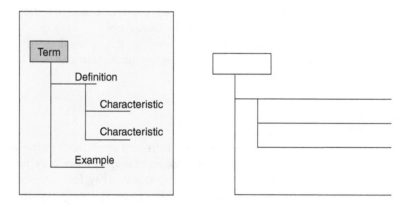

Description

Description is like listing; the characteristics that make up a description are no more than a definition or a simple list of details.

EXAMPLE CARIBBEAN

Caribbean America today is a land crowded with so many people that, as a region (encompassing the Greater and Lesser Antilles), it is the most densely populated part of the Americas. It is also a place of grinding poverty and, in all too many localities, unrelenting misery with little chance for escape.

—H. J. De Blij and Peter O. Muller,
Geography: Realms, Regions, and Concepts, 7th ed.

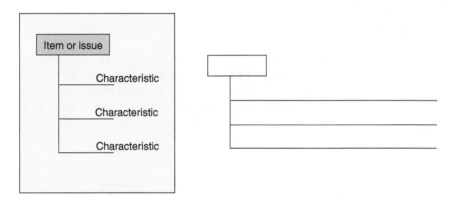

Time Order, Sequence, or Narration

Items are listed in the order in which they occurred or in a specifically planned order in which they must develop. In this case, the **time order** is important, and changing it would change the meaning. Narrative writing, which tells a story, is an example of writing in which time order is important.

Signal words that are often used for time order, sequence, or narration include *first, second, third, after, before, when, until, at last, next, later.* Actual time periods, such as days or years, also signal sequence and time.

EXAMPLE   **THE MORMON MOVEMENT**

The idea of the Mormon Church began when a young Joseph Smith, Jr., went into the New York woods in 1820 and was told by God that the true church of God would be reestablished. In 1823, another revelation led him to find buried golden plates and translate the *Book of Mormon.* Smith attracted thousands of followers and in the 1830s moved from Ohio to Missouri to Illinois to seek religious freedom for his group. In 1844 Smith was shot by an angry mob. After his death, a new leader, Brigham Young, led the Mormons to the Great Salt Lake.

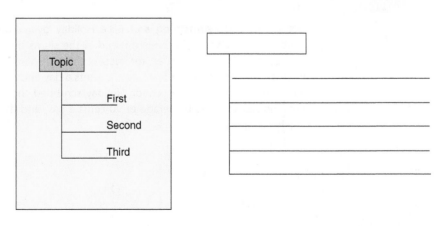

Contrast

With **contrast,** items are presented according to differences between or among them. Signal words that are often used for contrast include *different, in contrast, on the other hand, but, however, bigger than.*

EXAMPLE   ORANGES

An orange grown in Florida usually has a thin and tightly fitting skin, and it is also heavy with juice. Californians say that if you want to eat a Florida orange you have to get into a bathtub first. On the other hand, California oranges are light in weight and have thick skins that break easily and come off in hunks.

—John McPhee,
Oranges

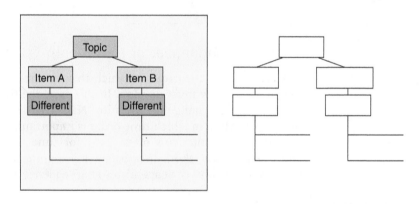

Comparison

With **comparison,** items are presented according to similarities between or among them. Signal words that are often used for comparison include *similar, in the same way, likewise, just like.*

EXAMPLE   JAZZ GREATS

Jazz greats Louis Armstrong and Billie Holiday overcame similar obstacles in their struggling early years. Both were raised in the slums by working mothers, and both learned the discipline needed for success through hard work. As a teen, Armstrong hauled coal from 7 A.M. to 5 P.M. for 75 cents a day and then practiced on his trumpet after work. Similarly, after school, Holiday scrubbed the white stone steps of neighbors' houses to earn an average of 90 cents a day, and then she came home to practice her singing.

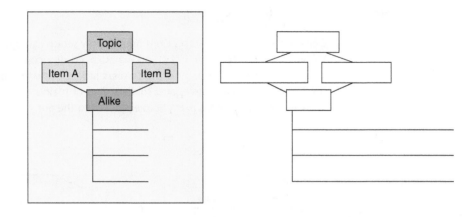

Comparison-Contrast

Some passages combine comparison and contrast into a single paragraph. This combination is called a **comparison-contrast** pattern and is demonstrated in the following examples.

EXAMPLE   **HISPANIC AMERICANS**

The primary groups in the rising new minority are Mexican Americans and Cuban Americans. Mexican Americans are heavily concentrated in the Southwest, whereas Cuban Americans are concentrated in Florida, particularly in the Miami area. Together the groups are called Hispanic Americans or Latinos. Although their histories are different, they share several similarities. They both speak the Spanish language and most of them, at least 85 percent, are Roman Catholic.

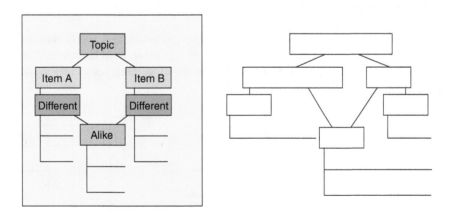

Cause and Effect

With **cause and effect,** an element is shown as producing another element. One is the *cause* or the "happening" that stimulated the particular result or *effect*. A paragraph may describe one cause or many causes, as well as one or many results. Signal words that are often used for cause and effect include *for this reason, consequently, on that account, hence, because.*

EXAMPLE   **WINTER CAMP AT VALLEY FORGE**

General George Washington's Continental army set up camp on the frozen grounds of Valley Forge in December 1777 and experienced dire consequences. The winter was particularly cold that year, and the soldiers lacked straw and blankets. Many froze in their beds. Food was scarce, and soldiers died of malnutrition. Because of the misery and disease in the camp, many soldiers deserted the army and went home.

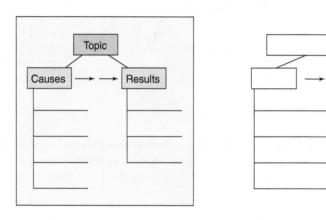

Classification

To simplify a complex topic, authors frequently begin introductory paragraphs by stating that the information that follows is divided into a certain number of groups or categories. The divisions are then named and the parts are explained. Signal words often used for **classification** include *two divisions, three groups, four elements, five classes, six levels, seven categories,* and so on.

EXAMPLE   **PREDATION**

Predation, the interaction in which one species kills and eats another, involves two groups. The predator, or consumer, must be alert and skillful to locate and capture the prey. The consumable group, or prey, constantly must adapt its behavior to defend against being eaten.

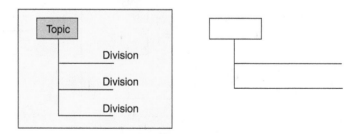

Addition

The addition pattern is used to provide more information related to something that has already been explained. Signal words are *furthermore, again, also, further, moreover, besides, likewise.*

EXAMPLE   **ENTREPRENEUR QUINCY JONES**

Not only is Quincy Jones the talented producer who helped drive Michael Jackson's "Beat It" to a number one hit and "Thriller" to the best-selling album of all time, he is also the founder of *VIBE* magazine and the co-owner of *SPIN* magazine. Furthermore, Jones, who has been awarded twenty-six Grammys and a Grammy Legend, is chairman and CEO of the Quincy Jones Media Group.

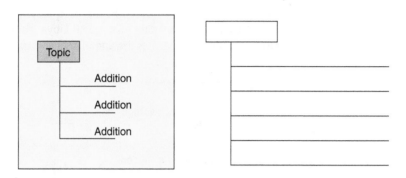

Summary

A **summary,** which usually comes at the end of an article or chapter, condenses the main idea or thesis into a short and simple concluding statement with a few major supporting details. Signal words are *in conclusion, briefly, to sum up, in short, in a nutshell.*

EXAMPLE   **WWII TOTAL WAR**

In conclusion, World War II was more of a total war than any previous war in history. Some 70 nations took part in the war, and fighting took place on the continents of Europe, Asia, and Africa. Entire societies participated, either as soldiers, war workers, or victims of occupation and mass murder.

—Adapted from James Kirby Martin et al.,
America and Its People

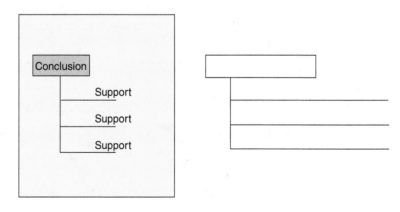

Location or Spatial Order

Location or **spatial order** identifies the whereabouts of a place or object. Signal words are *north, east, south, west, next to, near, below, above, close by, within, without, adjacent to, beside, around, to the right or left side, opposite.*

EXAMPLE   EGYPT

The Republic of Egypt is located in the northeastern corner of Africa. The northern border of Egypt is the Mediterranean Sea. Libya is the country to the west, and the Sudan lies to the south. Across the Suez Canal and to the east lies Israel.

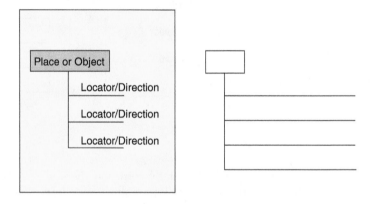

Generalization and Example

In the **generalization-and-example** pattern, a general statement or conclusion is supported with specific examples. Signal words include *to restate that, that is, for example, to illustrate, for instance.*

EXAMPLE   SMOKING

To restate it in simple terms, smoking kills. The American Cancer Society estimates that tobacco smoking is the cause of 30 percent of all deaths from cancer. Lung cancer is the leading cause of death from cancer in the United States, with 85 percent to 90 percent of these cases linked to smoking. Save your life by not smoking.

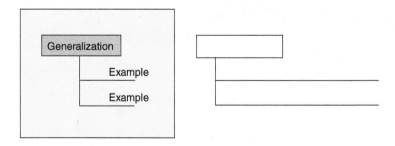

Reader's *Tip* ———— Patterns of Organization and Signal Words

➤ **Addition:** furthermore • again • also • further • moreover • besides • likewise
(provides more information)

➤ **Cause and Effect:** because • for this reason • consequently • hence • as a result • thus • due to • therefore
(shows one element as producing or causing a result or effect)

➤ **Classification:** groups • categories • elements • classes • parts
(divides items into groups or categories)

➤ **Comparison:** in a similar way • similar • parallel to • likewise • in a like manner
(lists similarities among items)

➤ **Contrast:** on the other hand • bigger than • but • however • conversely • on the contrary • although • nevertheless
(lists differences among items)

➤ **Definition:** can be defined • means • for example • like
(initially defines a concept and expands with examples and restatements)

➤ **Description:** is • as • is made up of • could be described as
(lists characteristics or details)

➤ **Generalization and Example:** to restate • that is • for example • to illustrate • for instance
(explains with examples to illustrate)

➤ **Location or Spatial Order:** next to • near • below • above • close by • within • without • adjacent to • beside • around • to the right or left side • opposite
(identifies the whereabouts of objects)

➤ **Simple Listing:** also • another • several • for example
(randomly lists items in a series)

➤ **Summary:** in conclusion • briefly • to sum up • in short • in a nutshell
(condenses major points)

➤ **Time Order, Sequence, or Narration:** first • second • finally • after • before • next • later • now • at last • until • thereupon • while • during
(lists events in order of occurrence)

exercise 5.3   Identifying Paragraph Patterns

Each of the following items presents the first two sentences of a paragraph stating the main idea and a major supporting detail. Select the letter that indicates the pattern of organization that you would predict for each.

_____ 1. Jim Vicary coined the term *subliminal advertising*, claiming that inserting messages like "Eat popcorn" and "Drink Coca-Cola" into movies would increase consumption. According to Vicary, the messages, flashed too fast for the human eye to recognize but registered in the brain, would prompt a rush to the snack bar.

   a. summary
   b. classification
   c. definition
   d. comparison-contrast

_____ 2. Now an integral part of the recruiting strategy, companies of all sizes are finding that e-cruiting, job recruiting over the Internet, has many benefits. To begin, the Internet is a fast, convenient, and inexpensive way to find prospective job candidates.

   a. description
   b. simple listing
   c. time order
   d. classification

_____ 3. Most prisons are designed to have three levels of custody: maximum, medium, and minimum. Maximum security prisons usually have a 25-foot wall surrounding the entire facility to prevent the escape of dangerous felons.

   a. classification
   b. cause and effect
   c. definition
   d. comparison

_____ 4. As a result of the Great Depression, Hollywood flourished. Cheap tickets, free time, and the lure of fantasy brought 60 million to 80 million Americans to the movies each week.

   a. comparison-contrast
   b. simple listing
   c. cause and effect
   d. description

_____ 5. Queens ruled England in the second half of the sixteenth century. In 1553, Mary I took the throne. She was followed in 1558 by Elizabeth I, who ruled for the next 45 years.

   a. summary
   b. contrast
   c. classification
   d. time order

_____ 6. The great white shark is a 6- to 7-meter predator. This most dangerous of all sharks gets extra power and speed from its warm muscles.

   a. description
   b. addition
   c. location or spatial order
   d. generalization and example

_____ 7. Although both artists lived in Spain, Pablo Picasso and Salvador
Dali had styles that differed dramatically. Picasso depicted his subjects in abstract terms, whereas Dali painted the stark reality of the
image.

   a. description
   b. comparison-contrast
   c. time order
   d. simple listing

_____ 8. Michelangelo depicted the creation of Eve on a panel that is almost
in the center of the Sistine Chapel ceiling. The Creation of Adam, a
larger and more famous panel, is located adjacent to it and toward
the back of the chapel.

   a. simple listing
   b. time order
   c. location or spatial order
   d. definition

_____ 9. In short, the Internet can be a source of dangerous misinformation.
Anyone can develop a Web site and fill it with distortions of the
truth and inflammatory accusations.

   a. classification
   b. summary
   c. definition
   d. time order

_____ 10. In case of a sprained ankle, you should first apply ice to constrict
the blood vessels and stop internal bleeding. Next, elevate your foot
above the level of your heart to further control bleeding by making
the blood flow away from the injured area.

   a. summary
   b. classification
   c. generalization and example
   d. sequence

exercise 5.4 **Patterns of Organization and Main Idea**

Read the following passages, and use the three-question system you learned in Chapter 4 to determine the author's main idea. In addition, indicate the dominant pattern of organization used by the author. Select from the following list:

classification	definition	description
example	cause and effect	comparison-contrast

Passage A

Also called ice pellets, sleet is formed when raindrops or melted snowflakes freeze as they pass through a subfreezing layer of air near Earth's surface. Sleet does not stick to trees and wires, and it usually bounces when it hits the ground. An accumulation of sleet sometimes has the consistency of dry sand.

—Frederick K. Lutgens and Edward J. Tarbuck,
The Atmosphere, 9th ed.

1. Who or what is this about? _____

_____

2. What are the major details? _____

_____

_____

_____

3. What is the overall pattern of organization? _____

4. What is the main idea the authors are trying to convey about the topic? _____

_____

_____

Passage B

A man bought his first new Lexus—a $45,000 piece of machinery. He took delivery of his new honey and started to drive it home. The lights, the windshield washer, the gizmo cup holder that popped out of the center console, the seat heater that warmed him on a cold winter morning—he tried them all. On a whim, he turned on the radio. His favorite classical music station came on in splendid quadrophonic sound. He pushed the second button. It was his favorite news station. The third button brought his favorite talk station that kept him awake on long trips. The fourth button was set to his daughter's favorite rock station. The customer was delighted.

—Adapted from Denny Hatch, "Delight Your Customers,"
Target Marketing, April 1, 2002

1. Who or what is this about? _____

_____

2. What are the major details? _____

_____

_____

_____

3. What is the overall pattern of organization? _____

4. What is the main idea the author is trying to convey about the topic? _____

_____

_____

_____

Passage C

There are so many types of water available to drink in the United States, how can we group them and distinguish among them? If we prefer to drink water with bubbles—carbonation—we can choose carbonated water. This type of water contains carbon dioxide gas that either occurs naturally or is added to the water. Mineral water is another beverage option. Mineral waters contain 250 to 500 parts per million of minerals. While many people prefer the unique taste of mineral water, a number of brands contain high amounts of sodium so they should be avoided by people who are trying to reduce their sodium intake. Distilled water is processed in such a way that all dissolved minerals are removed. This type of water is often used in steam irons, as it will not clog the iron with mineral buildup. Purified water has been treated so that all dissolved minerals and contaminants are removed, making this type of water useful in research and medical procedures. Of course, we can also drink the tap water found in our homes and in public places.

—Adapted from Janice Thompson and Melinda Manore,
Nutrition: An Applied Approach

1. Who or what is this about? _____

_____

2. What are the major details? _____

_____

_____

_____

3. What is the overall pattern of organization? _____

4. What is the main idea the authors are trying to convey about the topic?

_____

_____

_____

Passage D

The law of demand states that the quantity demanded will increase as the price is lowered as long as other factors that affect demand do not change. The makers of M&M candy conducted an experiment in the law of demand, holding the necessary demand-affecting conditions constant. Over a 12-month test period, the price of M&Ms was held constant in 150 stores while the content weight of the candy was increased. By holding the price constant and increasing the weight, the price (per ounce) was lowered. In the stores where the price was dropped, sales rose by 20 to 30 percent almost overnight. As a result of the law of demand, a reduction in prices caused the quantity demanded to rise.

—Adapted from Paul R. Gregory,
Essentials of Economics, 6th ed.

1. Who or what is this about? _____

_____

2. What are the major details? _____

_____

_____

_____

3. What is the overall pattern of organization? _____

4. What is the main idea the author is trying to convey about the topic? _____

_____

_____

_____

Passage E

One overlooked part of many presidents' emotional makeup has been their extraordinarily close relationship with their mothers. These mothers were strong, religious women who dominated the raising of their favorite sons. To illustrate the closeness of a few, Harry Truman had a portrait of his mom hung in the White House, and Calvin Coolidge died carrying a picture of his. In Richard Nixon's Watergate farewell address, he called his mother a "saint." Lyndon Johnson declared his mother "the strongest person I ever knew." Sara Roosevelt rented an apartment in Cambridge to be near Franklin at college. Years later when some New York political bosses asked him to run for office, he responded, "I'd like to talk with my mother about it first."

—Gary Wasserman,
The Basics of American Politics, 12th ed.

1. Who or what is this about? _____

_____

2. What are the major details? _____

_____

_____

_____

3. What is the overall pattern of organization? _____

4. What is the main idea the author is trying to convey about the topic? _____

_____

_____

_____

Passage F

I immediately noted differences in the early [basketball] practices. Girls' attention to directions was far superior to the boys', most of whom found it physically impossible not to be distracted by any movement anywhere in the gym. Whereas the boys generally either went deadpan or shot me the evil "how dare you" death stare when I corrected their play, the girls often sincerely apologized for any mistake. My stereotypically gawky center, when told not to leave her feet on defense, said, "I know. I'm sorry. I'm terrible." Strangest of all, they actually wanted to talk to me and the other coach, something teenage boys found equivalent to having their nose hairs individually plucked out in front of an audience.

—Brendan O'Shaughnessy,
"It's a Whole New Ballgame for Veteran Coach"

1. Who or what is this about? _____

_____

_____

_____

2. What are the major details? _____

_____

_____

_____

3. What is the overall pattern of organization? _____

4. What is the main idea the author is trying to convey about the topic? _____

_____

_____

_____

Mixed Organizational Patterns

Suppose you were writing an orientation article describing support services available at your own college. You could present the resources in a **simple listing** pattern, or you could discuss them in the **sequence** or **time order** in which a freshman is likely to need them or in terms of the most convenient geographic **locations** to students. Within your article, you might use a **description** or **definition** pattern to identify a relatively unknown service on campus, with **examples** of how it has helped others. You could demonstrate **cause and effect** with facts and statistics on how using services has helped students. You might also choose to **compare and contrast** a special service with that at another college.

You could supply **additional** information by presenting the qualifications of professional staff providing the services. To wrap things up, you could create an overall **summary** about the support services. Thus, one long article might have an overall **simple listing** pattern of organization yet contain individual paragraphs that follow other patterns.

exercise 5.5   **Identifying Combined Organizational Patterns**

Read the following textbook excerpts and answer the questions that follow. Note how combined organizational patterns may help you understand the main idea of a longer piece of writing. Signal words are set in bold type to help you identify a particular pattern.

Does the title suggest a pattern?

Passage 1
What Are Dust Devils?
A common phenomenon in arid regions of the world is the whirling vortex called the dust devil. Although they resemble tornadoes, dust devils are generally much smaller and less intense than their destructive cousins. Most dust devils are only a few meters in diameter and reach heights no greater than about 100 meters (300 feet). **By definition,** these whirlwinds are usually short-lived microscale phenomena. Most form and die out within minutes. In rare instances dust devils have lasted for hours.

Unlike tornadoes, which are associated with convective clouds, dust devils form on days when clear skies dominate. **In contrast,** these whirlwinds form from the ground upward, exactly opposite of tornadoes. Because surface heating is critical to their formation, dust devils occur most frequently in the afternoon when surface temperatures are highest.

Which pattern is suggested by the boldface words?

When the air near the surface is considerably warmer than the air a few dozen meters overhead, the layer of air near Earth's surface becomes unstable. In this situation warm surface air begins to rise, **causing** air near the ground to be drawn into the developing whirlwind. **As a result,** the rotating winds that are associated with dust devils are produced by the same phenomenon that causes ice skaters to spin faster as they pull their arms closer to their bodies. As the inwardly spiraling air rises, it carries sand, dust, and other loose debris dozens of meters into the air. It is this material that makes a dust devil visible. Occasionally, dust devils form above vegetated surfaces. Under these conditions, the vortices may go undetected unless they interact with objects at the surface.

—Adapted from Frederick K. Lutgens and Edward J. Tarbuck,
The Atmosphere, 9th ed.

1. Who or what is this about? _____

_____

2. What overall pattern is suggested by the title? _____

_____

3. What is the pattern of organization in the first paragraph? _____

_____

4. What is the pattern of organization in the second paragraph? _____

_____

5. What is the pattern of organization in the third paragraph? _____

_____

6. What is the main idea the authors are trying to convey about the topic?

_____

_____

_____

Passage 2
The Success of eBay

eBay is one of the most successful e-commerce businesses. **Unlike** Amazon.com, it does not need expensive warehouses and storage facilities. eBay earns its revenues by charging a small fee to sellers who list their products on eBay for sale. **While other** dot-com companies have suffered losses in recent years, eBay, **on the other hand,** has been consistently profitable, earning almost $150 million in annual profits.

eBay exists in all major countries (eBay Germany, eBay Austria, eBay Canada, and so on). It operates a worldwide virtual auction market in which registered sellers can list products and registered buyers can enter bids for them. Participants in this virtual market can follow the progress of bids online as each auction progresses. (Usually an ending time of each auction is listed.)

Products auctioned on eBay range from the ordinary to the unique or exotic. On a given day, wooden crates of rough jade ($15.95), a Tibetan bronze Buddha ($88), a 1913 Catholic dictionary ($204), a 1725 bible ($348), and an 1895 U.S. Navy steam launch engine ($2,025) can be found on auction.

eBay deals with problems of dishonesty. **That is,** eBay maintains bulletin boards of comments submitted by eBay subscribers, organized by the identification number of eBay buyers and sellers. These ratings provide information on records of past honesty and reliability. A "cheating" buyer or seller would not be able to buy or sell on eBay after disclosure of negative comments.

eBay **offers several** enormous **advantages** to buyers and sellers. **First,** the seller can gain access to a large number of potential buyers of unusual products by paying a small fee to eBay. **Second,** buyers have the opportunity to bid on thousands of products and services without leaving the comfort of their homes. Historically, exotic products such as Rembrandt paintings and Kennedy presidential memorabilia were auctioned by prestigious auction houses such as Sotheby's, which typically collected fees of 15 percent or more. It appears to be only a matter of time until rare and expensive items will be auctioned on eBay.

—Adapted from Paul R. Gregory,
Essentials of Economics, 6th ed.

1. Who or what is this about? _____

_____

2. What overall pattern is suggested by the title? _____

_____

3. What is the pattern of organization in the first paragraph? _____

_____

4. What is the pattern of organization in the second paragraph? _____

_____

5. What is the pattern of organization in the third paragraph? _____

_____

6. What is the pattern of organization in the fourth paragraph? _____

_____

7. What is the pattern of organization in the final paragraph? _____

_____

Summary *Points*

➤ **What are transitional words?**
Transitional or signal words connect parts of sentences and lead you to anticipate a continuation or a change in thoughts. They guide you through the logic of the message by showing the relationships of ideas within sentences, between sentences, and between paragraphs.

➤ **What is an organizational pattern, and how many types of patterns can be used in textbooks?**
An organizational pattern is the presentation plan, format, or structure of a message. It is a way to present ideas with logic. There are at least thirteen possible configurations or patterns for logically presenting details.

➤ **Why are several organizational patterns sometimes combined to develop a main idea?**
To fully present and explore the message, one long article may have a general overall pattern of organization yet contain individual paragraphs that follow other patterns.

selection 1 History

Contemporary *Focus*

Dr. Condoleezza Rice is the first African American woman to be secretary of state. She has brains, bravado, and a commanding presence. She loves foreign policy, fashion, and football. While growing up, Rice recalls that parental expectations were always high. In an interview she said, "My parents had me absolutely convinced that, well, you may not be able to have a hamburger at Woolworth's, but you can be president of the United States."

What Makes Condi Run

By Ann Reilly Dowd

AARP Magazine, September–October, 2005

Born in 1954 in Birmingham, Alabama, during the heart of racial darkness when little black girls couldn't eat at Woolworth's, Condoleezza—named after the Italian musical term *con dolcezza,* to perform "with sweetness"—has spent a half century breaking molds and busting stereotypes: child-prodigy pianist; competitive ice skater; top Soviet advisor at age 34 to President George H. W. Bush; Stanford University's youngest, first female, and first non-white provost; and George W's premier national-security and foreign policy advisor.

Condi's parents indulged their only child, who inherited her taste for fancy clothes from her mother, who loved to shop. She joined the Girl Scouts, took private language lessons (French and Spanish), and read stacks of books. And there was her music; even while Birmingham was plunged into racial torment, she was taking advanced classical piano at the Birmingham Conservatory—a first for a black youngster—and practicing hours a day. Even back then her discipline was extraordinary. At St. Mary's Academy in Denver, the first integrated school Condi attended, she was a straight-A student and a competitive ice skater. Her typical day: up at 4:30 A.M., hit the rink at 5,

practice until 7, then school, piano, back to the rink for an hour, then more piano.

But at 17, she found a new love: geopolitics and, in particular, all things Soviet—the language, the culture, the weaponry, the diplomacy (she even named her car Boris). Her inspiration was a political science professor at the University of Denver, where she was able to enroll at the age of 15, having skipped both first grade and seventh grade. He was former secretary of state Madeleine Albright's father, Czech diplomat and political refugee Josef Korbel. By then Condi had decided she was not a "phenomenal talent" as a pianist.

She still gets up early (5 A.M.) to lift weights or hit the treadmill, her headphones often blaring heavy metal legend Led Zeppelin. She also plays tennis and is taking golf lessons (really). And while she's had some awesome musical moments—playing a Brahms duet with cellist Yo-Yo Ma at Constitution Hall and now being wooed to play with the National Symphony Orchestra Pops by conductor and composer Marvin Hamlisch—she still finds time to play chamber music with a group of friends. And yes, she watches TV. Her favorite shows: *Law & Order* and *Cold Case Files.*

Collaborate on responses to the following questions:

➤ What is the job of the secretary of state?

➤ Who is Madeleine Albright?

➤ What other president did Condoleezza Rice work for, and what was her job?

Skill Development: Preview

Preview the next selection to predict its purpose and organization and to formulate your learning plan.

Activate Schema

Who was Sojourner Truth?
Why did the Civil War throw women into many leadership roles?

Establish a Purpose for Reading

Although history books tend to be mostly about the accomplishments of men, over time, women also have made contributions and pursued political and other professions. Who were some of the early women leaders? After recalling what you already know about women in history, read the selection to explain the contributions of individuals and groups toward changing the image of women.

Increase Word Knowledge

What do you know about these words?

restrictive	detriment	defiant	communal	hecklers
pursue	hygiene	incessant	convalescent	naive

Your instructor may give a true-false vocabulary review before or after reading.

Integrate Knowledge While Reading

Questions have been inserted in the margin to stimulate your thinking while reading. Remember to

Predict	Picture	Relate	Monitor	Correct

WOMEN IN HISTORY

THREE RADICAL WOMEN

Amelia Bloomer (1818–1894) published the first newspaper issued expressly for women. She called it *The Lily*. Her fame, however, rests chiefly in dress reform. For six or eight years she wore an outfit composed of a knee-length skirt over full pants

gathered at the ankle, which were soon known everywhere as "bloomers." Wherever
5 she went, this style created great excitement and brought her enormous audiences—
including hecklers. She was trying to make the serious point that women's fashions,
often designed by men to suit their own tastes, were too restrictive, often to the
detriment of the health of those who wore them. Still, some of her contemporaries
thought she did the feminist movement as much harm as good.

Why would Bloomer have hurt the movement?

10 Very few feminists hoped to destroy marriage as such. Most of them had husbands and lived conventional, if hectic, lives. And many of the husbands supported
their cause. Yet the feminists did challenge certain marital customs. When Lucy
Stone married Henry Blackwell, she insisted on being called "Mrs. Stone," a defiant
gesture that brought her a lifetime of ridicule. Both she and her husband signed a
15 marriage contract, vowing "to recognize the wife as an independent, rational being."
They agreed to break any law which brought the husband "an injurious and unnatural superiority." But few of the radical feminists indulged in "free love" or joined
communal marriage experiments. The movement was intended mainly to help
women gain control over their own property and earnings and gain better legal
20 guardianship over their children. Voting also interested them, but women's suffrage
did not become a central issue until later in the century.

Why was voting a later issue?

Many black women were part of the movement, including the legendary
Sojourner Truth (1797–1883). Born a slave in New York and forced to marry a man

Former slave Isabella Van Wagener became the abolitionist
Sojourner Truth.

MPI/Hulton Archive/Getty Images

approved by her owner, Sojourner Truth was freed when the state abolished slavery.
25 After participating in religious revivals, she became an active abolitionist and feminist. In 1851 she saved the day at a women's rights convention in Ohio, silencing
hecklers and replying to a man who had belittled the weakness of women:

> The man over there says women need to be helped into carriages and lifted
> over ditches, and to have the best place everywhere. Nobody ever helps me
> 30 into carriages or over puddles, or gives me the best place—and ain't I a
> woman? . . . Look at my arm! I have ploughed and planted and gathered
> into barns, and no man could head me—and ain't I a woman? I could work
> as much and eat as much as a man—when I could get it—and bear the lash
> as well! And ain't I a woman? I have borne thirteen children, and seen
> 35 most of 'em sold into slavery, and when I cried out my mother's grief, none
> but Jesus heard me—and ain't I a woman?

What makes this speech powerful? Read it aloud.

CHANGING THE IMAGE AND THE REALITY

The accomplishments of a few women who dared pursue professional careers had
somewhat altered the image of the submissive and brainless child-woman. Maria
Mitchell of Nantucket, whose father was an astronomer, discovered a comet at the
40 age of twenty-eight. She became the first woman professor of astronomy in the U.S.
(at Vassar in 1865). Mitchell was also the first woman elected to the American
Academy of Arts and Sciences and a founder of the Association for the
Advancement of Women. Elizabeth Blackwell applied to twenty-nine medical
schools before she was accepted. She attended all classes, even anatomy class, de-
45 spite the sneers of some male students. As a physician, she went on to make important contributions in sanitation and hygiene.

Why would there be sneers in anatomy?

By about 1860 women had effected notable improvements in their status.
Organized feminists had eliminated some of the worst legal disadvantages in fifteen
states. The Civil War altered the role—and the image—of women even more drasti-
50 cally than the feminist movement did. As men went off to fight, women flocked
into government clerical jobs. And they were accepted in teaching jobs as never before. Tens of thousands of women ran farms and businesses while the men were
gone. Anna Howard Shaw, whose mother ran a pioneer farm, recalled:

How did the Civil War force an image change?

> It was an incessant struggle to keep our land, to pay our taxes, and to live.
> 55 Calico was selling at fifty cents a yard. Coffee was one dollar a pound.
> There were no men left to grind our corn, to get in our crops, or to care for
> our livestock; and all around us we saw our struggle reflected in the lives of
> our neighbors.

Women took part in crucial relief efforts. The Sanitary Commission, the Union's
60 volunteer nursing program and a forerunner of the Red Cross, owed much of its
success to women. They raised millions of dollars for medicine, bandages, food, hospitals, relief camps, and convalescent homes.

North and South, black and white, many women served as nurses, some as
spies and even as soldiers. Dorothea Dix, already famous as a reformer of prisons
65 and insane asylums, became head of the Union army nurse corps. Clara Barton
and "Mother" Bickerdyke saved thousands of lives by working close behind the

front lines at Antietam, Chancellorsville, and Fredericksburg. Harriet Tubman led a party up the Combahee River to rescue 756 slaves. Late in life she was recognized for her heroic act by being granted a government pension of twenty dollars
70 per month.

Southern white women suffered more from the disruptions of the Civil War than did their northern sisters. The proportion of men who went to war or were killed in battle was greater in the South. This made many women self-sufficient during the war. Still, there was hardly a whisper of feminism in the South.

75 The Civil War also brought women into the political limelight. Anna Dickson skyrocketed to fame as a Republican speaker, climaxing her career with an address to the House of Representatives on abolition. Stanton and Anthony formed the National Woman's Loyal League to press for a constitutional amendment banning slavery. With Anthony's genius for organization, the League in one year collected
80 400,000 signatures in favor of the Thirteenth Amendment.

Once abolition was finally assured in 1865, most feminists felt certain that suffrage would follow quickly. They believed that women had earned the vote by their patriotic wartime efforts. Besides, it appeared certain that black men would soon be

Why was suffrage slow to come? →
85 allowed to vote. And once black men had the ballot in hand, how could anyone justify keeping it from white women—or black women? Any feminist who had predicted in 1865 that women would have to wait another fifty-five years for suffrage would have been called politically naive.

(1,102 words)

—From Leonard Pitt,
We Americans

Recall

Stop to self-test, relate, and react.

Your instructor may choose to give you a true-false comprehension review.

Write About the Selection

Have we been taught to believe that dynamic women are the exception rather than the rule in history? Is this idea confirmed when we see stories of women only in box inserts and footnotes in history textbooks? How did the actions of many early women "somewhat alter the image of the submissive and brainless child-woman"? Is that image still being altered?

Response Suggestion: List some dynamic women, and discuss how each has changed stereotypical thinking.

Contemporary *Link*

How does Condoleezza Rice continue to change the image of and the prospects for women? What characteristics do you admire about her? How would you compare her to the three radical women in the selection?

Skill Development: Identify Organizational Patterns

Fill in the organizational diagram to reflect the simple-listing pattern of the first part of the selection.

Check Your Comprehension

After reading the selection, answer the following questions with *a, b, c,* or *d*. To help you analyze your strengths and weaknesses, the question types are indicated.

Main Idea _____ 1. What is the best statement of the main point of this selection?

    a. Women made impressive gains because of their work during the Civil War.

    b. Many women made early contributions to changing the stereotypical image of the female role.

    c. Bloomer, Stone, and Truth changed a radical image into a reality.

    d. Women were slow to get the right to vote despite their efforts.

Detail _____ 2. In originating "bloomers," Amelia Bloomer's greatest concern was

    a. fashion.

    b. principle.

    c. expense.

    d. good taste.

Inference _____ 3. The major purpose of Sojourner Truth's quoted speech was to

    a. prove that women are stronger than men.

    b. reprimand men for social courtesy.

    c. dramatize the strengths of women.

    d. praise childbearing as a womanly virtue.

Detail _____ 4. Lucy Stone's major motive in retaining the name "Mrs. Stone" after marriage was to

    a. condone "free love" without marriage.

    b. de-emphasize the responsibilities of marriage.

    c. purchase property in her own name.

    d. be recognized as an independent person equal to her husband.

Detail _____ 5. The article explicitly states that women worked during the Civil War in all the following *except*

    a. farms and businesses.

    b. the military.

    c. government clerical jobs.

    d. the Red Cross.

Inference _____ 6. The author implies that the eventual assumption of responsible roles by large numbers of women was primarily due to

    a. the feminist movement.

    b. the determination and accomplishments of female professionals.

    c. a desire to give women a chance.

    d. economic necessity.

Inference _____ 7. The author believes that the Civil War showed southern women to be

     a. as capable as but less vocal than northern women.
     b. more capable than their northern sisters.
     c. capable workers and eager feminists.
     d. less able to assume responsible roles than northern women.

Inference _____ 8. The author's main purpose in mentioning the accomplishments of Maria Mitchell is to point out that

     a. she discovered a comet.
     b. her professional achievements in astronomy were exceptional and thus somewhat improved the image of women.
     c. she was the first woman professor of astronomy in the United States.
     d. she was a founder of the Association for the Advancement of Women.

Detail _____ 9. The article states or implies that all the following women worked to abolish slavery *except*

     a. Anna Howard Shaw.
     b. Harriet Tubman.
     c. Anna Dickson.
     d. Stanton and Anthony.

Inference _____ 10. In the author's opinion, the long wait by women after the Civil War for suffrage

     a. was predictable in 1865.
     b. would not have been expected in 1865.
     c. was due to the vote of black men.
     d. was justified.

Answer the following with *T* (true) or *F* (false).

Detail _____ 11. Women were granted the right to vote in 1920.

Detail _____ 12. Sojourner Truth had been a southern slave.

Inference _____ 13. The author implies that feminist leaders were more concerned with their own right to vote than with the abolition of slavery.

Detail _____ 14. From the very beginning, the right to vote was the focal point of the women's movement.

Detail _____ 15. Sojourner Truth had thirteen children.

Build Your Vocabulary

According to the way the italicized word was used in the selection, indicate *a, b, c,* or *d* for the word or phrase that gives the best definition. The number in parentheses indicates the line of the passage in which the word is located.

_____ 1. "were too *restrictive*" (7)
a. showy
b. expensive
c. complicated
d. confining

_____ 2. "to the *detriment* of" (8)
a. harm
b. anger
c. apology
d. objection

_____ 3. "a *defiant* gesture" (13)
a. unlucky
b. resistant
c. admirable
d. ignorant

_____ 4. "*communal* marriage experiments" (18)
a. permanent
b. living together in groups
c. illegal
d. uncommon

_____ 5. "silencing *hecklers*" (27)
a. soldiers
b. rioters
c. disciples
d. verbal harassers

_____ 6. "*pursue* professional careers" (37)
a. strive for
b. abandon
c. acknowledge
d. indicate

_____ 7. "sanitation and *hygiene*" (46)
a. garbage disposal
b. biology
c. preservation of health
d. mental disorders

_____ 8. "an *incessant* struggle" (54)
a. earlier
b. final
c. novel
d. unceasing

_____ 9. "*convalescent* homes" (62)
a. sanitary
b. government
c. reclaimed
d. recuperating

_____ 10. "called politically *naive*" (87)
a. unsophisticated
b. well informed
c. dishonest
d. unfortunate

Search the Net

Use a search engine such as Google, Yahoo, Ask.com, AltaVista, Excite, Dogpile, Yahoo, or Lycos to find information on Rosa Parks. Explain her pivotal role in the civil rights movement. For suggested Web sites and other research activities, go to http://www.ablongman.com/smith/.

Concept Prep for Art History

Why study art history?

Just as written history is a verbal record of the events and people of the past, fine art is a visual interpretation of reality and a reflection of past taste and values. Art tells us about people and their culture, as illustrated in the earliest primitive cave drawings depicting animals and hunters or in the elaborate tombs in the Egyptian pyramids, built for the pharaohs. Through art, we can glimpse a likeness of Elizabeth I, feel the power of a ship battle at sea, or view the majesty of the American frontier. Artists link us to the past through beauty, creativity, and emotion.

When we say "the arts," what do we mean?

The **arts** and the **fine arts** refer to creative works in painting, sculpture, literature, architecture, drama, music, opera, dance, and film. A work that is exceptionally well crafted is said to aspire to the level of fine art.

Museums, a word derived from Greek to mean places presided over by the Muses, display fine arts in paintings and sculpture. Some of the greatest museums in the world are the **Louvre** in Paris, the **Prado** in Madrid, and the **Metropolitan Museum of Art** in New York City.

Who are some of the great artists?

- One of the most extraordinary artists was **Leonardo da Vinci** (1452–1519). He was considered a **Renaissance man** because of his genius, insatiable curiosity, and wide interests in art, engineering, anatomy, and aeronautics. He painted the *Mona Lisa,* the world's most famous painting. This woman with the mysterious smile whose eyes seem to follow you is displayed in the Louvre behind several layers of bulletproof glass.
- **Michelangelo** (1475–1564) was a sculptor, painter, architect, and poet. Before he was 30 years old, he created the famous marble statue of *David,* which portrays the biblical king in his youth. Michelangelo was commissioned by the pope to paint the ceiling of the **Sistine**

Ram's Head, White Hollyhock-Hills (Ram's Head and White Hollyhock, New Mexico) by Georgia O'Keeffe, 1935. Oil on canvas, 20 × 36" (76.2 × 91.44 cm). Brooklyn Museum of Art. Bequest of Edith and Milton Lowenthal, 1992.11.28. © 2006 The Georgia O'Keeffe Foundation/Artist Rights Society (ARS), New York

Chapel in the Vatican in Rome. For four years, the artist worked on his back in the chapel to complete *The Creation of Adam,* which contains more than 400 individual figures.

- The founder and leading artist of the **impressionists** was **Claude Monet** (1840–1926). Critics said the feathery brushstrokes and play of light in his works conveyed the "impression" of a particular moment. Monet advocated getting out of the studio and painting outdoors, facing the subject. He painted many scenes of the gardens and water lily ponds surrounding his home in **Giverny** near Paris.
- **Vincent van Gogh** (1853–1890) borrowed from the impressionists but achieved another dimension in the swirling brushstrokes of his work to convey his unique vision. His sunflower paintings and *Starry Night* are among his most famous works, now popularized in mass reproductions, but in his lifetime van Gogh sold only one painting. He suffered from depression and spent his last years in a mental institution. In an argument with another artist,

he cut off his own ear, which he later sent to a prostitute.

- **Pablo Picasso** (1881–1973) is one of the most influential of all modern artists. Because traditional skills in painting were so easy for him, he looked for new modes of expression. He was the originator of cubism, an abstract style of painting that displays several perspectives of an object simultaneously. One of his most acclaimed paintings is *Guernica,* a haunting visual protest against the savagery of war.
- By the twentieth century, female artists were becoming more prominent. **Mary Cassatt** (1861–1914), an impressionist, holds a unique place in American art. She was one of the first women artists to succeed professionally. Cassatt began her work in Pennsylvania but later settled in Paris. Domestic scenes became her theme, and she portrayed women and children in intimate relationships.

- **Frida Kahlo** (1907–1954), a Mexican artist, is sometimes called the "portrait genie." She dramatized her life story in self-portraits, interweaving them with symbolism, myth, and surrealistic elements. Kahlo was studying to be a physician when a serious car accident hospitalized her. She took up painting and did not return to medicine. Her colorful creations reflect the endurance of life and the traditions of Mexico.
- **Georgia O'Keeffe** (1887–1986) was one of the first American artists to experiment with abstract form. She interpreted nature in beautiful geometric shapes. O'Keeffe combined the appearance of sculpture and photography in her paintings of flowers, sun-bleached animal bones, clouds, and surreal desert scenes. Her clear, bright colors reflect her love of the Southwest and her American independence.

Review Questions

After studying the material, answer the following questions:

1. What do works included in "the arts" have in common? _____
   _____
   _____

2. Where is the Louvre? _____
   _____

3. What is a Renaissance man? _____
   _____
   _____

4. What is unusually engaging about Mona Lisa's face? _____
   _____
   _____

5. What story is painted on the ceiling of the Sistine Chapel? _____
   _____
   _____

6. How did the impressionists get their name? _____

_____

_____

7. What scenes did Monet paint at Giverny? _____

_____

_____

8. Which painter advocated painting outdoors? _____

_____

9. How did Van Gogh disfigure himself? _____

_____

10. Why did Picasso turn to cubism? _____

_____

_____

Your instructor may choose to give a true-false review of these art history concepts.

selection 2 Business

Contemporary *Focus*

Did you know that 17 percent of all restaurants in our nation are pizza restaurants? Approximately 3 billion pizzas were sold in the United States in 2005. Pizza is a $30 billion per year business. Imagine the many other businesses that benefit from the pizza boom. For example, the pizza business affects the cheese, pepperoni, and tomato businesses. Is there still money to be made in inventing products that support the pizza industry?

Inventors Hope for Slice of Pizza Box Business

By Dave Hall

National Post's Financial Post & FP Investing, Canada, March 23, 2006

Tired of searching for plates or ripping strips of cardboard off pizza box lids, owners of a Windsor company have designed a revolutionary new environmentally friendly perforated lid that breaks up into slice-shaped pieces that replace plates.

The company hopes to corner a fraction of North America's multi-million-unit-per-month pizza box business.

"We're changing the way the world eats pizza," said Rob Tulk, one of the owners of the company. "It's a box with the plates on top."

Mr. Tulk said the idea originated with Chris Holden, his business partner, who was hosting an outdoor pizza party and ended up ripping the box apart to use as plates.

"We talked, and I sort of took the idea from there, worked with it, and came up with the idea we're now trying to market," said Mr. Tulk, who

said the new box has been patented and trademarked.

By reducing the need for paper, plastic, or foam plates, Mr. Holden believes the new box lids are environmentally friendly and will reduce waste.

The box, which has undergone a number of design changes in the past few years, costs no more to make than a regular box, and, despite the perforations, is strong enough to withstand a number of pizzas being piled on top without collapsing.

Ron Martinello, owner of Windsor's Pizza King, said, "The idea has merit, and the theory is good, especially for groups such as schools and workplaces, where you're always scrambling around for plates.

"At home, you might prefer to use a real plate, while guys sitting around eating pizza and drinking beer usually don't need napkins, much less plates," said Mr. Martinello, laughing.

COLLABORATE Collaborate on responses to the following questions:

➤ What kind of toppings do you order on your pizza?

➤ How do you select a pizza when many options are available?

➤ Why do you think the new pizza boxes could be successful?

➤ What new products would you suggest for the competitive pizza business?

Skill Development: Preview

Preview the next selection to predict its purpose and organization and to formulate your learning plan.

Activate Schema

Do you prefer pizzas from Domino's, Pizza Hut, or Papa John's?
If your dream could become a reality, what small business would you start?

Establish a Purpose for Reading

Downsizing, outsourcing, women's increasing presence in the workforce, and Internet technology are now shaping the American entrepreneurial spirit. The advantages and rewards of small business ownership are great, but so are the risks. What do you expect to learn from this selection about Papa John's and small businesses? After recalling what you already know about start-up businesses, read the selection to learn what defines a small business, why people open them, and why Papa John's is successful.

Increase Word Knowledge

What do you know about these words?

void	successive	droves	dominant	titans
novice	debut	vaulted	stagnant	heritage

Your instructor may give a true-false vocabulary review before or after reading.

Integrate Knowledge While Reading

Questions have been inserted in the margin to stimulate your thinking while reading. Remember to

Predict	Picture	Relate	Monitor	Correct

WHY IS PAPA JOHN'S ROLLING IN THE DOUGH?

Why are bubbles bad?

As a high school student working at a local pizza pub, John Schnatter liked everything about the pizza business. "I liked making the dough; I liked kneading the dough; I liked putting the sauce on; I liked putting the toppings on; I liked running the oven," recalls Schnatter. Obsessed with perfect pizza topping and bubble-free
5 melted cheese, Schnatter knew that something was missing from national pizza chains: superior-quality traditional pizza delivered to the customer's door. And his dream was to one day open a pizza restaurant that would fill that void.

Schnatter worked his way through college making pizzas, honing the techniques and tastes that would someday become Papa John's trademark. Shortly after gradu-
10 ating from Ball State University with a business degree, he faced his first business challenge. His father's tavern was $64,000 in debt and failing. So Schnatter sold his car, used the money to purchase $1,600 of used restaurant equipment, knocked out a broom closet in the back of his father's tavern, and began selling pizzas to the tavern's customers. Soon the pizza became the tavern's main attraction and helped turn
15 the failing business around. In 1985 Schnatter officially opened the first Papa John's restaurant. Then he set about opening as many stores as the market would bear.

But Schnatter needed a recipe for success. With Little Caesar's promoting deep discounts and Domino's emphasizing fast delivery, Papa John's needed a fresh approach to compete successfully with the big chains. If you were John Schnatter, how
20 would you grow a small pizza operation into one that could compete with national players? Would you franchise your concept? Would you remain a private enterprise or go public? Would you expand overseas? Where would you focus your efforts?

UNDERSTANDING THE WORLD OF SMALL BUSINESS

Many small businesses start out like Papa John's: with an entrepreneur, an idea, and a drive to succeed. In fact, the United States was originally founded by people in-
25 volved in small business—the family farmer, the shopkeeper, the craftsperson. Successive waves of immigrants carried on the tradition, launching restaurants and laundries, providing repair and delivery services, and opening newsstands and bakeries.

The 1990s were a golden decade of entrepreneurship in the United States. Entrepreneurs launched small companies in droves to fill new consumer needs.
30 *What companies succeeded?* → Many took advantage of Internet technologies to gain a competitive edge. Some succeeded; others failed. But the resurgence of small businesses helped turn the U.S. economy into the growth engine for the world.

Today, over 5.8 million small companies exist in the United States. But defining what constitutes a small business is surprisingly tricky, because *small* is a relative term.
35 One reliable source of information for small businesses is the Small Business Administration (SBA). This government agency serves as a resource and advocate for small firms, providing them with financial assistance, training, and a variety of helpful programs. The SBA defines a **small business** as a firm that (a) is independently owned and operated, (b) is not dominant in its field, (c) is relatively small in
40 terms of annual sales, and (d) has fewer than 500 employees. The SBA reports that 80 percent of all U.S. companies have annual sales of less than $1 million and that about 60 percent of the nation's employers have fewer than five workers.

FACTORS CONTRIBUTING TO THE INCREASE
IN THE NUMBER OF SMALL BUSINESSES

Three factors are contributing to the increase in the number of small businesses today: technological advances, an increase in the number of women and minority
45 business owners, and corporate downsizing and outsourcing.

TECHNOLOGY AND THE INTERNET

The Internet, together with e-commerce, has spawned thousands of new business ventures. ShippingSupply.com is one such firm. Karen Young, a collector of knick-
Do Internet companies have low start-up costs? → knacks, founded this small business when she was looking for affordable packing and shipping materials for her mail-order items. On a whim, Young decided to market

50 bubble wrap, plastic foam, and shipping tubes she purchased directly from manufacturers to eBay sellers. Today, ShippingSupply.com has eight full-time employees, occupies 7,000 feet of warehouse space, and has over 35,500 customers in its database.

RISE IN NUMBER OF WOMEN AND MINORITY SMALL-BUSINESS OWNERS

The number of women-owned small businesses has also increased sharply over the past three decades—from 5 percent to over 39 percent of all small businesses. These
55 businesses now employ more than 18.5 million people and ring up more than $3.1 trillion in annual sales. Women are starting small businesses for a number of reasons. Some choose to run their own companies so they can enjoy a more flexible work arrangement; others start their own businesses because of barriers to corporate advancement, known as the glass ceiling. Josie Natori is a perfect example of such a
60 scenario. By her late twenties, Natori was earning six figures as the first female vice president of investment banking at Merrill Lynch. But Natori knew that her chances of further advancement were slim in the male-dominated financial world. So she started her own lingerie line. Today, Natori is the owner of a multi-million-dollar fashion empire that sells elegant lingerie and evening wear.

DOWNSIZING AND OUTSOURCING

65 Contrary to popular wisdom, business start-ups soar when the economy sours. During hard times, many companies downsize or lay off talented employees, who then have little to lose by pursuing self-employment. In fact, several well-known companies were started during recessions. Tech titans William Hewlitt and David Packard joined forces in Silicon Valley in 1938 during the Great Depression. Bill
70 Gates started Microsoft during the 1975 recession. And the founders of Sun Microsystems, Compaq Computer, Adobe Systems, Silicon Graphics, and Lotus Development started their companies in 1982—in the midst of a recession and high unemployment.

Taro Yamasaki/Time Life Pictures/Getty Images

John Schnatter, founder and president of the Papa John's Pizza chain, makes a surprise check at one of his outlets.

selection

2

To make up for layoffs of permanent staff, some companies **outsource** or sub-
contract special projects and secondary business functions to experts outside the organization. Others turn to outsourcing as a way to permanently eliminate entire
company departments. Regardless of the reason, the increased use of outsourcing
provides opportunities for smaller businesses to serve the needs of larger enterprises.

Is this a cause and effect relationship?

BEHIND THE SCENES: PAPA JOHN'S PIPING HOT PERFORMANCE

John Schnatter did a remarkable job of expanding from a single pizza store he
started in his father's tavern. Three years after Schnatter opened his first Papa
John's, he expanded outside of the Louisville, Kentucky, area. He was no novice. He
knew the grass roots of the pizza business, he had an intuitive grasp on what customers wanted, and he knew how to make pizzas taste a little bit better than the
competition. Moreover, he had the qualities of an entrepreneur: driven, intense,
willing to make things happen, visionary, and very competitive.

John Schnatter used franchising to grow the business. Today about 75 percent of
Papa John's are franchised; the rest are company owned. He was encouraged by
Kentucky Fried Chicken, Long John Silver's, Chi Chi's, and other Kentucky-born
restaurants that had successfully taken their franchised restaurants national. Schnatter
thought, "What the heck, maybe I could do it too." But to keep growth under control,
Papa John's didn't just move into an area and open up 200 stores. Schnatter grew the
stores one at a time—spending up to six months to a year assessing an area's potential.

It wasn't long before Papa John's began grabbing business from such giants as Pizza
Hut, Little Caesar's, and delivery king Domino's. Then in 1999 Papa John's made its
European debut by acquiring Perfect Pizza Holdings, a 205-unit delivery and carryout
pizza chain in the United Kingdom. The acquisition gave Papa John's instant access to
proven sites that would have been difficult to obtain. Besides the real estate, Perfect
Pizza had a good management team that Schnatter could fold into his organization.

Today, Papa John's has vaulted past Little Caesar's to become the nation's
third-largest pizza chain. The company now boasts over 2,700 stores in 47 states
and 9 international markets. Annual sales have mushroomed to about $1.7 billion.
In spite of its tremendous growth, Schnatter insists on maintaining the highest quality standards. He does so by keeping things simple. About 95 percent of the restaurants are takeout only. The menu is simple—just two types of pizza, thin crust or
regular—no exotic toppings, no salads, no sandwiches, and no buffalo wings.
Owners are trained to remake pies that rate less than 8 on the company's 10-point
scale. If the cheese shows a single air bubble or the crust is not golden brown, out
the offender goes. Schnatter's attention to product quality has earned the company
awards. Papa John's was twice voted number one in customer satisfaction among all
fast-food restaurants in the American Consumer Satisfaction Index.

Does lack of diversity lower costs?

To keep things in order, Schnatter visits four to five stores a week, often unan-
nounced. He also trains managers how to forecast product demand. Stores project demand one to two weeks in advance. They factor in anything from forthcoming promotions to community events to the next big high school football game. If a big game is on
TV, Schnatter wants to make sure the store owners are ready for the surge in deliveries.

Still, like many companies today, Papa John's faces new challenges. It's becoming increasingly difficult to grow the company's share of the pie. Although
Americans consume pizza at a rate of 350 slices a second, the pizza industry is stagnant and highly competitive. Growth usually comes at the expense of a competitor's
existing business. Moreover, to keep profitability in line, Schnatter has scaled back
company expansion plans and even closed some unprofitable outlets. But Schnatter

is determined to succeed. And if one strength rises above the others in Schnatter's path to success, it's his ability to recruit and retain the right people. "There's nothing special about John Schnatter except the people around me," Schnatter says. "They

125 make me look better" and they make Papa John's what it is—committed to its heritage of making superior-quality, traditional pizza.

(1,640 words)

—Courtland Bovee, John Thill, Barbara Schatzman,
Business in Action

Recall

Stop to self-test, relate, and react.

Your instructor may choose to give you a true-false comprehension review.

Write About the Selection

What factors contribute to the opening of small businesses? Why did John Schnatter open his pizza business?

Response Suggestion: Discuss and explain the cause and effect relationship of at least five factors that prompt people to take risks and start something new.

Contemporary *Link*

Entrepreneurs could seek profits in the fast food pizza business through innovations that support the current industry or through expanding product offerings. Can you think of clever innovations, such as plate-boxes, or perhaps a new product? To counter the stiff competition in the pizza business, perhaps new items should be considered. For example, McDonald's did not always have breakfast and the Egg McMuffin. What menu items or services would you add to expand pizza restaurant sales, and why? What trend would you set, or what needs would you seek to meet?

Skill Development: Identify Organizational Patterns

Answer the following with *T* (true) or *F* (false).

_____ 1. The first and last sections are examples with anecdotal information about a real business.

_____ 2. The section "Understanding the World of Small Business" defines a small business.

_____ 3. The organizational pattern of the section "Factors Contributing to the Increase in the Number of Small Businesses" is simple listing.

_____ 4. The organizational pattern of the section "Downsizing and Outsourcing" is comparison-contrast.

Check Your Comprehension

After reading the selection, answer the following questions with *a, b, c,* or *d.* To help you analyze your strengths and weaknesses, the question types are indicated.

Main Idea _____ 1. Which is the best statement of the main idea of this selection?

    a. Through hard work, Papa John's has expanded globally and become the third-largest pizza company in the world.

    b. The golden decade for entrepreneurship has peaked but is not over, as proved by Papa John's Pizza.

    c. Current factors are contributing to a rise in the number of small businesses, and Papa John's Pizza is a glowing example of one such entrepreneurial success.

    d. The highly competitive pizza business requires more than good tomato sauce to turn dough into dollars.

Detail _____ 2. When John Schnatter started his pizza business, he had all the following *except*

    a. years of experience making pizza dough.

    b. a college degree in business.

    c. training in running the pizza ovens.

    d. restaurant equipment from his father's business.

Inference _____ 3. The author implies that John Schnatter

    a. pulled his father's business out of a $64,000 debt.

    b. closed his father's tavern to open his pizza parlor.

    c. was financed in the pizza business by his father.

    d. continued to use the formula of liquor sales with pizza.

Detail _____ 4. As defined by the Small Business Administration, a small business is all of the following *except*

    a. it has fewer than 500 employees.

    b. it is independently operated.

    c. it is owned by stock holders.

    d. it is not dominant in its field.

Inference _____ 5. The author suggests that Karen Young's ShippingSupply.com business is

    a. primarily a retail store that customers enter to buy supplies.

    b. a prime candidate for franchising.

    c. a mail-order knickknack venture.

    d. a firm that conducts business over the Internet, with supplies shipped from a warehouse.

Inference _____ 6. The author implies that a glass ceiling is

    a. a barrier to high-level corporate advancement.

    b. a more flexible work arrangement.

    c. an entry into investment banking.

    d. a barrier to male-dominated entry-level positions.

selection 2

Detail   _____ 7. Downsizing in a company means to

     a. fire incompetent workers.
     b. lay off valued employees.
     c. freeze hiring until profits improve.
     d. subcontract for special projects.

Inference   _____ 8. An example of outsourcing done by an American company would be

     a. selling products in India.
     b. hiring experienced European workers for an American company.
     c. contracting for payroll accounting to be done by a company in Ireland.
     d. buying coffee beans from Latin America and processing them in the United States.

Inference   _____ 9. The author suggests that Schnatter's success can be attributed to all the following *except*

     a. hiring good people.
     b. adding a variety of items to the menu.
     c. insisting on high-quality standards for pizzas.
     d. personally visiting stores to keep things in order.

Inference   _____ 10. The reader can conclude that of the company's 2,700 stores,

     a. most are owned by Schnatter.
     b. all but 340 stores are now franchised.
     c. the company owns about 675 of them.
     d. Perfect Pizza Holdings franchised 2,400 stores.

Answer the following with *T* (true), *F* (false), or *CT* (can't tell).

Detail   _____ 11. During a recession and times of high unemployment, few new businesses are started.

Detail   _____ 12. According to the Small Business Administration, over half of the small American businesses hire fewer than five workers.

Inference   _____ 13. Schnatter bought Perfect Pizza in the United Kingdom because it was poorly managed.

Inference   _____ 14. The author suggests that Papa John's plans to expand into salads and sandwiches.

Inference   _____ 15. The author suggests that the pizza industry is rapidly increasing its customer base and adding new patrons who have never tried pizza.

Build Your Vocabulary

According to the way the italicized word was used in the selection, select *a, b, c,* or *d* for the word or phrase that gives the best definition. The number in parentheses indicates the line of the passage in which the word is located.

_____ 1. "would fill that *void*" (7)
   a. goal
   b. empty space
   c. union
   d. demand

_____ 2. "*Successive* waves of immigrants" (26)
   a. one after another
   b. eager
   c. unsteady
   d. overwhelming

_____ 3. "launched small companies in *droves*" (29)
   a. efforts
   b. desperation
   c. reactions
   d. large numbers

_____ 4. "not *dominant* in its field" (39)
   a. growing
   b. foremost
   c. secure
   d. competitive

_____ 5. "Tech *titans*" (68)
   a. enthusiasts
   b. explorers
   c. giants
   d. hobbiests

_____ 6. "was no *novice*" (81)
   a. beginner
   b. pushover
   c. coward
   d. follower

_____ 7. "its European *debut*" (95)
   a. achievement
   b. marketing ploy
   c. market entry
   d. diversity

_____ 8. "has *vaulted* past Little Caesar's" (99)
   a. sneaked
   b. crawled
   c. leaped
   d. slowly moved

_____ 9. "pizza industry is *stagnant*" (118)
   a. nervous
   b. cutthroat
   c. small
   d. not growing

_____ 10. "committed to its *heritage*" (125)
   a. logo
   b. brand
   c. management
   d. tradition

Search the Net

Use a search engine such as Google, AltaVista, Excite, Infoseek, Dogpile, Yahoo, or Lycos to find information on the nutritional value of your favorite slice of pizza, as well as two other frequently consumed fast-food items. List the calories, carbohydrates, fats, and proteins for each. For suggested Web sites and other research activities, go to http://www.ablongman.com/smith/.

What is a CD?

When you put money into a **CD (certificate of deposit)** through a bank, you are essentially lending the bank money for a fixed interest rate and for a designated period, called the **maturity.** The CD matures for one month or up to five years, and the interest rate is higher for the longer maturities. Banks then lend out the money at a higher rate for people to buy cars or houses. With a CD, the return of your **principal** (original money) is guaranteed. You do not have to worry about losing your money.

What is a bond?

A **bond** is a loan to a government or a corporation. For example, many cities sell **municipal bonds** to finance infrastructure improvements or schools. When you buy bonds, you are lending the city money, and the taxpayers will pay you interest. The interest rate on bonds is usually higher than that on CDs, but the risk is greater. You have a promise that you will be paid back at **maturity** (a specified period), and you hope the city will be able to fulfill this promise. If you buy a **U.S. Treasury Bill** or a **savings bond,** you are lending money to the federal government, which uses the money to pay down the national debt. Because U.S. Treasury bills are backed by the federal government, they are safer investments than are municipal bonds.

What is a mutual fund?

A **mutual fund** is a company that pools the investment money of many individuals and purchases a **portfolio** (array of holdings) of stocks, bonds, and other securities. Each investor then shares accordingly in the profits or losses. Investors also pay a fee for professionals to manage the portfolio, which includes bookkeeping, researching, buying, and selling. All fees for management come out of profits before they are shared.

An advantage of mutual funds is that they offer instant **diversification.** With a $1,000 purchase, you can have a part ownership in many different stocks

John H. Johnson, the late former publisher of *Ebony* magazine, and his daughter, Linda Johnson Rice, company president, ran the fifty-year-old publishing business.

AP/Wide World Photos

or bonds. Also, if you do not have the expertise to research individual stocks, you can rely on the judgment of the professional money managers. Different mutual funds specialize in different areas such as large companies, small companies, or even IPOs, which are initial public offerings of stock. You would want to find one that matches your investment interests and also has a positive track record of growth.

What is a capital gain?

A capital gain is a profit on the sale of a property or a security. A **short-term capital gain** is a profit made on stocks or bonds owned for less than one year. This profit is taxed as ordinary income and may be as high as 40 percent for people in upper tax brackets. A **long-term capital gain,** on the other hand, is a profit on a property or security owned for over a year. On this, investors are taxed at a maximum of 15 percent.

Review *Questions*

After studying the material, answer the following questions:

1. Are CD rates better for a month or a year? _____
   _____

2. What does the bank do with your CD money? _____
   _____
   _____

3. What is your principal? _____
   _____
   _____

4. What is a municipal bond? _____
   _____
   _____

5. What are the advantages of a mutual fund? _____
   _____
   _____

6. Is tax greater on a short- or long-term capital gain? _____
   _____

7. How long must you hold a property before selling to achieve a long-term capital gain? _____

8. What is a portfolio? _____
   _____
   _____

9. For the safest choice, should you pick bonds, CDs, or a mutual fund? _____
   _____

10. What does diversification mean? _____
    _____
    _____

Your instructor may choose to give a true-false review of these business concepts.

213

6 Organizing Textbook Information

- What is study reading?
- What is annotating?
- What is the Cornell Method of note taking?
- What is outlining?
- What is mapping?

Guy Billout, *Maze*, 1995. Watercolor and airbrush. 4¹¹⁄₁₆ × 5 ⁹⁄₁₆ inches.

The Demands of College Study

If you are like most students, you have already confronted new challenges in college. Your courses may cover a great deal of information more rapidly than you are used to, and the study techniques you used in high school may not be as effective in college. In a sense, college textbook assignments are like the Olympics of reading. Can you train like an athlete to meet the challenge?

exercise 6.1 **Discovering Your Fitness as a Reader**

Take the following inventory to see how you already measure up. Check *yes* or *no* for your response.

What Kind of Reader Are You?

1. Do you mark your text while reading?   Yes——— No———
2. Do you make marginal notes while reading?   Yes——— No———
3. Do you take notes on paper while reading?   Yes——— No———
4. Do you differentiate between details and main ideas?   Yes——— No———
5. Do you stop to summarize while reading?   Yes——— No———
6. Do you have a purpose behind note taking?   Yes——— No———
7. Do you review your textbook notes?   Yes——— No———
8. Do you review class lecture notes within 24 hours?   Yes——— No———
9. Do you link old and new information to remember it?   Yes——— No———
10. Do you use maps or charts to condense notes for study?   Yes——— No———

If all your answers were yes, you are well on your way to becoming an Olympic champ in the college arena! If some of your answers were no, you will want to start training now.

Your first assignment in most college courses will be to read Chapter 1 of the assigned textbook. At that time, you will immediately discover that a textbook chapter contains an amazing amount of information. Your instructor will continue to assign the remaining chapters in rapid succession. Don't panic! Your task is to select the information that you need to remember, learn it, and organize it for future study for a midterm or final exam that is weeks or months away.

In a study of the demands on students in introductory college history courses during a ten-week period,[1] three professors analyzed the actual reading demands of classes they observed and found that students were asked to read an average of 825 pages over the course of each class. The average length of weekly assignments was more than 80 pages, but the amount varied both with

---

[1]J. G. Carson, N. D. Chase, S. U. Gibson, and M. F. Hargrove, "Literacy Demands of the Undergraduate Curriculum," *Reading, Research, and Instruction* 31 (1992): 25–30.

the professor and the topic. In one class, students had to read 287 pages in only ten days.

Students were expected to grasp relationships between parts and wholes, place people and events in historical context, and retain facts. Professors spent 85 percent of class time lecturing and 6 percent of the time giving tests, which often amounted to 100 percent of the final grade. In short, the demands were high and students were expected to work independently to organize textbook material efficiently and effectively to prepare for that crucial 6 percent of test-taking time.

The task is difficult, but you have seen many others succeed—and even earn A's. Train for the challenge by using the skills of a successful learner. Consciously build knowledge networks—your foundation for thought interaction—and organize your materials for learning.

Building Knowledge Networks

The old notion of studying and learning is that studying is an information-gathering activity. Knowledge is the "product" you can acquire by transferring information from the text to your memory. According to this view, good learners locate important information, review it, and then transfer the information to long-term memory. The problem with this model is that review does not always guarantee recall, and rehearsal is not always enough to ensure that information is encoded into long-term memory.

Experts now know that studying and learning involve more than review, rehearsal, and memorization; they require making meaningful connections. Cognitive psychologists focus on schemata, or prior knowledge, and the learner's own goals. To understand and remember, you must link new information to already existing schemata, creating networks of knowledge. As your personal knowledge expands, you create new networks. As the learner, you—not your professor—decide how much effort you need to expend, and you adjust your studying according to your answers to questions such as "How much do I need to know?" "Will the test be multiple-choice or essay?" and "Do I want to remember this forever?" In this way, you make judgments and select the material to remember and integrate into knowledge networks.

Organizing Textbook Information

In this chapter, we discuss four methods of organizing textbook information for future study: (1) annotating, (2) note taking, (3) outlining, and (4) mapping. Why four? In a review of more than five hundred research studies on organizing textbook information, two college developmental reading professors concluded that "no one study strategy is appropriate for all students in all study situations."[2] On the basis of these findings, they established guidelines encouraging students to develop a repertoire of skills in study reading. They felt that students need to know, for example, that underlining takes less time than note taking but that note taking or outlining can result in better test scores.

---

[2]D. Caverly and V. Orlando, *Textbook Strategies in Teaching Reading and Study Strategies at the College Level* (Newark, NJ: International Reading Association, 1991), pp. 86–165.

Your selection of a study-reading strategy for organizing textbook material will vary based on the announced testing demands, the nature of the material, the amount of time you have to devote to study, and your preference for a particular strategy. Being familiar with all four strategies affords a repertoire of choices.

The following comments on organizing textbook and lecture materials come from college freshmen taking an introductory course in American history. These students were enrolled in a Learning Strategies for History course that focused on how to be a successful student. Their comments probably address some of your experiences in trying to rapidly organize large amounts of textbook material.

From a student who earned an A:

Organization of my class notes is very important. The notes can be very easy to refer to if they are organized. This enables me to go back and fill in information, and it also helps me to understand the cycle of events that is taking place. I generally try to outline my notes by creating sections. Sections help me to understand the main idea or add a description of a singular activity. I usually go back and number the sections to make them easy for reference.

Taking notes can be very difficult sometimes. In class, if my mind strays just a few times, I can easily lose track of where my notes were going. Then again, when I am reading my textbook, I may read without even realizing what I just read. The difference in class and the textbook is that I can go back and reread the text.

It is very easy to overdo the notes that I take from the text. Originally, I tended to take too much information from the book, but now, as I read more, I can better grasp the main idea. Underlining also makes a big difference. When I underline, I can go back and reread the book.

From another student who earned an A:

I think that the best way to do it is to completely read the assignment and then go back over it to clear up any confusion. I would also recommend going over your lecture notes before starting your reading assignment, which is something I didn't do this past week. I also try to key in on words like "two significant changes" or "major factors." Sometimes you may go three or four pages without seeing anything like that. My question is, "What do you do then?" I think that you should write down the point or points that were repeated the most or stressed the most.

From a student who earned a B:

Taking notes is no longer something that you can just do and expect to have good and complete notes. I have learned that taking notes is a process of learning within itself.

From a student who earned a C:

In starting college, I have made a few changes in how I take notes. For instance, I am leaving a lot more space in taking notes. I find that they are easier to read when they are spread out. I have also been using a highlighter and marking topics and definitions and people's names. I make checks near notes that will definitely be on a test so I can go over them.

When I am reading, I have begun to do a lot of underlining in the book, which I would never do before because my school would not take back books if they were marked. I have also started to note important parts with a little star and confusing parts with a question mark.

All these students were successful in the history class, although the final grades varied. Each student's reflection offers sincere and sound advice. Regardless of the way you organize material—by annotating, note taking, outlining, or mapping—your goal should be to make meaning by making connections.

Annotating

Which of the following would seem to indicate the most effective use of the textbook as a learning tool?

1. A text without a single mark—not even the owner's name has spoiled the sacred pages
2. A text ablaze with color—almost every line is adorned with a red, blue, yellow, or green colored marker
3. A text with a scattered variety of markings—highlighting, underlines, numbers, and stars are interspersed with circles, arrows, and short, written notes

Naturally, option three is the best. The rationale for the first is probably for a better book resale value, but usually used books resell for the same price whether they are marked or unmarked. The reason for the second is probably procrastination in decision making. Students who highlight everything—the "yellow book disease"—rely on coming back later to figure out what is *really* important. Although selective highlighting in a light color such as yellow is a helpful strategy, highlighting everything is inefficient. The variety of markings in the third strategy enables you to pinpoint ideas for later study.

Why Annotate?

The textbook is a learning tool and should be used as such; it should not be preserved as a treasure. A college professor requires a particular text because it contains information vital to your understanding of the course material. The text places a vast body of knowledge in your hands, much more material than the professor could possibly give in class. It is your job to cull through this information, make some sense out of it, and select the important points that need to be remembered.

Annotating is a method of highlighting main ideas, major supporting details, and key terms. The word *annotate* means "to add marks." By using a system of symbols and notations rather than just colored stripes, you mark the text after the first reading so that a complete rereading will not be necessary. The markings indicate pertinent points to review for an exam. If your time is short, however, highlighting with a colored marker is better than not making any marks at all. The Reader's Tip on page 220 offers an example of annotation.

Marking in the textbook itself is frequently faster than summarizing, outlining, or note taking. In addition, since your choices and reactions are all in one place, you can view them at a glance for later study rather than referring to separate notebooks. Your textbook becomes a workbook.

Students who annotate, however, will probably want to make a list of key terms and ideas on their own paper to have a reduced form of the information for review and self-testing.

Reader's *Tip* — How to Annotate

Develop a system of notations. Use circles, stars, numbers, and whatever else helps you put the material visually into perspective. *Anything that makes sense to you is a correct notation.* Here is an example of one student's marking system:

Main idea	( )
Supporting material	————
Major trend or possible essay exam question	*
Important smaller point to know for multiple-choice item	✓
Word that you must be able to define	⬭
Section of material to reread for review	{ }
Numbering of important details under a major issue	(1), (2), (3)
Didn't understand and must seek advice	?
Notes in the margin	Ex., Def., Topic
Questions in the margin	Why signif.?
Indicating relationships	⌒
Related issue or idea	← R

When to Annotate

Plan to annotate after a unit of thought has been presented and you can view the information as a whole. This may mean marking after a single paragraph or after three pages; your marking will vary with the material.

When you are first reading, every sentence seems of major importance as each new idea unfolds, and you may be tempted to annotate too much. Resist this tendency, as overmarking wastes both reading time and review time. Instead, be patient and read through a passage or section until the end, at which point the author's complete thought will have been fully developed; and the major points will emerge from a background of lesser details. With all the facts at your fingertips and in your consciousness, you can decide what you want to remember. At the end of the course, your textbook should have that worn but well-organized look.

EXAMPLE The following passage is taken from a biology textbook. Notice how the annotations have been used to highlight main ideas and significant supporting details. This same passage will be used throughout this chapter to demonstrate each of the four methods of organizing textbook material.

Circulatory Systems

When we examine the systems by which blood reaches all the cells of an animal, we find two general types, known as open and closed circulatory systems.

Def. I

Open Circulatory Systems

The essential feature of the (open circulatory system) is that the blood moves through a body cavity—such as the abdominal cavity—and bathes the cells directly. The open circulatory system is particularly characteristic of insects and other arthropods, although it is also found in some other organisms.

In most insects the blood does not take a major part in oxygen transport. Oxygen enters the animal's body through a separate network of branching tubes that open to the atmosphere on the outside of the animal. (This type of respiratory system will be discussed in more detail in the next chapter.) Blood in an open circulatory system moves somewhat more slowly than in the average closed system. The slower system is adequate for insects because it does not have to supply the cells with oxygen.

Def. II

Closed Circulatory Systems

In a (closed circulatory system) the blood flows through a well-defined system of vessels with many branches. In the majority of closed systems the blood is responsible for oxygen transport. To supply all the body cells with sufficient oxygen, the blood must move quickly through the blood vessels. A closed circulatory system must therefore have an efficient pumping mechanism, or heart, to set the blood in motion and keep it moving briskly through the body.

Ex. 4

All vertebrates possess closed circulatory systems. Simple closed systems are also found in some invertebrates, including annelid worms. A good example of such a simple closed circulatory system can be seen in the earthworm.

Ex. R ⟶ regeneration?

exercise 6.2   **Annotating**

Using a variety of markings, annotate the following selection as if you were preparing for a quiz on the material. Remember, do not underscore as you read, but wait until you finish a paragraph or a section, and then mark the important points.

WORK SCHEDULES

Several work-scheduling trends are evident in the new millennium: flextime, job sharing, job splitting, permanent part-time workers, telecommuting, and employee leasing. Companies are increasing their use of these flexible approaches to work. For example, Merck has reported increased use of flextime, telecommuting, and job sharing. The composition of Merck's workforce is also illustrative of trends for the future, as women make up 52 percent of its U.S. employees while minorities account for 24 percent. More significantly, in its U.S. operations 32 percent of the company's managerial positions are held by women while minorities account for 16 percent. All of these trends present unique challenges and opportunities for supervisors.

Flextime allows people to vary their starting and ending times. A company may specify a core time, requiring all employees to be on the job from 10:00 A.M. until 1:00 P.M., but some may start as early as 6:00 A.M. or as late as 10:00 A.M. Some may go home as early as 1:00 P.M. Flexible scheduling appeals to working parents with school-age children and to a growing number of self-managing information workers. But such work schedules make it difficult for one supervisor to manage people who work over a span of 10 or more hours. **Compressed work weeks** of four 10-hour days also help organizations meet the needs of employees.

The Bechtel Group, a construction and engineering firm, has 27,800 employees worldwide. It offers a flexible schedule to its employees in Houston, Texas. Under the plan, employees work nine-hour days, Monday through Thursday each week. Each Friday, about half the employees work eight hours, and the other half have the day off. All employees work 80 hours in nine days. Management initially feared that longer work days would mean lower productivity, but productivity has improved. Employees seemed to be scheduling more of their personal business for their off time.

Job sharing allows two or more people to work at one full-time job. A growing number of people want to work part time, and a growing number of businesses want more part-time employees. The employer benefits in several ways. It gets double the creativity for each shared job. It may also cut benefit costs, which often add 30 to 40 percent to an employee's salary. People come to work refreshed and eager to perform and experience less fatigue and stress. Boring jobs can be more attractive when performed for fewer than 40 hours each week.

Permanent part-time workers usually work for small companies that do not have enough work for a full-timer to perform. Part-time work may be for any number of hours and days per week, up to 35 hours. Older individuals, such as those who may have retired from other jobs, provide a source of reliable employees who may be interested in permanent part-time work.

Temporary workers or contingent workers fill millions of jobs in the United States each year. The U.S. Bureau of Labor has estimated, using a broad definition of "contingent workers," that 4.4 percent of the employed population consists of contingent workers. A somewhat lower estimate is provided by the CEO of Manpower Inc., who has estimated that 2.5 percent of the U.S. workforce is made up of temporary workers. Temporary work agencies provide people to work part time for clients who need temporary help. Most come well trained for their jobs and work in skilled areas such as computer services, secretarial services, manufacturing, and accounting. Another view of the broad presence of temporary workers in the workforce is provided by the president of a temporary help firm that provides temporary employees to such employers as Sun Microsystems and Silicon Graphics: "There's not a single major company in the United States that doesn't have a substantial percentage of the work force as contingent workers."

Telecommuting allows a full- or part-time employee to work at home while remaining connected to the employer by telecommunications devices such as computers, e-mail, the Internet, and fax machines. Estimates of the number of telecommuters in the United States vary widely, with numbers ranging from 9 million to 24 million. More than half of the Fortune 500 companies reported that 1 to 5 percent of their employees are involved in telecommuting, and some companies have large numbers of telecommuters. For example, Merrill Lynch has 3,500 telecommuters. Nortel, one of the pioneers in this area, had 3,600 telecommuters at one point. In addition, AT&T has announced a telecommuting day, encouraging and making arrangements for any worker who can to telecommute. Telecommuters can increase their quality of life by living in geographic areas that are long distances from their offices and combining work at home with child care arrangements. In addition, major disasters quickly isolate people from their jobs and places of employment. The terrorist attack on the World Trade Center on September 11, 2001, earthquakes, floods, and hurricanes have highlighted the value of telecommuting—within hours, companies whose physical plants were in ruins were making alternative arrangements to meet their customers' needs, thanks to cellular communications.

—Charles R. Greer and W. Richard Plunkett,
Supervision: Diversity and Teams in the Workplace, 10th ed.

Review your annotations. Have you sufficiently highlighted the main idea and the significant supporting details?

Note Taking

Many students prefer **note taking,** or jotting down on their own paper brief sentence summaries of important textbook information. With this method, margin space to the left of the summaries can be used to identify topics. Thus, important topics and their explanations are side by side on notepaper for later study. To reduce notes for review and trigger thoughts for self-testing, highlight key terms with a yellow marker. The Reader's Tip on page 224 summarizes one note-taking method.

Why Take Textbook Notes?

Students who prefer note taking say that working with a pencil and paper while reading keeps them involved with the material and thus improves concentration. This method takes longer than annotating, but after annotating the text, you may at times feel an additional need—based on later testing demands, time, and the complexity of the material—to organize the information further into notes.

Reader's *Tip* How to Take Notes: The Cornell Method

One of the most popular systems of note taking is called the Cornell Method. The steps are as follows:

1. Draw a line down your paper two and one-half inches from the left side to create a two-and-one-half-inch margin for noting key words and a six-inch area on the right for sentence summaries.
2. After you have finished reading a section, tell yourself what you have read, and jot down sentence summaries in the six-inch area on the right side of your paper. Use your own words, and make sure you have included the main ideas and significant supporting details. Be brief, but use complete sentences.
3. Review your summary sentences and underline key words. Write these key words in the column on the left side of your paper. These words can be used to stimulate your memory of the material for later study.

You can use the Cornell Method to take notes on classroom lectures. The chart shown below, developed by Norman Stahl and James King, explains the procedure and gives a visual display of the results.

The example on pages 224–225 applies the Cornell Method of note taking to the biology passage on the circulatory system that you have already read (see page 221). Although the creators of this method recommend the writing of sentence summaries, you may find that short phrases can sometimes be as or more efficient and still adequately communicate the message for later study.

Taking Class Notes: The Cornell Method

← 2¹/₂ INCHES →	← 6 INCHES →
REDUCE IDEAS TO CONCISE JOTTINGS AND SUMMARIES AS CUES FOR RECITING.	*RECORD THE LECTURE AS FULLY AND AS MEANINGFULLY AS POSSIBLE.*
Cornell Method	This sheet demonstrates the Cornell Method of taking classroom notes. It is recommended by experts from the Learning Center at Cornell University.
Line drawn down paper	You should draw a line down your notepage about 2¹/₂ inches from the left side. On the right side of the line simply record your classroom notes as you usually do. Be sure that you write legibly.

After the lecture	After the lecture you should read the notes, fill in materials that you missed, make your writing legible, and underline any important materials. Ask another classmate for help if you missed something during the lecture.
Use the recall column for key phrases	The recall column on the left will help you when you study for your tests. Jot down any important words or key phrases in the recall column. This activity forces you to rethink and summarize your notes. The key words should stick in your mind.
Five Rs	The Five Rs will help you take better notes based on the Cornell Method.
Record	1. Record any information given during the lecture which you believe will be important.
Reduce	2. When you reduce your information you are summarizing and listing key words/phrases in the recall column.
Recite	3. Cover the notes you took for your class. Test yourself on the words in the recall section. This is what we mean by recite.
Reflect	4. You should reflect on the information you received during the lecture. Determine how your ideas fit in with the information.
Review	5. If you review your notes you will remember a great deal more when you take your midterm.
Binder & paper	Remember it is a good idea to keep your notes in a standard-sized binder. Also you should use only full-sized binder paper. You will be able to add photocopied materials easily to your binder.
Hints	Abbreviations and symbols should be used when possible. Abbrev. & sym. give you time when used automatically.

Circulatory System

Two types Open and closed	There are two types, the open and the closed, by which blood reaches the cells of an animal.
Open	In the open system, found mostly in insects and other arthropods, blood moves through the body and bathes the
Bathes cells	cells directly. The blood moves slower than in the closed system, and oxygen
Oxygen from outside	is supplied from the outside air through tubes.

(continued)

Closed Blood vessels Blood carries oxygen Heart pumps	In the <u>closed system</u>, blood <u>flows</u> <u>through</u> a system of <u>vessels</u>, <u>oxygen</u> is <u>carried</u> by the blood so it must move quickly, and the <u>heart</u> serves as a <u>pumping</u> mechanism. All vertebrates, as well as earthworms, have closed systems.

exercise 6.3   **Note Taking**

Using a variety of markings, annotate the following selection as if you were preparing for a quiz on the material. Remember, do not underscore as you read, but wait until you finish a paragraph or a section, and then mark the important points.

WHY THE FOOD PYRAMID HAS BEEN REVISED

The limitations of the USDA Food Guide Pyramid have resulted in serious criticisms about the effectiveness of the Pyramid as a tool and led nutrition experts to question its usefulness in designing a healthful diet. One major criticism is that it is overly simple and does not help consumers make appropriate food selections within each food group. For example, all the grains and cereals are grouped into one category with no distinction made between whole and refined grains or carbohydrates. A serving of Fruit Loops "counts" the same as a serving of oatmeal.

Yet nutritionists know that whole-grain foods contain important nutrients, such as fiber, vitamins, and minerals—nutrients that are typically lost when grains are refined. To help make up for this loss, some of these nutrients, but not all, are added back through a process called enrichment (or fortification). Whole grains are also high in fiber, increase the feeling of fullness, and are typically digested more slowly than refined grains, gradually releasing glucose into the blood. In contrast, refined-grain foods are low in fiber and typically high in simple sugars, causing a spike in blood glucose and contributing to increased hunger shortly after their consumption.

A second criticism is that the Pyramid makes a poor distinction between healthful and unhealthful fats. All the fats are lumped together at the tip of the Pyramid, and consumers are told to use them "sparingly." Not all fats have the same effect on health so they cannot be easily grouped together. We want to limit our intake of saturated and trans fats, while making sure our diets are adequate in the monounsaturated and polyunsaturated fats that are essential for good health and may protect against disease.

A third criticism is that the serving sizes suggested in the Food Guide Pyramid are unrealistic or do not coincide with typical serving sizes of foods listed on food labels. For instance, one serving of a muffin as defined in the Food Guide Pyramid is 1.5 ounces, but most muffins available to consumers range from 2 ounces to 8 ounces! The way that foods are packaged is also confusing to consumers. Unless people read food labels carefully, it is easy to consume an entire package of a food that contains multiple servings and assume that the entire package is equal to one serving. For example, it is common to find soft drinks sold in 20 fluid ounce bottles. Although the serving size listed on the label is 8 fluid ounces, and total servings per bottle is listed as 2.5, most people just drink the entire bottle in one sitting and assume they had one soft drink.

—Janice Thompson and Melinda Manore,
Nutrition: An Applied Approach

Review your annotations. Have you sufficiently highlighted the main idea and the significant supporting details?

exercise 6.4 **Note Taking**

In college courses, you will usually take notes on lengthy chapters or entire books. For practice with note taking here, use the passage "Work Schedules," which you have already annotated (see pages 222–223). Prepare a two-column sheet, and take notes using the Cornell Method.

exercise 6.5 **Note Taking**

For more practice with note taking, use the passage "Why the Food Pyramid Has Been Revised," which you have already annotated (see pages 226–227). Prepare a two-column sheet, and take notes using the Cornell Method.

Outlining

Outlining enables you to organize and highlight major points and subordinates items of lesser importance. In a glance, the indentations, Roman numerals, numbers, and letters quickly show how one idea relates to another and how all aspects relate to the whole. The layout of the outline is simply a graphic display of main ideas and significant supporting details.

The following example is a picture-perfect version of the basic outline form. In practice your "working outline" would probably not be as detailed or as regular as this. Use the tools of the outline format, *especially the indentations and numbers,* to devise your own system for organizing information.

I. First main idea
   A. Supporting idea
      1. Detail
      2. Detail

        3. Detail
           a. Minor detail
           b. Minor detail
     B. Supporting idea
        1. Detail
        2. Detail
     C. Supporting idea
II. Second main idea
     A. Supporting idea
     B. Supporting idea

Why Outline?

Students who outline usually drop the precision of picture-perfect outlines but still make good use of the numbers, letters, indentations, and mixture of topics and phrases to show levels of importance. A quick look to the far left of an outline indicates the topic, with subordinate ideas indented underneath. The letters, numbers, and indentations form a visual display of the parts that make up the whole. Good outliners use plenty of paper so the levels of importance are evident at a glance.

Another use of the outline is to organize notes from class lectures. During class, most professors try to add to the material in the textbook and put it into perspective for students. Since the notes taken in class represent a large percentage of the material you need to know to pass the course, they are extremely important.

How to Outline

While listening to a class lecture, you must almost instantly receive, synthesize, and select material and, at the same time, record something on paper for future reference. The difficulty of the task demands order and decision making. Do not be so eager to copy down every detail that you miss the big picture. One of the most efficient methods of taking lecture notes is to use a modified outline form—a version that adds stars, circles, and underlines to emphasize further the levels of importance.

Professors say that they can walk around a classroom and look at the notes students have taken from the text or from a lecture and tell how well each student has understood the lesson. The errors most frequently observed fall into the following categories. The Reader's Tip provides more details about how to outline.

1. Poor organization
2. Failure to show importance
3. Writing too much
4. Writing too little

Reader's *Tip* — Guidelines for Successful Outlining

The most important thing to remember when outlining is to ask yourself, *"What is my purpose?"* You don't need to include everything, and you don't need a picture-perfect version for study notes. Include only what you believe you will need to remember later, and use a numbering system and indentations to show how one item relates to another. There are several other important guidelines to remember:

- **Get a general overview before you start.**
  How many main topics do there seem to be?
- **Use phrases rather than sentences.**
  Can you state it in a few short words?
- **Put it in your own words.**
  If you cannot paraphrase it, do you really understand it?
- **Be selective.**
  Are you highlighting or completely rewriting?
- **After outlining, indicate key terms with a yellow marker.**
  Highlighting makes them highly visible for later review and self-testing.

EXAMPLE   Notice how numbers, letters, and indentations are used in the following outline to show levels of importance.

Circulatory System

I. Open circulatory system
  A. Blood moves through the body and bathes cells directly
  B. Examples—insects and other arthropods
  C. Oxygen supplied from outside air through tubes
  D. Slower blood movement since not supplying cells with oxygen
II. Closed circulatory system
  A. Blood flows through system of vessels
  B. Oxygen carried by blood so it must move quickly
  C. Heart serves as pumping mechanism
  D. Example—all vertebrates
  E. Example—earthworms

exercise 6.6   **Outlining**

Outline the key ideas in the following selection as if you were planning to use your notes to study for a quiz. You may want to annotate before you outline.

REACTING TO STRESS WITH DEFENSE MECHANISMS

Stress may occasionally promote positive outcomes. Motivated to overcome stress and the situations that produce it, we may learn new and adaptive responses. It is also clear, however, that stress involves a very unpleasant emotional component. **Anxiety** is a general feeling of tension or apprehension that often accompanies a perceived threat to one's well-being. It is this unpleasant emotional component that often prompts us to learn new responses to rid ourselves of stress.

There are a number of techniques, essentially self-deception, that we may employ to keep from feeling the unpleasantness associated with stress. These techniques, or tricks we play on ourselves, are not adaptive in the sense of helping us to get rid of anxiety by getting rid of the source of stress. Rather, they are mechanisms that we can and do use to defend ourselves against the *feelings* of stress. They are called **defense mechanisms.** Freud believed defense mechanisms to be the work of the unconscious mind. He claimed that they are ploys that our unconscious mind uses to protect us (our *self* or *ego*) from stress and anxiety. Many psychologists take issue with Freud's interpretation of defense mechanisms and consider defense mechanisms in more general terms than did Freud, but few will deny that defense mechanisms exist. It *is* true that they are generally ineffective if consciously or purposively employed. The list of defense mechanisms is a long one. Here, we'll review some of the more common defense mechanisms, providing an example of each, to give you an idea of how they might serve as a reaction to stress.

Repression. The notion of **repression** is the most basic of all the defense mechanisms. It is sometimes referred to as *motivated forgetting,* which gives us a good idea of what is involved. Repression is a matter of conveniently forgetting about some stressful, anxiety-producing event, conflict, or frustration. Paul had a teacher in high school he did not get along with at all. After spending an entire semester trying his best to do whatever was asked, Paul failed the course. The following summer, while walking with his girlfriend, Paul encountered this teacher. When he tried to introduce his girlfriend, Paul could not remember his teacher's name. He had repressed it. As a long-term reaction to stress, repressing the names of people we don't like or that we associate with unpleasant, stressful experiences is certainly not a very adaptive reaction. But at least it can protect us from dwelling on such unpleasantness.

Denial. **Denial** is a very basic mechanism of defense against stress. In denial, a person simply refuses to acknowledge the realities of a stressful situation. When a physician first tells a patient that he or she has a terminal illness, a common reaction is denial; the patient refuses to believe that there is anything seriously wrong.

Other less stressful events than serious illness sometimes evoke denial. Many smokers are intelligent individuals who are well aware of the data and the statistics that can readily convince them that they are slowly (or rapidly) killing themselves by continuing to smoke. But they deny the evidence. Somehow they are able to convince themselves that they aren't going to die from smoking; that's something that happens to other people, and besides, they *could* stop whenever they wanted.

Rationalization. **Rationalization** amounts to making excuses for our behaviors when facing the real reasons for our behaviors would be stressful. The real reason Kevin failed his psychology midterm is that he didn't study for it and has missed a number of classes. Kevin hates to admit, even to himself, that he could have been so stupid as to flunk that exam because of his own actions. As a result, he rationalizes: "It wasn't really *my* fault. I had a lousy instructor. We used a rotten text. The tests were grossly unfair. I've been fighting the darn flu all semester. And Marjorie had that big party the night before the exam." Now Susan, on the other hand, really did want to go to Marjorie's party, but she decided that she wouldn't go unless somebody asked her. As it happens, no one did. In short order, Susan rationalized that she "didn't want to go to that dumb party anyway"; she needed to "stay home and study."

Compensation. We might best think of **compensation** in the context of personal frustration. This defense mechanism is a matter of overemphasizing some positive trait or ability to counterbalance a shortcoming in some other trait or ability. If some particular goal-directed behavior becomes blocked, a person may compensate by putting extra effort and attention into some other aspect of behavior. For example, Karen, a seventh grader, wants to be popular. She's a reasonably bright and pleasant teenager, but isn't—in the judgment of her classmates—very pretty. Karen *may* compensate for her lack of good looks by studying very hard to be a good student, or by memorizing jokes and funny stories, or by becoming a good musician. Compensation is not just an attempt to be a well-rounded individual. It is a matter of expending *extra* energy and resources in one direction to offset shortcomings in other directions.

Fantasy. **Fantasy** is one of the more common defense mechanisms used by college students. It is often quite useful. Particularly after a hard day when stress levels are high, isn't it pleasant to sit in a comfortable chair, kick off your shoes, lie back, close your eyes, and daydream, perhaps about graduation day, picturing yourself walking across the stage to pick up your diploma—with honors?

When things are not going well for us, we may retreat into a world of fantasy where everything always goes well. Remember that to engage from time to time in fantasizing is a normal and acceptable response to stress. You should not get worried if you fantasize occasionally. On the other hand, you should realize that there are some potential dangers here. You need to be able to keep separate those activities that are real and those that occur in your fantasies. And you should realize that fantasy in itself will not solve whatever problem is causing you stress. Fantasizing about academic successes may help you feel better for a while, but it is not likely to make you a better student.

Projection. **Projection** is a matter of seeing in others those very traits and motives that cause us stress when we see them in ourselves. Under pressure to do well on an exam, Mark may want to cheat, but his conscience won't let him. Because of projection, he may think he sees cheating going on all around him.

Projection is a mechanism that is often used in conjunction with hostility and aggression. When people begin to feel uncomfortable about their own levels of hostility, they often project their aggressiveness onto others, coming to believe that others are "out to do me harm," and "I'm only defending myself."

Regression. To employ **regression** is to return to earlier, even childish, levels of behavior that were once productive or reinforced. Curiously enough, we often find regression in children. Imagine a four-year-old who until very recently was an only child. Now Mommy has returned from the hospital with a new baby sister. The four-year-old is no longer "the center of the universe," as her new little sister now gets parental attention. The four-year-old reverts to earlier behaviors and starts wetting the bed, screaming for a bottle of her own, and crawling on all fours in an attempt to get attention. She is regressing.

Many defense mechanisms can be seen on the golf course, including regression. After Doug knocks three golf balls into the lake, he throws a temper tantrum, stamps his feet, and tosses his three-iron in the lake. His childish regressive behavior won't help his score, but it may act as a release from the tension of his stress at the moment.

Displacement. The defense mechanism of **displacement** is usually discussed in the context of aggression. Your goal-directed behavior becomes blocked or thwarted. You are frustrated, under stress, and somewhat aggressive. You cannot vent your aggression directly at the source of the frustration, so you displace it to a safer outlet. Dorothy expects to get promoted at work, but someone else gets the new job she wanted. Her goal-directed behavior has been frustrated. She's upset and angry at her boss, but feels (perhaps correctly) that blowing her top at her boss will do more harm than good. She's still frustrated, so she displaces her hostility toward her husband, children, and/or the family cat.

Displacement doesn't have to involve hostility and aggression. A young couple discovers that having children is not going to be as easy as they thought. They want children badly, but there's an infertility problem that is causing considerable stress. Their motivation for love, sharing, and caring may be displaced toward a pet, nephews and nieces, or some neighborhood children—at least until their own goals can be realized with children of their own.

The list of defense mechanisms provided above is not an exhaustive one. These are among the most common, and this list gives you an idea of what defense mechanisms are like.

—Josh Gerow,
Psychology: An Introduction, 2nd ed.

exercise 6.7 **Outlining**

For additional practice, outline the selection on "Work Schedules" beginning on page 222. Use your annotations and notes to help.

exercise 6.8 **Outlining**

For further practice, outline the selection "Why the Food Pyramid Has Been Revised" beginning on pages 226–227. Use your annotations and notes to help.

Mapping

Mapping is a visual system of condensing material to show relationships and levels of importance. A map is a diagram of the major points, with their significant subpoints, that support a topic. The purpose of mapping as an organizing strategy is to improve memory by grouping material in a highly visual way.

Why Map?

Proponents of popular learning style theories (see the discussion of multiple intelligences in Chapter 1) would say that mapping offers a visual organization that appeals to learners with a preference for spatial representation, as opposed to the linear mode offered by outlining and note taking. A map provides a quick reference to overviewing an article or a chapter and can be used to reduce notes for later study. The Reader's Tip shows the steps in mapping.

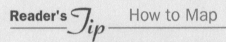

Reader's *Tip* ———— How to Map —————————————————

Use the following steps for mapping:

- **Draw a circle or a box** in the middle of a page, and in it write the subject or topic of the material.
- **Determine the main ideas** that support the subject, and write them on lines radiating from the central circle or box.
- **Determine the significant details,** and write them on lines attached to each main idea. The number of details you include will depend on the material and your purpose.

Maps are not restricted to any one pattern but can be formed in a variety of creative shapes, as the diagrams illustrate below.

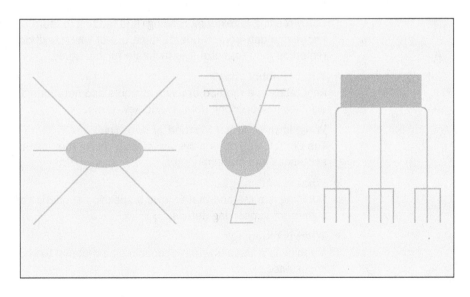

The following map highlights the biology passage on the circulatory system (see page 221). Notice how the visual display emphasizes the groups of ideas supporting the topic.

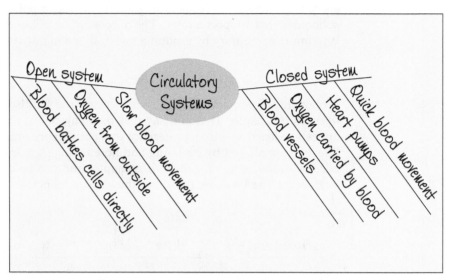

(see page 221)

exercise 6.9   **Mapping**

Return to Exercise 6.6 and design a map for the selection entitled "Reacting to Stress with Defense Mechanisms," which you previously outlined. Use your outline to help you design the map. Experiment with several different shapes for your map patterns on notebook or unlined paper. For additional practice, design maps for the selections in Exercises 6.2 and 6.3.

Summary *Points*

> **What is study reading?**
> Study reading is textbook reading. It is reading to learn and involves establishing knowledge networks. Students must select which textbook information to remember and organize it to facilitate further study.

> **What is annotating?**
> Annotating is a method of using symbols and notations to highlight main ideas, significant supporting details, and key terms.

> **What is the Cornell Method of note taking?**
> The Cornell Method is a system of note taking that includes writing summary sentences and marginal notes.

> **What is outlining?**
> Outlining is a method that follows a specified sequence of main ideas and significant supporting details.

> **What is mapping?**
> Mapping is a visual system of condensing material to show relationships and importance.

selection 1   Health

Contemporary *Focus*

The demands of college can certainly be stressful. With assignments, exams, work schedules, roommates, and personal responsibilities, life can become hectic, and your body and mind may be absorbing the trauma. What do you do to take care of your body and keep energized for studying?

Drink and Be Wary?

By Valerie Phillips
Deseret Morning News, April 26, 2006

Increasingly, people are looking for it in a can with revved-up names like AMP, Full Throttle, Adrenaline Rush, Socko! and Wired. "Energy drinks" are supposed to fuel a hectic lifestyle with quick bursts of energy.

But, while these gulp-and-go cocktails deliver nearly the same caffeine buzz as a cup of coffee, they're a poor substitute for proper rest and nutrition, according to Stacie Wing-Gaia, a University of Utah professor and sports dietitian, and Leslie Bonci, Director of the University of Pittsburgh Medical Center's Sports-Nutrition Department.

In an article for the Gatorade Sports Science Institute, Bonci concluded, "Being optimally 'energized' requires a suitable level of physical activity, adequate sleep, effective fueling and hydration strategies, and probably other unknown factors that affect neurochemicals in the brain. An energy drink alone will never make up for all of these elements."

Energy drinks are banned in France due to food safety concerns. But, in the rest of the world, the energy drink category has grown by 55 percent.

Wing-Gaia said energy drinks are a poor choice before or during strenuous exercise because their high carbohydrate content slows fluid absorption and delays hydration of the body. Sports drinks such as Gatorade or Powerade are only six to eight percent carbohydrate, with electrolytes added to enhance hydration.

COLLABORATE   Collaborate on responses to the following questions:

➤ What is your experience with energy or caffeine drinks?

➤ What is your typical sleep schedule? Does it create or reduce stress?

➤ Do cluttered surroundings make you feel unsettled and add to stress?

Skill Development: Preview

Preview the next selection to predict its purpose and organization and to formulate your learning plan.

Activate Schema

What causes stress for you, and what is your response to it?
What do you think of the low-carbohydrate diet craze that has swept the nation?

Establish a Purpose for Reading

Do you have bad habits that sabotage your energy? What can you do to attain a higher level of performance? After recalling what you already know about keeping your body healthy, read this selection to explain the scientific impact of nutrition, exercise, and stress on the body.

Increase Word Knowledge

What do you know about these words?

| attribute | crankiness | optimal | judiciously | mimic |
| aroused | prone | precursor | salient | euphoria |

Your instructor may give a true-false vocabulary review before or after reading.

Integrate Knowledge While Reading

Questions have been inserted in the margin to stimulate your thinking while reading. Remember to

| Predict | Picture | Relate | Monitor | Correct |

Skill Development: Note Taking

Use an informal outline to take notes for later study.

NUTRITION, HEALTH, AND STRESS

NUTRITION AND STRESS: RUNNING ON EMPTY

Good nutrition and eating habits contribute significantly to good health and stress resistance. They are especially important during high-stress times, but these may be the times when we are least likely to eat well! The cupboard is bare, we have no time to plan a shopping list and no money to go shopping, so we skip meals or grab
5 whatever fast food is closest at hand. Sometimes we depend on a dining hall whose
schedule doesn't match our own, or whose ideas of good nutrition and fine cuisine are limited to meat, potatoes, and overcooked vegetables with lots of butter. Dessert is usually the high point of every meal.

What should I eat?

The Image Bank/Getty Images

Exercising several times a week along with eating healthy food promotes emotional and physical well-being.

FOOD AND ENERGY: THE ROLE OF BLOOD SUGAR

Everyone has experienced the fatigue and irritability that can result from being
10 hungry. While many of the body's systems can make energy from fat, the central nervous system, including the brain, relies primarily on blood sugar, or glucose, for fuel. When blood sugar falls, these symptoms of fatigue result. Parents and people who work with children have observed the hungry-cranky connection on many oc-casions. As adults, we tend to attribute our moods to external events and ignore our
15 internal physiology, but hunger can cause crankiness in us just the same.

After you consume a meal, your blood glucose level rises as sugar enters the bloodstream from the digestive tract. A rising blood sugar level signals the pancreas to release **insulin.** Insulin is a hormone that allows sugar to enter the cells and be used for energy. As the glucose gradually leaves the bloodstream, blood glucose lev-
20 els begin to decrease.

Some people have more trouble regulating blood sugar than others and are prone to **hypoglycemia,** or low blood sugar, especially if they forget to eat or when they participate in physical activity. Symptoms of hypoglycemia include hunger, shakiness, nervousness, dizziness, nausea, and disorientation.
25 The following are recommendations for keeping your blood sugar at a healthful level without peaks and dips.

Do I have hypoglycemia?

Eat Regularly

Your body likes a regular schedule. Skipping meals means guaranteed hypoglycemia in people prone to this condition. Set up times for meals and snacks that are conve-nient for your schedule and stick to this routine as much as possible. This may mean
30 planning ahead and carrying snacks with you if you are at work or out running er-rands. Many people, including those with hypoglycemia, find that eating five or six small meals or snacks each day helps them feel more energetic than three large meals.

Include Protein Foods at Every Meal

Carbohydrate foods eaten without foods containing much protein are digested and enter the bloodstream quickly and are thus likely to challenge blood sugar regula-
35 tory processes in people prone to hypoglycemia. Protein slows digestion and allows blood sugar to rise more gradually. Protein servings may be small: a slice or two of meat or cheese; a half-cup of cottage cheese, yogurt, or tuna salad; small servings of fish or shellfish; a dish made with lentils or other legumes; or soy products like tofu.

Avoid Sugar Overload

When you eat a large amount of carbohydrates, blood sugar rises quickly. A high blood
40 sugar level calls forth a high insulin response, which in some people causes a sort of re-
bound effect: glucose enters the cells, and the blood sugar level drops quickly, causing hypoglycemia. While you may feel energized for a short period of time after too much sugar, you may eventually begin to feel tired, irritable, and hungry.

Do sweets work as snacks?

Drink Plenty of Fluids

Many people fail to maintain optimal levels of hydration. The next time you feel
45 tired, try drinking a glass of water. Dehydration causes fatigue and irritability. Thirst is not an adequate indicator of dehydration; you become dehydrated before you get thirsty. Nutritionists advise drinking at least eight cups of fluid each day, more with physical activity or hot weather. Caffeinated and alcoholic beverages don't count. Not only do they increase your stress, but they also dehydrate you and thus
50 increase your fluid needs. Your urine will be pale if you are adequately hydrated; dark-colored urine is a sign of dehydration.

Limit Caffeine

Caffeine is a **sympathomimetic** substance, which means its effects mimic those of the sympathetic nervous system and thus cause the fight-or-flight response. If you add caffeine to an already aroused sympathetic nervous system, the results can be
55 stressful and produce high levels of anxiety, irritability, headache, and stress-related illness. Most caffeine drinks, including coffee, tea, and cola soft drinks, can also cause stomachaches and nausea, which often get worse under stress.

One or two caffeinated beverages consumed judiciously at appropriate times during the day appear to do no harm for most people. Indeed, a little caffeine can
60 increase alertness. The problem with caffeine is that people are likely to overindulge in it when they are stressed. When summoning the energy necessary to get through the day feels like trying to squeeze water from a rock, they reach for a shot of caffeine. Caffeine cannot substitute for a good night's sleep, however. When you are truly fatigued, caffeine does not help you concentrate; it simply leaves you
65 wired, too jittery to sleep, and too tired to do anything productive.

Why do people consume too much caffeine?

EATING IN RESPONSE TO STRESS: FEEDING THE HUNGRY HEART

Few people look on eating and food only in terms of hunger and nutrition. Every culture in the world has evolved rituals around food and eating. Feasting and fasting carry layers of religious, cultural, and emotional overtones. As children, we learn to associate food with security, comfort, love, reward, punishment, anger, restraint. It's
70 no wonder that we eat for many reasons other than hunger: because we're lonely, angry, sad, happy, nervous, or depressed. Unlike alcohol, which we can give up if we are prone to a drinking problem, we must learn to live with food. If eating is the

Why do we celebrate with food?

only way we take the time to nurture ourselves, we eat more than we are really hungry for. In extreme cases, an inability to control eating can develop into an eat-
75 ing disorder, known as **compulsive overeating,** that often gets worse under stress.

FOOD AND MOOD: THE ROLE OF NEUROTRANSMITTERS

Most people feel relaxed and lazy after a big feast. For this reason many cultures have incorporated a siesta after the large midday meal, and professors who teach a class right after lunch or dinner rarely turn out the lights for a slide show. Why do we feel tired? Certainly our blood sugar should be adequate after eating all that
80 food. Changes in brain biochemistry may be the reason. The food we eat supplies the precursor molecules for manufacturing neurotransmitters that influence our emotions and mood. Some researchers believe that by selecting the right kinds of food we can encourage states of relaxation or alertness.

Big meals, especially those with a lot of fat, take a long time to digest, and with
85 a full stomach we feel like relaxing rather than working. On the other hand, smaller meals low in fat take less time and energy to digest and leave us feeling more ener-getic and alert.

Meals that are composed primarily of carbohydrates encourage production of the neurotransmitter *serotonin*, which makes us feel drowsy and relaxed. High-
90 carbohydrate meals are a prescription for relaxation and may be the reason some people overeat: it makes them feel good. A small, high-carbohydrate snack before bedtime can encourage sleep. Many people find that eating carbohydrates helps them feel less stressed and more relaxed. Some people find that a meal or snack with carbohydrate but little protein, especially in the middle of the day, leaves
95 them feeling tired.

What would be a great lunch for me?

Meals that include a small serving of protein foods, with or without carbohy-drates, encourage alertness by favoring production of neurotransmitters such as *dopamine* and *norepinephrine*. A small lunch that includes protein foods is best for students who need to stay alert for a 1:00 class.

PHYSICAL ACTIVITY AND STRESS RESISTANCE

100 Participation in regular physical activity is one of the most effective ways to in-crease your stress resistance. Countless studies comparing people with high and low levels of stress resistance have found exercise to be one of the most salient discrim-inators between these two groups. An important note is that the amount and inten-sity of exercise required to produce stress management benefits need not be over-
105 whelming. While many athletes enjoy extended periods of intense activity, other people find stress relief with a brisk walk, an hour of gardening, or a game of volley-ball on the beach.

Exercise High: Endorphins, Hormones, and Neurotransmitters

In addition to canceling the negative effects of stress, exercise may induce some positive biochemical changes. Many exercisers report feelings of euphoria and states
110 of consciousness similar to those described by people using drugs such as heroin. Such accounts have led to use of the term *runner's high*, since these descriptions first came primarily from long-distance runners. These reports have intrigued both exercise scientists and the lay public and have suggested the possibility that certain types of exercise, particularly vigorous exercise of long duration, may cause bio-
115 chemical changes that mimic drug-induced euphoria.

As scientists have come to understand something of brain biochemistry, some interesting hypotheses have emerged. The most publicized of these has focused on a group of chemical messengers found in the central nervous system (brain and spinal cord) called opioids, since they are similar in structure and function to
120 the drugs that come from the poppy flower: opium, morphine, and heroin. **Beta-endorphins** belong to this group. They not only inhibit pain but also seem to have other roles in the brain as well, such as aiding in memory and learning and registering emotions. It is difficult for scientists to measure opioid concentrations in the central nervous system of humans, but animal research has suggested that en-
125 dogenous (produced by the body) opioid concentrations increase with level of exercise: more exercise, more opioids.

Rhythmic Exercise: Relaxed Brain Waves

What will be my exercise regimen? → Rhythmic exercises such as walking, running, rowing, and swimming increase **alpha-wave** activity in the brain. The electrical activity of the brain can be monitored in the laboratory using an instrument called an **electroencephalograph**
130 **(EEG).** Alpha waves are associated with a calm mental state, such as that produced by meditation or chanting. The rhythmic breathing that occurs during some forms of exercise also contributes to an increase in alpha-wave activity. Rhythmic activity performed to music may be stress relieving in other ways as well.

(1,727 words)

—From Barbara Brehm,
Stress Management

Finding Your Life Stress Score

To assess your life in terms of life changes, check all the events listed that have happened to you in the past year. Add up the points to derive your life stress score.

Rank	Life Event	Life Change Unit Value	Your Points
1.	Death of spouse	100	_____
2.	Divorce	73	_____
3.	Separation from living partner	65	_____
4.	Jail term or probation	63	_____
5.	Death of close family member	63	_____
6.	Serious personal injury or illness	53	_____
7.	Marriage or establishing life partnership	50	_____
8.	Getting fired at work	47	_____
9.	Marital or relationship reconciliation	45	_____
10.	Retirement	45	_____
11.	Change in health of immediate family member	44	_____
12.	Pregnancy or causing pregnancy	40	_____
13.	Sex difficulties	39	_____

(continued)

Rank	Life Event	Life Change Unit Value	Your Points
14.	Gain of new family member	39	_____
15.	Business or work role change	39	_____
16.	Change in financial state	38	_____
17.	Death of a close friend (not a family member)	37	_____
18.	Change to different line of work	36	_____
19.	Change in number of arguments with spouse or life partner	35	_____
20.	Taking a mortgage or loan for a major purpose	31	_____
21.	Foreclosure of mortgage or loan	30	_____
22.	Change in responsibilities at work	29	_____
23.	Son or daughter leaving home	29	_____
24.	Trouble with in-laws or with children	29	_____
25.	Outstanding personal achievement	28	_____
26.	Spouse begins or stops work	26	_____
27.	Begin or end school	26	_____
28.	Change in living conditions (visitors, roommates, remodeling)	25	_____
29.	Change in personal habits (diet, exercise, smoking)	24	_____
30.	Trouble with boss	23	_____
31.	Change in work hours or conditions	20	_____
32.	Moving to new residence	20	_____
33.	Change in schools	20	_____
34.	Change in recreation	19	_____
35.	Change in religious activities	19	_____
36.	Change in social activities (more or less than before)	18	_____
37.	Taking out a loan for a lesser purchase (car or TV)	17	_____
38.	Change in sleeping habits	16	_____
39.	Change in frequency of family get-togethers	15	_____
40.	Change in eating habits	15	_____
41.	Vacation	13	_____
42.	Presently in winter holiday season	12	_____
43.	Minor violation of the law	11	_____
		LIFE STRESS SCORE:	_____

Adapted from the "Social Readjustment Rating Scale," by Thomas Holmes and Richard Rahe. The scale was first published in the *Journal of Psychosomatic Research*, vol. II, p. 214, Copyright 1967. Reprinted by permission of Elsevier, Inc., Philadelphia, PA.

Researchers Holmes and Rahe claim that there is a connection between the degree of life stress and major health problems. A person who scores 300 or more on the life stress test runs an 80 percent risk of suffering a major health problem within the next two years. Someone who scores 150 to 300 has a 50 percent chance of becoming ill.

Recall

Stop to self-test, relate, and react. Study your informal outline.

Your instructor may choose to give you a true-false comprehension review.

Write About the Selection

Explain how you can use the health and nutritional information in this selection to energize and stimulate your mental performance during exam week.

   Response Suggestion: List your energizing ideas with a purpose and examples for each.

Contemporary *Link*

During stressful times, some people eat more and some eat less. The "Freshman 15" refers not to an athletic team but to the 15 pounds that students often gain during the first year of college. Other students who are concerned with body image obsess about their weight and follow overly restrictive diets. How do you plan to use this information about nutrition, exercise, and stress to identify your needs and avoid unhealthy behaviors leading to excessive weight gain or loss?

Check Your Comprehension

After reading the selection, answer the following questions with *a, b, c,* or *d.* To help you analyze your strengths and weaknesses, the question types are indicated.

Main Idea _____ 1. Which is the best statement of the main idea of this selection?

   a. A balanced diet is the most effective way to decrease stress.
   b. Regular exercise and good eating habits contribute to stress reduction and both physical and emotional well-being.
   c. Stress negatively affects mental and physical performance.
   d. Avoiding sugar overload and including protein at every meal help regulate blood sugar.

Detail _____ 2. The pancreas is signaled to release insulin when

   a. protein is consumed.
   b. blood glucose levels rise.
   c. physical activity increases.
   d. blood sugar levels decrease.

Inference _____ 3. By using the term *fine cuisine,* the author suggests that

   a. "fine" meals include meat, potatoes, and vegetables.
   b. dessert is an important part of "fine dining."
   c. dining halls do not always serve good, nutritional meals.
   d. vegetables should be cooked without fats.

Detail _____ 4. People who experience symptoms of hypoglycemia should do all the following *except*

   a. eat three large meals per day and vary the times.
   b. combine proteins with carbohydrates.
   c. limit sugar intake.
   d. eat several small meals or snacks throughout the day.

Inference _____ 5. The implied similarity between drinking and eating problems is that

   a. many people who abuse alcohol are also prone to eating problems.
   b. compulsive eating is treated more easily than compulsive drinking.
   c. drinking alcohol and eating food sometimes are misguided responses to stress.
   d. the consumption of both food and alcohol releases endorphins, which reduce stress.

Detail _____ 6. The production of norepinephrine is stimulated by eating

   a. proteins.
   b. fats.
   c. carbohydrates.
   d. caffeine.

Detail _____ 7. The beta-endorphins believed to be released by exercise have all the following benefits *except*

  a. inducing feelings of euphoria.
  b. inhibiting pain.
  c. regulating blood sugar.
  d. aiding memory.

Inference _____ 8. The activity most likely to increase alpha-wave activity in the brain would be

  a. playing a game of chess.
  b. jogging.
  c. lifting weights.
  d. playing baseball.

Inference _____ 9. For a midnight snack before bed, the author would most likely recommend

  a. a bagel.
  b. cappuccino.
  c. peanuts.
  d. a chicken leg.

Detail _____ 10. The author's attitude toward the use of caffeine by most people is that

  a. caffeine can be used to decrease fear because it arouses the fight-or-flight response.
  b. light amounts of caffeine appear harmless and can increase alertness.
  c. caffeine should be avoided because it causes stomachaches, nausea, headaches, and irritability.
  d. when a person is truly fatigued, caffeine can increase concentration.

Answer the following with *T* (true) or *F* (false).

Detail _____ 11. Glucose provides the primary fuel for the brain.

Detail _____ 12. Thirst is an adequate indicator of the body's optimal hydration level.

Inference _____ 13. The term *hungry heart* implies a need that food cannot satisfy.

Detail _____ 14. A glass of cola can be counted toward the number of cups of fluid the body needs each day.

Inference _____ 15. The author suggests that serotonin is more important for effective studying than dopamine and norepinephrine.

Build Your Vocabulary

According to the way the italicized word was used in the selection, select *a, b, c,* or *d* for the word or phrase that gives the best definition. The number in parentheses indicates the line of the passage in which the word is located.

_____ 1. "to *attribute* our moods" (14)
    a. dissociate
    b. credit
    c. explain
    d. reject

_____ 2. "can cause *crankiness*" (15)
    a. rage
    b. irritability
    c. drowsiness
    d. fatigue

_____ 3. "*optimal* levels" (44)
    a. medium
    b. low
    c. most desirable
    d. regulatory

_____ 4. "its effects *mimic*" (52)
    a. distort
    b. imitate
    c. confuse
    d. falsify

_____ 5. "an already *aroused*" (54)
    a. excited
    b. not stimulated
    c. settled
    d. relaxed

_____ 6. "beverages consumed *judiciously*" (58)
    a. recklessly
    b. hastily
    c. cautiously
    d. carelessly

_____ 7. "we are *prone*" (72)
    a. damaged by
    b. inclined
    c. addicted
    d. connected

_____ 8. "the *precursor* molecules" (81)
    a. necessary
    b. final
    c. active
    d. forerunner

_____ 9. "*salient* discriminators" (102)
    a. noticeable
    b. instructive
    c. irrelevant
    d. damaging

_____ 10. "drug-induced *euphoria*" (115)
    a. insanity
    b. disorientation
    c. exhilaration
    d. serenity

Search the Net

Use a search engine such as Google, Yahoo, Ask.com, AltaVista, Excite, Dogpile, or Lycos to search for foods that can serve as remedies for specific ailments. Search for foods that help the body fight acne, cold sores, high blood pressure, and insomnia. For suggested Web sites and other research activities, go to http://www.ablongman.com/smith/.

Concept Prep for Health

What is blood pressure?

Blood pressure is the measure of the pressure exerted by the blood as it flows through the arteries. Blood moves in waves and is thus measured in two phases. The **systolic pressure** is the pressure at the height of the blood wave when the left ventricle of the heart contracts to push the blood through the body. The **diastolic pressure** is the pressure when the ventricles are at rest and filling with blood. The figures are expressed as the systolic "over" the diastolic pressure. The average blood pressure of a healthy adult is **120 over 80.**

What can happen to arteries as we age?

Cholesterol—a white soapy substance that is found in the body and in foods such as animal fats—can accumulate on the inner walls of arteries—blood vessels that carry blood away from the heart—and narrow the channels through which blood flows. Nutritionists recommend eating **unsaturated fats** such as vegetable or olive oils as opposed to **saturated fats** (animal fats), which are solid at room temperature.

Another condition that lessens the flow of blood through the arteries is hardening of the arteries or **arteriosclerosis.** A surgical technique called an **angioplasty** is used to clear the arteries. A catheter with a small balloon is inserted into the arteries around the heart to compress fatty deposits and restore the flow of blood.

What are some frequently discussed medical procedures?

- A **CAT scan** (computerized axial tomography) is a painless, noninvasive procedure that uses radiation to show a three-dimensional image of the body. The diagnostic procedure is used to detect tumors and other conditions. It shows differences in the density of soft tissue,

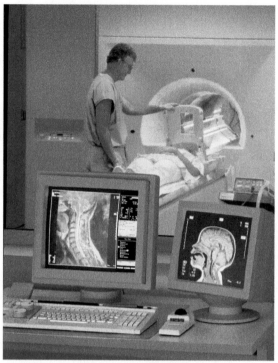

Radiologists are physicians who specialize in imaging technologies such as magnetic resonance imaging (MRI) for medical diagnosis.

Lester Lefkowitz/Taxi/Getty Images

with high-density substances appearing white and low-density substances appearing dark.
- An **MRI** (magnetic resonance imaging) uses magnetic fields and radio waves to detect hidden tumors and other conditions by mapping the vibration of atoms. An MRI is painless and does not use radiation.
- **Chemotherapy** is a treatment for cancer in which the patient receives chemicals that destroy cancer cells. Currently, more than 50 anticancer drugs are available for use. Temporary hair loss is a common side effect of chemotherapy.
- **Radiation** is another treatment for destroying malignant cancer cells. Unfortunately, it also destroys some healthy cells.

- A **mammogram** is an x-ray of the breast to detect tumors that are too small to be detected by other means.
- A **Pap test** is a procedure in which cells are taken from the cervical region and tested for cancer.
- **PSA** (prostate-specific antigen) levels in the blood are measured to detect prostate cancer in men. A **prostatic ultrasound** can also be used.

- A **sonogram** or **ultrasound** test uses high-frequency sound waves to detect abnormalities. It is a noninvasive procedure that can be used to view the size, position, and sex of a fetus.
- **Amniocentesis** is a procedure for detecting abnormalities in the fetus. Fluid is drawn from the liquid surrounding the fetus by a needle through the mother's stomach. The fluid contains cells of the fetus that can be analyzed.

Review Questions

After studying the material, answer the following questions:

1. What is the difference between systolic and diastolic pressure? _____

   _____

   _____

2. Which type of pressure should be higher? _____

   _____

3. How does cholesterol harm the body? _____

   _____

4. How can you distinguish saturated fats? _____

   _____

5. What does an angioplasty do? _____

   _____

6. What medical procedure uses drugs to cure cancer? _____

   _____

7. What procedure uses magnetic fields and radio waves to detect tumors and other conditions without radiation? _____

   _____

8. What test can indicate prostate cancer? _____

   _____

9. What procedure extracts fetal cells for diagnosis? _____

   _____

10. What type of x-ray is used to detect breast cancer? _____

   _____

Your instructor may choose to give a true-false review of these health concepts.

7 Inference

- What is an inference, and what does it mean to read between the lines?
- What is the connotation of a word?
- Why do authors use figurative language, and how can understanding it enhance comprehension?
- Why is prior knowledge needed for implied meaning?
- How does a reader draw conclusions?

Rafal Oblinski, *Graceful Dream of Poetic Glory*, 1995. Acrylic on canvas. 28 x 20 inches.

Copyright © 2008 by Pearson Education, Inc.

What Is an Inference?

At the first and most basic level of reading, the *literal level*—the level that presents the facts—you can actually point to the words on the page to answer a literal question. However, at the second and more sophisticated level of reading—the *inferential level*—you no longer can point to such an answer but instead must form it from clues and suggestions within the text.

EXAMPLE In the following passage from Michael Ondaatje's novel *The English Patient*, the author implies an activity, and the reader infers what is happening. Mark the point at which you understand the activity.

> She moves backwards a few feet and with a piece of white chalk draws more rectangles, so there is a pyramid of them, single then double then single, her left hand braced flat on the floor, her head down, serious. . . .
>
> She drops the chalk into the pocket of her dress. She stands and pulls up the looseness of her skirt and ties it around her dress. She pulls from another pocket a piece of metal and flings it out in front of her so it falls just beyond the farthest square.
>
> She leaps forward, her legs smashing down, her shadow behind her curling into the depth of the hall. She is very quick, her tennis shoes skidding on the numbers she has drawn into each rectangle, one foot landing, then two feet, then one again until she reaches the last square.[1]

EXPLANATION How many sentences did it take for you to infer that she is playing the game of hopscotch? You may have visualized the activity as early as the author's description of drawing "single then double then single"; or perhaps you caught on a bit later, when she jumps. In any case, you were able to make the inference when the clues from the text merged with your own prior knowledge.

Two different terms are used in discussing inferential thinking: the writer or speaker *implies* and the reader or listener *infers*. This merging of suggested thought is also figuratively called **reading between the lines.** Throughout this text, many of the thought questions, or think-alouds, appearing in the margins alongside the longer reading selections ask you to read between the lines.

At the inferential level, authors not only entertain readers but also subtly manipulate them. When you read, always consider what is left unsaid. This is true for the spoken word. For example, when asked, "How do you like your new boss?" you might answer, "She is always well dressed" rather than "I don't like her." By not volunteering information that directly answers the question, you convey your lack of approval or, certainly, your lack of enthusiasm. In some cases, this lack of information might send a damaging message. For example, when you graduate and look for that perfect position, you will need to ask professors and previous employers for job recommendations. Take care that the person you ask to recommend you is 100 percent on your team. The following exercise illustrates the power of what is left unsaid.

---

[1]As quoted in Stephanie Harvey and Anne Goudvis. *Strategies That Work* (Portland, ME: Stenhouse Publishers, 2000), p. 37.

exercise 7.1 **Reading Between the Lines**

Read the two recommendations and decide whom you would hire.

Carlos has been working as an assistant for one year and has been a valuable member of our team. He aggressively tackles new accounts, making calls after hours to track down customers and ship needed products. He excels in sales and follows through with the details in keeping customers satisfied. We want to keep Carlos but have no openings for advanced positions. I highly recommend him for the position at your company.

Roger has worked for our company for one year as an assistant. Our company sells chicken by-products, mostly thighs and legs that are not used in America, to Russia and third-world countries. Because of the international nature of our business, communication is extremely important. During his year with us, Roger has faithfully attended all meetings and has been friendly with our staff. We certainly wish him well.

Which one would you hire? Why? _____

_____

_____

_____

_____

_____

_____

_____

Any employer is wise enough to infer the meaning of a vaguely worded reference. Similarly, inferential skills are important in interpreting persuasive reports and arguments because facts that are detrimental to the supported position might be omitted to manipulate a reader's opinion. Such omissions send a "Reader Beware" signal. One of the most effective tools that selectively uses words and photos to send persuasive messages is advertising.

Cigarette advertisements, for example, entice the public through suggestion, not facts, to spend millions of dollars on a product that is known to be unhealthy. They use words and photos in a sophisticated way to lure consumers. Depending on the brand, smoking offers the refreshment of a mountain stream or the sophisticated elegance of the rich and famous. Never do the ads directly praise smoking or promise pleasure; instead, the ads *imply* smoking's positive aspects. The cigarette advertisers avoid lawsuits for false advertising by never putting anything tangible into print. The emotionalism of a full-page advertisement is so overwhelming that the consumer hardly notices the cautionary note in small print at the bottom of the page: "Warning: The Surgeon General Has Determined That Cigarette Smoking Is Dangerous to Your Health."

Implied Meaning in Advertisements

Advertisers can directly state that a detergent cleans, but the task of advertising other products can be more complicated. Look through magazines and newspapers to locate three advertisements: one each for cigarettes, alcoholic beverages, and fragrances. Answer the following questions about each:

1. What is directly stated about the product?
2. What does the advertisement suggest about the product?
3. Who seems to be the suggested audience or customer for the product? Why?

Authors and advertisers have not invented a new comprehension skill; they are merely capitalizing on a highly developed skill of daily life. Think, for example, of the inferences you make every day by noticing what people say or don't say, by examining what they do or don't do, and by interpreting what others say or don't say about them. In fact, if you lacked these skills, you would miss out on a lot of the humor in jokes, cartoons, and sitcoms.

Implied Meaning in Humor

Jokes and cartoons require you to read between the lines and make connections. They are funny not so much because of what is said but because of what has been left unsaid. When you "catch on" to a joke, it simply means that you make the connection and recognize the **implied meaning.** To enjoy the joke, you link prior knowledge to what is being said. If you are telling a joke and your listener lacks the background knowledge to which the joke refers, your attempt will fall flat because the listener cannot understand the implied meaning. Listeners cannot connect with something they don't know, so be sure to choose the right joke for the right audience.

Biting humor has two levels of implied meaning. On the surface the joke makes us laugh. At a deeper level, however, the humor ridicules our beliefs, practices, or way of life.

"**We built a snowperson!**"

EXAMPLE   What inference makes this joke funny?

> At an airline ticket counter, a small boy with his mother told the agent he was two years old. The man looked at him suspiciously and asked, "Do you know what happens to little boys who lie?"
>
> "Yes. They get to fly at half-price."

—Marleene Freedman
in *Chevron USA: Laughter, the Best Medicine*

EXPLANATION   The inference is that the boy and his mother had lied about his age so he could fly for half the price. Children tend to speak the truth.

exercise 7.3   **Implied Humor in Jokes**

Explain the inferences that make the following jokes funny.

Joke 1

"Take a pencil and paper," the teacher said, "and write an essay with the title 'If I Were a Millionaire.'"

> Everyone but Philip, who leaned back with arms folded, began to write furiously.
>
> "What's the matter?" the teacher asked. "Why don't you begin?"
>
> "I'm waiting for my secretary," he replied.

—Bernadette Nagy,
Laughter, the Best Medicine

Inference: _____

_____

_____

_____

Joke 2

Mel's son rushed in the door. "Dad! Dad!" he announced. "I got a part in the school play!"

> "That's terrific," Mel said proudly. "What part is it?"
>
> "I play the part of the dad."
>
> Mel thought this over. "Go back tomorrow," he instructed, "and tell them you want a speaking role."

—Darleen Giannini,
Laughter, the Best Medicine

Inference: _____

_____

_____

_____

Joke 3

A woman in Atlantic City was losing at the roulette wheel. When she was down to her last $10, she asked the fellow next to her for a good number. "Why don't you play your age?" he suggested.

The woman agreed, and then put her money on the table. The next thing the fellow with the advice knew, the woman had fainted and fallen to the floor. He rushed right over. "Did she win?" he asked.

"No," replied the attendant. "She put $10 on 29 and 41 came in."

—Christine L. Castner,
Laughter, the Best Medicine

Inference: _____

_____

_____

_____

exercise 7.4 **Implied Meaning in Cartoons**

Explain the inferences that make the following cartoons funny.

"Oh no, we're being spammed!"

Inference: _____

_____

_____

_____

THE FAR SIDE® BY GARY LARSON

"I've got it too, Omar ... a strange feeling like we've just been going in circles."

Inference: _____

_____

_____

_____

In cartoons, subtle expressions in the drawings, along with the words, imply meaning. In speech or writing, carefully chosen words imply attitude and manipulate the emotions of the reader.

Connotations of Words

Notice the power of suggested meaning as you respond to the following questions:

1. If you read an author's description of classmates, which student would you assume is smartest?

   a. A student annotating items on a computer printout
   b. A student with earphones listening to a CD
   c. A student talking with classmates about *The Sopranos*

2. Which would you find discussed in a vintage small town of the 1940s?

   a. Movies
   b. Cinema
   c. Picture shows

3. Who probably earns the most money?

   a. A businessperson in a dark suit, white shirt, and tie
   b. A businessperson in slacks and a sport shirt
   c. A businessperson in a pale-blue uniform

Can you prove your answers? It's not the same as proving when the Declaration of Independence was signed, yet you still have a feeling for the way each question should be answered. Even though a right or wrong answer is difficult to explain in this type of question, certain answers can still be defended as most accurate; in the preceding questions, the answers are *a*, *c*, and *a*. The answers are based on feelings, attitudes, and knowledge commonly shared by members of society.

A seemingly innocent tool, word choice is the first key to implied meaning. For example, compare the following sentences:

Esmeralda is skinny.

Esmeralda is slender or slim.

If she is skinny, she is unattractive; but if she is slender or slim, she must be attractive. All three adjectives might refer to the same underweight person, but *skinny* communicates a negative feeling, whereas *slender* or *slim* communicates a positive one. This feeling or emotionalism surrounding a word is called **connotation. Denotation,** on the other hand, is the specific meaning of a word. The connotative meaning goes beyond the denotative meaning to reflect certain attitudes and prejudices of society. Even though it may not seem premeditated, writers select words, just as advertisers select symbols and models, to manipulate the reader's opinions.

exercise 7.5 | **Recognizing Connotation in Familiar Words**

In each of the following word pairs, write the letter of the word with the more positive connotation:

_____ 1. (a) issue	(b) problem
_____ 2. (a) loneliness	(b) independence
_____ 3. (a) tolerant	(b) pushover
_____ 4. (a) difficult	(b) challenging
_____ 5. (a) pale	(b) fair
_____ 6. (a) direct	(b) rude
_____ 7. (a) cop	(b) officer
_____ 8. (a) take	(b) steal
_____ 9. (a) lazy	(b) easygoing
_____10. (a) unanswered	(b) ignored
_____11. (a) smart	(b) brilliant

_____ 12. (a) abandon   (b) leave

_____ 13. (a) know-it-all   (b) wise

_____ 14. (a) lead   (b) dominate

_____ 15. (a) make   (b) create

_____ 16. (a) mutt   (b) puppy

_____ 17. (a) late   (b) delinquent

_____ 18. (a) reasonable   (b) cheap

_____ 19. (a) call   (b) yell

_____ 20. (a) request   (b) beg

_____ 21. (a) tell   (b) command

_____ 22. (a) question   (b) interrogate

_____ 23. (a) gift   (b) solicitation

_____ 24. (a) discuss   (b) complain

_____ 25. (a) clever   (b) underhanded

exercise 7.6   **Choosing Connotative Words**

For each word listed, write a word with a similar denotative meaning that has a positive (or neutral) connotation and one that has a negative connotation.

	Positive	**Negative**
EXAMPLE eat	dine	devour
1. child	_____	_____
2. ruler	_____	_____
3. innocent	_____	_____
4. supportive	_____	_____
5. quiet	_____	_____

exercise 7.7   **Connotation in Textbooks**

For each of the underlined words in the following sentences, indicate the meaning of the word and reasons why the connotation is positive or negative.

EXAMPLE

While the unions fought mainly for better wages and hours, they also <u>championed</u> various social reforms.

—Leonard Pitt,
We Americans

<u>Championed</u>: Means "supported"; suggests heroes and thus a positive cause

1. The ad was part of the oil companies' program to sell their image rather than their product to the public. In the ad they <u>boasted</u> that they were reseeding all the disrupted areas with a newly developed grass that grows five times faster than the grass that normally occurs there.

   —Robert Wallace,
   Biology: The World of Life

   boasted: _____

   _____

2. At noon, a group of prominent bankers met. To stop the <u>hemorrhaging</u> of stock prices, the bankers' pool agreed to buy stocks well above the market.

   —James Kirby Martin et al.,
   America and Its People

   hemorrhaging: _____

   _____

3. Tinbergen, like Lorenz and von Frisch, entered retirement by continuing to work. Tinbergen was a hyperactive child who, at school, was allowed to periodically dance on his desk to let off steam. So in "<u>retirement</u>" he entered a new arena, stimulating the use of ethological methods in autism.

   —Robert Wallace,
   Biology: The World of Life

   "retirement": _____

   _____

4. The nation's capital is <u>crawling</u> with lawyers, lobbyists, registered foreign agents, public relations consultants, and others—more than 14,000 individuals representing nearly 12,000 organizations at last count—all seeking to influence Congress.

   —Robert Lineberry et al.,
   Government in America, Brief Version, 2nd ed.

   crawling: _____

   _____

5. Not since Wilson had tried to <u>ram</u> the League of Nations through the Senate had any president put more on the line.

   —Leonard Pitt,
   We Americans

   ram: _____

   _____

Euphemisms and Politically Correct Language

A **euphemism** is a substitution of a mild, indirect, or vague term for one that is considered harsh, blunt, or offensive. It is a polite way of saying something that is embarrassing or indelicate. In the funeral business, for example, euphemisms abound. In fact, one Web site lists 213 terms for *death* or *dying* such as *pass to the great beyond* or *big sleep*.

When used to hide unpleasant ideas in politics or social interaction, euphemisms are sometimes called doublespeak or **politically correct language.** For example, *collateral damage* refers to civilian casualties. Other examples are the janitor being called the *sanitation engineer,* a handicapped person being called *differently abled,* or someone with a missing tooth being called *dentally disadvantaged.*

EXAMPLE

Euphemism: My stomach feels unsettled.

Politically correct: The troops were hit by friendly fire.

Figurative Language

What does it mean to say "She worked like a dog"?

To most readers it means that she worked hard, but since few dogs work, the comparison is not literally true or particularly logical. **Figurative language** is, in a sense, another language because it is a different way of using "regular" words so that they take on new meaning. For example, "It was raining buckets" and "raining cats and dogs" are lively, figurative ways of describing a heavy rain. New speakers of English, however, who comprehend on a literal level, might look up in the sky for the descending pails or animals. The two expressions create an exaggerated, humorous effect, but on a literal level, they do not make sense.

Consider an example from a Shakespearean play. When Hamlet prepares to confront his mother, he says, "I will speak daggers to her, but use none." With an economy of expression, he vividly suggests his feelings. Much more is implied than merely saying, "I will speak sternly to her." No one expects he will use a knife on his mother, but the connotation is that the words will be sharp, piercing, and wounding. Words can be hurtful or enriching; and an author uses figurative language, sometimes called **imagery,** to stimulate readers' minds to imagine beyond the printed page by adding color, attitude, or wit.

Idioms

When first used, the phrases "works like a dog" and "raining cats and dogs" were probably very clever. Now they have lost their freshness but still convey meaning for those who are "in the know." Such phrases are called **idioms,** or expressions that do not make literal sense but have taken on a new, generally accepted meaning over many years of use.

EXAMPLE

She tried to keep a stiff upper lip during the ordeal.

His eyes were bigger than his stomach.

More Types of Inferences

Many types of text—not just advertising, humor, and poetry—demand that you read between the lines in order to understand the author's goals or meaning. You can make inferences based on facts, the voice of a narrator, descriptions, and actions.

Inferences from Facts

The way in which facts are juxtaposed can imply a certain message. For example, an author selected the following facts from issues of *Time* magazine and presented them consecutively to suggest an inference. No direct connection is stated, so the reader must thoughtfully reflect on the suggested message. This pause for thought adds power to the message.

EXAMPLE

28%   Proportion of public libraries in the United States that offered Internet access in 1996

95%   Proportion of libraries that offered Internet access in 2002

17%   Increase in library attendance between 1996 and 2002

Inference: _____

EXPLANATION   The inference is that library attendance has improved because many more libraries have Internet access. Before libraries buy more computers, however, specific data on daily use should be collected.

exercise 7.8   **Drawing Inferences from Facts**

400,000   Number of hot dogs ordered for the Winter Olympics

10   Number of days it took to go through the hot-dog supply

1. Inference: _____

     _____

     _____

     _____

1 billion   Number of birds killed by flying into glass windows in the United States each year.

121 million   Number of birds killed annually by U.S. hunters

2. Inference: _____

     _____

     _____

     _____

408	Species that could be extinct by 2050 if global warming trends continue.
6.6 tons	Average amount of greenhouse gases emitted annually by each American, an increase of 3.4% since 1990.

3. Inference: _____

_____

_____

_____

42%	Percentage of adults who say the toothbrush is the one invention they could not live without
6%	Percentage who say the personal computer is the one invention they could not live without.

4. Inference: _____

_____

_____

_____

1	Rank of Super Bowl Sunday, among all the days of the year, in pizza sales at the major U.S. pizza chains
20%	Increase in frozen-pizza sales on Super Bowl Sunday

5. Inference: _____

_____

_____

© *Time* Magazine, March 4, 2002; March 1, 2004;
January 19, 2004; February 3, 2003; February 2, 2004.

Using Prior Knowledge to Make Inferences

Just as a joke is funny only if you have the right background knowledge, college reading is easier if you have **prior knowledge** needed to grasp the details that are frequently implied rather than directly spelled out. For example, if a sentence began, "Previously wealthy investors were leaping from buildings in the financial district," you would know that the author was referring to the stock market crash of 1929 on Wall Street in New York City. The details fall into an already existing schema. Although the specifics are not directly stated, you have used prior knowledge and have "added up" the details to infer time and place.

exercise 7.9 **Inferring Time and Place**

Read the following passages and indicate *a*, *b*, or *c* for the suggested time and place. Use your prior knowledge of "anchor dates" in history to logically think about the possible responses. Underline the clues that helped you arrive at your answers.

Passage A

For disgruntled or abused women, divorce was sometimes available. Wives with grievances could sue for divorce in some colonies. For instance, although Puritan colonists preferred to keep couples together and often fined troublesome spouses or ordered them to "live happily together," they believed that some marriages could not be saved. Because Puritans viewed marriage as a legal contract rather than a religious sacrament, if one party violated the terms of a marital contract the marriage could be dissolved.

—Glenda Riley,
Inventing the American Woman: An Inclusive History,
3rd ed., vol. 1: To 1877

——— 1. The time period that this passage refers to is probably

   a. the 1600s–1700s.
   b. the 1800s–1900s.
   c. the 1900s–2000s.

——— 2. The part of colonial America discussed here is likely

   a. uncolonized territory in the west.
   b. the northeast.
   c. the southern colonies.

3. Underline the clues to your answers.

Passage B

Families at dinner were startled by the sudden gleam of bayonets in the doorway and rose up to be driven with blows and oaths along the weary miles to the stockade. Men were seized in their fields or going along the road, women were taken from their wheels and children from their play. In many cases, on turning for one last look as they crossed the ridge, they saw their homes in flames, fired by the lawless rabble that followed on the heels of the soldiers to loot and pillage. So keen were these outlaws on the scent that in some instances they were driving off the cattle and other stock of the Indians almost before the soldiers had fairly started their owners in the other direction. Systematic hunts were made by the same men for Indian graves, to rob them of the silver pendants and other valuables deposited with the dead. A volunteer, afterward a colonel in the Confederate service, said: "I fought through the Civil War and have seen men shot to pieces and slaughtered by thousands, but the Cherokee removal was the cruelest work I ever knew."

—James Mooney,
Myths of the Cherokee, 19th Annual Report,
Bureau of American Ethnology

_____ 4. The time period discussed is probably

     a. the 1600s.
     b. the 1700s.
     c. the 1800s.

_____ 5. The place is most likely

     a. the Great Lakes region of the United States.
     b. the southeastern United States.
     c. the Texas-Mexican border.

        6. Underline the clues to your answers.

Passage C

As unskilled workers, most found employment in the low-status, manual-labor jobs in the factories, mines, needle trades, and construction. At that time, workers had no voice in working conditions, for labor unions had not yet become effective. The 84-hour workweek (14 hours per day, 6 days per week) for low wages was common. Jobs offered no paid vacations, sick pay, or pension plans. Child labor was commonplace, and entire families often worked to provide a subsistence-level family income. Lighting, ventilation, and heating were poor. In the factories, moving parts of machinery were dangerously exposed, leading to numerous horrific accidents. There was no workers' compensation, although many laborers were injured on the job. A worker who objected was likely to be fired and blacklisted. Exploited by the captains of industry, the immigrants became deeply involved in the labor-union movement, so much so that to tell the story of one without the other is virtually impossible.

—Vincent N. Parrillo,
Strangers to These Shores: 8th ed. Published by
Allyn and Bacon, Boston, MA. Copyright © 2005 by Pearson
Education. Reprinted by permission of the publisher.

_____ 7. The time period discussed is probably

     a. the late 1600s.
     b. the late 1700s.
     c. the late 1800s.

_____ 8. The place is probably

     a. California.
     b. New York.
     c. Mississippi.

        9. Underline the clues to your answers.

Expanding Prior Knowledge

Your response on the previous passages depends on your previous knowledge of history and your general knowledge. If you did not understand many of the inferences, you might ask, "How can I expand my prior knowledge?" The answer is not an easy formula or a quick fix. The answer is part of the reason that you are in college; it is a combination of broadening your horizons, reading more widely, and being an active participant in your own life. Expanding prior knowledge is a slow and steady daily process.

Drawing Conclusions

To arrive at a conclusion, you must make a logical deduction from both stated ideas and from unstated assumptions. Using hints as well as facts, you rely on prior knowledge and experience to interpret motives, actions, and outcomes. You draw conclusions on the basis of perceived evidence, but because perceptions differ, conclusions can vary from reader to reader. Generally, however, authors attempt to direct readers to preconceived conclusions. Read the following example and look for a basis for the stated conclusion.

EXAMPLE   **UNDERGROUND CONDUCTOR**

Harriet Tubman was on a northbound train when she overheard her name spoken by a white passenger. He was reading aloud an ad which accused her of stealing $50,000 worth of property in slaves, and which offered a $5000 reward for her capture. She lowered her head so that the sunbonnet she was wearing hid her face. At the next station she slipped off the train and boarded another that was headed south, reasoning that no one would pay attention to a black woman traveling in that direction. She deserted the second train near her hometown in Maryland and bought two chickens as part of her disguise. With her back hunched over in imitation of an old woman, she drove the chickens down the dusty road, calling angrily and chasing them with her stick whenever she sensed danger. In this manner Harriet Tubman was passed by her former owner who did not even notice her. The reward continued to mount until it reached $40,000.

—Leonard Pitt,
We Americans

Conclusion: Harriet Tubman was a clever woman who became a severe irritant to white slave owners.

What is the basis for this conclusion?

_____

_____

EXPLANATION   Her disguise and subsequent escape from the train station provide evidence of her intelligence and resourcefulness. The escalating amount of the reward, finally $40,000, proves the severity of the sentiment against her.

Reader's *Tip* —— Making Inferences

- Consider the attitude implied in the author's choice of words.
- Think about what might have been left out.
- Unravel actions.
- Interpret motives.
- Use suggested meaning and facts to make assumptions.
- Draw on prior knowledge to make connections.
- Base conclusions on stated ideas and unstated assumptions.

exercise 7.10   **Drawing Conclusions**

Read the following passages. For the first passage indicate evidence for the conclusion that has been drawn. For the latter passages, write your own conclusion as well as indicate evidence. Use the suggestions in the Reader's Tip.

Passage A

Albert Einstein did not begin to talk until he was three years old, and he wasn't entirely fluent even by the time he was nine. His language skills were so poor that his parents seriously worried that he might be mentally retarded! Nevertheless, he eventually learned to speak not only his native German, but also French and English. However, he mixed German with his French, and he had a strong accent. His English, learned later in life, never became fluent—as countless satirists have noted, he made grammatical mistakes and had a heavy German accent.

—Stephen M. Kosslyn and Robin S. Rosenberg,
Psychology: The Brain, the Person, the World, 2nd ed.

Conclusion: Einstein's language skills were not an accurate reflection of his true intelligence.

What is the basis for this conclusion? _____

_____

_____

_____

_____

_____

Passage B

In Massachusetts, Nicola Sacco and Bartolomeo Vanzetti—an immigrant shoe-factory worker and a poor fish peddler—were charged with and convicted of robbery and murder in 1920. The prosecutor insulted immigrant Italian defense witnesses and appealed to the prejudices of a bigoted judge and jury. Despite someone else's later confession and other potentially exonerating evidence, their seven-year appeals fight failed to win them retrial or acquittal. They were executed in 1927. At his sentencing in 1927, Vanzetti addressed presiding judge Webster Thayer. At one point in his moving speech, he said,

"I would not wish to a dog or a snake, to the most low and misfortunate creature of the earth—I would not wish to any of them what I have had to suffer for the things that I am not guilty of . . . I have suffered because I was an Italian, and indeed I am an Italian."

—Vincent N. Parrillo,
Strangers to These Shores: 8th ed. Published by
Allyn and Bacon, Boston, MA. Copyright © 2005 by
Pearson Education. Reprinted by permission of the publisher.

Conclusion: _____

_____

_____

What is the basis for this conclusion? _____

_____

_____

_____

_____

_____

Passage C

A scientist wrote a report attesting to Mozart's musical ability and age. The proof that he was indeed a boy and not a midget came at the end of a rigorous series of musical examinations:

"While he was playing to me, a cat came in, upon which he immediately left his harpsichord, nor could we bring him back for a considerable time. He would also sometimes run about the room with a stick between his legs for a horse."

—Jeremy Yudkin,
Understanding Music, 4th ed.

Conclusion: _____

_____

_____

What is the basis for this conclusion? _____

_____

_____

_____

_____

Passage D

A seventy-five-year-old man who loved to square dance suddenly had a sharp pain in his left knee. He went to his doctor to find out what the trouble was. The doctor noted his age, gave his knee a fairly superficial examination, and said, "I can't find anything obviously wrong with your knee. It must be due to your age." The man asked the doctor to explain. The doctor launched into a discussion of various theories of aging and how they might explain his knee problem, and concluded, "Now do you understand?" The old man replied, "No, I don't, because my right knee is just as old as my left knee, and it's not giving me a bit of trouble!"

—Erdman Palmore,
The Facts on Aging Quiz, 2nd ed.

Conclusion: _____

_____

_____

What is the basis for this conclusion? _____

_____

_____

_____

_____

_____

Passage E

Many Irish were single women taking jobs as domestics or nannies for the native-born urban elite. In 1800, there was 1 domestic servant for every 20 families, but by 1840, the ratio had dropped to 1 servant for every 10 families. Unmarried Irish (and Scandinavian) young women often came first and worked in U.S. homes. Their daily typical workload was 16 hours of cooking, cleaning, tending to the children, and nursing the sick, six days a week. With little time to themselves, these women saved their earnings for passage money for other family members. Records from the Boston Society for the Prevention of Pauperism offer one illustration of the difficulties women had seeking jobs in a household compared to men finding work in labor gangs. Between 1845 and 1850, it received employment applications from 14,000 female foreigners in contrast to 5,034 male applications.

—Vincent N. Parrillo,
Strangers to These Shores:
Race and Ethnic Relations in the United States, 8th ed.

Conclusion: _____

_____

_____

What is the basis for this conclusion? _____

_____

_____

_____

exercise 7.11   **Building a Story Based on Inferences**

The following story unfolds as the reader uses the clues to predict and make inferences. To make sense out of the story, the reader is never told—but must figure out—who the main character is, what he is doing, and why he is doing it. Like a mystery, the story is fun to read because you are actively involved. Review the strategies for making inferences, and then use your inferential skills to figure it out.

CAGED

Emphatically, Mr. Purcell did not believe in ghosts. Nevertheless, the man who bought the two doves, and his strange act immediately thereafter, left him with a distinct sense of the eerie.

Purcell was a small, fussy man; red cheeks and a tight, melon stomach. He owned a pet shop. He sold cats and dogs and monkeys; he dealt in fish food and bird seed, and prescribed remedies for ailing canaries. He considered himself something of a professional man.

There was a bell over the door that jangled whenever a customer entered. This morning, however, for the first time Mr. Purcell could recall, it failed to ring. Simply he glanced up, and there was the stranger, standing just inside the door, as if he had materialized out of thin air.

The storekeeper slid off his stool. From the first instant he knew instinctively, unreasonably, that the man hated him; but out of habit he rubbed his hands briskly together, smiled and nodded.

"Good morning," he beamed. "What can I do for you?"

The man's shiny shoes squeaked forward. His suit was cheap, ill-fitting, but obviously new. A gray pallor deadened his pinched features. He had a shuttling glance and close-cropped hair. He stared closely at Purcell and said, "I want something in a cage."

"Something in a cage?" Mr. Purcell was a bit confused. "You mean—some kind of pet?"

"I mean what I said!" snapped the man. "Something alive that's in a cage."

"I see," hastened the storekeeper, not at all certain that he did. "Now let me think. A white rat, perhaps."

"No!" said the man. "Not rats. Something with wings. Something that flies."

"A bird!" exclaimed Mr. Purcell.

"A bird's all right." The customer pointed suddenly to a suspended cage which contained two snowy birds. "Doves? How much for those?"

"Five-fifty. And a very reasonable price."

"Five-fifty?" The sallow man was obviously crestfallen. He hesitantly produced a five-dollar bill. "I'd like to have those birds. But this is all I got. Just five dollars."

Mentally, Mr. Purcell made a quick calculation, which told him that at a fifty-cent reduction he could still reap a tidy profit. He smiled magnanimously. "My dear man, if you want them that badly, you can certainly have them for five dollars."

"I'll take them." He laid his five dollars on the counter. Mr. Purcell teetered on tiptoe, unhooked the cage, and handed it to his customer. The man cocked his head to one side, listening to the constant chittering, the rushing scurry of the shop. "That noise?" he blurted. "Doesn't it get you? I mean all this caged stuff. Drives you crazy, doesn't it?"

Purcell drew back. Either the man was insane, or drunk.

"Listen." The staring eyes came closer. "How long d'you think it took me to make that five dollars?"

The merchant wanted to order him out of the shop. But he heard himself dutifully asking, "Why—why, how long *did* it take you?"

The other laughed. "Ten years! At hard labor. Ten years to earn five dollars. Fifty cents a year."

It was best, Purcell decided, to humor him. "My, my! Ten years—"

"They give you five dollars," laughed the man, "and a cheap suit, and tell you not to get caught again."

Mr. Purcell mopped his sweating brow. "Now, about the care and feeding of—"

"Bah!" The sallow man swung around, and stalked abruptly from the store.

Purcell sighed with sudden relief. He waddled to the window and stared out. Just outside, his peculiar customer had halted. He was holding the cage shoulder-high, staring at his purchase. Then, opening the cage, he reached inside and drew out one of the doves. He tossed it into the air. He drew out the second and tossed it after the first. They rose like wind-blown balls of fluff and were lost in the smoky grey of the wintry city. For an instant the liberator's silent and lifted gaze watched after them. Then he dropped the cage. A futile, suddenly forlorn figure, he shoved both hands deep in his trouser pockets, hunched down his head and shuffled away. . . .

The merchant's brow was puckered with perplexity. "Now why," Mr. Purcell muttered, "did he do that?" He felt vaguely insulted.

—Lloyd Eric Reeve,
Household Magazine

1. Where had the man been? _____

2. How do you know for sure? Underline the clues. _____

   _____

3. When did you figure it out? Circle the clincher. _____

   _____

4. Why does he want to set the birds free? _____

   _____

5. Why should the shopkeeper feel insulted? _____

   _____

6. After freeing the birds, why is the stranger "a futile, suddenly forlorn figure,"

   rather than happy and excited? _____

   _____

Summary *Points*

➤ **What is an inference?**
The inferential level of reading deals with motives, feelings, and judgments. The reader must read between the lines and look for the implied meaning in words and actions. Understanding implied meaning can be the determining factor in a reader's comprehension of jokes, advertisements, poetry, and some prose.

➤ **What is the connotation of a word?**
The feeling or emotion surrounding a word is its connotation. The connotation reflects certain attitudes and prejudices that can be positive or negative. The author's choice of words can manipulate the reader.

➤ **What is figurative language?**
Figurative language creates images to suggest attitudes. It is a different way of using "regular" words so that the words take on new meaning. A simile is a comparison of two unlike things using the word *like* or *as,* whereas a metaphor is a directly stated comparison. A literary analogy includes both similes and metaphors. A euphemism is a more pleasant way of saying something that is embarrassing or indelicate. Hyperbole is a figurative exaggeration. Personification attributes human characteristics to nonhuman things. Verbal irony expresses a meaning the opposite of what is literally said.

➤ **Why is prior knowledge needed to grasp implied meaning?**
The reader must have background knowledge of a subject to understand the suggested or implied meaning.

➤ **How does a reader draw conclusions?**
The reader makes a logical deduction from hints, facts, and prior knowledge.

selection 1   Narrative Nonfiction

Contemporary *Focus*

What contributions did Malcolm X make to the civil rights movement? How did a hustler who spent years in prison rise to become a leader and spokesman for the cause?

Remembering A Civil Rights Hero

By Adil Ahmad
The Dartmouth via University Wire, Dartmouth College, April 12, 2004

Martin Luther King Jr. Day is celebrated every year. Unfortunately, a different hero of the Civil Rights Movement of the 1950s and '60s remains forgotten. That man is El-Hajj Malik El-Shabazz, or Malcolm X, as he is more commonly known.

Malcolm X was born Malcolm Little into a poor Baptist family in Omaha, Neb., on May 19, 1925. The son of a Baptist preacher and "outspoken promoter of social and economic independence for blacks" who was brutally murdered by white supremacists, Malcolm had political activism in his blood.

After his house was burned down by the Ku Klux Klan, Little and his siblings were forced into foster homes and reform schools. Little moved to Boston to live with his half-sister in 1941 after he dropped out of school at age 15, then fell into the underworld of Harlem, New York, at the age of 17. There, he turned to a life of crime and drug-addiction, committing armed robberies for a living.

At the age of 21, he was sentenced to 10 years in prison for a minor robbery. In prison, Little began to read with enthusiasm. He started to read about Elijah Muhammad and his mis-named Nation of Islam, a Black Nationalist organization whose followers were called Black Muslims. After his release from prison in 1952, Little went to Detroit to become a full member of the Nation of Islam.

He changed his name to Malcolm X, dropping the "slave name" of Little. With his dazzling oratorical and people skills, Malcolm X soon rose up the ladder of the Nation of Islam. He soon surpassed Elijah as the foremost spokesman of the Nation.

However, Malcolm X's high-profile, radical agenda, and popularity among black Muslims and whites alike put him in direct conflict with Elijah Muhammad, and Malcolm X was consequently disbarred from the Nation in 1964.

Soon after, he started a new organization to promote his own beliefs. In 1964, he made a pilgrimage to Mecca, Saudi Arabia, and visited several other African and Muslim nations in which he was treated as a hero. On this trip he realized that his theories of black supremacy were false, and that whites were not necessarily evil after all. He then converted to Sunni Islam and changed his name to El-Hajj Malik El-Shabazz. After his return to the United States, he created the Organization of Afro-American Unity (OAAU), a nationalist organization that sought to unite all black organizations fighting racism against blacks. He renounced his racism against whites and began to encourage blacks to vote, to participate in the political system, and to work with each other and with sympathetic whites and Hispanics for an end to all forms of racial discrimination.

Malik El-Shabazz was assassinated on February 21, 1965, by members of the Nation of Islam, who, under orders from Elijah Muhammad, felt that El-Shabazz was a danger to their organization.

Collaborate on responses to the following questions:

➤ What factors caused Malcolm X to end up in jail?

➤ How did Malcolm X's philosophy change with each of his name changes?

➤ Why was Malcolm X assassinated?

Skill Development: Preview

Preview the next selection to predict its purpose and organization and to formulate your learning plan.

Activate Schema

Why do we hear more about Martin Luther King Jr. than Malcolm X?
Why was Malcolm X considered controversial?

Establish a Purpose for Reading

Malcolm X was a strong voice in the civil rights struggle of the 1960s. With his background, how did he become an educated spokesperson for a movement? Recall what you already know about Malcolm X, and read the following selection to find out how he learned to read.

Increase Word Knowledge

What do you know about these words?

articulate	functional	emulate	riffling	burrowing
wedge	devour	engrossing	intervals	feigned

Your instructor may give a true-false vocabulary review before or after reading.

Integrate Knowledge While Reading

Inference questions have been inserted in the margin to stimulate your thinking and help you read between the lines. Remember to

Predict	Picture	Relate	Monitor	Correct

LEARNING TO READ: MALCOLM X

It was because of my letters that I happened to stumble upon starting to acquire some kind of a homemade education.

I became increasingly frustrated at not being able to express what I wanted to convey in letters that I wrote, especially those to Mr. Elijah Muhammad. In the
5 street, I had been the most articulate hustler out there—I had commanded attention when I said something. But now, trying to write simple English, I not only wasn't articulate, I wasn't even functional. How would I sound writing in slang, the way I would *say* it, something such as, "Look, daddy, let me pull your coat about a cat, Elijah Muhammad—"

10 Many who today hear me somewhere in person, or on television, or those who read something I've said, will think I went to school far beyond the eighth grade. This impression is due entirely to my prison studies.

It had really begun back in Charlestown Prison, when Bimbi first made me feel envy of his stock of knowledge. Bimbi had always taken charge of any con-
15 versations he was in, and I had tried to emulate him. But every book I picked up had few sentences which didn't contain anywhere from one to nearly all of the words that might as well have been in Chinese. When I just skipped those words, of course, I really ended up with little idea of what the book said. So I had come to the Norfolk Prison Colony still going through only book-reading motions.
20 Pretty soon, I would have quit even these motions, unless I had received the motivation that I did.

I saw that the best thing I could do was get hold of a dictionary—to study, to learn some words. I was lucky enough to reason also that I should try to improve my penmanship. It was sad. I couldn't even write in a straight line. It was both ideas
25 together that moved me to request a dictionary along with some tablets and pencils from the Norfolk Prison Colony school.

I spent two days just riffling uncertainly through the dictionary's pages. I'd never realized so many words existed! I didn't know *which* words I needed to learn. Finally, just to start some kind of action, I began copying.

How did he become so famous?

American civil rights leader Malcolm X speaks at an outdoor rally in 1963.

30   In my slow, painstaking, ragged handwriting, I copied into my tablet everything printed on that first page, down to the punctuation marks.

How did he read the defining words?

    I believe it took me a day. Then, aloud, I read back, to myself, everything I'd written on the tablet. Over and over, aloud, to myself, I read my own handwriting.

    I woke up the next morning, thinking about those words—immensely proud to 35 realize that not only had I written so much at one time, but I'd written words that I never knew were in the world. Moreover, with a little effort, I also could remember

How was he a strategic learner?

what many of these words meant. I reviewed the words whose meaning I didn't remember. Funny thing, from the dictionary's first page right now, that "aardvark" springs to my mind. The dictionary had a picture of it, a long-tailed, long-eared, 40 burrowing African mammal, which lives off termites caught by sticking out its tongue as an anteater for ants.

    I was so fascinated that I went on—I copied the dictionary's next page. And the same experience came when I studied that. With every succeeding page, I also learned of people and places and events from history. Actually the dictionary 45 is like a miniature encyclopedia. Finally the dictionary's A section had filled a whole tablet—and I went on into the B's. That was the way I started copying what eventually became the entire dictionary. It went a lot faster after so much practice helped me to pick up handwriting speed. Between what I wrote in my tablet, and writing letters, during the rest of my time in prison I would guess I 50 wrote a million words.

    I suppose it was inevitable that as my word-base broadened, I could for the first time pick up a book and read and now begin to understand what the book was saying. Anyone who has read a great deal can imagine the new world that opened. Let me tell you something: from then until I left that prison, in every free moment I 55 had, if I was not reading in the library, I was reading on my bunk. You couldn't have gotten me out of books with a wedge. Between Mr. Muhammad's teachings, my correspondence, my visitors, . . . and my reading of books, months passed without my even thinking about being imprisoned. In fact, up to then, I never had been so truly free in my life.

60   The Norfolk Prison Colony library was in the school building. A variety of classes was taught there by instructors who came from such places as Harvard

In what U.S. state was the prison?

and Boston universities. The weekly debates between inmate teams were also held in the school building. You would be astonished to know how worked up convict debaters and audiences would get over subjects like "Should Babies Be 65 Fed Milk?"

    Available on the prison library's shelves were books on just about every general subject. Much of the big private collection that Parkhurst had willed to the prison was still in crates and boxes in the back of the library—thousands of old books. Some of them looked ancient: covers faded, old-time parchment-looking binding. 70 Parkhurst . . . seemed to have been principally interested in history and religion. He had the money and the special interest to have a lot of books that you wouldn't have in a general circulation. Any college library would have been lucky to get that collection.

    As you can imagine, especially in a prison where there was heavy emphasis on 75 rehabilitation, an inmate was smiled upon if he demonstrated an unusually intense interest in books. There was a sizable number of well-read inmates, especially the popular debaters. Some were said by many to be practically walking encyclopedias.

How do values change in prison?

They were almost celebrities. No university would ask any student to devour literature as I did when this new world opened to me, of being able to read and *understand*.

80   I read more in my room than in the library itself. An inmate who was known to read a lot could check out more than the permitted maximum number of books. I preferred reading in the total isolation of my own room.

When I had progressed to really serious reading, every night at about ten P.M. I would be outraged with the "lights out." It always seemed to catch me right in the 85 middle of something engrossing.

Fortunately, right outside my door was a corridor light that cast a glow into my room. The glow was enough to read by, once my eyes adjusted to it. So when "lights out" came, I would sit on the floor where I could continue reading in that glow.

90   At one-hour intervals at night guards paced past every room. Each time I heard the approaching footsteps, I jumped into bed and feigned sleep. And as soon as the guard passed, I got back out of bed onto the floor area of that light-glow, where I would read for another fifty-eight minutes until the guard approached again. That went on until three or four every morning. Three or four 95 hours of sleep a night was enough for me. Often in the years in the streets I had slept less than that.

(1,245 words)

—From *The Autobiography of Malcolm X*
as told to Alex Haley

Recall

Stop to self-test, relate, and react.

Your instructor may choose to give you a true-false comprehension review.

Write About the Selection

If you did not know how to read at 21 years of age, what methods would you use to teach yourself? Would you copy the dictionary? How did Malcolm X use some of the learning tips in this textbook to remember the words on the dictionary pages? How did he seize an unfortunate circumstance and make it into an opportunity? How are his efforts at self-improvement inspirational?

Response Suggestion: Relate your own ideas to the path taken by Malcolm X.

Contemporary *Link*

Although Malcolm X changed, initially he opposed Martin Luther King Jr.'s movement to promote racial change through nonviolence. He wanted a black revolution rather than compromise. How do you think the background experiences of Malcolm X might have shaped his beliefs and pulled him more toward violence than peaceful change?

Response Suggestion: List the different events and influences on his life and learning. Suggest how each experience shaped his philosophy.

Skill Development: Implied Meaning

According to the implied meaning in the selection, answer the following with *T* (true) or *F* (false).

_____ 1. The phrase "let me pull your coat about a cat" probably means that we need to put a coat around the cat to keep it warm.

_____ 2. The phrase "let me pull your coat about a cat" is a simile.

_____ 3. The phrase "gotten me out of books with a wedge" is an idiom.

_____ 4. It is ironic that Malcolm X felt truly free in prison.

_____ 5. The Norfolk Prison Colony was probably in the Northeast.

Check Your Comprehension

After reading the selection, answer the following questions with *a, b, c,* or *d*. To help you analyze your strengths and weaknesses, the question types are indicated.

Main Idea _____ 1. Which is the best statement of the main idea of this selection?

   a. Malcolm X was motivated by educated prisoners to change his life.
   b. While in prison, Malcolm X learned to read by copying and studying the dictionary.
   c. Malcolm X spent his time in prison helping fellow prisoners.
   d. Although mistreated in prison, Malcolm X was able to go to the library to read.

Detail _____ 2. Malcolm initially began his reading program because

   a. he wanted to read the Parkhurst books in the library.
   b. he wanted to write letters to Elijah Muhammad.
   c. he wanted to debate Bimbi.
   d. he wanted to entertain himself at night during the long hours of "lights out."

Inference _____ 3. Malcolm X describes his learning as a "homemade education" because

   a. he started it at home.
   b. he made it up himself without professional help.
   c. it was designed by prison teachers.
   d. it was modeled after other efforts of prison education.

Detail _____ 4. Malcolm X described his reading at Charlestown Prison as

   a. knowing most words in the sentences.
   b. knowing at least half the words in sentences.
   c. not knowing one to all words in most sentences.
   d. not knowing half the words in a few sentences.

Inference _____ 5. Malcolm X would define book-reading motions as

   a. reading with understanding.
   b. reading aloud.
   c. reading without understanding.
   d. not bothering to try to read.

Detail _____ 6. Malcolm X's decision to copy each page of the dictionary was motivated by all the following *except*

   a. a desire to learn words.
   b. a desire to improve his handwriting.
   c. a proven method.
   d. not knowing with which words to begin.

Inference _____ 7. Malcolm X mentions *aardvark* because

    a. it is a funny word that he still remembers from the first page of the dictionary.

    b. he has used the word many times.

    c. he thinks that *aardvark* is an important word for all to know.

    d. he is still not sure what the word means.

Inference _____ 8. Malcolm X mentions the debate topic "Should Babies Be Fed Milk?" to show that

    a. the inmate debaters would get excited over any topic, even if it was irrelevant to them.

    b. the debaters were qualified on a wide range of subjects.

    c. the convicts took a special interest in family issues.

    d. it was a favorite topic with the inmate debaters and the audience.

Inference _____ 9. Malcolm X implies that prison officials

    a. encouraged education.

    b. discouraged education.

    c. were not concerned with rehabilitation.

    d. gave favors for good behavior but not for educational efforts.

Inference _____ 10. The reader can appropriately assume all the following *except*

    a. after "lights out," no reading was allowed.

    b. the glow of the corridor light after "lights out" was not strong enough to allow Malcolm to lie in his bunk and read.

    c. the night guards would object to Malcolm X's reading after "lights out."

    d. other prisoners would complain to the guards if Malcolm X read after "lights out."

Answer the following with *T* (true) or *F* (false).

Detail _____ 11. Malcolm X dropped out of school in the eighth grade.

Detail _____ 12. Malcolm X began his attempts at reading at Charlestown Prison before he went to Norfolk Prison Colony.

Inference _____ 13. Bimbi suggested that Malcolm X use a dictionary to learn words.

Inference _____ 14. Prisoners at Norfolk Prison Colony looked down on fellow inmates who were well read.

Inference _____ 15. Malcolm X suggests that university reading demands are insufficient.

selection

1

Build Your Vocabulary

According to the way the italicized word was used in the selection, select *a, b, c,* or *d* for the word or phrase that gives the best definition. The number in parentheses indicates the line of the passage in which the word is located.

_____ 1. "*articulate* hustler" (5)
  a. dangerous
  b. crafty
  c. unclear
  d. well-spoken

_____ 2. "wasn't even *functional*" (7)
  a. interested
  b. useful
  c. vocal
  d. determined

_____ 3. "tried to *emulate* him" (15)
  a. convince
  b. copy
  c. argue with
  d. advise

_____ 4. "*riffling* uncertainly through" (27)
  a. studying
  b. memorizing
  c. flipping
  d. reading

_____ 5. "*burrowing* African mammal" (40)
  a. tunneling
  b. insect-eating
  c. slow moving
  d. shy

_____ 6. "with a *wedge*" (56)
  a. bet
  b. tapered block
  c. hammer
  d. slap

_____ 7. "*devour* literature" (78)
  a. consume
  b. be assigned
  c. require
  d. discuss

_____ 8. "something *engrossing*" (85)
  a. absorbing
  b. confusing
  c. historical
  d. religious

_____ 9. "one-hour *intervals*" (90)
  a. watches
  b. reports
  c. walks
  d. periods

_____ 10. "*feigned* sleep" (91)
  a. begged for
  b. hoped for
  c. pretended
  d. accomplished

Search the Net

Use a search engine such as Google, Yahoo, Ask.com, Excite, Dogpile, or Lycos to find how Malcolm X's beliefs changed. Compare his initial beliefs with those he held when he died. For suggested Web sites and other research activities, go to http://www.ablongman.com/smith/.

"One of the difficult lessons we have learned," wrote Martin Luther King Jr., "is that you cannot depend on American institutions to function without pressure. Any real change in the status quo depends on continued creative action to sharpen the conscience of the nation." Although the equal protection clause in the Fourteenth Amendment has been a part of the Constitution since 1868, social reformers such as Malcolm X and Martin Luther King Jr. challenged and changed the interpretation of that amendment. Civil rights activists maintained that the Constitution was color-blind, and court decisions supported that policy.

What is the U.S. Constitution?

The **Constitution** is a document that defines the structure of our government and the roles, powers, and responsibilities of public officials. It was signed in Philadelphia in 1787. Before the Constitution, the **Declaration of Independence** in 1776 affirmed our independence from England. The **Articles of Confederation** were written to govern the resulting new union of states that joined to fight for freedom and forge a new democracy. The articles created a loose union and left most of the authority with the individual states. After the Revolution, as economic conflicts arose and more central control was needed, the Constitution was written to give more power to the federal government, replacing the Articles of Confederation. Our country is still governed by this same Constitution of 1787, which also guarantees our civil liberties and civil rights, including freedom of expression, due process, and equal protection.

Because no document is perfect, the writers of the Constitution allowed for amendments, and the Constitution has been amended 27 times.

What are the three branches of government?

The Constitution divides the federal government into the executive, legislative, and judicial branches.

- The **executive branch** consists of the president, whose powers include approving or vetoing (refusing to sign) laws passed by Congress, and the **president's cabinet,** an advisory group of 13 government department heads appointed by the president. For example, Madeleine Albright was a member of former president Bill Clinton's cabinet.
- The **legislative branch** of the government consists of the two houses of Congress: the Senate and the House of Representatives. The **Senate** with 100 members (two from each state) and the **House of Representatives** with 435 members (apportioned to each state according to population) pass federal laws and serve on committees that investigate problems and oversee the executive branch.
- The **judicial branch** consists of a system of federal courts, the highest of which is the **Supreme**

Voters using electronic voting machines cast ballots.

Bob Daemmrich/PhotoEdit Inc.

Court. It consists of a chief justice and eight associate justices who are appointed by sitting presidents. The Supreme Court ensures uniformity in the interpretation of national laws.

Each of the three branches has checks and balances over the other branches so that power is shared.

What are political parties?

- Our president, senators, and representatives are nominated for office by a political party, an organization formed to support and elect candidates who uphold the views and beliefs of the group. Over the years, political parties have changed and some have disappeared. Today the two major parties are Republican and Democrat.
- The **Republican Party,** also called the GOP, for "Grand Old Party," began in 1854. Its symbol is the elephant, and Abraham Lincoln was the first Republican president. The party tends to be against expanding the size and responsibilities of the federal government and to support private enterprise. The party image is **conservative,** an ideology or set of beliefs that prefers the existing order and opposes change.
- The **Democratic Party** was organized by Thomas Jefferson in the late eighteenth century, and its first elected president was Andrew Jackson. The party tends to support the expansion of federal programs and a tax system with a greater burden on the rich and corporations. Its symbol is the donkey. The party image is **liberal,**

an ideology that supports the strong role of government in economic and social issues.

Before elections, both parties pay organizations such as **Gallup** to conduct **polls,** questioning voters about the most important issues and sampling public opinion on voting preferences.

What are capitalism, communism, and socialism?

- **Capitalism** is an economic system based on a free market for goods and services. Production centers such as factories seek profits and are owned by individuals as well as corporations and their stockholders, not the government. The United States has a capitalist economy, although it is not purely capitalistic since government does impose regulations on business.
- **Communism** is almost the opposite of capitalism. It is an economic, political, and social system in which there is no individual ownership. The government controls businesses, and goods and property are owned in common by all citizens. Goods are available to all people as they are needed. The communist system was envisioned by Karl Marx and is associated with the former Soviet Union and China.
- **Socialism** is an economic system advocating government or collective ownership of goods, rather than private ownership. In Karl Marx's theory, it represents the transition between capitalism and communism in which people are paid according to work done. Communists are socialists, but not all socialists are communists.

Review *Questions*

After studying the material, answer the following questions:

1. Why were the Articles of Confederation replaced? _____

_____

_____

_____

2. How does the Declaration of Independence differ from the Constitution? ____

_____

_____

_____

3. Which branch of the government has the fewest appointed members? _____

_____

4. In which branch of the government do members of the cabinet serve? ____

_____

5. Which branch of the government has the most elected members? _____

_____

6. In which house of Congress does each state have the same number of representatives? _____

_____

7. How do Republican and Democratic views on federal government expansion differ? _____

_____

_____

_____

8. Would a push to reduce corporate taxes most likely be a liberal or conservative cause? _____

9. Would a dynamic business owner prefer capitalism or socialism? _____

_____

10. In theory, under which system—capitalism or communism—does a worker share equally in goods regardless of the work he or she does? _____

_____

Your instructor may choose to give a true-false review of these political science concepts.

8 Point of View

- Is a textbook influenced by the author's point of view?
- What is the author's point of view?
- What is the reader's point of view?
- What is the difference between a fact and an opinion?

Eyvind Earl, *Horses by the Sea*. 1981, 40 x 30 inches.

Textbooks and the Author's Point of View

If you are like many people, you might assume that textbooks contain facts rather than opinions, that historical accounts are based on fact and do not vary from one author to another, and that textbooks are free from an author's bias. Nothing could be further from the truth. Textbooks are replete with interpretation, opinion, and slanted—rather than balanced—views. In short, they reflect the author's point of view and the "politically correct" winds of change.

For example, in your world civilization textbook, you will read about the wealthy and cosmopolitan Persian Empire, whose kings were righteous rulers believed to be elected by the gods. About 2,500 years ago, the Persian Empire was at its height, with spectacular public buildings and palaces at the capital, Persepolis, located in what is now Iran. Yes, *you* will read about the splendor of the empire, but twenty-first-century inhabitants of the region will not. Read what one textbook author has to say about the way historical facts about that region are treated:

> Islam denigrates the earlier cultures of its converts, just as it was noted that Christianity can. Everything before Islam was, in Arabic, *jahiliya*, "from the age of ignorance." This leaves little room in these peoples' historical consciousness for their pre-Islamic past, so they often lack interest in it. For example, despite Persia's brilliant antique history, for contemporary Iranians the glory began with the coming of Islam. Many people in Muslim countries view their own ancient cultural landscapes without interest. They may even discourage tourists from viewing pre-Islamic ruins.
>
> Edward Bergman and William Renwick,
> *Introduction to Geography*, 2nd ed.

In other violent changes of regime, such as the communist takeover of the Russian Empire, new leaders have also thrown out the old history books and written new ones to reflect the new political thinking. Even in American history books, you now see more about women and minorities—not because historical records have recently been unearthed, but in response to public demand. Thus, no purity rule applies to textbook writing.

The slant may start with, but is not limited to, what is included in the book; it continues with the author's interpretation. For example, the view of government in political science texts varies with liberal and conservative authors. Global warming, cloning, and stem cell replacement therapy can be opinion-laden topics in biology texts. And although the name of the first U.S. president does not vary from one American history book to another, the emphasis on the importance of Washington's administration might vary, depending on the author's point of view.

In short, *everything you read is affected by the author's point of view, purpose, tone, and presentation of facts and opinions.*

What Is the Author's Point of View?

An author's opinions and theories concerning factual material will influence the presentation of the subject matter. Although the author of a British textbook might describe American history during Revolutionary times as a colonial uprising on a

distant continent, an American author would praise the heroic struggle for personal freedom and survival. Each of the two authors would write from a different **point of view** and express particular opinions because they have different ways of looking at the subject.

Recognizing the author's point of view is part of understanding what you read. Sophisticated readers seek to identify the beliefs of the author to know "where he or she is coming from." When the point of view is not directly stated, the author's choice of words and information provide clues for the reader.

What Is Bias?

The terms *point of view* and *bias* are very similar and are sometimes used interchangeably. When facts are slanted, though not necessarily distorted, to reflect the author's personal beliefs, the written material is said to reflect the author's bias. Thus, a **bias** is simply an opinion or position on a subject. As commonly used, however, *bias* has a negative connotation suggesting narrow-mindedness and prejudice, whereas *point of view* suggests thoughtfulness and openness. Perhaps you would like to refer to your own opinion as a point of view and to those of others, particularly if they disagree with you, as biases!

EXAMPLE Read the following passage and use the choice of information and words to identify the author's point of view or bias.

> As president, Richard Nixon enjoyed the pomp and circumstance of office. He liked to listen to the presidential song, "Hail to the Chief," and to review at strict attention ranks of marching soldiers. Nixon's vaguely royal pretensions seemed harmless enough initially, but after Watergate many people began to feel that an all-too-royal president was endangering democratic practice.
>
> —Morris Fiorina and Paul Peterson,
> *The New American Democracy*, 3rd ed.

What is the author's point of view? Underline clues that support your answer.

[EXPLANATION] The author feels that former President Nixon began to think that he was king of the country rather than president of a democracy. This is suggested by the passage and by words such as *pomp and circumstance, royal pretensions, all-too-royal* and *endangering democratic practice*.

exercise 8.1   **Recognizing an Author's Point of View**

Read the following passages, and use the choice of information and words to identify the author's point of view or bias.

Passage 1

Commercial fishing vessels, which can catch massive amounts of fish using dragnets, have emptied coastal waters of fish, often with the help of government subsidies. No longer is the sea an inexhaustible source of food, as 60 percent of all fishing regions are now showing a decline in catch.

—Christian Goergen,
Politics in a Globalized World

What is the author's point of view? Underline clues that support your answer.

_____

_____

_____

Passage 2

"I suppose that I need not tell you that as regards Hawaii I take your views absolutely, as indeed I do on foreign policy generally. If I had my way we would annex those islands tomorrow. If that is impossible I would establish a protectorate over them."

—David Goldfield et al.,
The American Journey: A History of the United States,
vol. II, 3rd ed.

What is the point of view of the person quoted? Underline clues that support your answer. _____

_____

_____

Passage 3

Unless you are willing to argue that single mothers are lazier than others, it will be hard to deny that circumstances and government policies matter for poverty. Single mothers are the largest group among the poor, because they are caught between a rock and a hard place. They need to take care of their children—often without support from a father—but without support from others, they also need to work to make money. Especially if they are young and do not have a good education, it will be very hard to find a job that pays enough for childcare and a decent living. Thus, many women are forced to rely on the welfare system.

—Christian Goergen,
Politics in a Globalized World

What is the author's point of view? Underline clues that support your answer.

_____

_____

_____

exercise 8.2   **Comparing Points of View of Different Authors**

Read the following two descriptions of Mary Stuart, queen of Scotland, from two different history books. Although both include positive and negative comments, the second author obviously finds the subject more engaging and has chosen to include more positive details.

Portrait of Mary Stuart, Queen of Scots, Anonymous, 16th Century.

Passage A

Mary Stuart returned to Scotland in 1561 after her husband's death. She was a far more charming and romantic figure than her cousin Elizabeth, but she was no stateswoman. A convinced Catholic, she soon ran head-on into the granitelike opposition of Knox and the Kirk. In 1567 she was forced to abdicate, and in the following year she fled from Scotland and sought protection in England from Elizabeth. No visitor could have been more unwelcome.

—Joseph R. Strayer et al.,
The Mainstream of Civilization, 4th ed.

Passage B

Mary Stuart was an altogether remarkable young woman, about whom it is almost impossible to remain objectively impartial. Even when one discounts the flattery that crept into descriptions of her, one is inclined to accept the contemporary evidence that Mary was extraordinarily beautiful, though tall for a girl—perhaps over six feet. In addition to beauty, she had almost every other attractive attribute in high degree: courage, wit, resourcefulness, loyalty, and responsiveness, in short everything needful for worldly greatness save discretion in her relations with men and a willingness to compromise, if need be, on matters of religion. She was a thoroughgoing Roman Catholic, a good lover, and a magnificent hater.

—Shepard B. Clough et al.,
A History of the Western World

1. How are the two descriptions alike? _____

   _____

2. How do the two descriptions differ? _____

   _____

3. Which do you like better, and why? _____

4. Which clues signal that the author of the second description is more biased

   than the first? _____

   _____

5. What is the suggested meaning in the following phrases:

   a. "no stateswoman" _____

   b. "A convinced Catholic" _____

   c. "granitelike opposition" _____

   d. "more unwelcome" _____

   e. "save discretion in her relations with men" _____

   f. "thoroughgoing Roman Catholic" _____

   g. "magnificent hater" _____

What Is the Reader's Point of View?

Thus far we have considered only the author's point of view. However, to recognize a point of view, a reader must know enough about the subject to realize that there is another opinion beyond the one being expressed. Therefore, prior knowledge and a slightly suspicious nature will open the mind to countless other views and alternative arguments.

On the other hand, prior knowledge can lead to a closed mind and rigid thinking. Existing opinions affect the extent to which readers accept or reject what they read. If their beliefs are particularly strong, sometimes they refuse to hear what is said or they hear something that is not said. Research has shown that readers will actually "tune out" new material that expresses views drastically different from their own. For example, if you were reading that the AIDS virus should not be a concern for most middle-class Americans, would you be "tuned in" or "tuned out"?

EXAMPLE Read the following passage on smoking from the point of view of a non-smoker. Next, reread it from the point of view of a smoker. Finally, answer the questions.

> Smoke can permanently paralyze the tiny cilia that sweep the breathing passages clean and can cause the lining of the respiratory tract to thicken irregularly. The body's attempt to rid itself of the smoking toxins may produce a deep, hacking cough in the person next to you at the lunch counter. Console yourself with the knowledge that these hackers are only trying to rid their bodies of nicotines, "tars," formaldehyde, hydrogen sulfide, resins, and who knows what. Just enjoy your meal.
>
> —Robert Wallace,
> *Biology: The World of Life*

1. Is the author a smoker? Underline the clues suggesting your answer. _____

2. What is your view on smoking? _____

3. Reading this passage in the guise of a nonsmoker, what message is conveyed to you? _____

4. Assuming the role of a smoker, what message is conveyed to you? _____

5. What is the main point the author is trying to convey? _____

EXPLANATION Although it is possible that both the smoker and nonsmoker would get exactly the same message, it is more likely that the nonsmoker would be disgusted by the health risks, whereas the smoker would find the author guilty of exaggeration and discrimination. The main point is that smoking causes permanent physical damage. The attitude suggests that the author is probably not a smoker.

exercise 8.3 **Identifying Points of View**

Read the following passages and answer the questions about point of view.

Passage A: Columbus

On August 3, 1492, Columbus and some ninety mariners set sail from Palos, Spain, in the *Niña, Pinta,* and *Santa Maria.* Based on faulty calculations, the Admiral estimated Asia to be no more than 4500 miles to the west (the actual distance is closer to 12,000 miles). Some 3000 miles out, his crew became fearful and wanted to return home. But he convinced them to keep sailing west. Just two days later, on October 12, they landed on a small island in the Bahamas, which Columbus named San Salvador (holy savior).

A fearless explorer, Columbus turned out to be an ineffective administrator and a poor geographer. He ended up in debtor's prison, and to his dying day in 1506 he never admitted to locating a world unknown to Europeans. Geographers overlooked his contribution and named the Western continents after another mariner, Amerigo Vespucci, a merchant from Florence who participated in a Portuguese expedition to South America in 1501. In a widely reprinted letter, Vespucci claimed that a new world had been found, and it was his name that caught on.

—James Kirby Martin et al.,
America and Its Peoples

1. Which paragraph sounds more like the Columbus you learned about in elementary school? _____

   _____

2. What is the author's position on Columbus? Underline clues for your answer.

   _____

   _____

3. What is your view of Columbus? What has influenced your view? _____

   _____

   _____

4. What is the main point the author is trying to convey? _____

   _____

   _____

Passage B: Mexican Cession

The tragedy of the Mexican cession is that most Anglo-Americans have not accepted the fact that the United States committed an act of violence against the Mexican people when it took Mexico's northwestern territory. Violence was not limited to the taking of the land; Mexico's territory was invaded, her people murdered, her land raped, and her possessions plundered. Memory of this destruction generated a distrust and dislike that is still vivid in the minds of many Mexicans, for the violence of the United States left deep scars. And for Chicanos—Mexicans remaining within the boundaries of the new United States territories—aggression was even more insidious, for the outcome of the Texas and Mexican-American wars made them a conquered people. Anglo-Americans were the conquerors, and they evinced all the arrogance of military victors.

In material terms, in exchange for 12,000 lives and more than $100,000,000, the United States acquired a colony two and a half times as large as France, containing rich farm lands and natural resources such as gold, silver, zinc, copper, oil, and uranium which would make possible its unprecedented industrial boom. It acquired ports on the Pacific which generated further economic expansion across that ocean. Mexico was left with its shrunken resources to face the continued advances of the expanding capitalist force on its border.

—Rodolfo Acuña,
Occupied America: A History of Chicanos

1. What is the author's point of view? Underline clues. _____

_____

_____

2. How does this author's view differ from what you would expect in most American history texts? _____

_____

_____

3. What is your point of view on the subject? _____

_____

_____

4. What is the main point the author is trying to convey? _____

_____

_____

Passage C: Surviving in Vietnam

Vietnam ranks after World War II as America's second most expensive war. Between 1950 and 1975, the United States spent $123 billion on combat in Southeast Asia. More importantly, Vietnam ranks—after our Civil War and World Wars I and II—as the nation's fourth deadliest war, with 57,661 Americans killed in action.

Yet, when the last U.S. helicopter left Saigon, Americans suffered what historian George Herring terms "collective amnesia." Everyone, even those who had fought in 'Nam, seemed to want to forget Southeast Asia. It took nearly ten years for the government to erect a national monument to honor those who died in Vietnam.

Few who served in Vietnam survived unscathed, whether psychologically or physically. One of the 303,600 Americans wounded during the long war was 101st Airborne platoon leader James Bombard, first shot and then blown up by a mortar round during the bitter Tet fighting at Hue in February 1968. He describes his traumatic experience as

> feeling the bullet rip into your flesh, the shrapnel tear the flesh from your bones and the blood run down your leg. . . . To put your hand on your chest and to come away with your hand red with your own blood, and to feel it running out of your eyes and out of your mouth, and seeing it spurt out of your guts, realizing you were dying. . . . I was ripped open from the top of my head to the tip of my toes. I had forty-five holes in me.

Somehow Bombard survived Vietnam.

Withdrawing U.S. forces from Vietnam ended only the combat. Returning veterans fought government disclaimers concerning the toxicity of the defoliant Agent Orange. VA hospitals across the nation still contain thousands of para- and quadriplegic Vietnam veterans, as well as the maimed from earlier wars. Throughout America the "walking wounded" find themselves still embroiled in the psychological aftermath of Vietnam.

—James Divine et al.,
America: Past and Present

1. What is the author's own view of the war? Underline clues for your answer.

   _____

   _____

2. What is your own position on the Vietnam War? _____

   _____

   _____

3. What is the purpose of Bombard's quotation? _____

   _____

   _____

4. How do you feel about war after reading this passage? _____

   _____

   _____

5. What is the main point the author is trying to convey? _____

   _____

   _____

What Are Fact and Opinion?

For both the reader and the writer, a point of view is a position or belief that logically evolves over time through gained knowledge and experience and is usually based on both facts and opinions. For example, what is your position on city curfews for youth, on helping the homeless, and on abortion? Are your views on these issues supported solely by facts? Do you recognize the difference between the facts and the opinions used in your thinking?

Both facts and opinions are used persuasively to support positions. You have to determine which is which and then judge the issue accordingly. A **fact** is a statement based on actual evidence or personal observation. It can be checked objectively with empirical data and proved to be true. By contrast, an **opinion** is a statement of personal feeling or judgment. It reflects a belief or an interpretation of evidence, rather than evidence itself; it cannot be proved true. Adding the quoted opinion of a well-known authority to a few bits of evidence does not improve the data, yet this is an effective persuasive technique. Even though you may believe an opinion is valid, it is still an opinion.

EXAMPLE

Fact: Freud developed a theory of personality.

Fact: Freud believed that the personality is divided into three parts.

Opinion: Freud constructed the most complete theory of personality development.

Opinion: The personality is divided into three parts: the id, the ego, and the superego.

Authors mix facts and opinions, sometimes in the same sentence, to win you over to a particular point of view. Persuasive tricks include quoting a source of facts who then voices an opinion or hedging a statement with "It is a fact that" and attaching a disguised opinion. Recognize that both facts and opinions are valuable, but be able to distinguish between the two. The questions listed in the Reader's Tip can help you.

Reader's *Tip* ——— Questions to Uncover Bias

- What is your opinion on the subject?
- What is the author's opinion on the subject?
- What are the author's credentials for writing on the subject?
- What does the author have to gain?
- Does the author use facts or opinions as support?
- Are the facts selected and slanted to reflect the author's bias?

---

exercise 8.4   **Differentiating Beween Facts and Opinions**

Read each statement, and indicate *F* for fact and *O* for opinion.

_____ 1. Regarding the drugs that can cause death from overdose, the dangers have been blown wildly out of proportion.

—Jeffrey Reiman,
*The Rich Get Richer and the Poor Get Prison:
Ideology, Class, and Criminal Justice*, 7th ed.

_____ 2. Jefferson was feared, honestly feared, by almost all Federalists.

—Morton Borden,
America's Eleven Greatest Presidents.

_____ 3. A misdemeanor is a crime punishable by less than one year in prison.

—Adapted from John J. Macionis,
Social Problems, 2nd ed.

_____ 4. The most controversial tax is a general sales tax, which is levied by all but a few states on the sale of most goods, sometimes exempting food and drugs.

—Adapted from David B. Magleby et al.,
Government by the People, Teaching and
Learning Classroom Edition, 6th ed.

_____ 5. Phosphorus, found in detergents, causes an overgrowth of algae, which then consume all the available oxygen in the water, making it incapable of supporting any flora or fauna.

—Ricky W. Griffin and Ronald J. Ebert,
Business, 8th ed.

_____ 6. Witnesses who identify culprits (from photos or police lineups) within 10 seconds are 90% accurate, whereas those who take longer than 12 seconds are only 50% accurate.

—Lester A. Lefton and Linda Brannon,
Psychology, 9th ed.

_____ 7. When you feel anger, your heart rate increases and so does the temperature of your skin; and when you feel fear, your heart rate increases but your skin temperature actually decreases.

—Stephen M. Kosslyn and Robin S. Rosenberg,
Psychology: The Brain, the Person, the World, 2nd ed.

_____ 8. Today colleges and universities increasingly tend to circumvent the courts and bury serious criminal cases in their own judicial systems.

—John Silber,
"Students Should Not Be Above the Law,"
New York Times, May 9, 1996.

_____ 9. Convicted juveniles, like adult offenders, often gain early and undeserved release from jail.

—Judy Sheindlin,
*Don't Pee On My Leg and Tell Me It's Raining:
America's Toughest Family Court Judge Speaks Out*

_____ 10. In all states, compulsory-attendance laws forbid students to drop out until they turn 16 and sometimes until they turn 18 or even older.

—Jackson Toby,
"Obsessive Compulsion: The Folly of Mandatory High School Attendance."

_____ 11. Repairing the meetinghouse, building a school, aiding a widowed neighbor—such were the proper uses of wealth.

—Gary B. Nash et al.,
The American People, 6th ed., vol. 1

_____ 12. If you are like most people in the United States, you eat only about 2 servings of fruits or vegetables each day, a figure below the 5 to 9 recommended servings.

—Janice Thompson and Melinda Manore,
Nutrition: An Applied Approach

_____ 13. Although there are a large number of Web browsers, some developed by Internet giants such as Microsoft, the dominant Web browser is Google, which has gained dominance by offering the most efficient search engine on the Web.

—Paul R. Gregory,
Essentials of Economics, 6th ed.

_____ 14. Americans are poorly informed about politics.

—Gary Wasserman,
The Basics of American Politics, 12th ed.

_____ 15. Bach was by no means considered the greatest composer of his day, though he was recognized as the most well-known organist, harpsichordist, and improviser (one who creates music at the same time it is performed).

—Roger Kamien,
Music: An Appreciation, Brief 5th ed.

exercise 8.5   ## Discerning Fact and Opinion in Textbooks

The following passage from a history text describes Sigmund Freud. Notice the mixture of facts and opinions in developing a view of this scientist. Mark the items that follow with *F* for fact and *O* for opinion.

Passage A

Sigmund Freud was a disciplined man, precise and punctual in his habits. In many ways, his life was typical of the life of a Viennese bourgeois professional at the end of the nineteenth century. His day was like a railway timetable, scheduled to the minute—whether seeing patients, dining with his family, or taking his daily constitutional. He even calculated his pleasures, counting as his only indulgence the 20 cigars he smoked every day.

The order in Freud's life seemed curiously at odds with his dedication to the study of disorder. He was a man of science, a medical doctor specializing in *organic* diseases of the nervous system. Early in his career, he began to question *physiological* explanations for certain nervous disorders and to search for another reason for the disorders of the mind. His exploration took him to Paris in 1885 to study with the leading French neurologist, Jean Martin Charcot (1825–1893), whose work on hysteria had won him an international reputation.

Surrounded by hysterics in Charcot's clinic, Freud wondered whether organic physical illnesses could be traced to psychological problems. Freud explored the value of hypnosis as a technique for uncovering the secret workings of the mind. He learned that emotions alone could produce physical symptoms such as blindness and paralysis. By hypnotizing patients, Freud caught glimpses of the world of the unconscious as a vast and hidden terrain. He approached the new territory as an explorer.

Freud created a new science of the unconscious, psychoanalysis, when he rejected physiological causes for nervous disorders in favor of psychological ones. He intended psychoanalysis as a theory of personality and a method of treatment or therapy. That was a dramatic break with existing theories of madness and mental disorder. On his seventieth birthday, Freud looked back over his own career and described his achievement: "The poets and philosophers before me discovered the unconscious; what I discovered was the scientific method by which the unconscious can be studied."

—Mark Kishlansky et al.,
Civilization in the West, 6th ed.

_____ 1. Freud smoked 20 cigars each day.

_____ 2. He lived the life of a typical Viennese professional of his era.

_____ 3. The order in Freud's life was at odds with his dedication to the study of disorder.

_____ 4. Freud was a medical doctor specializing in organic disorders of the nervous system.

_____ 5. Freud created the science of psychoanalysis.

The following passage from a business text discusses Winston Churchill's leadership capabilities. Notice the mixture of facts and opinions in developing a view of this former British leader. Mark the items that follow with *F* for fact and *O* for opinion.

Passage B

Successful leaders often have the experience of prevailing in the face of adversity and learning from earlier failures. Leaders' skills also must match the circumstances. Winston Churchill's career provides a classic example.

Churchill began his remarkable political career in 1901 when he became a member of the House of Commons at the age of 26. Prior to his entry into Parliament he had seen combat as a cavalry officer in India, Cuba, and the Sudan and was awarded several medals for valor. He rose quickly in politics and governmental service, becoming the First Lord of the Admiralty (civilian head of the British Navy) in 1911. One of Churchill's decisions about deployment of naval forces in 1915 during World War I resulted in failure and marked the end of his fast-track career. Churchill returned to combat, serving as an infantry officer in 1917. After World War I Churchill returned to public office but was essentially relegated to the sidelines of politics. His calls for rearmament, warnings about the intentions of the Nazis between 1933 and 1939, and criticisms of the government's attempts to appease the Nazis were ignored. When things looked the worst in May 1940, the country turned to the 65-year-old Churchill for leadership as Prime Minister. It is said that Churchill "stood out as the one man in whom the nation could place its trust."

In June 1940 Britain had been at war with Germany for a year. British soldiers had been driven out of France and narrowly escaped capture through an evacuation from Dunkirk. France surrendered on June 22, and the United States had not yet entered World War II. The Battle of Britain, which involved heavy bombing of Britain's major cities, was about to begin, and it appeared that Germany would invade Britain. The outcome looked bleak. Churchill's hats, cigars, and two-fingered "v" for victory signs were distinctive, as well as symbolic, and endeared him to his followers. There were other qualities about Churchill as well that made him well-suited for the challenges of leadership during these difficult times. Two specific examples of his personal risk-taking are described as follows:

> Churchill as Prime Minister frequently and deliberately ran terrible personal risks. But the people admired him for it, and loved his offhand disregard for danger. Once, when a German bomb landed near his car and nearly tipped it over, he joked, "Must have been my beef that kept the car down"—a reference to his pudginess.
>
> Windston Churchill was another who liked to leave his underground air-raid shelter in Whitehall for the streets the moment bombs began falling. Attempts were made to stop him, because the risk of getting one's head blown off or losing a limb from shrapnel was great. . . . "I'll have you know," thundered Churchill, "that as a child my nursemaid could never prevent me from taking a walk in the Green Park when I wanted to do so. And, as a man, Adolf Hitler certainly won't."

At the end of World War II in 1945, Churchill lost his bid for reelection because he was unresponsive to the needs for social change after the war. He returned to office again as Prime Minister from 1951 to 1955, but his performance was limited by age and health problems. In general, his service as a peace-time Prime Minister did not measure up to his service during war time.

—Charles R. Greer and W. Richard Plunkett,
Supervision: Diversity and Teams in the Workplace, 10th ed.

_____ 1. The skills of leaders must also match their circumstances.

_____ 2. Churchill began his political career at the age of 26 in the House of Commons.

_____ 3. Things looked the worst for England in May of 1940.

_____ 4. France surrendered to Germany on June 22, 1940, but the United States had not yet entered the war.

_____ 5. Churchill wore hats, smoked cigars, and made the two-finger "v" for victory sign.

_____ 6. Churchill was unresponsive to social issues after World War II.

_____ 7. Churchill was a frequent and deliberate risk-taker.

_____ 8. Churchill was a better leader during the war than during peacetime.

selection 1 Essay

selection 1

Contemporary *Focus*

Is life as a twenty-something filled with questions and uncertainty? After college, is the path predictable? What are the crucial questions confronting college graduates and young working adults?

Growing Up Is Taking Longer Than It Used To

By Jordan Capobianco
The Oracle, University of South Florida, May 15, 2006

Where's my $100,000 Mercedes S-Class?

As spoiled as that question may sound, it's a tune that more and more young adults are humming. The 18-to-35 crowd wants everything from true love to a high-paying, enjoyable job.

And they want it plenty.

The problem is that most emerging adults aren't exactly sure how to get it. Graduating from college and being employed by a company for the entirety of one's working life is less possible now than it was when the parents of this generation were emerging into adulthood. Choosing one career path and sticking to it is also less

desirable today and borders on boring. With all of the options that are available, doing so is like going to a large Chinese buffet and just eating the fried rice.

However, there is a problem: When young adults find themselves in such a position of not knowing what to do or how to get what they want, they flounder. It's referred to as a "quarter-life crisis," and it's a phenomenon occurring in many places. It is not a disease, nor is it indicative of a lack of values. It is merely a change in the way life is led, and every new generation experiences such changes to some degree.

Collaborate on responses to the following questions:

➤ How is attending school a goal setting, structured experience?

➤ How do you find a job that is more than a paycheck?

➤ How often can you change jobs and still have a respectable employment record?

Skill Development: Preview

Preview the next selection to predict its purpose and organization and to formulate your learning plan.

Activate Schema

What do you predict will be your first job as a college graduate?
How long will you stay in your first job?
How do you plan to meet friends after college?

Establish a Purpose for Reading

Much attention has been given to the midlife crisis. What is a quarterlife crisis? Read to learn the challenges facing young adults as they seek to establish their careers and social networks.

Increase Word Knowledge

What do you know about these words?

inevitable	scorned	ponder	relevant	devastating
chaotic	stagnancy	desperation	trepidation	barrage

Your instructor may give a true-false vocabulary review before or after Readings.

Integrate Knowledge While Reading

Questions have been inserted in the margin to stimulate your thinking and help you read between the lines. Remember to

Predict	Picture	Relate	Monitor	Correct

WHAT IS THE QUARTERLIFE CRISIS?

Jim, the neighbor who lives in the three-story colonial down the block, has recently turned 50. You know this because Jim's wife threw him a surprise party about a month ago. You also know this because, since then, Jim has dyed his hair blond, purchased a leather bomber jacket, traded in his Chevy Suburban for a sleek Miata, and
5 ditched the wife for a girlfriend half her size and age.

Yet, aside from the local ladies' group's sympathetic clucks for the scorned wife, few neighbors are surprised at Jim's instant lifestyle change. Instead, they nod their heads understandingly. "Oh, Jim," they say. "He's just going through a midlife crisis. Everyone goes through it." Friends, colleagues, and family members excuse his
10 weird behavior as an inevitable effect of reaching this particular stage of life. Like millions of other middle-aged people, Jim has reached a period during which he

Do women also have midlife crises?

believes he must ponder the direction of his life—and then alter it. Jim's midlife crisis is relevant to you because it is currently the only age-related crisis that is widely
recognized as a common, inevitable part of life. The midlife crisis, however, is not
15 the only age-related crisis that we experience.

This other crisis can be just as, if not more, devastating than the midlife crisis. It
can throw someone's life into chaotic disarray or paralyze it completely. It may be
the single most concentrated period during which individuals relentlessly question
their future and how it will follow the events of their past. It covers the transition
20 from the academic world to the "real" world—an age group that can range from late
adolescence to the mid-thirties but is usually most intense in twentysomethings. It
is what we call the quarterlife crisis, and it is a real phenomenon.

The quarterlife crisis and the midlife crisis stem from the same basic problem,
but the resulting panic couldn't be more opposite. At their cores, both the quarter-
25 life and the midlife crisis are about a major life change. Often, for people experiencing a midlife crisis, a sense of stagnancy sparks the need for change. During this period, a middle-aged person tends to reflect on his past, in part to see if his life to
date measures up to the life he had envisioned as a child (or as a twentysomething).
The midlife crisis also impels a middle-aged person to look forward, sometimes
30 with an increasing sense of desperation, at the time he feels he has left.

What causes the quarterlife crisis? → In contrast, the quarterlife crisis occurs precisely because there is none of that
predictable stability that drives middle-aged people to do unpredictable things.
After about twenty years in a sheltered school setting many graduates undergo
some sort of culture shock. In the academic environment, goals were clear-cut and
35 the ways to achieve them were mapped out distinctly. To get into a good college or
graduate school, it helped if you graduated with honors. To graduate with honors,
you needed to get good grades. To get good grades, you had to study hard. If your
goals were athletic, you worked your way up from junior varsity or walk-on to varsity
by practicing skills, working out in the weight room, and gelling with teammates
40 and coaches. The better you were, the more playing time you got, the more impres-
sive your statistics could become.

Twenty-somethings may become disillusioned with their life's path.

Royalty Free/Corbis

But after graduation, the pathways blur. In the "real world," there is no definitive way to get from point A to point B, regardless of whether the points are related to a career, financial situation, home, or social life. The extreme uncertainty that twenty-somethings experience after graduation occurs because what was once a solid line that they could follow throughout their series of educational institutions has now disintegrated into millions of different options. The sheer number of possibilities can certainly inspire hope. That is why people say that twenty-somethings have their whole lives ahead of them. But the endless array of decisions can also make a recent graduate feel utterly lost.

Would there be a crisis if fewer choices existed?

WHY WORRY ABOUT A QUARTERLIFE CRISIS?

The whirlwind of new responsibilities, new liberties, and new choices can be entirely overwhelming for someone who has just emerged from the shelter of twenty years of schooling. We don't mean to make graduates sound as if they have been hibernating since they emerged from the womb; certainly it is not as if they have been slumbering throughout adolescence (though some probably tried). They have in a sense, however, been encased in a bit of a cocoon, where someone or something—parents or school, for example—has protected them from a lot of the scariness of their surroundings. As a result, when graduates are let loose into the world, their dreams and desires can be tinged with trepidation. They are hopeful, but at the same time they are also, to put it simply, scared silly.

Why are people at midlife and twentysomethings the most likely groups to experience a crisis?

The revelation that life simply isn't easy is one of the most distressing aspects of the quarterlife crisis, particularly for individuals who do not have large support networks or who doubt themselves often. It is in these situations that the quarterlife crisis can become hazardous. Depression is one common result of the quarterlife crisis. That is why it is so important to acknowledge this transition period.

Another way the quarterlife crisis can show up is in a feeling of disappointment, of "This is all there is?" Maybe the job turns out to be not so glamorous after all, or maybe it just doesn't seem to lead anywhere interesting. Perhaps the year of travel in Europe was more of a wallet buster than previously imagined. Or maybe the move to a hip, new city just didn't turn out to be as fabulous a relocation as expected.

What are some strategies twentysomethings might use to combat the crisis?

Twenty-somethings are particularly vulnerable to doubts. They doubt their decisions, their abilities, their readiness, their past, present, and future. But most of all, they doubt themselves. The twenties are a period of intense questioning. The questions can range from seemingly trivial choices—"Should I really have spent $100 to join that fantasy baseball league?"—to much larger decisions—"When is the right time for me to start a family?"

But if the questioning becomes constant and the barrage of doubts never seems to cease, twenty-somethings can feel as if it is hard to catch their breath, as if they are spiraling downward. Many times the doubts increase because twenty-somethings think it is abnormal to have them in the first place. No one talks about having doubts at this age, so when twentysomethings do find that they are continuously questioning themselves, they think something is wrong with them.

(1,092 Words)

—Alexandra Robbins and Abby Wilner,
from *Quarterlife Crisis*

Recall

Stop to self-test, relate, and react.

Your instructor may choose to give you a true-false comprehension review.

Write About the Selection

Is there a legitimate quarter life crisis? What factors merge for twentysomethings to cause this uncertainty?

Response Suggestion: List and explain the causes of the crisis.

Armed with information about a looming quarterlife crisis, what can you do to lessen the impact? What questions would you ask the authors of this selection?

Skill Development: Explore Point of View

Form a collaborative group to discuss the following questions:

- What is the author's point of view on the quarterlife crisis?
- What is your point of view on the quarterlife crisis?
- Why should people feel disappointed to be out of school?
- How do expectations for school and expectations for work differ?
- After graduating from college, how do you become your own boss?

Check Your Comprehension

After reading the selection, answer the following questions with *a, b, c,* or *d*. To help you analyze your strengths and weaknesses, the question types are indicated.

Main Idea _____ 1. What is the best statement of the main idea of this selection?

    a. People who have a quarterlife crisis will most likely not have a midlife crisis.

    b. Graduating from college does not prevent a quarterlife crisis.

    c. The quarterlife crisis is an extension of the predictable academic plan for the future.

    d. The quarterlife crisis is a time of uncertainty as twenty-somethings chart paths for the future.

Inference _____ 2. The authors suggest that each of the following is true *except*

    a. many people are familiar with the term "midlife crisis."

    b. many people tend to change their values in a midlife crisis.

    c. the midlife crisis involves reflection and change.

    d. the midlife crisis is experienced only by men.

Detail _____ 3. The quarterlife crisis

    a. marks the transition from the academic world to the "real" world.

    b. occurs in late adolescence as college draws near.

    c. lasts longer than a midlife crisis.

    d. is seldom an intense experience.

Inference _____ 4. An important difference between the midlife crisis and the quarterlife crisis is that

    a. the midlife crisis is stressful.

    b. the midlife crisis is triggered by the long established and predictable routine of one's life.

    c. the quarterlife crisis involves looking forward.

    d. the quarterlife crisis is age-related.

Inference _____ 5. The authors discuss the connections between schools, grades, and studying most likely in order to

    a. indicate that the stress of the quarterlife crisis is due to school, grades, and studying.

    b. suggest that academic success can reduce the severity of a quarterlife crisis.

    c. illustrate that in the academic world, the rules and goals are clear.

    d. indicate that there are few connections between academic success and career success.

selection **1**

Detail _____ 6. According to the selection, a significant source of stress for people experiencing a quarterlife crisis is that

    a. parental expectations conflict with the expectations of twenty-somethings.

    b. there are no clear directions to follow.

    c. good grades are required to get into graduate school.

    d. the unemployment rate is increasing, and job security is decreasing.

Inference _____ 7. The authors suggest that the sheer number of possibilities facing people after graduation

    a. can both inspire and overwhelm.

    b. is an indication of our improving standard of living.

    c. is not a factor in the quarterlife crisis.

    d. should make young people feel confident of success.

Inference _____ 8. The authors suggest that college contributes to the quarterlife crisis because it

    a. protects students from much of the "real" world.

    b. fails to provide skills that can be used in the "real" world.

    c. costs so much that graduates have no financial resources left to start a career.

    d. leads students to believe that few employment activities will be structured.

Inference _____ 9. By saying, "People have to invent their own road map," the authors mean that presently young people must

    a. study hard and get a good job.

    b. seek security in a job and satisfaction will follow.

    c. think creatively in choosing from the many options for success.

    d. follow a predictable path without the guarantee of financial success.

Inference _____ 10. The authors suggest that

    a. the twenties are not necessarily the best years of one's life.

    b. decisions made in one's twenties are usually not realistic.

    c. most people in their twenties suffer from job-related depression.

    d. twentysomethings should travel in Europe before getting a job.

Answer the following with *T* (true) or *F* (false).

Detail _____ 11. The authors suggest that the "cocoon" in which twentysomethings have previously been encased is a web of addiction, anxiety, and depression.

Inference _____ 12. The tone of the statement "It is not as if they have been slumbering throughout adolescence (though some probably tried)" is humorous and a little sarcastic.

Inference _____ 13. Doubt can be a major problem for people experiencing a quarterlife crisis.

Inference _____ 14. The authors suggest that figuring out the meaning of life before you're fifty will alleviate the stress of a midlife crisis.

Inference _____ 15. People in a quarterlife crisis often think they are the only ones who feel the way they do.

Build Your Vocabulary

According to the way the italicized word was used in the selection, select *a, b, c,* or *d* for the word or phrase that gives the best definition. The number in parentheses indicates the line of the passage in which the word is located.

_____ 1. "the *scorned* wife" (6)
    a. endangered
    b. intelligent
    c. disrespected
    d. liberated

_____ 2. "*inevitable effect*" (10)
    a. uncertain
    b. unavoidable
    c. silly
    d. normal

_____ 3. "*ponder* the direction" (12)
    a. discard
    b. overlook
    c. think about
    d. reject

_____ 4. "crisis is *relevant*" (13)
    a. significant
    b. commonplace
    c. entertaining
    d. refreshing

_____ 5. "can be just as, if not more, *devastating*" (16)
    a. thought provoking
    b. distressing
    c. meaningful
    d. lonely

_____ 6. "*chaotic* disarray" (17)
    a. harmful
    b. disorderly
    c. faster
    d. needed

_____ 7. "sense of *stagnancy*" (26)
    a. standing still
    b. moving rapidly
    c. uncertainty
    d. dissatisfaction

_____ 8. "sense of *desperation*" (30)
    a. despair
    b. unknowing
    c. isolation
    d. guilt

_____ 9. "tinged with *trepidation*" (59)
    a. hopefulness
    b. delight
    c. eagerness
    d. uneasiness

_____ 10. "*barrage* of doubts" (79)
    a. rapid outpouring
    b. feeling
    c. conversation
    d. argument

selection 2 Essay

Contemporary *Focus*

Does personal appearance affect the way people are treated? If you like a person, does that affect your view of the person's attractiveness? Do attractive people have more advantages than their less attractive counterparts? If so, is this a form of discrimination that can be measured and proven?

The Beauty Premium

By Sarah Boyd
The Dominion Post (Wellington, New Zealand), June 4, 2005

The advantages of being attractive have long been explored and measured by psychologists, with various levels of precision. Ideas about what constitutes beauty differ, but there are general rules that appear to be cross-cultural about the wide appeal of symmetrical faces. Even three-month-old babies, according to several studies, prefer beautiful faces to plainer ones, and teachers favor better-looking kids.

Recent, though disputed, Canadian research suggests parents may even take better care of pretty children than they do of ugly ones. It studied how parents treated their children on trips to the supermarket and observed that less attractive children were allowed to wander farther and engage in potentially dangerous activities. Afterwards, they were less likely to be buckled into the car.

A much-quoted U.S. study by economist Daniel Hammermesh found plain people earned less than people with average looks, who earned less than the good looking. The penalty for plainness is 5–10 percent, and the effect is slightly stronger for men than for women.

COLLABORATE Collaborate on responses to the following questions:

➤ Do beautiful people get special treatment?

➤ Why do we think friends look better than strangers might judge them to look?

➤ If we willingly engage in discrimination according to looks, is this an issue worth worrying about? Why or why not?

Skill Development: Preview

Preview the next selection to predict its purpose and organization and to formulate your learning plan.

Activate Schema

Why are most politicians good looking?
Did looks help Arnold Schwarzenegger become governor of California?

Establish a Purpose for Reading

Recall a time when you might have discriminated against a person or people on the basis of appearance. Then reflect on whether you have been discriminated against because you were not nicely dressed. Do well-groomed customers receive better service from sales people and restaurant staff? Read the selection to discover how we subconsciously favor good looks.

Integrate Knowledge While Reading

Questions have been inserted in the margin to stimulate your thinking while reading. Remember to

Predict	Picture	Relate	Monitor	Correct

THE IMPORTANCE OF BEING BEAUTIFUL

Unlike many people, I was neither shocked nor surprised when the national Israeli TV network fired a competent female broadcaster because she was not beautiful. I received the news with aplomb because I had just finished extensive research into "person perception," an esoteric branch of psychology that examines the many ways
5 in which physical attractiveness—or lack of it—affects all aspects of your life.

Unless you're a 10—or close to it—most of you will respond to my findings with at least some feelings of frustration or perhaps disbelief. In a nutshell, you can't overestimate the importance of being beautiful. If you're beautiful, without effort you attract hordes of friends and lovers. You are given higher school grades than
10 your smarter—but less appealing—classmates. You compete successfully for jobs against men or women who are better qualified but less alluring. Promotions and pay raises come your way more easily. You are able to go into a bank or store and cash a check with far less hassle than a plain Jane or John. And these are only a few of the many advantages enjoyed by those with a ravishing face and body.

15 "We were surprised to find that beauty had such powerful effects," confessed Karen Dion, a University of Toronto social psychologist who does person perception research. "Our findings also go against the cultural grain. People like to think that success depends on talent, intelligence, and hard work." But the scientific evidence is undeniable.

20 In large part, the beautiful person can attribute his or her idyllic life to a puzzling phenomenon that social scientists have dubbed the "halo effect." It defies human reason, but if you resemble Jane Fonda or Paul Newman it's assumed that you're more generous, trustworthy, sociable, modest, sensitive, interesting, and sexually responsive than the rest of us. Conversely, if you're somewhat physically
25 unattractive, because of the "horns effect" you're stigmatized as being mean, sneaky, dishonest, antisocial, and a poor sport to boot.

The existence of the halo/horns effect has been established by several studies. One, by Dion, looked at perceptions of misbehavior in children. Dion provided 243 female university students with identical detailed accounts of the misbehavior of a
30 seven-year-old school child. She described how the youngster had pelted a sleeping

Is this all true? Is it fair?

95 motivated, and more likely to improve than their less attractive counterparts. Pam Ennis, the consultant, commented, "Because the doctor feels that beautiful patients are more likely to respond to his treatment, he'll give them more time and attention."

We like to think we have moved beyond the era when the most desirable woman was the beauty queen, but we haven't. Every day we make assumptions
100 about the personality of the bank teller, the delivery man, or the waitress by their looks. The way in which we attribute good and bad characteristics still has very little to do with fact. People seldom look beyond a pleasing façade, a superficial attractiveness. But the professors of person perception are not discouraged by this. They want to educate us. Perhaps by arming us with the knowledge and awareness
105 of why we discriminate against the unattractive, we'll learn how to prevent this unwitting bigotry. Just maybe, we can change human nature.

Should you fight this or use it?

(1,371 words)

—From Sidney Katz,
in *Motives for Writing*, 3rd ed., ed. Robert Miller

Recall

Stop to self-test, relate, and react.

Your instructor may choose to give you a true-false comprehension review.

Skill Development: Think Critically

Apply the four-step format for evaluating the argument. Use the perforations to tear this page out for your instructor.

- **Step 1.** Identify the position on the issue. State the main point the author is arguing.

  _____

  _____

- **Step 2.** Identify the support in the argument. Make a lettered list of the major assertions of support.

  _____

  _____

  _____

  _____

  _____

  _____

  _____

_____

_____

- **Step 3.** Evaluate the support. Comment on weaknesses in relevance, believability, and consistency for the assertions you listed in step 2. Label the fallacies. What support do you feel is missing?

_____

_____

_____

_____

_____

_____

_____

- **Step 4.** Evaluate the argument. What is your overall evaluation and why?

_____

_____

_____

What is your opinion on the issue? _____

_____

_____

Write About the Selection

How do you plan to use the ideas from this selection to your benefit and apply the author's documented awareness of discrimination according to looks?

Response Suggestion: Discuss this from two points of view: the way you manage yourself and the way you perceive and assess others.

Contemporary *Link*

Authors of both selections seek to prove their arguments by quantifying or measuring. Devise a research study of your own to prove or disprove the argument that attractive students get better grades than their smarter but less attractive counterparts. Design your study to account for different levels of ability. Also, consider the level of attractiveness and grades of a student who was previously known by the professor.

Check Your Comprehension

Answer the following questions about the selection:

1. Why do we like to believe that success depends on talent, intelligence, and hard work? _____

   _____

   _____

   _____

2. How does the study of the misbehaving seven-year-old prove the existence of the halo/horns effect? _____

   _____

   _____

   _____

3. What does the statement, "you get the top score" mean? _____

   _____

   _____

   _____

4. What evidence shows that the beautiful are treated differently in legal matters? _____

   _____

   _____

   _____

5. Why do you think tall men are assumed to be born leaders? _____

   _____

   _____

   _____

6. What does the author mean by "Beauty makes it easier to establish rapport"?

   _____

   _____

   _____

7. For the elderly, why can looks be a life-and-death matter? _____

   _____

   _____

   _____

selection 3   Essay

Contemporary *Focus*

Do you believe that boys and girls are brought up to express themselves differently? Are boys and girls rewarded differently at a young age? How is a typical male defined in American culture?

Boys' Perceptions of the Male Role

By Randolph H. Watts Jr. and L. DiAnne Borders
The Journal of Men's Studies, January 31, 2005

Participants for this study were a sample of high school aged boys currently enrolled in North Carolina public schools who were members of a local youth organization.

Participants robustly supported the gender role conflict theme of restricted affectionate behavior between men. Many of the participants said that they could not share their feelings of affection with their friends for fear of criticism. "You would never know if a guy liked another guy 'cause they would never talk about it," said one participant. If feelings were shared, "People would tease him or something." Another participant said, "I know that if I share with some of my friends, they just laugh in my face. And be like, 'Man, you're gay.' "

One participant articulated the reason why boys might fear expressing feelings to one another: "'Cause they've developed that unspoken code, you know. They know, if I do this to this guy, pat him on the back or something, some people might look at it in a different light and make some assumptions."

Some participants said that they simply did not have feelings of affection for male friends. "Well, yeah. I don't really have like . . . emotions for other guys. I mean . . . Or, yeah, friendship. But like, love? I don't love any guys!" Other participants were willing to share feelings of affection, but said that they did so knowing that there would be retribution or ridicule. One boy, who claimed that he was pretty open about sharing his emotions, said that he would share his feelings with another boy: "And when I share with him, for example, he'll just laugh at me."

COLLABORATE   Collaborate on responses to the following questions:

➤ Are boys taught not to show affection? If so, how?

➤ What purpose do fraternities serve in college?

➤ How do males bond?

Skill Development: Preview

Preview the next selection to predict its purpose and organization and to formulate your learning plan.

Activate Schema

What happy memories do you have of your childhood?
Who were the class bullies when you were in school?

Establish a Purpose for Reading

The author is making an argument about how boys become men. Read to understand his argument, weigh the support, and to determine your position on the issue.

Integrate Knowledge While Reading

Questions have been inserted in the margin to stimulate your thinking while reading. Remember to

Predict	Picture	Relate	Monitor	Correct

HOW BOYS BECOME MEN

Two nine-year-old boys, neighbors and friends, were walking home from school. The one in the bright blue windbreaker was laughing and swinging a heavy-looking book bag toward the head of his friend, who kept ducking and stepping back. "What's the matter?" asked the kid with the bag, whooshing it over his head. "You chicken?"

5   His friend stopped, stood still and braced himself. The bag slammed into the side of his face, the thump audible all the way across the street where I stood watching. The impact knocked him to the ground, where he lay mildly stunned for a second. Then he struggled up, rubbing the side of his head. "See?" he said proudly. "I'm no chicken."

Is this definition of manhood learned or genetically programmed?

10   No. A chicken would probably have had the sense to get out of the way. This boy was already well on the road to becoming a *man*, having learned one of the central ethics of his gender: Experience pain rather than show fear.

Women tend to see men as a giant problem in need of solution. They tell us that we're remote and uncommunicative, that we need to demonstrate less 15 machismo and more commitment, more humanity. But if you don't understand something about boys, you can't understand why men are the way we are, why we find it so difficult to make friends or to acknowledge our fears and problems.

Boys live in a world with its own Code of Conduct, a set of ruthless, unspoken, and unyielding rules:

20   Don't be a goody-goody.
Never rat. If your parents ask about bruises, shrug.
Never admit fear. Ride the roller coaster, join a fistfight, do what you have to do. Asking for help is for sissies.

Does this code of conduct cross cultural boundaries?

Empathy is for nerds. You can help your best buddy, under certain cir-25 cumstances. Everyone else is on his own.
Never discuss anything of substance with anybody. Grunt, shrug, dump on teachers, laugh at wimps, talk about comic books. Anything else is risky.

Paul A. Souders/Corbis

A soccer game turns violent.

Boys are rewarded for throwing hard. Most other activities—reading, befriending girls, or just thinking—are considered weird. And if there's one thing boys don't
30 want to be, it's weird.

More than anything else, boys are supposed to learn how to handle themselves. I remember the bitter fifth-grade conflict I touched off by elbowing aside a bigger boy named Barry and seizing the cafeteria's last carton of chocolate milk. Teased for getting aced out by a wimp, he had to reclaim his place in the pack. Our fistfight, at
35 recess, ended with my knees buckling and my lip bleeding while my friends, sympathetic but out of range, watched resignedly.

When I got home, my mother took one look at my swollen face and screamed. I wouldn't tell her anything, but when my father got home I cracked and confessed, pleading with them to do nothing. Instead, they called Barry's parents, who re-
40 stricted his television for a week.

The following morning, Barry and six of his pals stepped out from behind a stand of trees. "It's the rat," said Barry.

I bled a little more. *Rat* was scrawled in crayon across my desk.

They were waiting for me after school for a number of afternoons to follow. I
45 tried varying my routes and avoiding bushes and hedges. It usually didn't work.

I was as ashamed for telling as I was frightened. "You did ask for it," said my best friend. Frontier Justice has nothing on Boy Justice.

In panic, I appealed to a cousin who was several years older. He followed me home from school, and when Barry's gang surrounded me, he came barreling toward
50 us. "Stay away from my cousin," he shouted, "or I'll kill you."

After they were gone, however, my cousin could barely stop laughing. "You were afraid of *them*?" he howled. "They barely came up to my waist."

Is there an age at which male friendships do change and become more supportive?

Men remember receiving little mercy as boys; maybe that's why it's sometimes difficult for them to show any.

55 "I know lots of men who had happy childhoods, but none who have happy memories of the way other boys treated them," says a friend. "It's a macho marathon from third grade up, when you start butting each other in the stomach."

"The thing is," adds another friend, "you learn early on to hide what you feel. It's never safe to say 'I'm scared.' My girlfriend asks me why I don't talk more about 60 what I'm feeling. I've gotten better at it, but it will *never* come naturally."

You don't need to be a shrink to see how the lessons boys learn affect their behavior as men. Men are being asked, more and more, to show sensitivity, but they dread the very word. They struggle to build their increasingly uncertain work lives but will deny they're in trouble. They want love, affection, and support but don't 65 know how to ask for them. They hide their weaknesses and fears from all, even those they care for. They've learned to be wary of intervening when they see others in trouble. They often still balk at being stigmatized as weird.

Some men get shocked into sensitivity—when they lose their jobs, their wives, or their lovers. Others learn it through a strong marriage, or through their 70 own children.

It may be a long while, however, before male culture evolves to the point that boys can learn more from one another than how to hit curve balls. Last month, walking my dog past the playground near my house, I saw three boys encircling a fourth, laughing and pushing him. He was skinny and rumpled, and he looked 75 frightened. One boy knelt behind him while another pushed him from the front, a trick familiar to any former boy. He fell backward.

When the others ran off, he brushed the dirt off his elbows and walked toward the swings. His eyes were moist and he was struggling for control.

"Hi," I said through the chain-link fence. "How ya doing?"

80   "Fine," he said quickly, kicking his legs out and beginning his swing.

(995 words)

—Jon Katz,
Reprinted by permission of SLL/Sterling Lord Literistic, Inc.
Copyright 1993 by Jon Katz. Originally published in *Glamour.*

Recall

Stop to self-test, relate, and react.

Your instructor may choose to give you a true-false comprehension review.

Skill Development: Think Critically

Apply the four-step format for evaluating the argument. Use the perforations to tear out this page for your instructor.

- **Step 1.** Identify the position on the issue. State the main point the author is arguing.

  _____

  _____

  _____

- **Step 2.** Identify the support in the argument. Make lettered lists of the major assertions of support.

    I. Boys grow up under a ruthless code of conduct that includes the following:

    A. _____

    _____

    B. _____

    _____

    C. _____

    _____

    D. _____

    _____

    E. _____

    _____

    F. _____

    _____

    G. _____

    _____

    II. As a consequence of the code of conduct, men exhibit the following behaviors:

    A. _____

    _____

    B. _____

    _____

    C. _____

    _____

    D. _____

    _____

- **Step 3.** Evaluate the support. Comment on weaknesses in relevance, believability, and consistency for the assertions you listed in step 2. Label the fallacies. What support do you feel is missing?

    _____

    _____

    _____

    _____

- **Step 4.** Evaluate the argument. What is your overall evaluation and why?

_____

_____

_____

_____

What is your opinion on the issue? _____

_____

_____

Write About the Selection

How might men get shocked into sensitivity through loss or marriage or children? Can this happen to women also?

Response Suggestion: Discuss an example of this kind of shock. What kind of sensitivity resulted?

Contemporary *Link*

If boys are indeed taught and rewarded differently, how is this later reflected in parenthood when affection is part of nurturing? How do boys learn to become good fathers? What cultural biases operate against fatherhood?

Check Your Comprehension

Inference _____ 1. What is the best statement of the main idea of this selection?

    a. It is more difficult for boys than for girls to learn how to become responsible and fair-minded adults.

    b. Boys in today's world face a set of unspoken rules that put them in conflict with their parents.

    c. Boys grow up learning a code of conduct that affects adult male behavior.

    d. Boys in today's world are much more likely to break the unspoken rules because the rules limit their personal growth.

Inference _____ 2. In telling the story of the two nine-year-old boys, the narrator is trying to explain

    a. what it is like to walk home from school with a friend.

    b. that courage is not easy to explain to school-age children.

    c. the kind of experiences that make boys into less sensitive men.

    d. why boys often behave with violence toward one another.

Inference _____ 3. When the narrator mentions the "central ethics of his gender," he is referring to

    a. traditions of justice and honor for men.

    b. fundamental rules of male behavior.

    c. assessments of male moral character.

    d. rules that govern his own adult life.

Inference _____ 4. The narrator indicates that the "Code of Conduct" is a set of rules that

    a. fathers teach to their sons.

    b. are unwritten yet understood.

    c. teach leadership and commitment.

    d. are emphasized by teachers.

Detail _____ 5. According to the narrator, one of the worst things a boy can do is be

    a. different.

    b. uncommunicative.

    c. aggressive.

    d. friendly.

Inference _____ 6. The narrator tells the story about himself in fifth grade primarily to illustrate that

    a. he had been an unusually fearful boy.

    b. his cousin liked protecting him from other boys.

    c. he had violated the Code of Conduct and suffered the consequences.

    d. his school had a lot of boys who picked on him.

Inference _____ 7. The narrator says "I was as ashamed for telling as I was frightened" to illustrate that he

    a. grew tired of getting beaten up by classmates.
    b. thought his parents would get mad at him.
    c. felt pressure to live by the Code of Conduct.
    d. knew he had started it all by elbowing Barry.

Inference _____ 8. The narrator uses the phrase "macho marathon" to suggest that the way boys treat each other in school

    a. seems to be never-ending.
    b. is physically exhausting.
    c. feels like a kind of workout.
    d. is ultimately channeled into organizational sports.

Detail _____ 9. According to the author, men are most likely to

    a. readily admit when they are in trouble.
    b. hide weaknesses.
    c. intervene when others are in trouble.
    d. communicate feelings.

Inference _____ 10. The story the narrator tells at the end, about the four boys on the playground, seems meant to show that the

    a. narrator had been shocked into sensitivity.
    b. narrator feels that male culture is evolving.
    c. boys of today are like boys have always been.
    d. boys who were playing were not really hurt.

Answer the following with *T* (true) or *F* (false).

Inference _____ 11. The author concludes that men who learn not to fear pain as they are growing up build strong moral character in the process.

Inference _____ 12. The narrator realized that the best solution was for Barry's father to be contacted about the fight.

Inference _____ 13. The selection suggests that men dislike talking about their feelings because they learned not to talk about feelings when they were boys.

Detail _____ 14. According to the author, although progress is slow, male culture is clearly evolving and becoming generally more sensitive.

Inference _____ 15. The word "Fine" in the last line of the selection indicates that the young boy understands the "central ethic of his gender."

Search the Net

Use a search engine such as Google, Yahoo, Ask.com, Excite, Dogpile, or Lycos to find more information about the ways both boys and girls are taught their gender roles. How are these messages relayed to them, how do these messages differ, and are the messages only harmful or can they be beneficial as well? For suggested Web sites and other research activities, go to http://www.ablongman.com/smith/.

9 Graphic Illustrations

- What do graphics do?
- What is a diagram?
- What does a table do?
- What is most helpful on a typical map?
- What does a pie graph represent?
- How do you read a bar graph?
- What is a line graph?
- What information does a flowchart convey?

Rafal Olbinski, *Castles Around the Baltic*, 1997. Acrylic on canvas. 32 x 22 inches.

What Graphics Do

If a picture is worth a thousand words, a graphic illustration is worth at least several pages of facts and figures. Graphics express complex interrelationships in simplified form. Instead of plodding through repetitious data, you can glance at a chart, a map, or a graph and immediately see how everything fits together as well as how one part compares with another. Instead of reading several lengthy paragraphs and trying to visualize comparisons, you can study an organized design. The graphic illustration is a logically constructed aid for understanding many small bits of information.

Graphic illustrations are generally used for the following reasons:

1. **To condense.** Pages of repetitious, detailed information can be organized into one explanatory design.
2. **To clarify.** Processes and interrelationships can be more clearly defined through visual representations.
3. **To convince.** Developing trends and gross inequities can be forcefully dramatized.

Reader's *Tip* ———— How to Read Graphic Material

- **Read the title to get an overview.** What is it about?
- **Look for footnotes and read introductory material.**
  Identify the who, where, and how.
  How and when were the data collected?
  Who collected the data?
  How many persons were included in the survey?
  Do the researchers seem to have been objective or biased?
  Taking all this information into account, does the study seem valid?
- **Read the labels.**
  What do the vertical columns and the horizontal rows represent?
  Are the numbers in thousands or millions?
  What does the legend represent?
- **Notice the trends and find the extremes.**
  What are the highest and lowest rates?
  What is the average rate?
  How do the extremes compare with the total?
  What is the percentage of increase or decrease?
- **Draw conclusions and formulate future exam questions.**
  What does the information mean?
  What purpose does the information serve?
  What wasn't included?
  What else is there to know about the subject?

There are five kinds of graphic illustrations: (1) diagrams, (2) tables, (3) maps, (4) graphs, and (5) flowcharts. All are used in textbooks, and the choice of which is best to use depends on the type of material presented. This chapter contains explanations and exercises for the five types of graphic illustrations. Read the explanations, study the illustrations, and respond to the questions as instructed. The Reader's Tip gets you started by summarizing how to read graphics to get the most information from them.

Diagrams

A **diagram** is an outline drawing or picture of an object or a process. It shows the labeled parts of a complicated form, such as the muscles of the human body, the organizational makeup of a company's management and production teams, or the flow of nutrients in a natural ecological system.

exercise 9.1   **Diagrams**

The diagrams display the major structures of the human ear. Refer to the diagram to respond to the following statements with *T* (true), *F* (false), or *CT* (can't tell).

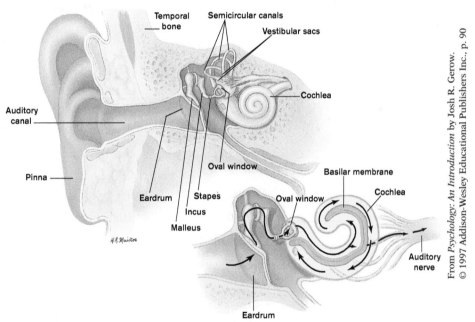

From *Psychology: An Introduction* by Josh R. Gerow. © 1997 Addison-Wesley Educational Publishers Inc., p. 90

Major Structures of the Human Ear

_____ 1. Sound enters the ear through the auditory canal.

_____ 2. The cochlea can be seen by looking through the auditory canal.

_____ 3. Sound travels through the cochlea to the auditory nerve.

_____ 4. Most hearing problems result from damage to the eardrum.

_____ 5. The nerves in the pinna conduct sound directly to the oval window.

_____ 6. The basilar membrane is a part of the cochlea.

_____ 7. The malleus, incus, and stapes are positioned to transmit sound from the eardrum to the oval window.

_____ 8. According to the diagram, the semicircular canals contain the basilar membrane.

_____ 9. If punctured, the eardrum cannot be adequately repaired.

_____ 10. The cochlea could be described as snail-like in appearance.

11. The purpose of each diagram is _____

_____

Tables

A **table** is a listing of facts and figures in columns and rows for quick and easy reference. The information in the columns and rows is usually labeled in two different directions. First read the title for the topic and then read the footnotes to judge the source. Determine what each column represents and how they interact.

exercise 9.2 **Tables**

Refer to the table shown on page 327 to respond to the following statements with _T_ (true), _F_ (false), or _CT_ (can't tell).

_____ 1. Of the salad greens listed, a cup of watercress has the fewest calories.

_____ 2. A cup of chicory has over three times as much vitamin A as a cup of spinach.

_____ 3. Arugula has three times as much vitamin A as iceberg lettuce.

_____ 4. All of the salad greens listed contain calcium and potassium.

_____ 5. Of the salad greens listed, chicory is highest in all categories.

_____ 6. Iceberg lettuce is the most popular salad green served in the United States.

_____ 7. Of the salad greens listed, iceberg lettuce is the lowest in all categories.

_____ 8. Much of the calcium in spinach is not available for use in the body.

_____ 9. For those who do not like chicory, red cabbage is the next best salad green choice for potassium.

10. The purpose of this chart is _____

_____

ADDING MORE SALADS TO YOUR DIET

Salads add variety to your diet and balance out the average American's meat-and-potatoes diet. Use this information to choose healthful salad greens and toppings for your salad.

NUTRITIONAL COMPARISON OF SALAD GREEN SERVINGS

Salad Green	Calories	Vitamin A (IU)	Vitamin C (mg)	Potassium (mg)	Calcium (mg)
Arugula (rocket, roquette)	5	480	3	74	32
Butterhead lettuce (Boston, Bibb)	7	534	4	141	18
Cabbage, red	19	28	40	144	36
Chicory	41	7,200	43	756	180
Endive	8	1,025	3	157	26
Fennel	27	117	10	360	43
Iceberg lettuce	7	182	2	87	10
Leaf lettuce	10	1,064	10	148	38
Romaine lettuce	8	1,456	13	162	20
Spinach	7	2,015	8	167	30*
Watercress	4	1,598	15	112	41

Note: Serving size is one cup; IU = International Units, mg = milligrams

*Much not available to body for use

Source: Rebecca Donatelle, *Access to Health*, 8th ed.

Maps

Traditional **maps,** such as road maps and atlas maps, show the location of cities, waterways, sites, and roads, as well as the differences in the physical terrain of specified areas. A modern use of the map as a visual aid is to highlight special characteristics or population distributions of a particular area. For example, a map of the United States might highlight all states with gun control laws in red and all states without gun control laws in blue.

Begin reading a map by noting the title and source. The legend of a map, which usually appears in a corner box, explains the meanings of symbols and shading.

exercise 9.3   **Maps**

Read the following passage about national exports and state economies. Then use the legend on the map shown on page 328 to help you respond to the subsequent statements with *T* (true), *F* (false), or *CT* (can't tell).

STATE ECONOMIES

All states are affected by the global economy, but some states are more dependent on it. Exports are a larger fraction of their economies. For example, the state of Washington, with its aerospace, fishing, and logging industries, depends most heavily on trade with other countries. Exports account for nearly 20 percent of Washington State's economy.

Most of the top exporting states are located on the nation's borders, which gives them easier access to other countries. For example, the state of Washington abuts Canada, and its seaports are a departure point for goods destined for Asia.

Thomas E. Patterson, *We the People: A Concise Introduction to American Politics*, 5th ed., p. 561 (2004). Reprinted by permission of The McGraw-Hill Companies.

_____   1. The western states bordering the Pacific Ocean are all among the highest exporters in the nation.

_____   2. Each island state exports more than 5 percent of its total economy.

_____   3. Each state bordering the Atlantic Ocean exports 3 percent or more of its total economy.

_____   4. Nevada does not export more than 5 percent of its total economy because gambling is legal in Nevada.

_____   5. Each state bordering Canada exports 3 percent or more of its total economy.

_____   6. Each state bordering Mexico exports 3 percent or more of its total economy.

_____   7. Florida and Maine export the same dollar amount of goods.

_____   8. Only 18 states export more than 5 percent of their total economies.

_____   9. Although the map shows they export the same percentage, California and Arizona could differ on the actual dollar amounts exported because their total state economies could be different.

_____ 10. Tennessee and Kentucky are higher exporters than New York and Pennsylvania.

11. The purpose of the map is to _____

_____

_____

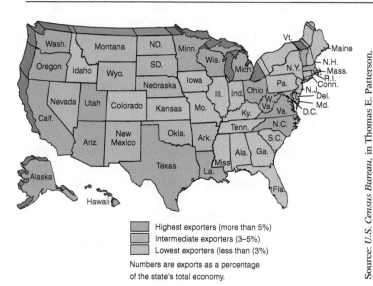

Highest exporters (more than 5%)
Intermediate exporters (3–5%)
Lowest exporters (less than (3%)

Numbers are exports as a percentage of the state's total economy.

National Exports and State Economies

Source: *U.S. Census Bureau*, in Thomas E. Patterson, *We the People: A Concise Introduction to American Politics*, 5th ed., p. 561 (2004). Reprinted by permission of The McGraw-Hill Companies.

exercise 9.4   **Geographic Review**

Use the map below to test your knowledge of world geography.

CITIZENS OF THE WORLD SHOW LITTLE KNOWLEDGE OF GEOGRAPHY

In the spring of 1988, twelve thousand people in ten nations were asked to identify sixteen places on the following world map. The average citizen in the United States could identify barely more than half. Believe it or not, 14 percent of Americans tested could not even find their own country on the map. Despite years of fighting in Vietnam, 68 percent could not locate this Southeast Asian country. Such lack of basic geographic knowledge is quite common throughout the world. Here is the average score for each of the ten countries in which the test was administered.

Country	Average Score	Country	Average Score
Sweden	11.6	United States	8.6
West Germany	11.2	Britain	8.5
Japan	9.7	Italy	7.6
France	9.3	Mexico	7.4
Canada	9.2	Former Soviet Union	7.4

How would you do? To take the test, match the numbers on the map to the places listed.

—Robert L. Lineberry et al.,
Government in America

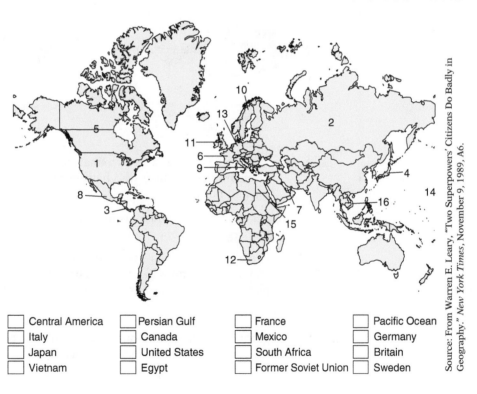

☐ Central America	☐ Persian Gulf	☐ France	☐ Pacific Ocean
☐ Italy	☐ Canada	☐ Mexico	☐ Germany
☐ Japan	☐ United States	☐ South Africa	☐ Britain
☐ Vietnam	☐ Egypt	☐ Former Soviet Union	☐ Sweden

Source: From Warren E. Leary, "Two Superpowers' Citizens Do Badly in Geography." *New York Times,* November 9, 1989, A6.

Pie Graphs

A **pie graph** is a circle divided into wedge-shaped slices. The complete pie or circle represents a total, or 100 percent. Each slice is a percentage or fraction of that whole. Budgets, such as the annual expenditure of the federal or state governments, are frequently illustrated by pie graphs.

exercise 9.5   **Pie Graphs**

Refer to the pie graphs shown here to respond to the following statements with *T* (true), *F* (false), or *CT* (can't tell). Note that the figures are percentages rather than actual numbers.

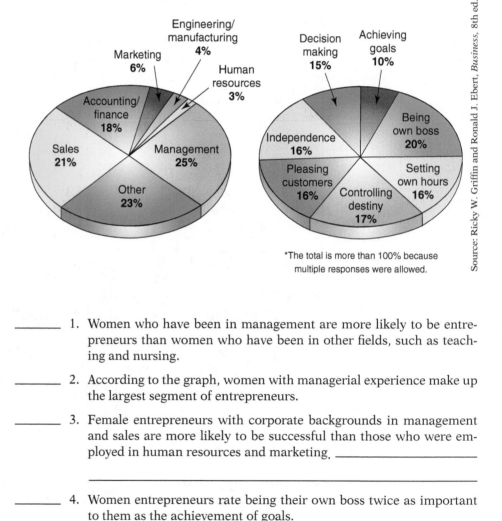

Profiles of Women Entrepreneurs

Corporate Backgrounds

Responsibility Preferences*

*The total is more than 100% because multiple responses were allowed.

Source: Ricky W. Griffin and Ronald J. Ebert, *Business*, 8th ed.

_____   1. Women who have been in management are more likely to be entrepreneurs than women who have been in other fields, such as teaching and nursing.

_____   2. According to the graph, women with managerial experience make up the largest segment of entrepreneurs.

_____   3. Female entrepreneurs with corporate backgrounds in management and sales are more likely to be successful than those who were employed in human resources and marketing. _____

_____   4. Women entrepreneurs rate being their own boss twice as important to them as the achievement of goals.

_____ 5. Women entrepreneurs value making decisions slightly more than their ability to control their own destiny at work.

_____ 6. There are over three times as many female entrepreneurs from accounting/finance backgrounds as there are from engineering/manufacturing fields.

7. The purpose of the pie graphs is to _____

_____

_____

Bar Graphs

A **bar graph** is a series of horizontal or vertical bars in which the length of each bar represents a particular amount or number of what is being discussed. A series of different items can be quickly compared by noting the different bar lengths.

exercise 9.6   **Bar Graphs**

Refer to the bar graph shown on page 332 to respond to the following statements with *T* (true), *F* (false), or *CT* (can't tell)

_____ 1. No more than seven professions and technical fields are listed in which women make up the majority of workers.

_____ 2. Fewer than one-third of computer systems analysts are women.

_____ 3. College teachers are more likely to be male than female.

_____ 4. The fields of social work and vocational/educational counseling have approximately the same percentage of male workers.

_____ 5. More females are accountants than are auditors.

_____ 6. According to the graph, the actual number of female elementary school teachers is greater than the number of female health technicians.

_____ 7. Women make up only one-quarter of the workers who are natural scientists.

_____ 8. A greater percentage of men teach in high school than teach elementary students.

_____ 9. Men make up a lower percentage of workers in the field of nursing than in any other profession listed.

_____10. Of the total workers in the field, the percent of women who are medical doctors exceeds the percent who are dentists.

11. The purpose of the bar graph is _____

_____

_____

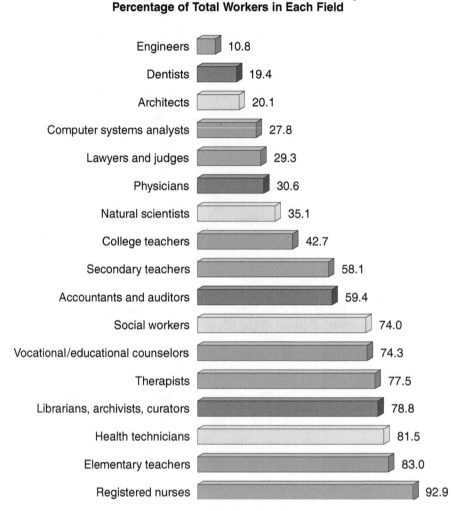

Female Professional and Technical Workers, by Percentage of Total Workers in Each Field

Engineers 10.8
Dentists 19.4
Architects 20.1
Computer systems analysts 27.8
Lawyers and judges 29.3
Physicians 30.6
Natural scientists 35.1
College teachers 42.7
Secondary teachers 58.1
Accountants and auditors 59.4
Social workers 74.0
Vocational/educational counselors 74.3
Therapists 77.5
Librarians, archivists, curators 78.8
Health technicians 81.5
Elementary teachers 83.0
Registered nurses 92.9

Source: In Vincent N. Parrillo, *Strangers to These Shores*, 8/e. Published by Allyn and Bacon, Boston, MA. Copyright © 2005 by Pearson Education. Reprinted by permission of the publisher.

Cumulative Bar Graphs

Both bar graphs and line graphs can be designed to show cumulative effects in which all the lines or segments add up to the top line or total amount. Rather than having multiple bars or lines, the groups are stacked on top of each other to dramatically show differences. The bar graph shown here illustrates a cumulative effect.

exercise 9.7 **Cumulative Bar Graphs**

Refer to the cumulative bar graph on page 333 to respond to the following statements with *T* (true), *F* (false), or *CT* (can't tell).

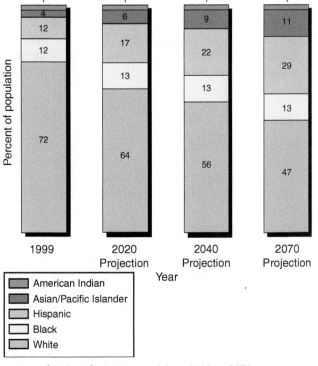

Source: Modified from the U.S. Census Bureau, National Projections, 2020–2070, in Les Rowntree et al., *Diversity Amid Globalization*, 2nd ed.

Projected U.S. Ethnic Composition, 1999 to 2070

_____ 1. From 1999 to 2070, the percentage of the population of American Indians is expected to shrink.

_____ 2. In each projected year, the percentage of the population that is white decreases.

_____ 3. From 1999 to 2070, the percentage of Hispanics in the population more than triples.

_____ 4. The black percentage of the population decreases between 2020 and 2070.

_____ 5. Asian/Pacific Islanders as a percentage of the total population increase at a higher rate than blacks from 1999 to 2070.

_____ 6. The number of African Americans in the population is not projected to increase from 2020 to 2070.

_____ 7. In 2070, whites and Asian/Pacific Islanders are projected to comprise more than half the population.

8. The purpose of the bar graph is _____

_____

_____

_____

Line Graphs

A **line graph** is a continuous curve or frequency distribution in which numbers are plotted in an unbroken line. The horizontal scale measures one aspect of the data and the vertical line measures another aspect. As the data fluctuate, the line will change direction and, with extreme differences, will become very jagged.

exercise 9.8 **Line Graphs**

Read the following passage from a psychology text, and then examine the line graph to respond to the subsequent questions with *T* (true), *F* (false), or *CT* (can't tell). Notice that the graph's horizontal axis indicates age, and the vertical axis measures the average self-esteem score on a 5-point scale.

SELF-ESTEEM

In a cross-sectional study of self-esteem a large, diverse sample of 326,641 individuals between the ages of 9 and 90 was assessed. About two-thirds of the participants were from the United States. The individuals were asked to respond to the item, "I have high self-esteem," on the following 5-point scale:

—Adapted from John W. Santrock, *Life-Span Development*, 9th ed.

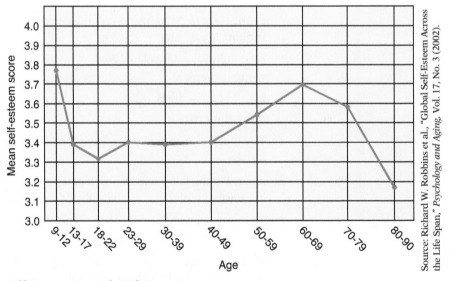

Self-Esteem Across the Life Span

_____ 1. Teenagers report lower self-esteem than do adults in their sixties.

_____ 2. The decline in self-esteem measures from the ages of 9–12 to 13–17 is slightly less than the drop from the ages of 70–79 to 80–90.

_____ 3. According to the graph, the two groups with the highest self-esteem ratings are adults of ages 60–69 and those of ages 70–79.

_____ 4. Self-esteem measures show little variation from the ages of 23 to 49.

_____ 5. Self-esteem ratings increase after graduation from college because students have proved to themselves that they are capable of obtaining a degree and getting a job.

_____ 6. Adult self-esteem ratings peak at ages 60–69.

_____ 7. Self-esteem rises at approximately the same rate from the years 40–49 to 50–59 as it does from the years 50–59 to 60–69.

_____ 8. On average, self-esteem ratings for all groups were more positive than negative.

9. The purpose of the line graph is _____

_____

_____

Flowcharts

A **flowchart** shows the sequence of a set of elements and the relationships among them. Flowcharts were first used in computer programming. Key ideas are stated in boxes, and supporting ideas are linked by arrows. In the flowchart shown on page 336, arrows point toward a progression of steps required for a bill to become a law in the United States.

exercise 9.9   **Flowcharts**

Bills introduced in the U.S. House of Representatives or Senate follow a specific path before being passed into laws. Refer to the flowchart on page 546 to respond to the following statements with _T_ (true), _F_ (false), or _CT_ (can't tell).

_____ 1. If a bill is introduced in the Senate, the chart indicates that it can be debated in the House before it is passed in the Senate.

_____ 2. After both the House and Senate vote on a bill, it goes to the Conference Committee.

_____ 3. The House has a Rules Committee action stage that the Senate does not have.

_____ 4. The president can veto and override a bill that has been passed and approved by both the House and Senate.

_____ 5. Full Senate debate on a bill occurs before the full committee report.

_____ 6. If a bill has solid support from both the House and Senate, the president usually signs the bill into law.

7. The purpose of the flowchart is _____

_____

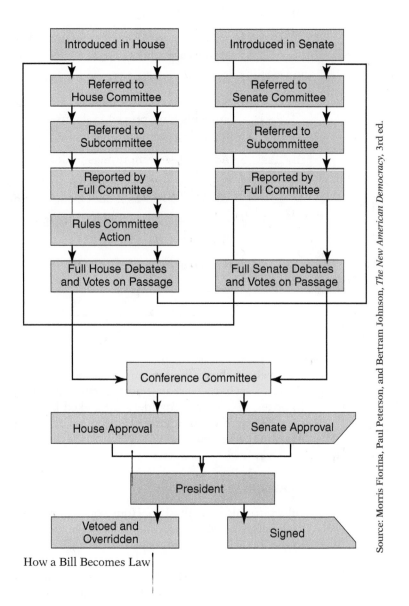

How a Bill Becomes Law

Source: Morris Fiorina, Paul Peterson, and Bertram Johnson, *The New American Democracy*, 3rd ed.

Summary *Points*

➤ **What do graphics do?**
Graphic illustrations condense, clarify, and convince. They express complex interrelationships in simplified form.

➤ **What is a diagram?**
A diagram is an outline drawing or picture of an object or a process with labeled parts.

➤ **What does a table do?**
A table lists facts and figures in columns for quick and easy reference. You must determine what the columns represent and how they interact.

➤ **What is most helpful on a typical map?**
The legend on a map of a geographic area explains the symbols and shading used to convey information.

➤ **What does a pie graph represent?**
A pie graph depicts a total, or 100 percent, divided into wedge-shaped slices.

➤ **How do you read a bar graph?**
You must determine what the length of each horizontal or vertical bar represents.

➤ **What is a line graph?**
A line graph represents a frequency distribution. To read a point on the continuous line, you must identify what the horizontal and vertical scales measure.

➤ **What information does a flowchart convey?**
A flowchart provides a diagram of the relationship and sequence of events of a group of elements. Key ideas usually appear in boxes, and arrows are used to connect the elements.

selection 1 Science

Contemporary *Focus*

San Francisco lies on the San Andreas Fault and is expected to have another major earthquake. Although new buildings are constructed to withstand tremors, older homes, built above garages or shopfronts, have little structural support. Part of the city is built on reclaimed land that was under water fifty years ago; this land would turn to quicksand during an earthquake. What can be done to avert a major disaster and save the city of San Francisco?

Shock Tactic That Could Save a City

By Peter Sheridan
The Express, UK, April 18, 2006

Exactly 100 years ago an enormous earthquake flattened San Francisco and killed thousands. Today, as scientists fear another one is set to do the same, they're ready to take an extraordinary gamble—by blowing up the San Andreas fault.

The 1906 San Francisco earthquake remains one of America's greatest disasters—and a repeat of it is guaranteed. "The question isn't if, but when," says Jeffrey Mount, director of the Watershed Centre at the University of California in Davis, who predicts that the consequences of the inevitable 21st-century San Francisco earthquake will be "diabolical."

Diabolical possibilities perhaps call for diabolical measures. Drilling holes along the San Andreas fault, stuffing them with explosives and then blowing them up certainly doesn't seem like the work of sanity. Yet a small group of scientists believe that while they can't stop the next seismic tremor any more than King Canute could hold back the waves, this may be how they will be able to predict where it will cause the most damage.

An estimated 1,500 people in the city would be killed by falling buildings and fires, and in the Bay Area about 6,000 would die. Thousands would be injured, and almost 360,000 would be made homeless. Nearly 40 percent of private buildings could be destroyed because the majority were built before anti-earthquake building codes of the seventies came in.

COLLABORATE Collaborate on responses to the following questions:

➤ Why do people live in San Francisco if an earthquake is predicted?

➤ How would blowing up the fault with explosives ever be a viable consideration?

➤ What are earthquake building codes?

Skill Development: Preview

Preview the next selection to predict its purpose and organization and to formulate your learning plan.

Activate Schema

Have you ever felt an earthquake? What happened?
Why is fire a hazard after an earthquake?

Establish a Purpose for Reading

Rather than the earth opening up and swallowing people, as in the movies, the reality of an earthquake is different, but just as frighteningly destructive. Read to learn what happens as the result of an earthquake. What causes the destruction?

Increase Word Knowledge

What do you know about these words?

topple	debris	sediment	eliminated	triggered
loess	displacement	subsidence	unsettling	precede

Your instructor may give a true-false vocabulary review before or after reading.

Integrate Knowledge While Reading

Questions have been inserted in the margin to stimulate your thinking while reading. Remember to

Predict	Picture	Relate	Monitor	Correct

EFFECTS OF EARTHQUAKES

Ground motion is the trembling and shaking of the land that can cause buildings to vibrate. During small quakes, windows and walls may crack from such vibration. In a very large quake the ground motion may be visible. It can be strong enough to topple large structures such as bridges and office and apartment buildings. Most
5 people injured or killed in an earthquake are hit by falling debris from buildings. Because proper building construction can greatly reduce the dangers, building codes need to be both strict and strictly enforced in earthquake-prone areas. Much of the damage and loss of life in recent Turkey, El Savador, and India earthquakes were due to poorly constructed buildings that did not meet building codes. As we
10 have seen, the location of buildings also needs to be controlled. Buildings built on soft-sediment are damaged more than buildings on hard rock.

Why are buildings on soft sediment more vulnerable?

Fire is a particularly serious problem just after an earthquake because of broken gas and water mains and fallen electrical wires. Although fire was the cause of most of the damage to San Francisco in 1906, changes in building construction and im-
15 proved fire-fighting methods have reduced (but not eliminated) the fire danger to modern cities. The stubborn Marina district fires in San Francisco in 1989 attest to modern dangers of broken gas and water mains.

An Indonesian woman surveys the wreckage of her home after a devastating earthquake shook the region.

Landslides can be triggered by the shaking of the ground. The 1959 Madison Canyon landslide in Montana was triggered by a nearby quake of magnitude 7.7.
20 Landslides and subsidence caused extensive damage in downtown and suburban Anchorage during the 1964 Alaskan quake (magnitude 8.6). The 1970 Peruvian earthquake (magnitude 7.75) set off thousands of landslides in the steep Andes Mountains, burying more than 17,000 people. In 1920 in China over 100,000 people living in hollowed-out caves in cliffs of loess were killed when a quake collapsed
25 the cliffs. The 2001 El Salvador quake resulted in nearly 500 landslides, the largest of which occurred in Santa Tecla where 1,200 people were missing after tons of soil and rock fell on a neighborhood.

What is loess?

A special type of ground failure caused by earthquakes is liquefaction. This occurs when a water-saturated soil or sediment turns from a solid to a liquid as a result of earthquake shaking. Liquefaction may occur several minutes after an earth-
30 quake, causing buildings to sink and underground tanks to float as once-solid sediment flows like water. Liquefaction was responsible for much of the damage in the 1989 Loma Prieta quake and contributed to the damage in the 1906 San Francisco, the 1964 Alaska, the 1995 Kobe, Japan, and the 2001 Puget Sound,
35 Washington, and Gujarat, India quakes.

Permanent displacement of the land surface may be the result of movement along a fault. Rocks can move vertically, those on one side of a fault rising while those on the other side drop. Rocks can also move horizontally, those on one side of a fault sliding past those on the other side. Diagonal movement with both vertical
40 and horizontal components can also occur during a single quake. Such movement can affect huge areas, although the displacement in a single earthquake seldom exceeds 8 meters. The trace of a fault on Earth's surface may appear as a low cliff, called a scarp, or as a closed tear in the ground. In rare instances small cracks open during a quake (but not to the extent that Hollywood films often portray). Ground
45 displacement during quakes can tear apart buildings, roads, and pipelines that cross faults. Sudden subsidence of land near the sea can cause flooding and drownings.

Why is development allowed along faults?

Aftershocks are small earthquakes that follow the main shock. Although aftershocks are smaller than the main quake, they can cause considerable damage, particularly to structures previously weakened by the powerful main shock. A long period
50 of aftershocks can be extremely unsettling to people who have lived through the
main shock. Foreshocks are small quakes that precede a main shock. They are usually less common and less damaging than aftershocks but can sometimes be used to
help predict large quakes (although not all large quakes have foreshocks).

Make a list of effects.

(678 words)

—From Diane H. Carlson, Charles C. Plummer, and David McGeary,
Physical Geology: Earth Revealed, 6th Edition. Copyright © 2006 by
The McGraw-Hill Companies, Inc. Reproduced with permission.

Recall

Stop to self-test, relate, and react.

Your instructor may choose to give you a true-false comprehension review.

Write About the Selection

What are the effects of an earthquake? List and explain how damage occurs.
   Response Suggestion: Focus on three major types of damage. Give an explanation and an example of each.

Contemporary *Link*

*What precautions can people who live in earthquake-threatened areas realistically take?
How vulnerable is your area? How would you prepare if you lived in San Francisco?*

Skill Development: Graphics

Refer to the designated graphic on page 342 and answer the following items with
T (true) or *F* (false).

_____ 1. The total number of earthquakes reported in 2001 was greater than
that reported in 2000.

_____ 2. The only deaths reported from U.S. earthquakes in the listed years
occurred in 2003.

_____ 3. The total number of earthquakes in the U.S. based on the graphic
for 2006 was 891.

_____ 4. In 2005 the largest number of U.S. earthquakes had a magnitude of
3.0 to 3.9.

_____ 5. In the years listed in the report, Alaska had over half of the earthquakes that were 7.0 or higher.

Magnitude	2000	2001	2002	2003	2004	2005	2006

NUMBER OF EARTHQUAKES IN THE UNITED STATES FOR 2000–2006 LOCATED BY THE US GEOLOGICAL SURVEY NATIONAL EARTHQUAKE INFORMATION CENTER

Magnitude	2000	2001	2002	2003	2004	2005	2006
8.0 to 9.9	0	0	0	0	0	0	0
7.0 to 7.9	0	1	1	2	0	1	0
6.0 to 6.9	10	5	5	7	2	4	1
5.0 to 5.9	60	45	70	54	25	49	13
4.0 to 4.9	287	294	538	541	284	345	107
3.0 to 3.9	913	834	1525	1303	1362	1471	377
2.0 to 2.9	657	646	1228	704	1336	1738	380
1.0 to 1.9	0	2	2	2	1	2	4
0.1 to 0.9	0	0	0	0	0	0	1
No Magnitude	415	434	507	333	540	73	8
Total	2342	2261	3876	2946	3550	3683	891
Estimated Deaths	0	0	0	2	0	0	0

Red values indicate the earthquakes occurred in Alaska.
Source: United States Geological Survey as of June 2, 2006

Check Your Comprehension

After reading the selection, answer the following questions with *a*, *b*, *c*, or *d*. To help you analyze your strengths and weaknesses, the question types are indicated.

Inference _____ 1. Which is the best statement of the main idea of this selection?

a. Earthquakes cause many types of dangerous ground motion.
b. Earthquakes may change a city landscape permanently.
c. Earthquakes are most dangerous when landslides occur.
d. Earthquakes can cause damage in many different ways.

Detail _____ 2. The author indicates that of all the types of ground failure caused by earthquakes, the one that is least likely to occur is a

a. closed tear.
b. scarp.
c. surface crack.
d. landslide.

Inference _____ 3. The author's main purpose in discussing fires and landslides is to show that

a. fires and landslides that usually follow earthquakes can cause many thousands of deaths.
b. fires and landslides are more likely to kill people than liquefaction is.

    c. problems caused by earthquakes can be deadlier than the actual earthquakes themselves.

    d. problems that are created by earthquakes can destroy whole neighborhoods or cities.

Inference   _____ 4. The author refers to liquefaction as a ground failure because during liquefaction the ground

    a. is noticeably torn.

    b. changes consistency.

    c. moves horizontally.

    d. becomes heated.

Inference   _____ 5. The reader can conclude that the word *fault*, when used to discuss an earthquake, refers to

    a. a building code error.

    b. a crack in the earth.

    c. damage to a building.

    d. deaths from a quake.

Inference   _____ 6. The reader can infer that a *scarp* is created by rocks that move

    a. vertically from a fault.

    b. horizontally along a surface.

    c. diagonally into buildings.

    d. slowly over large areas.

Detail   _____ 7. According to the passage, during earthquakes the structures that would predictably receive the least damage are those that are built on

    a. sediment.

    b. soil.

    c. rock.

    d. loess.

Detail   _____ 8. The selection indicates that, compared to aftershocks, earthquake foreshocks are less

    a. damaging.

    b. noisy.

    c. predictable.

    d. unsettling.

Inference   _____ 9. The purpose of this selection is to

    a. warn people of the dangers of earthquakes and explain precautions.

    b. argue for preventive building code enforcement for earthquakes.

    c. record the worldwide damage caused by earthquakes since 1906.

    d. explain how damage results from earthquakes.

Inference   _____ 10. The reader can reasonably infer that the ground motion referred to in the selection's first sentence is the result of

    a. falling debris.

    b. collapsing buildings.

    c. liquefaction of some types of soil.

    d. movement of rocks underground.

Answer the following with *T* (true) or *F* (false).

Detail _____ 11. Most earthquake deaths are caused by a type of ground failure called liquefaction.

Detail _____ 12. Earthquake aftershocks tend to be more dangerous than earthquake foreshocks because of previously weakened structures.

Detail _____ 13. The author feels that the way that Hollywood movies depict earthquakes is fairly accurate.

Detail _____ 14. Of all the effects of earthquakes described in this selection, the greatest loss of human life was caused by landslides in China occurring after earthquakes.

Detail _____ 15. With the improvements in modern building techniques, fire is no longer a dangerous by-product of earthquakes.

Build Your Vocabulary

According to the way the italicized word was used in the selection, indicate *a, b, c,* or *d* for the word or phrase that gives the best definition. The number in parentheses indicates the line of the passage in which the word is located.

_____ 1. "*topple* large structures" (4)
   a. build
   b. view
   c. collapse
   d. survive

_____ 2. "falling *debris*" (5)
   a. fragments
   b. windows
   c. rain
   d. snow

_____ 3. "soft-*sediment*" (11)
   a. concrete
   b. residue
   c. cotton
   d. wood

_____ 4. "but not *eliminated*" (15)
   a. established
   b. started
   c. abolished
   d. escaped

_____ 5. "can be *triggered*" (18)
   a. started
   b. stopped
   c. targeted
   d. measured

_____ 6. "cliffs of *loess*" (24)
   a. clay
   b. sand
   c. minerals
   d. gravel

_____ 7. "Permanent *displacement*" (36)
   a. distress
   b. distance
   c. disposal
   d. dislocation

_____ 8. "Sudden *subsidence* of land" (46)
   a. swelling
   b. swaying
   c. sinking
   d. shrinking

_____ 9. "extremely *unsettling*" (50)
   a. calming
   b. disturbing
   c. powerful
   d. lucky

_____ 10. "*precede* a main shock"
   (51)
   a. go before
   b. go after
   c. follow
   d. stop

Search the Net

Use a search engine such as Google, Yahoo, Ask.com, Excite, Dogpile, or Lycos to find more information about the relationship between the earth's plates and earthquakes and volcanoes. Locate maps that show the land formations caused by plate tectonics. For suggested Web sites and other research activities, go to http://www.ablongman.com/smith/.

selection 2 Sociology

Contemporary *Focus*

Research shows that each Minnesotan now produces 1.16 tons of garbage every year, which is almost twice the amount of 15 years ago. By 2050 Africa's population will more than double to almost two billion. What are the effects on the environment of growing consumption in industrialized nations and surging population in poor nations?

Water Crisis Will Worsen Plight

The East African, March 28, 2006

Right now, Africa is facing a serious water shortage. The statistics are grim. Two out of every three people in the world will be facing water shortages by 2025, according to a report entitled "Running on Empty." Just over 1 billion people today have no access to safe drinking water, and 2.5 billion have no basic sanitation.

Consumption of water rose six-fold between 1990 and 1995, more than twice the population growth. While the United Kingdom and other prosperous nations of the world can cope with dwindling water supplies owing to efficient water management, poorer countries, especially from Africa, are already suffering massively, making it pretty hard to escape the ravages of drought and poverty.

This crisis is caused partly by the depletion of forest cover and unprecedented encroachment on the environment. Furthermore, supplies of water have been stretched to the limit due to rising populations, rising agricultural use, poor management and the effects of global warming.

With the current water scarcity, the poor of Africa cannot have the full enjoyment of the right to water. Yet it is estimated that about $100 billion is spent each year on bottled water.

COLLABORATE Collaborate on responses to the following questions:

➤ Why is Africa particularly vulnerable to a water shortage?

➤ What is the source for water in your city?

➤ What are the politics of water in arid areas such as Los Angeles and Las Vegas?

Skill Development: Preview

Preview the next selection to predict its purpose and organization and to formulate your learning plan.

Activate Schema

Where is the waste in your city dumped?
Who uses the highest percentage of water in your region?

Why do people in poor nations have more children than people of industrialized nations?

Establish a Purpose for Reading

Humans are damaging nature with waste and overconsumption, as well as depleting natural resources. Read to learn how humans are changing the planet.

Increase Word Knowledge

What do you know about these words?

migration	deficit	predictable	surging	affluent
abundance	disposable	decompose	arid	finite

Your instructor may give a true-false vocabulary review before or after reading.

Integrate Knowledge While Reading

Questions have been inserted in the margin to stimulate your thinking while reading. Remember to

Predict	Picture	Relate	Monitor	Correct

TECHNOLOGY AND THE ENVIRONMENT

Grandma Macionis, we always used to say, never threw anything away. Born in Lithuania—the "old country"—she grew up in a poor village, an experience that shaped her life even after she came to the United States as a young woman.

5   Her birthday was an amusing occasion for the rest of the family. After opening a present, she would carefully put aside the box, refold the wrapping paper, and roll up the ribbon; all this meant as much to her as the gift itself. Probably more, because Grandma never wore the new clothes given to her, and she was never known to go shopping for herself. Her kitchen knives were worn down from decades of sharpening, and every piece of furniture she ever bought stayed with her to the end
10 of her life (I still eat at the same table she had in her kitchen seventy-five years ago).

Why did Grandma Macionis save everything?

As curious as Grandma Macionis was to her grandchildren, she was a product of her culture. A century ago, there was little "trash." Grandma Macionis never thought of herself as an environmentalist. But she was: She lived simply, using few resources and creating almost no solid waste.

THE RISING POWER OF TECHNOLOGY

15 Our earliest ancestors—hunters and gatherers—had only simple technology, so they had a very little effect on the environment. Nature ruled much of their way of life: They lived according to the migration of animals, the changing of the seasons, and natural events such as fires, floods, and droughts.

Paul Marcus/Studio SPM, Inc.

The painting, *Day Dreaming*, by Paul Marcus depicts the pollution and environmental damage from unrestricted factories.

20 When the Industrial Revolution replaced muscle power with combustion engines that burn fossil fuels (coal and, later, oil), societies began changing the environment much more, by consuming energy resources and by releasing pollutants into the atmosphere. As a result of technological power, humans have brought more change to this planet in the last two centuries than over the last billion years. The typical adult in the United States consumes about one hundred times more energy 25 each year than the average person in the world's poorest nations.

What were the effects of the Industrial Revolution?

THE ENVIRONMENTAL DEFICIT

A short look at human history teaches an important lesson: By using more powerful technology to improve living standards, people put the lives of future generations at risk. The evidence is mounting that we are running up an **environmental deficit,** *profound and long-term harm to the environment caused by humanity's focus on short-* 30 *term material affluence.*

How are we harming the environment?

POPULATION INCREASE

Consider that, 2,000 years ago the entire world's population was about 300 million—about the population of the United States today.

Once humans developed industrial technology, higher living standards and improved medical treatments sharply decreased the death rates in Western Europe. 35 The predictable result was a sharp upward spike in world population. By 1800, global population had soared to 1 billion.

Most experts predict that the world population will reach 8 to 9 billion people by 2050. The most rapid population growth is occurring in the poorest regions of the world. In 2003, the world's population was about 6.3 billion. Although the rate 40 of increase is slowing, we are adding 80 million people to the world's total each year (218,000 every day).

Rapid population growth makes the problem of poverty worse. This is because a surging population offsets any increase in productivity so that living standards stay the same. If a society's population doubles, doubling its productivity
45 amounts to no gain al all. But poverty also makes environmental problems worse.
Because they are preoccupied with survival, poor people have little choice but to
consume whatever resources are at hand, without thinking about long-term environmental consequences.

Now imagine the consequences of rising population and advancing technology
50 *together*. That is, what would happen if poor societies suddenly industrialized? An
affluent India, for example, would suddenly be a nation with more than 1 billion
additional cars on its streets. What effect would that have on the world's oil reserves
and global air quality?

Simply put, if people around the world lived at the level of material abundance
55 the people in the United States take for granted, the natural environment would
soon collapse even if birth rates were to drop. From an environmentalist point of
view, our planet suffers from economic underdevelopment in some regions and economic overdevelopment in others.

SOLID WASTE: THE DISPOSABLE SOCIETY

One environmental problem is waste—or, more precisely, too much of it. The aver-
60 age person in the United States discards about five pounds of paper, metal, plastic,
and other disposable materials daily; over a lifetime, that comes to 50 tons.

The problem of solid waste stems from a simple fact: The United States is a
disposable society. Not only is this country materially rich, but its people value convenience. As a result, we consume more products than any nation on Earth, and
65 many of these products come with excessive packaging. The most familiar case is
the cardboard, plastic, and Styrofoam containers that we buy with our fast food and
throw away within minutes.

We like to say that we "throw things away." But the two-thirds of our solid waste
that is not burned or recycled never really "goes away." Rather, it ends up in landfills.
70 These dumping grounds are a threat to the natural environment for several reasons.

First, the sheer volume of discarded material is filling up landfills all across
the country. Already the United States is shipping trash to other countries to be
discarded. Second, the material in landfills contributes to water pollution.
Although the laws in most localities now regulate what can go in a landfill, the
75 Environmental Protection Agency has identified 30,000 dump sites across the
United States containing hazardous materials that are polluting water both above
and below the ground. Third, what goes into landfills all too often stays there,
sometimes for centuries. Tens of millions of tires, diapers, and plastic utensils do
not readily decompose and will be an unwelcome environmental burden for gen-
80 erations to come.

INADEQUATE WATER SUPPLY

In much of North America and Asia, people look to rivers rather than rainfall for
their water, making supply a problem. In some U.S. regions, the main source is
groundwater, water underground that supplies wells and springs. In many regions,
the supply is running low. For example, the Ogallala aquifer runs below ground
85 across seven states from South Dakota to Texas; it is now being pumped so rapidly
that some experts fear it could run dry within several decades.

How would rising populations in industrial societies impact the environment?

Compare our disposable society to Grandma Macionis' times.

> *How can we work together with other cities, states, and countries to preserve local and world water supplies?*

Nowhere is water supply a bigger problem than in the Middle East. In Egypt, an arid region of the world, people depend on the Nile River for most of their wa-ter. But because of population increases, Egyptians make do with one-sixth as much
90 water per person as they did in 1900. Experts project that the supply may shrink by half again by 2015. Throughout the Middle East and Africa, where populations are rising rapidly, experts predict that as many as 1 billion people may lack necessary water by 2030.

In light of such developments, we must face the reality that water is a finite re-
95 source. Greater conservation of water by individuals (the average person consumes 10 million gallons in a lifetime) is part of the answer. However, individuals in house-holds around the world account for just 10 percent of all water use. We need to curb consumption by industry, which is responsible for 25 percent of global water use, and by farming, which consumes nearly two-thirds of the total for irrigation.

(1,233 words)

—From John J. Macionis,
Social Problems, 2nd ed.

Recall

Stop to self-test, relate, and react.

Your instructor may choose to give you a true-false comprehension review.

Write About the Selection

How are humans changing the planet, and what are the consequences?

Response Suggestion: Focus on one major change, such as population growth or waste disposal. How does it affect us now? How might it affect us fifty years from now?

Contemporary *Link*

Will water become the oil of tomorrow? If so, who will get rich, and who will pay the price? Describe a worldwide scenario in which water demands a price equivalent to that of oil. How would this change our lives?

Skill Development: Graphics

Refer to the global map on page 351 and answer the following items with *T* (true) or *F* (false).

_____ 1. Africa has the largest number of countries of any continent with very high water consumption in comparison to the natural supply.

_____ 2. North America has the lowest consumption of water as a percentage of the natural supply of any continent.

_____ 3. The water consumption as a percentage of the natural supply is higher in India than it is in Mexico.

_____ 4. Argentina and Australia both have a similarly low water consumption as a percentage of their natural supply.

_____ 5. Both Brazil and Indonesia contain tropical rain forests.

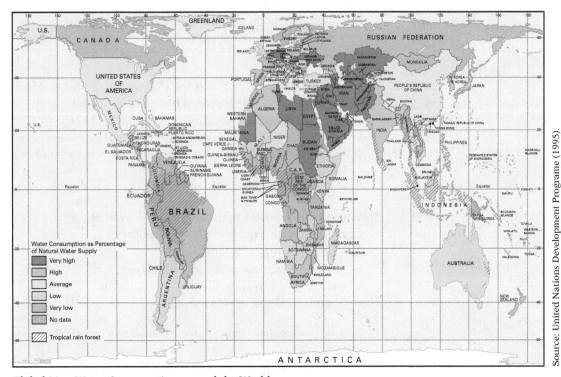

Source: United Nations Development Programe (1995).

Global Map Water Consumption around the World
This map shows each country's water consumption in relation to available resources. Nations near the equator consume only a tiny share of their available resources and do not face fresh water shortages. Northern Africa and the Middle East are a different story, however, with dense populations drawing on very limited water resources. As a result, in Libya, Egypt, Saudi Arabia, and other countries there is a serious problem of too little fresh water, especially for the poor.

Check Your Comprehension

After reading the selection, answer the following questions with *a, b, c,* or *d.* To help you analyze your strengths and weaknesses, the question types are indicated.

Main Idea _____ 1. Which is the best statement of the main idea of this selection?

a. Social problems cause poverty and suffering around the world today.
b. Advances in technology are destined to worsen rather than solve environmental problems.
c. The environment is suffering from overpopulation and poverty.
d. Several factors contribute to the environmental problems we face today.

Inference _____ 2. The reader can conclude that the story about Grandma Macionis is used to introduce this selection because the author

a. feels that Grandma Macionis was ecologically aware.
b. needs to provide an example of how social problems originate.
c. sees Grandma Macionis as someone from whom humans today could learn.
d. feels Grandma Macionis was careful in spending her money.

Detail _____ 3. The author indicates that our very earliest ancestors did not appreciably alter their environment because they

a. rejected the use of technology.
b. lived simply in cooperation with nature.
c. were affected by fires, floods, and droughts.
d. migrated during the seasons.

Inference _____ 4. The author implies that the world's environmental deficit is in direct proportion to

a. the material demands of humanity and population growth.
b. technological research.
c. the dreams of future generations.
d. toxicity of pollutants.

Detail _____ 5. The author says that the "spike in world population" in the years leading up to 1800 was predictable because

a. there were great advances in medicine.
b. the world's population was fairly small.
c. there were no major wars taking place.
d. productivity was growing rapidly.

Detail _____ 6. The author claims that those who live in poverty

a. seek to destroy the environment.
b. damage the environment out of necessity.
c. take little from the environment.
d. consider long-term consequences.

selection
2

Inference _____ 7. The author indicates that from an environmentalist perspective, world economic development is not

a. fair.
b. efficient.
c. balanced.
d. obvious.

Detail _____ 8. The author describes the United States as a *disposable society* because it is a society that

a. attempts unsuccessfully to recycle.
b. sends waste to foreign countries.
c. is regulated by the Environmental Protection Agency.
d. values convenience over ecological concerns.

Inference _____ 9. When the author says that the materials our society throws away don't actually go away, he means that they do not

a. get recycled.
b. fully disappear without a trace.
c. get burned.
d. go to landfills.

Inference _____ 10. In the section "Inadequate Water Supply," the author observes that the world's future water supply problems will be mainly caused by

a. a lack of rain.
b. used-up aquifers.
c. rising populations.
d. pollutants in rivers.

Answer the following with *T* (true) or *F* (false).

Detail _____ 11. Most of the world's water is used for agricultural purposes.

Detail _____ 12. The more industrially advanced an economy, the more likely its industries are to cause pollution.

Detail _____ 13. If a society's population doubles, its productivity automatically doubles.

Detail _____ 14. Unlike the Nile River, the Ogallala aquifer runs underground and thus is not endangered by overconsumption.

Detail _____ 15. Two-thirds of our solid waste goes into landfills, therefore it does not "go away."

Build Your Vocabulary

According to the way the italicized word was used in the selection, indicate *a, b, c,* or *d* for the word or phrase that gives the best definition. The number in parentheses indicates the line of the passage in which the word is located.

_____ 1. "*migration* of animals" (17)
    a. reproduction
    b. courtship
    c. breeding
    d. movement

_____ 6. "material *abundance*" (54)
    a. prosperity
    b. misfortune
    c. consequence
    d. development

_____ 2. "environmental *deficit*" (28)
    a. shortage
    b. technology
    c. condition
    d. design

_____ 7. "*disposable* society" (63)
    a. collecting
    b. throw-away
    c. consumer
    d. expensive

_____ 3. "*predictable* result" (35)
    a. disappointing
    b. anticipated
    c. wonderful
    d. scientific

_____ 8. "readily *decompose*" (79)
    a. sell
    b. break down
    c. multiply
    d. survive

_____ 4. "*surging* population" (43)
    a. poverty-stricken
    b. lively
    c. increasing
    d. shrinking

_____ 9. "*arid* region" (88)
    a. wet
    b. mountainous
    c. historical
    d. dry

_____ 5. "*affluent* India" (51)
    a. industrial
    b. wealthy
    c. technologically advanced
    d. growing quickly

_____ 10. "*finite* resource" (94)
    a. knowledgeable
    b. limited
    c. expensive
    d. endless

Search the Net

Use a search engine such as Google, Yahoo, Ask.com, Excite, Dogpile, or Lycos to find information about environmental issues such as global warming and the shrinking water supply. Find the factors that contribute the most to both of these environmental challenges and search for suggested solutions to fixing these problems. For suggested Web sites and other research activities, go to http://www. ablongman.com/smith/.

10 Test Taking

- Can being testwise improve your score?
- How should you prepare before a test?
- What should you notice during a test?
- What are the major question types?
- What hints help with multiple-choice items?
- How do you answer an essay question?

Victor Bregeda, *Transformation.*

Can Being Testwise Improve Your Score?

Are you preparing for a midterm or another important exam? Is it a multiple-choice or essay test? Can test-taking tricks help you get a higher score?

Research shows that gimmicks, such as schemes involving length of responses or the likelihood of *b* or *c* being the right answer, don't work.[1]

However, insight into the testing experience can help. High scores depend on preparation, both mental and physical.

The purpose of this chapter is to help you gain points by being aware. You can improve your score by understanding how tests are constructed and what is needed for maximum performance. Study the following and do everything you can both mentally and physically to gain an edge.

Strategies for Mental and Physical Preparation

Before Taking a Test

Get Plenty of Sleep the Night Before. How alert can you be with inadequate sleep? Would you want a surgeon operating on you if he had slept only a few hours the night before? The mental alertness you derive from a good night's sleep can add as much as six points to your score and mean the difference between passing or failing. Why gamble by staying up late? Prioritize tasks and budget your time during the day so you can go to bed on time.

Arrive Five or Ten Minutes Early and Get Settled. If you run into class flustered at the last second, you will spend the first five minutes of the test calming yourself rather than getting immediately to work. Avoid unnecessary stress by arriving for the test early. Find a seat, get settled with pen or pencil and paper, and relax with a classmate by making small talk.

Know What to Expect on the Test. Ask beforehand if the test will be essay or multiple choice so that you can anticipate the format when you study. Both stress main ideas, and research shows that one is not easier than the other.[2]

Have Confidence in Your Abilities. Achieve self-confidence by being well prepared. Be optimistic, and approach the test with a positive mental attitude. Lack of preparation breeds anxiety, but positive testing experiences tend to breed confidence. Don't miss quizzes; research shows that students who have frequent quizzes during a course tend to do better on the final exam.[3]

---

[1]W. G. Brozo, R. V. Schmelzer, and H. A. Spires, "A Study of Test-Wiseness Clues in College and University Teacher-Made Tests with Implications for Academic Assistance Centers," *College Reading and Learning Assistance*, Technical Report 84–01 (ERIC 1984), ED 240928.

[2]P. M. Clark, "Examination Performance and Examination Set," in D. M. Wark, ed., *Fifth Yearbook of the North Central Reading Association* (Minneapolis: Central Reading Association, 1968), pp. 114–22.

[3]M. L. Fitch, A. J. Drucker, and J. A. Norton, "Frequent Testing as a Motivating Factor in Large Lecture Classes," *Journal of Educational Psychology* 42 (1951): 1–20.

Know How the Test Will Be Scored. If the test has several sections, be very clear on how many points can be earned from each section so you can prioritize your time and effort. Determine if some items are worth more points than others. Find out if there is a penalty for guessing and, if so, what it is. Because most test scores are based on answering all the questions, you are usually better off guessing than leaving items unanswered. Research shows that educated guessing can add points to your score.[4]

Plan Your Attack. At least a week before the test, take an inventory of what you need to do and make plans to achieve your goals. Preparation can make a difference for both standardized tests and with content area exams. The Reader's Tip lists the elements of a sound test preparation strategy.

Reader's *Tip* — Preparing for a Test

Professors report that students gain awareness before content area exams by writing truthful answers to questions like the following:

- **How will the test look?** How many parts will the test have? What kinds of questions will be asked? How will points be counted?
- **What material will be covered?** What textbook pages will the test cover? What lecture notes will be included? Will outside reading be significant?
- **How will you study?** Have you made a checklist or study guide? Have you read all the material? Will you study notes or annotations from your textbook? Will you write down answers to potential essay questions? Will you include time to study with a classmate?
- **When will you study?** What is your schedule the week before the test? How long will you need to study? How much of the material do you plan to cover each day? What are your projected study hours?
- **What grade are you honestly working to achieve?** Are you willing to work for an A, or are you actually trying to earn a B or C?

During the Test

Concentrate. Tune out internal and external distractions and focus your attention on the test. Visualize and integrate old and new knowledge as you work. Read with curiosity and an eagerness to learn something new. Predict, picture, relate, monitor, and use correction strategies. If you become anxious or distracted, close your eyes and take a few deep breaths to relax and get yourself back on track.

On a teacher-made test, you may have a few thoughts that you want to jot down immediately on the back of the test so you don't forget them. Do so, and proceed with confidence.

---

[4]R. C. Preston, "Ability of Students to Identify Correct Responses Before Reading," *Journal of Educational Research* 58 (1964): 181–83.

Read and Follow Directions. Find out what to do and then do it. On a multiple-choice test, perhaps more than one answer is needed. Perhaps on an essay exam you are to respond to only three of five questions.

Schedule Your Time. Wear a watch and use it. When you receive your copy of the test, look it over, size up the task, and allocate your time. Determine the number of sections to be covered, and organize your time accordingly. As you work through the test, periodically check to see if you are meeting your time goals.

On teacher-made tests, the number of points for each item may vary. Do the easy items first, but spend the most time on the items that will yield the most points.

Work Rapidly. Every minute counts. Do not waste the time that you may need later by pondering at length over an especially difficult item. Mark the item with a check or a dot and move on to the rest of the test. If you have a few minutes at the end of the test, return to the marked items for further study.

Think. Use knowledge, logic, and common sense in responding to the items. Be aggressive and alert in moving through the test.

If you are unsure, use a process of elimination to narrow down the options. Double-check your paper to make sure you have answered every item.

Ignore Students Who Finish Early. Early departures draw attention and can create anxiety for those still working, but reassure yourself with the knowledge that students who finish early do not necessarily make the highest scores. Rapid workers do not necessarily work more accurately. If you have time, carefully review test items that you found yourself answering with less confidence. If your reassessment leads you to another response, change your answer to agree with your new thoughts. Research shows that scores can be improved by making such changes.[5]

After the Test

Analyze Your Preparation. Question yourself after the test, and learn from the experience. Did you study the right material? Do you wish you had spent more time studying any particular topic? Were you mentally and physically alert enough to function at your full capacity?

Analyze the Test. Decide if the test was what you expected. If not, what was unexpected? Did the professor describe the test accurately or were there a few surprises? Why were you surprised? Use your memory of the test to predict the patterns of future tests.

Analyze Your Performance. Most standardized tests are not returned, but you do receive scores and subscores. What do these scores tell you about your strengths and weaknesses? What can you do to improve?

---

[5]F. K. Berrien, "Are Scores Increased on Objective Tests by Changing the Initial Decision?" *Journal of Educational Psychology* 31 (1940): 64–67.

Content area exams are usually returned and reviewed in class. Ask questions about your errors. Find out why any weak responses did not receive full credit. Look for patterns of strengths and weaknesses in planning for the next test.

Meet with your professor if you are confused or disappointed and ask for suggestions for improvement. Find out if tutorial sessions or study groups are available for you to join. Ask to see an A paper. Formulate a plan with your professor for improved performance on the next test.

Strategies for Multiple-Choice Items

Consider All Alternatives Before Choosing an Answer

Read all the options. Do not rush to record an answer without considering all the alternatives. Be careful, not careless, in considering each option. Multiple-choice test items usually ask for the best choice for an answer, rather than any choice that is reasonable.

EXAMPLE   Choose the best answer.

_____   Peter was most likely called a "moronic booby" because

a. he neglected Catherine.
b. he drank too much.
c. he disliked German customs.
d. he played with dolls and toys.

EXPLANATION Although the first three answers are true and reasonable, the last answer seems to be most directly related to that particular name.

Anticipate the Answer and Look for Something Close to It

As you read the beginning of a multiple-choice item, anticipate what you would write for a correct response. Develop an answer in your mind before you read the options, and then look for a response that corroborates your thinking.

EXAMPLE   Before choosing from among *a, b, c,* and *d,* try to anticipate the correct response. Note the reader's thought process in italics.

_____   The author suggests that Catherine probably converted to the Russian Orthodox church because . . . *she wanted to rule the country and wanted the people to think of her as Russian, rather than German.*

a. she was a very religious person.
b. Peter wanted her to convert.
c. she was no longer in Germany.
d. she wanted to appear thoroughly Russian to the Russian people.

EXPLANATION The last answer most closely matches the kind of answer you were anticipating.

Avoid Answers with 100 Percent Words

All and *never* mean 100 percent, without exceptions. A response containing either word is seldom correct. Rarely can a statement be so definitely inclusive or exclusive. Here are some other 100 percent words to avoid:

no	none	only	every	always	must

EXAMPLE   Answer the following with *true* or *false:*

_____   Catherine the Great was beloved by all the Russian people.

EXPLANATION   *All* means 100 percent and thus is too inclusive. Surely one or two Russians did not like Catherine, so the answer must be *false.*

Consider Answers with Qualifying Words

Words like *sometimes* and *seldom* suggest frequency but do not go so far as to say *all* or *none.* Such qualifying words can mean more than *none* and less than *all.* By being so indefinite, the words are difficult to dispute. Therefore, qualifiers are more likely to be included in a correct response. Here are some other qualifiers:

few	much	often	may
many	some	perhaps	generally

EXAMPLE   Answer the following with *true* or *false:*

_____   Catherine was beloved by many of the Russian people.

EXPLANATION   The statement is difficult to dispute, given Catherine's popularity. An uprising against her occurred, but it was put down, and she maintained the support of many of the Russian people. Thus, the answer would be *true.*

Choose the Intended Answer Without Overanalyzing

Try to follow logically the thinking of the test writer rather than overanalyzing minute points. Don't make the question harder than it is. Use your common sense and answer what you think was intended.

EXAMPLE   Answer the following with *true* or *false:*

_____   Catherine was responsible for Peter's murder.

EXPLANATION   This is false in that Catherine did not personally murder Peter. On the other hand, she did "tacitly consent" to his murder, which suggests responsibility. After seizing power, it was certainly in her best interest to get rid of Peter permanently. Perhaps without Catherine, Peter would still be playing with his toys, so the intended answer is *true.*

True Statements Must Be True Without Exception

A statement is either totally true or it is incorrect. Adding an incorrect *and, but,* or *because* phrase to a true statement makes the statement false and thus an unacceptable answer. If a statement is half true and half false, mark it *false.*

EXAMPLE   Answer the following with *true* or *false:*

_____   Catherine was an enlightened despot who did her best to improve the lot of all her people.

EXPLANATION   It is true that Catherine was considered an enlightened despot, but she did very little to improve the lot of the serfs. In fact, conditions for the serfs worsened. The statement is half true and half false, so it must be answered *false.*

If Two Options Are Synonymous, Eliminate Both

If *both* is not a possible answer and two possible answers say basically the same thing, then neither can be correct. Eliminate the two and spend your time on the others.

EXAMPLE   Choose the correct answer, watching for synonyms.

_____   The purpose of this passage is

a. to argue.
b. to persuade.
c. to inform.
d. to entertain.

EXPLANATION   Because *argue* and *persuade* are basically synonymous, you can eliminate both and move to the other options.

Strategies for Content Area Exams

Almost all professors would say that the number one strategy for scoring high on content area exams is to study the material. Although this advice is certainly on target, there are other suggestions that can help you gain an edge.

Multiple-Choice Items

Multiple-choice, true-false, or matching items on content area exams are written to evaluate factual knowledge, conceptual comprehension, and application skill. *Factual questions* tap your knowledge of names, definitions, dates, events, and theories. *Conceptual comprehension* questions evaluate your ability to see relationships, notice similarities and differences, and combine information from different parts of a chapter. *Application questions* provide the opportunity to generalize from a theory to a real-life illustration; these are particularly popular in psychology and sociology.

To study for a multiple-choice test, make lists of key terms, facts, and concepts. Quiz yourself on recognition and general knowledge. Make connections and be sure you know similarities and differences. Finally, invent scenarios that depict principles and concepts.

EXAMPLE The following is an example of an application question from psychology:

_____ An illustration of obsessive-compulsive behavior is

    a. Maria goes to the movies most Friday nights.
    b. Leon washes his hands more than a hundred times a day.
    c. Pepe wants to buy a car.
    d. Sue eats more fish than red meat.

EXPLANATION The second response is obviously correct, but such questions can be tricky if you have not prepared for them. Use your own knowledge, plus the previous suggestions for multiple-choice tests, to separate answers from distractors.

Short-Answer Items

Professors ask short-answer questions because they want you to use your own words to describe or identify. For such questions, be sure that you understand exactly what the professor is asking you to say. You do not want to waste time writing more than is needed, but on the other hand, you do not want to lose points for not writing enough. Study for short-answer items by making lists and self-testing, just as you do when studying for multiple-choice items. For history exams, especially, be prepared to identify who, what, when, where, and why.

Essay Questions

Essay answers demand more effort and energy from the test taker than multiple-choice items. On a multiple-choice test, all the correct answers are before you. On an essay exam, however, the only thing in front of you is a question and a blank sheet of paper. This blank sheet can be intimidating to many students. Your job is to recall appropriate ideas, organize them under the central theme designated in the question, and create a response in your own words. The following suggestions can help you respond effectively.

Translate the Question. Frequently, an essay "question" is not a question at all but a statement that you are asked to support. When you see this type of question on a test, your first step is to read it and then reread it to be sure you understand it. Next, reword it into a question. Even if you begin with a question, translate it into your own words. Simplify the question into terms you can understand. Break the question into its parts.

Convert the translated parts of the question into the approach that you will need to use to answer each part. Will you define, describe, explain, or compare? State what you will do to answer. In a sense, this is a behavioral statement.

EXAMPLE The following example demonstrates the translation process.

- **Statement to support.** It is both appropriate and ironic to refer to Catherine as one of the great rulers of Russia.
- **Question.** Why is it both appropriate and ironic to refer to Catherine as one of the great rulers of Russia?
- **Translation:** The question has two parts:
  1. What did Catherine do that was great?
  2. What did she do that was the opposite of what you would expect (irony) of a great Russian ruler?
- **Response approach.** List what Catherine did that was great and then list what she did that was the opposite of what you would expect of a great Russian ruler. Relate her actions to the question.

Answer the Question. Make sure your answer is a response to the question that is asked, rather than a summary of everything you know about a particular subject. Write with purpose so that the reader can understand your views and relate your points to the subject. Padding your answer by repeating the same idea or including irrelevant information is obvious to graders and seldom appreciated.

EXAMPLE The following is an inappropriate answer to the question "Why is it both appropriate and ironic to refer to Catherine as one of the great rulers of Russia?"

> Catherine was born in Germany and came to Russia as a young girl to marry Peter. It was an unhappy marriage that lasted seventeen years. She . . .

EXPLANATION This response does not answer the question; rather, it is a summary.

Organize Your Response. Do not write the first thing to pop into your head. Take a few minutes to brainstorm and jot down ideas. Number the ideas in the order that you wish to present them, and use the plan shown on the opposite page as your outline for writing.

In your first sentence, establish the purpose and direction of your response. Then list specific details that support, explain, prove, and develop your point. Reemphasize the points in a concluding sentence, and restate your purpose. Whenever possible, use numbers or subheadings to simplify your message for the reader. If time runs short, use an outline or a diagram to express your remaining ideas.

> I. _Appropriate_
> 1. Acquired land
> 2. Art, medicine, buildings
> 3. 34 years
> 4. Political skill & foreign diplomacy
>
> II. _Ironic (opposite)_
> 1. Not Russian
> 2. Killed Peter
> 3. Serfs very poor
> 4. Revolt against her

EXAMPLE To answer the previous question, think about the selection on Catherine and jot down the ideas that you would include in a response.

Use an Appropriate Style. Your audience for this response is not your best friend but your learned professor who is giving you a grade. Be respectful. Do not use slang. Do not use phrases like "as you know," "like," or "well." They may be appropriate in conversation, but they are not appropriate in formal writing.

Avoid empty words and thoughts. Words like *good, interesting,* and *nice* say very little. Be more direct and descriptive in your writing.

State your thesis, supply proof, and use transitional phrases to tie your ideas together. Words like *first, second,* and *finally* help to organize enumerations. Terms like *however* and *on the other hand* show a shift in thought. Remember, you are pulling ideas together, so use phrases and words to help the reader see relationships.

EXAMPLE Study the following response to the question for organization, transition, and style.

> Catherine was a very good ruler of Russia. She tried to be Russian but she was from Germany. Catherine was a good politician and got Russia seaports on the Baltic, Caspian, and Black Sea. She had many boyfriends and there was gossip about her. She did very little for the Serfs because they remained very poor for a long time. She built nice buildings and got doctors to help people. She was not as awesome as she pretended to be.

EXPLANATION Notice the response's lack of organization, weak language, inappropriate phrases, and failure to use transitional words.

Be Aware of Appearance. Research has shown that, on the average, an essay written in a clear, legible hand receives a score that is one grade level higher than does the essay written somewhat illegibly.[6] Be particular about appearance and considerate of the reader. Proofread for correct grammar, punctuation, and spelling.

Predict and Practice. Predict possible essay items by using the table of contents and subheadings of your text to form questions. Practice brainstorming to answer these questions. Review old exams for an insight both into the questions and the kinds of answers that received good marks. Outline answers to possible exam questions. Do as much thinking as possible to prepare yourself to take the test before you sit down to begin writing. The Reader's Tip shows the range of demands you might encounter in essay exams for your courses.

---

[6]H. W. James, "The Effect of Handwriting upon Grading," *English Journal* 16 (1927): 180–85.

Reader's *Tip* — Key Words in Essay Questions

The following key words of instruction appear in essay questions.

- **Compare:** List the similarities between things.
- **Contrast:** Note the differences between things.
- **Criticize:** State your opinion and stress the weaknesses.
- **Define:** State the meaning so that the term is understood, and use examples.
- **Describe:** State the characteristics so that the image is vivid.
- **Diagram:** Make a drawing that demonstrates relationships.
- **Discuss:** Define the issue and elaborate on the advantages and disadvantages.
- **Evaluate:** State positive and negative views and make a judgment.
- **Explain:** Show cause and effect and give reasons.
- **Illustrate:** Provide examples.
- **Interpret:** Explain your own understanding of a topic that includes your opinions.
- **Justify:** Give proof or reasons to support an opinion.
- **List:** Record a series of numbered items.
- **Outline:** Sketch out the main points with their significant supporting details.
- **Prove:** Use facts as evidence in support of an opinion.
- **Relate:** Connect items and show how one influences another.
- **Review:** Write an overview with a summary.
- **Summarize:** Retell the main points.
- **Trace:** Move sequentially from one event to another.

View Your Response Objectively for Evaluation Points. Respond to get points. Some students feel that filling up the page deserves a passing grade. They do not understand how a whole page written on the subject of Catherine could receive no points.

Although essay exams seem totally subjective, they cannot be. Students need to know that a professor who gives an essay exam grades answers according to an objective scoring system. The professor examines the paper for certain relevant points that should be made. The student's grade reflects the quantity, quality, and clarity of these relevant points.

Unfortunately, essay exams are shrouded in mystery. Sometimes the hardest part of answering an item is to figure out what the professor wants. Ask yourself, "What do I need to say to get enough points to pass or to make an A?"

Do not add personal experiences or extraneous examples unless they are requested. You may be wasting your time by including information that will give you no points. Stick to the subject and the material. Demonstrate to the professor that you know the material by selectively using it in your response.

The professor scoring the response to the question about Catherine used the following checklist for evaluation:

Appropriate	Ironic
1. Acquired land	1. Not Russian
2. Art, medicine, buildings	2. Killed Peter
3. 34 years	3. Serfs very poor
4. Political skill and foreign diplomacy	4. Revolt against her

The professor determined that an A paper should contain all the items. To pass, a student should include five of the eight categories covered. Listing and explaining fewer than five would not produce enough points to pass. Naturally, the professor would expect clarity and elaboration in each category.

After the Test, Read an A Paper. Maybe the A paper will be yours. If so, share it with others. If not, ask to read an A paper so that you will have a model from which to learn. Ask your classmates or ask the professor. You can learn a lot from reading a good paper; you can see what you could have done.

When your professor returns a multiple-choice exam, you can reread items and analyze your mistakes to figure out what you did wrong. However, you cannot review essay exams so easily. You may get back a C paper with only a word or two of comment and never know what you should have done. Ideally, essay exams should be returned with an example of what would have been a perfect A response so that students can study and learn from a perfect model and not make the same mistakes on the next test, but this is seldom, if ever, done. Your best bet is to ask to see an A paper.

EXAMPLE Study the following response to the previous question. The paper received an A.

> To call Catherine one of the great rulers of Russia is both appropriate and ironic. It is appropriate because she expanded the borders of Russia. Through her cunning, Russia annexed part of Poland and expanded the frontier to the Black, Caspian, and Baltic seas. Catherine professed to be enlightened and formed an art academy and a college of pharmacy, and she imported foreign physicians. She built many architecturally significant buildings, including the Hermitage. For thirty-four years she amazed the Russian people with her political skill and diplomacy.
>
> On the other hand, Catherine was not a great Russian, nor was she an enlightened leader of all the people. First, she was not Russian; she was German, but she had worked hard to "russify" herself during the early years of her unhappy marriage. Second, and ironically, she murdered the legitimate ruler of Russia. When she seized power, she made sure the tsar quickly died of "hemorrhoidal colic." Third, she did nothing to improve the lot of the poor serfs and after a bloody uprising in 1773, she became even more despotic. Yet, Catherine was an engaging character who, through her cunning and intellect, has become known to the world in history books as "Catherine the Great."

EXPLANATION Note the organization, logical thinking, and effective use of transitions in this response.

Locus of Control

Have you ever heard students say, "I do better when I don't study," or "No matter how much I study, I still get a C"? According to Julian Rotter, a learning theory psychologist who believes that people develop attitudes about control of their lives, such comments reflect an *external locus of control* regarding test taking.[7] People with an external locus of control, called "externalizers," feel that fate, luck, or other people control what happens to them. Because they feel they can do little to avoid what befalls them, they do not face matters directly and thus do not take responsibility for failure or credit for success.

On the other hand, people who have an *internal locus of control* feel that they, not "fate," have control over what happens to them. Such students might evaluate test performance by saying, "I didn't study enough" or "I should have spent more time organizing my essay response." "Internalizers" feel their rewards are due to their own actions, and they take steps to be sure they receive those rewards. When it comes to test taking, be an internalizer: Take responsibility, take control, and accept credit for your success.

[7]Julian Rotter, "External Control and Internal Control," *Psychology Today* 5, no. 1 (1971): 37–42.

Summary *Points*

➤ **Can being testwise improve your score?**
Test taking is a serious part of the business of being a college student. Preparation and practice—being testwise—can lead to improved scores on both standardized reading tests and content area exams.

➤ **How should you prepare before a test?**
Study according to the type of test you are taking. Plan your study times to avoid having to cram. Arrive rested and alert.

➤ **What should you notice during a test?**
Read the directions, and keep up with the time.

➤ **What strategies should you use to read a comprehension passage?**
Items on standardized reading tests tend to follow a predictable pattern and include five major question types. Learn to recognize these types and the skills needed for answering each.

➤ **What are the major question types?**
They are (1) main idea, (2) details, (3) inference, (4) purpose, and (5) vocabulary.

➤ **What hints help with multiple-choice items?**
Be careful, not careless; consider all options; notice key words; and use logical reasoning.

➤ **How do you answer an essay question?**
Be sure you understand the question, brainstorm your response, organize your thoughts, and write in paragraphs with specific examples.

11 The Writing Process

Write-O-Matic
The write-o-matic takes pure thought
And funnels it into, A cylinder where it's transformed
To something bright and new.
From deep within, this strange machine
Puffs out an orange vapor,
Then spits out from the other end
A smooth, well-written paper.

Unfortunately, the verse on the chapter opener page describes something that does not exist. There is no write-o-matic; there is only the writing process—easy to talk about, but not always easy to do. However, the more familiar you become with the writing process, the more you experiment with your own strategies for writing and practice the ones in this book, the easier and more automatic writing will become for you.

Writing is not a single act, but a process composed of several steps. As with most processes—in-line skating, playing the clarinet, or surfing the Internet—it is sometimes easier to do than to analyze. When people try to analyze how they write, their descriptions of the process are uniquely their own. Yet from a sea of individual accounts, the same steps emerge.

One writer, Nick, describes the process this way:

I think first. It's not like it pops out of me; it brews in me for a while. The next thing I do is to begin writing ideas down, good or bad. Once I get the ideas down in rough form—I wouldn't call it an outline necessarily—I write it out from beginning to end. Then the revision process begins, because I'm always unhappy with the first thing I write. It's a thorough examination: cutting, connecting thoughts, shifting ideas around, adding new ideas. I really go back to the beginning, because every time I revise, I have to think more. Then I write out the second draft from beginning to end. I don't worry about punctuation or spelling. I keep revising until I think I've got it, then I start worrying about periods and commas. Then it's ready for another reader.

Reader's *Tip* — Focus on the Writing Process: Completing the Steps

Think of the steps that went into making and putting up this sign. Someone planned it right down to the style of the letters and the black border. A company manufactured it and passed it through quality control. A city, state, or county purchased the signs and put them up. Yet clearly, something went wrong during the process.

Taking shortcuts in any process, including the writing process, can result in embarrassing mistakes. So even if "Dash it off and hand it in" has been your motto up until now, give the writing process a chance, and allow yourself time to complete all the steps. That way, whatever you are writing—a paper for school, a memo for work, a purchasing request, a legal document—will reflect your best effort.

Reflect on It

1. Write down something you do that requires several steps.
2. List the steps in the order in which you do them.
3. Is it a flexible process, like the writing process, in that you can go back to a previous step if you need to? Or is it a process more like cooking, in that once the cake is in the oven, it's too late to add another egg?
4. Finally, think about the importance of each step in your process. What would happen if you left out a step?

The Writing Process

Although everyone approaches writing a little differently, most of us follow a process similar to the one just described. The writer in the example above is, in fact, following all of the steps in the **writing process:** prewriting, planning, drafting, revising, and proofreading.

Prewriting

"I think first."

Prewriting covers a range of activity from casually thinking about your topic to doing a prewriting exercise to get your thoughts on paper. You will find that you prewrite throughout the writing process. When you are sitting at a traffic light and an example to illustrate one of your points pops into your head, you are prewriting. When you realize that a paragraph isn't working the way you planned and you stop to figure out another approach, you are prewriting. Prewriting *is* thinking, and the more thought you put into your paper, the stronger it will be.

Planning

"I get the ideas down in rough form—I wouldn't call it an outline."

Careful and thoughtful **planning** makes an essay easier for you to write and easier for your readers to read. Your plan may include a thesis statement, a statement of the main idea. Because it states the main idea, the thesis statement is the cornerstone of your essay. It may change more than once as your essay takes shape; still, it is important to have a main idea and to keep it in sight. After all, if you are not certain of your main point, you can be sure that your readers won't be, either. Besides a thesis, your plan will probably include an informal outline. Don't be afraid that planning will waste your time. Careful planning—or lack of it— always shows in the final draft.

Drafting

"I write it out from beginning to end."

Drafting your essay can be easy or difficult. Sometimes your ideas flow freely. At other times, your thoughts grind to a standstill, and you become frustrated and think you have nothing to say. Both situations are a normal part of the creative process. If you get stuck during the drafting process, don't quit in frustration. What is happening to you happens to all writers. Write through the problem or, if necessary, return to the planning or prewriting stage.

The best advice on drafting is "don't procrastinate." Do your planning and prewriting early. If you have a project that involves research or outside reading, do those things early to give them time to sink in before you write. Writing is easier if you plan ahead, and getting an early start prevents last-minute panic. Then if you get stuck during the drafting process, you will have time to work out the problem rather than going into emergency mode because your paper is due the next day.

As you draft your essay or paragraph, don't worry about grammar, spelling, or punctuation. Stopping to look up a comma rule will only distract you. Concentrate on ideas and save proofreading for later.

If your word processing program is one that highlights or underlines mistakes as you write, then turn the spelling and grammar checker off until you are ready to proofread. You will appreciate your word processing software much more if it does not interrupt you as you write.

Revising

"I'm always unhappy with the first thing I write."

In its Latin roots, the word revising means "seeing again." Revising is difficult because it is hard to see your work with the eyes of a reader. Writers often see what they meant to say rather than what they really said. Sometimes they take for granted background knowledge that the reader may not have. To overcome these difficulties, put your draft aside for a day or so before trying to revise it. With twenty-four hours between writing and revising, you will see your paper more clearly. It is also helpful to let someone else look at your work—a friend, classmate, or relative. Ask the person to focus on the content of your paper rather than on grammar, spelling, or punctuation. Ask which ideas are clear and which ones need more explanation. Ask how well your examples illustrate the points you have made. A reader's comments can help you see your paper in a new light.

Don't be afraid of making big changes during revision. Throwing a whole paragraph out and starting over may keep an essay on track. Changing the paragraph order sometimes gives your message just the emphasis you want. Or you may find a first draft contains just a seed of what you really want to say. Don't be afraid to start over. The first words you write are not written in stone.

One word of advice—if you don't know how to use a computer, learn. Taking an essay through multiple drafts and major changes is much easier on a computer. Once you learn to write on a computer, the essays, term papers, and reports you write in college will look less intimidating.

Proofreading

"Then I start worrying about periods and commas."

Proofreading is the final polish that you put on your paragraph. When you proofread, consider such matters as grammar, spelling, and word choice. Replace vague words with specific words, and mercilessly cut words that are not carrying their weight. Look at connections, making sure ideas flow smoothly from one sentence to the next. Because the stages of the writing process overlap, you have probably done some minor proofreading along the way. Before the final proofreading, set the piece of writing aside for a time. Then proofread it once more to give it the polish of a finished piece.

An Important Point

If you go through the writing process expecting a series of sequential steps like those involved in changing your car's oil, you may think the process is not working for you. However, writing a five-hundred-word essay is not a sequential process but a repetitive one, more like driving a car than changing its oil.

If you take a five-hundred-mile trip, the steps you follow might be described as "Turn on the ignition. Put the car in drive. Accelerate. Brake. Put the car in park. Turn off the ignition." Yet it is not that simple. During a five-hundred-mile journey, you repeat each step not once but several times, and sometimes you stop for rest or fuel.

Writing an essay works the same way. You may list the steps as "prewrite, plan, draft, revise, proofread," but again, it is not that simple. You may change the order of paragraphs as you write the first draft or correct a spelling mistake as you revise. Sometimes you repeat a step several times. You probably even stop for rest or fuel. Eventually, both processes—driving and writing—take you where you want to go.

exercise 11.1   ## The Writing Process

Answer the following questions to review your knowledge of the writing process.

1. The five steps in the writing process are ——————, ——————, ——————, —————— , and ——————.

2. The "thinking step" in the writing process is called ——————.

3. The part of the writing process that involves correcting grammar and punctuation is called ——————.

4. Major changes would most likely be made during the —————— step in the writing process.

5. —————— True or false? The steps in the writing process often overlap.

The Writing Process: Carla's Essay

This section follows the development of one writer's essay from start to finish. In writing her essay, Carla went through several forms of prewriting and made two different outlines. She talked with members of her writing group and her instructor, and she wrote two rough drafts. (Only the first rough draft is shown here because the final draft reflects all of the changes made.) Before turning in her final draft, Carla also proofread the essay once from top to bottom and twice from bottom to top. Then she asked a member of her writing group to look over the final draft for any mistakes she had overlooked.

The steps that Carla goes through are steps that you will take as you learn the writing process. You will also share some of her frustrations. But like Carla, you will probably find that what seems difficult at first is attainable, one step at a time.

Carla's Assignment Carla's instructor handed out a list of three essay topics. Carla chose to write on this one:

> Write an essay about one of your roles in life and the emotions it makes you feel. Discuss positive aspects, negative aspects, or both, but be sure to tie your discussion to specific emotional reactions.

Carla's instructor suggested that the students try one or more forms of prewriting, then make an outline. Earlier, the class had been divided into writing groups of four or five people who would critique and support one another during the term. The instructor suggested that the writing groups meet to discuss each student's outline. Then, each student would write a rough draft to bring to an individual writing conference with the instructor.

Carla's Prewriting

Working on a computer, Carla tried a form of prewriting called invisible writing. (For more information on invisible writing and other forms of prewriting, see Chapter 12.) In this prewriting, Carla did not worry about grammar or spelling. Instead, she focused on gathering ideas. Her prewriting is reproduced here without correction.

> Roles, roles. I have many roles in life. I am a student, a worker, a mother, a daughter, a friend. And I have roles within those roles. With my daughter I am a teacher, a doctor, a disciplinarian, a playmate. With my mother I am sometimes child, sometimes adult. At work I feel competent and at school I often feel lost. As a modern woman I have to do it all, work, school, motherhood, the whole bit and still stay sane. It's juggling roles that gives me such headaches. I get so stressed sometimes when I have to study for a test and I am beat from working all day and Alisa needs her bath and a story. There is so much to say I don't know where to start. And what about the emotions connected with all that. Sometimes I am happy, sometimes I am too tired to feel anything, sometimes I am proud of all I do and sometimes I could just cry from exhaustion and frustration. I don't know what else to say and I don't feel any closer to getting an essay written. I am afraid this is not working for me.

Later, Carla followed up her invisible writing by brainstorming, focusing on her role as a mother.

> Role—Mother
> Everything I do is for Alisa
> school
> work
> reading to her
> tucking her in at night
> asking about her day
> spending time with her
> making sure she knows her grandparents, has a family connection
> working hard so her future can be secure
> want to be someone she can look up to
> give up a lot but get a lot in return

Carla's Outline As she looked over her brainstorming, Carla saw that many of the duties of her role as a mother were focused on her child's present needs, and others on Alisa's future. She also saw a possible connection to the past through Alisa's grandparents. She decided to structure her outline around her child's past, present, and future.

> Outline
> Thesis: As a mother, it is my job to see that my daughter is connected to the past, has her present needs met, and is ready for the future.
> Paragraph 1—Connect her to the past:
>   1. Teach her what I have learned
>   2. Make sure she is connected to a previous generation through grandparents
> Paragraph 2—Take care of her present needs:
>   1. Work to see that she is provided for
>   2. Spend time with her
> Paragraph 3—The future:
>   1. Go to school to take care of her future
>   2. Make sure her future needs are met and that she can go to college

Carla's Writing Group Meets

Next, Carla met with her writing group. A transcript of the portion of the session dealing with Carla's outline appears here.

Transcript: Writing Group Session, Wednesday, October 3, 2:10 p.m.

Brenda: Okay, who wants to go first? Antonio?

Antonio: Not me. Carla?

Carla: Well, I just brought an outline. I'll go first. (Carla passes out copies of her outline, and the group reads.)

Antonio: I like it. I like the way you include past, present, and future. It gives the outline a good flow.

Carla: You're just saying that because I got you off the hook. You didn't have to go first. (Laughter.)

Thanh: I like the chronological order, too. But there's one thing I don't see. Where's the emotion?

Carla: What?

Thanh: Remember the assignment said to connect the role to the emotions it made us feel?

Carla: Oh, no! That's right. Now, after all the work I've done, I'll have to change it. Maybe I can just go back and put in how I feel about teaching, working, and going to school.

Kelly: How do you feel about it?

Carla: I feel good. It makes me happy to know that I'm doing all I can for her.

Antonio: No tough times? No bad emotions?

Carla: (laughs) Plenty. I am always tired—no energy, no money. Sometimes it gets me down.

Brenda: Tell me about it. My kids are grown, but I remember. But I wouldn't raise a kid today for anything. The world is too scary.

Carla: I know. Sometimes I lie awake at night and worry about all the things that could happen.

Thanh: Well, why don't you put some of that in. You know, reality. Tell us what it's really like.

Brenda: I agree. That will make it more interesting.

Carla: Okay. I'll try it. What about my three points? Should I keep them?

Brenda: Maybe. Or you could make the emotions your three points.

Antonio: But don't get rid of that past, present, and future part. I like that.

Carla: Thanks, everybody. You've really helped. Okay, Antonio, now it's your turn.

Carla's Journal Entry and New Outline

After talking to her writing group, Carla wrote a journal entry, then made a new outline.

I can't believe I forgot that the assignment said the essay should be about my emotions. Well, let's see. What are the emotions I feel about being a mother? First of all, I feel an overwhelming and protective love for my daughter. I never knew I could feel that way about any living thing. But I also feel discouraged and downhearted many times. I work hard and just barely get by. I can't remember the last time I bought a new outfit for Alisa or for myself. Financial troubles are the worst. And like Brenda said, it is scary raising a child these days. Some nights I lie awake terrified about what could happen to her or what could happen to me that would keep me from taking care of her. I also feel angry when I hear people talk about single parents not being able to raise their children with the right values. This is not a perfect world I did not create it, but I have to live in it and I do the best I can. If they haven't walked in my shoes, they can't judge me.

So far, the emotions I can pick out are happiness, love, discouragement, terror and anger. Maybe I can write about some of those.

Carla's new outline:

Thesis:
Since my daughter Alisa was born, I have lived with the joy, the pain, and often, the sheer terror of raising a child alone.
Joy:
   1. Seeing her at birth
   2. Watching her grow and form a personality
Pain:
   1. Being a single parent
   2. Not having enough money
   3. Working long hours along with going to school

> Terror:
> 1. Something could happen to me—illness or whatever—and keep me from taking care of her.
> 2. Things that could happen to her

Carla's Rough Draft with Notes From her new outline, Carla wrote a rough draft. Then she met with her instructor for a conference on her draft. Carla's rough draft, with notes she made at the conference with her instructor, follows.

Since my daughter Alisa was born, I have lived with the joy, the pain, and also the sheer terror of raising a child alone. Being a single parent can happen to anyone but I never thought it would happen to me. I had dreams of a marriage that would last forever and of strong, healthy children who would always feel secure in the love of two full-time parents.

> Move the thesis to the end of the introduction.

Raising my daughter Alisa is a joy that I would not trade for anything. The first time I saw her, I thought she was beautiful even though to anyone else, she probably was not much to look at. Watching her grow into a real little human being with a personality that is not mine or her grandparents' or her father's but uniquely her own has been a delight. Seeing her develop as a person has been and will always continue to be my chief joy in life.

> Add description. What did she look like? How did the sight of her affect me? What is her personality like? Make the last sentence less wordy.

At first, I was unhappy not having her father to share the joy of Alisa's first word or to sit up with me through the night when she had a fever. But that kind of pain goes away. What remains is the constant weight of struggling to keep up financially. I wait for child support checks that may or may not come, and if they do not come, I do without. Between school and work, my day often lasts twelve hours. But I know the rewards of building a life for myself and my daughter will one day outweigh the pain I have endured.

> Add a topic sentence to this paragraph. Add more support about the ways I cope.

Parenthood has brought with it feelings of terror. No matter how loving and watchful I am, there are so many things that are beyond my control. Sometimes, I wake in the lonely hours before dawn and think, What if something happens to me? What if I die or am in an accident and can't take care of Alisa? Worse yet, is the thought that something could happen to her. Every time I hear of a child who is seriously ill or who has been badly hurt, my heart freezes. When I see television news stories about trusted scout leaders, teachers, or pastors being arrested for child molestation or child pornography, I am reminded that I can take nothing for granted. Fortunately, the business of daily living usually keeps those thoughts away, otherwise, I don't know how I would stay sane.

> *No major changes.*

Raising a child is joy even though it is a full-time job, and it is even harder when money is scarce and the world seems uncertain. Still, I would not trade the joys of raising my daughter for all the wealth and security in the world.

> *Conclusion is okay.*

CARLA'S FINAL DRAFT

Sandoval 1

Carla Sandoval
English 101
Professor De Luca
7 May 2007

My Feelings about Motherhood

Being a single parent can happen to anyone, but I never thought it would happen to me. I had dreams of a marriage that would last forever and of strong, healthy children who would always feel secure in the love of two full-time parents. But life is not a fairy tale, and dreams don't always come true. Since my daughter Alisa was born, I have lived with the joy, the pain, and the sheer terror of raising a child alone.

Raising my daughter Alisa is a joy that I would not trade for anything. The first time I saw her red, wrinkled face, swollen eyes, and the thin fuzz of hair plastered to her tiny head, I was certain that I would do anything to protect her and keep her safe. Watching her personality develop has been a delight. From the start, she has had incredible focus. At two months, she peered at people

(continued)

intently, as if she were memorizing their faces. At two years, that intentness turned into a stubborn insistence on exploring every cabinet and emptying every drawer and shelf she could reach. Now, at five, she still has that same focus. I see it when she stacks her blocks or looks at her books, shutting out the world in her concentration on the task. She is my joy.

Along with joy, single parenthood holds special pain. Alisa's father was not there to share the joy of Alisa's first word or to sit up with me through the night when she had a fever. But that kind of pain goes away. What remains is the constant weight of financial struggle. I wait for child support checks, and if they do not come, I do without. I scour yard sales for good used clothing for the two of us and stretch my paycheck so that I can still buy groceries at the end of the month. I leave Alisa at my mother's and head out for a day that, between school and work, often lasts twelve hours. If it weren't for Alisa, I don't know how I could endure those long grinding days. But I know the rewards of building a life for myself and my daughter will one day outweigh the pain I have endured.

Parenthood has brought with it feelings of terror that are even more intense because I am raising my child alone. I know that no matter how loving and watchful I am, many things are beyond my control. Sometimes, I wake in the lonely hours before dawn and think, "What if I die or am in an accident and can't take care of Alisa?" Worse yet is the thought that something could happen to her. Every time I hear of a child who is seriously ill or who has been badly hurt, my heart freezes. When I see television news stories about trusted scout leaders or pastors being arrested for child molestation or child pornography, I am reminded that I can take nothing for granted. Fortunately, the daily rush usually keeps those thoughts away; otherwise, I don't know how I would stay sane.

Raising a child is a full-time job, and it is even harder when money is scarce and the world seems uncertain. Still, I would not trade the joys of raising my daughter for all the wealth and security in the world.

Carla's Approach to Writing—and Yours Carla's final draft is the product of many hours' thought and work, and is at least partly a result of her willingness to listen to the advice and comments of others. It is also a result of her willingness to discard ideas that don't work.

Writing is a process of trial and error—sometimes it feels like mostly error. Even experienced writers often find writing difficult, often wonder each time they write if they have anything worthwhile to say or the ability to say it. In addition, the very act of writing makes the writer vulnerable. Your words and experiences are a part of you, and putting them on paper for others' examination can make you feel exposed. So why should you bother to write? You should bother because, at its best, writing can give you power and joy and the ability to move others. Fortunately, writing is a skill that improves with practice, and if you give it serious effort, you will amaze yourself. The following list, "Five Quick Takes on Writing," may help you put the task of writing in perspective.

Reader's *Tip*   Five Quick Takes on Writing

1. **Take it a step at a time.** Writing is often a slow process, and it always requires thought.
2. **Take it seriously.** The ability to write clearly and well will benefit you academically, professionally, and personally throughout your life.
3. **Take it easy.** Don't expect yourself to be perfect.
4. **Take it to the limit.** Stretch the limits of your imagination. Refuse to limit yourself by labeling yourself a poor writer.
5. **Take it with you.** Writing is a vital part of the real world. Make it a part of your life.

exercise 11.2   **The Ideal Conditions for Writing**

In a group of three or four, discuss the ideal conditions for writing. Think about questions such as these: What tools do you enjoy working with? Do you write best with music or in absolute silence? Do you like having others around, or do you prefer to be alone? Do you need coffee or snacks when you write? Do you need room to pace, or do you think best seated in front of a desk or computer? After each group member has contributed, see what differences and similarities exist among members of your group. Have a spokesperson report your group's findings to the rest of the class.

If You Hate the Thought of a Step-by-Step Approach . . .

This section is for those of you who rebel at the idea of a step-by-step approach like the one described in this chapter and outlined in the writing assignments at the end of the chapter. Although prewriting, planning, drafting, revising, and proofreading are identifiable steps in the writing process, there's no law that says everyone has to approach them in exactly the same way.

For some people, a step-by-step approach does not come naturally. These people have a thinking style that is most often called "right-brained" or "holistic." The human brain is divided into two halves, or hemispheres, and most people are wired to rely heavily on the left hemisphere—the half responsible for logical, sequential, step-by-step thinking. Some people, however, rely more heavily on the right half of the brain, the part responsible for seeing the whole, for thinking in images, and for flashes of insight.

The following questions may help you decide if you are a right-brained thinker.

1. If you were asked to analyze how you write, would your answer be, "I don't know. I just do it"?
2. When you are required to turn in an outline, do you do it last, after you have written the paper?

3. If you were asked to describe your usual prewriting technique, would you say, "I never prewrite"?
4. Do you often arrive at the right answer to math problems without following the steps?
5. Do you have a hard time getting detail into your writing?
6. Are you a "big picture person" rather than a "detail person"?

If you answered yes to three or more of these questions, you may have sometimes been seen as a rebel because you don't always follow a step-by-step, conventional approach to your work. But the chances are that whatever other characteristics you possess, you are also a right-brained writer.

Right-brained people are often intuitive, seeing the big picture before others do. They have a strong creative streak. They sometimes grasp ideas easily without knowing why or understanding how. But unlike their methodical, list-making, left-brained brothers and sisters, right-brained people often have trouble with the details. Planning isn't in their natures, and they tend not to have systems or specific steps to rely on. Whatever the task is, they "just do it."

If you are right-brained, does that mean that the methods in this text won't work for you? No. They *will* work. But you may have to work at them a bit harder. Give them a chance. Don't count them out until you have had enough experience with them to determine whether they work for you or not.

There are additional strategies you can use. Unlike more conventional methods, the following tips for right-brained writers were crafted with you in mind. These ideas may give you the extra boost you need to harness your creativity and let your right-brained way of thinking work for you, not against you. If your thinking style is left-brained, read on anyway. There may be something here that you can use along with the logical, step-by-step approach that works so well for you.

Tips for Right-Brained Writers Find your most creative time and use it for writing. Some people find that they are at their best in the mornings. Others find that their creative juices begin to flow around 9:00 or 10:00 P.M. Writing will be easier if you schedule it during your natural period of creativity.

Use your rough draft as your prewriting. Because you think in terms of the whole, you may find it easier to do a rough draft than to prewrite. Consider your rough draft a form of prewriting, to be extensively revised before you turn it in.

Give your brain an assignment. When you have writing to do, let your right brain work on it while you are doing other things. At the beginning of the day, for instance, look over the assignment for a few minutes. Then come back to it in the evening and reap the benefits of having worked on the topic subconsciously. Or think about your topic before you go to sleep at night and write in the morning. This technique can work not only in prewriting but also in revising.

Realize that doing the grunt work is a necessary evil. Right-brained people are less likely to put in the time it takes to master the basics because doing so may be tedious and boring to them. They are also less likely to plan. But even the most creative people need self-discipline. It's a hard lesson to learn, but mastering the basics is essential to creative work. Singers spend endless time on breath control and scales. Artists learn anatomy and basic drawing. It is those efforts that set them free to do their best work. The payoff in mastering the basics is that once you learn them, you can forget about them. They will be second nature. The same goes for planning. Once you have made a plan, you are free to do the creative work. Doing the grunt work now always pays off in more freedom later.

Make a commitment to writing. Many professional writers are right-brained and face the same resistance that you do. Invariably, they say that the only way they can maintain the extended effort it takes to write books, plays, or novels is to have a routine and to write every day.

Review of the Paragraph

This text will guide you step by step through the process of writing an essay. Before you begin essay writing, take the time to briefly review the single-paragraph composition.

A paragraph has a topic sentence that gives it direction and lets the reader know where the paragraph is headed. It has strong support for the topic sentence in the form of details and examples, all of which contribute to paragraph unity by supporting the topic sentence. Each sentence flows smoothly into the next, providing coherence. Often, the paragraph ends with a summary sentence that restates the topic sentence and brings the paragraph to a strong close.

The Topic Sentence

A topic sentence does two things. First, it presents the **general topic** of the paragraph. Then it makes a **specific point** about that topic.

EXAMPLE

 topic   specific point about that topic
Balancing school and family life can be difficult.

 topic   specific point about that topic
My sense of humor often gets me in trouble.

The Supporting Sentences

A topic sentence provides direction—the road map for a paragraph—but supporting sentences supply the scenery. While topic sentences are broad and general, large enough to encompass the entire paragraph, supporting sentences are specific, giving details and examples.

The Summary Sentence

A summary sentence ends the paragraph. Sometimes it sums up the points made in the paragraph, sometimes it restates the topic sentence, but it always brings the paragraph to a graceful and definite close.

A Model Paragraph

Reader's *Tip* ———— People-Watching at the Convenience Store

Topic sentence ———— My part-time job as a convenience store clerk allows to me to observe a fascinating variety of people. If I work the morning shift, my

First supporting point ———— customers are mostly neatly dressed office workers rushing to work. They stop to buy gas for their morning commute or to grab a cup of coffee on the way to the office. They dash up to the register in a cloud of aftershave or perfume, pay for their purchases, and quickly leave. In the early afternoon, the store fills with children who attend a nearby el-

Second supporting point ———— ementary school. They flock into the store in giggling groups and head straight for the candy aisle. The children take their time choosing fruit-flavored bubble gum, sour candies, and chocolate bars. They bring their purchases and their money to the register, then noisily flock out again, happy to be out of school for the day. If I work the late afternoon shift, I see laborers, grimy and exhausted, buying a single can of beer

Third supporting point ———— or a lottery ticket. They are young men with old, tired eyes, yet most of them offer a smile or make a joke as they count out crumpled dollar bills with callused hands. With such a wide variety of customers, my

Summary sentence ———— job at the convenience store is never dull.

Writing Assignment 1 Writing and You Write a paragraph describing your attitudes toward writing. Use the following steps.

Prewrite: Jot down a few of the words that come to mind when you think of writing. Think of any significant experiences you have had that have shaped your attitude toward writing. Consider your writing habits. Are you organized? Do you procrastinate?

Plan: Look over your prewriting. Try to sum up your attitude toward writing in a single word or phrase, and then construct an opening sentence for your paragraph using that word or phrase. Use one of the following sentences, filling in the blank with your word or phrase, or construct your own sentence.

- My attitude toward writing is —————.
- When I think about writing, I feel —————.
- My feelings about writing have always been ————— ones.

Once you have constructed an opening sentence, decide how to organize your paragraph. A couple of possibilities are listed here.

1. Take a historical approach, describing the influences that have shaped your writing. Use chronological (time) order.
2. Take a step-by-step approach, describing what you do and how you feel as you go through a writing assignment.

Finally, complete the planning stage by making an outline that briefly lists the points you plan to make in support of your opening sentence.

Draft: Write out a rough draft of your paragraph. Focus on expressing your ideas rather than on grammar and punctuation.

Revise: Read over your rough draft. Have you left out anything important? Is each idea clearly expressed? Does the paragraph flow smoothly? Is the sequence of ideas logical and effective? If possible, ask a classmate to look over your rough draft with the same questions in mind. Then revise your paragraph, incorporating any necessary changes.

Proofread: Check your paragraph for mistakes in spelling, grammar, or punctuation. Look at each sentence individually. Then proofread once more. You have now completed all the steps in the writing process.

Writing Assignment 2   Reasons for Attending College   People go to college for many reasons. Some attend college to fulfill lifelong goals, others to escape a dead-end job, still others to fulfill their families' expectations. What has brought you to college?

Write a paragraph discussing your reasons for attending college, using the follo-wing steps.

Prewrite: Take a sheet of paper and begin with the words "When I . . . " Write for five or ten minutes without stopping, then look to see what you have. Does your prewriting focus more on the past (When I was a child, I used to line up my dolls and pretend they were students . . .) or on the future (When I receive my nursing degree, I will be able to fulfill many of my dreams . . .)? Seeing whether your focus is on the past or on the future will help you to decide on the direction your paragraph should take.

Plan: Look over your prewriting and underline the most important words and ideas. Then construct an opening sentence that states the central idea you want to express in your paragraph. Some typical opening sentences follow.

- All of my reasons for attending college are rooted in the past.
- Attending college is one way I can ensure a brighter future for my children
- Attending college will help me to realize my dream of becoming a nurse.
- For me, attending college is a way out of a dead-end job.

Once you have constructed an opening sentence, decide how to organize your paragraph. A couple of possibilities are listed here.

1. Take a historical approach, describing the influences that shaped your deci-sion to attend college. Use chronological (time) order.
2. Take a point-by-point approach, listing your reasons one by one.

Finally, complete the planning stage by making an outline that briefly lists the points you plan to make in support of your opening sentence.

Draft: Write out a rough draft of your paragraph. Focus on expressing your ideas rather than on grammar and punctuation.

Revise: Read over your rough draft. Have you left out anything important? Is each idea clearly expressed? Does the paragraph flow smoothly? Is the sequence of ideas logical and effective? If possible, ask a classmate to look over your rough draft with the same questions in mind. Then revise your paragraph, incorporating any necessary changes.

Proofread: Check your paragraph for mistakes in spelling, grammar, or punctuation. Look at each sentence individually. Then proofread once more. You have now completed all the steps in the writing process.

12 Preparing to Write

Dream
　　　Invent
Play
　　　Discover
Imagine
　　　Reflect
Consider

Prewriting

Prewriting is the first step in the writing process. It is the act of gathering your thoughts on a topic. Depending on the assignment you are given, it may also include narrowing your topic to a manageable size. Prewriting begins the moment you receive an assignment. Immediately, a part of your mind begins to gather information. However, it usually takes a bit of effort to bring that information to the surface. The prewriting methods in this chapter are designed to jump-start the writing process by helping you collect your thoughts on a topic and get them on paper.

Reader's _Tip_ — Focus on Preparing to Write:
Finding Inspiration

 When Emilio Estevez was in the process of writing Bobby, a screenplay about the day Robert F. Kennedy was shot in the kitchen of the Ambassador Hotel, he allowed writer's block to stop him from writing the script for a year. Finally, Estevez checked into a hotel in Pismo Beach, California, to finish the job. He casually mentioned the project to a check-in clerk, who told him that she had been in the kitchen of the Ambassador Hotel on that day. Her story gave him the inspiration he needed to create a new character and finish the script.

When you write, do you sometimes have difficulty coming up with ideas, or, like Emilio Estevez, get stuck after you come up with the idea? Unlike Estevez, you don't have years to do your writing projects. You need a reliable way of generating ideas. This chapter will help you find various ways to tap into your imagination so you can get your ideas on paper.

Reflect on It

Whether you are taking a class or pursuing a career, you need ideas. Think about how you best generate ideas. Is your mind most open to new ideas when you are talking with others or when you are alone? Do you need to "sleep on it" to get good ideas, or do they come to you quickly? Think about a time when you solved a problem with a creative idea. How did you come up with it?

Source:
http://www.urbancinefile.com.au/home/view.asp?a=12867&s=Interviews

Why Prewrite?

It's tempting to skip prewriting. After all, why take the time to prewrite when you can just sit down and start writing? The answer is that taking a few extra minutes to prewrite is more efficient than not prewriting. Prewriting is worth your time for several reasons.

- *Prewriting opens a doorway to your thoughts.* Your mind does not offer instant access to its content. Bits of memory and stored knowledge reveal themselves gradually, one by one. Prewriting allows your mind time to reveal its knowledge on the subject.
- *Prewriting helps prevent writer's block.* Prewriting can never be wrong, so the process of prewriting gives you a certain immunity to writer's block, the paralysis that comes from feeling that every word must be perfect and every sentence correct.
- *Prewriting builds confidence.* By the time you finish prewriting, you will probably find that you have more to say about your subject than you imagined. Therefore, you will write more strongly and confidently.
- *Prewriting sparks creativity.* When you are not worried about whether your ideas are right or wrong, you are more likely to think creatively and let your thoughts flow freely.
- *Prewriting tells you when to quit.* If you just can't get a topic going, maybe it's not worth pursuing. Try something else.

Prewriting Methods

The aim of all **prewriting methods** is the same: to help you get ideas on paper. At this point in the writing process, it is not the quality of ideas that counts, but the quantity.

When you are ready to prewrite, sit at the computer or in a comfortable spot with pen and paper. Relax your mind and body, and remind yourself that prewriting is a playful exercise of imagination and that it is okay to write down anything that comes to mind. As for the part of your mind that automatically jumps in to criticize what you think and say, give it some time off. Your purpose in prewriting is to put down every thought on your topic, no matter how ridiculous it seems. Later, you can discard what is not usable. But while you are prewriting, there is no good or bad, no right or wrong.

Some of the methods may feel awkward at first, but try them all. One will be right for you.

Brainstorming

Brainstorming, a listing technique, is one of the easiest prewriting techniques. To brainstorm, take a few minutes to list whatever comes to mind on your topic, no matter how strange it seems. Your purpose is not to censor or come up with the "right" items for your list, but to generate ideas.

EXAMPLE   Here's how one writer, Tamiko, approached a brainstorming exercise on clothing.

stores	department stores
fashion models	occasions
slick magazines	job interviews
anorexia	professional dress
expensive	uniforms
name brands	proms
my red dress	my favorites—old jeans
designer labels	and T-shirts
even children are fashion-conscious	"Clothes make the man" (or woman!)
secondhand stores	

When Tamiko looked over her prewriting, she decided that the part of it that most interested her was the quotation "Clothes make the man." She wasn't quite sure which side she was on, so she did a two-sided brainstorming. Though Tamiko used brainstorming, she could have chosen any form of prewriting to explore both sides of the issue. Her brainstorming follows.

EXAMPLE

Clothes make the man (or woman).

Agree	Disagree
People judge us by the outside	It's what's inside that counts
Clothing tells people about us	
Tells our economic status	Clothing can hide the truth
Sometimes reveals professional status	People who can't look beyond clothing are shallow
Shows our sense of style	
Different dress for different ages	
Helps us express our personality	
Tells how much we care about appearance	
It's all people have to go on until they know us	

When she looked at her brainstorming, Tamiko was surprised to find that her evidence favored the "agree" side of the issue. "I thought I looked beyond superficial things like clothes," she said, "but I really have more evidence to support the statement than to disagree with it."

Like Tamiko, you may find that willingness to explore both sides of an issue leads you in an unexpected direction.

exercise 12.1   ## Brainstorming

Brainstorm on one of the following topics, then see if you have a focus for a possible essay. Feel free to explore more than one side of your idea.

1. Do credit cards do more harm than good?
2. Is it better to be a leader or a follower?
3. Are manners necessary in the modern world?
4. Do video surveillance systems protect people or violate their privacy?
5. If two people are in love, should large differences in their ages matter?

Freewriting

Freewriting is nonstop writing on a topic for a set period of time. The point of freewriting is that your flow of words never ceases; your pen never stops moving. If you have nothing to say, repeat your last thought again and again until a new thought replaces it. Do not worry about spelling, about clarity, or about whether your thoughts are logically connected. Just write.

EXAMPLE   Burt's freewriting on goals draws on his own experience.

> I am supposed to do a freewriting on goals and I can't think of anything to say. I should talk about my goals, I guess, but I haven't even decided on a major yet. My goal has mostly been to get through each day. My sociology professor said that one characteristic of poverty is a focus on today. A poor person wonders, "What will I eat today?" not "How will I provide for my future?" People who are poor can't afford to think of tomorrow because today is such a struggle. I am goal-poor. I have accomplished so little in my life that I feel afraid to set goals.
>
> I guess I fear failure. I am even afraid to commit to a major for fear I won't be able to do it. I can set little goals, like making an A on a test or studying for two hours in the evening, but I just don't set big goals. I can still hear my father saying, "You will never accomplish anything." Maybe it's not too late. I am going in the right direction by starting school.

exercise 12.2   **Freewriting**

Freewrite on one of the following topics, then see if you have a focus for a possible essay.

1. children
2. friendship
3. morality
4. television
5. physical appearance

Focused Freewriting

Focused freewriting helps you to zoom in on a topic and to bring ideas into closer focus. Rather than ranging outward in all directions, a focused freewriting examines a narrow topic. Use focused freewriting when the assigned topic is a specific question or when you have narrowed your topic through a previous prewriting. A focused freewriting is just like any other freewriting, but with a narrower range.

EXAMPLE   Here is how one writer, Eric, handled a focused freewriting on the question "What rules of etiquette are important today?" His finished essay appears in Chapter 19.

> Some people today totally ignore manners, as if they are not important. Some of the old rules are gone but new ones replace them. Just like that old guy in the health club who said he never opened doors for women. He seemed to think that he didn't have to be polite anymore. That's wrong. Manners is just basic consideration for other people. Maybe there was a time when it was which fork to use, that kind of thing, but now that the world is so crowded, that stuff matters less and respecting people's space matters more. New rules come up for new situations, too. There are rules for computers and email and rules for cell phones and beepers. All the old stereotypes are out and manners are just practical ways of getting along in the world.

exercise 12.3   **Focused Freewriting**

Do a focused freewriting on one of the following topics.

1. What kinds of risks are good to take?
2. Why are people superstitious?

3. What kinds of music do you enjoy?
4. What one characteristic is most important in a friend?
5. Is family more or less important than it was in your grandparents' day?

Invisible Writing: A Computer Technique

Invisible writing is a freewriting technique especially for writing on a computer. Turn on your computer and, once you have a blank screen in front of you, type the words "Invisible Writing" at the top of the page. Then turn your monitor off or adjust the contrast until the words are no longer visible and your screen is completely dark.

Freewrite for five or ten minutes. It is especially important not to worry about spelling errors. With this method, you can hardly avoid them. At first, you may feel strange, even anxious, pouring your words into the dark computer screen. Soon, though, your fingers and your thoughts will fly.

exercise 12.4 | **Invisible Writing**

If you have access to a computer, do an invisible writing on one of the following topics. Then see if you have a focus for an essay.

1. transportation
2. competition
3. grades
4. newspapers
5. littering

Clustering

Clustering is a technique designed to boost your creativity by stimulating both hemispheres, or halves, of your brain. The left brain is the part used in logical tasks that move in 1-2-3 order. When you count to ten, write a sentence, or make an outline, you are using your left hemisphere. Your right hemisphere, on the other hand, specializes in tasks involving imagery or intuition. Since clustering involves both listing (a left-brain task) and drawing (a right-brain task), it allows you to tap both your logical side and your creative side.

To cluster, begin with a circled word—your topic. From there, "map out" associations. Some people branch ideas from the central word like quills on a porcupine. Others group ideas when they cluster, with smaller clusters branching out from larger ones. When this type of cluster is finished, it resembles a biology textbook's diagram of a molecule.

What your diagram looks like does not matter. In clustering, what matters is that you get your thoughts on paper using both images and words.

Look at the following examples of clustering.

EXAMPLE   Here is Kelly's "porcupine" cluster on the topic "If you could change one aspect of your personality, what would it be?"

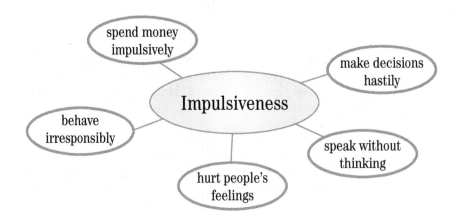

EXAMPLE   Jemal's "molecule" cluster is on the topic "computers."

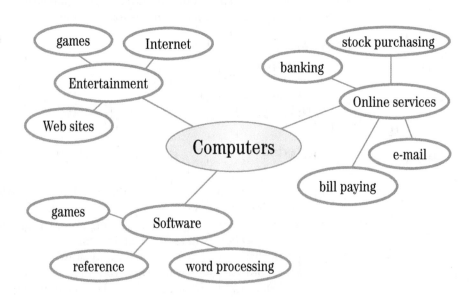

exercise 12.5   **Clustering**

Do a cluster diagram on one of the following topics.

1. managing anger
2. fitness
3. making sacrifices to reach a specific goal
4. automobiles
5. bad habits

Narrowing Your Topic: The Topic-Subtopic Method

If you are given a specific topic such as "Discuss the best way to make a positive impression on your instructor during the first week of class," your prewriting task is relatively easy. You can just begin thinking about the ways to make a good impression in class. In other words, you can begin thinking about supporting your paragraph or essay. However, if you are given a general assignment such as "Write about jobs," or "Write a paragraph about money," or even "Write an essay about a topic of your own choosing," then your task is a much larger one. Entire books have been written about employment, and books and magazines about money take up considerable shelf space in any bookstore. Therefore, you need to narrow and focus the topic so that it is manageable in a short composition.

For some writers, narrowing a topic becomes a natural part of the prewriting process. Others prefer to narrow a topic in a separate step or series of steps.

One way to narrow a topic in a step-by-step fashion is with a simple method called the *topic-subtopic method*. The steps are listed here.

Step 1: Write down the topic.
Step 2: List possible subtopics.
Step 3: Look over the list of subtopics and pick the one you are most interested in. If the subtopic you have chosen is still too broad, then do another narrowing using the same method.

In the following example, Melissa takes a general topic, "college," through three narrowings. In the first narrowing, shown here, she has made a list of subtopics. From that list, she chooses the subtopic "costs." From there, she will repeat the process until she has narrowed the topic to the right size for the paragraph she wants to write.

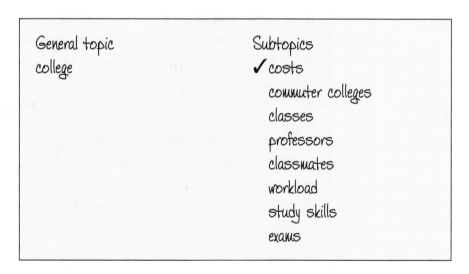

"College costs" is a narrower topic than "college," but it is still a very broad topic. So Melissa does a second narrowing, this time with "college costs" as the general topic.

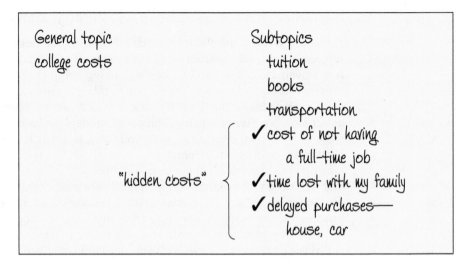

Melissa decides to focus on the last three items in her list, which she labels the "hidden costs" of college. Now, to flesh out the details of her paragraph, she does a freewriting, which follows.

The Hidden Costs of College

When people think about costs of college, they usually think about tuition, books, and the other costs they pay directly from their pockets. But the larger costs may really be the "hidden costs" of college. For example, I could be working at a full-time job and bringing in four times what I make at my part-time job. And because I work and go to school, I seem to have very little time to spend with my husband and my family—my mother and sisters. My grandmother in Seattle died just at the time of finals last winter, and I did not have the time or money to go to her funeral. That's something I regret, but it can never be undone. I also have to consider in those hidden costs the fact that my husband and I could probably be buying a house now if I had a full-time job. It's not that I'm complaining. If I didn't think it would be worth it in the long run, I wouldn't be here. But most people don't realize that you pay not just the direct costs of college, but a lot more when you make the decision to attend.

exercise 12.6   **Narrowing a Topic**

Take one of the following broad topics and narrow it, following the topic-subtopic method previously shown. Take your topic through as many narrowings as are needed to bring it down to paragraph or essay size.

1. the environment
2. alcohol
3. education
4. money
5. commercials

Outlining

Outlining is often the last step in the prewriting process. Once you have used one or more of the other prewriting methods, organizing your thoughts into outline form takes you one step further in the writing process. Forget about the formal outline with its array of Roman numerals, ABCs, and 123s. A short essay calls for a short outline. Your outline may be just a few words jotted on a page, or it may include a thesis statement, topic sentences, and a brief listing of support for each topic sentence. Following are two sample outlines on the same topic.

Outline 1

Benefits of Karate

1. Confidence
    physical confidence
        walk taller and straighter
        not as klutzy
        feel more comfortable with my physical self
    mental confidence
        believe more in my ability to do things
2. Self-discipline
    plan study time and make better grades
    do my homework on weekdays to leave most of the weekend free
    keep my work area neater
3. New view of life
    helps me see life as something I control, not something that controls me
    helps me see that hard work turns desire to succeed into success
    new hopes for future

Outline 2

Thesis:

Karate has given me confidence, self-discipline, and a new view of life.

Topic Sentence 1:

Karate has helped me to become mentally and physically confident.

Topic Sentence 2:

The self-discipline I bring to karate has helped me to be more disciplined in other areas.

Topic Sentence 3:

Seeing my hard work pay off has given me a new view of life and of my future.

exercise 12.7   **Outlining**

Choose one of your practice prewritings and make an outline for a paragraph or essay.

Journal Writing

The word *journal* comes from *jour*, the French word for *day*. **Journal writings,** then, are "daily writings." Journals are usually composed of informal writings on a variety of subjects. A journal allows you to experiment with the techniques you are learning in your writing class. In a journal, the only form of writing you should avoid is "diary mode." An "I-got-up-I-fed-the-dog-I-went-to-school" format makes for dull writing and even duller reading. Write about issues that matter to you. Tell your dreams. Describe your grandfather's tool shed. Work toward detailed writing that follows a logical pattern.

Whether you receive credit for it in class or not, make journal writing a habit. Practice is the only thing that is guaranteed to make you a better writer. Courses and texts are of limited value without time spent alone with a word processor or pen and paper. If you think, "It won't matter because I'll never be a good writer," ask yourself this: How good a driver would you be if the only driving you had done was in a driver education course? You *can* be a better writer. Daily writing in your journal will start you on your way.

Journal Topics
1. What are some reasons for keeping a journal or diary?
2. What are the characteristics of a good student?
3. Discuss a person who has been a mentor or role model to you.
4. A poem by Paul Laurence Dunbar begins, "We wear the mask/That grins and lies . . . " Discuss some of the masks that you wear.
5. Should every able citizen of the United States be required to do some sort of paid public service (not necessarily military service) for a set period of time?
6. What are the reasons some people are unsuccessful in school or at work?
7. Is it necessary for you to own an automobile?
8. Do Americans spend too much time watching television?
9. Is year-round school a good idea?

10. If you could know any one thing about your future, what would you want to know?
11. Have you ever had a dream that was so vivid it seemed real? Describe it.
12. If you could live anywhere in the world, where would you live?
13. If you could visit any historical period, which would you choose?
14. Although responsibilities are sometimes burdens, they also help tell us who we are. Which of your responsibilities is most important to you?
15. Is it better to have a determined, forceful "Type A" personality or a relaxed, easygoing "Type B" personality?

Progressive Writing Assignment

How the Progressive Writing Assignment Works

One of the following topics will serve as the basis for your first essay. In this chapter, you will complete prewriting for the essay. Throughout the next five chapters, each progressive assignment will take you a step further toward a completed essay. By the time you have finished the assignment at the end of Chapter 17, you will have completed all the steps in the writing process and will have a finished essay.

Progressive Writing Assignment: Prewriting

In this chapter, your progressive assignment is a prewriting assignment. Choose one of the topics below and follow the instructions.

Topic 1: Discuss three obstacles to your education.
Tips for Prewriting Use any of the methods outlined in this chapter to prewrite on the topic "Discuss three obstacles to your education." As you prewrite, consider all factors that surround those obstacles. What is the nature of the obstacles? Are they physical, emotional, financial, academic? Does family or work play a role? Are there obstacles you have already overcome? How have you managed to overcome them? Are there obstacles that remain to be conquered? How will you do it?

What Now? After you have completed your prewriting, you should have more material than you will be able to use. To prepare for the next step in the Progressive Writing Assignment, choose the three obstacles that you want to focus on in your essay.

Topic 2: Discuss your short-term goals, long-term goals, or both.
Tips for Prewriting Use any of the methods outlined in this chapter to prewrite on the topic "Discuss your short-term goals, long-term goals, or both." As you prewrite, consider all factors that surround those goals. What are they? Are they new goals or lifelong ambitions? Is goal-setting easy for you because you have practiced it all your life, or is it difficult because you have not been a goal-oriented person? What is the nature of your goals? Are they academic goals, career goals, physical goals, spiritual goals, family goals? How do you plan to reach them? How are they related to one another? How will they change your life?

What Now? After you have completed your prewriting, you should have more material than you will be able to use. Decide which ideas you want to focus on. Recall that you can discuss long-term goals, short-term goals, or both. To prepare for the next step in the Progressive Writing Assignment, choose three goals to focus on in your essay.

Topic 3: Discuss the values you have learned by observing members of your family.
Tips for Prewriting Use any of the methods outlined in this chapter to prewrite on the values reflected in the behavior of your family. Most people learn *values*—ideas about what is important and how we should conduct ourselves—from family members. Often, these values are learned from parents who stress the importance of honesty, hard work, and other positive traits. In this essay, however, you are to consider the values you learned through *observation* of your family members, not through what they have told you. For example, your grandfather may never have said a word to you about the value of hard work, but if he got up before dawn, worked twelve hours a day, and spent his weekends repairing the plumbing in his house or tending to his yard, he didn't need to tell you. He showed you. Think about members of your family and write down the things they do to show you what is important in life. Be as specific as possible.

Another Possible Approach Another approach to this topic is possible. Perhaps you look at certain members of your family and see negative values that you want to avoid. You can present these negative influences as examples you do not want to follow, changing the names if you wish to protect your relatives' privacy.

What Now? After you have completed your prewriting, you should have more material than you will be able to use. To prepare for the next step in the Progressive Writing Assignment, decide which ideas you want to focus on in your essay.

Topic 4: Discuss your methods of coping with stress.
Tips for Prewriting Everyone experiences stress from many sources, such as overwork, family problems, pressure to excel in school, or even boredom. In this essay, you will write about your ways of coping with stress. Begin by brainstorming or freewriting about some of the sources of your stress. Then explore the coping strategies that you use for each source of stress. Think in detail about those methods and about how well they work.

What Now? After you have completed your prewriting, you should have more material than you will be able to use. To prepare for the next step in the Progressive Writing Assignment, decide which three coping strategies to focus on in your essay.

13 Building a Framework: Thesis and Organization

Built into the framework—
A splash of sunlight across the floor,
The velvety embrace of an old recliner,
The stench of wet dog,
A shout of children's laughter—
Things that make a house a home.

When you are ready to begin writing an essay, you are ready to think about its framework. Just as a builder lays a foundation and builds a framework before building a house, you will set up the framework of your essay through its thesis and organization. You know the subject of your essay, and you have decided, through prewriting, what points your essay will cover. Perhaps you have even made a scratch outline. Now, you are ready to write a thesis statement. Several ways of writing a thesis are presented in this chapter, but at heart, a thesis is very simple: It is the main idea of your essay. Once you have stated the main idea clearly and effectively, you are ready to organize your essay to best advantage.

Reader's *Tip* — Focus on Building a Framework: Finding Direction in Your Writing

The picture shows a sextant, a navigational instrument invented by Isaac Newton around the turn of the eighteenth century. This tool allowed sailors to measure a star against the horizon to help gauge where their ship was on a nautical chart. Without a sextant, sailors had to use what they knew of the ocean, land, and stars and hope for the best. With sextants, sailors had a much better idea where they were and how to get where they were going.

A thesis statement functions much like a sextant: It provides direction to your readers so that they will know where your essay is going. Without a thesis, both you and your readers may feel lost in a vast ocean of words. An effective thesis statement will ensure smooth sailing for your readers as you guide them through your essay.

Reflect on It

A thesis statement is your statement of the main idea. It sums up your essay in a sentence and lets the reader know where the essay is going.

But a thesis statement is more than just a sentence in a college essay. When you have learned to write a good thesis statement, you have learned to capture a large idea in very few words.

How will you find capturing the gist of an idea useful in your future career? What kinds of documents will you write that will benefit from the inclusion of a single statement of the main idea before you go into the details? These may be emails, reports, or proposals. But whatever your career, you'll have to write something to someone. Write down at least one detailed example of a document you will write that will benefit from a thesis statement.

The Structure of an Essay

Before constructing a thesis, study the diagram of a typical essay on the next page. Then read the following essay, noticing how it corresponds to the diagram. A well-planned thesis statement is an important step in writing a well-structured essay.

Structure of an Essay

Title
- Concisely conveys the topic of the essay

Introduction
- Begins with an interesting opening sentence
- Introduces the topic
- Ends with a thesis that presents the main idea and that may list the points that will be covered

First Body Paragraph
- Begins with a topic sentence that introduces the first point of discussion
- Presents examples and details that develop the first point
- May close with a summary sentence that restates the first

Second Body Paragraph
- Begins with a topic sentence that introduces the second point of discussion
- Presents examples and details that develop the second point
- May close with a summary sentence that restates the second

Third Body Paragraph
- Begins with a topic sentence that introduces the third point of discussion
- Presents examples and details that develop the third point
- May close with a summary sentence that restates the third

Conclusion
- Provides a two- to four-sentence ending for the essay
- May sum up the points made in the essay
- Ends on a note of finality

A Model Essay

THE ADVANTAGES OF INTERNET SHOPPING

Standing in a line at a huge discount store on the Saturday before Christmas, I felt grumpy and impatient. The line had been at a standstill for five minutes, and the toddler behind me in his mother's shopping cart had started to wail loudly. Hunger was beginning to gnaw at the edges of my stomach. When had shopping become such a pain? Recently, however, I have discovered Internet shopping. Convenience, choice, and savings are the reasons I now prefer to do my shopping online.

Convenience is the main advantage of shopping over the Internet. If I want to, I can shop at the same large discount store where I shopped on that miserable Saturday afternoon, with no long lines and no squalling babies. On the Internet, I do not have to circle a huge parking lot searching for a space. I can shop in the quiet and convenience of my own home, with jazz playing softly on the CD player and a cup of hot chocolate in my hand. "No shirt, no shoes, no service" does not apply on the Internet. My flannel pajamas and fuzzy bunny slippers are well within the dress code. And if it's midnight, I can still shop. The Internet is open all night.

A second advantage to Internet shopping is choice. Living in a medium-sized city, I don't have access to the full range of shops that a large metropolitan area would offer. However, the Internet connects me in minutes with a full range of retailers. Since the online environment offers a wide range of stores, from Walmart to Tiffany's, I am sure to find something within my price range. In addition, a wide variety of merchandise is available. I can shop for CDs and listen to samples of music at online music stores. I can buy gifts, flowers, candy, and personalized T-shirts for Christmas, birthdays, or Mother's Day. I can even buy textbooks for my classes at an online textbook outlet. With the variety of merchandise offered on the Internet, I can almost always find what I need.

Finally, shopping on the Internet saves both money and time. I don't have to buy gas for my car before I shop online, nor do I buy lunch as I might if I were at a mall. In addition, since online retailers don't need a brick-and-mortar store, they have lower overhead and often, lower prices. I recently saved $200 on a laser printer by purchasing it online, and shipping was free. Shopping online also takes less time than shopping in a store. Driving around and shopping at malls or discount stores can easily take the better part of a Saturday. Shopping online usually takes less than an hour, even if I visit multiple sites to compare prices. Saving money and time is a big advantage of online shopping.

Internet shopping has many advantages, including convenience, choice, and savings. Next Christmas, I will not drive to a crowded discount store and wear out my feet and my patience looking for a gift; I will turn on my computer instead. I hear that even Santa surfs the Net these days.

Constructing the Thesis Statement

A **thesis statement**, usually placed at the end of your introductory paragraph, states the main idea of your essay, often states or implies your attitude or opinion about the subject, and gives your essay **direction. Direction** means that the thesis sets the course that the essay will follow. In an essay, the thesis statement is the controlling force behind every sentence and every word. It is a promise to your reader that you will discuss the idea mentioned in the thesis statement and no other.

Types of Thesis Statements

A thesis statement presents the main idea of an essay. Sometimes, it also presents the points that will be covered in the essay. When you construct your thesis statement, you will decide whether to write a thesis that lists points of developments or one that does not.

As you write, you will find that some topics lend themselves to listing points while others do not. Your writing habits can also help you decide which type of thesis to use. Careful, organized writers can usually work with either type. Writers who tend to skip steps, however, find that listing points forces them to be more thorough and organized.

The Thesis with Points Listed

A *thesis with points listed* presents the main idea along with the points of development. These points are listed in the order in which they will be discussed in the essay. The thesis listing points of development has a long tradition in college writing. Listing thesis points provides a road map that lets the reader see where the essay is headed.

 EXAMPLE

My formula for a successful lawn care business includes *clever advertising, competitive prices,* and *reliable service.*

Price, performance, and *fit* are factors to consider when shopping for athletic shoes.

Advantages of a Thesis with Points Listed

1. Listing thesis points forces you to plan your essay carefully. If you habitually skim over the prewriting and planning stages, then listing points forces you to think through your topic before you write the essay.
2. Listing thesis points conveys an impression of careful organization. Your reader sees concrete evidence that you have planned before writing.
3. Listing thesis points aids clarity by giving the reader a road map to the development of your essay.
4. Listing thesis points keeps you on track. Your thesis serves as a mini-outline for you to follow as you write.

Three Ways to Write a Thesis Listing Points When you write a thesis listing points, you may list the points at the end of the thesis statement, at the beginning of the thesis statement, or in a separate sentence.

Points listed at the end of the thesis statement. One way of writing a thesis statement is to present the main idea first and then list the points of development.

EXAMPLE

thesis   point 1   point 2

I enjoy fishing because it relaxes me, it challenges me, and

point 3

it occasionally feeds me.

The writer's thesis, or main idea, is that fishing relaxes him, challenges him, and occasionally feeds him. Notice that the thesis also conveys the writer's attitude toward his subject: He enjoys fishing. Even without the word *enjoys*, the positive nature of the points conveys the writer's attitude. Also notice the parallel structure of the thesis points. Each point follows the same pattern.

it relaxes me

it challenges me

it (occasionally) feeds me

Although perfect parallel structure will not be possible in every thesis, try to make thesis points as parallel as possible. For more information on parallel structure, see Chapter 30, "Parallel Structure."

Points listed at the beginning of the thesis statement. Listing points first is a bit out of the ordinary. With this technique, you can create a thesis that will not look like everyone else's.

EXAMPLE

point 1   point 2   point 3

Too little time, a shortage of money, and a lack of belief in my abilities

thesis

made me postpone my college education.

Points listed in a separate sentence. Listing points separately works well for longer thesis statements. If you find your thesis statement becoming long and cumbersome, try listing the points separately.

EXAMPLE

thesis

AIDS is changing the dating habits of American men and women.

point 1   point 2

People are becoming reluctant to engage in casual sex, choosy about

point 3

the men or women they date, and more likely to remain monogamous.

exercise 13.1   **Analyzing Thesis Statements**

Analyze the three thesis statements below by answering the questions that follow.

1. Good students are likely to attend class regularly, participate enthusiastically, and study often.

   a. What is the topic of the essay? _____

   b. Are the points of development listed first, last, or separately? _____

   _____

   c. List the points in the order of presentation. Notice the parallel structure.

   _____

   _____

   _____

2. Pride in my accomplishment, the opportunity to help others, and the ability to support my family will be the rewards of earning my nursing degree.

   a. What is the topic of the essay? _____

   b. Are the points of development listed first, last, or separately? _____

   _____

   c. List the points in the order of presentation. Notice the parallel structure.

   _____

   _____

   _____

3. Singing with a jazz band gives me an outlet for my creativity, a source of extra income, and a more active social life.

   a. What is the topic of the essay? _____

   b. Are the points of development listed first, last, or separately? _____

   _____

   c. List the points in the order of presentation. Notice the parallel structure.

   _____

   _____

   _____

exercise 13.2   **Completing Thesis Statements**

Complete the following thesis statements, making sure to list the points in parallel structure.

1. The convenient parking, the _____, and the _____ are advantages of shopping in a mall.

2. Classmates who talk in class, _____, and _____ _____

3. _____, _____, and _____ are the main ingredients for a party.

4. Any employer would be fortunate to hire me. I would bring enthusiasm, _____, and _____ to my job.

5. I would like living in a small town. Small towns are _____, _____, and _____.

exercise 13.3   **Writing a Thesis Statement Listing Points**

Write a thesis listing points on three of the following topics. Include one thesis with points listed first, at least one with points listed last, and at least one with points listed separately. Remember to use parallel structure.

1. What are the keys to maintaining good health?

    _____

    _____

2. If you could possess any one talent or ability, what would you choose? Why?

    _____

    _____

3. What are some differences between high school and college classes?

    _____

    _____

4. Do you prefer working alone or in a group?

    _____

    _____

5. Do you enjoy being outdoors? Why or why not?

    _____

    _____

The Thesis without Points Listed

The *thesis without points listed* presents the central idea of the essay without listing the points of development. A thesis that does not list points requires you to plan carefully to keep yourself and your reader on track. Without the road map that listing your points provides, it is even more important that your essay flow logically and smoothly. Thus topic sentences require careful planning so that they are clearly connected to the thesis. When you plan a thesis without points, it is a good idea to plan each topic sentence, too, to ensure that you stay on track. Remember, not listing points does not mean that you do not plan them; it simply means you do not list them.

EXAMPLE   Working in a chicken processing plant was a sickening experience.

When I look back ten years from now, I will see that my choice to attend college was the best decision I ever made.

Advantages of a Thesis without Points Listed

1. A thesis without points allows you to state your main idea simply and concisely.
2. A thesis without points works well when the points are long and cumbersome or difficult to write in parallel structure.
3. A thesis without points eliminates the worry that your topic sentences will echo the wording of your thesis too closely.
4. The thesis without points is considered a more advanced technique and is more often the choice of professional essayists.

Following are examples of thesis statements that do not list points, along with possible topic sentences for each body paragraph.

EXAMPLE   *Thesis:* On the college level, the proper punishment for those caught cheating is expulsion.

Topic sentences:

Body paragraph 1: Expulsion is a severe penalty that will make potential cheaters think twice before being dishonest.

Body paragraph 2: Expelling cheaters will reassure responsible students that honesty really is the best policy.

Body paragraph 3: Most important, a college's refusal to tolerate cheating ensures that a college degree will retain its value.

EXAMPLE   *Thesis:* Year-round attendance at public schools is a good idea.

Topic sentences:

Body paragraph 1: For working parents, a longer school year would ease summer child-care problems.

Body paragraph 2: Year-round school attendance would prevent "brain drain" during summer vacation.

Body paragraph 3: A longer school year would lead to higher student achievement.

exercise 13.4   **Writing a Thesis Statement without Points Listed**

Write a thesis that does not list points on three of the following topics.

1. Do you prefer to write on a computer or with pen and paper?

   _____

   _____

2. Some are promoting the day after Thanksgiving, traditionally a big day for retailers, as "Buy Nothing Day," a day of awareness about consumer habits. Would you participate in "Buy Nothing Day"?

   _____

   _____

3. If you could have an all-expenses-paid trip to anywhere for two weeks, where would you go? Why?

   _____

   _____

4. If you were building a house and had enough in your budget for just one porch, would you choose to build a front porch or a back porch? Why?

   _____

   _____

5. Is it better to grow up in a small family or a large family? Why?

   _____

   _____

Evaluating Your Thesis Points

After you construct your thesis, the next step is to evaluate your thesis points. Specifically, your thesis points should not overlap, should not be too broad, and should not be too narrow.

Avoiding Overlap When two or more of your points overlap, you risk making the same point more than once. Evaluating the thesis for overlap means making sure that your points of development are distinct, separate points that do not cover the same territory. The following examples show thesis statements with overlapping points.

                        thesis   point 1

Taking out an auto loan has helped me to be responsible in making

             point 2   point 3

payments, to handle money wisely, and to obtain reliable transportation

that I could not otherwise afford.

Analysis: Points 1 and 2 overlap because making payments is a part of handling money wisely. The writer needs to evaluate the support she plans to use for each point and modify the thesis accordingly.

Revision Taking out an auto loan has helped me to handle my finances responsibly, to establish a good credit rating, and to obtain reliable transportation that I could not otherwise afford.

Analysis: The writer has eliminated the overlap by combining the overlapping points and adding a new point: establishing a credit rating.

exercise 13.5   **Eliminating Overlap**

Each of the following thesis statements contains one point that overlaps with another point. Cross out that point and write in one that does not overlap with any other point.

1. Although I enjoy my job, I sometimes tire of the long hours, the stress, and pressure.

    _____

2. Our college's snack bar is a place to meet friends, a place to study, and a place to gather.

    _____

3. Trustworthiness, honesty, and a sense of humor are qualities I look for in a friend.

    _____

4. I broke off my engagement because I needed to finish college before marrying, the timing was not right, and I was not ready for a long-term commitment.

    _____

5. People on public assistance should work for the money they receive. Such work would prepare them for the job market, make them feel good about themselves, and give them experience that might help them find future employment.

_____

Avoiding Ideas That Are Too Broad Ideas that are too broad are too large to develop in a single paragraph. Often, they are also vague because the writer has not taken the time to consider exactly what the paragraph will be about.

EXAMPLE

A nursing degree will give me a chance to work at a challenging career, to support my family well, and to make the world a better place.

Analysis: The third point, "to make the world a better place," is too broad. Narrowing the idea to cover only the writer's community and relating the idea to the writer's field of study makes the point narrower, more realistic, and easier to support.

Revision A nursing degree will give me a chance to work at a challenging career, to support my family well, and to educate my community on health issues.

exercise 13.6   **Eliminating Points That Are Too Broad**

Each of the following thesis statements contains one point that is too broad. Cross out that point and write in a point that can be developed within one paragraph.

1. Spending a year or two on a job before going to college can provide a student the opportunity to earn money toward a college education, to see what the real world is like, and to learn responsible work habits.

_____

2. I like Ms. Brennan, my supervisor, because of her fairness, her sense of humor, and her good qualities.

_____

3. For me, the ideal job provides on-site child care, up-to-date equipment, and great working conditions.

_____

4. Losing weight, controlling my temper, and improving myself are some New Year's resolutions I am trying to keep this year.

_____

5. I dislike driving at night because of poor night vision, fear of something happening to me, and the possibility of a breakdown.

   _____

Avoiding Ideas That Are Too Narrow Ideas that are too narrow may not produce a paragraph's worth of support. Often, these ideas are better used as supporting detail. When an idea is too narrow, see if it is related to a larger idea that could be used as a topic sentence. If the idea cannot be broadened, discard it and look for another.

EXAMPLE

My grandmother, the owner of Sally's Frame Shop, has all the characteristics of a good businesswoman. She works hard, says "hello" to customers, and provides quality service.

Analysis: The second point, "says 'hello' to customers," is too narrow to develop as a paragraph. However, saying "hello" is part of a larger issue: treating customers with courtesy.

Revision My grandmother, the owner of Sally's Frame Shop, has all the characteristics of a good businesswoman. She works hard, treats customers courteously, and provides quality service.

exercise 13.7   **Eliminating Points That Are Too Narrow**

Each of the following thesis statements contains one point that is too narrow. Cross out that point and write in a point that is large enough to develop within a paragraph.

1. Growing up with three sisters has taught me to stand up for myself, to share my hair dryer, and to cherish my family ties.

   _____

2. I enjoy my job at First National Bank because the working conditions are pleasant, I make $12.80 per hour, and my coworkers are helpful.

   _____

3. The latest safety devices, a medium blue color, and reliability are features I look for in a car.

   _____

4. My dog is playful, protective, and named Butch.

   _____

5. We enjoyed the lake because of its eighty-degree water temperature, its long, sandy beach, and its abundant plant and animal life.

Organizing Your Essay

As you construct your thesis statement, think about the order of the supporting paragraphs within your essay. Four possible ways of organizing your essay are emphatic order, reverse emphatic order, sandwich order, and chronological order. Above all, choose a method of organization that is logical to you and to your readers.

Emphatic Order

One logical way to present your ideas is in **emphatic order, or order of importance.** Leading up to a strong idea with emphatic order gives your essay a "snowball effect": The essay becomes more convincing as it goes along.

You may also wish to experiment with **reverse emphatic order,** beginning with your most important idea and leading to the less important ideas. This type of organization suggests that your strongest idea carries such weight that it demands to be heard first. Your lesser points shore up that idea and lend your thesis further support.

Whether you choose emphatic order or reverse emphatic order, your technique will be sound. The first and last body paragraphs are always strong points of emphasis because readers are more likely to remember points that come first or last.

EXAMPLE **EMPHATIC ORDER**

Thesis: Both parents should share equally in raising their children.

Topic sentence 1: Since economic necessity usually forces both parents to work, sharing child-care duties is a matter of fairness.

Topic sentence 2: Sharing responsibility allows fathers to enjoy a closer relationship with their children.

Topic sentence 3: Most important, shared responsibility gives children the active support of both parents.

EXAMPLE **REVERSE EMPHATIC ORDER**

Thesis: When I bought a new car recently, I looked for cars with the features that were most important to me.

Topic sentence 1: When I began my search for a new car, the most important factor was cost.

Topic sentence 2: After finding cars in my price range, I looked at crash test data to find the cars that were safest.

Topic sentence 3: Finally, I checked *Consumer Reports* to see which cars were most reliable.

exercise 13.8   **Using Emphatic Order**

Develop a thesis statement and topic sentences on two of the following four topics. Use emphatic order for one of your chosen topics and reverse emphatic order for the other.

1. Why are people afraid of aging?
2. What do you hope to accomplish within the next five years?
3. What skills—academic or nonacademic—should everyone have?
4. People usually regard anger as destructive and unproductive. Is anger ever useful?

Your Answers

Emphatic Order

Thesis _____

_____

Topic sentence 1 (least important idea) _____

_____

Topic sentence 2 (second most important idea) _____

_____

Topic sentence 3 (most important idea) _____

_____

Reverse Emphatic Order

Thesis _____

_____

Topic sentence 1 (most important idea) _____

_____

Topic sentence 2 (second most important idea) _____

_____

Topic sentence 3 (least important idea) _____

_____

Sandwich Order

The points you develop within an essay are not always equally strong. When one of your points is weaker than the others, try **sandwich order**, placing your weaker point between the two stronger ones. This method employs the same psychology that is at work when you use emphatic order. If ideas are presented in a sequence, people remember the first and last ideas more strongly than those presented in the middle. Thus the first and last body paragraphs become the "showcase positions" in the essay, the positions to place the material that you want readers to remember.

EXAMPLE

Thesis: Children benefit from attending day-care centers.

Topic sentence 1: At day-care centers, children benefit from interaction with peers.

Topic sentence 2: Children who attend day-care centers learn rules of behavior and basic skills.

Topic sentence 3: Perhaps most important, day care helps a child to become self-reliant.

Analysis: Point 2 is the weakest point because skills and knowledge children will need in school could also be acquired at home. Point 1 is strong because exposure to many other children is more likely at a day-care center than at home. Point 3 is strong because at a day-care center, without parents to cling to, children are more likely to become independent.

exercise 13.9   **Using Sandwich Order**

Develop a thesis and topic sentences for two of the following topics. Decide which point is weakest and sandwich it in the middle of your thesis. Be prepared to explain the logic you used to your instructor and classmates.

1. What can parents do to prepare their children for school?
2. What do people reveal about themselves by the way they speak?
3. Is there any college course you would refuse to take? Why?
4. If you controlled pay scales, what job would pay the highest salary? Why?

Answers

1. Thesis _____

   _____

   Topic sentence 1 (strong point) _____

   _____

   Topic sentence 2 (weak point) _____

   _____

   Topic sentence 3 (strong point) _____

   _____

2. Thesis _____

   _____

   Topic sentence 1 (strong point) _____

   _____

   Topic sentence 2 (weak point) _____

   _____

   Topic sentence 3 (strong point) _____

   _____

Chronological Order

Chronological order, also called *time order* or *order of occurrence,* is most often used in narratives and storytelling. But chronological order is also useful in essays. In writing about the hassles of being a first-year student, you would probably discuss problems with registration before discussing the first day of class, because registration occurred first. If you were discussing your lifelong love of music, you would probably begin with your childhood piano lessons and end with your participation in your college's community chorus. Chronological order fulfills your reader's expectation to have events described in the order in which they occur.

EXAMPLE

Thesis: My first day of classes was difficult.

Topic sentence 1: Finding a parking place on the first day of class was more difficult than I expected.

Topic sentence 2: Finding my way around an unfamiliar campus was frustrating.

Topic sentence 3: After dashing into class late, I was embarrassed to realize that I was in the wrong room.

exercise 13.10   **Using Chronological Order**

Using chronological order, develop a thesis and three topic sentences for two of the following topics.

1. What should a job candidate do to make a good impression in an interview?
2. What three people have had the greatest influence on your life?
3. Discuss how you became involved in a hobby that you enjoy.
4. If you had an entire day to spend any way you wanted, what would you do?

Answers

1. Thesis _____

   _____

   Topic sentence 1 _____

   _____

   Topic sentence 2 _____

   _____

   Topic sentence 3 _____

   _____

2. Thesis _____

   _____

   Topic sentence 1 _____

   _____

Topic sentence 2 _____

_____

Topic sentence 3

_____

_____

Progressive Writing Assignment

Progressive Writing Assignment: Thesis and Outline

If your instructor has assigned the Progressive Writing Assignment, you have already completed your prewriting for one of the following topics. In this chapter, you will complete your thesis and outline. Recall that each assignment takes you a step further toward an essay.

Topics and Tips for Writing a Thesis and Outline

The Topics

Topic 1: Discuss three obstacles to your education.
Topic 2: Discuss your short-term goals, long-term goals, or both.
Topic 3: Discuss the values you have learned by observing members of your family.
Topic 4: Discuss your methods of coping with stress.

Tips for Writing a Thesis and Outline

- Develop a thesis and outline from your prewriting, but don't be afraid to add new material if you have new ideas.
- Decide on the points you will cover in your essay and the order in which you will present them. Then write a tentative thesis.
- If you have listed your thesis points, check to make sure they are parallel and do not overlap.
- Finally, make an outline by writing a topic sentence for each body paragraph and, if you wish, briefly jotting down a couple of the major points you will discuss in the essay.

14 Introducing the Essay

Temptation

You have just opened a chocolate shop on a busy street. You have only one small display window to catch your customers' attention. What do you do with that bare window, which right now holds only a dead fly? Do you throw in a few boxes of chocolate, unopened, along with a big red **SALE** sign? Of course not. You clean the window, dispose of the fly, and put down a luxurious velvet cloth. You cover silver trays with lace doilies and artfully arrange the chocolates. You make the display so irresistible that those passing by are drawn into your shop.

Temptation. It works on readers, too. No one *has* to buy your chocolates or read your essay. Your job is to make them want to do those things. An artfully placed image, an exciting story, or a carefully chosen quotation can be irresistible, pulling a reader into your essay. However, an introduction is more than just a way to draw a reader in. It does several jobs that no other part of the essay could do quite so effectively.

Reader's *Tip* — Focus on Introducing the Essay:
A Look at the Hook

Famous first lines from novels:

Ships at a distance have every man's wish on board.
—Zora Neale Hurston, *Their Eyes Were Watching God* (1937)

All this happened, more or less.
—Kurt Vonnegut, *Slaughterhouse-Five* (1969)

Once upon a time, there was a woman who discovered she had turned into the wrong person.
—Anne Tyler, *Back When We Were Grownups* (2001)

As any novelist knows, the first line of any book is crucial, Joseph Heller's "It was love at first sight" in *Catch-22* or Herman Melville's "Call me Ishmael" in *Moby-Dick* are among some of the most famous. They demonstrate how first lines can hook a reader into reading the next sentence, and the next, and the next.

An introduction to an essay does the same thing. A strong and compelling introduction will capture your readers' attention and prepare them for the essay to come.

Reflect on It

Look through the Readings section of this book and essay with a first line that interests you. Read the essay. Then fill in the information below.

Essay you choose: _____

First line: _____

Did the first line hook you? _____

Was the essay as good as its first line? Explain. _____

Purposes of an Introduction

1. **An introduction draws your reader into the essay.**

The first sentence of your introduction should be as irresistible as a box of French chocolates. True, it won't always turn out that way. Aim high anyway. A reader who is drawn in by the first sentence is more likely to read the second and the third.

2. **An introduction advances the general topic of your essay.**

Have you ever noticed how people approach a topic of conversation? They don't just walk up and say, "The colonization of space may become an increasingly important goal as the world's population increases," or "May I borrow twenty dollars?" Instead, they ease into the conversation, giving their listeners time to make a mental shift to the topic before bringing up the main point.

Your reader needs to make a similar mental shift. When you ease into the thesis by bringing up your general topic first, your reader has time to turn her thoughts away from whatever is on her mind—the price of gas or what to eat for lunch—and to get in the mood to listen to what you have to say.

3. **An introduction provides necessary background.**

Background information is not always necessary. But if it is, the introduction is a good place for it. Background information tucked into the introduction gives the necessary details without intruding on the rest of the essay. In an essay about your job, for instance, the introduction should include where you work and what you do. Then you won't have to include the information as an afterthought. In an essay about a short story or novel, your introduction should include the title and author's name. If you are writing about an event in your life, use the introduction to establish background details such as your age at the time, where it happened, and who else was involved.

4. **An introduction presents your essay's thesis.**

The most important job of an introductory paragraph is to present your essay's thesis. Every sentence in the introduction should follow a path of logic that leads directly to your thesis, which will be the last sentence of your introduction. Once you have stated the thesis, stop. Your body paragraphs will flow naturally from a thesis that comes at the end of the introduction.

Types of Introduction

Introductions that draw a reader in don't just happen; they are carefully crafted. Following are several types of introduction. Try them all, using the examples as models.

Broad to Narrow

The **broad-to-narrow** introduction is a classic style of introduction. Sometimes called the *inverted triangle introduction*, it funnels your reader from a broad statement of your topic to the narrowest point in the introduction: your thesis.

EXAMPLE

During registration week, tables offering MasterCard or Visa applications litter college campuses like autumn leaves. Gifts are offered just for completing an application, and the promise of easy credit is tempting. Once that shiny piece of plastic is in hand, the way it is used can mean the difference between starting out after graduation with a good credit record and starting out under a mound of debt. Establishing a set of simple rules can help to make a credit card an asset instead of a liability.

exercise 14.1   ### A Broad-to-Narrow Introduction

Arrange the following numbered sentences into a broad-to-narrow introduction, ending with the thesis.

1. Among the skillet meals, frozen dishes, boxed dinners, and canned cuisine, one convenience food stands out.

2. Manufacturers have developed a variety of convenience foods for people who do not have the time or the desire to prepare food from scratch.

3. Microwaveable frozen meals offer superior variety, nutrition, and ease of preparation.

4. Most people enjoy eating, but not everyone enjoys cooking.

   The sentences should be arranged in the following order: _____,
   _____, _____, _____.

Narrow to Broad

The **narrow-to-broad introduction** is just the opposite of the broad-to-narrow introduction. Instead of beginning with a statement of your general topic, the narrow-to-broad introduction begins at a point that is smaller than your thesis and expands toward that thesis. With this method, you can create an unusual and intriguing opening.

EXAMPLE

Thousands of feet above the earth, a small crystal traces a zigzag path to the bleak landscape below. It is the first snowflake of the season, soon to be followed by many more that will blanket the earth in a layer of white. Winter is my favorite of all the seasons. I love its beauty, I enjoy the opportunity to ski, and, like a kid, I can never wait for Christmas to arrive.

exercise 14.2   **A Narrow-to-Broad Introduction**

Arrange the following numbered sentences so that they form a narrow-to-broad introduction, ending with the thesis.

1. Seeing my father dying without dignity only reinforces my belief that physicians should be allowed to assist the suicides of terminally ill patients.

2. His eyes show no sign of recognition as I enter the room and say, "Hello, Dad."

3. As I stand in the doorway, I see my father, his hand curled like a fallen leaf and tied to the bed's metal safety bar with a Velcro wrist cuff.

4. When he became terminally ill, my father begged for enough pills to kill himself, but Dr. Abercrombie refused to prescribe them.

The sentences should be arranged in the following order: _____,

_____, _____, _____.

Quotation

A **quotation** adds sparkle to your introduction and spares you the work of crafting just the right words for your opening—someone else has already done it for you. You do not necessarily have to quote a book, a play, or a famous person. You may quote your best friend, your mother, or your great-aunt Sally. You may quote a commercial, a bumper sticker, or a popular song. You may quote an expert on your subject to lend authority to your words. For a ready-made source of quotations, consult the reference section of your college library for collections of quotations, such as *Bartlett's Familiar Quotations*.

When opening with a quotation, you need to know how to use quotation marks and how to paraphrase a quotation. It is also important to give credit to the author or, if you do not know who originally said it, to acknowledge that the quotation is not your own. In addition, a quotation cannot just hang in space, unconnected to your essay. You need a transition that shows your reader the connection between the quotation and your thesis.

EXAMPLE   QUOTATION OPENING—KNOWN AUTHOR:

Mark Twain wrote, "Few things are harder to put up with than the

transition to thesis
annoyance of a good example." He must have had a brother just like mine.

All my life I have tried to live up to the example of a brother who is

more athletic, more studious, and more at ease socially than I am.

QUOTATION OPENING—UNKNOWN AUTHOR:

acknowledgement of outside source
A habit has been defined as "a shackle for the free." This statement seems

transition to thesis
particularly relevant to the habit of smoking. A person who smokes is no

longer free but is chained to a habit that is expensive, socially unacceptable,

and dangerous.

PARAPHRASED QUOTATION—AUTHOR AND EXACT WORDS UNKNOWN:

acknowledgement of outside source   paraphrased quotation
I once heard someone say that we get old too soon and smart too late.

transition to thesis
That statement is certainly true in my case. I have just begun to

understand that my parents were right when they told me I should go to

college. At seventeen, I disregarded their advice. Now, at thirty-two, I

realize that I need a college education to make a comfortable living, to

reach my career goals, and to set the right example for my children.

exercise 14.3   **Opening with a Quotation**

Choosing from the list of quotations below, follow the directions for each numbered part of the exercise.

QUOTATIONS

The only way to have a friend is to be one.
—Ralph Waldo Emerson, *Essays, First Series: Friendship*

The real problem is not whether machines think but whether men do.
—B. F. Skinner, *Contingencies of Reinforcement*

In spite of everything, I still believe that people are really good at heart.
—Anne Frank, *Anne Frank: The Diary of a Young Girl*

Everyone is a moon and has a dark side which he never shows to anybody.
—Mark Twain, *Following the Equator*, Vol. 1

Wisdom is not bought.
—African proverb

Show me someone not full of herself, and I'll show you a hungry person.
—Nikki Giovanni, "Poem for a Lady Whose Voice I Like"

Beware of all enterprises that require new clothes.
—Henry David Thoreau, *Walden*

1. Write an opening sentence using an exact quotation and the author's name.

    _____

    _____

2. Write an opening sentence using an exact quotation but pretending you do
    not know the author's name.

    _____

    _____

3. Write an opening sentence paraphrasing one of the quotations and pretend-
    ing you do not know the author's name.

    _____

    _____

4. Write a transitional sentence connecting the quotation to the thesis in the fol-
    lowing introduction.

    "The brain is like a muscle," Carl Sagan said. "When we use it, we feel good."
    (Transitional sentence) _____

    _____

    My experiences in a college classroom have made me more self-reliant, more
    certain of my abilities, and less fearful of being wrong.

5. Write an introduction that opens with a quotation and leads with a transitional
    sentence into one of the following thesis statements (or one of your own).

    a. People reveal a lot about themselves by the way they dress.

    b. Every first-year student needs to know how to form new relationships dur-
        ing the first term at a new college.

    c. The aspects of my personality that I like least are my impatience, my stub-
        bornness, and my tendency to procrastinate.

    _____

    _____

    _____

    _____

Anecdote

An **anecdote** is a brief story that illustrates a point. Brief is the key word. Introductions should be short, so keep your story to a few sentences and be sure to include a transition that connects the anecdote to the thesis.

EXAMPLE   When she saw her front door standing open, the woman knew there had

been another break-in. She took her five-year-old daughter next door and

returned with a neighbor and a borrowed baseball bat. Hesitantly, she

entered. Vulgar graffiti covered the walls, and the sofa had been slashed.

transition to thesis
In neighborhoods like this one where crime is out of hand, residents often

feel powerless. But community involvement in the form of neighborhood

watches, neighbor patrols, and insistence on a strong police presence can

help residents of high-crime neighborhoods reclaim their streets.

exercise 14.4   **An Anecdotal Introduction**

Read the following anecdotal introduction, then answer the questions that follow.
    ¹Last night, my sister Karen picked at her dinner, eating only her salad and her green beans. ²Before bed, she did fifty stomach crunches, then stood at the mirror critically eyeing her waist, which is approximately the same size as her hips. ³When I asked what she was doing, she said she was too fat and had to lose weight. ⁴Karen is only nine years old, but she is already in pursuit of a goal that is impossible and unhealthy. ⁵The modern obsession with having a reed-thin body is encouraged by the fashion industry, the media, and even the manufacturers of food.

1. How many sentences does the anecdote contain? _____
2. Which sentence contains the transition to the thesis? _____

Contrasting Idea

Gold placed on black velvet in a jeweler's window takes on extra luster against the contrasting background. Through the drama of contrast, your ideas, too, can shine. Starting with a **contrasting idea** is an easy and effective technique to use, but there are two elements that must not be left out. The first is a change-of-direction signal. When switching from one idea to its opposite, you need a word such as *but* or *however* to signal the change. The second required element is a clear, strong contrast.

EXAMPLE

When I hit a home run in the bottom of the ninth to win the game for the McDuffie's Auto Parts Tigers, my dad was not there. He missed many family activities because he believed his first duty was to his job. After I graduate from college, I will have a career, but it will not be my only priority. I hope to have a well-rounded life with time for career, time for family, and time for activities that interest me.

exercise 14.5   ## Opening with Contrasting Ideas

In the blank below each introduction, write the word that serves as a change-of-direction signal.

1. One of my professors says that students who see college simply as preparation for a career are in the wrong place. College, she says, is for those who want to become well-rounded and educated. I hate to tell her, but if all this place had to offer were wisdom, there would be an abundance of empty seats in the lecture halls. Colleges should replace classes in art appreciation and French with career skills courses, additional courses in the student's major field, and internships in various career fields.

   _____

2. I used to believe in accepting coworkers as they were. I did my job and minded my own business. If my coworkers goofed off, that was their business. Lately, however, I am becoming increasingly intolerant of people who arrive late, gossip, or don't carry their share of the load.

   _____

Historical

The **historical introduction** gives the reader background information—the "history" behind your essay. Historical introductions have two functions—to *establish authority* or expertise on a subject or to *set the stage* for your discussion.

Historical Introduction to Establish Authority   Background material can help you establish your authority or expertise on a particular subject. If you are giving advice on car maintenance, for instance, it might help your reader to know that you've worked summers and weekends at Ace's Auto Repair for the last four years, or that your own car is nearing the 200,000-mile mark on the odometer. Readers are more likely to accept advice from those who have some experience or expertise in a particular area.

EXAMPLE

Through my parents' divorces and subsequent remarriages, I have acquired one stepfather, two stepmothers, three sets of step-grandparents, three stepsisters, two stepbrothers, and assorted step-aunts, uncles, and cousins. I speak with the voice of experience when I say that getting along with stepfamilies requires compromise, respect of others' privacy, and willingness to share.

Historical Introduction to Set the Stage Another reason to use a historical introduction is to give the background that sets the stage for your essay. Information that the reader needs to understand the rest of the essay should be placed in the introduction. If you write about neighbors who donated food, clothing, and money to your family, don't wait until the last paragraph to tell about the house fire that prompted their generosity. Establish those details in the introduction.

EXAMPLE

My dad was a car enthusiast and, almost from the time I could walk, I followed him around on Saturdays, carrying things and being "helpful." He encouraged my love of cars, and when I was fourteen, he bought me an old junker to rebuild. Restoring cars and working on engines has brought enjoyment, won the respect of other car enthusiasts, and helped me to earn extra income.

exercise 14.6 **Historical Introductions**

Look at each of the following thesis statements and decide whether the writer needs to use a historical introduction (1) to establish authority or (2) to set the stage. Write your choice in the blank beneath each question and be prepared to give reasons for your answer.

1. If you are not satisfied with a product or service, complain immediately, complain to the right person, and suggest a solution to the problem.

   _____

2. Moving away from home has made me more independent, more confident in my abilities, and more appreciative of my parents.

   _____

3. Helpful coworkers, a pleasant workplace, and an understanding boss make my job enjoyable.

   _____

4. Setting up your computer and printer is easier than you think.

   _____

5. To get a good bargain in a used car, you must do the proper research, have the car checked by a professional, and know how to negotiate with the dealer.

   _____

Progressive Writing Assignment

Progressive Writing Assignment: Introducing the Essay

If your instructor has assigned the Progressive Writing Assignment, you have already completed your prewriting and written a thesis and an outline. In this chapter, you will write your introduction. Recall that each assignment takes you a step further toward an essay, and that you are now one chapter closer to a complete essay.

Topics and Tips for Introducing the Essay

The Topics

Topic 1: Discuss three obstacles to your education.
Topic 2: Discuss your short-term goals, long-term goals, or both.
Topic 3: Discuss the values you have learned by observing members of your family.
Topic 4: Discuss your methods of coping with stress.

Tips for Introducing Your Essay

- Carefully consider which type of introduction would be most effective for your topic. Ask yourself if there is a quotation or anecdote that might be particularly effective with your topic. See if there is a contrasting idea that you could use or a way to lead into your thesis with a broad-to-narrow introduction. Once you have thought through each method of introduction, ask which one would work best with your topic and be most appealing to a reader.
- Place your thesis at the end of your introduction. Then make sure that the sentence that leads into the thesis does its job smoothly, providing a smooth, logical transition from your lead-in to your main idea.

15 Developing Body Paragraphs

Sparkle

A jeweler judges the quality of a diamond by "The Four C's"—color, cut, clarity, and carat weight. Evaluating by these four standards, the jeweler can determine the value of the gem.

Wouldn't it be nice if there were similar standards we could apply to writing? Direction, unity, coherence, and support are the standards that measure paragraph and essay writing. Check your essays against these standards to see if you have written a real gem—or at least a diamond in the rough.

A paragraph is the smallest multiple-sentence unit of communication in our language. But simply lumping sentences together does not make them a paragraph. A **body paragraph** is a paragraph that supports a larger idea: the thesis statement of an essay. An effective body paragraph has four characteristics: direction, unity, coherence, and support.

Reader's *Tip* —— Focus on Developing Body Paragraphs: Considering the Details

Cartoons take an incredible amount of time to create. Joe Rhodes, columnist for *Entertainment Weekly* online, says, "It takes six months to complete a half hour episode of *The Simpsons*" because "there are 24 frames for every second, 24 minutes in every show. The mechanics of a simple eye blink can take half a page of instructions" ("The Making of *The Simpsons*," www.ew.com). Imagine the detail each of those frames must take so that the audience watches seamless programming.

You may not plan to create cartoons for a living, but undoubtedly your career will require attention to detail. If you design clothing, every element of the design must work together in a unified manner. If you are a trial lawyer, you will need to review every piece of evidence to present a coherent case to the jury. As in an essay, the details work together to form a unified and coherent whole.

Reflect on It

Think about the career you plan to pursue. What details will you have to weave into a coherent and unified whole?

Characteristics of an Effective Body Paragraph

1. **Direction** means that the body paragraph has a strong topic sentence that states the main idea and sets the course that the paragraph will follow.
2. **Unity** means that the paragraph makes one main point and sticks to that point.

3. **Coherence** means that the ideas in the paragraph are logically connected and easy to follow.
4. **Support** means that the paragraph contains specific and detailed discussion of the idea stated in the topic sentence.

Direction: Shaping the Topic Sentences of Body Paragraphs

A **thesis statement** gives an essay its overall direction and sometimes provides a road map for the reader by listing points. The **topic sentences** extend that function by charting each leg of the journey as the essay moves through each body paragraph. Each topic sentence outlines one thesis point, thus providing direction for each body paragraph.

The following list outlines the functions of the topic sentences of body paragraphs.

Functions of the Topic Sentence of a Body Paragraph

1. The topic sentence of a body paragraph provides a **thesis link** by mentioning the *general subject* of the essay.
2. The topic sentence of a body paragraph mentions the *specific thesis point* that will be developed within the paragraph.
3. The topic sentence may also provide *transitions* from one paragraph to the next.

Look at the following thesis statements and their topic sentences. Notice that the topic sentences provide a thesis link by mentioning the general subject of the essay. The topic sentences also present the specific thesis points. Notice that if supporting points are listed in the thesis, topic sentences follow the same order.

EXAMPLE

general subject (thesis link)   point 1
Thesis: A commuter college is a good choice for students with children,

point 2   point 3
students on a budget, and students with full-time jobs.

point 1
Topic sentence 1: Students who have children find that

general subject (thesis link)
a commuter college allows them to be students and parents, too.

general subject (thesis link) (transition)   point 2
Topic sentence 2: A commuter college also helps students fit the costs

of college into a tight budget.

point 3
Topic sentence 3: Students who work during the day often prefer to

general subject (thesis link)
attend night school at a commuter college.

EXAMPLE

general subject   no points listed
Thesis: Making a daily schedule helps me use my time efficiently.

general subject (thesis link)   point 1
Topic sentence 1: A daily schedule helps me to set priorities.

general subject (thesis link)   point 2
Topic sentence 2: <u>By using a daily schedule</u>, I can <u>avoid committing</u>

<u>myself to too many activities.</u>

(transition) general subject (thesis link)   point 3
Topic sentence 3: Finally, <u>my daily schedule</u> helps to <u>keep my day</u>

<u>organized.</u>

exercise 15.1 ### Completing Topic Sentences

A list of incomplete topic sentences follows each of the following thesis statements. Fill in the blanks in each topic sentence. Topic sentences should follow the same order suggested in the thesis.

1. For me, an ideal vacation spot will offer me the opportunity to lie in the sun, to exercise, and to eat a variety of food.

   a. When I am on vacation, I enjoy _____.
   b. Vacation also gives me the opportunity to _____.
   c. One of the activities I enjoy most on vacation is _____

   _____.

2. My favorite piece of furniture is my grandfather's desk. I love it for its beauty, usefulness, and sense of family history.

   a. I admire the desk for its _____.
   b. Not only is the desk attractive, it is also _____.
   c. The link to my _____, however, is the main reason the desk is important to me.

3. I am attending college so that I can become an accountant, support my children, and make my family proud.

   a. With a college education, I can _____.
   b. A degree will also help ensure _____.
   c. As a first-generation college student, I _____.

4. At my favorite hangout, the Sand Crab, I enjoy the casual atmosphere, the unique blend of music, and the company of friends.

   a. The Sand Crab has a/an _____ that I enjoy.

b. The combination of old and new _____ makes the Sand

Crab unique.

c. Best of all, _____ also enjoy gathering at the Sand Crab.

5. When parents go through a divorce, children may be plagued by guilt, divided loyalty, and insecurity.

a. When parents divorce, children may _____.

b. Especially if the parents' divorce is a bitter one, children may _____

_____.

c. Children of divorce may also experience _____.

The Thesis Link

A **thesis link** is a word or phrase that links the topic sentence directly to the central idea of the essay. It is not always enough for the topic sentence to state a thesis point. Linking the topic sentence to the general subject of the essay or to your attitude about that subject reminds your reader that the paragraph is part of a larger whole. At the same time, a thesis link aids coherence by relating the specific point to the thesis. Notice in the examples that each topic sentence contains a word or phrase that links the paragraph to the thesis.

EXAMPLE

thesis
Thesis statement: I have achieved higher grades this term by improving

point 1   point 2   point 3
my study habits, organizing my time, and cutting back my work hours.

point 1   thesis link
Topic sentence 1: Better study habits have been a key to my improved grades.

point 2   thesis link
Topic sentence 2: Planning has also helped me improve my grades.

thesis link
Topic sentence 3: The step that has most affected my GPA was reducing

point 3
my work hours.

EXAMPLE

point 1   point 2
Thesis: An unreasonable boss, inconvenient work hours, and

point 3   thesis
unpleasant duties make me dislike my job at Sadie's Donut Heaven.

point 1   thesis link
Topic sentence 1: Sadie, my boss, makes my job so unbearable

at times that I'm sure her name must be short for "Sadist."

thesis link   point 2
Topic sentence 2: <u>Another unpleasant part of my job</u> is <u>my work schedule.</u>

point 3   thesis link
Topic sentence 3: The <u>work itself</u> <u>makes Donut Heaven anything</u>

<u>but heavenly.</u>

EXAMPLE

thesis
Thesis: I have benefited from subscribing to an online computer service.

Although the points are not listed in the thesis, the writer presents them in the topic sentences. The thesis link in each topic sentence will be a reference to the idea of *the benefits of an online computer service.* Points 1, 2, and 3 will be *those specific benefits.*

thesis link   point 1
Topic sentence 1: <u>My computer service</u> <u>brings me the news before it</u>

<u>appears in the newspaper.</u>

thesis link   point 2
Topic sentence 2: <u>Through my link to the Internet,</u> <u>I can visit an art</u>

<u>museum without moving from my chair.</u>

thesis link   point 3
Topic sentence 3: <u>Another benefit of an online service</u> is <u>the opportunity to</u>

<u>"meet" people from all over the country</u> through computer chat rooms

and bulletin boards.

exercise 15.2 **Providing Thesis Links**

Following are five thesis statements and topic sentences that relate to them. Circle the letter of the topic sentence that does not have a thesis link, that is, the sentence that does not mention the general subject of the essay. Then rewrite the sentence, linking it to the thesis.

1. *Thesis:* The size, the location, and the design of my house make it an ideal place to live.

   a. My house is easy to enjoy because it's small enough to take care of easily.
   b. Out in the country, my nearest neighbor is five miles away.
   c. The convenient layout and many windows in my home suit my casual lifestyle.

   _____

   _____

2. *Thesis:* Many people over twenty-five hesitate to return to school because of the demands of their jobs, their commitment to their children, or their fear of returning to the classroom.

   a. Many jobs are demanding.
   b. The demands of parenthood often keep older students from continuing their education.
   c. Perhaps the number one reason older students postpone a return to school is fear.

   _____

   _____

3. *Thesis:* Dieting is difficult for me because I usually eat substantial meals, snack in the evenings, and nibble when I am nervous.

   a. My lifelong habit of eating "three squares a day" defeats any diet I start.
   b. Snacks usually accompany my evening reading or television viewing.
   c. Even if a diet is going well, stress often sends me running to the refrigerator.

   _____

   _____

4. Thesis: Some students are a pain to have as classmates. These include students who never come prepared, those who are noisy, and those who monopolize the class discussion.

   a. Coming to class unprepared is a common occurrence.
   b. Even worse than the unprepared student is the student who distracts the class with unnecessary noise.
   c. Most tiresome of all is the student who monopolizes the class discussion.

   _____

   _____

5. Thesis: In recent years, the public has become increasingly unwilling to report crimes.

   a. Many people fear that reporting a crime will provoke retaliation from the criminal.
   b. Some citizens don't want to get involved.
   c. Other crimes go unreported because crime victims believe the police can do nothing to help.

   _____

   _____

Unity: Sticking to the Point of the Essay

An essay with **unity** is like a completed jigsaw puzzle. Every piece is necessary, and each does its part to contribute to the big picture. Each paragraph, each sentence, fits perfectly to support the thesis. When one piece does not fit, the essay lacks unity. Lack of unity occurs within a paragraph when one or more sentences do not support the paragraph's topic sentence. Likewise, when an entire paragraph does not support the thesis of the essay, the essay lacks unity.

Read the paragraph in the example below and see if you can spot the three sentences that interfere with the unity of the paragraph.

EXAMPLE
[1]I have heard that inside every fat person, there is a thin person waiting to get out, but I believe that just the opposite is true. [2]Inside every thin person, a fat person is waiting to take control. [3]For most people, maintaining thinness requires self-control at mealtime. [4]A thin person may say "no" to the extra helping of cottage cheese and measure the fat-free salad dressing carefully because it too contains calories. [5]But somewhere inside, an inner, fat self is craving ice cream with chocolate sauce for dessert. [6]Staying thin also requires exercise. [7]The thin person may have plans to attend evening aerobics after work, but the fat person inside would rather curl up in front of a fire with a book and a cup of hot cocoa. [8]The thin person who gets up at 5:30 a.m. to jog has to silence the fat self's inner voice, which is whining for just an extra half-hour's sleep. [9]Of course, thin people are better off staying thin. [10]Studies have shown that in general, people who eat less live longer. [11]In addition, people who exercise are healthier and more likely to maintain flexibility and mobility well into old age. [12]All it would take is a moment of weakness for the fat person inside to burst forth, no longer held in by the tight cocoon of thinness.

Were you able to spot the sentences that did not fit? The paragraph lacks unity because sentences 9, 10, and 11 do not support the topic sentence of the paragraph.

exercise 15.3 **Spotting Problems with Unity**

Read the following essay. Find and identify

    a. the body paragraph that does not support the thesis statement, and
    b. the body paragraph that contains two sentences that do not support its topic sentence.

CHOOSING A VETERINARIAN

That squirming, tail-wagging furball that you bring home from the pound or pet store needs more than just love and kibble. Good veterinary care is also essential. If you know what to look for, finding the right veterinarian for your pet can be a simple process.

[1]The first step is to evaluate the veterinarian's office. First, consider its location. It should be close enough to your home to be convenient. In an emergency, you should be able to get there in a few minutes. Next, look at the physical facility itself. Cleanliness is a must. The waiting room should be clean and pleasant, and it should be standard practice for the staff to disinfect the tables in the exam rooms before each use. Finally, make sure that the facility's services meet your needs. Some veterinary clinics provide boarding, grooming, and bathing. Some clinics require appointments, while others provide service on a first come, first served basis. The clinic you choose should be convenient, clean, and provide the services that you need.

[2]Once you have found a clinic you like, the next step is to evaluate the veterinarian and the staff. They should be kind to you and to your pet. Watch the way your pet is handled. Is he handled gently yet confidently, called by name, and spoken to in a kind tone? The vet's approach to your pet should make you smile. If your pet is treated roughly, find another vet. Your vet's treatment of you should pass muster, too. Good veterinarians do not simply treat animals; they also educate owners. They tell you why and how an illness can occur, signs to look for as the pet gets better, and signs that indicate you should bring the pet back. Caring for a sick pet can be difficult because a pet cannot talk to you like a human can. The pet cannot tell you where it hurts or what is wrong.

[3]Even with good veterinary facilities and a competent, caring vet, chances are that the veterinary clinic will not be your pet's favorite place to visit. Many pet owners report that their pets have an uncanny sixth sense about visits to the vet. When it's time to go to the vet, these apparently psychic pets disappear under beds, into closets, or behind refrigerators. Repeated calling does not bring them out, and they must finally be hunted down and dragged out of hiding. In the car, cats yowl and dogs whine, and some fearful pets even have "accidents" on the way, losing control of their bowel or bladder functions. At the vet's office, most become quiet and docile as the veterinarian handles them. Rarely, animals become aggressive, growling or snapping. But although the visits may be traumatic, they are necessary to a pet's good health.

Ensuring good veterinary care is easier if you know how to pick the right vet for your dog or cat. Good veterinary care is one way you can repay the love, loyalty, and companionship your pet provides.

The paragraph that is entirely off the topic is body paragraph _____.

The paragraph that contains two sentences that do not support the topic sentence is body paragraph _____.

Coherence: Holding the Essay Together

An essay with **coherence** is an essay with solid and strong connections between paragraphs and ideas. To achieve coherence, you must first make sure that the ideas you set down are logically related and well thought out. Coherence between ideas can also be aided by transitional words and expressions.

Following is a list of transitional words and expressions, organized by their function within the sentence.

Some Common Transitional Words and Expressions
* Transitions of Time

after	during	later	now	suddenly	when
as	first	meanwhile	often	temporarily	while
before	immediately	next	previously	then	yet

* Transitions of Space

above	beside	down	next to	toward
around	between	in	on	under
behind	by	near	over	

* Transitions of Addition

also	finally	furthermore	in addition	next
another	first			

* Transitions of Importance

as important	essential	major	primary
equally important	just as important	most important	significant

*Transitions of Contrast

although	even though	in contrast	instead	on the other hand
but	however	in spite of	nevertheless	yet

*Transitions of Cause and Effect

a consequence of	because	since	therefore
as a result	consequently	so	thus

*Transitions of Illustration or Example

for example	for instance	including	such as

Making Transitions between Body Paragraphs When you move from one body paragraph to the next, **transitional words** act as signposts. In the first body paragraph, often no transition is needed. If you use a transitional word or expression, a simple "first of all," or "one reason . . ." usually works well. But avoid a mechanical "first, second, third" approach. Instead, vary your transitional techniques. In the second and third body paragraphs, transitional words create a bridge between paragraphs that suggests that you have discussed a related idea in the preceding paragraph. Because you are adding an idea to the ones you have already discussed, the transitional words you use will be transitions of addition: *also, another, next, an additional (reason, factor, way).*

EXAMPLE Doing something for someone else is *another* way to shake a bad mood.

Some teenagers' unwillingness to use birth control *also* contributes to the high rate of teen pregnancy.

The *first* step in resolving a conflict is to define the issues involved.

exercise 15.4 ## Using Transitional Expressions in Topic Sentences

Rewrite the following topic sentences using a transitional word or phrase. The word or phrase you choose will depend on whether you see each sentence as the topic sentence for the first body paragraph, the second body paragraph, or the last body paragraph, but it should be a *transition of addition.*

1. Newspapers are a better source of news than television because the stories go

   into more detail.

   _____

   _____

2. It is important to find a family doctor after moving to a new town.

   _____

   _____

3. The tailgater is a type of bad driver.

   _____

   _____

4. Using public transportation is cheaper than owning a vehicle.

   _____

   _____

5. Good communication skills are essential in a job interview.

   _____

   _____

Making Transitions within Paragraphs Within paragraphs, transitional words keep your reader oriented in time and space and aware of relationships between ideas. Within a single paragraph, you may need several types of transitional words to move your reader smoothly from one idea to the next.

exercise 15.5   ### Using Transitional Expressions within Paragraphs

In the following paragraph, provide the indicated type of transition in the blank.

> [1] _____ (time) the Fresh-Food Supermart was robbed, Shawna had the bad luck to be the only cashier on duty. The robber came in about 7:00 a.m., [2] _____ (time) the store opened. She noticed him right away [3] _____ (cause-effect) his baseball cap was pulled low over his eyes and he wore a jacket [4] _____ (contrast) the morning was warm. He loitered for a while [5] _____ (space) the door, [6] _____ (time) he walked up to her register. She must have suspected him [7] _____ (cause-effect) she suddenly remembered Mr. Monroe, the store manager, saying: "If you are ever robbed, remember that your life is worth more than whatever is in that cash drawer. Stay cool and hand over the money." [8] _____ (time) the robber leaned [9] _____ (space) her and mumbled, "I have a gun. Put the money in a bag." Remembering Mr. Monroe's words, Shawna quickly withdrew the money from the register. [10] _____ (time) she reached for a bag, she was surprised at the words that automatically fell from her lips: "Paper or plastic?" Much [11] _____, (time) Mr. Monroe teased that not only had she remembered his instructions, she had [12] _____ (addition) remembered to offer her "customer" a choice.

The Transitional Topic Sentence The **transitional topic sentence** takes a backward glance at the topic of the preceding paragraph before moving on to the topic of the paragraph it leads into. Since the first body paragraph presents the first point of discussion, transitional topic sentences are not used there. Transitional topic sentences can be used only in the second and third body paragraphs of a five-paragraph essay. They are an effective way of moving between paragraphs, but like any other technique, they should not be overdone. One per essay is probably enough. Some examples of transitional topic sentences follow.

EXAMPLE

Not only do illegal drugs pose a health risk, they can also land the user in jail.

Discussion: The writer has discussed the health risks posed by illegal drugs in the preceding paragraph and is now going to discuss the possibility that the user may spend time in jail.

EXAMPLE

A lifetime sentence to the prison of addiction is often the worst consequence of drug use.

Discussion: This variation of the first example merely hints at the topic of the preceding paragraph (the possibility of serving time in jail). The hint provides a connection between paragraphs.

EXAMPLE

Although rock music suits my happy, energetic moods, I turn to the sound of blues when I am depressed.

Discussion: This transition outlines a movement from a paragraph about rock music to a paragraph about blues.

exercise 15.6 **Writing Transitional Topic Sentences**

The following outlines show a thesis and three topic sentences. For each outline, rewrite topic sentences 2 and 3 as transitional topic sentences. The first one is done for you.

1. *Thesis:* I prefer renting videos to going to a movie theater. When I rent a movie, I watch it when I want to, avoid crowds, and spend less money.

   Topic sentence 1: One advantage of renting a video is that I can watch it whenever I want to, not when the theater schedules it.

   Topic sentence 2: I also like being able to avoid crowds at the theater.

   Rewritten transitional topic sentence 2: <u>In addition to setting my own</u> <u>schedule, I like being able to avoid the crowded theater.</u>

   Topic sentence 3: Saving money is another important advantage of renting a video.

   Rewritten transitional topic sentence 3: <u>Avoiding crowds is good, but</u> <u>saving money by renting a video is even better.</u>

2. *Thesis:* Automated answering systems, telephone sales pitches, and repeated wrong numbers have made me hate the telephone.

Topic sentence 1: When Alexander Graham Bell invented the telephone, he never foresaw the horror of automated answering systems.

Topic sentence 2: Telephone sales pitches are another reason I hate the telephone.

_____

_____

Topic sentence 3: Answering wrong numbers at all hours is an inconvenience of having a telephone.

_____

_____

3. *Thesis:* In my spare time, I enjoy tennis, woodworking, and reading.

Topic sentence 1: Tennis is one of my favorite spare-time activities.

Topic sentence 2: Another of my hobbies is woodworking.

_____

_____

Topic sentence 3: Reading is one of my favorite leisure activities.

_____

_____

Support: Using Specific Detail

Support is the heart of any piece of writing. Even a grammatically perfect essay falls flat without strong, specific support. If a thesis or topic sentence is a promise to the reader to discuss a specific topic, then an essay without solid support makes that thesis an empty promise. No matter how good it sounds, there is nothing behind it.

Although few writers deliberately set out to make empty promises, many do so because providing strong support is one of the most difficult dimensions of writing body paragraphs. It takes practice, thought, and the ability to recognize and to construct specific examples and details.

Why It's Hard to Be Specific   Quick, what did you eat for lunch yesterday?

If you are like most people, you answered with a broad term—*fast food, a sandwich, a microwaveable dinner*—rather than with a specific description, such as *a tuna-salad sandwich on rye toast.*

Being specific does not come naturally because the human brain is programmed to think in categories. This ability to lump things together by function saves you time. It also gives your brain an orderly way to store the information it receives every day. Without the ability to categorize, a football and a baseball would seem to have as little in common as a dandelion and a Phillips screwdriver. Bits of information would be scattered throughout your brain like confetti, impossible to retrieve.

But the ability to categorize can work against you when you write. Most people would complete the sentence "Harold drove to work in his _____" with the word <u>car</u> or <u>truck</u>. Few would fill in *beat-up Chevrolet Caprice that had seen its best days fifteen years ago* or *ten-year-old Volvo without a single scratch or dent.* Such specific examples do not come to mind easily because the human brain, programmed to categorize, looks first at the big picture.

To write rich, detail-packed paragraphs, train yourself to move beyond general categories and to look for the details. This skill is similar to the one that police officers develop when they learn to observe sharply and to remember detail. Police officers, however, receive special training on developing observational skills. Writers are on their own. The exercises in this section are designed to help you move beyond general categories. When you can do that, you will be able to provide examples and details and become a writer who delivers on your promises.

Essay Development Technique 1: Supporting with Specific Examples **Examples** are one of the best ways to get a point across because they provide a concrete illustration of your point. If you say your father is sentimental, your reader will get the general idea. If you say he gets teary-eyed over Hallmark commercials, you are giving specific support to the general idea. Examples, then, are specific illustrations, exact instances. Using an example is like making a word or phrase more specific, but on a larger scale since examples range in length from a single word to multiple paragraphs. With an example, you are usually giving your reader both the general idea and a specific example of that idea.

An Example in a Word or Phrase   Examples expressed in a word or phrase are usually used when the author wants to illustrate an idea briefly and then move on. Look at the use of short examples in the following process paragraph.

EXAMPLE

Cleaning the grout in a ceramic tile floor is a laborious process. Begin by diluting a liquid cleaner with bleach, <u>such as Clorox Clean-Up or Comet Gel,</u> to half strength. Then, using the squeeze bottle that the cleaner came in, squeeze cleaner directly into the grout line. After doing a small patch, about a <u>three-foot by six-foot square,</u> allow the cleaner to penetrate for five to ten minutes. Then, using a <u>wire scrub brush, toothbrush, or another small, stiff-bristled brush,</u> scrub the grout clean. Be sure to keep the area properly ventilated and to walk outside the room from time to time for air, especially if you are cleaning a small area <u>such as a bathroom.</u> After the entire floor is complete and the area is completely dry, you are ready to seal the grout.

exercise 15.7   **Providing Examples**

Provide an example of each of the following ideas in a word or a phrase.

1. music

   _____

2. game

   _____

3. book

_____

4. luxuries

_____

5. food

_____

6. problems at school

_____

7. metals

_____

8. injury

_____

9. entertainment

_____

10. bad habit

_____

The Sentence-Length Example Sometimes, you need more than just a word or phrase to illustrate an idea. In such cases, try giving an example in a sentence or two. The example needs to be a specific, detailed illustration of the general idea you are discussing, not just a vague restatement.

EXAMPLE

✗   _Idea + vague restatement:_ The new disk jockey on the morning show is really obnoxious. He has an unpleasant attitude that makes listening to his show a bad experience.

✓   _Idea + specific example:_ The new disk jockey on the morning show is really obnoxious. He tries to humiliate listeners who call in, and his jokes border on the offensive.

EXAMPLE

✗   _Idea + vague restatement:_ The new grocery store has added whimsical touches to some of its departments. It's enjoyable to shop in a store that is entertaining.

✓   _Idea + specific example:_ The new grocery store has added whimsical touches to some of its departments. In the produce department, thunder rolls and "lightning" flashes above the vegetable bins before the automatic vegetable sprinkler turns on. On the dairy aisle, recordings of mooing cows and clucking hens amuse passing shoppers.

exercise 15.8   **Weeding Out Vague Examples**

Circle the letter of the sentence that is a general restatement of the idea, not a specific example.

1. We needed a break, so we decided to stop and have something to drink.

   a. I ordered coffee, and Marcie had iced tea.
   b. We chose from the restaurant's wide selection of refreshing beverages.
   c. I went to the kitchen and fixed hot herbal tea with honey and lemon.

2. A conflict broke out.

   a. Fists and plates flew as restaurant patrons scuffled over the last yeast roll.
   b. Apparently, some sort of disagreement caused an altercation to take place.
   c. John accused Myra of taking his parking place, and the two began to argue.

3. My friends are all trying to be thriftier.

   a. Emily tries to save wherever she can. She knows the value of a dollar.
   b. Tom has decided to bring his lunch instead of eating out every day.
   c. Khara clips coupons and checks grocery store specials before shopping.

4. Kay worked hard sprucing up her yard this weekend.

   a. Wearing heavy gloves, she pulled weeds from the flowerbed in front of the house.
   b. She toiled laboriously on the lawn.
   c. Soaked with sweat, she pushed the mower through tall grass for more than an hour.

5. Researchers have found that many of our grandmothers' home remedies really work.

   a. Chicken soup, the all-time favorite home remedy, eases congestion and aids breathing.
   b. Warm milk really does induce sleep.
   c. It seems that Grandma may have known what she was talking about after all.

exercise 15.9 Providing Specific Support

For each of the following general ideas, provide a sentence or two of specific support.

1. The kitchen was a mess.

   _____

   _____

2. Without my glasses, I find it difficult to see.

   _____

   _____

3. In the hallway, two students complained about their English assignment.

   _____

   _____

4. The police found plenty of evidence that the accident had been Darren's fault.

_____

_____

5. When I met Fern, I knew immediately that she was a heavy smoker.

_____

_____

6. The two brands of orange juice are quite different in taste and appearance.

_____

_____

7. The package was damaged when it arrived in the mail.

_____

_____

8. One look at the teacher's face told the students he was angry.

_____

_____

9. The mailbox contained nothing but junk mail.

_____

_____

10. Litter is becoming a problem on Sanford Road.

_____

_____

The Extended Example Sometimes you may wish to develop an entire paragraph with an extended, paragraph-length example. In this case, your topic sentence will state the general idea, and the rest of the paragraph will provide a detailed example. In this sort of paragraph, it is important to end with a summary sentence that connects the specific example back to the general idea, as in the following paragraph.

EXAMPLE

topic sentence

One of the most annoying and time-consuming technological advances is the

automated telephone system. Recently, I called a government agency to ask a

simple question, but instead of being greeted by a human voice, I reached a

recorded menu. "Press 1 if you need directions on filling out forms," the voice

extended example {

began. After listening to the menu and finding no information that I needed,

I pressed a number at random. Once I reached a human being, I reasoned,

I could find out what I needed to know. Instead, I was connected to yet

another recording, which reeled off information, then hung up. I dialed

again. Finally, I reached a part of the menu that said, "For permission to

speak to an agent, press 4." I pressed the key, astounded that a taxpaying

citizen would need permission to speak to someone at a government office.

At last I heard the ringing of a phone that I hoped would connect me to a

human voice. But it was another recording, saying "For permission to speak

to an agent, please hold." Soothing music played in the background as my

blood pressure reached new heights. After fifteen minutes on hold, I hung up.

summary sentence
I had decided that writing a letter might be the easiest way to bypass the

technological obstacles that stood between me and the answer to my question.

Although the example in the preceding paragraph is a personal example, examples do not necessarily have to be from direct personal experience. Look at the next paragraph for a different kind of extended example, one that is not based on personal experience but on the writer's knowledge of how test anxiety works.

EXAMPLE

topic sentence
Sometimes, factors totally unrelated to study can interfere with performance

on a test. Test anxiety is an excellent illustration. It often strikes students who

have prepared adequately and who set high standards for themselves. Test

extended example {

anxiety goes beyond the mild jitters that plague almost every student the night

before a test. It holds its victims in a paralyzing grip. Typically, the student

with test anxiety looks at the first question on the test, and all the carefully

studied material seems to evaporate in a haze of panic. The student knows the material before entering the examination room and may recall both

questions and answers after the test has ended, but in the pressure cooker of

summary sentence
the test environment, the answers do not come. <u>As the example of test anxiety</u>

<u>shows, poor test performance is not always an indication that no studying</u>

<u>took place.</u>

exercise 15.10 **Writing Extended Examples**

Write an extended example to support one of the three following topic sentences. Don't forget to write a summary sentence connecting the example back to the idea in the topic sentence.

Topic sentence 1: Instead of hoping that a problem will go away, the best way to deal with it is to confront it head-on.

Topic sentence 2: Sometimes an opportunity comes along at exactly the right time.

Topic sentence 3: Telephone salespersons can be an annoyance.

_____

_____

_____

_____

_____

_____

_____

_____

_____

Essay Development Technique 2: Adding Detail through Comparisons One way to express ideas is by comparing the familiar with the unfamiliar. If your doctor tells you that a centrifuge separates the liquid parts of your blood sample from the solid by centrifugal force, you may not understand. If she says that a centrifuge separates plasma from solid blood components just as a washer on the spin cycle separates water from clothes, then you will understand more readily.

Like an example, a comparison may be brief or extended. Although entire essays are developed using comparison, you may use comparison techniques in any essay to make your writing more specific.

Comparisons Using *Like* or *As* When you make brief comparisons, you may find the words *like* and *as* useful. A comparison using *like* or *as* is called a *simile*.

EXAMPLE
- ✓ Nina moved across the dance floor like a skater on ice.
- ✓ The car was crumpled like a used tissue.
- ✓ Nina moved across the dance floor as gracefully as a skater on ice.
- ✓ The car was as crumpled as a used tissue.

When you make a comparison, it is usually more useful to compare unlike things than like things. If you say, for instance, "When Billy opened the presents at his eighth birthday party, he looked like a kid at Christmas," the comparison is not very useful. After all, Billy *is* a child and he *is* opening presents, just as he might at Christmas. However, look at what happens if you compare two unlike things: "When Smitty dealt the hand, Jack picked his cards up one by one and arranged them carefully, looking like a kid at Christmas." The comparison reveals two things about Jack that a reader would not know from the rest of the sentence: He has been dealt a good hand, and he is probably not a very good card player—his face reveals too much.

EXAMPLE
- ✗ Bill's old Ford truck runs like a Chevrolet pickup.
- ✓ Bill's old Ford truck runs like a Maytag washer.
- ✗ The car was dented only slightly, but Sam reacted like a typical car enthusiast.
- ✓ The car was dented only slightly, but Sam squawked like a bird whose baby had fallen from the nest.

exercise 15.11   **Matching Comparisons**

Match each of the following phrases with one of the sentences to form a logical comparison.

a. seats in a stadium
b. socks left too long at the bottom of a gym bag
c. gravestones in an old cemetery
d. spilled candy
e. needles
f. the sound of computer keys
g. a job interview
h. the rising tide engulfing the shore
i. cats' eyes in the dark
j. hot dogs browning on a grill

———— 1. His car smelled unpleasant, like _____.

———— 2. Next to the pool, the sunbathers lay side by side, like _____.

———— 3. With her dentures, the old woman made a muted clicking noise, like _____.

———— 4. Calvin's meeting with a date's parents was more like _____ than a social occasion because they asked so many questions.

———— 5. His eyes were as piercing as _____.

————— 6. Pebbles of all colors were scattered at the shoreline as carelessly

as _____.

————— 7. On the side of the road, beer cans glinted like _____.

————— 8. Sleep came over her gradually, like _____.

————— 9. The new shelf organizers that Tina bought are tiered like _____.

————— 10. Scarred desks lined the empty classroom in orderly, silent rows

like _____.

exercise 15.12   **Making Comparisons**

Use your own comparisons to complete each sentence.

1. Throughout the ceremony, the groom looked bored, like a _____.

2. The small, gray-haired grandmother marched into the mayor's office like

_____.

3. When the tired-looking server brought my sandwich, it was as tasteless

as _____.

4. Marcia's old car was as reliable as _____.

5. Emerging from the dark theater, Brian felt disoriented, like _____.

6. After Elton's wife left him, he drifted from job to job and from town to town

like _____.

7. I hoped the class would have a relaxed atmosphere, but it was as formal

as _____.

8. Just before final exams, students burst into a frenzy of activity, like

_____.

9. "When I came into this business, I had visions of limos, champagne, and ador-

ing fans," said the actor. "Instead, I'm working as hard as _____."

10. Looking at the test in front of him, the student sat like _____.

Progressive Writing Assignment

Progressive Writing Assignment: Writing Body Paragraphs

If your instructor has assigned the Progressive Writing Assignment, you have already completed your prewriting, your thesis and outline, and your introduction. In this chapter, you will complete your body paragraphs. Recall that each assignment takes you a step further toward an essay.

Topics and Tips for Writing Body Paragraphs

The Topics

Topic 1: Discuss three obstacles to your education.

Topic 2: Discuss your short-term goals, long-term goals, or both.

Topic 3: Discuss the values you have learned by observing members of your family.

Topic 4: Discuss your methods of coping with stress.

Tips for Writing Body Paragraphs

The Topic Sentence: Tips for Direction

- Make sure that each topic sentence mentions the subject of the paragraph and that each topic sentence links back clearly to the thesis with key words. For example, if you chose Topic 1, "Discuss three obstacles to your education," the key words *education* and *obstacles* (or a synonym such as *barriers*) should appear in each topic sentence. A typical topic sentence might read "One of the obstacles to my education is my financial situation."

Transitions: Tips for Coherence

- Use a transitional word such as *also* or *another* in the topic sentences of body paragraphs 2 and 3. (*Another* of my long-term goals is to start my own business.)
- Make one of the topic sentences a transitional topic sentence. (*After I start my accounting business,* my next long-term goal is to start a family.)
- Check each paragraph to make sure it flows logically and has transitional expressions where needed.

Staying on Track: Tips for Unity

- Check each paragraph to make sure that every sentence supports the topic sentence.

Examples and Details: Tips for Support

- Make sure that your language is specific. Have you used words that create pictures by appealing to the reader's sense of sight, hearing, touch, taste, and smell?
- Check to see that you have supported your paragraphs with specific examples. If you are writing on Topic 4, "Discuss your methods of coping with stress," you might use a *specific example* that describes what happened on a particular occasion (Last Tuesday, when I was nervous and worried about a job interview the next day . . .). However, you might also decide to use a *typical example* that describes something that customarily occurs (Every evening when I come home from work, I put on my exercise clothing . . .).

16 Concluding the Essay

True horror
COMING SOON
to an essay near you?

Endings are difficult. Courses end with the pressure of exams. Weekends end with Monday mornings. And for many writers, the ending of an essay is the hardest part to write. However, the etiquette of concluding an essay, like that of ending a telephone conversation, is simple: Keep the goodbye short and don't introduce any new information that keeps the other person hanging on too long.

After the specific and detailed support of the body paragraphs, the first sentence or two of the conclusion should take your reader once again to a broad, thesis-level view of the topic. This broader statement may take the form of a summary, a recommendation, or a prediction.

Then comes the closing statement, harder to write but vital because it is the last impression your reader takes away from the essay. The key requirement of a closing statement is that it should *sound* like a closing statement. It should sound as final as the slam of a door.

Reader's *Tip* ——— Focus on Concluding the Essay:
Thinking about Endings

Think of the endings to *The Shawshank Redemption* and *The Silence of the Lambs*. In *The Shawshank Redemption*, Red (Morgan Freeman) finally gets to the beach in Mexico and to his friend Andy (Tim Robbins), who has successfully—and brilliantly—escaped from prison. The ending of this movie wraps everything up neatly, and the audience gets the sense that the characters will live the rest of their days in relative happiness. Now think of *The Silence of the Lambs*. The vicious and cannibalistic Hannibal Lecter (Anthony Hopkins) has escaped, and he calls FBI agent Clarice Starling (Jodie Foster) to let her know that she will be safe from him. As he hangs up, he casually says, "I'm having an old friend for dinner." The audience knows that when Hannibal Lecter *has a friend for dinner,* the friend is likely to be on the menu. Nothing is resolved, and Hannibal Lecter roams free to kill again.

Though these movies have different kinds of endings, each ending works. Audiences are satisfied to see Red and Andy together again, and titillated to think of Hannibal Lecter having a friend for dinner, perhaps with a side of fava beans. The same is true with conclusions in essays; you want the ending to fit with the paper in order to satisfy your audience's expectations.

Reflect on It

Whenever you end something, be it a project or a paper, you want to do it with style. But how do you know when you have the right ending? Try this: Think of a movie you have seen recently and imagine a totally different ending to it. How does the ending work? Does it feel right, or was the original ending better? Why does a single change make such a big difference? This exercise may illustrate that sometimes you have to "try on" different endings before you get it right. Don't be afraid to experiment!

Methods of Conclusion

To bring your essay to a solid, satisfying close, try one of the following methods of conclusion.

Summary

A **summary conclusion** is the simplest and easiest type of conclusion to write. In the first sentence or two, recap the main points of your essay, making sure to use different wording than you used in your thesis and topic sentences. Your final sentence brings the essay to a close.

In the following example, the writer recaps the major points, then ends with a strong, final-sounding statement.

EXAMPLE

During my tour of duty with the Air Force, I received hands-on experience in electronics, furthered my education, and developed confidence in my ability to handle my own life. I never piloted a plane while I was in the Air Force, but in many ways, I learned to soar.

exercise 16.1   **Analyzing a Summary Conclusion**

1. From the above summary conclusion, try to determine the major points of the essay it concludes. In what order were they most likely presented?

    _____

    _____

    _____

2. Consider the following possible versions of the ending sentence. Which do you think is strongest? Which is weakest? Why?

    a. I never piloted a plane while I was in the Air Force, but in many ways, I learned to soar. (original version)

    b. I learned to soar in many ways although I never piloted a plane while I was in the Air Force.

    c. I never piloted a plane, and while I was in the Air Force, I learned to soar in many ways.

    _____

    _____

Recommendation

A **recommendation conclusion** suggests a solution to a problem raised in the essay. A logical way to end an essay that discusses a problem is to offer a solution or suggest that one is on the horizon.

EXAMPLE

It does not matter whether the shot is fired in the commission of a robbery, in the heat of an argument, or by accident. The result is the same: A life is lost. The logical solution is the one already implemented by more enlightened countries—to outlaw handguns. Outlawing handguns is a major step toward a safer, saner, less fearful society.

exercise 16.2 **Writing a Recommendation Conclusion**

Imagine that you have written an essay discussing the causes of one of the following social problems. Write a brief conclusion (two to four sentences) making general recommendations about working toward a solution.

teenage suicide
violence in the schools
poverty among the elderly

_____

_____

_____

_____

_____

_____

_____

_____

Prediction

A **prediction conclusion**—a look toward the future—is another good way of ending an essay. In the following example, the writer has discussed society's growing dependence on providers of personal service. The ending is a simple yet effective prediction.

EXAMPLE

A society of graying baby boomers, working parents, and two-income families is becoming increasingly dependent on service providers. In the twenty-first century, hiring help with housecleaning, lawn maintenance, and child care will no longer be a luxury for many Americans, but a necessity.

exercise 16.3 **Writing a Prediction Conclusion**

You have written an essay suggesting that the solution to reducing the unwanted pet population is to require that every cat and dog be spayed or neutered within five years. Financial help is available for those who cannot afford the procedure, and exemptions are available for pets too old or ill to withstand the operation. Those who wish to breed their animals may purchase a special breeding license at a cost of $500 per animal.

Write a conclusion of two to four sentences predicting the changes that will occur over the next five years as your plan goes into effect.

_____

_____

_____

_____

_____

_____

_____

_____

Full Circle

A **full circle conclusion** incorporates a word or image from the introduction as a theme in the conclusion, thus bringing the essay full circle to end where it began. This type of conclusion is surprisingly powerful and satisfying.

EXAMPLE

Following is an introduction paired with a conclusion that comes full circle, ending with an image from the introduction.

Introduction

The photograph in the magazine showed a laboratory rat with a human ear growing out of its back. The strange-looking creature was part of an experiment in the re-growth of human cartilage through genetic engineering. I immediately thought of my neighbor Otis Needham, who lost an ear to cancer. Genetic engineering is a relatively new field, but it promises quantum leaps in organ and tissue replacement, cure of dis-ease, and prevention of birth defects.

Conclusion

In a laboratory somewhere, a little white rat, burdened with an ear he cannot use, her-alds a brighter future for the Otis Needhams of the world. Thanks in part to this little rat and others like him, human beings will live longer and healthier lives through the promise of genetic engineering.

exercise 16.4   **Completing a Full Circle Conclusion**

Step 1: Read the following introduction.

I stood in the bookstore line, staring glumly at a green book entitled *Understanding Psychology*. I could not believe my bad luck. Not only was Psychology 101 the only social science elective left, but I had to take it with Nortenson, the toughest psychology professor on campus. Before the quarter was over, however, I was thankful for the luck that led me to Dr. Nortenson's psychology class.

Step 2: Complete the conclusion by writing a first sentence that brings in the image of the book. Notice that the second sentence, beginning "Every time I look at it . . ." makes a transition that suggests that the book is someplace where you see it often. Perhaps the sentence you write could tell where it is.

Conclusion

_____

_____. Every time I look at it, I think of what I might have missed if I had been able to get the courses I really wanted last fall. Thanks to my bad luck, I discovered an inspiring teacher, a fascinating field of study, and my future career.

Quotation

A **quotation conclusion** can help you bring your point home solidly and effectively. For the strongest effect, make the quotation your closing statement.

EXAMPLE

I had always planned to go to college "someday." But it took a loaded gun to make me realize how much of my life I had squandered behind the counter of the Kwik-Stop #7. The day after the robbery, I gave my notice and filled out a college application. At the time, I had never heard of Cervantes, but his words express a truth I realized that day: "By the streets of someday, one arrives at the house of never."

exercise 16.5 **Ending with a Quotation**

Write a conclusion that ends in a quotation. Use a topic and quotation of your own choosing or choose from the list that follows.

_____

_____

_____

_____

_____

_____

_____

_____

_____

_____

_____

_____

_____

QUOTATIONS

When poverty comes in at the door, love flies out the window.
—Seventeenth-century saying

Our life is frittered away by detail. . . . Simplify, simplify.
—Henry David Thoreau, *Walden*

Lost time is never found again.
—Ben Franklin, *Poor Richard's Almanac*

It is not the man who has too little, but the man who craves more, who is poor.
—Lucius Annaeus Seneca, *Epistles*

Turn your face to the sun, and the shadows fall behind you.
—Maori proverb

Life sucks—and then you die.
—Bumper sticker, circa 1990

A place for everything, and everything in its place.
—Isabella Mary Beeton, *The Book of Household Management*

Have a place for everything and keep the thing somewhere else. This is not advice, it is merely custom.
—Mark Twain, *Notebooks*

The cat in gloves catches no mice.
—Ben Franklin, *Poor Richard's Almanac*

I have often regretted my speech, but never my silence.
—Publius Syrus, *Maxim*

Topics
- In what situations is it most important to be assertive?
- An optimist has been defined as a person who sees the glass as half full, while a pessimist sees it as half empty. Is it wiser to be an optimist or a pessimist?
- Do you consider yourself an organized person?
- What is your biggest regret?
- How important are wealth and material things to you?

Traps to Avoid

Sermonizing

One trap that some otherwise good writers fall into is lecturing a reader who should be assumed to be on their side of the issue. After a thoughtful, well-reasoned essay on why people turn to drugs, for instance, a writer might be tempted to end the essay with a statement like "Stay away from drugs—you'll be glad you did." Such a statement insults the reader, who should always be counted among the "good guys."

The only type of essay that should end with direct advice to the reader is one in which direct advice is given throughout, such as an essay entitled "How to Shop for a Used Car."

Starched Prose

Writers who speak in a natural voice throughout an essay sometimes stiffen up at the conclusion. They write starched prose like "As I have proven in this essay by discussing the above-mentioned points. . . ." These writers may simply be feeling the awkwardness of saying goodbye, or they may feel that an announcement of the conclusion is needed. It isn't. Even "in conclusion" is probably too much. Readers know when a writer is concluding because the writer stops developing specific points and begins to look once again at the big picture.

Armed with a set of specific concluding techniques, you can avoid the traps that snare some writers as they go about the difficult task of ending an essay.

Progressive Writing Assignment

Progressive Writing Assignment: Concluding the Essay

If your instructor has assigned the Progressive Writing Assignment, you have already completed your prewriting, a thesis and outline, an introduction, and three body paragraphs. In this chapter, you will write your conclusion. Recall that each assignment takes you a step further toward an essay and that you are now only a chapter away from a complete essay.

Topics and Tips for Concluding the Essay

The Topics

Topic 1: Discuss three obstacles to your education.
Topic 2: Discuss your short-term goals, long-term goals, or both.
Topic 3: Discuss the values you have learned by observing members of your family.
Topic 4: Discuss your methods of coping with stress.

Tips for Concluding Your Essay

- For any of the topics in this assignment, a summary of the main points would be an appropriate concluding strategy, but consider other alternatives, too.
- If you used an anecdote or a particularly striking image in your introduction, consider using a full circle conclusion.
- Topics 1 and 2 might lend themselves to a prediction conclusion—a vote of confidence that you will overcome the obstacles to your education or will reach your goals.
- Check to make sure that you have not introduced any new material in your conclusion.

17 Revising, Proofreading, and Formatting

A doggone good revision

Revising, proofreading, and formatting provide a final opportunity to shape your essay into the exact form you want it to take. These three final steps in the writing process can help you close the gap between what your essay is and what you want it to be. Revising helps you capture your ideas more vividly and accurately, while proofreading helps you express them grammatically and with proper punctuation. Finally, formatting gives your essay the visual polish that your readers expect to see.

Reader's *Tip* Focus on Revising, Proofreading, and Formatting: Revision in Real Life

North Wind Picture Archives

On first seeing the Declaration of Independence in draft form, some people wonder why the Founding Fathers would put something so important into the hands of a person who made so many mistakes. People see the messiness of the emerging Declaration and don't stop to think that Thomas Jefferson, like any other writer, went through multiple drafts.

The truth is that all writers revise—even Thomas Jefferson. No—make that *especially* Thomas Jefferson. After all, when you're doing something as important as building a country, you are not going to rely on the first thing that pops out of your head. The more important the document, the more important it is to think through it and revise it multiple times.

Reflect on It

Think about something that you do that requires revision, checking and double-checking, or attention to format. For example, you might "revise" an outfit before going out for an important interview. You might "proofread" your appearance in a mirror before you step into the interviewer's office. As you shake the interviewer's hand, it might boost your confidence to notice that your formatting is just right: She is wearing a gray suit, too. What else in your life requires revision, proofreading, or formatting?

Revising

In your mind, an idea may seem perfect. Yet when you try to get it on paper, it tumbles onto the page like a load of rough gravel. **Revising** can help you do justice to your ideas and to restore the sparkle that made you want to express them in the first place.

Beyond matters of style, there are practical reasons for revision, reasons that have their roots in the difference between writing and conversation. Conversation is constantly under revision. When your listener says, "What do you mean?" and you explain, you are revising. In conversation, revision is a response to the listener. But in writing, response and revision must take place before your essay meets its reader. Therefore, you must try to see your work through the eyes of a reader.

The word *revise* combines the Latin root meaning *to see* with the prefix meaning *again*. In its most literal sense, to revise means *to see again*, and seeing again is exactly what you need to do as you revise.

To see your work again, you need to create a mental distance between yourself and the work. You can best achieve this mental distance with time. Lay the writing aside for at least twenty-four hours. When you return to it, words that are not precise, sentences that are not clear, and explanations that do not explain enough will be easier to spot.

It may also help to have someone else look at your work. Ask your reader to focus on content and to question any point that does not seem clear. Because the written word carries no facial expression, no gesture, and no tone of voice, it is more open to misinterpretation than face-to-face communication. Discussing your work with a reader can help to close the gap between your intention and your reader's understanding.

In addition to letting your work "cool" for a day or so and enlisting the help of a reader, you can also check your essay point by point to make sure that it fulfills the purpose you had in mind. The following revision checklist will help you to go through your essay section by section to make sure each part is doing the job you intend it to do.

Checklist for Revision

The Introduction
✓ Does the introduction draw the reader in?
✓ Does the introduction provide background information, if needed?

The Thesis
✓ Is the thesis the last sentence of the introduction?
✓ If the thesis does not include points of development, does it state the main idea broadly enough to include all the points you raise in your body paragraphs?
✓ If the thesis lists points of development, does it list three separate and distinct points that do not overlap?

Topic Sentences
✓ Does each topic sentence raise one separate and distinct thesis point?
✓ Is each topic sentence clearly linked to the thesis with a reference to the general subject or to your attitude about the subject?
✓ If your thesis lists points of development, are body paragraphs arranged in the same order as the thesis points?

The Body

✓ Does each body paragraph provide specific detail and examples for each thesis point?

✓ Have you provided enough specific support for each thesis point?

✓ Does each sentence of each body paragraph support the topic sentence?

The Conclusion

✓ Is the first sentence of the conclusion a broad, thesis-level statement?

✓ Is the conclusion short, with no new information introduced?

✓ Is the last sentence satisfying and final-sounding?

Checking Coherence

✓ In the introduction, is there a clear transition between introductory material and the thesis?

✓ Have you used transitional words or transitional topic sentences to link the second and third body paragraphs to the rest of the essay?

✓ Have you used transitions within the paragraph effectively?

exercise 17.1   **Analyzing Two Versions of an Essay**

Read the two versions of the essay "My War on Insects." Using the preceding Checklist for Revision as your guide, decide which version is the revision and which is the rough draft.

Version 1

MY WAR ON INSECTS

I once read that if a nuclear war wipes out all humanity, insects are the only species that would survive. I believe it. My war on various kinds of insects has shown me that they usually win. Over the years, my battle with insects has caused me to feel disgust, pain, and awe.

I fought a battle with the most disgusting insect of all, the cockroach, when I lived in my first apartment. The apartment was the renovated attic of a seventy-five-year-old house. For seventy-five years the house had stood, and for seventy-five years the cockroaches had made it their own. In spite of the landlord's monthly visits with an industrial-sized canister of bug spray, the cockroaches held on tenaciously. I was embarrassed to invite friends up to the apartment after an evening out. The first flip of the light switch always revealed brown insects slithering across the yellow walls of the kitchen into temporary hiding. The kitchen was so infested with roaches that I kept all my food in the refrigerator, even bread and cookies, and I washed plates and utensils before I used them. When I finally moved out of that apartment, I imagined the cockroaches listening from the walls, waiting to reclaim their territory.

My next insect battleground had no cockroaches; instead, I fought a painful battle with vicious, stinging wasps. My husband and I moved into an upstairs apartment with a curved iron staircase leading to a postage-stamp yard below. I had visions of planting tomatoes in that small yard. Eagerly, I ran down the steps to examine it. Halfway down the stairs, I was attacked by a horde of stinging wasps. Their painful stings raised red, itchy welts that lasted for weeks. I was reluctant to try those stairs again though my husband had emptied a can of wasp spray on the nests underneath the stairs. I never did plant that tomato garden. Once again, the insects won the battle.

The most recent insect conflict has been a war with ants, creatures I can only regard with awe. The sandy soil that our house sits on is honeycombed with ant tunnels, and as long as the ants stay outside, I am willing to coexist peacefully. In recent months, however, they have ventured inside the house in search of food. I am amazed at the way a few scouter ants can become a battalion, marching in a purposeful column toward the food, then retreating with bits of food held like triumphant flags above them. Because I dislike pesticides, I tried using organic remedies such as vinegar and hot sauce around doors and cracks in the wall to repel the ants. But one evening, when I found a twenty-pound bag of cat food transformed into a writhing mass of ants, I decided that the time for more potent weapons had arrived. A pest control agency recommended ant baits, so I purchased a few and laid them out for the ants to find. For now, the ants are gone. I won't say I have won the battle, though, because I have learned that ants are amazingly persistent.

It seems that anywhere I have lived, I have had to fight insects. I can't help noticing that in most of my battles with them, I am the loser. It makes me wonder if I should trade in my can of Black Flag for a white flag, and simply surrender.

Version 2

MY WAR ON INSECTS

I once read that if a nuclear war wipes out all humanity, insects are the only species that would survive. Over the years, my battle with insects has caused me to feel disgust and pain.

I fought a battle with the most disgusting insect of all, the cockroach, when I lived in my first apartment. The apartment was the renovated attic of a seventy-five-year-old house. For seventy-five years the house had stood, and for seventy-five years the cockroaches had made it their own. In spite of the landlord's monthly visits with an industrial-sized canister of bug spray, the cockroaches held on tenaciously. My neighbors complained, too, saying that their apartments were overrun with cockroaches. Mrs. Higgins, who lived in the apartment downstairs, said she called the landlord at least twice a month to complain. When I finally moved out of that apartment, I imagined the cockroaches listening from the walls, waiting to reclaim their territory.

My next insect battleground had no cockroaches; instead, I fought a painful battle with vicious, stinging wasps. My husband and I moved into an upstairs apartment. Under the back stairs, the wasps had found a quiet home. Unfortunately, I disturbed their peace, and the resulting encounter was quite a painful one for me. In spite of my husband's efforts to rid the back stairs of the stinging pests, I never felt comfortable going down those stairs again. Once again, the insects won the battle.

Ants are creatures I can only regard with awe. The sandy soil that our house sits on is honeycombed with ant tunnels, and as long as the ants stay outside, I am willing to coexist peacefully. In recent months, however, they have ventured inside the house in search of food. I am amazed at the way a few scouter ants can become a battalion, marching in a purposeful column toward the food, then retreating with bits of food held like triumphant flags above them. Because I dislike pesticides, I at first tried using organic remedies such as vinegar and hot sauce around doors and cracks in the wall to repel the ants. But one evening, when I found a twenty-pound bag of cat food transformed into a writhing mass of ants, I decided that the time for more potent weapons had arrived. A pest control agency recommended ant baits, so I purchased a few and laid them out for the ants to find. For now, the ants are gone. I won't say I have won the battle, though, because I have learned that ants are amazingly persistent.

It seems that anywhere I have lived, I have had to fight insects. I haven't even mentioned the troubles I've had with aphids on my tomatoes and fleas on my cats. It makes me wonder if I should trade in my can of Black Flag for a white flag, and simply surrender.

The version of the essay that has been revised is version _____.

exercise 17.2   **Examining an Unrevised Essay**

Examine the essay that you believe is the unrevised version of "My War on Insects" and circle the best answer to each of the following questions.

1. The introduction lacks

   a. an attention-getting statement.
   b. a transition to the thesis.
   c. a thesis.

2. The point covered in the essay but not mentioned in the thesis is the point discussed in

   a. body paragraph 1.
   b. body paragraph 2.
   c. body paragraph 3.

3. In body paragraph 1, which two sentences do not support the paragraph's topic sentence?

   a. sentences 3 and 4
   b. sentences 4 and 5
   c. sentences 5 and 6

4. The topic sentence that does not link the paragraph to the thesis statement by mentioning the general subject of the essay is in

   a. body paragraph 1.
   b. body paragraph 2.
   c. body paragraph 3.

5. The body paragraph that lacks specific detail is

   a. body paragraph 1.
   b. body paragraph 2.
   c. body paragraph 3.

6. A problem in the conclusion is that

   a. it does not start with a broad, thesis-level statement.
   b. it introduces new information.
   c. it is too short.

Proofreading

Think about the last time you saw a misspelling in a newspaper. The minute you saw it, your thoughts moved away from the story itself and focused on the error. Similarly, errors in your writing take a reader's focus away from your ideas and put emphasis on grammar, spelling, or punctuation. Naturally, you want your ideas to stand in the foreground while grammar, spelling, and punctuation remain in the background. Proofreading, then, is an essential last step. Although proofreading is usually a chore, it is a necessary chore.

After you have completed the last revision of your essay, you should proofread it at least twice, once from the top down and once from the bottom up. If you have a special problem area, such as comma splices or subject-verb agreement, you should do at least one extra proofreading focused on those skills.

The Top-Down Technique

The first proofreading should go from the top of the essay down. As you proofread from the top down, check to make sure the connections between ideas are smooth and solid and that the sentences and paragraphs flow smoothly into one another. Check for parallel structure, clear pronoun reference, and appropriate transitional expressions. After correcting any problems you find in the top-down proofreading, move to the second type of proofreading, the bottom-up proofreading.

The Bottom-Up Technique

The bottom-up proofreading technique is more labor-intensive and more focused than top-down proofreading. When you read from the bottom up, you are no longer reading your essay as a single piece of writing but as disconnected sentences that do *not* flow into one another. Because your focus is on a single sentence, you can look at it closely, as if it is a sentence in a grammar exercise. Read it carefully, correct any errors you find, and then move to the preceding sentence.

The Targeting Technique

If you have a "favorite error"—one that you seem to make more often than any other—try doing an additional proofreading to target that error. Following are some common errors and shortcuts to finding those errors. As you become more experienced, you will devise your own strategies to target problem areas.

Subject-verb agreement. Check each subject-verb sequence. Look for present-tense verb forms and make sure they agree with their subjects. Remember that in the present tense, if the subject ends in -*s*, the verb usually does not. If the verb ends in -*s*, the subject usually does not. Exceptions occur when a singular subject ends in -*s* (for example, *boss speaks*) or when a plural subject does not *(children play)*.

Comma splices and run-ons.
Target long sentences; they are more likely to be run-ons. Target commas, too. If there is a complete sentence on both sides of the comma, you have found a probable comma splice.

Other comma errors. Target each comma and question its reason for being. If you aren't sure why you used it, maybe it doesn't belong.

Pronoun agreement. Look for the plural pronouns *they* and *their*. Make sure that they have a plural, not a singular, antecedent.

Sentence fragments. Using the bottom-up technique, read each sentence to see if it could stand on its own. If you suspect a fragment, check for a subject and a verb. If it lacks either one, it is a fragment.

Proofreading the Word-Processed Essay

Spelling and grammar checkers can be helpful in proofreading, but they are no substitute for knowledge and judgment. A spelling or grammar checker can find possible errors and suggest possible solutions. However, it is up to you to decide what, if anything, is wrong and how to fix it.

Even when you use spelling and grammar checkers, you should do at least two separate proofreadings. The following sentence, in which all words are spelled correctly, may illustrate the need:

Weather or knot ewe use a spelling checker, you knead too proof reed.

Whether to proofread on the screen or print out a hard copy to proofread is a personal choice. Some writers find it easier to scroll up and down on the computer screen, viewing the essay in small segments. Others swear that they cannot see their errors until they hold the printed copy in their hands. Find out what works best for you.

exercise 17.3   **Proofreading an Essay Confident? Go solo!**

Each of the forty sentences in the following essay contains an error. Form a small proofreading team with two or three of your classmates. Pooling your knowledge, see how many errors you can identify and correct. The first twenty errors are underlined. Record your corrections in the spaces provided or use your own paper.

AN URBAN LEGEND

[1]Around a carefully tended fire that kept the predators at bay until morning, our cave-dwelling ancestors told tale of the hunt. [2]In the american West, the power of a good yarn drew cowboys around the fire, a circle against the darkness. [3]Today, the folk tale lived on in what is often called the "urban legend." [4]Urban legends are those stories that many has heard but none can verify. [5]Stories of alligators in sewers and narrow escapes in lovers' lanes. [6]One modern folk tale, "Gunshot Wound," exemplifies the urban legend in it's themes of danger, individual power, and reprieve.

[7]Like many urban legend, "Gunshot Wound" plays on modern fears. [8]The story opens in a supermarket parking lot as a female shopper pulls in and notices a woman apparently past out in a car. [9]Afread of the dangers that lurk even in supermarket parking lots, the woman walks on into the store. [10]When she come out, she notices the

woman in the car, clutching the back of her head with both hands. ¹¹The woman's face is etched with terror the shopper offers help. ¹²"I've been shot", the woman says, "and I can't open the car door. ¹³The back of my skull has been blowed off, and I'm afraid to take my hands away." ¹⁴In horror, the shopper notices the blood on the womans hair and the doughy mass protruding through her tightly clasped fingers. ¹⁵By presenting horror in a ordinary setting, the opening section of this tale brings the listener face to face with the modern nightmare of random violence.

¹⁶The next part of the tale deals with the power of the individual by showing what 1 person can do. ¹⁷But in this present-day folk tale, the finger in the dike have been replaced by the finger on the button. ¹⁸The shopper's call to 911 brings ambulances fire trucks, and police cars screaming into the parking lot. ¹⁹"Dont worry, Ma'am," says a police officer. ²⁰"The Med-Evac chopper is here any minute." ²¹In this phase of the tale, a individual's ability to cope with disaster has been reinforced. ²²It do not matter that, in the tradition of Aladdin, the woman has called on more powerful forces to aid her. ²³Its enough that they come when summoned.

²⁴The final phase of the tale deal with rescue and reprieve. ²⁵a rescue team breaks into the injured woman's car. ²⁶And carefully removes her. ²⁷A paramedic bends over her she clutches the spongy, bloody mass at the back of her head. ²⁸As a chopper appears in the distance, the Paramedic, looking puzzled, pulls what appears to be a metal disk from her head. ²⁹A spongy mass cling to the disk. ³⁰Ma'am, he says, are your groceries in the back seat? ³¹"Yes", says the woman. ³²The paramedic begin to laugh. ³³"Ma'am, it looks like a biscuit can explodes in your grocery bag. ³⁴It must of sounded like a gunshot. ³⁵The metal disk from the can nicked your scalp bad, and biscuit dough and blood covered the back of your head. ³⁶A superficial wound." ³⁷To make a long story short and not to beat around the bush, the ending of this urban folk tale provokes relieved laughter. ³⁸Then a dawning realization that if innocent people were not shot every day, the tale would not be so compelling.

³⁹Despite their modern flavor, urban folk tales like "Gunshot Wound" still warn, reassure, and are entertaining. ⁴⁰In a way, they transport us too that ancestral fire where we huddle together in temporary safety, a circle against the darkness.

Corrections

1. _____
2. _____
3. _____
4. _____
5. _____
6. _____
7. _____
8. _____
9. _____
10. _____
11. _____
12. _____
13. _____
14. _____
15. _____
16. _____
17. _____
18. _____
19. _____
20. _____
21. _____
22. _____

23. _____   33. _____

24. _____   34. _____

25. _____   35. _____

26. _____   36. _____

27. _____   37. _____

28. _____   _____

29. _____

30. _____   _____

    _____   38. _____

31. _____   39. _____

32. _____   40. _____

33. _____

Formatting

You have heard it all your life: First impressions count. The document you hand to your instructor, the resumé you hand to a prospective employer, or the letter you send to the editor of a newspaper has the ability to present a positive first impression or a negative one. When an instructor sees a word-processed or neatly handwritten paper, with no smudges, crossovers, or dog-eared edges, the instructor expects that paper to be a good one, written as carefully as it was prepared. On the other hand, a hastily scrawled document smudged with eraser marks or heavily laden with Wite-Out suggests that the writer did not take the time to create a good impression—or to write a good paper.

Manuscript format is so important that entire books have been written about it. An instructor who asks you to use MLA style, APA style, or Chicago style is referring to styles outlined in books published by the Modern Language Association, the American Psychological Association, and the University of Chicago, respectively.

If you are given instructions for formatting a document, follow those instructions carefully. If you have no specific instructions, use the guidelines in the following section. They will help you to format a document effectively, whether that document is written in class or out of class, by hand or on a word processor.

Handwritten Documents

Paragraphs and Essays For handwritten paragraphs and essays, use lined white 8½ × 11-inch white paper and blue or black ink. Write on one side of the paper only and leave wide margins.

In the upper right-hand corner of the page, put your name and the date. If you wish, include your instructor's name and the name of the class for which you are preparing the assignment. Center your title, if any, on the first line of the paper, but do not underline the title or put it in quotation marks. Indent each paragraph about ¾ inch. In a handwritten document, do not skip lines unless your instructor specifically requests it. If you make an error, draw a single line through the error and rewrite your correction above the crossed-out error. Put a single paper clip, not a staple, in the upper left corner to join the pages.

Essay Tests When you take an essay test, you may be required to use a "blue book" or to write on the test itself. If you are allowed to use your own paper, use lined paper and write on one side only.

Answers to questions on essay tests should be written in blue or black ink. Because time is too limited for a rough draft, take a moment to organize your thoughts, and then answer the question. Indent each paragraph that you write ¾ inch to 1 inch. Just as in any paragraph or essay, state your main idea first.

If you misspell a word or make a mistake, cross through it with a single line. Be sure to write clearly and legibly, and if your handwriting is difficult to read, try printing instead.

Word-Processed Documents

Setting Up the Word-Processing Software Choose a font and a font size that are easily readable, such as Times New Roman in a 12-point size. Do not use a bold or italic font.

Margins should be 1 inch all around. One-inch margins are the default on most word processors, so you probably will not have to set the margins at all. Set the word processor to double-space the text. Leave the right edge ragged rather than justifying it. (To justify means to line up in a straight edge, like a newspaper column. Most word processors have settings that allow you to justify, but these settings are not commonly used for academic work.)

Formatting the Document Put your name and the date in the upper right corner of the page. Other information, such as the name of your instructor or the class for which you are preparing the assignment, is optional. Center the title and indent each paragraph as shown in the sample that follows. A title page is not necessary unless your instructor asks for one.

Derek Smith

April 1, 2004

Format Reform

I am ashamed to say that I used to be a format abuser. I used strange fonts such as Adolescence and Space Toaster. I tried to make my papers look longer by using 2-inch margins with 14-point font. At my lowest point, I turned in a report on lime-green paper printed in 15-point Star Trek font. A caring instructor saw that I had a problem and helped me to turn my formatting around. Now, I know how to format a document perfectly.

The first step in formatting a document is setting up the word processor. Margins should be set at 1 inch all around—left, right, top, and bottom. Make sure

Printing and Presenting Your Document   When the document has been revised and proofread, print it on good-quality 8½ × 11-inch white paper. To hold the pages together, place a single paper clip in the upper left corner. Do not staple your document or put it in a report cover.

Progressive Writing Assignment

Progressive Writing Assignment: Revising, Proofreading, and Formatting

If your instructor has assigned the Progressive Writing Assignment, you are almost finished. All that remains is to revise the essay, proofread it carefully, and put it in the proper format.

Topics and Tips for Revising, Proofreading, and Formatting

The Topics

Topic 1: Discuss three obstacles to your education.
Topic 2: Discuss your short-term goals, long-term goals, or both.
Topic 3: Discuss the values you have learned by observing members of your family.
Topic 4: Discuss your methods of coping with stress.

Tips for Revising, Proofreading, and Formatting

- Ask someone else to look at your essay and to tell you if any point is not clear or if any idea needs further explanation.
- Evaluate your essay using the Checklist for Revision in this chapter.
- Use your word processor's spelling and grammar checkers, but don't forget to proofread the document at least three times yourself.
- Check the formatting of your essay against your instructor's instructions or against the guidelines in this chapter. Improper formatting can be distracting to a reader, while proper formatting allows your essay to shine.

18 Showing and Telling: Description, Narration, and Example

"I was this far away when the mailman threw his bag at me and started running. All I could see were legs and letters . . ."

The essays you write and the stories you tell come alive when you use description, narration, and example. Descriptive techniques help you show your reader what you see, hear, smell, touch, or taste. Narrative techniques help you concisely tell a reader a story that makes a point. Examples supply specific illustrations and instances in many types of writing. Description, narration, and example provide the foundations for many other types of essay writing.

Reader's *Tip* — Focus on Showing and Telling: Looking at Description, Narration, and Example

The little gecko pictured here may well be a relative of a more famous gecko featured in commercials. GEICO's clever commercials make an impact using the appealing lizard, an angst-ridden caveman, and guest celebrities who entertainingly help real people explain their insurance needs.

Advertisers know that the way in to consumers' minds, hearts, and pocketbooks is through their effectiveness with description, narration, and example. GEICO commercials use cute animals and clever hooks to sell their products, but they also employ description, narration, and example.

The "caveman" commercials illustrate the use of all three techniques. The descriptive element lies in the use of effective visual images that viewers are likely to remember—a cavemen perfectly at home in modern settings like an airport or a therapist's office. The narrative element rests on his ongoing story: Wherever he goes, he is confronted by GEICO's portrayals of caveman as primitive and stupid, but even his therapist does not understand why he finds these stereotypes so disturbing. And if viewers need an example of why GEICO is a good choice, they need only listen to the slogan, "So easy a caveman could do it."

Reflect on It

Find another commercial on TV or in a magazine that does absolutely nothing to sell the product other than trying to use description, narration, and example. Is the ad effective? Would consumers buy this product? How do description, narration, and example help with the sale of this product?

Description, Narration, and Example in Action

In this chapter, you will have the opportunity to examine and use the techniques of description, narration, and example. To help you become skilled in using these techniques, the text analyzes and explains each one separately. In reality, they are rarely used that way. Instead, authors combine techniques, using the ones that best suit their purpose for writing.

Before looking at description, narration, and example separately, look at how a professional writer uses all three techniques together. The following essay is by Maya Angelou, noted writer, poet, and activist. It is an excerpt from *Wouldn't Take Nothing for My Journey Now*, one of Angelou's several autobiographical books.

The essay embodies all three of the writing techniques featured in this chapter. The predominant technique of the essay is **narration,** or storytelling. Notice how the author highlights her narrative with **dialogue,** or conversation, to help the reader understand the characters she describes.

In the second and third paragraphs, Angelou uses **examples,** exact instances or illustrations of a particular type. Notice how these paragraphs provide specific examples of complainers, showing exactly how they behave.

Finally, the author uses **description** to paint a picture so that the reader can visualize the people in her story. Because humans perceive the world through our senses of sight, hearing, touch, taste, and smell, describing in terms of the five senses is an effective way to make a subject real and concrete to readers.

Complaining

MAYA ANGELOU

1 When my grandmother was raising me in Stamps, Arkansas, she had a particular routine when people who were known to be whiners entered her store. Whenever she saw a known complainer coming, she would call me from whatever I was doing and say conspiratorially, "Sister, come inside. Come." Of course I would obey.

2 My grandmother would ask the customer, "How are you doing today, Brother Thomas?" And the person would reply, "Not so good." There would be a distinct whine in the voice. "Not so good today, Sister Henderson. You see, it's this summer. It's this summer heat. I just hate it. Oh, I hate it so much. It just frazzles me up and frazzles me down. I just hate the heat. It's almost killing me." Then my grandmother would stand stoically, her arms folded, and mumble, "Uh-huh, uh-huh." And she would cut her eyes at me to make certain that I had heard the lamentation.

3 At another time a whiner would mewl, "I hate plowing. That packed-down dirt ain't got no reasoning, and mules ain't got good sense. . . . Sure ain't. It's killing me. I can't ever seem to get done. My feet and my hands stay sore, and I get dirt in my eyes and up my nose. I just can't stand it." And my grandmother, again stoically with her arms folded, would say, "Uh-huh, uh-huh," and then look at me and nod.

4 As soon as the complainer was out of the store, my grandmother would call me to stand in front of her. And then she would say the same thing she had said at least a thousand times, it seemed to me. "Sister, did you hear what Brother So-and-So or Sister Much to Do complained about? You heard that?" And I would nod. Mamma would continue, "Sister, there are people who went to sleep all over the world last night, poor and rich and white and black, but they will never wake again. Sister, those who expected to rise did not, their beds became their cooling boards, and their blankets became their winding sheets. And those dead folks would give anything, anything at all for just five minutes of this weather or ten minutes of that plowing that person was grumbling about. So you watch yourself about complaining, Sister. What you're supposed to do when you don't like a thing is change it. If you can't change it, change the way you think about it. Don't complain."

Thinking about the Essay

1. Examples provide specific instances that help a reader understand a more general point. Look at the two specific examples of complainers: Brother Thomas in the second paragraph and an unnamed whiner in the third paragraph. How do those specific examples help you understand what a whiner does in general? In other words, if you were the proverbial visitor from another planet where whining did not exist, how would you describe a whiner after reading about the two whiners in Angelou's essay?

2. Narration helps essay writers make a point by telling a story. Although the point may become evident as the story unfolds, writers often reinforce the point at the end of the story. Based on the last paragraph, what is the point of Angelou's story? Which character is used to convey the point?

3. Description helps readers understand an essay in the same way that they understand the world: through sight, hearing, taste, touch, and smell. Look at the words used at the beginning of paragraphs 2 and 3 to describe the voices of the whiners. Then, look at the description of the grandmother's body language at the end of paragraphs 2 and 3. What do these descriptions show you about the character of the whiners as opposed to the character of the grandmother, Sister Henderson?

Description

"You can't miss it. It's the big yellow house on the corner."

"Officer, he was bald with a tattoo of a turtle on the top of his head."

"I just asked to borrow a pen, and she gave me a look that would freeze hot coffee on a July day."

Where would we be without description? It is used every day to communicate the essentials of life and to add the embellishments that keep listeners hanging on every word.

In writing, too, description helps readers understand your point and keeps them waiting for the next detail. Descriptive essays often answer questions such as the ones that follow.

- What is your favorite season of the year?
- What one place, for you, is "heaven on earth"?
- Describe a place that causes (or caused) you to feel uncomfortable or unhappy.

Laying the Groundwork for Descriptive Writing

Visualizing Look at the photograph of the building with the sign "Cocktails" on the front. Then use your imagination to visualize the interior. Is it large and airy or small and intimate? Is the lighting bright or soft? Are the colors warm or cool? How is it furnished and decorated? How are the people dressed? What music would you hear? What kinds of food and drink are served?

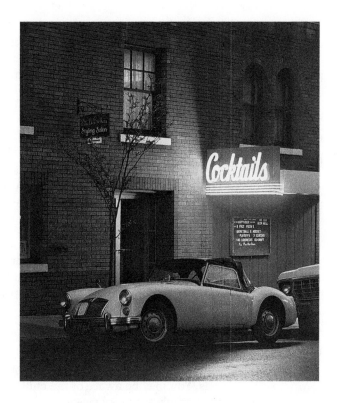

Planning You have visualized the décor, the people, the music, and the food and/or beverages that you might find inside the building. Decide which three elements you would include in an essay on this topic. What order would you place them in? Why?

Writing Write a paragraph about one of the elements you have chosen in the "Planning" section. Your challenge in this assignment is to make everything you describe seem so real that the reader can almost see it, hear it, touch it, taste it, and smell it.

Elements of Descriptive Writing

Effective descriptive writing paints a picture for the reader. Just as artists use canvas, brushes, and paints, writers use their tools of the trade to create a more effective picture. Your tools as a writer of descriptive paragraphs and essays include sense impressions, spatial order, and a dominant impression.

Sense Impressions

Every scrap of information we collect about the world around us comes through our five senses: sight, hearing, smell, taste, and touch. It is logical, then, that descriptions painted using sense impressions present a more vivid picture to your reader.

Sight In writing, descriptive imagery is most often visual. Visual impressions are strong and lasting. Psychological studies confirm that people are more likely to rely on what they see than on what they hear. For example, you would not be fooled by a clerk's "Thank you" if his facial expression said, "I hate my job." If it is true that seeing is believing, then creating a visual picture for the reader is particularly important in descriptive writing.

Hearing Our sense of hearing also gives us information about the world around us. We are warned by the blast of a horn, energized by the driving beat of rock music, or soothed by the thunder of the ocean. Imagery that appeals to a reader's sense of hearing is an essential dimension of descriptive writing.

Smell The sense of smell has a powerful connection to memory. The smell of freshly popped popcorn may summon the claustrophobic feel of a dark, crowded movie theater. A whiff of furniture polish can bring back an aunt's stately dining room. Using imagery related to smell can help to complete the picture you create for your reader.

Touch The sense of touch is a backdrop for all experience. As you sit reading this, you may feel beneath you the hard surface of a wooden chair or the softness of sofa cushions. You may be aware of the chill of air conditioning or the warmth of sunlight, the scratch of a wool sweater or the cottony feel of an old pair of jeans. Imagery that brings out textures and temperatures adds a special touch to the picture you draw for your reader.

Taste Taste imagery may play a smaller role in your writing unless you are writing about food. However, used sparingly, references to taste add spice to your descriptive writing.

exercise 18.1 **Recognizing Words of the Senses**

In the following paragraph, underline words and phrases that draw on the senses of sight, hearing, smell, touch, and taste.

ROCKING-CHAIR SATURDAY

Our screened porch is a peaceful place to read and relax on a Saturday afternoon. Sitting in a creaking wooden rocker, I look through the gauzy wire screen into the back yard. From the top of a pine tree, a mockingbird scolds. In the distance, I hear the sleepy drone of a neighbor's mower. A slight breeze wafts the tempting aroma of grilling hamburgers toward me. Prudence, my calico cat, pads out to join me, stretching out in a warm patch of sun near the screen door. I scoop her warm, furry body into my arms as she rumbles her approval. She settles into my lap, content to sit with me and enjoy the peace of the back porch.

exercise 18.2   **Writing Sensory Descriptions**

Write a phrase that describes each of the following words in sensory terms. Then note whether you are describing the word through sight, hearing, smell, touch, or taste. The first one is done for you.

1. stone

    a smooth, heavy stone (touch)
    _____

2. milk

    _____

3. wrapping paper

    _____

4. sunlight

    _____

5. glove

    _____

6. coin

    _____

7. french fries

    _____

8. voice

    _____

9. leaves

    _____

10. bark (tree or dog's, your choice)

    _____

Spatial Order

Spatial order helps you to write about anything that takes up space. Use spatial order to present physical objects in a way that makes sense: bottom to top, left to right, background to foreground, or outside to inside. A partial list of words commonly used when referring to space follows.

above	beyond	near	right
ahead	by	next to	south
around	down	north	toward
behind	east	on	under
beside	in	over	underfoot
between	left	overhead	west

exercise 18.3   **Recognizing Effective Use of Spatial Order**

Look at the following short paragraphs. In which paragraph is spatial order used in a more organized way?

Paragraph 1

The singer looked as if he had just stepped out of the 1960s. His hair, twisted into thick dreadlocks, fell almost to his shoulders. On his feet were chunky leather sandals. A small golden ring pierced his left nostril. His hands, clasped around the microphone in front of his chest, were ringed in silver and turquoise. He wore a faded pair of jeans that flared into a wide bell over his ankles. Over his shirt, he wore a soft leather vest that ended at his waist in a beaded fringe. His shirt, open at the neck, revealed a silver and turquoise necklace. He wore a small golden earring on one ear. He looked as though he belonged on a Woodstock poster.

Paragraph 2

The model walking down the runway looked like a movie actress from the 1940s. Her hair curved under just above her shoulders and dipped across one eye as she turned her head. Her eyebrows were arched and penciled, and her lipstick was a deep red. The jacket of her gray pinstriped suit was padded at the shoulders and nipped in at the waist. Her skirt hugged her hips and legs tightly and flared below the knee. She wore dark stockings with seams up the back, and stiletto heels that looked impossible to walk in. She looked as though she had stepped out of an old black-and-white movie.

The paragraph that uses spatial order more effectively is paragraph _____.

Establishing a Dominant Impression

Description is more than just a tangle of unrelated details. In a descriptive essay, every detail should join in conveying a single **dominant impression.** A dominant impression helps to convey your attitude toward the subject and aids in the unity of your description. If you are writing a description of a house that you pass every day, your description should show more than shutters, bricks, and roofing tiles. What is your overall impression of that house? Is it cheerful? Eerie? Prim? Dignified? The word that you choose to describe the house conveys your dominant impression. As you describe the house, each detail should contribute to the dominant impression.

When you write a descriptive paragraph or essay, it is helpful to include the dominant impression in the topic sentence of your paragraph or in the thesis statement of your essay. Stating the dominant impression helps you keep the paragraph or essay on track by reminding you of the impression that each detail should create. It also lets your reader know what to expect.

If you are describing a house that is eerie, include details designed to send chills up the reader's spine: the loose, creaking shutters and the blankly staring windows. If cheerful dandelions bloom in the yard, let them bloom unseen. Details that do not reinforce the dominant impression do not belong in your description.

The topic sentences below illustrate different ways of stating a dominant impression.

Examples

The classroom was uncomfortably warm.

The car was a joy to drive.

The instructor looked more like a homeless person than a college professor.

The office was obviously a place where serious work was done.

exercise 18.4   ## Supporting the Dominant Impression

In each list below, circle the letter of the detail that would not support the dominant impression of the topic sentence.

1. The house on the corner is dignified.

   a. stately columns on the porch
   b. well-trimmed bushes lining the driveway
   c. crumpled beer can on the lawn
   d. dark green shutters framing curtained windows

2. The kitchen was messy.

   a. dirty dishes piled in the sink
   b. cat food spilled on the floor
   c. overflowing trash can
   d. shiny coffeepot stored neatly on a shelf

3. Greta seems studious.

   a. studies in the library every evening
   b. enjoys playing poker
   c. makes good grades
   d. takes good notes in class

4. The garage was a fire hazard.

   a. oily rags and newspapers stacked three feet high
   b. space heater with frayed cord plugged into a wall outlet
   c. rusty mower blades and chainsaw blades thrown into an open box
   d. boxes of old fireworks, open bags of quick-start charcoal, and dented aerosol cans piled haphazardly on shelves

5. The town seemed prosperous.

   a. many large new homes
   b. new school under construction
   c. boarded-up stores downtown
   d. large manufacturing plant on outskirts of town

Wordsmith's Corner: Examples of Descriptive Writing

Following are two student examples of descriptive essays. Read each essay and answer the questions that follow.

Descriptive Essay 1

The writer of this essay describes a store's produce department. Notice the imagery appealing to sight, sound, smell, touch, and taste.

A GARDEN OF TEMPTATION

Harry's Farmer's Market is more than just a grocery store. It is a storehouse of temptation. At Harry's, a shopper can find breads and pastries, ethnic delights from a variety of countries, and a selection of candies that would unravel the strongest will. But when it comes to temptation, nothing at Harry's can rival the produce section.

The vegetable bins at Harry's are a feast for the senses. Row upon row of green, musty-smelling cabbages temptingly hint of cabbage rolls and coleslaw to come. Beyond the green cabbages are bins of the purple, curly-leafed variety, piled like basketballs in a sporting goods store. Next come potatoes in all shapes and sizes. Large, long Idahos weigh in the hand like a stone and bake up fluffy and dry. The yellow-fleshed Yukon Golds can be sliced into golden medallions and topped with cheese. Farther along the aisle, carrots beckon like slender fingers and plump squash nestle comfortably in neat bins. At the end of the aisle, mountains of waxy purple eggplant lie in lush array. The vegetable bins at Harry's provide a feast for the eyes as well as for the taste buds.

Beyond the vegetables lie the fruits in a patchwork of geographic and seasonal variety. Bananas, pineapples, mangoes, and limes flaunt tropical hues. Their exotic aromas hint of balmy breezes, marimba bands, and sweet summer nights. Across the aisle, the season is fall. Apples, crisp as a New England day, stir the air with the fragrance of autumn. Their red and yellow colors and even their names—Crispin, Pippin, Granny Smith, Ginger Gold—suggest brisk autumn days, the crunch of leaves underfoot, and a cozy hearth. Farther on, yellow grapefruit, bright as the California sun, suggest a return to summer. Beside them, giant navel oranges add a hint of citrus to the air. In this section of Harry's, time and place blend in a fruit-basket turnover.

For customers who can't wait until they are out of the store to sample the delights of Harry's fruits and vegetables, the juice bar offers instant gratification. Thirsty shoppers can drink in the tartness of a California grapefruit or taste the sweetness of freshly squeezed orange juice. For something different, customers can sample apricot juice in hues of rich dusky amber or exotic papaya flavored with coconut milk. Vegetable lovers can sip a cool, pale celery drink, rich red tomato juice, or carrot juice so brightly orange that many shoppers swear their eyesight improves just by looking at it. There's no better way to end a trip through Harry's produce department than by drinking it in.

Grocery shopping can be a chore, but at Harry's, it is more often a delight. A trip through the produce department is a tempting tour through a garden where every vegetable is in season and no fruit is forbidden.

Questions?

1. What is the dominant impression of the essay?

   _____

2. The introduction of the essay is

   a. an anecdote
   b. broad to narrow
   c. narrow to broad
   d. quotation

3. Write the thesis statement on the line below. Are the points listed?

   _____

   _____

4. Write the topic sentences on the lines that follow.

   _____

   _____

   _____

   _____

   _____

5. Underline the sense impressions in the essay. Can you find imagery of all five senses? Write five images below that evoke each of the senses.

   a. sight _____

   b. hearing _____

   c. smell _____

   d. touch _____

   e. taste _____

Descriptive Essay 2

An unusual museum exhibit inspired this essay. Notice how the writer moves the reader through the exhibit.

JUKE JOINT

I hear a rising laugh, like notes played on a piano, as I approach the doorway marked "Little Grocery." By day, the Little Grocery sold milk, bread, cereal, and cigarettes—the stuff of everyday life. At night, under a pungent haze of smoke, the jukebox played "Slip Away" or "Mr. Big Stuff" to the clink of bottles of illegal liquor. But I am not worried about a police raid, for I am in the Tubman African American Museum, looking at artist Willie Little's re-creation of his father's North Carolina juke joint. The setting, the music, and the life-size figures are nostalgic reminders of an earlier era.

As I enter the doorway, I step into a setting from the past. The sawdust-covered floor leads to an old-fashioned glass-topped counter. On the counter, beside a gallon jar of pickled pig's feet, sits an empty bottle labeled "Sun-Drop Golden Cola—As Refreshing as a Cup of Coffee." Behind the glass are old-fashioned bottles of White Rain shampoo and a half-filled box of individually wrapped Moon Pies. A card offers "Mystery Edge Razor Blades, 4 blades 10¢." To the left of the counter, a sawdust trail leads to a large yellow cooler emblazoned with the words "Royal Crown Cola" in red. Above the cooler, a rectangular metal sign advertises "Viceroy Filter Tip Cigarettes—Filtered Smoke with the Finest Flavor." Beside the cooler sits a jukebox.

The old-fashioned jukebox pulses with light and music, taking me back to the sixties. I walk toward it, passing a tall thin figure whose upraised fingers, the color of mahogany, look as though they are holding an invisible harmonica. As I move closer, I can make out the name "Wurlitzer Zodiac" on the front of the jukebox. I look at the selections. If I had a quarter, I could hear "Jimmy Mack" by Martha and the Vandellas, "Mercy, Mercy Me" by Marvin Gaye, or Aretha Franklin's "Respect." A museum employee walks by, opens the jukebox, and presses a button. I hear the machine clicking through the selections, and more music fills the air. "How Sweet It Is to Be Loved by You" is followed by "Midnight Hour" and "Mr. Pitiful," songs that must have once filled the smoky air in "Mr. Charlie's" juke joint.

The artist has also brought the past to life with re-creations of the people who danced, drank, and laughed in his father's juke joint. Beside me, a slim, chocolate-colored figure in jeans dances with outstretched arms, her head a mass of pink curlers. Across from the jukebox, a sad-looking figure of a man with a goiter sits on an old church pew, his hat resting on his knee, his tie undone. Beside him, a female figure, an unlit cigarette clenched between her lips, extends an empty pack of Pall Malls. Her polyester pantsuit is pink and glittery, her blouse a satiny sky blue. Beyond them, a figure labeled "Sara Carroway" holds a parasol above her head. She is wearing soiled Keds, and stockings are knotted under her knobby knees. Despite her shabby attire, her bearing is formal and prim. As I look more closely, I see that her tight, pressed curls are created with round seed pods. In a shadowed corner at the back of the exhibit, two figures embrace. A long-haired figure of a woman in harlequin glasses stands against the wall, her short skirt hiked around her hips. Her lover, a light-skinned, impassioned-looking male figure, stretches out his hand as if to reach under her skirt. Feeling like an intruder, I back away. As I leave, I notice the male's pants, unbuckled and falling below slim hips.

As I leave the exhibit, I hear again the rising laughter. It comes from a small group of students touring the museum. Yet it seems to me to echo the laughter that once floated above the haze of cigarette smoke in the Little Grocery in the 1960s.

Questions?

1. Which two senses does the essay emphasize most strongly?

2. Write the thesis statement on the following line. Does it list the points to be discussed in the essay?

3. What is the dominant impression? Is it stated in the thesis and topic sentences?

4. List the topic of each body paragraph.

5. Underline the sense impressions in the essay. Can you find imagery of all five senses?

    a. sight _____

    b. hearing _____

    c. smell _____

    d. touch _____

    e. taste _____

Topics for Descriptive Writing
Descriptive Assignment 1: The Cockroach
Journal Entry

You are a cockroach. Within the walls where you live it is dark and cool and safe, and the still air is sterile and dry. Noise and light from outside the wall warn you that the large creatures that live beyond the wall are still stirring about. You are hungry, and you long to go toward the yellow light where the moist air is fragrant with the smell of food. But you know you must wait. Finally, the noise subsides outside the wall, and the yellow light that filters in through the cracks mutes to a soft, deep gray. All is quiet. Describe what happens next, focusing on your five senses.

Descriptive Assignment 2: Describing a Place
Essay

Write an essay describing a place. It can be a store, office, nightclub, park, beach, street, parking lot, church sanctuary, stadium, or any place of your choosing. In your thesis statement, state the dominant impression in one word, choosing a word from the following list or thinking up your own word. Make sure all details of your description reinforce that dominant impression. *Hint:* Your thesis statement will follow this pattern:

The _____(place)_____ was/is (dominant impression).

cheerful	colorful	filthy	orderly
cluttered	disgusting	spotless	chaotic
serene	dull	crowded	lonely
bleak	gloomy	eerie	noisy
messy	elegant	exciting	calm
shabby	depressing	impersonal	cozy

Descriptive Assignment 3: Describing a Person
Essay

Write an essay describing a person. It can be someone you know well, such as a friend or relative, or someone you see often but don't really know, such as a library worker or a fellow student. Be sure that you state a dominant impression in your thesis; a few possibilities are listed below. Make sure that all the details in your essay support the dominant impression. Focus on sense impressions, details that can be expressed through sight, hearing, smell, touch, and taste. Don't simply *say* that someone has bad breath; let your reader *smell* it: "His breath reeked with the sour, sharp odor of cigarettes, unbrushed teeth, and onions he had eaten the night before."

arrogant	easygoing	graceful	neat
dignified	elegant	gruff	unhappy
disorganized	forbidding	messy	upbeat

Descriptive Assignment 4: Vacation in Paradise
Essay

What is your idea of the perfect vacation spot? Describe the spot, including details like the climate and landscape; the hotel, campsite, or cabin you would stay in; and the attractions you would visit.

Descriptive Assignment 5: Essay-Based Topic—A Strong Influence
Essay

Reread Maya Angelou's essay, "Complaining," at the beginning of this chapter. Sister Henderson, Angelou's grandmother, was obviously a strong influence in her life. Write an essay describing an adult who influenced you when you were a child. Focus on the traits of character and personality in your role model that helped to make you the person you are today. Try, as Angelou does, to show the character of the person you describe through the person's actions and words.

Descriptive Assignment 6: Real-World Topic—Secret Shopper
Essay

Many times, people ask how writing essays will help them in the "real world." This real-world assignment gives just one example of how descriptive writing might be used outside the classroom.

Stores or restaurants often hire "secret shoppers" who are asked to write reports about their experiences in a particular store or restaurant. The reports focus first on the store or restaurant environment: Is it clean, neat, and inviting? Next come the employees: Are you greeted immediately? Are employees friendly and professional? Next, what about the merchandise or the food? If it is merchandise, is it logically and invitingly arranged? Can you find what you want easily? If the establishment is a restaurant, is the food invitingly presented? Is it hot and fresh? How does it taste?

For this assignment, choose a store or restaurant—it may be the college bookstore or cafeteria if you wish—and pretend you are a secret shopper hired to evaluate the place from a customer's point of view.

Example

Examples give your reader a specific illustration of an idea. A good example is never a generalization but a crisp and specific picture that shows exactly what the sentence it illustrates means. An example is a shortcut, providing a vivid and direct way to get your meaning across to your reader. Because examples are used to illustrate a point, they often include narration or description.

Examples can be used in almost any type of essay. However, essays supported by examples alone might be used to answer questions such as the ones that follow.

- What would cause you to end a friendship?
- Discuss some of the ways that an individual can help the environment.
- How has attending college affected your eating habits?

Example   **487**

Reader's *Tip* ———— Building Connections
───

You have seen the way brief anecdotes—small narratives—can be used to introduce an essay. Anecdotes can often serve as examples, too. For instance, if you need an example of rude behavior to illustrate an essay, tell a story. Maybe you recently encountered a gum-chewing clerk in a convenience store who talked on a cell phone during your entire transaction, or perhaps a rude driver cut you off in traffic. A supporting anecdote can add life to your example essay.

Laying the Groundwork for Writing Using Examples

Visualizing Look at the photograph of the "Beach Closed" sign; then use your imagination to generate several examples of dangers that might have closed this beach.

Planning Plan a paragraph, and choose whether you will give several examples of dangers that could close a beach, devoting a sentence or two to each, or just one example of a danger that might close a beach.

Writing Write a paragraph that follows the plan you set up. Take one of the examples and write it up in detail, describing all of the circumstances that led to the closing.

exercise 18.5 **Using Examples Effectively**

To get an idea of how examples help you to get your meaning across, look at the following paragraphs. Which presents a clearer picture?

Paragraph A

A person who visits another country should be prepared for more than just a change in climate and language. Even such a simple thing as taking a drive can result in culture shock if a tourist is not prepared for different driving customs in the country he is visiting. Nothing can prepare a person for some of the strange driving customs of other countries. Not everyone drives the way we do in the United States. Even though road signs are supposed to be international in meaning, driving customs are not. An American visiting another country may put himself in danger or, at the very least, risk confusion simply by taking a drive. For their own safety and that of others, tourists to other countries should become familiar with driving customs before getting behind the wheel.

Paragraph B

A person who visits another country should be prepared for more than just a change in climate and language. Even such a simple thing as taking a drive can result in culture shock if a tourist is not prepared for the different driving customs in different countries. In Great Britain, for example, a car's steering wheel is on the right side of the car, and people drive on the left-hand side of the road. An American used to driving on the right-hand side may put himself in danger or, at the very least, risk confusion simply by taking a drive. In Cairo, Egypt, drivers navigate the city's streets at night with their lights off. Like bats flying into the dusk, these drivers steer by sound, tooting their horns every few minutes to warn approaching drivers of their presence. Driving with the lights on, it is widely believed, will drain a car's battery whether the car is running or not. Is maneuvering a car down dark streets and highways dangerous without headlights? Perhaps it is. But in that city, it might be even more dangerous to turn headlights on and risk blinding other drivers on the dark, noisy streets. For their safety and that of others, tourists to other countries should become familiar with driving customs before getting behind the wheel.

The paragraph that makes its point more clearly through examples is paragraph

_____.

exercise 18.6 **Short and Extended Examples**

As you saw in Chapter 15, a paragraph may be supported by a series of short examples or by one long, extended example. Look at the following paragraphs. Which is supported by a series of examples, and which by an extended example?

Paragraph A

My roommate Charlotte is excessively neat. She makes her bed up military style, with the covers so tight she could bounce a battalion of quarters from the taut surface. If I shower after her, it is as if I am the first one in the bathroom. The shower stall and mirrors are wiped dry. Her wet towel has been whisked into the hamper, and a dry towel,

Example   **489**

neatly folded, hangs from the towel rack. Her hair dryer hangs neatly on its hook, and her toothbrush stands soldierlike in its holder. Of course, the cap is back on her toothpaste tube, which is neatly rolled up from the end, not squeezed in the middle. In her closet, skirts and jackets, as fresh as if they had just been brought from the dry cleaner, fall neatly from hangers spaced exactly one inch apart. Her CDs are arranged in alphabetical order, as are the books on her shelves. I admire neatness; I even strive for it. But Charlotte takes neatness a step too far.

Paragraph B

Social service agencies sometimes do more harm than good. A recent story in the local newspaper provides a good example. A young woman went to a hospital's emergency room because of complications from the recent birth of her child. Because she had no one to keep the child, she brought him with her to the emergency room. When a decision was made to admit her to the hospital, she told hospital personnel that she had no family in the United States, and there was no one to take care of her baby. Trying to help her, hospital officials called a state social services agency to get temporary care for the child. When the child's mother was released from the hospital five days later, she was told that she would have to prove she was a fit mother before regaining custody of her child. The woman was angry and did not understand why her fitness as a mother was being questioned. A spokesperson for the social services agency said its personnel were simply following procedure. In this case, the agency did more harm than good, making the woman a victim instead of giving her the help she needed.

The paragraph that is supported by a series of examples is paragraph

_____.

The paragraph that is supported by a single extended example is paragraph

_____.

Wordsmith's Corner: Examples of Writing Supported by Example

Below are two student essays supported by example. Read each and answer the questions that follow.

Example Essay 1

It's on the dinner plate now, but what was its life like before? The writer of this essay shows the reader through examples.

CRUEL PORTION

My grandmother was nine years old when her pet chicken, Belle, showed up on the table at Sunday dinner or, to be more precise, *as* Sunday dinner. Grandma did not eat chicken that Sunday or for many Sundays thereafter. These days, most of us have no such intimate contact with our food before we eat it. Chicken comes from the Colonel or from the Shop-Rite down the street. We have lost touch with the way that animals are treated before they reach our plate. All too often, animals raised for food are treated cruelly—like crops instead of creatures.

While chickens in Grandma's time were allowed to flap, squawk, and strut around the chicken yard until that fateful dinner invitation came, today's chickens lead unnatural lives. They are born in hatcheries, raised in cages on special diets, then crated like cantaloupes and trucked to the processing plant. Who has not seen those trucks, with chickens huddled several to a cage, and cage piled upon cage? Feathers fly as the truck ferries its terrified cargo down the highway, and by the time it reaches its destination many chickens are already dead. Why should we worry when the chickens are going to die anyway? We should worry because we have, it seems to me, a minimal ethical responsibility to give any animal we use for food a decent life.

Some farm animals seem to have decent lives, but often we do not see the whole picture. Cattle graze peaceably in fragrant pastures and gather under trees to escape the summer sun. Yet many cattle never see those fragrant pastures. Some dairy cows are kept permanently in stalls, their engorged udders rubbed raw by the milking machine. The white flesh of veal is the flesh of calves that are deliberately weakened and kept in cages their entire short lives, calves that never rise on unsteady legs to follow their mothers through the clover. These animals live their lives behind barn doors, where no one can see their plight.

Finally, consider the lobster, perhaps the worst-treated of all our food. Once caught, it is doomed to spend the rest of its life in a small fish tank in the fluorescent-lit seafood department of a grocery store. Its claws are closed with heavy rubber bands, and it is crowded together with its fellows at the bottom of the tank. Is it fed, I wonder, or does it slowly starve as it waits to be eaten? Peered at by children, ignored by adults until it is finally bought, it ends its miserable life being boiled alive. Isn't there a more humane way to keep it and to cook it?

After the hunt, the Cherokee had a custom of thanking an animal for its sacrifice. They did not forget that it was a fellow creature, that it had the right to walk the earth and roam the forests. We, too, owe a debt to the animals we raise for food. At the very least, we can treat them like creatures and not like crops.

Questions?

1. Write the thesis statement and each of its topic sentences in the following space.

    _____

    _____

    _____

    _____

    _____

    _____

    _____

    _____

2. Which body paragraph uses two short examples rather than an extended example? _____

Example   **491**

3. What type of introduction does the essay have?

    a. broad to narrow
    b. anecdote
    c. narrow to broad

4. Write two descriptive details from the essay that appeal to the reader's sense of sight.

    _____

    _____

    _____

    _____

Example Essay 2

Who are the heroes of today? One student writer provides three examples.

QUIET HEROES

Movie stars and athletes are often held up as heroes and role models because they lend their names to a cause or visit a child in the hospital, followed, of course, by a convoy of reporters. These "heroes" are showered with media attention and admiration. But in every community, there are also quiet heroes. I know several of these quiet heroes, ordinary people of all ages who work to make their community a better place.

One of my heroes is Deb, an outgoing grandmother of three who works with Habitat for Humanity. Deb can wield a hammer with the best of them, but it is her talent for feeding people that makes her contribution special. Deb spends the morning chopping, slicing, and mixing in a kitchen filled with delicious aromas. By 11:30, she is on the road to the construction site. In winter, she may bring hot vegetable soup or Brunswick stew. On warm days, lunch may be homemade pimento cheese sandwiches, fruit, and iced tea. But day after day, Deb uses her money, time, and talent to keep the Habitat crew going.

Then there is Pete, an accountant, who uses his clear, expressive voice to share the joys of reading. He is a member of the Rolling Readers, a group that visits elementary schools to interest children in reading. Pete reads every week to a class he has adopted. To keep the children reading over the summer, he gives each child a book furnished by the Rolling Readers program. Pete also shares his love of reading by volunteering for the Radio Reading Service for the blind and print-handicapped. Once a week, he gets up at six a.m. and drives to a small recording studio. He takes the morning paper and selects the articles he will read from each section of the paper, judging from experience when he has enough to fill the hour. Then, he goes into a recording booth and reads, editing out mistakes as he goes along. By reading to others, Pete manages to turn what is usually a solitary activity into a shared joy.

Another hero is Andrea, a high school junior who has organized a "Friendship Brigade" to serve senior citizens. The Friendship Brigade mows lawns, runs errands, and does chores for low-income senior citizens that it has "adopted." The brigade has also sought business sponsorship to provide for various needs such as wheelchair ramps and smoke detectors. Andrea says that her reward is knowing that she and her friends are helping older people live more independent lives.

To me, a hero is not necessarily a movie star who jets in for a personal appearance accompanied by a hair stylist, a personal trainer, and an appointment secretary. More often, heroes are ordinary people who, without fanfare, work to improve their community and their world.

Questions?

1. Write the thesis statement and each of its topic sentences below.

   _____

   _____

   _____

   _____ .

   _____

   _____ .

   _____

   _____ .

2. How many examples of "quiet heroes" does the writer provide? _____

3. What type of introduction does the essay have? Circle the correct answer.

   a. broad to narrow
   b. anecdote
   c. contrast

4. What type of conclusion does the essay have? Circle the correct answer.

   a. full circle
   b. recommendation
   c. prediction

Topics for Writing with Examples
Example Assignment 1: Quotation Station
Journal Entry or Essay

Choose one of the following quotations and write a journal entry or essay agreeing or disagreeing with it. Provide specific examples to support your argument.

QUOTATIONS

To be loved, be lovable.
—Ovid, *Amores II*

Hope is a good breakfast but a bad supper.
—Francis Bacon, *Apothegms*

Example   **493**

If there is anything disagreeable going on, men are sure to get out of it.
—Jane Austen, *Persuasion*

The female of the species is more deadly than the male.
—Rudyard Kipling, "The Female of the Species"

Less is more.
—Robert Browning, "Andrea del Sarto"

When we stop to think, we often miss our opportunity.
—Publius Syrus, *Maxim 185*

It is your concern when the wall next door is on fire.
—Horace, *Epistles, Book I*

One of the greatest pains to human nature is the pain of a new idea.
—Walter Bagehot, *Physics and Politics*

To him who is afraid, everything rustles.
—Sophocles, *Acrisius*, Fragment 58

Example Assignment 2: Is Your Campus Student-Friendly?
Essay

Computer programs are often described in terms of their user friendliness. What about your college campus? Is it a student-friendly place to acquire an education? Support your answer with specific examples that prove your point.

Example Assignment 3: (S)hopping Mad!
Essay

When you shop, what are your pet peeves? Provide extended examples or a series of short examples of the things that make shopping a pain. A few suggestions are provided to get your thoughts flowing.

the customer ahead of you in line who can't find her checkbook, pen, or credit card

the clerk who is too busy with a phone conversation to wait on you

the salesperson who follows you as if she has just seen your picture on the FBI's "Ten Most Wanted" list

the shopping cart sitting in the middle of the parking place where you would like to park

the grocery store shopper who waits until the total has been rung up and then says, "Oh, I have coupons here . . . somewhere"

the clothing store with locked dressing rooms and no one on duty to open them

Example Assignment 4: Essay-Based Assignment—It Takes All Kinds
Essay

In her essay, "Complaining," featured at the beginning of this chapter, Maya Angelou wrote about one type of person she observed while helping her grandmother in a store. Write an essay about one type of person that you have observed in a particular situation and would or would not want to be like. Like Angelou, you will be giving multiple examples of a single type. You may have observed this type of person at work, at school, or in a social situation. Reread Angelou's essay to see how she uses language and narrative to make her examples vivid and real.

Some adjectives that describe people's attitudes are listed below to start you off:

optimistic	grumpy
pessimistic	amiable
considerate	timid
rude	brave
efficient	lazy
inefficient	hardworking

Example Assignment 5: Real-World Topic—Safety Measures Essay

Many times, people ask how writing essays will help them in the "real world." This real-world assignment demonstrates how writing with examples might be used outside the classroom.

You are the director of security for a large mall. Many employees leave after dark, and recently, a female store manager was a victim of a carjacking as she left alone, late at night. You want to remind all employees of the mall, both male and female, of basic safety procedures they can take to stay safe from carjackings and other types of crimes. You want to mention and give examples of such safety measures, which might include using a buddy system, riding to one's car with a security guard, being observant, having keys ready and cell phone dialed to security, and other measures you might think of.

Consider the tone of your message. You do not want employees to be unduly alarmed, but you wish them to be cautious and to watch out for themselves and one another.

Reader's *Tip*   Building Connections
_____

Methods of development are tools of a writer's trade. Like a carpenter's hammer, saw, and sander, they each do a specific job. Which one should you use? It depends on the job you have to do. Some pieces of writing will require just one method, but most will require you to use more than one of your tools of the trade.

Topics for Combining Methods of Development

Description, narration, and example are methods of showing or telling a reader exactly what you mean. Combining the methods adds even more power to your writing. The assignments that follow ask you to combine two or more of the methods of development discussed in this chapter.

Example   **495**

Mixed Methods Assignment 1: Strong at the Broken Places
Essay: Narration and Example
Popular wisdom holds that adversity makes people stronger, that it is only in hard times that a person's inner strength comes through. Write a narrative and example essay describing how hard times have made you (or someone you know) a stronger person.

You may wish to make the essay primarily a narrative of a difficult time in your life, supported by examples of the way you (or the person you are writing about) became stronger. Alternatively, you may wish to write an example essay showing three different tough situations that made you (or the person you are writing about) stronger. If your essay is primarily an example essay, then at least one of your examples should be an anecdote, a brief story that demonstrates your point.

Mixed Methods Assignment 2: A Day in the Life
News Story: Narration, Description, and Example
You are a newspaper reporter. Your editor has assigned you to write a human interest story on a day in the life of a person whose life or job is difficult—a homeless person, a single parent, a person with Alzheimer's, a firefighter, a fast-food worker—the choice is yours. Your job in this human interest story is to allow your reader to get to know the person through narration, description, and example. You may write about someone you know or you may simply use your imagination to create a day in the life of a fictional person.

A human interest story is structured differently from an essay. The first paragraph is an introduction that tells who, what, when, and where. Since you are writing about a day in a person's life, the basic structure of your essay will be narrative, but you will also describe the person and give examples of problems that he or she encounters as the day goes on.

A human interest story should be immediate and fresh, so journalists often write them in the present tense.

Consider using an opening like the one that follows.

> Crossing the living room, Charlotte McCabe shuffles to the door in her bedroom slippers. Her shoulders are hunched, and her thin white hair is cut short. Clutching her robe around her with one hand, she tries the doorknob with the other. Her daughter looks at me and whispers apologetically, "I have to keep it locked. She wanders if I don't." Charlotte McCabe is 78 years old, and a day in her life is filled with the confusion and frustration of Alzheimer's disease.

Mixed Methods Assignment 3: Movie Time
Movie Review: Description, Narration, and Example
You are a movie critic. Your assignment is to write a review describing the best or worst movie you have ever seen. You may describe the acting, the music, the plot, or any other aspect of the movie that you particularly like or dislike. At least one of your paragraphs should contain a narrative example (a retelling) of one of the scenes in the movie.

19 Limiting and Ordering: Definition, Classification, and Process

4,362 of a kind

As a writer, you have probably found that your ideas are sometimes hard to pin down—they prefer to roam free. Writing an essay can be a bit like herding sheep into a pen—finding ideas that go together, separating them from their natural environment, and confining them within the fences of an essay. The techniques of definition, classification, and process help to fence in your ideas—to limit and order information and to answer the questions *What is it? How many different types exist?* and *How does it work?* Although this chapter presents each technique in isolation, you may eventually find yourself using the three techniques together to define an idea, show its different variations, and describe how it works.

Reader's *Tip* — Focus on Limiting and Ordering: Thinking about Definition, Classification, and Process

Who is the man in the photo? As the police officer searches his pockets, he has the resigned look of someone who has been through it all before. Is he a career criminal? A gangster? No, he is Lenny Bruce, a comedian who was arrested repeatedly during the 1960s for the content of his comedy act. Like many comedians today, Bruce considered any topic fair game for comedy, and his act was often raunchy and profane.

Society was less tolerant then, and Bruce was charged with obscenity in a trial that became famous in the 1960s. Celebrities testified on his behalf and newspapers reported every detail. Ultimately, Lenny Bruce was convicted of obscenity.

Lenny Bruce's trial provides a real-world example of the use of the writing techniques outlined in this chapter: definition, classification, and process. First, prosecutors had to define obscenity. Next, material from Lenny Bruce's act had to be reviewed to see if they could be classified as obscene. Finally came the process of laying out the evidence in a courtroom trial.

Reflect on It

Every profession limits and orders in some way. Think about your own profession. What part of your job might require you to define something, classify something to show how it fits into a larger picture, or explain a process?

Source: http://en.wikipedia.org/wiki/Lenny_Bruce

Definition, Classification, and Process in Action

In this chapter, you will have the opportunity to examine and use the techniques of definition, classification, and process. In this text, each technique is explained separately, although writers seldom use them in isolation. Just as an aspiring tap dancer would learn and practice the ball change, the shuffle-flap, and the hop-step separately before employing them together to do the Shim Sham Shimmy, so is it useful for writers to learn and practice techniques of writing separately before using them together in a composition.

Before looking at definition, classification, and process separately, look at how a professional writer uses all three techniques together. The following essay is by Letty Cottin Pogrebin, writer, founding editor of Ms. magazine, and activist in feminist and Jewish causes.

The essay embodies all three of the writing techniques featured in this chapter. Mainly, the essay shows the **process** through which the author acquired her superstitions and passed them on to the next generation. Notice how Pogrebin moves through the process in chronological order, starting with her childhood and ending with an anecdote about her own child.

The author also employs **definition** in her essay. In the first paragraph, Pogrebin makes it clear that her definition of her topic will be a personal one. Notice that Pogrebin cites examples of traditional superstition before moving on to a discussion of her own brand of superstition, a common technique in definition essays.

In the third through sixth paragraphs, the author also employs **classification** as she outlines the various types of behavior that might allow the "Evil Eye" to inflict harm. Writers often use examples to illustrate classification. Notice Pogrebin's clear and sharp examples as she discusses forbidden behaviors.

Superstitious Minds

LETTY COTTIN POGREBIN

1 I am a very rational person. I tend to trust reason more than feeling. But I also happen to be superstitious—in my fashion. Black cats and rabbits' feet hold no power for me. My superstitions are my mother's superstitions, the amulets and incantations she learned from her mother and taught me.

2 I don't mean to suggest that I grew up in an occult atmosphere. On the contrary, my mother desperately wanted me to rise above her immigrant ways and become an educated American. She tried to hide her superstitions, but I came to know them all: Slap a girl's cheeks when she first gets her period. Never take a picture of a pregnant woman. Knock wood when speaking about your good fortune. Eat the ends of bread if you want to have a boy. Don't leave a bride alone on her wedding day.

3 When I was growing up, my mother would often tiptoe in after I seemed to be asleep, making odd noises that sounded like a cross between sucking and spitting. One night I opened my eyes and demanded an explanation. Embarrassed, she told me she was excising the "Evil Eye"—in case I had attracted its attention that day by being especially wonderful. She believed her kisses could suck out any envy or ill will that those less fortunate may have directed at her child.

4 By the time I was in my teens, I was almost on speaking terms with the Evil Eye, a jealous spirit that kept track of those who had "too much" happiness and zapped them with sickness and misery to even the score. To guard against this mischief, my mother practiced rituals of interference, evasion, deference, and above all, avoidance of situations where the Evil Eye might feel at home.

5 This is why I wasn't allowed to attend funerals. This is also why my mother hated to mend my clothes while I was wearing them. The only garment one should properly get sewn into is a shroud. To ensure that the Evil Eye did not confuse my pinafore with a burial outfit, my mother insisted that I chew thread while she sewed, thus proving myself very much alive. Outwitting the Evil Eye also accounted for her closing window shades above my bed whenever there was a full moon. The moon should only shine on cemeteries, you see; the living need protection from the spirits.

6 Because we were dealing with a deadly force, I also wasn't supposed to say any words associated with mortality. This was hard for a 12-year-old who punctuated every anecdote with the verb "to die," as in, "You'll die when you hear this!" or "If I don't get home by ten, I'm dead." I managed to avoid using such expressions in the presence of my mother until the day my parents brought home a painting I hated and we were arguing about whether it should be displayed on our walls. Unthinking, I pressed my point with a melodramatic idiom: "That picture will hang over my dead body!" Without a word, my mother grabbed a knife and slashed the canvas to shreds.

7 I understand all this now. My mother emigrated in 1907 from a small Hungarian village. The oldest of seven children, she had to go out to work before she finished the eighth grade. Experience taught her that life was unpredictable and often incomprehensible. Just as an athlete keeps wearing the same T-shirt in every game to prolong a winning streak, my mother's superstitions gave her a means of imposing order on a chaotic system. Her desire to control the fates sprang from the same helplessness that makes the San Francisco 49ers' defensive team more superstitious than its offensive team. Psychologists speculate that this is because the defense has less control; they don't have the ball.

8 Women like my mother never had the ball. She died when I was 15, leaving me with deep regrets about what she might have been—and a growing understanding of who she was. Superstitious is one of the things she was. I wish I had a million sharp recollections of her, but when you don't expect someone to die, you don't store up enough memories. Ironically, her mystical practices are among the clearest impressions she left behind. I honor this matrilineal heritage—and to symbolize my mother's effort to control her life as I in my way try to find order in mine—I knock on wood and do not let the moon shine on those I love. My children laugh at me, but they understand that these tiny rituals have helped keep my mother alive in my mind.

9 A year ago, I awoke in the night and realized that my son's window blinds had been removed for repair. Smiling at my own compulsion, I got a bed sheet to tack up against the moonlight and opened his bedroom door. What I saw brought tears to my eyes. There, hopelessly askew, was a blanket my son, then 18, had taped to his window like a curtain.

10 My mother never lived to know David, but he knew she would not want the moon to shine upon him as he slept.

Thinking About the Essay

1. A personal definition is often quite different from a traditional definition. In what ways does Pogrebin's definition of superstition vary from a more traditonal definition?

2. When writers describe a process, they use sequential or chronological order. As Pogrebin describes how she acquired her superstitions, she uses chronological order. Look at the essay and identify three stages of Pogrebin's life that were touched by superstition.
3. Classification of ideas deals with types or kinds. In the essay, Pogrebin outlines various types of behavior that allowed the Evil Eye to operate. What types of behavior does she mention? What do they have in common?

Definition Write a personal definition of superstition. You have seen Letty Cottin Pogrebin's essay on superstition on page 499. She saw superstition as a way of remaining close to her mother. You see it in a different way. Perhaps you think superstition is silly. Perhaps you see it as a way of exerting control over situations in which you feel helpless. Perhaps you connect it with a particular activity, such as athletics. Prewrite to discover your thoughts on superstition, and then write an essay defining it.

Classification Look at Letty Cottin Pogrebin's essay, "Superstitious Minds," on page 499 of this chapter. Write an essay in which you classify different types of superstition. You might classify superstitions according to the objects or ideas that they center on. For example, some superstitions involve numbers (fear of the number 13, lucky number 7), others involve animals (black cats crossing one's path), and still others involve household items (breaking a mirror). Alternatively, you could classify superstitions by the situations they are thought to affect. For instance, some superstitions concern ways to affect love; others, money; and still others, travel. Another possibility is to classify superstitions according to who accepts them as true. If you have a superstitious family, superstition may be generational: Your superstitions may be different from your mother's or your grandmother's. Write your essay using one of these bases for classification or your own basis for classification.

Process Look at Letty Cottin Pogrebin's essay, "Superstitious Minds," on page 499 of this chapter. She details in chronological order the process by which superstition entered her mind. Write an essay describing the process or processes through which superstition takes hold. For instance, it might be passed on by family, as Pogrebin's superstitions were. It might come about when a person notices that good things happen when he wears a particular sweater or performs a particular action. It might be passed on by cultural beliefs. For example, most people know that the number 13 is supposed to be unlucky. Some people might reject that belief, while others might accept it. You can perhaps think of other ways that superstition takes hold.

In this process essay, you may write in first person about your own superstitions, as Pogrebin did. Alternatively, you may write objectively in third person about how people come to acquire superstition. In either case, support your process essay with clear, detailed examples of specific superstitions.

Definition

When you think of definitions, you probably think of the dictionary. If you want to know the definition of *curmudgeon* or the difference between an *ectomorph* and an *endomorph*, you turn to the dictionary for definitions. Similarly, when you want to define an idea or concept in detail, you may write a definition essay.

A dictionary entry provides a good example of a definition. Examine the sample dictionary definition of the word *burden*, and then answer the questions that follow.

Sample Dictionary Definition

bur'den (ber'dan) *n.* **1,** something carried; a load. **2,** something borne with difficulty, as care, grief, etc. **3,** an encumbrance. **4,** a main theme; a refrain.

(from *The New American Webster Handy College Dictionary, New Third Edition*)

Questions?

1. Would you characterize the definition as brief or extended?
2. Does the entry provide any clue about how the person writing the entry felt about the subject, or is it strictly factual?
3. Does the dictionary definition include any examples?

As you noticed, a dictionary definition is extremely brief and entirely factual. However, there are two very brief examples in definition 2—*care* and *grief*.

A definition essay is like a dictionary definition in some ways. For example, a definition essay, like a dictionary definition, attempts to capture the essence of something—an object, a feeling, or a task—in words.

However, unlike the writer of a dictionary definition, you have the luxury of using many words in your definition essay. Instead of a four-word definition, you may have a four-hundred-word definition.

A definition essay might answer questions like the following:

- What is a status symbol?
- What are the characteristics of a leader?
- What does the word *duty* mean to you?

Classification

Whether you know it or not, **classification** comes naturally to you. From the time you are born, you explore. You discover that some things are pleasurable and others are painful, that some things are edible and others are not. Those are your first lessons in classification.

By the time you reach adulthood, you divide people, articles of clothing, words, teachers, and ways of behaving into different types or categories so automatically that you are barely aware of it. When you answer a classmate's question, "What kind of teacher is Dr. Burton?" or reply to a friend who asks what kind of day you have had, you are classifying.

Writing a classification essay allows you to use your categorizing skills to answer questions like the ones that follow.

- What kinds of extracurricular activities benefit students most?
- What types of students do you least enjoy having as classmates?
- How would you classify the fans that you see at a football game?

Laying the Groundwork for Writing Classification Papers

Visualizing Look at the photograph of the dangerous curve in the road. Imagine cars going around that curve. Some drivers are cautious, others speed; some clutch the steering wheel with a death grip, others casually drape one hand across it. Look at the drivers in your mind; see their faces, anxious or relaxed or gleefully demonic.

Planning Think about the drivers you have visualized and other kinds of drivers you have encountered. What different types are there? What specific term would you use for each?

Writing In a paragraph, describe how two of the types of drivers you have listed might approach the dangerous curve at night.

Establishing a Basis for Classification

In the following list, which item does not belong?

Kinds of Teachers
a. the drill sergeant
b. the comedian
c. the sociology teacher

If you chose c, you are right. You have recognized, consciously or subconsciously, that the first two have the same basis for classification—teaching style. The third item has a different basis for classification—subject matter.

Reader's *Tip* ——— Building Connections ————————————————

Classifications, especially those that are your own invention, may often begin with a definition. For example, if you classified *teacher* into three groups—the drill sergeant, the comedian, and the prima donna—you might begin each body paragraph with a definition: "The drill sergeant is a professor who runs the classroom as if it were boot camp."

When you write a classification essay, it is important that your classification have a single basis or underlying principle. If it does not, then your categories of classification may be so close that they overlap or so far-flung that they seem to have no connection with one another.

In the example above, "sociology teacher" overlaps all three categories since sociology teachers have a variety of teaching styles. A single basis for classification ensures that your categories of classification are separate and distinct.

Categories of classification that are too diverse can be illustrated with a different example. A writer who has listed "airplane" and "bus" under the heading "types of transportation" would not be likely to add "camel" to the list, even though a camel can be transportation in some parts of the world. The other two types are modern forms of mass transportation, so "camel" does not fit in.

exercise 19.1   **Classifying Items in a List**

Fill in the blanks with the appropriate words to classify each list of items.

1. Kinds of _____   Basis for classification: _____

   a. dalmatian
   b. Labrador retriever
   c. cocker spaniel
   d. poodle

2. Kinds of _____   Basis for classification: _____

   a. French
   b. Italian
   c. ranch
   d. blue cheese

3. Kinds of _____ Basis for classification: _____

   a. heavy metal
   b. rap
   c. country
   d. pop

4. Kinds of _____ Basis for classification: _____

   a. carving
   b. fillet
   c. steak
   d. pocket

5. Kinds of _____ Basis for classification: _____

   a. rocky road
   b. Neapolitan
   c. fudge ripple
   d. coffee

6. Kinds of _____ Basis for classification: _____

   a. pepperoni
   b. sausage
   c. cheese
   d. mushrooms

7. Kinds of _____ Basis for classification: _____

   a. dining
   b. coffee
   c. end
   d. card

8. Kinds of _____ Basis for classification: _____

   a. skim (fat free)
   b. 1%
   c. 2%
   d. 4%

9. Kinds of _____ Basis for classification: _____

   a. rollerball
   b. ballpoint
   c. felt-tip
   d. fountain

10. Kinds of _____ Basis for classification: _____

    a. bow ties
    b. elbows
    c. angel hair
    d. twists

exercise 19.2   **Finding a Basis for Classification**

Part 1: Circle the letter of the item that does not belong in the following lists. Then write the basis for classification of the other items in the blank.

1. Cars   Basis for classification: _____

   a. Ford
   b. Mazda
   c. sports car
   d. Nissan

2. Cats   Basis for classification: _____

   a. tiger
   b. tabby
   c. snow leopard
   d. cheetah

3. Restaurants   Basis for classification: _____

   a. Mexican
   b. Italian
   c. Thai
   d. fast food

4. Schools   Basis for classification: _____

   a. fewer than 200 students
   b. 201–500 students
   c. high school
   d. 501–1000 students

5. Dances   Basis for classification: _____

   a. tango
   b. Macarena
   c. senior prom
   d. electric slide

Part 2: As entry *d* in each list, add one item that fits the basis for classification.

6. Drugs

   a. caplet

   b. liquid

   c. patch

   d. _____

7. Games

   a. solitaire

   b. hearts

   c. go fish

   d. _____

8. Books

   a. geography

   b. biology

   c. history

   d. _____

9. Tools

   a. trowel

   b. shovel

   c. hedge clippers

   d. _____

10. Hair

   a. brown

   b. black

   c. red

   d. _____

exercise 19.3   **Finding the Point That Does Not Fit**

The following paragraph contains one point that is on a different basis for classification than the other two. Read the paragraph, then answer the questions that follow.

KINDS OF EXERCISERS

At the gym where I work out, three types of exercisers stand out from the crowd. The first type, the struggler, breaks into a sweat just at the sight of an exercise bike. Strugglers walk five laps around the track, then stop, huffing and puffing, to rest on a bench before attempting another few laps. In contrast to strugglers are the fashion plates, who always have the latest in exercise wear. Exercising in front of the mirror, fashion plates can admire their colorful leotards, smartly cut shorts, or new athletic shoes. Even when they exercise, fashion plates never have limp, straggly hair or sweat-stained clothing. They always look their best. Finally, there are the athletes, who do not mind working up a sweat and are dedicated to fitness. In aerobics class, they bounce higher than anyone else even after an hour on the treadmill. Before they leave, they may swim a few laps in the pool just to cool off. Whether they are suffering strugglers, self-absorbed fashion plates, or dedicated athletes, these exercisers are fun to watch as I struggle through my own workout.

1. Which type of exerciser is not classified on the same basis as the others?

   _____

2. What is the basis for classification of the other two points?

   _____

Wordsmith's Corner: Examples of Writing Developed through Classification

Following are two student essays developed through classification. Read each and answer the questions that follow.

Classification Essay 1

Drawing on observation and her own experience as a shopper, this writer divides shoppers into different categories.

KINDS OF SHOPPERS

"Why do women love to shop?" my husband asks. I point out that it's a strange question from a man who, when it comes to pulling out a credit card, is quicker on the draw than a gunslinger in the Old West. I am convinced that men, despite their protests to the contrary, enjoy shopping as much as women do. But as a woman, I know female shoppers and I believe I know what motivates them. Some are bargain hunters, some are pleasure seekers, and others are social shoppers.

For bargain hunters, shopping is a game of strategy and skill, and saving money is the motivation. My friend Renee is a perfect example of a bargain hunter. She never shops without a plan. Her motto is, "Never pay full price for anything." This past October, when the breeze picked up and the temperature dropped, we went shopping. I watched her bypass the tables of long-sleeved shirts and racks of dresses in deep colors with names like "pumpkin" and "eggplant." On a clearance table, she found marked-down shorts and tank tops in tropical colors. Then we went to the men's department, where she expertly searched through a picked-over display of short-sleeved shirts and khaki pants to find her husband's sizes. Buying clothes at the end of the season, she says, lets her buy twice the clothes at half the price.

Unlike the bargain hunter, a pleasure seeker shops because it feels good. Shopping is therapy, celebration, and comfort. I admit to being a pleasure seeker. If I am feeling down, the cure is a trip to the mall for aromatherapy at Lotions and Potions. Placing strawberry-guava shower gel, cucumber-mint facial masque, or mango-honey lip pomade into a wicker shopping basket, I feel my mood lift, and by the time I present my Visa card at the register, I am feeling downright cheerful. Celebrations call for a soft velour dress or just the right pair of earrings. Even an ordinary Saturday becomes special if I can pick up a novel or a few magazines and stop by Candyland for a treat to enjoy as I read. Shopping is always a mood enhancer for me.

For the last type of shopper, shopping is a social act. Social shoppers travel in pairs or threes or even groups of five or six. Laughing and chatting, they flit through the stores, fingering cashmere, modeling hats, and spritzing colognes on one another. Since the purpose of the trip is mainly social, making purchases is optional. One sub-group of the social shopping group, however, shops seriously, usually in pairs. These shoppers don't need a mirror; they have one another. Their voices ring through the dressing room: "Lydia, what do you think of this peach color on me?" "Mom, does this bathing suit make me look fat?" "Ooo-wee, girl, that skirt looks good on you!" If the shopping trip is fruitful, so much the better. If not, the social shopper is un-daunted. There is, after all, a food court and a sit-down restaurant that serves yummy pumpernickel croutons with its salad. The social shopper almost never has a shopping trip she doesn't enjoy, unless she has to shop alone.

Why do so many women love to shop? The reasons are as varied as the individu-als themselves. As long as money, pleasure, and companionship motivate humans, the bargain hunter, the pleasure seeker, and the social shopper will keep the cash registers humming at malls everywhere.

Questions?

1. What type of introduction does this essay have?

   a. narrow to broad

   b. historical

   c. anecdote

   d. contrast

2. In the space below, write the thesis statement of the essay and the topic sen-tence of each body paragraph.

   _____

   _____

   _____

   _____

   _____

   _____

3. What is the basis for classification in this essay on types of shoppers?

   a. amount of money spent

   b. motivation for shopping

   c. type of merchandise bought

   d. type of store visited

4. Which body paragraph begins with a transitional topic sentence?

   _____

5. What type of conclusion does the essay have?

   a. prediction

   b. recommendation

   c. summary

   d. quotation

Classification Essay 2
The writer of this essay explores people's attitudes toward life.

ATTITUDES TOWARD LIFE

I have always heard it said that people are the same under the skin, and in many ways it's true. People have similar impulses, hopes, and dreams. However, people vary widely in their attitudes toward life.

A person with a negative attitude puts a pessimistic twist on life, even when good things happen. If she has front-row center seats at the concert, she complains that her neck hurts from sitting so close or that the music is too loud. If he has a new job, he complains that the hours are too long and the benefits inadequate. When I congratulated my friend Tim on his new job, his response was typically negative. "It's okay, I guess," he said, "but the money and the chances for advancement aren't that great. I'm just biding my time until something else comes along." Negative people can turn even good fortune into bad luck.

A positive person, on the other hand, can find the good in almost anything. My coworker Mario always says, "Something good is going to happen today." At first, I thought Mario's good cheer was just a false front. But I have worked with him for a while now and I have begun to see that there is nothing fake about his optimism. He really does look for good things to happen, and he sees failure as an incentive to work harder. Any doubt I had about Mario's attitude evaporated when he confided that his wife has cancer. "It's made me realize what's important in my life," he said, "and it's made me closer to her than ever before." Even tragedy has its positive side to a positive person like Mario.

The person with a wait-and-see attitude withholds judgment on everything. If you ask him how he is today, he may cautiously reply, "So far, so good." He sees no point in committing himself when unexpected disaster or great good fortune may befall him at any time. My elderly neighbor is a classic example of the wait-and-see person. The last time I saw her, I asked about her children and grandchildren. She told me that her daughter and son-in-law had just celebrated their twenty-fifth wedding anniversary. When I commented on how long their marriage had lasted, my neighbor shrugged. "Yes, I guess it's a good marriage," she said. "Time will tell."

Attitudes toward life shape the way we see the world. A negative person finds the bad in everything, while a positive person looks for the good. And the person with a wait-and-see attitude, like someone watching a play, sits back and waits for the next act to unfold.

Questions?

1. What two techniques are used in the introduction?

    a. narrow to broad and contrast

    b. quotation and contrast

    c. anecdote and quotation

    d. anecdote and contrast

2. In the following space, write the thesis statement of the essay and the topic sentence of each body paragraph.

    _____

    _____

    _____

    _____

    _____

    _____

    _____

3. What basis does the author use to classify people's attitudes?

    a. gender of the person

    b. how the attitude was acquired

    c. type of attitude.

    d. age of the person

4. Which body paragraph contains three short examples?

    a. body paragraph 1

    b. body paragraph 2

    c. body paragraph 3

Topics for Writing Using Classification
Classification Assignment 1: Kinds of People
Journal Entry

Write a journal entry classifying and describing one of the following categories of people.

gum chewers	doughnut eaters	cell phone users
complainers	speakers	grocery shoppers

Classification Assignment 2: Relationship in Ruins
Essay
Discuss the kinds of problems that can ruin a relationship. It is up to you to decide what the relationship is—it may be a romance, a friendship, a marriage, a student-teacher relationship, a relationship with a coworker, or a relationship with a neighbor. Choose the type of relationship that you wish to discuss, then write an essay about the types of problems that might ruin it.

Classification Assignment 3: Classy Classification
Essay
Write an essay classifying one of the following items having to do with classes.

assignments	tests
desks	schedules
professors	textbooks
classmates	note takers

Classification Assignment 4: It Takes All Kinds
Essay
Write a classification essay categorizing one of the types of people below.

pet owners	parents
drivers	neighbors
dates	sports fans
friends	coworkers
teachers	classmates

Classification Assignment 5: Real-World Topic—
Designing a New Program
Many times, people ask how writing essays will help them in the "real world." This real-world assignment demonstrates how writing using classification might be used outside the classroom.

You are part of a human resources team at a medium-sized company. Profits have been so good that the company has set aside five million dollars to fund a program that will benefit employees and the company. Each team member has been asked to come up with ideas about the kinds of programs that might be offered. The only restrictions are that both the company and the employees should benefit from the programs. For example, wellness programs such as exercise, weight loss, or stop-smoking clinics would benefit both the employee, who would be healthier, and the company, which would theoretically benefit because healthier employees would use less sick leave and incur lower health insurance costs. Incentive programs offering rewards for increased productivity would similarly benefit both the rewarded employees and the company, which would benefit from the increased productivity.

Write an essay describing three types of programs that might be developed. Give examples of how each program would work and describe how it would benefit both the employees and the company.

Process

When you write a **process** essay, you describe how to do something or how it works. Process writing surrounds you. Recipes, instruction manuals, and any of the many self-help books that offer advice on how to become fit, lose weight, save money, or lead a more satisfying life are all examples of process writing. A chapter in your American government text that tells you how a bill becomes a law, the page in your biology text on the life cycle of the fruit fly, and the fine print on the back of your credit card statement that explains how interest is applied are also examples of process writing.

Process essays typically answer questions like the ones that follow.

- What is the best way to handle a broken relationship?
- What is your recipe for an enjoyable vacation?
- Describe an effective process for setting and reaching goals.

Laying the Groundwork for Process Writing

Visualizing Look at the photograph of the young man and woman. What is happening in the photograph? How might it end?

Planning What process are these two individuals engaged in? What are the steps in this process? Do the steps usually occur in a different order, or is the order the same every time? Which stage of the process is the couple in?

Writing In a paragraph, list the steps in the process in a logical order, giving a one-sentence explanation of what happens in each step.

Organizing the Process Essay

Some processes are **fixed** processes—that is, ones in which the order of the steps cannot vary. If you tell someone how to change the oil in a car, for instance, you can't place the step "add new oil" before the step "drain old oil." If you explain how a bill becomes a law, you can't place "goes to president for signing or veto" before "approved by both houses of Congress." If you are describing a fixed process, list the steps in chronological order or step-by-step order.

Other processes are **loose** processes. They have no fixed, predetermined order. Loose processes include such things as handling money wisely or becoming physically fit. In describing these processes, it is up to the writer to choose the most logical order.

Imagine that you are writing a paper on handling money wisely. You decide that the steps involved include paying down debt, developing a spending plan, and saving for the future. Developing a spending plan seems logical as a first point, but you can't decide whether to place "saving" or "paying down debt" next in the order. You may say, "It's impossible to save any meaningful amount until debts are paid. Therefore, paying debt before saving is logical." Or you may reason like this: "Most people stay in debt for most of their lives. If it's not a credit card, it's a car loan or a mortgage. The important thing is to pay yourself first, no matter what." Either order is logical. What is important is that you have thought about it and chosen the order that best suits your own philosophy.

Reader's *Tip* Building Connections

As you analyze the process you plan to write about, you will find yourself breaking the process into pieces in a way that feels a lot like classification. Process and classification have a lot in common and can often be combined. An essay called "The Road to Alcoholism," for instance, might mainly describe the process by which someone became an alcoholic. However, it would probably also break the process into definite stages—a form of classification.

One important point to remember when organizing the "how-to" process paper is that many processes require tools or must be done under certain conditions. Ideally, a "how-to" paper should be written so clearly and logically that the reader could carry out the process on the first read-through. Usually, then, the first step of your process will direct the reader to gather tools and make preparations. Whether you're telling how to make a pastry or how to defuse a bomb, your reader won't appreciate being led to a crucial point and then being instructed to use a tool that isn't handy.

Introducing the Process Essay

If you are explaining a process with wide appeal to readers, almost any of the types of introduction discussed in Chapter 14 will serve your purpose. However, if you are writing about a process of more limited interest, you may find it useful to motivate a specific audience and explain the value of or reason for the process.

When you motivate a specific audience, you think about who might find your process useful. If you are writing about study strategies, your target audience would be students. If your topic is "choosing a day-care center," your target audience would be parents of young children. Once you have identified your audience, think about how the process will benefit that audience. Readers are more likely to be motivated to read your essay if you can show them that the process has value for them.

EXAMPLE   **INTRODUCTION TO MOTIVATE**

> Choosing the right day care for your child can mean the difference between a happy child who looks forward to the fun and friends at day care and a child who hangs back in the mornings, reluctant to leave the house. A child's attitude toward day care is often a precursor to his or her attitude about school. Because the choice of day care is so vital, it pays to know what to look for in a day-care center.

Concluding the Process Essay

The conclusion of a process paper should answer the question, *What is the value of the process?* If your paper is a "how-to" process paper, the answer to the question may motivate the reader to carry out the process. If the paper is an explanation of how something works, the conclusion serves as a reminder of the value of or reason for the process.

EXAMPLES   **CONCLUSION TO MOTIVATE**

> Getting your finances in order is hard work. But consider the rewards. You will no longer be feeding money into the black hole of credit card debt to pay for long-forgotten purchases. And when you get mail from the bank, it will be your savings statement, not an overdraft notice.

CONCLUSION TO EXPLAIN THE VALUE OF THE PROCESS

> As the hatchlings make their way instinctively toward the sea, some are plucked from the sand and eaten by hungry gulls. Turtles that survive that crucial journey to the sea may one day return to this very beach to deposit their eggs and begin the cycle of life anew.

Wordsmith's Corner: Examples of Process Writing

Following are two student process essays. Read each and answer the questions that follow.

Process Essay 1

This essay describes a process of self-discovery as the writer confronts a learning disability.

DISCOVERING MY ABILITIES

On my report cards, my teachers used to write, "Erica doesn't apply herself" or "Erica lacks motivation." When I decided to go to college, I thought I had the motivation I needed. But I still had trouble finishing what I started, and I always felt frustrated, disorganized, and ten steps behind the rest of the class. In desperation, I visited the college's counseling center and began a process of self-discovery that turned my life around.

My journey to self-discovery began the day I walked into the counseling center. I came in shyly, just planning to pick up a few brochures. But the counselor, Dr. Fordham, invited me into her office and asked me about my study problems. I told her that I would start writing an essay and find myself playing solitaire on the computer. I would get most of the work done on a term paper, and then resistance would set in and I would find excuses not to finish. I habitually lost assignment sheets, syllabi, and library books. I was my own worst enemy. After we had talked a bit longer, Dr. Fordham said that some of the habits I mentioned could be symptoms of attention deficit disorder, or ADD. I told her I did not have a learning disability; I was just lazy and disorganized. Dr. Fordham did not press, but along with the study skills brochures she gave me an information sheet on ADD.

The next step in my process of self-discovery involved overcoming denial. When I read the brochure, I recognized myself immediately. However, I was not about to be labeled "learning disabled" at my age. But I reasoned that getting more information could not hurt, so I searched the Internet. Along with other information about ADD, I found an adult ADD checklist. The checklist said that experiencing twenty or more of the symptoms could indicate a tendency toward ADD. I had checked forty-six of them. It was becoming harder for me to deny that I had a problem.

The most difficult step in the process was getting up the courage to be tested. I finally talked to my parents. "So what if you have a learning disability?" my practical mother said. "It's not going to change who you are." My father did some research, and told me that Einstein had a learning disability. Finally, I overcame my reluctance and went to an ADD center that Dr. Fordham recommended. The tests confirmed that I had ADD. Somehow, knowing the truth lifted a weight from my shoulders. Now I was ready to do something about my problem. When a doctor at the center suggested Ritalin, I was doubtful. I had always thought it was some sort of tranquilizer for unruly kids. Dr. Sims told me it was actually a stimulant that helped many people with ADD to focus. After talking with Dr. Sims, I agreed to try it. I also scheduled a visit with a counselor to learn coping techniques. Accepting my learning disability and finding ways of coping was the last step in my process of self-discovery.

Now, dealing with school is much easier. Last term, for the first time, I made the dean's list. It is as if I have discovered my abilities, not my disability. I know that I am not lazy and unmotivated, but a smart and determined person. Now, though, I'm able to show it.

Questions?

1. In the space below, write the thesis statement of the essay.

   _____

   _____

2. In the space below, write the topic sentence of each body paragraph.

   _____

   _____

   _____

   _____

   _____

   _____

3. What were the steps the writer followed in accepting her disability?

   _____

   _____

   _____

Process Essay 2

A job in a bakery, an ambition to start a business, and a bit of observation helped the writer of this essay to learn about the process of pleasing a customer.

A LESSON IN CUSTOMER SERVICE

As a full-time college student majoring in business administration, I have hopes of owning my own business someday. As a part-time worker in a bakery, I see what a hassle owning a business can be. Business owners have to worry about making a profit and keeping employees happy and productive. Most of all, they have to worry about keeping customers, even when they can't always deliver what the customer wants. The other day, I watched Herschel, our bakery manager, deal with a difficult customer. Herschel's behavior showed me how to handle a customer complaint.

The first thing that Herschel did was to accept full responsibility. The customer had been told that there were no angel food cakes. The last two had been thrown out that morning because they were out of date. She was upset. Why hadn't they been marked down? My answer would have been, "Sorry, it's company policy." Herschel took responsibility. He said, "When you buy a cake, I want you to have the freshest one available. If I sell merchandise that is out of date, I know I'm not giving you my best." The woman was still not happy. "Other stores sell out-of-date products at a reduced price," she said. "If I get it for a reduced price, I don't expect it to be as fresh."

As I watched, I was getting a little irritated with the woman, but Herschel explained his position patiently. He spoke of his pride in his products and his belief that every customer was entitled to quality. He spoke calmly and casually, as if the customer were a friend. He leaned forward, his body language saying that their conversation was of great interest. "If you take home a cake or a loaf of bread and you don't eat any for four days," he said, "it should still be good when you open it." The customer said, "Okay, I understand," and started to leave.

I would have probably shrugged and let her walk away, but Herschel took a little extra time to make her feel important. He walked with the woman around the bakery, squeezing loaves of bread and chatting. He pointed out fat-free muffins and raisin bread, and told her how much he liked the carrot cake. It was trivial conversation, but the point was not what he said. The point was that his willingness to take time with her suggested that she was a valuable customer. When she left, she was smiling and carrying a loaf of raisin bread with her.

Instead of taking the easy way out, Herschel accepted responsibility for company policies, took the time to explain, and made the woman feel like a valued customer. I believe he won a customer for life. As for me, I received a lesson in customer service that I will remember when I am running my own business.

Questions?

1. In the space below, write the thesis statement of the essay.

   _____

   _____

2. In the space below, write the topic sentence of each body paragraph.

   _____

   _____

   _____

   _____

   _____

3. What are the steps involved in handling a customer complaint, according to the writer?

   _____

   _____

Topics for Process Writing
Process Assignment 1: An Everyday Task
Journal Entry
Write a process journal entry telling your reader how to do a simple, everyday task. Describe it so well and so completely that a reader could complete the process based on your directions alone. Be sure to include at the beginning of the paper any tools that the reader will need. A few suggestions follow.

tying a shoe	putting on and buttoning a shirt
brushing your teeth	feeding a pet
making toast	putting on makeup
making coffee	shaving
starting a car	reading a newspaper

Process Assignment 2: The Way You Do the Things You Do
Essay

Write an essay telling your reader how to do something that you do well. It might be a physical skill, like pitching a baseball, driving a car, or doing an aerobic exercise routine. It might be a social skill, like making people feel comfortable or mediating an argument. Or it might be a practical skill or a craft, like getting the most for your money at the grocery store or making a stained-glass window.

Process Assignment 3: The Process of Change
Essay

Change can be difficult, and the process of coping with it is not always easy. Think of a change or transition that was difficult for you and describe in a five-paragraph essay your process of coping with it.

Process Assignment 4: The Right Start
Essay

Write an essay directed at someone who is just getting started in one of the following processes.

starting a physical fitness program
beginning college
setting up a budget
trying to lose or gain weight

Process Assignment 5: Real-World Topic—
Performing a Job-Related Task
Essay

Describe one of the tasks involved in your job. Describe it step by step, so well that someone who had the necessary tools and knowledge could do the job from your description.

Consider your audience. Will you describe this task for a person who possesses job skills and knowledge similar to your own, or will you write it for someone who is not familiar with the terminology of your field? Consider your tone. Descriptions of a task can convey much more than the bare bones of the task itself, as two essays from the Readings section of this book demonstrate. In "Two Ways of Seeing a River," Mark Twain describes, to some extent, the tasks of piloting a steamboat, but he also writes of how his job has affected the way he sees the river. In "Letting in Light," Patricia Raybon describes window-washing in such a way as to thread together generations of women who are linked by this humble task.

Topics for Combining Methods of Development

Definition, classification, and process are methods of showing the limits of a topic—the borders that define it—and of ordering it into steps, stages, or types. The following assignments ask you to combine one or more methods of development.

Mixed Methods Assignment 1: Stress
Essay: Definition and Classification

In this essay, your job is to define the term stress and to divide it into types. Your definition must be broad enough to cover all the types of stress that you explore in your essay. As a suggestion for organizing your essay, try defining the broad term stress in the introduction. Then, list and define each type of stress in a topic sentence. Since classification essays often incorporate examples, you may wish to support your body paragraphs with examples that give the reader a clear picture of each type of stress.

Mixed Methods Assignment 2: Problems and Solutions
Consultant's Report: Definition, Classification, and Process

You are a consultant. A large organization—it could be a school, a mall, a grocery store, a church, or some other organization that serves many people—has hired you to look at its problems and determine how the organization can fix those problems. It is up to you to choose the organization and define and classify its problems. Just to give some examples, a mall might find that many people with handicaps have trouble moving freely about the mall. They can't climb the stairs, the aisles in some of the stores are too narrow to navigate in a wheelchair, and the food court tables are too close together for them to navigate the food court. You might classify these as "mobility problems." That same mall might find that teenagers, who traditionally have high disposable incomes, are not spending their money. Instead of making the mall stores profitable by buying clothing, CDs, or video games, they are hanging out in the food court with friends or flirting with other teenagers. How can the mall lure these teenagers into the stores to spend money? These problems might be classified as "profitability problems." Or perhaps existing parking is not adequate and there is no land available adjacent to the mall to create more parking—a parking problem. Your first task, then, is to decide on the organization you want to write about and to define and classify its problems.

Once you have listed the problems and classified them into groups, your job is to come up with a process by which the organization can solve its problems.

This report can easily be organized like a traditional essay. The thesis will state the problems faced by the organization, and each body paragraph will define and classify a problem and suggest a process for solving it.

Mixed Methods Assignment 3: What It Is, How It Works
Essay: Definition and Process

Everyone develops ways of doing things—of completing everyday processes—that work for them. Some people even name their systems—Andrea's Clothing Coordination System, Raoul's Never-Fail Approach to Getting a Date, Betty's Efficient Grocery Shopping Method. What's your system? In this essay, your job is to define a process that works well for you, pointing out its advantages over conventional methods. Then, describe the process, step by step, so that a reader could easily follow your directions and use your process.

20 Examining Logical Connections: Comparison-Contrast, Cause-Effect, and Argument

Back to back
Not eye to eye,
We disagree
And don't know why.
We are the same,
Yet poles apart,
Perhaps my words
Can reach your heart.

Reader's *Tip* — Focus on Examining Logical
Connections: Thinking about Logic

Look at the sign pictured here. Is it illogical under the circumstances?

Evidence of illogical thinking is everywhere. Often, that lack of logic comes from forced comparisons, faulty cause-effect relationships, or ill-formed arguments. It's not enough just to compare two things or say that an effect happened or to argue without evidence. It's also necessary to show the logical connections between the two things that are being compared, explain how an effect clearly stemmed from a cause, or provide evidence that supports an argument.

Reflect on It

Find a sign somewhere that you think has some sort of logical flaw. Describe your sign (or better yet, take a picture of it), and explain why it is logically flawed.

When you compare one alternative with another, when you look for causes and effects, or when you argue for a particular course of action, you are using logic to explore connections between ideas. If your logic is thin or your connections weak, your reader will notice. The methods in this chapter call for rational thought and careful planning. The skills that go along with these methods of development—pinpointing differences and similarities, discovering reasons, predicting results, and arguing an issue logically—are essential. These higher-order tools of thought can help you in the college classroom and beyond.

Comparison Contrast, Cause-Effect, and Argument in Action

In this chapter, you will have the opportunity to examine and use the techniques of comparison-contrast, cause-effect, and argument. The text explains the techniques separately so that you can become thoroughly familiar with them and learn to use them successfully. Later, you will mix techniques to suit your purpose for writing.

Before looking at definition, classification, and cause-effect separately, look at how a professional writer uses all three techniques together. The following essay is by Liz Pulliam Weston, a personal finance writer for MSN.com and author of two books on personal finance.

The essay embodies all three of the writing techniques featured in this chapter. The first technique that the writer incorporates is **comparison-contrast.** Mainly, the essay compares the ways that people spent money in the 1970s with the way they spend it today. We could also say that the essay *contrasts* the ways that people spent money in the 1970s with the way they spend it today and be just as correct. The term *comparison* also includes contrast; that is, we may compare two things and find them similar, or we may find them quite different. The term *contrast,* however, always suggests that a difference will be found.

The author also uses **cause-effect** to suggest the effect that emulating the spending of the 1970s might have on the reader's overall spending. After comparing the areas of spending in the two decades, Weston tells us exactly how much money might be saved by reverting to the spending habits of the 1970s.

Finally, the entire essay constitutes an argument for dialing back spending a few decades. Argumentation, sometimes called *persuasion* or *persuasive writing,* comes in all strengths, from "gentle nudge" to "baseball bat over the head." Weston's argument is on the gentler end of the scale. How can we tell? First, touches of humor spice the essay throughout with gentle jabs at the 1970s. In addition, Weston's tone is helpful rather than dictatorial; that is, she presents her ideas as helpful suggestions. She is considering her audience, which consists of people who have chosen to read her personal-finance column and are therefore predisposed to accept what she says. Although Weston does not suggest that her readers give up modern conveniences (she even admits that she would not give up her iPod), she does suggest that a pullback toward an earlier decade would help to fatten the reader's wallet.

Save Big with the Flashback Budget

LIZ PULLIAM WESTON

Last week's innovation becomes yesterday's luxury, which quickly becomes today's necessity.

Just think of air conditioners. Or televisions. Or microwave ovens. Or personal computers.

Each started as a novelty. Now each is considered a requirement of daily living by a majority of Americans, according to a recent Pew Research Center survey. (Cell phones almost made the necessity list; 49% considered them so.)

But clearly, people lived rich, fulfilling, functional lives before any of these gadgets came along. So we here at MSN Money thought it would be fun to dial the Way Back Machine to one of those times, to see how much money we could save.

PERCENT OF ADULTS POLLED WHO RATE THE FOLLOWING ITEMS AS NECESSITIES:			
Car	91%	Home computer	51%
Clothes washer	90%	Cell phone	49%
Clothes dryer	83%	Dishwasher	35%
Home air conditioning	70%	Cable/satellite TV	33%
Microwave	68%	High-speed Internet	29%
TV set	64%	Flat-screen TV	5%
Car air conditioning	59%	iPod	3%

Source: Pew Research Center, December 2006

Those were the days . . . of "Muskrat Love"

We picked the 1970s—era of Watergate and disco, "The Brady Bunch" and pet rocks, streaking and "Muskrat Love" (if you have to ask, you really, really don't want to know). It's the era when I grew up, and I have photos of the frizzy, Barbra-Streisand-in-"A-Star-Is-Born" perm to prove it.

And here's what we found:

We were living small

The average new home in 1970 took up less than 1,500 square feet. Today, new homes average more than 2,400 square feet, and there are fewer people living in them (about one person fewer, compared with the 1970s). Smaller homes cost less to buy, insure, heat, cool, and maintain. Since the typical American household spent $15,167 on shelter and related costs in 2005, trimming even 10% of that bill would save you more than $1,500 a year. (If you could actually save a proportional amount—1970s homes were about 40% smaller—that would be about $6,000 in savings.)

We drove smaller, too

The 1973–74 oil crisis led to lines at the gas pumps and a new interest in fuel-efficient vehicles. But most households didn't have multiple tanks to fill. At the start of the 1970s, only 31% of households had more than one car, according to the U.S. Census Bureau; more than a quarter had no vehicles at all. By 1995, 60% of households had more than one car and only 8% were carless. The AAA tells us the average car costs about $7,800 a year to finance and operate, so one fewer vehicle could save you a tidy sum.

We ate at home

Food in general used to take up a lot more of our budgets. Food costs declined from 20.2% of the average family's expenditures in 1960 to 16.3% in 1972 to 12.8% in 2005. But even as food costs have dropped, the portion of our budgets we spend on eating out has grown considerably. That jibes with my family memories; eating out used to be a fairly rare treat. Eating out just one less night a week could save a whopping $1,560 a year (and that's in today's dollars).

We vacationed closer to home, too

U.S. airlines weren't deregulated until 1978, and before then flying was a pricey proposition. Most of my family's vacations were camping trips to national forests within a day's drive of our Washington State home, with an occasional train trip to visit relatives in the Midwest or (O glorious day!) Disneyland in California. You don't need to give up Southwest Airlines for the Greyhound bus—for all I know, Southwest is cheaper—but if you skipped just one flight a year, you'd save $300 to $400 a person.

Phones and entertainment

"We don't care. We don't have to. We're the phone company."

If you got that reference, then you remember Lily Tomlin's obnoxious Ernestine the Operator character from the hit show "Laugh-In," which ran from 1968 to 1973. (She reprised the character for "Saturday Night Live" a few years later.) The joke was on us, since back then we all rented our telephones from one big monopoly—AT&T—and paid through the nose, especially for long-distance calls. A federal judge ordered the breakup of AT&T in 1984, and clearly life is better now that we can choose from several phone companies that don't care. I wouldn't suggest returning to Ma Bell era, but you could realize some savings if you recreated the days when families had one phone number, rather than half a dozen. Figure $360 or so in savings for every line you drop.

Entertaining yourself

As one of the 3% who consider iPods necessities (or at least close to it), I wouldn't dream of telling you to swap yours for an eight-track player. There are some sacrifices no one should have to make. But downsizing your expectations as far as your television could save you some serious bucks. Back then, a 27-inch screen was considered huge, and most of us watched three (count 'em, three) network channels with maybe a public broadcast station thrown in. TV was free; most people picked up stations with an antenna attached to the roof. Cable television didn't really take off until the late 1970s, and it wasn't until the 1990s that most folks paid for TV. VCRs weren't introduced until the late 1970s, either, although we did have video games like Pong and Tank (ask your grandpa, kids). I won't insist you get a black-and-white set, since by 1972 half of U.S. homes had a color television. I'll just note that ours wasn't one of them; I didn't realize the "Star Trek" crew had different-colored uniforms until I was in college. Anyway, unplug cable for a year and you'd save $600 or so.

Had enough? I certainly have. Living through the '70s once was more than enough. And now I can't get "Muskrat Love" out of my head.

Thinking about the Essay

1. Why do you think the author compares the budgets of the 1970s with today's budgets, rather than simply advising her readers to budget for items as if it were the 1970s? In other words, what is it about this topic that calls for using comparison-contrast?

2. This essay shows the effects of cutting back a household budget to resemble a 1970s budget. Name one area in which 1970s budgeting would have an effect. What would such budgeting do, according to Weston's article? The essay also describes changes that have taken place over the decades since 1970. Name one of these changes. What has been the result?

3. Weston argues that taking a household budget back to the 1970s is a way to save money. Does she base her argument on fact or opinion? Give an example.

Comparison-Contrast

One of the most effective ways of describing an unfamiliar situation or object is by comparing or contrasting it with something familiar. When you make a **comparison**, you show how two things are similar. If a friend asks you about a class you are taking, you may describe it by comparing it to a class that the two of you have taken together. When you **contrast** two things, you show how they are different. If you are asked on a political science exam to discuss the legislative and judicial branches of the government, you may find yourself contrasting the ways each branch shapes the country's laws. In an English class, you may find yourself using both comparison and contrast to show how two writers develop similar themes in different ways. Used alone or used together, comparison and contrast are useful tools for any writer.

Comparison-contrast techniques are useful in answering questions such as those that follow.

- What are some of the differences between high school and college classes?
- Discuss the similarities and/or differences between your values and those of your parents.
- A line from the movie *Forrest Gump* says, "My mama always said life was like a box of chocolates. You never know what you're going to get." A line from an old song says, "Life is just a bowl of cherries." Now it's your turn to fill in the blank: Life is like a _____. Discuss three ways in which life is like the word or phrase you chose.

Laying the Groundwork for Comparison-Contrast Writing

Visualizing Look at the photograph of the homeless man and his dog. Think about a day in the life of this dog. How might this dog's life be different from the life of a dog that lives in a house? How might it be the same? How might the relationship between the man and his dog be different from the relationship of a homeowner and her dog? How might it be the same?

Planning List three points of comparison or contrast between a dog owned by a homeless person and a dog owned by a person who has a home.

Writing Write a paragraph comparing or contrasting the lives of two dogs: one belonging to a homeless person and one belonging to a homeowner. Use one of the two beginnings that follow, or make up your own. Note that in the second opening, the dogs are named. It takes a sentence to establish the names, but cumbersome repetition is avoided.

> Opening 1: A homeless person's dog lives much like any other dog.
> Opening 2: Banjo and Cadet are mixed-breed dogs who are much loved by their owners. But the similarity ends there, because Banjo travels the open road with his homeless owner while Cadet lives with his family in a three-bedroom ranch house with a yard.

Setting Up a Comparison-Contrast Paper

The first step in setting up a comparison-contrast composition is to choose your points of comparison or contrast and decide whether to compare or contrast. One way to decide is to prewrite. That way, you can see whether your primary focus is on comparison or on contrast. Following is a sample brainstorming for a paragraph or essay.

Brainstorming—Two Teachers

Kimball	Bettman
extremely good teacher	excellent teacher
liked by students	liked by students
✓ funny but disorganized	✓ organized lectures—hints about lectures, test questions
✓ multiple-choice tests	✓ essay tests
✓ group project assignment	✓ research paper
easy to talk to	approachable and friendly

Though there are several points of comparison, the contrasting points "lectures," "tests," and "assignments" may make a more interesting paragraph than the points of comparison. These points will also be more valuable to a reader who is trying to decide which class to take.

The next step in planning the comparison-contrast paper is to decide whether to use a point-by-point pattern or a block pattern to discuss the points. In a point-by-point pattern, each point of comparison or contrast is considered separately. Following is a **point-by-point outline** that could be developed into a paragraph or essay.

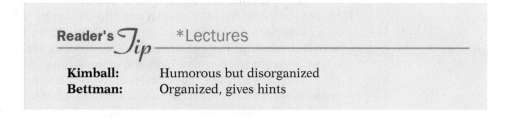

Reader's *Tip* ───── *Lectures

Kimball: Humorous but disorganized
Bettman: Organized, gives hints

Reader's Tip _____ *Tests

| Kimball: | Multiple choice, tricky questions |
| Bettman: | Essay questions require creative thought |

Reader's Tip _____ *Outside Projects

| Kimball: | Group presentation |
| Bettman: | Research paper |

In a block pattern, information about one subject is presented in one big block, followed by information about the other subject in a second big block. A **block outline** is shown here.

Reader's Tip _____

Kimball:	Delivers humorous but disorganized lectures
	Gives tricky multiple-choice tests
	Assigns a group project
Bettman:	Delivers organized, hint-packed lectures
	Gives essay exams that require creative thought
	Assigns a term paper

exercise 20.1 **Recognizing Comparison-Contrast Patterns**

Following are two paragraphs written from the outlines above. Read each paragraph and decide which is the point-by-point paragraph and which is the block paragraph.

Paragraph A

Mr. Kimball and Dr. Bettman are both excellent sociology teachers, but they are different in the way they lecture, test, and make assignments. Mr. Kimball makes jokes during class and throws out silly puns that make the class groan. He speaks quickly, so taking accurate notes can be difficult. Sometimes he gets sidetracked and forgets what he was talking about. Dr. Bettman does not tell jokes, but she is extremely organized. Her lectures are practically in outline form, and as she lectures, she gives hints about what might be on the test. The testing styles of the two teachers are also different. Mr. Kimball's tests are multiple choice, and he words questions so that students must read carefully. Dr. Bettman's tests are in essay format, and she expects students to use their knowledge in new and creative ways. The two instructors also differ in their assign-ment of outside projects. Mr. Kimball requires a group project and presentation. He asks for a typed list of references but no formal paper. Dr. Bettman, on the other hand, requires a research paper complete with a bibliography. Both are able instructors, but each approaches lecturing, testing, and outside projects in a different way.

Paragraph B

Mr. Kimball and Dr. Bettman are both excellent sociology teachers, but they are differ-ent in the way they lecture, test, and make assignments. During his lectures, Mr. Kimball makes jokes and throws out silly puns that make the class groan. He speaks quickly, so taking accurate notes can be difficult. Sometimes he gets sidetracked and forgets what he was talking about. His tests are multiple choice, and he words ques-tions so that students must read carefully. Mr. Kimball requires a group project and presentation at the end of the term rather than a traditional term paper. In contrast, Dr. Bettman's style and classroom requirements are quite different. She does not joke during class, and she is extremely organized. Her lectures are almost in outline form, and she gives little hints about what might be on the test. Dr. Bettman's tests are in es-say format, and she expects students to use their knowledge in new and creative ways. At the end of the term, she requires a research paper, complete with a bibliography. Both Mr. Kimball and Dr. Bettman are able instructors, but each approaches lecturing, testing, and outside projects in a different way.

1. The paragraph organized in point-by-point format is paragraph _____.

2. The paragraph organized in block format is paragraph _____.

3. Look at the two paragraphs. In which paragraph do you find more transitions?

_____

Why?

_____

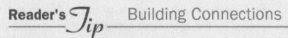

Reader's *Tip* ——— Building Connections ———

When you make comparisons or draw contrasts, *examples* are often useful in making the similarities or differences clear to your reader.

Wordsmith's Corner: Examples of Writing Using Comparison-Contrast

In the following essays, see how two student writers use comparison-contrast. Read each essay and answer the questions that follow.

Comparison-Contrast Essay 1

This essay contrasts home ownership and apartment living. At what point in the essay are you certain which one the writer prefers?

THE ADVANTAGES OF APARTMENT LIVING

The other day, a friend asked, "When are you going to buy a house?" When I told him that my wife and I were happy in our apartment, he shook his head. "You don't know what you're missing," he said. I think I do. Natalie and I have talked about buying a house, but we always come to the same conclusion. Apartment living offers many advantages over home ownership.

First of all, apartment living gives us luxuries we could never afford if we owned a home. If we bought a home, it would be a small home in a modest neighborhood. We would be lucky to have a postage-stamp yard for recreation. Our security system would probably consist of a deadbolt lock on the door. Any home in our price range would certainly not have lighted tennis courts, a pool, and 24-hour security. In our apartment complex, we have all of those things. Anytime I like, I can go over to the courts for a set or two of tennis. Afterward, I can cool off in the clear blue water of our apartment complex's swimming pool. At night, I can sleep well, knowing that if thieves or vandals venture into the complex, there is on-site security to take care of them. Only apartment living can give me so many luxuries for such a small price.

As apartment dwellers, we are also more mobile than homeowners. If Natalie and I owned a home and one of us were offered a dream job in a distant city, we would have to put our home on the market and worry about whether it would sell. If it had not sold by the date of our move, we could entrust it to a real estate agent, or one of us could stay behind and try to sell it. In any case, it would be a burden to us until someone else bought it. Living in an apartment, we have none of those worries. The worst that could happen is that we would have to forfeit our deposit if we did not give adequate notice. If we had to move, we could leave right away and focus on settling into a new job and a new community.

Perhaps most important, apartment living frees us from the chores of home ownership. If the water heater, the air conditioner, or the refrigerator in our apartment breaks down, I don't pull out the owner's manual and call the parts store. I call the resident manager, who sends over a repair person. If the roof develops a leak or the outside of the building needs a coat of paint, I don't risk my neck climbing a shaky ladder, as a homeowner might. I know that the apartment complex will hire a roofer or painter to take care of the problem. And on Saturdays, when my homeowning friends are mowing lawns, cleaning gutters, or trimming shrubbery, I am relaxing in front of the television or enjoying a game of tennis. For an apartment dweller, routine chores are handled by the apartment complex's maintenance staff.

Some people enjoy home ownership in spite of the hassles that go along with it. But I prefer the luxury, mobility, and freedom from chores that apartment living offers.

Questions?

1. In the following space, write the thesis statement of the essay.

   _____

2. In the following space, write the topic sentence of each paragraph.

   _____

   _____

   _____

   _____

   _____

3. Does the essay compare or contrast? What is being compared or contrasted?

   _____

   _____

   _____

4. In this essay, two of the three body paragraphs are in block format.

   Which paragraph is presented point by point? _____

Comparison-Contrast Essay 2

The writer of this essay uses comparison-contrast to show the world of work, past and present.

WORKING—THEN AND NOW

When a reader wrote to the advice columnist Ann Landers saying he could not find a job in spite of a college degree and work experience, Ann suggested that perhaps the man's attitude was to blame. An avalanche of mail told Ann that she was behind the times. In the decades since Ann Landers began writing her column, the job market has undergone a mixed bag of changes. Today's workplace is more diverse, more demanding, and less secure than the workplace of the 1960s.

The most positive change in the workforce is that it has become more diverse. In the 1960s, executive jobs went mostly to white males, while women and minorities were steered toward secretarial or janitorial jobs. Today, an ever-widening crack in the door to the executive suite is admitting all ethnic groups and both genders. Minorities have moved from the mail room to the board room, and females from the typing pool to the executive suite. There is likewise a diversity in mindset. Once, the "corporation man" was esteemed because his values and his ideas were likely to be in line with those of upper management. Now, however, employees are no longer expected to be yes-men or yes-women. Corporations now have become more creative and competitive, so the employee with a different slant on things is useful. Greater diversity has made today's workplace stronger and more vital.

Today's workplace also makes more demands on its workers' time than the workplace of the sixties. In those days, "nine to five" was the rule rather than the exception, and if a worker took an hour for lunch, the true workday was only seven hours long. The work week spanned Monday through Friday, and weekends were for rest. Today, split shifts, extended shifts, and brown-bag lunches at the desk are common. The downsized workforce of today means that the average worker simply has more to do, even if that work has to be done on weekends or after hours.

The most profound change in today's workplace is a change in the level of job security. When a college graduate from the class of 1965 went to work for a company like IBM, he expected to retire thirty-five years later with a gold watch and a fat pension. He could be assured that if he did his job reasonably well, he would not be fired. Today, however, the first job after college is seldom a permanent one. It is an item for the résumé, a stepping-stone to other jobs. Pensions have changed as well. Once totally financed by employers, pensions have evolved into 401(k)s and IRAs that are at least partially financed by employees themselves. The worst aspect of today's workplace is that good employees with many years of service have no guarantee of keeping their jobs. If the company downsizes to cut costs, the worker's job may be eliminated regardless of years of service.

Since the 1960s, the job market has changed drastically. Today's workers face a workplace that is more diverse, more demanding, and much less secure.

Questions?

1. In the space below, write the thesis statement of the essay.

   _____

   _____

2. In the space below, write the topic sentence of each paragraph.

   _____

   _____

   _____

   _____

   _____

   _____

   _____

3. Does the essay compare or contrast? What is being compared or contrasted?

   _____

   _____

4. In this essay, two of the three body paragraphs are in block format. Which paragraph is presented point by point?

   _____

   _____

Topics For Comparison-Contrast Writing
Comparison-Contrast Assignment 1: Two by Two
Journal Entry
Write a comparison-contrast journal entry on one of the following topics.

two brands of pizza	two times of day or days of the week
two classrooms	two sports teams

Comparison-Contrast Assignment 2: Optimism and Pessimism
Essay
In an essay, discuss the differences in the way an optimist and a pessimist might approach life. It might help to select three areas, such as work, school, relationships, finances, or religion, and write a paragraph comparing and contrasting each point.

Comparison-Contrast Assignment 3: School Days
Essay
Write an essay explaining some of the differences between high school and college.

Comparison-Contrast Assignment 4: Today and Tomorrow
Essay

In five years, how will your life be different from the way it is today? In this essay, be sure to contrast the present and the future rather than simply discussing your plans for the future.

Comparison-Contrast Assignment 5: Essay-Based Topic—Budgeting by the Decade
Essay

Re-read Liz Pulliam Weston's essay on page 523 of this chapter. Then pick three of the six spending areas (homes, cars, food, vacations, telephones, and entertainment) that she discusses in her essay. Compare or contrast your own spending in that area to the spending of today's consumer or to the spending of a 1970s consumer, as described in Weston's essay.

Comparison-Contrast Assignment 6: Real-World Topic—
Going the Extra Mile
Essay

You are applying for a small-business startup grant for the business of your choice. The application asks you to compare your business to other, similar businesses and show how yours meets a need or needs in the community that are not filled by other businesses in the same category. In other words, if you are opening a dry cleaning shop, how is it different from all the others? Do you deliver to meet the needs of senior citizens or busy working people? Are your hours extended to meet a need that other dry cleaners do not meet? Do you offer some other service that other dry cleaners do not? Dry cleaning is just an example; use any business you wish and write an essay applying for the grant.

Cause and Effect

When you look for the **causes** of an event, you are looking for the reasons it happened. In other words, you are looking for answers to "why" questions. Why did your last romantic relationship end badly? Why is your Uncle Leroy's car still humming along at 150,000 miles? Why are so many high schools plagued by violence?

When you look for the **effects** of an action, you are looking for its results. You are answering the question "What would happen if . . . ?" What would happen if every community had a Neighborhood Watch? What would happen if you decided to devote just one hour a day to an important long-term goal? What is the effect of regular maintenance on an automobile?

When you explore both **cause and effect,** you look at both the reason and the result. You may explore actual cause and effect, as in "Uncle Leroy performs all scheduled maintenance on his car and changes the oil every 3,000 miles; as a result, his car is still going strong at 150,000 miles." You may also explore hypothetical cause and effect, as in "Many members of my generation are bored and cynical because everything—material possessions, good grades, and even the respect of others—has come to them too easily."

A cause-effect essay might be written in response to any of the following questions.

What are the causes of violence in schools?

What are the major effects of stress?

What are some of the reasons that people fear growing old?

Laying the Groundwork for Cause-Effect Writing

Visualizing Look at the photograph of the burning house on the next page. Visualize the flames inside, licking at furniture and consuming the belongings of a family.

Planning Write down four possible causes of the fire. If you were writing a paper, how would you develop a paragraph about those causes? Would you use examples? Would you explain a process?

Next, think about the effects of the fire. How many different people or groups might it affect? List them. If you were writing a paper about the effects of the fire, how would you set it up?

Writing Write a paragraph on the causes or effects of a house fire. If you wish, you may focus on just one cause or just one effect in your paragraph.

Identifying Causes and Effects

A cause is a *reason*. If you are asking a "why" question, the answer is probably a cause. Why do toilets flush in a counterclockwise spiral north of the equator and in a clockwise spiral south of it? Why did I do so poorly on my history test? Why did the chicken cross the road? From the scientific to the silly, these "why" questions can be answered by finding reasons or causes.

An effect is a *result*. If you ask "What will happen if . . . " or "What were the results of . . . ," then your answer is an effect. What would the results be if the speed limit were lowered by ten miles per hour? What would happen if I set aside an hour a day to exercise? What would happen if I threw these new red socks into the washer with my white underwear? When you answer these and other "what if" questions, your answer is an effect.

exercise 20.2   ## Causes or Effects?

For each topic listed, indicate whether an essay or paragraph on the topic would involve a discussion of causes (reasons) or effects (results).

———— 1. Why do so many people enjoy watching action-adventure films?

———— 2. What would the results be if private ownership of automobiles were phased out over a ten-year period?

———— 3. Why are so many American children overweight?

———— 4. Describe your reasons for attending college.

———— 5. What would happen if so-called recreational drugs were made legal for adult use and regulated in the same way as alcohol?

———— 6. What would happen if private ownership of handguns were banned?

———— 7. What bad habit have you broken lately? Why did you decide to break it?

———— 8. Do you recycle? Why or why not?

———— 9. What would be the effects of a mandatory parenting course for every first-time parent?

———— 10. What would be the effect if all nonviolent, first-time criminals had the option of performing community service and undergoing counseling as an alternative to prison?

Wordsmith's Corner: Examples of Writing Using Cause and Effect

Following are two examples of student writing dealing with causes and effects. Read each essay and answer the questions that follow.

Cause-Effect Essay 1
Our movement toward a twenty-four-hour society provided inspiration for the writer of this essay.

OPEN ALL NIGHT

There was a time when the world woke with the sun and slept when darkness fell. In some places it is still that way, but in modern America, the line between night and day is becoming blurred. In the trend toward a twenty-four-hour society, the average American is being caught up in a cycle of unceasing activity.

For most Americans, the movement toward a twenty-four-hour society means that "nine to five" is no longer the rule at work. As factories install expensive technology that must run twenty-four hours a day to be cost effective, many workers find themselves pulling the night shift, twelve-hour shifts, or even split shifts. They become exhausted trying to maintain family relationships, attend school functions with their children, and catch a few hours' sleep during the day. The problem does not occur only among shift workers. Executives who used to leave their work behind them at the office now are given the mixed blessing of laptop computers, cell phones, and home fax machines that keep them in constant touch and make it harder to leave work behind. Americans increasingly complain that they are giving more and more of their lives up for work.

As America moves toward a twenty-four-hour society, people of all ages are playing harder and longer than ever before. A greater awareness of fitness means that many people get up before dawn to struggle to six A.M. aerobics or head for the gym for an evening tai chi class. For those seeking entertainment, the search can continue around the clock. All-night restaurants, skating rinks, movie houses, and miniature golf courses light up the night. Even child's play no longer stops at dusk. Little League fields are lighted for night games that sometimes start as late as 8:00 or 8:30 and last long past the time when children used to be in bed. Midnight basketball, which arose in cities as a way to keep teens off the streets and out of trouble, has become increasingly popular.

With the movement toward a twenty-four-hour society, there is also more to do at home than ever before. Decades ago, television and radio stations went off the air at midnight, but even at 3:00 A.M., today's couch potatoes can choose from a performance of Handel's *Messiah,* a Three Stooges film, or a rerun of *Green Acres.* No matter what time it is, there is no reason to put off Christmas shopping or filing income taxes. Catalog companies often have twenty-four-hour order lines, and the Internet is open twenty-four hours a day for shopping or downloading tax forms. And why shouldn't a homeowner go grocery shopping or start a painting project at 2:00 A.M.? The grocery store and the discount store are open twenty-four hours a day.

Now that the world never shuts down for rest, many people feel they must constantly seek some pleasurable or productive activity. These days, more Americans are living faster and enjoying it less.

Questions?

1. In the space below, write the thesis statement of the essay.

   _____

   _____

2. In the space below, write the topic sentence of each paragraph.

   _____

   _____

   _____

   _____

   _____

   _____

3. Does the essay emphasize causes or effects? _____

4. Identify the cause(s) and effect(s) discussed in the essay.

   _____

   _____

   _____

   _____

Cause-Effect Essay 2

In this essay, the writer discusses the burden of perfectionism.

THE EFFECTS OF PERFECTIONISM

Some people urge themselves to better performance with slogans like "Practice makes perfect." However, I am a perfectionist, and I have to remember another slogan: "Sometimes good is good enough." I stay away from proverbs that urge perfection. Over the years, I have noticed that the effects of perfectionism are mostly negative.

First of all, my perfectionism makes me anxious about high-pressure situations. In school, I worry about taking tests. The pressure is on because there is no way to go back or change my performance. As I enter the classroom on test day, I feel my hands becoming clammy and I worry that I will forget everything I have studied. Socially, I worry when I have to go to parties or meet new people. I am afraid that I will be dressed too casually or too formally, that I will forget someone's name, or that I won't be able to make small talk. Before I met my girlfriend's parents, I spent a week worrying about what I would say and how I would act. First impressions count, and with my perfectionistic nature, it was important to me make a good impression.

Trying to do things perfectly often means that I do not do them quickly enough. Once, my perfectionism cost me my summer job at a car wash. On my first day, I was issued a T-shirt with a slogan on the back: "If you can read this, I'm moving too slowly." My job was to detail the cars after they came out of the automated washer. I would wipe the water from the car and polish the tires and rims, while my partner, Grady, cleaned the inside of the windows, polished the dash, and vacuumed the seats. Grady always finished before I did and had to help me with the rims and tires. When the manager thought we weren't working quickly enough, he would yell, "Hustle it up, guys!" But hurrying meant that dirt was left on the rims, watermarks on the car, and gray streaks on whitewalls, and my perfectionistic nature shrank from doing less than my best. I was forced to turn in my T-shirt before the month was over.

Perfectionism also makes me my own worst critic. I know that others do not see me as negatively as I see myself. To my teachers, I seem like a serious student who usually does well. To my friends and acquaintances, I am a funny, likeable guy, and to their parents, I am a well-mannered young man. Even my boss at the car wash could not deny that I worked hard. But I see only my failures. I see the question I missed on a test, not the ones I answered correctly. I notice my social blunders, not the times when I handle myself well. Perfectionism magnifies my faults and shrinks my good qualities. It means that no matter how hard I try or how well I do, there is one person that I can never please—myself.

Perfectionism affects my performance in high-pressure situations, the speed of my work, and the way I see myself. It may be true that nobody is perfect, but unfortunately, that has not stopped me from trying.

Questions?

1. In the space below, write the thesis statement of the essay.

   _____

   _____

2. In the space below, write the topic sentence of each paragraph.

   _____

   _____

   _____

   _____

   _____

   _____

3. Does the essay emphasize causes or effects? _____

4. Identify the cause(s) and effect(s) discussed in the essay.

   _____

   _____

   _____

5. What two introductory techniques are used in this essay?

   a. anecdote and quotation
   b. quotation and contrast
   c. broad to narrow and quotation

Topics For Practicing Cause-Effect Writing
Cause-Effect Assignment 1: Just Causes
Journal Entry

In a journal entry, discuss the causes of one of the following problems.

suicide among the elderly	homelessness
shoplifting	rudeness
stress or burnout	distrust between generations

Cause-Effect Assignment 2: A Milestone
Essay

Write an essay discussing the effects of an important event in your life. Some possibilities include the addition of a family member, the death of someone close to you, or a surprising discovery about yourself or someone you love.

Cause-Effect Assignment 3: A Painful Decision
Essay

Write an essay discussing the reasons for a painful decision in your life. A decision to divorce, to have an abortion or to give up a child for adoption, to break off a friendship, or to quit a job are some possibilities.

Cause-Effect Assignment 4: Healthful Effects
Essay

Write an essay describing the effects of exercise on a person's health, energy level, and self-esteem.

Cause-Effect Assignment 5: Essay-Based Topic—The Necessities of Life
Essay

Look at Liz Pulliam Weston's essay on page 523 of this chapter. She identifies several items that at least some percentage of the population identified as necessities. The list includes the following items

Car	Home computer
Washer	Cell phone
Dryer	Dishwasher
Home air conditioner	Cable/satellite TV
Microwave	High-speed internet
TV set	Flat screen TV
Car air conditioner	iPod

From this list or from your own experience, choose three items that you would classify as necessities. These should be technology-based items that were not available in an earlier era. Write an essay showing why these items are necessities in your life. In other words, show the effects that these items have on your everyday life that make you consider them necessary.

Cause-Effect Assignment 6: Real-World Topic—Ending Unprofessional Conduct
Essay

You are the manager of a resort hotel, part of a large chain. Recently, in a guest poll covering the entire chain, your hotel was cited among the rudest. Guests reported desk clerks hanging up on them, screaming matches between employees in the hall, and housekeeping employees who rudely shoved towels at them and stalked off down the hall. The hotel chain regards this very seriously, and though no one has said so, you feel your job may be on the line. Your supervisor has asked you to write an action plan that will turn your employees from surly to polite and improve your hotel's image. The action plan is to be very specific, with each action described in detail along with its expected result . For instance, if you say that you plan to train employees, describe specifically what you plan—role-playing games in which employees act out handling problems with customers, punitive actions or conferences with problem employees, or whatever—and then describe the expected result and why you think it will work. The more specific and detailed your plan is, the safer your job will likely be.

Argument

Though the word **argument** is sometimes used to mean a heated discussion or shouting match, the argument you make in an essay is of a cooler sort. Using pen and paper to explain your stand on an issue has its advantages—no one will interrupt you or try to outshout you. However, a good argument is more than just your opinion on an issue. It is your convincing, well-supported opinion. What matters is not which side you take, but how well and how strongly you support your views. Logic, a strong regard for truth, and solid examples are your allies in an argument essay.

Argument essays answer questions like the ones that follow.

- Is television a harmful influence on children?
- Should courses in consumer finance be required in high school?
- Is capital punishment an appropriate sentence for serious crimes?

Laying the Groundwork for Writing an Argument

Visualizing Look at the photograph of the woman using a mobile phone underneath a sign forbidding the use of mobile phones. What is she talking about? Is her conversation urgent or casual? Is she aware that she is breaking a rule?

Planning Make a list of reasons that some places ban the use of cell phones. Then make another list of reasons, this time a list of arguments a cell phone user might use to support her right to use a cell phone.

Writing Write a paragraph arguing for or against a cell phone user's right to use a telephone in most public places.

Taking Sides

It has been said that there are two sides to every argument. Your essay, however, should favor just one side. In an argument essay, it is important to make your position clear and not waffle. Starting on the "pro" side of an argument and switching to the "con" side will not work. If you feel it is necessary to acknowledge the other side of the argument, try doing so in the introduction.

Introducing an Argument Essay

An introduction to an argument essay can be a **historical introduction** that provides background for your argument. It might also be a **contrast introduction** in which you briefly summarize the opposing view and then present your own. A third type of introduction that works well for an argument essay is the **concession,** or "yes-but" introduction. In a yes-but introduction, you acknowledge the opposition's strong points before bringing in your own argument. This type of introduction makes your essay seem fair and balanced. In the following example, the writer concedes the strong points of the opposition's argument, then states his own thesis.

EXAMPLE   **CONCESSION OR YES-BUT INTRODUCTION**

> Many a reluctant student is pulled from a warm bed for an eight o'clock class by a college attendance policy that limits the number of absences a student may accumulate. Such policies have the advantage of ensuring that the professor is not talking to an empty room at 8:00 a.m. on a frosty Monday morning. They also help many marginal students make it through a class. But these policies do more harm than good by treating college students like kindergartners, forcing students who know the material to sit in class anyway, and unfairly penalizing students who may be absent for legitimate reasons.

Fact or Opinion?

Opinions are statements that, in an essay, need to be supported by facts or examples. It is important to be able to distinguish fact from opinion. Fact can be defined as a statement that is ultimately provable. In other words, you can look it up in an encyclopedia, you can observe it for yourself, or you can measure it against some objective standard.

However, you can expect even facts to be slippery because of differences in people's perceptions. Any police officer who has taken down eyewitness statements can describe the immense differences in the accounts of people who have all witnessed the same event. Facts can also be slippery because of the differences in the way people see the world. Does the sun rise in the east every morning, travel across the sky, and set in the west? While most of us might say yes, a scientist or a literal-minded person might remind us that the sun does not travel at all, but remains fixed while the earth moves. In other words, while facts may be ultimately provable (or disprovable), they are not indisputable.

exercise 20.3   **Group Exercise**

Individually, write down three facts and three opinions. Mix them up and do not label them. In groups of three, trade papers and mark each statement as F (fact) or O (opinion). If there are any differences of opinion, write the disputed statement on a sheet of paper and hand it to the instructor for discussion by the entire class.

exercise 20.4   **Fact or Opinion?**

In the blank to the left of each statement, mark each statement as fact (F) or opinion (O).

———— 1.   The wall in the classroom is ugly.

———— 2.   The wall in the classroom is green.

———— 3.   The wall in the classroom is an ugly green.

———— 4.   The president of the United States is doing a good job.

———— 5.   The president promised in a campaign speech that he would not raise taxes.

———— 6.   The school café needs to add more menu choices.

———— 7.   The school café serves no salads and only two kinds of sandwiches.

———— 8.   Killing another human being is never justifiable.

———— 9.   Private ownership of handguns should be outlawed in the United States.

————10.   Locking away firearms is one way of preventing tragic accidents.

————11.   According to historians, Abraham Lincoln's Gettysburg Address was not really written on the back of an envelope.

————12.   Martin Luther King, Jr.'s "I Have a Dream" speech was delivered in Washington, D.C.

————13.   King's "I Have a Dream" and Lincoln's Gettysburg Address are two of the greatest speeches ever delivered in the United States.

————14.   Writing essays is the only way to become a better thinker and writer, and to express oneself more effectively.

————15.   One way to diet is to cut carbohydrates.

————16.   The death penalty for murder is always justified in cases where the victim is a child or a police officer.

————17.   It is fair to charge overweight passengers for two airline tickets if they take up two seats.

————— 18. Some airlines charge overweight passengers for two tickets if they take up two seats.

————— 19. The justice system in the United States is fair.

————— 20. The level, two-mile trail can be walked in less than an hour by anyone who is in reasonably good physical condition.

Supporting an Opinion Essay A good opinion essay is always a mixture of fact and opinion. Factual support for opinions can take the form of examples, facts, and even anecdotes. The opinions themselves are not only supported by facts, they are logically connected to the facts. In other words, a person in possession of only the facts might logically draw the same conclusion from them that the writer does—and the key word is *might*. Again, facts can be slippery, and the same facts can often be used to support two different conclusions. For example, look at the following set of facts about the parking situation at a hypothetical school.

1. There are three types of parking: red zone parking (closest to the classroom buildings, for faculty only); green zone parking (near classroom buildings, for commuter students); and blue zone parking (near on-campus housing, for students who live on campus).
2. Each automobile is issued a red, blue, or green numbered sticker to indicate where it is to park.
3. Shuttle buses take students who live on campus from housing to the classroom buildings.
4. Many people pay no attention to the parking regulations—students park in faculty spaces, and on-campus students park in commuter spaces.
5. Tickets are given when security staff can be spared to patrol the parking lots.
6. No penalty is assessed for those who do not pay the fines.

Opinion 1, from a Commuter Student

Obviously, the current system is not working. We have three clearly marked parking zones, but people park wherever they choose and security staff patrol only when they have nothing else to do. The school needs to hire someone full-time to patrol the parking lots. If fines are collected, perhaps people will obey the rules. If fining does not work, stiffer penalties need to be enforced. The parking regulations themselves need no change. It is fair that faculty park close to the classroom buildings, and students housed on campus, who have the benefits of a shuttle to the campus buildings, park farthest away if they choose to drive.

Opinion 2, from a Student Who Lives on Campus

Obviously, the current system is not working. The three parking zones are a joke, since no one is ever fined and security rarely patrols. In fact, security personnel have more important things to do than to patrol the parking lots, and this petty task should be removed entirely from their duty roster. The parking regulations themselves are the problem. Faculty and commuter students get privileged parking, while those of us who pay extra to live on campus get the leftovers. The system is inherently unfair. A first-come, first-serve parking system would be fair to everyone.

Opinion 3, from a Faculty Member

Obviously, the current system is not working. Students complain about faculty having special parking privileges, but they don't realize that we may have day and evening classes, meetings in the afternoon, and all manner of class materials to bring from our vehicles. It is only fair that we get the spaces closest to the classroom buildings. However, since the current system is not enforced, faculty need a gated parking lot that can be entered only with a key card.

The three previous examples make it clear that the facts can lead different people to different conclusions. The only thing that all parties agree on in the previous examples is that change is needed. Because the same facts can be used to support more than one conclusion or more than one opinion, a good opinion paper usually contains both fact and opinion, skillfully woven together.

Look at the following paragraph. Fact and opinion are woven together in it to make a convincing argument.

opinion   opinion
Professor Smith is not a good teacher. His lectures are impossible to

fact
understand because he stands with his head in his notes and mumbles at

opinion
the lectern instead of talking to the class. He always seems to be in a hurry,

fact   opinion
rushing through his notes and speaking rapidly, making it difficult to take

fact
notes. When one student asked him to go more slowly, he said, "Sorry, we

opinion
have to get through this material." Personally, I would rather cover less

opinion
material and understand it more. He also does not like to respond to

fact
questions. When students ask questions, he asks us to save them until the

end of the period, but he never stops lecturing early enough for us to ask

opinion   fact
questions. His tests are also clearly unfair. When it was time for us to take

the midterm exam, we had covered only chapters 1–10, but the midterm

fact
covered chapters 1–12. He told us we would just have to read Chapters 11

fact
and 12 on our own because he had already made out the midterm.

I would not advise anyone to take a class with Professor Smith.

exercise 20.5 **Recognizing Fact and Opinion**

Underline and label the fact and opinion in the following paragraph.

Dr. Greentree is an excellent teacher. Her lectures are clear and are supplemented by PowerPoint outlines that help the class take notes. She knows how to keep the class's attention by injecting humorous stories into her lectures and varying the pitch of her voice. She helps us understand by asking questions frequently and encouraging us to ask questions. In addition, she cares about students who may be falling behind. She maintains office hours and encourages class members to come by if they have questions or concerns. I would advise anyone to take a class with Dr. Greentree.

Will You Change Anyone's Mind?

A good argument is aimed at changing people's views. On some topics, a convincing argument may change someone's mind. On other topics, though, you will find it next to impossible to sway an opinion that may have been molded by a lifetime of experience. Particularly on such hot-button issues as abortion, assisted suicide, and the death penalty, the best you can realistically hope for is to open a window to your viewpoint. In this case, success means coaxing your reader to look through that window long enough to say, "I see what you mean, and I understand your point of view."

Reader's *Tip* Building Connections

Arguing a point often involves *contrast* and *cause-effect*. Making an argument sometimes involves contrasting one side with another. An argument favoring a particular course of action (for example, making handgun ownership illegal) often involves examining the positive effects of that action.

Wordsmith's Corner: Examples of Writing Using Argument

Following are two student essays that argue a point. Read each essay and answer the questions that follow.

Argument Essay 1

Is it time to bench college athletes and let the scholars take the field? In this essay, one student speaks out.

GIVING ACADEMICS THE EDGE

College athletic programs offer obvious benefits. Games bring money and recognition to the school. Athletic teams promote school pride and unity, and going to games can be fun. In spite of these benefits, the attention given to athletics shortchanges the majority of the students and forces scholarship to take a back seat. It is time for colleges to take the spotlight away from athletics and give academics the edge.

Special treatment for athletes sends the wrong message to other students. At some colleges, athletes are given their own dorms and a separate dining hall that provides special meals to help them reach the peak of physical condition. Coaches and staff watch over them carefully. If their grades lag, they are given tutoring and encouragement. These special privileges send the wrong message. College should be about academics, not athletics. If there are special dorms, they should be for students who are on academic scholarships. If there are special dining halls, they should serve "brain food" to students on the dean's list. And colleges should have a way of watching over every student. If an ordinary "C" student begins to lag behind, help and encouragement should be as immediate for her as it would be for a star athlete. The special privileges athletes enjoy should be spread among all students.

Expensive athletic facilities and equipment should not be used only by the teams. At the college level, sports should stress fitness and the joy of competition and should include everyone. It's time to open the basketball courts, unlock the weight rooms and saunas, and bring out the track and field equipment for everyone to enjoy. If students are to focus on academics, they need a healthy outlet for their energy. Encouraging every student—even the clumsy or the overweight, even the couch potatoes and the party people—to use these facilities for exercise would contribute to healthier bodies and minds for the whole student body.

Perhaps the worst consequence of shining the spotlight on athletics is that it takes the focus away from scholarship. Many talented students write computer programs, conduct experiments in physics or psychology, or write poems, stories and plays. The attention, however, is not on these students, but on the few who manage to move a pigskin-covered ball a few yards down a green field or who use their height and coordination to dunk a ball through a hoop. A focus on academics would give bright, successful students the attention they deserve. Then other students, seeing the recognition that scholarship brought, would be inspired to make the most of their own intellectual talents.

Sports programs have their place. However, when a school is more recognized for its athletic program than its academics or when athletes are seen as heroes by fellow students while scholars are dismissed as geeks and nerds, something is wrong. It's time for colleges to draft a new game plan, one that places the focus on academics.

Questions?

1. In the space below, write the thesis statement of the essay.

   _____

   _____

2. In the space below, write the topic sentence of each paragraph.

   _____

   _____

   _____

   _____

   _____

   _____

3. The type of introduction used is

   a. contrast.
   b. concession (yes-but).
   c. broad to narrow.

4. List the three arguments that the writer makes against college athletic programs.

   _____

   _____

5. Do you agree or disagree with the writer's argument? If you agree, what further points could you make in support of it? If you disagree, what arguments would you make against it?

   _____

   _____

   _____

Argument Essay 2
The writer of this essay is willing to share the road, but thinks that truckers—and their rigs—should be held to a higher standard.

CURBING THE TRUCKING INDUSTRY

Truckers have been called "the knights of the road," and for the most part, it's true. Drivers of the big rigs will usually change lanes to let a car onto the interstate, radio for help for a stalled car, or flash lights in a friendly warning that a speed trap lies ahead. Yet trucks cause problems, too. The trucking industry and the government should join forces to curb unsafe drivers, control pollution, and keep truckers away from residential areas.

The keys to controlling unsafe drivers are education and enforcement. Education for truckers should go beyond load limits and gear ratios. It should stress professional conduct. Most automobile drivers know the terror of having twenty tons of steel and cargo inches from their bumper, and quite a few have seen sleep-deprived truckers driving erratically. Education is one way to eliminate such dangerous behavior. For those who will not be educated, enforcement is the answer. Heavier penalties for speeding and reckless driving should be enacted and enforced. Drivers who drive under the influence of drugs or alcohol should face a mandatory minimum license suspension of one year and mandatory counseling. Those who repeat the offense should never be allowed behind the wheel of an eighteen-wheeler again. Education and enforcement will put dangerous truckers out of business and help the image of those who are already safe and courteous drivers.

Measures also need to be taken against two types of truck pollution: air pollution and ear pollution. Automobile emissions are strictly regulated, but "truck yuck" continues to pollute the air over interstates and cities. Like automakers, truck manufacturers should be required to develop and install better pollution control devices. Trucks that do not belch clouds of black, foul-smelling diesel smoke will be much more welcome on the road. Noise pollution is another problem that should be controlled. Many cities are filled with the deafening roar of large trucks, and the low rumble of an interstate highway is audible for miles in some places. Noise barriers around interstates and the development of quieter engines are two possible ways to mute the deafening roar of large trucks.

Finally, truck traffic through residential areas needs to be strictly limited. As cities and towns become more spread out and roads become better, trucks are encroaching on residential areas. They move cargo over roads that are not built for heavy vehicles. Their noise and pollution disturb the peace of the neighborhood, and their speed endangers children who play or ride their bikes in the streets. Laws are needed to preserve the peace of residential neighborhoods by keeping heavy trucks on the interstates and major roadways that are built to withstand truck traffic.

The trucking industry is essential, but like any other industry, it must be regulated to preserve safety, prevent pollution, and preserve the peace of residential neighborhoods.

Questions?

1. In the space below, write the thesis statement of the essay.

_____

_____

_____

2. In the space below, write the topic sentence of each paragraph.

_____

_____

_____

_____

_____

3. What three changes would the writer like to see in the trucking industry?

    _____

    _____

4. What type of introduction does the writer use?

    a. anecdote
    b. historical
    c. concession (yes-but)

Topics For Writing Using Argument
Argument Assignment 1: Seeing Both Sides
Journal Entry

Choose any controversial issue that you feel strongly about and write a journal entry supporting your belief. Then, as an exercise in objectivity, write a journal entry supporting the opposing viewpoint.

Argument Assignment 2: Dangerous Drugs
Essay

In an essay, support your position on one of the following issues.

1. Should physicians be allowed to prescribe lethal doses or combinations of drugs to assist terminally ill patients in suicide?
2. Should the growing of marijuana for medical or personal use be legal?

Argument Assignment 3: School Days, Rule Days
Essay

Does your school have a policy or rule that makes you angry? If so, write an essay giving your reasons why the policy is unwise. Some students object to policies limiting the number of absences, while others fret at library policies that say a book may be checked out for only two weeks. Still others object to exams that all students must pass before graduating: sometimes these are tests of reading and writing ability, and at other times they are senior comprehensive exams in a student's major field. Brainstorming with other students will help to get your thoughts focused on your school's policies.

Argument Assignment 4: At Liberty
Essay

What is the most important freedom you have? Why is it important to you? Some of the freedoms that people in the United States take for granted are freedom to practice the religion of their choice; freedom to speak their mind, even against their government; freedom to move from place to place; and freedom to pursue any career they wish. Discuss in your essay one of these freedoms or any other that you value.

Argument Assignment 5: Essay-Based Assignment—Living in the Past
Essay

Look at Liz Pulliam Weston's essay on page 523 of this chapter. She argues that budgeting as if it were the 1970s can be financially beneficial. Would changing our lifestyle to that of an earlier era be beneficial in other ways, too? Write an essay in which you argue that living as if it were the 1970s (or any decade of your choice) would be beneficial or, alternatively, that it would be harmful. Think of specific examples that help your argument and use them as support.

Argument Assignment 6: Real-World Assignment—The Next Step Up Essay

You are one of several paraprofessional teacher's aides in an elementary school. You have the opportunity to apply for a full scholarship to a college of education to become a teacher. (Feel free to alter the occupation, but make sure that the scholarship provides a step up in the profession—licensed practical nurse to registered nurse, and so on.) You must write a letter to the scholarship committee detailing your experience and accomplishments as a teacher's aide as well as other experiences with children in the community (scout leader, coach, and so on). You are being judged on what you have already done, not on what you plan to do, so give concrete and specific examples of your accomplishments.

Topics For Combining Methods of Development

Comparison-contrast, cause-effect, and argument are methods of looking at the logical connections between ideas. How are they alike? How do they differ? How does one affect another, and what logical arguments can be made for or against an idea? The following assignments ask you to combine one or more methods of development.

Mixed Methods Assignment 1: Transportation
Essay: Contrast and Argument

Imagine that you are faced with one of the following decisions regarding transportation:

- Should I buy or lease a car?
- Should I buy a used car or a new car?
- Should I buy a car, or should I use public transportation?

First, choose one of the three questions as the basis for your essay. Contrast the two alternatives and make a recommendation (an argument) for the best alternative.

As you write each body paragraph, you may find advantages and disadvantages to each alternative. For example, in terms of monthly payment, leasing a car is better than buying. However, buying a car may cost less in the long run since you own it when the payments are finished. If you have mixed results such as these, your conclusion will be a "decision paragraph" in which you weigh the arguments for and against each alternative and make a recommendation.

Mixed Methods Assignment 2: Argument For or Against
Legalizing Marijuana
Argument before the State Senate: Argument, Comparison-Contrast, and Cause-Effect

You are a state senator. One of your fellow legislators has placed a bill before the state senate advocating the legalization of marijuana for personal use. You are preparing a speech to argue for or against this proposal. In your argument, you may also want to compare or contrast marijuana with alcohol, a legal substance with similar effects. You may also wish to discuss the effects that legalizing marijuana may have on the people of your state.

Organize your paper as a speech, with an introduction mentioning the proposal to legalize marijuana and stating your position for or against the legalization of marijuana. The body of your speech will contain your arguments for or against the proposal. You should provide at least three strong arguments. Conclude by strongly urging your fellow senators to vote for or against the proposed law.

Mixed Methods Assignment 3: Poor Child, Poor Adult
Report: Comparison-Contrast, Cause-Effect, and Argument

Is it harder to be poor as a child or to be poor as an adult? In this essay, you will answer the question with an argument—that is, your thesis will state that it is harder to be poor as a child or that it is harder to be poor as an adult. Although the larger structure of the essay will be one of argument, you will also explore the effects of poverty on children and adults and contrast them to see which group would probably find poverty more difficult, thus bringing cause-effect and comparison-contrast techniques into your essay.

This is a surprisingly complex topic with strong arguments to be made for both sides. Before you write, prewrite thoroughly to explore the differing ways in which adults and children might experience poverty.

21 Writing a Summary

It usually takes a long time to
find a shorter way.
—Author Unknown

Although the saying on the chapter opening page is probably intended as a warning against shortcuts, it could just as easily apply to writing a summary. Summarizing is a painstaking process. It involves fully understanding the material to be summarized, determining the most important ideas, and condensing those ideas in your own words. A summary may be a shorter way of saying something, but writing one is a time-consuming process.

Reader's *Tip* ── Focus on Writing a Summary:
Looking at Summary

 Think of the last movie you saw. In a sentence or two, what was it about? If someone were to ask you, for example, to explain what *Pirates of the Caribbean* was about, would you simply say, "It was a great movie" or "Don't bother seeing it"? No. You would describe the events of the movie as concisely as possible.

You are constantly summarizing information to other people. You may replay your day to a significant other, describe movies or TV shows to friends, or explain situations to your boss. The better you are at summarizing, the greater the chances that your significant others will actually listen, that your friends will be entertained, and that your boss will think you do your job well.

Reflect on It

Think of your favorite movies and choose one to summarize in no more than four sentences. Your first sentence should tell the movie's title and general subject. The next two sentences should present the movie's central problem and how it is solved. The final sentence should summarize the movie's overall message. With a limit of four sentences, you will need to emphasize only the major details and leave out minor ones. It's not as easy as it may seem!

Writing a Summary

A **summary** condenses and presents information, often from a single source. When you write a summary, your goal is to concisely present information from an essay, article, or book so that your reader understands the main points. A summary ordinarily presents the author's ideas objectively, without criticism or evaluation. At the end of your summary, if the assignment calls for it, write a brief evaluation of the essay or article you are summarizing.

Five Steps in Writing a Summary

The following section shows you the steps in summarizing an essay or article.

Step 1: Choose a Topic and Find Sources of Information

Your instructor may assign a topic or area of investigation or you may be asked to choose your own. Choose a topic that interests you about which information is readily available.

Articles on your topic may be found in periodicals, databases, or on Internet sites. An overview of each type of information source follows.

Periodicals are publications such as newspapers, magazines, and scholarly journals that are published on a regular basis—daily, monthly, or quarterly, for example. Newspapers and magazines are written for the general public, while journals are written for scholars in a particular field.

Subscription and CD-ROM Databases Periodical articles are also available through subscription databases or CD-ROM databases. Most college libraries subscribe to databases such as ABI/INFORM, Academic Search Premier, ERIC, and Research Library. These databases may contain full-text articles from journals, newspapers, or magazines, or they may contain article abstracts. **Full-text articles** are complete articles, exactly as originally published. **Article abstracts** are summaries intended to help you decide if a particular article is appropriate for your purposes. If it is, you will need to find the original article in the periodical in which it originally appeared.

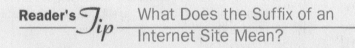

Reader's *Tip* — What Does the Suffix of an Internet Site Mean?

An Internet site's suffix can tell you a bit about the person or group behind the site. Here's a key to decoding Internet suffixes.

.org: A nonprofit organization
.edu: A college or university
.gov: A U.S. government site
.com: A business or private individual

Internet Sources Some websites may contain articles previously published in print sources; others may contain articles written for and published on the Internet. Internet sources vary widely in quality; it is up to you to evaluate the credibility of each site you visit.

Step 2: Evaluate Sources of Information

Once you have found articles on your chosen topic, evaluate them to make sure they are suitable for your summary. Use the following criteria for evaluation to find suitable articles.

Reader's *Tip* — Advice for Online Researchers

Go Online

Research used to mean poring through stacks of books and periodicals. Today, it usually means sitting in front of a computer screen. Even print sources must be located through online catalogs, indexes to periodicals, and databases. Even if you are comfortable using a computer, these resources may seem alien to you at first. If you need help, do not hesitate to ask for it.

Find a Friend

Find someone in class who will agree to be your research partner. You don't need an expert, nor do you need someone who is working on the same topic. All you need is someone who is willing to go through the process with you. The two of you can work side by side and handle the rough spots together.

Ask a Librarian

Librarians are experts in finding information, and they are there to help. Explain your project and the kind of information you are looking for, and a librarian will point you in the right direction.

Print the Information

When you find useful articles online, print them so that you will not have to find them again. Documentation of online sources requires that you note the database you are using and the date you accessed the information.

Be Patient

Be patient with yourself and with the process of finding information—it always takes longer than you think it will.

- *Length.* If an article summary covers all the major points in the article, it will probably be 25 to 50 percent of the length of the article. Therefore, if you are assigned a five-hundred-word summary, choose an article of between one thousand and two thousand words. These figures are only an approximation. The idea is not to choose an article so short that a few sentences can summarize it or one so long that you cannot summarize the entire article.
- *Readability.* In any article that you choose, expect to find unfamiliar terminology and concepts that are new to you. After all, the purpose of research is to learn something new. However, some articles are written for experts in the field and may be hard for a layperson to understand. If you read the article three times and still feel as though you are trying to comprehend ancient Egyptian hieroglyphics, choose another article.

- *Publication date.* A publication date helps you to evaluate the timeliness of the source. In fields where change is rapid, such as medicine or computer technology, finding up-to-date sources is essential.
- *Author.* Is the author an authority in the field? If not—if the author is a journalist, for example—does the author consult and quote credible, authoritative sources? These questions help you evaluate the authority and credibility of your source.

Step 3: Read the Article Thoroughly

Before taking any notes, read the article through once or twice. Then, highlighter in hand, look for the following information.

- *Main and major ideas.* Read through the article, highlighting main and major ideas. Remember, main ideas are often found at the beginning of an article and repeated at the end. Major ideas are often stated at the beginning of a paragraph or after a headline, and they are often supported by examples. Don't worry if finding and highlighting main and major ideas takes more than one reading.
- *Examples and supporting details.* Once you have found the main and major ideas, go back and highlight the supporting details and examples that most directly support those ideas. A summary contains a minimum of the detail that fleshes out the main ideas, so be selective and choose only necessary and important details.
- *Information for the works cited list.* The final step in taking notes from your source is to write down the information you will need for your works cited list. In a summary of a single article, you have only one work to cite, but it is important to cite it correctly. A list of information needed for your works cited list follows.

For all sources
- Author
- Title of article
- Title of the magazine, journal, or newspaper in which the article was published
- Date of publication
- Volume and issue number of periodical, if available
- Page numbers

For online sources, note the following additional information
- Date of access
- The URL (Universal Resource Locator, or complete Web address) of an article from a website
- The name of the database for articles accessed from subscription databases through a college (or other) library.

Step 4: Draft Your Summary

Drafting a summary report is similar to drafting an essay. Your draft should contain the following elements:

- *Introduction.* The introduction includes the author's name, the title of the article, and the central idea of the article.

Sample Introduction to a Summary

For many, the Internet is an increasingly vital part of everyday life. Senior citizens, however, are often less willing to embrace technology and reap the benefits the Internet might provide. In her article, "Bringing the Internet to Seniors," Ima Wizzard argues that an Internet connection can make a vast difference in quality of life for many senior citizens.

- *Body Paragraphs.* The body paragraphs outline the most important points in the article. The topic sentence of each body paragraph should state the idea that the paragraph will develop and incorporate a reference to the author.

Sample Topic Sentence in a Body Paragraph of a Summary

✓ Wizzard points out that the Internet can connect seniors to a larger community.
✓ For many seniors, Wizzard stresses, an Internet connection can mean the difference between loneliness and a sense of community.

The inclusion of the author's name in each topic sentence makes it perfectly clear to the reader that you are still discussing the ideas of another person rather than your own ideas.

The body paragraph itself will paraphrase the author's ideas; that is, you will state the ideas in your own words. Quoting the author is also permissible, but use quotations sparingly. Most of the summary should be in your own words.

Sample Body Paragraph of a Summary

The Internet can also connect seniors to a world of information. Wizzard names many websites designed specifically for senior citizens. For many seniors, Wizzard stresses, an Internet connection can mean the difference between loneliness and a sense of community. The Internet can provide connections to family and friends through e-mail.

- *Conclusion.* The conclusion sums up the author's ideas and presents your evaluation of or reaction to the article. Placing your evaluation in the conclusion is a way of clearly separating your reaction to the article from the summary, but if your evaluation is lengthy, you may place it in a final body paragraph before beginning the conclusion.

Step 5: Format, Proofread, and Cite Your Source

The final draft of your paper will include proper formatting and a works cited page. Use the documentation style recommended by your instructor. (Brief guides to APA and MLA style appear later in this chapter.) Your instructor may also ask you to provide a copy of the article you are summarizing.

Reader's *Tip* — Making the Switch to Academic Writing

As you move from personal writing to academic writing, you need a new set of strategies. Here are five helpful strategies for academic writing.

A Learning Approach

While personal writing allows you to write about the things you know best, academic writing requires a willingness to read, understand, and evaluate the ideas of others.

Objectivity

Personal writing is *subjective*—that is, it allows you to express your own feelings and opinions. Academic writing, on the other hand, is *objective*. It requires you to put aside your own opinions and to look without bias at the ideas of another person—even if you disagree with those ideas.

Knowledge of Key Terms

When you read and write about academic subjects, understanding key terms is essential. Make an effort to learn the meanings of unfamiliar terms. This essential step will help your comprehension of the article you are reading and will help you to use the terms knowledgeably in your writing.

Use of Third Person

When you write from personal experience, you often use the *first-person* pronouns *I, me,* or *my*. In academic writing, *third person* is preferred, even when you are expressing your own opinion. Thus you would write, "Several of Emily Dickinson's poems reflect an obsession with death," not "I think that Emily Dickinson's poetry reflects an obsession with death."

Careful Acknowledgment of Others' Work

If you are quoting or using the ideas of other writers, it is important to acknowledge your sources both informally within the text of your paper and formally through parenthetical references and a works cited page. Failure to acknowledge sources is called **plagiarism** and is considered cheating.

Paraphrasing and Summarizing: Essential Research Skills

One of the most difficult tasks of writing a research paper is to put an author's ideas in your own words. When you *paraphrase,* you rephrase a sentence or paragraph using your own sentence structure and your own words. A *summary* involves exactly the same skills—capturing ideas in your own words—but with a longer piece of source material. You would normally paraphrase a sentence or a short paragraph but summarize a longer paragraph, a section of an article, or a chapter in a book. A paraphrase can usually capture an idea a bit more closely. When you have only a sentence or a short paragraph to paraphrase, you can express the author's idea fully in your own words. A summary of a chapter or of a long section of an article will be more general and will leave out the details. Both a paraphrase and a summary must be properly referenced as someone else's work.

Paraphrasing

A **paraphrase** captures an idea expressed in a short piece of writing, such as a sentence or paragraph. It is an author's idea expressed in your own words. Here are some pointers to help you when you paraphrase:

- It is always permissible to repeat key terms. If the author uses the term *geriatric medicine,* there is no need to rephrase it as "medical care of old people."
- Unusual phrasing should be rephrased. If the author refers to a spider web as "a spider's gossamer trap," a paraphrase should simply call it a spider web.
- A paraphrase is usually a bit shorter than the source material, but it captures the entire idea.
- The sentence structure of a paraphrase should vary from that of the original material.

exercise 21.1 | **Recognizing Effective Paraphrases**

For the two numbered items below, circle the letter of the better paraphrase.

1. Original material:

   Unlike extroverts, introverts become worn out or at times overstimulated by the company of others. Therefore, introverts will seek solitude to regain their equilibrium and replenish their energy.

   a. Because being with people is sometimes too exhausting or too exciting for introverts, they often need time alone to restore their energy and their balance.
   b. Unlike outgoing people, introverts become fatigued or overexcited from the presence of other people. Therefore, introverts will search for seclusion to recover their balance and recapture their vigor.

2. Original material:

   Email is less formal than a business letter or memo, but that does not mean that no rules apply. Sending email without a subject line, sending crude jokes or lewd pictures, or sending mass emailings about free kittens or lost earrings are no-nos in the corporate world.

   a. Email is more informal than some other forms of business communication, yet that does not mean that rules do not apply. Not having a subject line, sending dirty jokes or pornographic pictures, or emailing employees about lost glasses or free puppies is not proper in the world of business.
   b. Email is an informal method of communication, but in a business situation, it is still inappropriate to send potentially offensive material or to mass mail messages that do not relate to business.

exercise 21.2 **Paraphrasing Short Passages**

Paraphrase the following passages.

1. Many workers no longer receive a paycheck. Instead, their employers issue a plastic card that looks something like a credit card. Each payday, the employee's pay is made available electronically through any ATM.

   _____

   _____

   _____

2. Though the custom of "giving away" the bride now is strictly symbolic, among the ancient Romans it had a legal purpose. A Roman patriarch literally owned a daughter for a lifetime, even after she was married, unless he chose to formally transfer her and her possessions to her husband. To moderns, the ceremony may seem to exchange one kind of bondage for another, but ancient Romans probably saw it as liberating a daughter to live her own life as a married woman.

   _____

   _____

   _____

   _____

   _____

   _____

Summarizing

A **summary** is a statement of the main idea of a longer portion of a work. Like a paraphrase, a summary should restate the author's idea in your own words. Unlike a paraphrase, a summary does not need to capture the details of the paragraph or section of the work that you are summarizing. Therefore, a paragraph summary might be just a sentence or two, and a summary of a chapter might be just a paragraph or two.

exercise 21.3 **Recognizing Effective Summaries**

For the two numbered items below, circle the letter of the better summary.

1. Original material:

   Convenience is the main advantage of shopping over the Internet. If you shop at a mall, you have to shop during the mall's hours of business. To do that, you have to get dressed, drive your car, use your gas, and find a parking space. With e-commerce, if you feel like shopping at midnight in pajamas and fuzzy bunny slippers, you can go right ahead. Get a cup of hot chocolate, sit at your computer, and shop at your convenience, not someone else's.

a. Convenience is the main advantage of shopping over the Internet. While wearing fuzzy slippers, a person can sit at the computer with a cup of cocoa and shop at his or her convenience.

b. Internet shopping at home is more convenient than mall shopping because one can shop without worrying about getting dressed, driving to a mall, or making it to a store before closing time.

2. Original material:

Almost everyone has encountered a surly waiter or a rude clerk and wondered, "What is his problem?" The answer may lie in the amount of control the worker feels. Polite workers are most often those who feel they are in charge of their jobs and of their lives. They realize that life is what they make it, and they may as well make it pleasant. Impolite workers, on the other hand, may feel controlled. They feel manipulated and used by other people and by their employers. The only way they can retaliate is to be surly and rude.

a. Workers who feel in control of their jobs and lives are more likely to be polite than those who feel manipulated by employers.

b. Surly waiters and rude clerks are retaliating in the only way they know.

exercise 21.4 **Summarizing Short Passages**

Summarize the following passages in a sentence or two.

1. Migraine researchers have recently confirmed what many *migraineurs,* or migraine sufferers, have known all along: Weather can affect migraines. Specifically, falling barometric pressure can trigger a migraine in many people. People who possess what one sufferer terms a "weather head" often feel symptoms as a thunderstorm rolls in and the barometric pressure begins to fall. "I should have been a weather forecaster," jokes one longtime migraine sufferer. "I always know when a storm is coming."

_____

_____

2. What is the scientific method? The scientific method is a process of gathering and testing information. The four steps in the scientific method are observation, formulation of a hypothesis, prediction, and experimentation. The first step, observation, involves observing a particular phenomenon, usually over a period of time. In the second step, the scientist constructs a hypothesis that

explains something about the phenomenon. In the third step, the hypothesis is then used to make a prediction about the phenomenon, an "educated guess" that the scientist must prove through the fourth step, experimentation. The experiment must be set up so that it can be repeated by the same scientist or by others to verify the results. If the experiment confirms the prediction consistently, the hypothesis becomes a theory, an assumption about the way the phenomenon works.

_____

_____

_____

Using Documentation Styles

When you write a college research paper, you will likely be asked to use one of three documentation styles: APA (American Psychological Association) style, MLA (Modern Language Association), or Chicago (University of Chicago) style, also called *Turabian* style after Kate Turabian, who developed it for the University of Chicago. In general, MLA style is used in the fields of English language and literature, media studies, and cultural studies. APA style is used in the fields of psychology, sociology, business, economics, nursing, and criminal justice. Chicago style is used in the fields of art and art history, music, theology, and women's studies.

Why Use a Documentation Style?

Documentation styles help you document, or cite, sources that you use in your research. Naturally, you must cite your sources properly to avoid accidentally plagiarizing. But use of documentation styles goes beyond the need to avoid plagiarism. Documentation styles have their own methods of formatting, titling, and spacing.

The driving force behind documentation styles is the need for consistency. If a journal or other publication in, for instance, the field of economics receives ten papers to review for publication, it is important that those papers all be in the same format and use the same method of documenting sources. That way, editors (and later on, readers) will not get bogged down worrying about why Professor X used in-text citations and Professor Y used footnotes. They can direct their focus to the content of the papers.

In the same way, by requiring you to use a particular format for your papers, your professors are ensuring that style remains a background issue and content moves to the foreground. Imagine if spelling were as inconsistent today as it was in Shakespeare's day, when even Shakespeare's name had several variants, including "Shakspear" and "Shaxberd." It would be easy to become sidetracked wondering about different spellings of a word or name and to lose sight of the content entirely.

In addition, when your instructors require you to use a particular style or format, they are preparing you for a time when you might be a writer in a particular field yourself and be required to use those styles. At the very least, your instructors are preparing you for a time when you will be required to adapt your writing to a particular style or format on the job. Every workplace has a format for writing memos, letters, and reports. Again, consistency keeps the focus on the content of those documents. In addition, just as academic writing has certain conventions that must be followed, workplaces, too have particular writing styles. A police report would never say, "The low-down slimeball tried to get away from me, so I grabbed the sucker and got him in a headlock." Instead, an officer would choose factual, un-emotional words, such as "The subject attempted to escape and was restrained."

In addition to requiring a particular format, each documentation style requires a list of sources. The list of sources is an important part of your research paper. Ideas are the currency of the academic community, and a list of references in a standardized style makes it easier to share those ideas. You list sources so that other researchers in your field can go back to the original source, read it, and form their own conclusions.

Using Online Sources

You will probably do much of your research on the Internet through various academic databases. Accessing online sources allows you to search beyond the print holdings of your college's library. It also allows you the convenience of researching from a remote location through your college library's website.

Documenting online sources is more complex than documenting print sources. The content of a print source will not change, but online sources often change and evolve. When a website is updated, its previous content may disappear forever. A site may move to a new server and change its Web address entirely, or a library may drop its subscription to one database and pick up another. Because of these complexities, extra documentation is necessary for online sources of information.

The online researcher needs to document when and where source material was viewed. The date that material was accessed, the name of the library that was used to access a subscription database, and the address of a website are necessary for the works cited list. For that reason, printing out material accessed online is strongly recommended. The date, the database used, and most other relevant information will be on the printed copy for easy reference.

Many databases provide the convenient option of mailing a full-text article to yourself. In addition, you often have the option of copying or sending yourself a citation for your works cited or references page in the style you wish to use. Two words of caution are necessary. First, if you use the citation option, be sure that you select the correct style from the drop-down menu. That seems obvious, but it is easy to forget. Second, be aware that differences and errors occur in citations among various databases, so check the citation against this text or against another reliable source.

Brief Guide to MLA (Modern Language Association) Style

The following section outlines a few basic principles of MLA style. For complete information on MLA style, consult the *MLA Handbook for Writers of Research Papers*, available in most college libraries and bookstores.

Formatting Your Paper

- Double-space the paper, including the works cited page.
- Use one-inch margins.
- Indent paragraphs one-half inch.
- Do not use a title page. Instead, put your name, your instructor's name, your course name, and the date at the top of the first page, each on a separate line, each line flush with the left margin. Center the title above the first paragraph. This material, like the rest of your paper, should be double-spaced.

Price 1

Ferris Price
Dr. Ruby S. Acres
Business Administration 101
22 April 2003

Summary of "The Interview: Rights and Wrongs"

Referencing Sources Within Your Paper

Within your paper, MLA style requires parenthetical references, not footnotes. For a paragraph in which you mention the author's name, the only parenthetical reference necessary is a page number placed at the end of the paragraph. If you use a direct quotation, place a page number after the quotation.

    ✓   According to Steven Pinker, the idea that parents are at fault if children turn out badly is an outgrowth of the "tabula rasa" or "blank slate" theory. This theory holds that cultural influence, not genetics, determines personality and character (16).

The Works Cited List

Use the following model entries as a guide to preparing your works cited list.

Journal Article
Shipman, Harry L. "Hands-on Science, 680 Hands at a Time." Journal of College Science Teaching 30.5 (2001): 318–21.

Magazine Article
Pinker, Steven. "The Blank Slate." Discover Oct. 2002: 34–40.

Newspaper Article
Hummer, Steven. "Surviving the Sweet Science." Atlanta Journal-Constitution 13 Oct. 2002: E-9.

Article on a Website

Dunleavy, M. P. "Twenty Ways to Save on a Shoestring." <u>MSN/Money</u> 29 Dec. 2001. 16 Oct. 2002. <http://moneycentral.msn.com/articles/smartbuy/basics/8677.asp.>

Note that the date of publication is followed by the date of access. The complete Internet address of the article is enclosed within carets.

Article Accessed from an Online Database

Zimbardo, Phillip G. "Time to Take Our Time." <u>Psychology Today</u> 35: 2 Mar/Apr 2002 <u>Psychology and Behavioral Sciences Collection.</u> EbscoHost. 10 Oct. 2002. Metro College Library.

Include the name of the database through which you accessed the article, the date of access and the library where you accessed it (if applicable).

Jackson, Carol D., and R. Jon Leffingwell. "The Role of Instructors in Creating Math Anxiety in Students from Kindergarten through College." <u>Mathematics Teacher</u> 92.7 (1999). <u>ERIC.</u> EbscoHost. 2 May 2003. GALILEO.

If your college is part of a larger university system that has a systemwide set of databases, reference that systemwide set of databases rather than the individual library.

A Model Summary Report

For her summary report, Sandra chose an article dealing with the evolutionary reasons behind negative emotions such as fear and anxiety. The article, along with Sandra's highlighting and annotations, appears below, followed by the final draft of her summary report.

THE FEARS THAT SAVE US
DIANNE ACKERMAN

main idea

Anxiety, dread, panic, aversion, depression—a small demonology of our age. It makes one anxious just to name them, and most people will eagerly perform any ritual, intone any magic that might keep such demons at bay. But, despite the disruptions that they cause us today, these demons once had a life-saving purpose. Just as physical pain warns us of potential damage to the body, emotional pains helped us avoid more complicated threats to life and limb.

Indeed, the full bouquet of our cherished traits and tastes, as well as the bestiary of our negative behaviors, evolved at a time when humans lived in small bands of hunter-gatherer scavengers. To us, their lives seem arduous and uncertain, but heaven knows what they would make of ours. The only thing is, we still navigate by their maps, still respond according to their instincts, still act like hunter-gatherers, though we grapple with problems they would not have encountered, understood, or valued.

anxiety—major point

example—usefulness of anxiety

Anxiety, that masochistic terrier of one's own devising, played a life-saving role in our ancestors' lives by alerting them to potential threats so they could plan a response. "A tiger may be in that grass," one instinctive train of thought might go. "It looks like the same sort of tall grass tigers hide out in. If a tiger is hiding there and attacks me, what would I do? Did I just see the grass move? Maybe not. On the other hand, maybe I'd better check again." Obsessive worry about nonexistent tigers might burn up needed calories, interfere with work and damage the body by flooding the tissues with cortisol, a stress hormone. Costly strategy, that, but one hungry tiger could result in instant death.

Evolution wagers risk against advantage. Better to agonize at every opportunity about a tiger than be wrong that one lethal time. The grinding down of one's spirit, hope, health, and sense of well-being doesn't matter; only one's ability to survive long enough to launch heirs. We face profound and trivial uncertainties: the possible effects of fluoride, a nuclear test in the South Pacific, deciding what to wear on a first date. Our penchant for anxiety doesn't sift what's important from that civilized heap. Worry kicks in even when we don't need it, want it or know how to stop it.

another type of anxiety

example—usefulness of r'ship anxiety

Anxiety about a relationship feels the worst of all, but ultimately it's a lifesaver. When you're faced with hunger, the elements, and wild animals, belonging to a loyal family group is your only hope. Not belonging is one of those things to dread and worry endlessly about. You keep checking to be sure you won't be abandoned, won't be sacrificed if wild animals attack, won't be left to starve. Most of the time, these may be unfounded neurotic fears, but misread the situation once, overlook a warning sign, and you're dead.

Small wonder that loneliness frightens us. Even though being excluded isn't deadly today, the nerve it touches stretches down the arms of time to a world of distant relations who left us a bag of tricks we barely understand but which we enjoy, puzzle over and often misuse.

depression—major point

usefulness of depression

Faced with horrible adversity or nameless anxiety, the more vulnerable among us become depressed. In a sense, it's a form of temporary hibernation. Overloaded, a person winds down to a low-energy state, speaks and moves very little. Famine produces the same inert, energy-saving response. Depression also elicits concern and nurturing, and people tend to make allowances for the depressed person who may ignore the normal give-and-take of society, not meet the same schedules or obligations. "I'm helpless as a child," the posture says. "Protect me, embrace me, tell the world I'm not available for a while."

low self-esteem—major point

usefulness of low self-esteem—

We think of low self-esteem as an affliction, but it had important benefits too. Self-esteem helps one seize opportunities. But if our ancestors had been confident in every circumstance, they would have taken too many risks—like venturing alone into the wilderness—or they might have been tempted to pick fights, challenge leaders, not bother negotiating or create some other social havoc.

point—fewer positive emotions

possible reason

Besides serenity, joy, excitement, thrill and desire, it may seem that we've evolved few positive emotions, or at least a wider and subtler range of negative ones. That may be because, when things are going well, only a few responses are needed. Everything is dandy, and we get on with tracking happiness like the elusive quarry it is.

(continued)

How odd to live in a country whose Constitution guarantees us the right to pursue happiness. In a recent study of thirty-nine cultures reported in *Psychology Today,* the U.S. ranked twelfth in perceived happiness. Citizens of Denmark, Finland, Norway, and Sweden were the happiest despite their gloomy weather. Surprisingly, people in France and Japan said they were among the least happy. Many cultures don't expect to be happy, though they're thankful for its state of grace. In collectivist countries such as China, an individual's wishing to be happy is thought selfish and therefore not a high priority. But we expect happiness, pursue it, feel wretched in its absence and experience sadness as a failure.

usefulness of happiness

We sometimes feel serene, quiet, at rest—what we label "happy." When you're happy, the world is breaking someone else's heart. Of course, it may be nothing more than a sort of biological idle, the body being thrifty with its limited energy. Negative feelings burn up precious calories, so not to be in pain or at red alert feels good.

What continues to amaze me is how such mind-binding forces, ancient and powerful as glaciers, can be modified by circumstance to produce quirky individuals living unique and unpredictable lives. However tempting it may be to think evolution stopped with us—its crowning glory—in the grand scheme of things, we're newcomers. Our evolution isn't happening fast enough to be visible in our lifetime, but it's still under way as we eat, sleep, play, lust, worry, learn, work, dream. Heaven only knows what we will become.

prediction—more evolution—dry changes

---

1 inch ↕

1/2 inch ↕

Lopez 1

Sandra Lopez
Psychology 1101
Dr Wilder
7 February 2004

Double-spaced throughout

Title Centered ———————————— **Article Summary: "The Fears That Save Us"**

Most people have heard of the "fight or flight" response, the rush of adren alin that is blamed for everything from road rage to panic attacks. Most people have also heard that this response is left over from prehistoric days when a tiger might attack at any moment and a quick response could save a life. In her article, "The Fears That Save Us," Diane Ackerman takes the idea even further. She believes that a whole range of negative emotions can be traced to the pre historic past, and that those emotions were once necessary to the survival of our earliest ancestors.

The first emotion that Ackerman discusses in terms of evolutionary value is anxiety. While constant worry may not seem useful today, our ancestors needed it. Ackerman points out that anxiety wastes time that might be used on more valuable pursuits, floods the body with stress hormones, and wears down an individual's sense of well-being. How could such a negative emotion have been

Lopez 2

useful to our ancestors? Ackerman suggests that constant anxiety about a tiger hiding in tall grass might have a big payoff if, just once, there really was a tiger and the watchfulness caused by anxiety saved a life. Ackerman also points out that anxiety over relationships can be traced to a very real threat. In prehistoric times, a person left alone might not survive.

Ackerman also has evolutionary explanations for depression and low self-esteem. Depression is an emotional retreat from the world, but it also saves the body's energy and brings a nurturing response from others, both of which could make survival more likely. Low self-esteem, seen as negative today, could have helped groups stay together by making it less likely that someone would challenge authority or fight.

Ackerman points out that, compared to the wide range of negative emotions, we seem to have developed few positive emotions. She suggests that positive emotions are not necessary for survival—when things are going fine, there's no need for a response. Happiness may be nothing more than a form of "biological idle"—a way of saving energy when there is no imminent danger. These responses are not the end of the evolutionary road, according to Ackerman. Evolution is a slow process, and while we will not see changes in our lifetime, they are certain to come.

Ackerman's article was valuable to me because it helped me to see negative emotions in a new light. This article also makes me wonder if I should evaluate my own negative emotions in terms of their usefulness. If I am worrying over a test or over a relationship, maybe that anxiety is a sign that I should take some action—or maybe not. Diane Ackerman's article, "The Fears That Save Us," was a fascinating look at how negative emotions may actually have had survival value for our earliest ancestors.

Lopez 3

Centered ——————————— **Works Cited**

First line is flush with left margin; any subsequent lines are indented one-half inch.
Ackerman, Diane. "The Fears That Save Us." Parade 26 Jan. 1997: 18.

Summary Report Assignments

Summary Report Assignment 1: Summarizing an Article about Your Career or Major

Write a summary of an article that deals with some aspect of your chosen career or major. The article may be one about job opportunities in your field, or it may focus on a particular issue central to your field. Follow the step-by-step process outlined in this chapter to find your article, evaluate it, read it to find the main ideas, and write your summary.

Summary Report Assignment 2: Summarizing an Article That Solves a Problem

Write a summary of an article that helps you solve a problem in your life. Whether you are trying to find ways to save more money, impress an interviewer, organize your time, choose an automobile, or eat more nutritiously, dozens of articles await you in the library or on the Internet. Because articles of this type vary widely in length, be sure to choose an article substantial enough to lend itself to summarizing. Follow the step-by-step process outlined in this chapter to find your article, evaluate it, read it to find the main ideas, and write your summary.

Summary Report Assignment 3: Summarizing an Article That Explores a Social Issue

Write a summary of an article that explores a current social problem. You will find articles on homelessness, drug abuse, domestic violence, school violence, and many more issues of current concern in the library or on the Internet. Articles may vary in length, so be sure to choose an article substantial enough to lend itself to summarizing. Follow the step-by-step process outlined in this chapter to find your article, evaluate it, read it to find the main ideas, and write your summary.

22 Verbs and Subjects

A Journalist's Questions
~~Who?~~
~~What?~~
When?
Where?
Why?

If there were no verbs or subjects, the top two items in the list of traditional journalist's questions would be eliminated. Verbs tell what was done, while subjects tell *who* or *what* the sentence is about.

The **verb** of a sentence carries the action, if any, and directs that action to and from the other words in the sentence. Some verbs, called **linking verbs,** function as connectors for related words.

A **subject** is what the sentence is about. It is usually a noun or a pronoun. It is probably not the only noun or pronoun in the sentence, but it is the only one that enjoys such a direct grammatical connection to its verb. If you ask, "Who or what _____?" putting the verb in the blank, the answer to your question is always the subject of the sentence.

Action and Linking Verbs

Verbs work in two ways within a sentence. Some verbs show the action, physical or mental, of the subject of the sentence. These verbs are called *action verbs*. Other verbs link the subject with other words in the sentence. These verbs are called *linking verbs*.

Action Verbs

Action verbs show physical or mental action performed by a subject. Look at the following action verbs, highlighted in italic print.

EXAMPLE
- ✓ Rachel *drove* to the doughnut shop. (physical action)
- ✓ She *bought* a dozen doughnuts and ate two on the way home. (physical action)
- ✓ She *wondered* why she found sweets irresistible. (mental action)

practice 22.1 **Recognizing Action Verbs**

Underline the action verbs in the following sentences.

1. The judge's decision sparked controversy in the small community.
2. The twins' vivid red hair draws everyone's attention.
3. James worried about Monday's history test.
4. The cat leaped to the safety of the tree's lower branches.
5. The old car puttered along like a windup toy.

Linking Verbs

A **linking verb** links its subject with a word that describes it. The most common linking verb in English is the verb *to be,* in all its various forms: *is, are, was, were, has been, will be, could have been,* and so on. Look at the following examples to see how the verb *to be* functions as a linking verb.

EXAMPLE
- ✓ The dog *is* hungry.

The verb *is* links the subject, *dog,* with an adjective describing it.

✓   Ann *has been* a police officer for ten years.

The verb *has been* links the subject, *Ann,* with a phrase, *police officer,* that tells more about her.

✓   Tomorrow *will be* the last day to drop a class without penalty.

The verb *will be* links the subject, *tomorrow,* with a noun, *day,* that tells more about it.

Other common linking verbs include the verbs *to seem, to appear, to grow,* and *to become.* Verbs of the senses, such as *to smell, to taste, to look, to sound,* and *to feel,* can be action or linking verbs, depending on how they are used.

EXAMPLE

L   The dog *seems* friendly. (The verb links *dog* with the adjective *friendly.*)

L   The gym socks *smelled* terrible. (*Smelled* is a linking verb—the socks are performing no action.)

A   Monica *smelled* the perfume sample. (The verb *smelled* shows Monica's physical action.)

L   The pumpkin pie *looks* tasty. (The verb links *pie* with the adjective *tasty.*)

A   The dog *looks* forlornly at every passerby, hoping for a handout. (The verb shows the dog's physical action.)

The Linking Verb Test   To tell if a verb is a linking verb, see if you can substitute *is* or *was* in its place. If the substitution works, the verb is probably a linking verb.

EXAMPLE

?   The crowd *grew* quiet as the conductor stepped onto the podium.

L   The crowd ~~grew~~ *was* quiet as the conductor stepped onto the podium.

The substitution makes sense; therefore, *grew* is used here as a linking verb.

?   The vines grew until they covered the cottage.

A   The vines ~~grew~~ *were* until they covered the cottage.

The substitution does not makes sense; therefore, *grew* is used as an action verb.

?   Michael stayed home from work because he *felt* sick.

L   Michael stayed home from work because he ~~felt~~ *was* sick. (linking verb)

?   Barbara *felt* the stress of the day dissolve as she stepped through the door of her apartment.

A   Barbara ~~felt~~ *was* the stress of the day dissolve as she stepped through the door of her apartment. (action verb)

practice 22.2   **Recognizing Action and Linking Verbs**

Underline the verbs in the following sentences. In the blank to the left of each sentence, write *A* if the verb is an action verb, *L* if it is a linking verb.

———   1. Sharon is in a sour mood today.

———   2. Emilio smelled the container to determine its contents.

———   3. The bologna smells spoiled.

———   4. The terrier leaped with joy as Nancy entered the house.

———— 5. Kim studied her sociology notes carefully before the test.

———— 6. The committee decided to postpone its meeting until Wednesday at noon.

———— 7. The small post office branch handles a large volume of mail.

———— 8. The ground is parched from lack of rain.

———— 9. The advertisement seems appealing.

————10. Too many drivers fail to use turn signals.

————11. Hisako grew tomatoes in a container on the patio.

————12. The audience grew restless when the singer was late.

————13. Yesterday Rozell tasted tiramisu, a layered Italian dessert, for the first time.

————14. The dessert tasted creamy and delicious.

————15. The burglar fled with over two thousand dollars in cash.

————16. Bernard felt sleepy all afternoon.

————17. Alanna pounded loudly on the door.

————18. The baker felt the silky texture of the flour between her fingers.

————19. On the upper right-hand corner of the envelope, Alex carefully pasted the stamp.

————20. Sandra looked through the tiny window at the front of the house.

Recognizing Verbs and Subjects

Finding the Verb

Finding the subject and verb of a sentence is easier if you look for the verb first. Here are some guidelines to help you spot the verb in a sentence.

1. **A verb may show action.**

   ✓ The ancient elevator <u>groaned</u> to a stop on the second floor.

   ✓ Larry <u>wondered</u> if he should take the stairs.

2. **A verb may link the subject to the rest of the sentence.**

   ✓ The inspection sticker <u>was</u> three years out of date.

   ✓ The old lion <u>looked</u> sleepy.

3. **A verb may consist of more than one word. Some verbs include a main verb and one or more *helping verbs*.**

   ✓ Jemal <u>has been taking</u> flute lessons for six years.

   ✓ Katherine <u>has</u> not <u>found</u> the keys she lost yesterday.

   ✓ Gwen <u>might have been going</u> to the library when we saw her this morning.

4. **Some verbs are compound verbs. Some subjects have more than one verb. When more than one verb goes with the same subject, the verb is called a *compound verb*.**

   ✓ The meteorologist <u>pointed</u> to a low-pressure system on the weather map and <u>predicted</u> rain.

   ✓ The teller <u>counted</u> the bills twice and <u>handed</u> them to the customer.

   ✓ I <u>ate</u> the asparagus and avocado casserole but <u>did</u> not <u>like</u> it.

5. **An infinitive (*to* + present tense verb) cannot act as a verb in a sentence.**

   ✗ Paulo wanted <u>to accept</u> the award on his brother's behalf.

   The phrase *to accept* is an infinitive and cannot be the main verb of the sentence. The verb in this sentence is *wanted*.

   ✓ Paulo <u>wanted</u> to accept the award on his brother's behalf.

   ✗ The actor's hair looked too smooth and full <u>to be</u> real.

   The phrase *to be* is an infinitive, not the verb of the sentence. The verb in this sentence is *looked*.

   ✓ The actor's hair <u>looked</u> too smooth and full to be real.

6. **A verb form ending in *-ing* cannot act as a verb in a sentence unless a helping verb precedes it.**

   ✗ From the street came sounds of children <u>playing</u>.

   Playing cannot be the verb because a helping verb does not precede it. The verb in this sentence is *came*.

   ✓ From the street <u>came</u> sounds of children playing.

   ✗ The <u>setting</u> sun sank below the horizon.

   Setting cannot be the verb because a helping verb does not precede it. The verb in this sentence is *sank*.

   ✓ The setting sun <u>sank</u> below the horizon.

   ✓ A crowd <u>was gathering</u> at the scene of the accident.

   The verb in this sentence is *was gathering* (helping verb + main verb).

   ✓ James <u>has been thinking</u> about changing his major.

   The verb in this sentence is *has been thinking* (helping verb + main verb).

practice 22.3   **Finding Verbs**

Underline the verbs in each of the following sentences.

1. A strong breeze filled the sails of the small boat, pushing it toward the shore.
2. For her computer, Joy wants a wireless mouse and a flat-screen monitor.
3. Iced tea tastes refreshing on a hot day.

4. Mrs. Binks sat on her porch and waited for the mail to arrive.
5. I have been listening to the radio, hoping to hear my favorite song.
6. A person has a better chance of being struck by lightning than of winning the lottery.
7. Maud wondered why she had bought the black T-shirt with tarantulas on it.
8. Every morning, Anthony reads the comics page of the paper first.
9. Grandpa said the baby looked like him—bald and toothless.
10. Inch by inch, the tiny kitten climbed up the side of the bed.

Finding the Subject

Now that you can find the verb of a sentence, you can more easily find the subject of the verb. The easiest way to find the subject of a sentence is to find the verb first and work from there.

A subject answers the question "Who or what _____?" The verb fills in the blank. Be sure that the words *who* or *what* are stated before the verb, or you may find the object of the verb rather than its subject.

✓ The telephone <u>rang</u>, startling Raoul.

Who or what rang? The <u>telephone</u> rang. *Telephone* is the subject of the verb *rang*.

✓ The tour group <u>will fly</u> to Toronto on the six P.M. flight.

Who or what will fly? <u>The tour group</u> will fly. *Group* is the simple subject of the verb *will fly*. (The words *the* and *tour* are modifiers and are part of the complete subject.)

✓ Cedric and Joseph <u>sat</u> on the bench waiting for their mother.

Who or what sat? <u>Cedric and Joseph</u> sat. *Cedric and Joseph* is the compound subject of the verb *sat*.

✓ Carefully, Sandra <u>measured</u> the cinnamon and raisins and <u>folded</u> them

into the bread dough.

Who or what measured? <u>Sandra</u> measured. *Sandra* is the subject of the verb *measured*. Who or what folded? <u>Sandra</u> folded. *Sandra* is the subject of the verb *folded*.

✓ Carefully, Sandra <u>measured</u> the cinnamon and raisins, and Brian <u>folded</u>

them into the bread dough.

Who or what measured? <u>Sandra</u> measured. *Sandra* is the subject of the verb *measured*. Who or what folded? <u>Brian</u> folded. *Brian* is the subject of the verb *folded*.

practice 22.4 **Recognizing Verbs and Subjects**

Find the verb in each sentence below and underline it twice. Then find the subject by asking "Who or what _____?" Underline the subject once.

1. *Casablanca* is Adrienne's favorite movie.
2. Exhaustion showed in Hank's face.
3. Ophelia's college diploma hung on the wall of her office.

4. Dust clung stubbornly to the computer screen.
5. Tracy drove to the post office and mailed her package.

Recognizing Prepositional Phrases

A subject will not be part of a prepositional phrase. In many sentences, prepositional phrases intervene between subject and verb.

✓ The rim *of the glass* is chipped.

When we pick out the subject of the verb by asking "What is chipped?" it is tempting to say, "The glass is chipped." But *glass* cannot be the subject of the verb in this sentence. Grammatically, it already has a job: It is the object of the preposition. The subject of this sentence is *rim*. To avoid mistakes in picking out the subject of the sentence, cross out prepositional phrases before picking out subject and verb.

Reader's *Tip* ——— Famous Prepositional Phrases

The following prepositional phrases have been used as titles for songs, television shows, movies, and books. How many do you recognize? Can you think of others?

Above Suspicion	In Living Color
Against the Wind	Of Mice and Men
Around the World in Eighty Days	On Golden Pond
At Long Last Love	On the Waterfront
At the Hop	Over the Rainbow
Behind Closed Doors	Under the Boardwalk
Behind Enemy Lines	Under the Yum Yum Tree
Beneath the Planet of the Apes	Up a Lazy River
Beyond the Sea	Up on the Roof
In Cold Blood	Up the Down Staircase

- **Prepositional phrases always begin with a preposition.** Prepositions are often short words like *of, to, by, for,* or *from.* They are often words of location, such as *behind, beside, beneath, beyond,* or *below.* A list of common prepositions follows.

Frequently Used Prepositions

about	beneath	in	to
above	beside	into	toward
across	between	like	under
after	beyond	near	underneath
along	by	next to	until
along with	down	of	up
around	during	off	upon
at	except	on	with
before	for	outside	within
behind	from	over	without

- **Prepositional phrases always end with a noun or pronoun.** The object of a preposition, always a noun or pronoun, comes at the end of a prepositional phrase: of the *mongoose,* beside a sparkling *lake,* with *them,* to *James and Harlow,* within five *minutes.*
- **Prepositional phrases often have a three-word structure.** Often, prepositional phrases have a three-word structure: preposition, article *(a, an,* or *the),* noun. Thus phrases like *of an employee, under the car,* and *with a gift* become easy to recognize. But prepositional phrases can also be stretched with modifiers and compound objects: *beside Katie's bright blue dance shoes and pink-and-purple designer leotard.* More often, though, the three-word pattern prevails.

practice 22.5 | **Eliminating Prepositional Phrases**

Cross out the prepositional phrases in the following sentences.

1. The vivid colors of the flowers in the blue bowl on the table brighten the room.
2. Outside the office, on the busy street, swarms of happy vacationers were leaving for weekend trips.
3. The point of Mr. Smith's remarks to the class was lost on Kendall, who dozed peacefully in the back row.
4. For dessert, I'll have a cup of coffee and a slice of that gooey, rich pecan pie.
5. The smell of freshly brewed coffee and frying bacon wafted through the open door of the small restaurant on the corner of Poplar and Main.

Reader's *Tip* ——— *Real-World Writing: Is It Okay to End a
Sentence with a Preposition?

How else would you say, "Will you pick me up?" or "I feel left out"?

Sometimes, what seems to be an objection to a preposition at the end of a sentence is really an objection to an awkward or redundant construction. "Where are you at?" will bring a scowl to any English teacher's face—not because it ends in a preposition, but because it is redundant: "where" and "at" are both doing the same job—indicating location.

But by all means, say "I have nothing to put this in" or "The dog wants to go out." Except in the most formal writing, ending sentences with prepositions is something almost everyone can live with.

Regular and Irregular Verbs

Regular verbs follow a predictable pattern in the formation of their **principal parts.** Every verb has four principal parts: the present-tense form, the past-tense form, the past participle (used with helping verbs), and the present participle (the *-ing* verb form used with helping verbs). Regular verbs add ed to form their past tense and past participles. Some examples of regular verbs follow.

Examples of Regular Verbs

Present	Past	Past Participle	Present Participle
add	added	(have) added	(are) adding
change	changed	(have) changed	(are) changing
pull	pulled	(have) pulled	(are) pulling
walk	walked	(have) walked	(are) walking

Irregular verbs, on the other hand, follow no predictable pattern in their past and past participle forms. Sometimes a vowel changes: *sing* in the present tense becomes *sang* in the past tense and *sung* in the past participle. Sometimes an *n* or *en* will be added to form the past participle: *take* becomes *taken, fall* becomes *fallen.* Some verbs, such as the verb *set,* do not change at all. Others change completely: *buy* in the present tense becomes *bought* in the past and past participle.

Some common irregular verbs and their principal parts follow. If you are unsure about a verb form, check this list or consult a dictionary for the correct form.

Principal Parts of Common Irregular Verbs

Present	Past	Past Participle	Present Participle
be (am, are, is)	was (were)	(have) been	(are) being
become	became	(have) become	(are) becoming
begin	began	(have) begun	(are) beginning
blow	blew	(have) blown	(are) blowing
break	broke	(have) broken	(are) breaking
bring	brought	(have) brought	(are) bringing
burst	burst	(have) burst	(are) bursting
buy	bought	(have) bought	(are) buying
catch	caught	(have) caught	(are) catching
choose	chose	(have) chosen	(are) choosing
come	came	(have) come	(are) coming
cut	cut	(have) cut	(are) cutting
do	did	(have) done	(are) doing
draw	drew	(have) drawn	(are) drawing
drink	drank	(have) drunk	(are) drinking
drive	drove	(have) driven	(are) driving
eat	ate	(have) eaten	(are) eating
fall	fell	(have) fallen	(are) falling
feel	felt	(have) felt	(are) feeling
fight	fought	(have) fought	(are) fighting
find	found	(have) found	(are) finding
fly	flew	(have) flown	(are) flying
freeze	froze	(have) frozen	(are) freezing
get	got	(have) gotten (or got)	(are) getting
give	gave	(have) given	(are) giving
go	went	(have) gone	(are) going
grow	grew	(have) grown	(are) growing

Present	Past	Past Participle	Present Participle
have	had	(have) had	(are) having
hear	heard	(have) heard	(are) hearing
hide	hid	(have) hidden	(are) hiding
hold	held	(have) held	(are) holding
hurt	hurt	(have) hurt	(are) hurting
keep	kept	(have) kept	(are) keeping
know	knew	(have) known	(are) knowing
lay (put)	laid	(have) laid	(are) laying
lead	led	(have) led	(are) leading
leave	left	(have) left	(are) leaving
lend	lent	(have) lent	(are) lending
lie (recline)	lay	(have) lain	(are) lying
lose	lost	(have) lost	(are) losing
put	put	(have) put	(are) putting
ride	rode	(have) ridden	(are) riding
rise	rose	(have) risen	(are) rising
run	ran	(have) run	(are) running
see	saw	(have) seen	(are) seeing
set (place)	set	(have) set	(are) setting
sing	sang	(have) sung	(are) singing
sit (be seated)	sat	(have) sat	(are) sitting
speak	spoke	(have) spoken	(are) speaking
swim	swam	(have) swum	(are) swimming
take	took	(have) taken	(are) taking
tear	tore	(have) torn	(are) tearing
throw	threw	(have) thrown	(are) throwing
write	wrote	(have) written	(are) writing

practice 22.6 **Using the Correct Form of Irregular Verbs**

Fill in the blank with the correct form of the verb shown to the left of each question. For help, consult the list of irregular verbs above.

(become) 1. James has _____ an accomplished pianist.

(break) 2. Ellen hopes she has not _____ her computer keyboard.

(drink) 3. The dog _____ all the water in her bowl before we came home.

(eat) 4. Have you _____ dinner?

(go) 5. James has _____ to pick up his daughter.

(lead) 6. The mother duck _____ her ducklings across the busy intersection.

(lend) 7. The bank _____ Miguel the money to buy a car.

(run)   8. Alisha _____ across the street, hoping to catch the bus.

(see)   9. When Greg _____ his test grade, he felt relieved.

(swim)   10. When Tamiko had _____ for half an hour, she got out of the pool.

Puzzling Pairs

Some irregular verbs are easily confused with other words. The following section will help you make the right choice between *lend* and *loan, lie* and *lay,* and *sit* and *set.*

Lend and Loan *Lend* is a verb meaning "to allow someone to borrow," as in "*Lend* me ten dollars until payday," or "She *lent* her book to another student." *Loan* is a noun meaning "something borrowed," as in "He went to the bank for a mortgage *loan.*"

EXAMPLE

✗   I was not sure the bank would *loan* me the money.

✓   I was not sure the bank would *lend* me the money.

✗   Mrs. Timmons *loaned* her son the money for tuition.

✓   Mrs. Timmons *lent* her son the money for tuition.

Reader's *Tip* ——— *Real-World Writing: Lend? Loan? Who Cares!

People who care about English also care about the distinction between *lend* and *loan.* Though the use of *loan* as a verb is widespread, it is not considered acceptable by careful writers and speakers of English.

Therefore, it's best to avoid such constructions as "Loan me a quarter for the telephone," or "He loaned me his car."

practice 22.7   **Using *Lend* and *Loan***

For each sentence, choose the correct word.

1. I promised my grandmother I would pay back the (lend, loan), but she said, "Consider it a gift."
2. Derek tries not to (lend, loan) books he wants to keep.
3. Shakespeare wrote, "Friends, Romans, countrymen, (lend, loan) me your ears."
4. Amy is irresponsible with money; she needs a (lend, loan) before each payday.
5. Would you mind (lending, loaning) me a hand?

Lay* and *Lie *Lay* and *lie* are often confused, partly because their forms overlap. The present tense of the verb *lay* and the past tense of *lie* are both the same: *lay.* Look at the following chart to see the different forms of each verb.

Present	Past	Past Participle	Present Participle
lay (put)	laid	(have) laid	(are) laying
lie (recline)	lay	(have) lain	(are) lying

- The verb *lay* means to *put* or *place*. It always takes an object; that is, there will always be an answer to the question, "Lay what?"

EXAMPLE

✓ Horace lays his work problems aside before he walks into his house.

✓ Jessica laid her duffel bag on a bench in the locker room.

✓ Spiros has laid the brick for his patio, and he promised he would help me with mine.

✓ Preston and I are laying the groundwork for our project.

- The verb *lie* means to *recline*. It does not take an object.

EXAMPLE

✓ Since Anna broke her ankle, she lies around watching soap operas all day.

✓ The turtle lay upside down in the middle of the highway, unable to right itself.

✓ I have lain on that soft couch for too long; now my back is aching.

✓ The flashlight was lying on the mantel where Kaya had left it.

practice 22.8   **Using *Lay* and *Lie***

Underline the correct verb forms in the following paragraph.

Before the sun rose, Martin went out to pick up the newspaper that was ¹(laying, lying) in his driveway. Because it was dark, he did not even see the small shape that ²(laid, lay) in the street just past his mailbox. Inside the house, he ³(lay, laid) the paper on the kitchen counter, fixed a bowl of cereal for himself, and opened a can of food for his golden retriever, Bart. But when he went to the back door to call Bart, the dog did not come. "He must have jumped the fence again," Martin thought. "I'll have to ⁴(lay, lie) down the law to that crazy dog." But when Martin pulled out of his driveway to go to work, he saw Bart ⁵(laying, lying) beside the road. The dog ⁶(lay, laid) so still that Martin thought he was dead. As he bent down, Martin heard a soft whine, so he picked the dog up and gently ⁷(lay, laid) him in the back seat of the car. At the vet's office, Dr. Jordan said, "I'll have to ⁸(lay, lie) it on the line. Bart's injuries are serious, and it will be twenty-four hours before we can make any real predictions." That night, Martin ⁹(lay, laid) awake for a long time. When he called Dr. Jordan the next morning, the vet said, "Bart's a strong dog. I think he's going to make it." As he ¹⁰(lay, laid) the telephone receiver back in its cradle, Martin breathed a sigh of relief. It would not be a day for goodbyes.

Sit* and *Set The verb *sit* means to take a seat or to be located. It does not take an object.

EXAMPLE

✓   verb
    The house <u>sits</u> on a hill overlooking the lake.

✓   verb
    Phooey <u>sat</u> beside her bowl wearing a look that said "feed me."

✓   verb
    The children <u>have sat</u> in front of the television for too long.

✓   verb
    The Arnolds' car <u>is sitting</u> in the driveway, so they must be at home.

- *Set* means to put or place. The verb *set* always takes an object; that is, you will always find an answer to the question, "Set what?"

EXAMPLE

✓   verb   object
    <u>Set</u> the <u>groceries</u> on the counter.

✓   verb   object
    On New Year's Eve, Janis <u>set</u> her <u>goals</u> for the year.

✓   verb   object
    I believe I <u>have set</u> the <u>tomato plants</u> too close together.

✓   verb   object
    The students believe the teacher <u>is setting</u> <u>standards</u> that they

    cannot meet.

practice 22.9   **Using *Sit* and *Set***

Underline the correct verb forms in the following sentences.

1. The cat (sits, sets) in the window, entertained for hours by the sparrows outside.
2. The letter carrier (sat, set) the package beside the door.
3. While the grownups were (sitting, setting) on the porch, Billy scrawled abstract designs on the living room wall.
4. (Sitting, setting) at the table, Bonita (sat, set) her goals down in writing.
5. Craig's bread machine has (set, sat) on the shelf ever since he bought it.

Review Exercises

Complete the Review Exercises to see how well you learned the skills addressed in this chapter. As you work through the exercises, go back through the chapter to review any of the rules you do not understand completely.

exercise 22.1 **Finding Subjects and Verbs**

Cross out prepositional phrases in the following sentences. Then underline the subject once and the verb twice.

1. In many homes, the kitchen is the hub of family activity.
2. The television has been blaring loudly in the living room almost all day.
3. The kite sailed majestically upward, then spiraled to earth.
4. The coffee in this pot tastes bitter and strong.
5. The meeting of the planning committee might be rescheduled.
6. The dog has been drinking from your glass of water.
7. The lack of space in my office may force me to dispose of some of my books.
8. Anita longed for a new car to replace her unreliable old clunker.
9. Computers were supposed to create a "paperless office."
10. Instead, they generate even more paper.

exercise 22.2 **Finding Subjects and Verbs**

Cross out prepositional phrases in the following sentences. Then underline subjects once and verbs twice.

1. The sleeping cat woke when Mattie went into the kitchen.
2. Some of the leftovers in this refrigerator should be thrown out.
3. The dictionary's cover was tattered and worn.
4. The sound of the gong reverberated throughout the auditorium.
5. Selenium is believed to play a role in cancer prevention.
6. Tim glanced in the mirror at his shaggy hair and decided to get a haircut after work.
7. The company's apology came too late for Claire.
8. Jake and Mike are fraternal twins and do not look much alike.
9. The melon, grown in poor, sandy soil, barely reached the size of a baseball.
10. The witness could not recollect the color of the robber's shoes.

exercise 22.3 **Puzzling Pairs**

Choose the correct form of the following verbs.

1. (Sit, Set) down and make yourself comfortable.
2. In the summer, Kristen enjoys (laying, lying) on the beach.
3. James was sorry he had (lent, loaned) his circular saw to Matt.
4. Pablo has promised to (lend, loan) his expertise when we paint the set.
5. A shining ribbon of discarded cans (lay, laid) alongside the road.

6. The rivals shook hands and (lay, laid) their differences aside.
7. Barbara has (laid, lain) in the sun too long.
8. Joan called and asked, "Are you busy or are you just (sitting, setting) around?"
9. Can you (loan, lend) me a pencil?
10. The compact disks, removed from their cases, were (laying, lying) on the table.

exercise 22.4 **Using Irregular Verbs**

Fill in the blank with the correct form of the verb shown to the left of each question. For help, consult the list of irregular verbs in this chapter.

(lie) 1. Nicole walked along the stretch of sand, occasionally stopping to pick up one of the shells that _____ scattered along the shoreline.

(burst) 2. The child stood in the supermarket aisle, crying because his balloon had _____ .

(fly) 3. The nest was deserted; the nestlings had long since _____ .

(put) 4. Howard brought the groceries in and _____ them away immediately.

(fall) 5. When Alison _____ on the track, everyone rushed over to ask if she was hurt.

(begin) 6. It is distracting when people enter the theater after a performance has _____.

(tear) 7. An hour ago, the cat _____ out of the house, and I haven't seen him since.

(spend) 8. I _____ $35 and left the grocery store with just one small bag.

(fight) 9. When they were young, the sisters _____ continually.

(throw) 10. Quinton _____ the ball too hard and pulled a shoulder muscle.

exercise 22.5 **Using Irregular Verbs**

Fill in the blank with the correct form of the verb shown to the left of each question. For help, consult the list of irregular verbs in this chapter.

(bring) 1. After she was hired, the new manager _____ a measure of stability to the department.

(rise) 2. After the dough had _____ , Mary shaped it into loaves.

(ride) 3. Mr. Smith said he had not _____ a bicycle since he was a child.

(see) 4. Yesterday I _____ a wasp's nest in our garage.

(drink) 5. Who _____ all the diet cola?

(lay) 6. Harriet _____ a blanket across the sleeping child.

(break) 7. The company _____ with tradition by adding athletic shoes to its line.

(go) 8. Betty _____ to work before the sun rose.

(lose) 9. Adam has _____ the combination to the safe.

(drive) 10. Four police cars have _____ past within the last hour.

23 Subject-Verb Agreement

Singular with singular
Will need no referee,
And plural paired with plural is
In perfect harmony.

In grammatical relations,
Achieve tranquility
By using combinations
That never disagree.

In Standard English, subjects and verbs must always agree. This does not necessarily mean that they shake hands, as in the drawing that opens this chapter. In grammatical terminology, **agreement** always means that singular is paired with singular and plural with plural. All of the rules for subject-verb agreement presented in this chapter have the same idea behind them: **A singular subject requires a singular verb, and a plural subject requires a plural verb.**

The Basic Pattern

Because most subject-verb agreement problems occur in the present tense, let's begin by looking at a present-tense verb as it moves through the first, second, and third person.

	Singular	**Plural**
First person	I walk	we walk
Second person	you walk	you walk
Third person	he, she, it walks	they walk

practice 23.1 **Conjugating a Verb**

All regular verbs follow the pattern above. Using the sample above as a model, fill in the forms of the verb *call* in the spaces below.

	Singular	**Plural**
First person	I ————	we ————
Second person	you ————	you ————
Third person	he, she, it ————	they ————

Did you remember to put the *s* on the third-person singular form? Notice that it is only in the third person that the singular form is different from the plural form. Notice, too, that the third-person verb pattern is exactly the opposite of the pattern you see in nouns. When you look at the noun *cat*, you know that it is singular and that the plural form is *cats*. But verbs in the third person, present tense, work in exactly the opposite way. The third-person singular form of the verb ends in *s*, not the plural form. When you see the verb *walks*, you know it is singular because it ends in *s*.

EXAMPLE A third-person singular subject and verb usually follow the pattern shown below:

The *cat walks.* (The singular noun does not end in *s;* the singular verb does end in *s.*)

A third-person plural subject and verb usually follow this pattern:

The *cats walk.* (The plural noun ends in *s;* the plural verb does not end in *s.*)

Reader's *Tip* ———— * Memory Jogger

If you have trouble with third-person verbs, remember the following verse.

The Singular S

When verbs are in the present tense,
You never need to guess.
The singular third-person verb
Always ends in s.

practice 23.2

Conjugating Verbs

On your own paper, fill in the first-, second-, and third-person forms of the following regular verbs: *inspire, locate, dance, resist, type.* Remember to add the *s* to the third-person singular form.

Verbs Ending in *-s*

Look at the regular verb *confess* in the present tense. Here, when the verb already ends in *s*, the third-person singular form also changes, adding an *es*.

	Singular	**Plural**
First person	I confess	we confess
Second person	you confess	you confess
Third person	he, she, it confess**es**	they confess

Using Third Person

Third person is sometimes confusing. One reason is that it is the only person for which the verb form changes. The biggest reason, however, is that third person includes much more than just the pronouns *he, she, it,* and *they.* Third-person singular also includes any noun or pronoun that can be replaced by *he, she,* or *it. James, Ms. Smith, cat, table, child, one, bank teller,* and *Abraham Lincoln* are all third-person singular. Thus, each requires a present-tense verb ending in *s* or *es.*

Any noun or pronoun that can be replaced by *they* is third-person plural. The *Joneses, both, washer and dryer, beds, automobiles,* and *several* are words that could be replaced by *they.* Thus, all are third-person plural and require a present-tense plural verb, the form that does not add *s* or *es.*

The Verb *to be*

Now look at the most common irregular verb, the verb *to be.*

	Singular	**Plural**
First person	I am	we are
Second person	you are	you are
Third person	he, she, it is	they are

Notice that the pattern still holds: The third-person singular form of the verb always ends in *s* or *es*.

A Fundamental Rule

Knowing the pattern that present-tense verbs follow should make it a bit easier to apply the fundamental rule of subject-verb agreement:

A singular subject requires a singular verb, and a plural subject requires a plural verb.

EXAMPLE

      S   V

Susan takes a walk every morning before leaving for work. (singular subject, singular verb)

       S   V

A hurricane spins in a huge spiral around a central eye. (singular subject, singular verb)

          S V

Ice cream shops do most of their business during the summer months. (plural subject, plural verb)

                   S   V

In the kitchen of the new restaurant, crates of dishes and glassware wait to be unpacked. (plural subject, plural verb)

practice 23.3 ## Making Subjects and Verbs Agree

Underline the correct verb form in each of the following sentences.

1. Roberto (insists, insist) on biking every day, rain or shine.
2. If Karen (impress, impresses) the interviewer, she will have a good chance to get the job.
3. The cuckoo clock (squawks, squawk) loudly on the hour and half hour.
4. The names of Trevor's goldfish (is, are) Moe, Larry, and Curly.
5. The speckled jellybeans (tastes, taste) like buttered popcorn.
6. The cat had found the jellybeans, and they (was, were) scattered across the floor.
7. An airline's reputation (suffers, suffer) when one of its planes crashes.
8. Because the sisters (is, are) so busy, they rarely see one another.
9. Ms. Roberts (quiz, quizzes) her students on grammar every week.
10. For breakfast, Lauren (insist, insists) on eating sugary cereal with multicolored marshmallows.

Problems in Subject-Verb Agreement

Prepositional Phrase Between Subject and Verb

One problem in subject-verb agreement occurs when a prepositional phrase comes between a subject and a verb, making it easy to make mistakes. Crossing out prepositional phrases will help you remember this important rule:

The subject of a verb is not found in a prepositional phrase.

EXAMPLE

Consider the following problem in subject-verb agreement:

The members of the softball team (practices, practice) every afternoon until five.

Which verb is correct? If you look for the subject by asking the question, "Who or what *practices* or *practice?*" it might seem logical to say, "The *team* practices, so *team* is the subject of the sentence and *practices* is the verb." However, *team* cannot be the subject of the sentence because it already has a job: It is the object of a preposition, and *the subject of a sentence is never found in a prepositional phrase.*

Incorrect Solution

✗ The members of the <u>softball team</u> <u>practices</u> every afternoon until five.

Correct Solution

Cross out prepositional phrases to find the subject.

✓ The <u>members</u> ~~of the softball team~~ (practices, <u>practice</u>) ~~every afternoon until five.~~

EXAMPLE

✓ The <u>color</u> ~~of the draperies~~ <u>matches</u> the stripe woven ~~into the fabric of~~ the sofa.

The verb agrees with its subject, *color,* not with the object of the preposition.

practice 23.4   ## Eliminating Prepositional Phrases

In the following sentences, cross out prepositional phrases to find the subject of the sentence. Then, underline the subject and double-underline the correct verb.

1. The hands on the clock (seems, seem) to have stopped.
2. The layers of grime on the old desk (obscures, obscure) its beautiful finish.
3. The loudness of the music in the aerobics room of the fitness center (makes, make) Yolanda's head ache.
4. As the stairs of the escalator (disappears, disappear) into the floor, a child stands watching in amazement.
5. The computers in the library of the college (attracts, attract) many students.

Indefinite Pronouns as Subjects

Problems in subject-verb agreement are also likely to occur when the subject is an **indefinite pronoun,** a pronoun that does not refer to a specific person or thing. The following indefinite pronouns are always singular and require singular verbs.

each	everybody	everyone	anything
either	nobody	one	everything
neither	somebody	someone	nothing
anybody	anyone	no one	something

Reader's *Tip* ———— * Memory Jogger ————————

Remember the singular indefinite pronouns more easily by grouping them:

Each, either, neither
All the bodies (anybody, everybody, somebody, nobody)
All the ones (anyone, everyone, someone, one, no one)
All the things (anything, everything, something, nothing)

EXAMPLE   If <u>no one</u> <u>comes</u> to their yard sale, Pat and Amy will donate the goods to charity.

The subject *no one* is singular, as is the verb *comes*.

<u>Each</u> ~~of the party guests~~ <u>has been asked</u> to bring an inexpensive gag gift.

The singular verb *has been asked* agrees with the singular subject *each*. The plural object of the preposition, *guests*, does not affect the verb.

practice 23.5   **Making Verbs Agree with Indefinite Pronouns**

In each of the following sentences, cross out prepositional phrases and underline the verb that agrees with the indefinite pronoun subject.

1. Neither of the contestants (was, were) prepared to lose.
2. Everybody on the street (pass, passes) the homeless man without a backward glance.
3. No one in any of my classes (has, have) taken a class from Dr. Mason.
4. Something on the bottom of Sidney's shoes (makes, make) them stick to the floor as he walks.
5. Everything on the table (looks, look) good to me.

Subject Following the Verb

Problems in subject-verb agreement are also likely to occur when a subject follows the verb. In most English sentences, the subject comes before the verb. However, the subject follows the verb in these situations:

1. when the sentence begins with *here* or *there*
2. when the sentence begins with a prepositional phrase that is immediately followed by a verb
3. when the sentence is a question

EXAMPLE   There <u>are</u> no more <u>tissues</u> left ~~in the box~~.

The plural subject *tissues* requires the plural verb *are*. The word *there* is not the subject of the sentence.

On top of the refrigerator <u>sit</u> my lost <u>keys</u>.

The prepositional phrases *on top* and *of the refrigerator* are immediately followed by a verb. Because the subject is never found in a prepositional phrase, it must be somewhere after the verb. The plural verb *sit* agrees with the plural subject *keys*.

What <u>was</u> the <u>answer</u> to the first question?

The singular subject *answer* follows the singular verb *was*.

What <u>were</u> the <u>answers</u> to the first two questions?

The plural subject *answers* follows the plural verb *were*.

practice 23.6   **Making Verbs Agree with Subjects That Come after Verbs**

Cross out prepositional phrases in each of the following sentences. Then underline the subject and double-underline the correct verb.

1. Nestled in the little valley (was, were) a cluster of houses.
2. Why (is, are) Trevor's parents moving to Detroit?
3. Here (is, are) the study guides you asked for, Jonathan.
4. (Does, Do) Angelica know that her paper is due on Friday?
5. There (wasn't, weren't) any newspapers left at the bookstore.

Compound Subjects

Compound subjects, subjects joined by *and, or, either/or* or *neither/nor,* may also cause confusion in subject-verb agreement. The rules for subject-verb agreement with compound subjects are outlined in the sections that follow.

Compound Subjects Joined by *and* Because *and* always joins at least two elements, compound subjects joined by *and* require a plural verb. Remember this rule:

Compound subjects joined by *and* require a plural verb.

Look at the following sentence:

Keisha and her brother (is, are) scheduled to arrive today.

If you look at the sentence and ask *how many* will arrive, subject-verb agreement should be easy. *More than one* will arrive, so the logical choice is the plural verb *are*.

<u>Keisha</u> and her <u>brother</u> <u>are</u> scheduled to arrive today.

EXAMPLE   A good <u>book</u> *and* a warm <u>fire</u> <u>are</u> ideal companions on a winter night.

<u>Patience</u> *and* <u>persistence</u> <u>pay</u>.

A bent <u>umbrella</u>, an old <u>chair</u>, *and* a discarded <u>mop</u> <u>sit</u> forlornly beside the trash can.

Tall <u>pines</u> *and* scrub <u>oaks</u> <u>dot</u> the landscape.

practice 23.7 | **Making Verbs Agree with Subjects Joined by *And***

Cross out prepositional phrases, then underline the verb that agrees with each compound subject.

1. A bright-eyed Raggedy Ann doll and a tattered bear (adorns, adorn) the bookshelf in Kim's room.
2. Cold pizza and a moldy scrap of cheese (was, were) the only food in Foster's refrigerator.
3. A bowl of cold ice cream and a hot bath (awaits, await) Kim at the end of the day.
4. Two plates of spaghetti with meatballs, two salads, a glass of iced tea, and one cup of coffee (costs, cost) less than ten dollars at the Coffee Cup Cafe.
5. A monster truck show and a trip to the drive-through window of a fast food restaurant (was, were) not Gayle's idea of a good time.

Compound Subjects Joined by *or, either/or,* or *neither/nor* When subjects are joined by *or, either/or,* or *neither/nor,* it is not always possible to use logic to determine whether the verb will be singular or plural. Therefore, one rule applies to all compound subjects joined by *or, either/or,* or *neither/nor.*

> **When a compound subject is joined by *or, either/or,* or *neither/nor,* the verb agrees with the part of the subject closer to it.**

Consider the following sentence:

> Keisha or her brother (is, are) scheduled to arrive today.

How many will arrive today? *Just one* will arrive: either Keisha *or* her brother, so using the singular verb *is* makes logical sense. The singular verb *is* also agrees with *brother,* the part of the subject closer to the verb.

> <u>Keisha</u> or her <u>brother</u> <u>is</u> scheduled to arrive today.

Now, let's change the sentence a bit.

> Keisha's brothers or her parents (is, are) scheduled to arrive today.

How many will arrive? In this sentence, *more than one*—either *brothers* or *parents.* It makes sense, then, to use a plural verb. The plural verb *are* also agrees with *parents,* the part of the subject closer to the verb.

Keisha's <u>brothers</u> or her <u>parents</u> <u><u>are</u></u> scheduled to arrive today.

The next two sentences do not respond to logical examination.

Keisha or her parents (is, are) scheduled to arrive today.

Keisha's parents or her brother (is, are) scheduled to arrive today.

How many will arrive? There is no way to tell. Simply follow the rule and make the verb agree with the part of the subject closer to it.

Keisha or her <u>parents</u> <u><u>are</u></u> scheduled to arrive today.

Keisha's parents or her <u>brother</u> <u><u>is</u></u> scheduled to arrive today.

EXAMPLE   A term <u>paper</u> *or* an oral <u>report</u> <u><u>is</u></u> required ~~in Mr. Hanson's class~~.

A term <u>paper</u> *or* two oral <u>reports</u> <u><u>are</u></u> required ~~in Mr. Hanson's class~~.

Either two oral <u>reports</u> *or* a term <u>paper</u> <u><u>is</u></u> required ~~in Mr. Hanson's class~~.

Neither the <u>cats</u> *nor* the <u>dog</u> <u><u>shows</u></u> any interest ~~in the parakeet~~.

~~Among the requirements~~ <u><u>was</u></u> <u>listed</u> an associate's <u>degree</u> *or* <u>five years</u> ~~of experience~~.

practice 23.8   **Making Verbs Agree with Subjects Joined by *Or, Either/Or,* or *Neither/Nor***

Cross out prepositional phrases, then underline the verb that agrees with each compound subject.

1. Garlic bread or dinner rolls (is, are) served with the meal.
2. Either the neighbors or my mother (watches, watch) my house while I am on vacation.
3. Neither Ms. Pitts nor Mr. Shaw (possesses, possess) the qualities that the personnel director looks for in a manager.
4. A thunderstorm or a hailstorm (is, are) expected later this afternoon.
5. Neither going to a movie nor eating at a trendy restaurant (appeal, appeals) to Jenae.

Review Exercises

Complete the Review Exercises to see how well you learned the skills addressed in this chapter. As you work through the exercises, go back through the chapter to review any of the rules you do not understand completely.

exercise 23.1 Underline the correct verb in each of the following sentences.

1. The persistent ringing of the alarm clock (wakes, wake) Shawn every morning at six.
2. Books from the library (is, are) an inexpensive form of entertainment.
3. Each of the kittens (has, have) found a good home.
4. Neither of the witnesses to the crime (tells, tell) the same story.
5. The shampoo and the conditioner (smells, smell) good, but neither is worth five dollars.
6. The flowers and the grass (has, have) dried out in the dry weather.
7. Neither Benjamin nor his professors (was, were) told that he would receive the award.
8. In an emergency, salt or baking soda (substitutes, substitute) for toothpaste.
9. How (does, do) Angela and Dennis get away with being late every day?
10. There (is, are) few students remaining on campus after exams are over.

exercise 23.2 Write *correct* in the blank if the italicized verb agrees with its subject. If the verb is incorrect, write the correct form in the blank.

———— 1. The potholes in the parking lot *make* driving difficult.

———— 2. The purpose of the two assignments *was* not clear to the students.

———— 3. One of the librarians *are* holding a book for me.

———— 4. Everybody in the front of the classroom *seem* to make good grades.

———— 5. A bowl of cereal and a chocolate-chip cookie *is* all I have eaten today.

———— 6. Apples and bananas *was* at the top of Avery's shopping list.

———— 7. Beatrice's uncle or her aunt always *comes* to her rescue when she runs out of money.

———— 8. The blue notebook or the two red ones *belongs* to Mickey.

———— 9. Why *has* class *been canceled* today?

————10. Here *is* the assignments for the next two weeks.

exercise 23.3 In each set of sentences, cross out the two verbs that do not agree with their subjects. Then write the correct verb forms on the lines provided.

1. The two quizzes in math class was not difficult, but the test was very hard. However, the last two problems on the test was for extra credit.

   Sentence 1: _____   Sentence 2: _____

2. Not one of the animals in that pet shop look very healthy. An animal adopted through the Humane Society cost much less, and spaying or neutering is included in the fee.

   Sentence 1: _____   Sentence 2: _____

3. Neither Tanya nor her friends was able to find a job as a grocery store cashier. Neither of the grocery stores were hiring.

Sentence 1: _____   Sentence 2: _____

4. A college diploma or a technical school certificate are required by most employers these days. As a result, people of all ages is attending these schools.

Sentence 1: _____   Sentence 2: _____

5. "Why is the lines always so long in this bank?" Stephanie complained. "There is just not enough tellers to help all of the customers."

Sentence 1: _____   Sentence 2: _____

exercise 23.4   In each set of sentences, cross out the two verbs that do not agree with their subjects. Then write the corrected verbs on the lines provided.

1. One of the purposes of children's games are to teach. I sometimes wonder what the violence in so many video games teach children.

Sentence 1: _____   Sentence 2: _____

2. Keith and Valerie always budgets carefully and cut out coupons from the Sunday paper to save a few extra dollars. But it seems as if bills or an unexpected emergency take whatever they manage to save.

Sentence 1: _____   Sentence 2: _____

3. Our neighborhood used to be quiet and peaceful, but now that there is a gas station and a shopping center two miles down the road, traffic has increased. Why have the city's zoning board approved commercial development so close to quiet residential districts?

Sentence 1: _____   Sentence 2: _____

4. When an outbreak of influenza occurs, attendance at the elementary schools always drop. Some parents keep their kids at home just to ensure that the children doesn't come in contact with anyone who is infected.

Sentence 1: _____   Sentence 2: _____

5. Neither the cat nor the dog have been fed this morning. What is the chances of running out of cat food and dog food at the same time?

Sentence 1: _____   Sentence 2: _____

exercise 23.5   Find and correct the ten subject-verb agreement errors in the following paragraph.

[1]My friend Helen believe that she is addicted to shopping. [2]She says that whenever she feels depressed or disappointed, the neon lights and large department stores

of the local mall seems to draw her right in. ³As she wanders around the department stores, displays of stylish clothing catches her eye, and she starts to forget her problems. ⁴On the racks in front of her hang the answer to her problems. ⁵By the time one of the salesclerks offer to show her to a dressing room, her mood has improved considerably. ⁶As she tries on clothing, she begins to feel that a new dress or a pair of jeans are just what she needs. ⁷Before she knows it, she is standing at the register with an armload of clothes, and there are a charge slip or a check in front of her waiting to be signed. ⁸As she walks to her car, pleasure and satisfaction washes over her, and everything is right with the world. ⁹But by the time she gets home, the logical part of her mind have begun to take over. ¹⁰She realizes she has bought unnecessary items and know she will be back at the store tomorrow to return them.

1. _____   6. _____

2. _____   7. _____

3. _____   8. _____

4. _____   9. _____

5. _____   10. _____

24 Coordination and Subordination

It's good to have choices.

Writing Effective Sentences

Imagine a world without choices. What if everyone were named John or Jane? What if everyone ate oatmeal for breakfast, wore green clothing, and drove a white Chevrolet? What if every sentence had to start with the subject and one verb and contain only one idea? Here's a paragraph from that world:

> My name is Jane. I got up this morning. The sky was blue. The sun was shining. I put on my green slacks. I put on my green shirt. I put on my green shoes. I ate oatmeal. I ate it for breakfast. I drove my white Ford. I drove it to school.

Fortunately, the real world is abundant with choices in names, food, cars, and sentence structure. Here's what it really looks like.

> Hi, I'm Isabella. When I got up this morning, the sun was steaming through my window from a clear blue sky. I threw on a pair of jeans, a pink sweater, and a pair of gray athletic shoes. My stomach was rumbling, so I sliced a ripe banana into a bowl, poured milk over it, and ate it standing at the counter. Then I stepped into the sunlight, cranked up my silver Toyota, and headed for school.

When you learned to write, you started by expressing one idea per sentence. Now, your ideas are more complex. Your sentence structure, too, has become more sophisticated to handle those complex ideas. This chapter will help you polish your sentence structure with the tools of **coordination** and **subordination** and may even help you add a few new tricks to your repertoire.

Connecting Ideas through Coordination

Often, ideas expressed in short, simple sentences can be joined to make a more effective sentence. One way to connect sentences is called *coordination*. Coordination can be done in two ways: by using a comma and a FANBOYS conjunction, or by using a semicolon and a joining word.

Comma and FANBOYS

FANBOYS conjunctions, more commonly called *coordinating* conjunctions, are used with a comma to connect two independent clauses. Remember that a **clause** is a grammatical unit that contains a subject and a verb and that an **independent clause** can stand alone as a sentence. The nonsense word FANBOYS stands for all seven coordinating conjunctions: **f**or, **a**nd, **n**or, **b**ut, **o**r, **y**et, **s**o.

This is the pattern used when a FANBOYS conjunction is used with a comma to connect two independent clauses. The comma goes before the FANBOYS conjunction.

Independent clause, and independent clause.

EXAMPLE

S   V
Luis scanned the small auditorium. (independent clause)

S   V
He did not see his friend Kathy. (independent clause)

The preceding two independent clauses can be connected with a FANBOYS and a comma:

Luis scanned the small auditorium, **but** he did not see his friend Kathy.

practice 24.1   **Connecting Sentences with Fanboys**

Connect each of the following sentence pairs with a comma and a FANBOYS.

1. In the quiet classroom, a cell phone began to ring.

   Someone quickly silenced it.

   _____

   _____

2. Austin's girlfriend tells him that he is lazy.

   Austin says he's just an expert at conserving energy.

   _____

   _____

3. Cars packed the parking lot of the new restaurant.

   A long line of customers waited to get in.

   _____

   _____

4. Vanessa's family used to travel as far as they could on vacation. Rising gas prices have compelled them to vacation closer to home.

   _____

   _____

5. Shane hopes to move out of his parents' house and into his own place. He works and saves as much as possible.

   _____

   _____

Semicolon and Joining Word

Another method of coordination is using a semicolon and a joining word. As with a comma and **FANBOYS** conjunction, a complete sentence (an independent clause) will appear on both sides of the semicolon.

Independent clause; therefore independent clause.

EXAMPLE ✔ Shakira thought she would have money left over at the end of the month.

✔ She did not anticipate having to buy a new tire.

The two separate sentences can be combined with a semicolon and a joining word.

✔ Shakira thought she would have money left over at the end of the month; **however,** she did not anticipate having to buy a new tire.

The joining words also function as *transitional expressions,* underscoring the relationship between the two clauses. A list of joining words commonly used with semicolons follows.

Joining Words Used with a Semicolon

accordingly	furthermore	meanwhile
also	however	nevertheless
as a result	in addition	of course
besides	in fact	on the other hand
finally	instead	therefore

practice 24.2 **Connecting Sentences with a Semicolon and Joining Word**

Connect each of the following sentence pairs with a semicolon, a joining word from the preceding list, and a comma.

1. Mallory knew her paper was due on Friday.

   She resisted the temptation to go out shopping with her friends.

   _____

   _____

2. Diego agreed to help Clara move to her new apartment.

   He did not realize she had so much furniture.

   _____

   _____

3. The woman who sat next to DeShawn on the plane insisted on telling him her life's story.

   He pretended to go to sleep to avoid her chatter.

   _____

   _____

4. Snow swirled against the windshield, obscuring Natalie's view. She slowed down and drove with extreme caution.

   _____

   _____

5. Vehicles in the southbound lanes of the highway crawled to a halt because of an accident ahead. Traffic in the northbound lanes flowed smoothly and quickly.

_____

_____

Connecting Ideas through Subordination

Another way of connecting ideas is through **subordination.** Placing a **dependent word** such as *because, although, if, when,* or *after* in front of an independent clause makes it a **dependent** or **subordinate clause,** one that can no longer stand on its own as a sentence. It must be connected to another idea that is stated as a complete sentence. It will then *depend on* the sentence it is attached to and can no longer be separated from it. Two examples are shown here using the dependent word *because.*

EXAMPLE   The fuel gauge in Rashid's car was broken.

He never knew for certain when he was running low on gas.

If the dependent clause acts as an introductory clause, a comma follows it.

Because <u>dependent clause</u>, <u>independent clause</u>.

✔ **Because** the fuel gauge in Rashid's car was broken, he never knew for certain when he was running low on gas.

EXAMPLE   The weathercaster told her audience to break out the barbeque grills and the sunscreen.

The weekend would be sunny and hot.

<u>Independent clause</u> *because* <u>dependent clause</u>.

✔ The weathercaster told her audience to break out the barbeque grills and the sunscreen **because** the weekend would be sunny and hot.

A list of dependent words is shown next.

Dependent Words

after	even though	what
although	if	whatever
as	once	when
as if	since	whenever
as long	so that	where
as soon as	that	wherever
as though	though	which
because	unless	while
before	until	who

practice 24.3 **Connecting Sentences with Dependent Words**

Choosing from the preceding list of dependent words, connect each sentence pair using the following pattern:

Dependent word <u>dependent clause</u>, <u>independent clause</u>.

The first one is done for you.

1. Ruth searched through her purse for her debit card.

   The customer in line behind her sighed dramatically.

   <u>As Ruth searched through her purse for her debit card, the customer in line behind</u>
   <u>her sighed dramatically.</u>

2. Movies and televison have romanticized the excitement and danger of detective work.

   Police detectives say their work is ninety-five percent routine and five percent terror.

   _____

   _____

   _____

3. Thomas Edison invented the electric light bulb in 1879.

   He paved the way for society to function 24 hours a day instead of stopping at sunset.

   _____

   _____

4. The holiday weekend promised beautiful weather.

   The lake was crowded with picnickers, boaters, sunbathers, and swimmers.

   _____

   _____

5. Jake sat on a park bench eating his lunch.

   Bold pigeons strutted and pecked around his feet, hoping to share his meal.

   _____

   _____

practice 24.4   **Connecting Sentences with Dependent Words**

Choosing from the preceding list of dependent words, connect each sentence pair using the following pattern:

Independent clause *dependent word* dependent clause.

The first one is done for you.

1. Security was tight at the university's graduation.

   The vice president of the United States was expected to give the commencement address.

   <u>Security was tight at the university's graduation because the vice president of the</u>
   <u>United States was expected to give the commencement address.</u>

2. Maria had just sat down to eat.

   The doorbell rang, causing her to sigh with impatience.

   _____

   _____

3. Jason watched in dismay.

   The cup of coffee he had just bought slipped from his hand and fell to the floor, splashing coffee on his pants.

   _____

   _____

4. Susan's muscles were sore and tired.

   She had spent the afternoon swimming laps in the campus pool.

   _____

   _____

5. Ashley changed her mind about teaching young children.

   She spent a week assisting with a preschool class.

   _____

   _____

Creating Emphasis through Subordination

Dependent words also act as transitional words, showing the relationship between the ideas. Using dependent clauses helps to downplay one idea while emphasizing another. Usually, the idea expressed in the independent clause is of greater importance, while the idea in the dependent clause is of lesser importance.

EXAMPLE

emphasis on the pay

✔ Although police work is important and often dangerous, the pay is surprisingly small.

emphasis on the danger

✔ Police work is important and often dangerous although the pay is surprisingly small.

emphasis on the cheer

✔ A cheer went up from the crowd as the home team scored the winning run.

emphasis on the run

✔ The home team scored the winning run as a cheer went up from the crowd.

practice 24.5 **Using Dependent Words to Emphasize Ideas**

Choosing from the preceding list of dependent words, connect each sentence pair. The idea that is given less emphasis should be introduced by a dependent word. The first one is done for you.

1. Valerie could barely cover her monthly expenses.

   She decided to look for a second job. ✔ *Emphasize this idea.*

   Because Valerie could barely cover her monthly expenses, she decided to look for a

   second job.

2. Orlando looked forward to having an entire week off. ✔ *Emphasize this idea.*

   He had no money for a vacation.

   _____

   _____

   _____

3. The endless expanse of blue sky passed by the plane's window unnoticed.

   Sameera headed back to India for her father's funeral. ✔ *Emphasize this idea.*

   _____

   _____

4. The flowers were already shedding their petals all over the kitchen table.

   ✔ *Emphasize this idea.*

   Julia had picked them from her garden just yesterday.

   _____

   _____

5. James was celebrating his twenty-first birthday.

   He broke his leg in a Jet Ski accident. ✔ *Emphasize this idea.*

   _____

   _____

Review Exercises

exercise 24.1 | **Connecting Sentences Using Coordination**
Connect each sentence pair using *coordination*. Use a comma and a FANBOYS *or* a semicolon, a joining word, and a comma.

1. Alonzo put his portable music player on shuffle.

   He began to jog though the park, listening to his favorite tunes.

   _____

   _____

2. Roxanne knew that traffic would be heavy in Phoenix.

   She had not bargained for drivers who were speeding, weaving in and out of traffic, and following an inch from her bumper.

   _____

   _____

3. Heavy winter clothing was crowded onto the rod in the closet.

   The entire rod eventually fell under its weight.

   _____

   _____

4. The rich, warm sound of the violin used to be produced by strings made of sheep's intestines.

   Today's synthetic strings stay in tune longer and produce a sound that is just as rich.

   _____

   _____

5. People used to have to wait for a daily paper or for the six o'clock news program for a news update.

   News is now available twenty-four hours a day on the Internet and on television.

   _____

   _____

exercise 24.2 **Connecting Sentences Using Subordination**
Connect the two sentences using *subordination*.

1. Tina does her grocery shopping after most people have gone to bed.

   The store is never crowded late at night.

   _____

   _____

2. Kim's children were bored.

   She took them to the miniature golf course on Saturday morning.

   _____

   _____

3. Sanjay carefully removed the casserole dish from the oven.

   It slipped from his fingers and shattered on the floor.

   _____

   _____

4. Nick had always wanted to try carpentry.

   He signed up for a woodworking class.

   _____

   _____

5. The applicant seemed charming and capable at the job interview.

   She proved to be undependable and careless.

   _____

   _____

exercise 24.3   **Connecting Sentences Using Coordination or Subordination**
Connect each sentence pair using *coordination* or *subordination.*

1. A little stress can enhance a person's ability to perform a task.

   Too much stress can impair performance.

   _____

   _____

2. Most people go through life with the name their parents gave them.

   In Hong Kong, some people drop their given names and go by exotic names

   such as Komix, Zeus, Boogie, or Maverick.

   _____

   _____

3. The coffee was brewing.

   The pleasant aroma filled the kitchen.

   _____

   _____

4. Arlene came to work after a two-week vacation.

   She had 147 email messages waiting for her.

   _____

   _____

5. Laney had trouble concentrating on her work.

   The room was too hot and muggy.

   _____

   _____

25 Run-on Sentences

Two cars spin in a crazy dance
And spiral to a stop,
Locked in a less-than-fond embrace
Both destined for the shop.

And so it is with sentences
When they're too closely linked.
It's up to you to put them right
And make them each distinct.

A fender-bender is an unfortunate incident. Aside from the damage to the cars, there's the red tape of insurance claims, and maybe even a costly traffic ticket. Run-on sentences are similarly unfortunate. Aside from the damage to sentence structure, there's red ink on your poor essay, and maybe even a grade penalty. Run-on sentences can be corrected or avoided, and this chapter will show you how.

What Is a Run-on Sentence?

A **run-on sentence** is not one sentence, but two or more, run together without proper punctuation. The following sentence is a type of run-on that is often called a **fused sentence** because two thoughts are fused together with no punctuation to separate them. In this text, the fused sentence type of run-on is simply referred to as a *run-on.*

   ✗ Two pieces of paper slipped out of Desmond's notebook a student walking by picked them up and ran down the hall after Desmond.

By examining the sentence, you can probably decide where the first thought ends and the second begins—between *notebook* and a *student.* Grammatically, too, you can figure out why the thoughts should be separate. Each has a subject and a verb and is an **independent clause,** a clause that can stand alone as a sentence or that can be combined with other clauses in specific patterns.

Another type of run-on is called a **comma splice** because two independent clauses are spliced, or joined, with a comma.

   ✗ Two pieces of paper slipped out of Desmond's notebook, a student walking by picked them up and ran down the hall after Desmond.

The first step toward writing paragraphs and essays that are free of run-on sentences is to learn to recognize run-ons and comma splices. When you see a sentence that you believe is a run-on, test it. Read the first part. Is it a sentence that could stand alone? If your answer is yes, read the second part, asking the same question. If your answer is again yes, the sentence is probably a run-on.

practice 25.1 | **Recognizing Run-ons and Comma Splices**

In each sentence, underline the spot where the run-on occurs. Mark *RO* in the blank to the left of the sentence if the sentence is a run-on (fused sentence), *CS* if it is a comma splice.

_____ 1. An old, bent woman trudged alongside the busy highway she wore several layers of clothing and pushed a shopping cart laden with her belongings.

_____ 2. The computer screen was hard to read, light from the window created a reflection on the screen's surface.

_____ 3. Fitness is important to Sandra, she jogs every morning.

_____ 4. "What does it take to be successful?" Anthony asked his boss Ms. Gray told him, "You have to be willing to make a lot of mistakes."

_____ 5. Vanessa's brother goes to the university her sister attends a technical school.

_____ 6. The store will open in the morning, it is closed for inventory today.

_____ 7. Yesterday's meeting was supposed to last for an hour one hour and forty-five minutes later, it was still in progress.

_____ 8. Maureen had a part-time job, an active social life, and a full load of courses after she received her first test grade, she decided she needed to spend more time on her coursework.

_____ 9. No matter how many times Antwan went by his instructor's office, she wasn't there after a while, he decided he needed to make an appointment.

_____ 10. The microwave's buzzer sounded dinner was ready.

Correcting Run-ons

Five methods of correcting run-ons are presented in the following sections. The first three methods are simple; the remaining two are more complex. Learning all five methods will give you more than just ways to correct run-ons; it will give you a variety of sentence patterns and transitional words to use in your writing.

Method 1: Period and Capital Letter

Correcting a run-on with a period and capital letter is the easiest method to use. The hard part is knowing when and how often to use it. Short, single-clause sentences can emphasize ideas by setting them apart. Too many short sentences can make your writing seem choppy and disconnected.

Pattern: Independent clause. Independent clause.

Put a period between the two sentences. Use a capital letter to begin the new sentence.

EXAMPLE

✗ The technician flipped a switch red and green lights blinked on the control panel.

✔ The technician flipped a switch. Red and green lights blinked on the control panel.

practice 25.2   **Correcting Run-ons with a Period and Capital Letter**

In each sentence, underline the spot where the run-on (fused sentence) or comma splice occurs. Write *RO* in the blank to the left of the sentence if it is a run-on, *CS* if it is a comma splice. Then correct each sentence using a period and a capital letter.

_____ 1. Nonessential water usage has been banned, people are asked not to wash their cars or water their lawns until the drought ends.

_____

_____ 2. Rosie walked over to a display of books she picked up a novel by Stephen King.

_____

_____ 3. In the checkout line, Olivia dropped a quarter it rolled across the floor until an elderly man placed his foot on it to stop its progress.

_____

_____ 4. Wearing his bathrobe, Lou sleepily walked to the end of the driveway, he picked up the newspaper and headed back toward the house.

_____

_____ 5. Americans are becoming more aware of the need to exercise the sale of treadmills, stationary bikes, and weight training equipment has increased over the last decade.

_____

Method 2: Comma and FANBOYS Conjunction

Coordinating conjunctions, or FANBOYS conjunctions, are among the most useful and powerful connecting words in the English language. If you can remember the nonsense word FANBOYS, you can remember the seven coordinating conjunctions: **f**or, **a**nd, **n**or, **b**ut, **o**r, **y**et, **s**o.

   Pattern: Independent clause, and independent clause.

When a FANBOYS conjunction is used with a comma to separate two clauses, the comma goes before the FANBOYS conjunction.

EXAMPLE   ✗ Andrea had the day off, she went shopping.

   ✔ Andrea had the day off, so she went shopping.

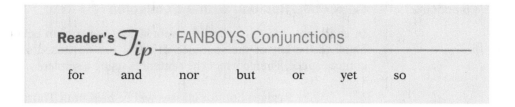

practice 25.3 **Correcting Run-ons with a *Fanboys* Conjunction**

In each sentence, underline the spot where the run-on (fused sentence) or comma splice occurs. Write *RO* in the blank to the left of the sentence if it is a run-on, *CS* if it is a comma splice. Correct each run-on or comma splice by using a comma and a FANBOYS conjunction.

_____ 1. The house was painted brown the shutters and trim were red.

_____

_____ 2. The letter carrier had never seen the two dogs before, she approached them cautiously.

_____

_____ 3. The park was overgrown with weeds the city workers were on strike.

_____

_____ 4. Eating raw eggs used to be considered healthy now people worry about the dangers of salmonella.

_____

_____ 5. Karen is a grouch when she first wakes up, after her first cup of coffee, she feels human again.

_____

Method 3: Semicolon

Using a semicolon to join clauses works best with ideas that are closely connected and need no transitional word to explain the connection between them. The semicolon is the grammatical equivalent of a period, but the first letter of the clause after the semicolon is *not* capitalized.

> **Pattern:** <u>Independent clause</u>; <u>independent clause</u>.

The semicolon goes between the two clauses.

EXAMPLE

✗ The book section is to the right as patrons enter the library, journals and periodicals are to the left.

✔ The book section is to the right as patrons enter the library; journals and periodicals are to the left.

practice 25.4   **Correcting Run-ons with a Semicolon**

In each sentence, underline the spot where the run-on occurs. Write *RO* in the blank to the left of the sentence if it is a run-on (fused sentence), *CS* if it is a comma splice. Then correct the sentences using a semicolon alone.

_____   1. Registration for classes will be held until Thursday the late registration period runs through Monday.

_____

_____   2. Stephanie bought a five-year-old Toyota, newer cars were too expensive.

_____

_____   3. Marcy fell from a swing and broke her arm at recess, the school could not immediately reach either of her parents.

_____

_____   4. Jason buys a lottery ticket every week, he calls it his retirement plan.

_____

_____   5. Books lined the shelves in the small classroom, maps were displayed on the walls.

_____

Method 4: Semicolon and Transitional Expression

A run-on sentence may also be corrected with a connecting word or phrase that functions as a transitional expression, underscoring the relationship between the two clauses.

> **Pattern:** <u>Independent clause</u>; therefore, <u>independent clause</u>.

A semicolon precedes the transitional expression and a comma follows it. With the words *thus* and *then*, the comma is often omitted.

EXAMPLE

✗ Traffic was heavy the rain made it almost impossible to see the road.

✔ Traffic was heavy; furthermore, the rain made it almost impossible to see the road.

Commonly Used Dependent Words

accordingly	furthermore	nevertheless
after	how	what
also	however	of course
as a result	in addition	on the other hand
besides	in fact	then
finally	instead	therefore
for example	meanwhile	thus
for instance	namely	

practice 25.5   **Correcting Run-ons with a Semicolon and Transitional Expression**

In each sentence, underline the spot where the run-on occurs. Write *RO* in the blank to the left of the sentence if it is a run-on (fused sentence), *CS* if it is a comma splice. Then correct the sentence using a semicolon and an appropriate transitional expression.

_____ 1. Denice thought she could get by without studying, her grades suffered.

_____

_____ 2. The lake was beautiful and clear, cans, bottles, and fast-food wrappers littered the beach alongside it.

_____

_____ 3. Philip looked at expensive stereo equipment for hours, he decided that what he had was good enough.

_____

_____ 4. Dogs have lost their position as the most popular pet, more Americans now have cats than dogs.

_____

_____ 5. In relatively wealthy countries, people can afford to have pets in some countries, dogs and cats are used as food.

_____

Method 5: Dependent Word

Placing a dependent word in front of an independent clause makes it a dependent clause, a clause that can no longer stand on its own as a sentence. It now *depends* on the sentence it is attached to and can no longer be separated from it.

EXAMPLE   Each of the independent clauses shown below stands on its own as a sentence.

independent clause   independent clause
The orchestra began to play. Fireworks appeared in the night sky.

When the word *as* is added to the first clause, it becomes a *dependent clause*. Now, it cannot stand on its own but must depend on—or remain attached to—the independent clause.

dependent clause   independent clause
As the orchestra began to play, fireworks appeared in the night sky.

Two Patterns Using the Dependent Clause Sentences containing dependent clauses take on various patterns. Two of those patterns are shown below. In the first pattern, the dependent clause introduces the sentence and is followed by a comma. In the second pattern, the dependent clause ends the sentence.

Pattern 1: Dependent clause as an introductory clause

As dependent clause, independent clause.

When the dependent clause acts as an introductory clause, a comma follows it.

   ✗   Margaret walked into her office, the phone began to ring.

     ✔   As Margaret walked into her office, the phone began to ring.

Pattern 2: Dependent clause last

Independent clause as dependent clause.

When the dependent clause comes last in the sentence, no comma is used.

✔   Margaret walked into her office as the phone began to ring.

Commonly Used Dependent Words

after	because	that	whenever
although	before	though	where
as	even though	unless	wherever
as if	if	until	which
as long	once	what	while
as soon as	since	whatever	who
as though	so that	when	

practice 25.6   **Correcting Run-ons with a Dependent Word**

In each sentence, underline the spot where the run-on occurs. Write *RO* in the blank to the left of the sentence if it is a run-on (fused sentence), *CS* if it is a comma splice. Correct the following sentences, using a different dependent word with each.

_____   1. The throbbing in Charles's jaw became worse he picked up the phone to call the dentist.

    _____

_____   2. The setting sun painted the lake red-gold, the breeze ruffled its mirrored surface.

    _____

_____   3. A water shortage developed the city imposed a ban on outdoor watering.

    _____

_____   4. The women's softball team has won every game this season, the men's team has turned in its worst performance ever.

    _____

_____   5. Helen won tickets to the concert she is looking for someone to go with her.

    _____

Five Ways to Correct Run-on Sentences

Method 1: Period and Capital Letter

Pattern: Independent clause. Independent clause.

Method 2: Comma and FANBOYS Conjunction

Pattern: Independent clause, and independent clause.

A comma goes before the FANBOYS conjunction in this pattern.

FANBOYS Conjunctions

for	and	nor	but	or	yet	so

Method 3: Semicolon

Pattern: Independent clause; independent clause.

Method 4: Semicolon and Joining Word

Pattern: Independent clause; therefore, independent clause.

A semicolon goes before the joining word and a comma follows it. With the words *thus* and *then*, the comma is often omitted.

Joining Words Used with a Semicolon

also	however	of course
as a result	in addition	on the other hand
besides	in fact	then
finally	instead	therefore
for example	meanwhile	thus

Method 5: Dependent Word

Pattern: Although dependent clause, independent clause.

When a dependent word begins the sentence, a comma is used between the dependent and independent clause.

Pattern: Independent clause when dependent clause.

When the dependent clause ends the sentence, a dependent word separates the clauses.

Dependent Words

although	because	that	whenever
as	before	though	where
as if	if	unless	wherever
as long	once	until	which
as soon as	since	whatever	while
as though	so that	when	who

A Special Case: The Word *That*

Occasionally, the dependent word *that* is implied rather than stated in a sentence. The sentence may look like a run-on, but it is not.

EXAMPLE

✔ The mechanic didn't think he could fix the car.

This sentence could be mistaken for a run-on. "The mechanic didn't think" has a subject, *mechanic,* and a verb, *did think,* and is not preceded by a dependent word. It could stand alone as a sentence. "He could fix the car" also has a subject, *he,* and a verb, *could fix.* It, too, could stand alone as a sentence. But is the sentence a run-on? No. The two thoughts are connected by the implied dependent word *that.* The meaning of the sentence is "The mechanic did not think *that* he could fix the car." Sentences in which the dependent word *that* is implied do not need correction—it is not even necessary to insert the word *that.*

practice 25.7   **Recognizing an Implied *That***

Write *OK* by the sentences that contain the implied word *that.* Write *RO* by the run-ons.

_____ 1. The lawyer had a feeling her client was withholding information.

_____ 2. On the desk sat a mystery novel Becky had not read.

_____ 3. On the desk sat a mystery novel Becky had not read it.

_____ 4. Last night Andrew dreamed he had forgotten to take his final exams.

_____ 5. Jason was afraid his instructor would find out he had cheated on the exam.

_____ 6. In the parking lot, Lauren ran over a nail it went through the bottom of her tire and out the sidewall.

_____ 7. The technician at the tire store told her it would be too dangerous to patch the sidewall.

_____ 8. Lauren had planned to buy a new pair of shoes she bought a tire instead.

_____ 9. As the police officer wrote the ticket, she reminded Bryan his driver's license would need to be renewed in a month.

_____ 10. The ceiling fan cooled the room an air conditioner would have done a better job.

Review Exercises

Complete the Review Exercises to see how well you have learned the skills addressed in this chapter. As you work through the exercises, go back through the chapter to review any of the rules you do not understand completely.

exercise 25.1   Correct the ten run-on sentences below, using each of the five methods at least once. Rewrite the corrected portion of each sentence on the line provided.

1. The bus was late this morning the driver was delayed by a wreck on Miller's Hill Road.

   _____

2. Zandra likes her unusual name she wonders how some parents can saddle their children with names like "Bob" or "Ann."

   _____

3. We met our new neighbors today, their names are Gary and Vicki.

   _____

4. Vijay worked for two hours on his research paper then he went out for pizza with his friends.

   _____

5. The shallow lake near the college is a popular gathering place everyone calls it Lake Knee Deep.

   _____

6. In the clear night sky, the Belt of Orion shone brightly Tasha could not find the Big Dipper.

   _____

7. The Andersens didn't have time for a camping trip, they pitched their tent in the back yard for a weekend mini-vacation.

   _____

8. Sonya's job in the Gaslight Grill pays less than minimum wage her tips, however, more than compensate for her low wages.

   _____

9. The gym was crowded at 6:00 P.M., Bert had to wait fifteen minutes for a treadmill.

   _____

10. Seven fragile cups sat in a row on the cupboard shelf, the eighth lay in pieces on the tile floor.

    _____

exercise 25.2   Correct the ten run-on sentences below, using each of the five methods at least once. Rewrite the corrected portion of each sentence on the line provided.

1. Chandra is a vegetarian her husband complains he has not seen a hamburger for months.

_____

2. Alex answered the telephone only silence greeted him on the other end.

_____

3. Jan likes blues and rock, her husband prefers Beethoven and Bach.

_____

4. Highlighters are useful for marking textbooks experts say only 10 to 20 percent of the material should be highlighted.

_____

5. Orientation and study skills courses are a good way to learn to adjust to the demands of college many students say they benefit from such courses.

_____

6. A roll of pennies contains fifty pennies a roll of nickels contains only forty nickels.

_____

7. Bank tellers count money rapidly they always count it twice to make sure the amount is correct.

_____

8. Smoke billowed from the forest fire the sky turned a muddy brown.

_____

9. Annette always forgot to water the plants on her porch they eventually died.

_____

10. Tyler is an optimist he always looks at the positive side of any situation.

_____

26 Sentence Fragments

A mirror breaks, and someone screams
In horror and in fright.
Must be your English teacher,
Who thinks fragments are a blight.

The woman in the photograph on chapter opener seems horrified by the fragments of broken mirror that reflect her image. Perhaps she is superstitious and believes that a broken mirror will bring seven years' bad luck. Of course, she could also be an English professor, suddenly reminded of the horror of sentence fragments.

What Is a Sentence Fragment?

A **sentence fragment** is an incomplete sentence. It may be a dependent clause that cannot stand on its own, or it may lack a subject, a verb, or both. If you read a fragment by itself, without the other sentences that surround it, you will usually recognize that it does not express a complete thought. It is only a part, or fragment, of a sentence.

EXAMPLE

✗ Many animals hibernate in winter. *Including woodchucks, ground squirrels, and frogs.*

✗ On Saturday morning, Alvin spent an hour raking leaves. *And sweeping them from his carport.*

The italicized word groups are sentence fragments—pieces of sentences that cannot stand alone.

Dependent Clause Fragments

✗ Jarrod said he did not finish his term paper. *Because his computer had crashed.*

✗ *When Alice arrived at 10:15.* The exam had already started.

Each of the italicized fragments above is a **dependent clause fragment.** A dependent clause fragment always begins with a dependent word. To fix a dependent clause fragment, attach it to a complete sentence. Removing the dependent word will also fix the fragment, but the dependent word may be necessary to strengthen the logical connection between two ideas.

✔ Jarrod did not finish his term paper because his computer had crashed.

✔ Jarrod did not finish his term paper. His computer had crashed.

✔ When Alice arrived at 10:15, the exam had already started.

✔ Alice arrived at 10:15. The exam had already started.

Reader's *Tip* — Punctuation Pointer

Use a comma to attach a dependent clause fragment at the beginning of a sentence.

Commonly Used Dependent Words

after	how	what
although	if	when
as	once	whenever
as if	since	where
as long as	so that	wherever
as soon as	that	which
because	though	while
before	unless	who
even though	until	whoever

practice 26.1

Correcting Dependent Clause Fragments

Correct the dependent clause fragments in the following exercise by attaching them to an independent clause. Write the corrected portion of each sentence on the line provided.

1. Tamika complained that her car did not run well. Unless she used premium gasoline.

   _____

2. Ray wondered what was wrong with the compact disc changer. That he had bought just two weeks ago.

   _____

3. Since Andrea is cold-natured and her roommate is not. They are always battling over the thermostat.

   _____

4. If Jeff did not set his clock fifteen minutes fast. He might never be on time.

   _____

5. The suspect admitted that she had shot her husband. Because the poison she was giving him had not worked quickly enough.

   _____

Verbal Phrase Fragments (*to*, -*ing*, and -*ed*)

✗ *To relax and to develop her creative abilities.* Ann decided to take an art class.

✗ Anita's dog was a familiar sight in the neighborhood. *Running through yards and tearing up flowerbeds.*

✗ *Bored by his job in a warehouse.* Evan bought a lawn mower and cut grass to earn money.

The examples above are **verbal phrase fragments.** A verbal phrase fragment begins with a verb form that is not used as a main verb. Verbal phrase fragments include *to* fragments, *-ing* fragments, and *-ed/-en* fragments.

Correct verbal phrase fragments by attaching them to a complete sentence.

✔ Anita's dog was a familiar sight in the neighborhood, running through yards and tearing up flowerbeds.

✔ To relax and to develop her creative abilities, Ann decided to take an art class.

✔ Bored by his job in a warehouse, Evan bought a lawn mower and cut grass to earn money.

to **Fragments** Correct *to* fragments by connecting them to a sentence or by adding a subject and verb, as shown in the examples below.

EXAMPLE

✗ The auto repair shop has begun to open on weekends. To accommodate customers who work during the week.

✔ The auto repair shop has begun to open on weekends to accommodate customers who work during the week.

✗ To ensure that we would not forget to tip him. The server asked, "Do you want change back?"

✔ To ensure that we would not forget to tip him, the server asked, "Do you want change back?"

✗ James programmed his VCR before he left the house. To make sure he would not miss even one inning of the ball game.

✔ James programmed his VCR before he left the house. He wanted to make sure he would not miss even one inning of the ball game.

Reader's Tip —— Punctuation Pointer ————————

A *to* fragment attached to the beginning of a sentence is followed by a comma because it is an introductory phrase. A *to* fragment connected to the end of the sentence needs no comma.

---

practice 26.2 **Correcting *to* Fragments**

Underline and correct the *to* fragments in the following exercise. Write the corrected portion of each sentence on the line provided.

1. To give his students plenty of writing practice. The teacher assigned journals.

   _____

2. To give herself a break from the computer. Nora took her dog for a walk.

   _____

3. Samuel was surprised. To see the package outside his door.

_____

4. To mark his place in his book. Henry used a dollar bill.

_____

5. Radio stations often hold contests. To keep listeners tuned in.

_____

-ing Fragments

To correct an -*ing* fragment, connect it to the rest of the sentence with a comma. You may also correct it by adding a subject and a helping verb.

✗ Peering out the window and checking her watch every five minutes. Charlene waited for her guests to arrive.

✔ Peering out the window and checking her watch every five minutes, Charlene waited for her guests to arrive.

✗ Rachel spent the afternoon at home. Listening to her new CD and reading magazines.

✔ Rachel spent the afternoon at home, listening to her new CD and reading magazines.

Sometimes, the -*ing* word may be the second or third word in the fragment.

✗ James hopped into his car and left the restaurant's parking lot. Not realizing that he had left his bucket of chicken on top of the car.

✔ James hopped into his car and left the restaurant's parking lot, not realizing that he had left his bucket of chicken on top of the car.

Reader's _Tip_ ——— Punctuation Pointer

Usually, -*ing* fragments can be connected to the rest of the sentence with a comma. When the -*ing* fragment acts as an introductory element, place a comma after it. When you add it to the end of a sentence, lead into it with a comma.

---

practice 26.3 | **Correcting -ing Fragments**

Underline and correct the -*ing* fragments in the following exercise. Write the corrected portion of each sentence on the line provided.

1. Puffing as if she had run a marathon. Bonita completed her first lap on the circular track.

_____

2. The vines grew thick on the abandoned house. Obscuring the windows and part of the front door.

_____

3. Riding in the back of the pickup truck. The dog wobbled unsteadily as his owner rounded a curve.

_____

4. Sneaking cigarettes, playing her music too loud, and visiting a male resident after curfew. Aunt Matilda has broken most of the nursing home's rules.

_____

5. Leslie complains that her neighbor's children are allowed to run wild. Playing loudly in the street until past midnight.

_____

-ed and -en Fragments Another kind of fragment begins with an -ed or -en verb form, or past participle. If the verb is a regular verb, the verb form will end in -ed, like the verbs *walked, called,* and *plotted.* If the verb is irregular, then the verb form will end in -en or in another irregular ending. *Broken, grown, found, bought,* and *written* are some of these forms. (For other examples, see the list of irregular verbs in Chapter 22.) This type of fragment is usually corrected by connecting it to a complete sentence.

✗ Spaced evenly and set in rows. The desks seemed ready for the fall term.

✔ Spaced evenly and set in rows, the desks seemed ready for the fall term.

✗ Everyone looked at the white rabbit. Held by the top-hatted magician.

✔ Everyone looked at the white rabbit held by the top-hatted magician.

✗ Caught with his car full of stolen property. The thief could only confess.

✔ Caught with his car full of stolen property, the thief could only confess.

practice 26.4 **Correcting -ed and -en Fragments**

Underline and correct the -ed and -en fragments in the following exercise. Write the corrected portion of each sentence on the line provided.

1. Next week, students are invited to a career fair and resumé workshop. Presented by the college's career counseling office.

_____

2. Cleaned and pressed at the local cleaners. Eldon's old sport coat looked like new.

_____

3. Drawn by the smell of food. The dog decided to join our picnic.

_____

4. Kevin has kept his old model trains. Stored on a shelf in a closet in his parents' house.

_____

5. Encouraged by her parents. Dawn decided to apply for the scholarship.

_____

Missing-Subject Fragments

Fragments beginning with a joining word such as *and, or, but,* or *then* followed by a verb are **missing-subject fragments.** The subject of the verb is usually in a previous sentence. Connect the fragment to the sentence or add a subject to begin a new sentence.

✗ Woodrow held up his prize fish and posed for the camera. Then fell off the end of the fishing pier.

✔ Woodrow held up his prize fish and posed for the camera, then fell off the end of the fishing pier.

✗ The hurricane changed course and seemed to falter. But gathered strength again before it hit the coast.

✔ The hurricane changed course and seemed to falter but gathered strength again before it hit the coast.

✔ The hurricane changed course and seemed to falter. But it gathered strength again before it hit the coast.

practice 26.5   **Correcting Missing-Subject Fragments**

Underline and correct the missing-subject fragments in the following exercise. Write the corrected portion of each sentence on the line provided.

1. The cat ate the hamburger. But refused the bun.

_____

2. The baseball player emerged from the dugout. And waved his cap to acknowledge the cheering fans.

_____

3. At the side of the road, the collie looked both ways. Then crossed the street.

_____

4. On her days off, Ebony reads a book. Or surfs the Internet on her computer.

_____

5. Every morning, a wily squirrel bounds into Maurice's backyard and heads for the bird feeder. Then eats the food Maurice has put out for the birds.

_____

Reader's *Tip* ——— Real-World Writing: Is it Okay to Start a Sentence with *But?*

Yes and no. Grammatically, it is correct to start a sentence with *but* or any other **FANBOYS** conjunction. However, your instructors may discourage the practice for two good reasons.

1. Beginning a sentence with *but* is an informal technique. It may work in personal essays but should not be used in formal compositions such as research papers. (This text, you may have noticed, takes an informal, conversational approach, addressing you directly and occasionally using a **FANBOYS** conjunction to begin a sentence.)
2. Using *but* to begin a sentence can be addictive. *But* is the strongest contrast signal in our language, and it's easy to overuse.

The bottom line: Use conjunctions to begin sentences only if your instructor gives the green light, and then use them sparingly.

Example and Exception Fragments

Fragments often occur when a writer decides to add an example or note an exception. Example fragments often begin with *such as, including, like, for example,* or *for instance.* Exception fragments often begin with *not, except, unless, without,* or *in spite of.* To fix the fragment, connect it to the sentence with which it logically belongs. If the fragment begins with *for example* or *for instance,* it is often best to make the fragment into a separate sentence.

✗ Hollis becomes nervous in high-pressure situations. Such as exams and interviews.

✔ Hollis becomes nervous in high-pressure situations, such as exams and interviews.

✗ Lindsay is trying to put herself through college. Without any help from her parents.

✔ Lindsay is trying to put herself through college without any help from her parents.

✗ Classes with labs require more time than other classes. For example, biology and French.

✔ Classes with labs require more time than other classes. For example, biology and French take more of my study time than history or math.

Reader's $\mathcal{T}ip$ ── Punctuation Pointer

Usually, you can connect fragments beginning with *such as, including, not, especially,* and *in spite of* with a comma, and fragments beginning with *except, unless, without,* and *like* with no punctuation.

A fragment beginning with *for example* or *for instance* may be attached with a comma if it immediately follows the idea it illustrates: **The chef enjoyed cooking with beans, for example, lima beans, garbanzo beans, and kidney beans.** If the idea that the example illustrates is expressed earlier in the sentence, place the example in a new sentence: **Beans are the specialty of the house at Rizzoli's Restaurant. For example, the chef makes delicious dishes from lima beans, garbanzo beans, and kidney beans.**

practice 26.6   ## Correcting Example and Exception Fragments

Underline and correct the example and exception fragments in the following exercise. Write the correction on the line provided.

1. Natalie sets aside specific times to study and lets nothing interfere with her plans. Unless something more interesting comes along.

   _____

2. Leonard complained that nothing grew in his garden. Except weeds.

   _____

3. Thirty years ago, office workers had to get along without modern equipment. Such as computers, copiers, and fax machines.

   _____

4. On New Year's Eve, Alexandra vowed to give up all sweets. Especially chocolate.

   _____

5. If everyone would cooperate, it would be easy to solve some of the community's problems. For example, litter on public streets.

   _____

Prepositional Phrase Fragments

A prepositional phrase, alone or within a series, cannot function as a sentence. Correct a prepositional phrase fragment by connecting it to a sentence with which it logically belongs.

✗ Hamilton finally found his lost history book. In a large mud puddle on the street beside the student union.

✔ Hamilton finally found his lost history book in a large mud puddle on the street beside the student union.

✗ On her way to a three o'clock job interview at Stanfield Corporation. Melanie became lost.

✔ On her way to a three o'clock job interview at Stanfield Corporation, Melanie became lost.

Reader's *Tip* ──── Punctuation Pointer
──

Use a comma behind introductory prepositional phrases. No punctuation is required to connect a prepositional phrase to the end of a sentence.

---

practice 26.7 **Correcting Prepositional Phrase Fragments**

Underline and correct each of the following prepositional phrase fragments. Write your correction on the line provided.

1. After searching frantically for half an hour, Amanda finally found her lost keys. Under a bunch of bananas on the kitchen counter.

   _____

2. In a hanging philodendron on the front porch. The bird had built her nest.

   _____

3. On a sandy beach with a frosty strawberry slush in her hand. Morgan found contentment.

   _____

4. Because she had stayed up all night to study, Deb fell asleep. During the exam.

   _____

5. In a pond beyond the city limits. James and his father fish on the weekends.

   _____

Review Exercises

Complete the Review Exercises to see how well you have learned the skills addressed in this chapter. As you work through the exercises, go back through the chapter to review any of the rules you do not understand completely.

exercise 26.1   Underline and correct each fragment in the following exercise. Write your correction on the line provided.

1. In their cabin beside the lake. The Millers displayed photos of fish they had caught and released.

_____

2. Because of numerous complaints. The city council passed a law prohibiting obscene bumper stickers.

_____

3. Tom enjoys all aspects of cooking. Except chopping onions and garlic.

_____

4. Uncle Walter raised his parrot lovingly. Giving it affection and teaching it to curse in seven languages.

_____

5. It took three people to carry the prize-winning pumpkin. Which weighed almost 100 pounds.

_____

6. The preschool teacher says jokingly that Sharma is a born rebel. Because she always colors outside the lines.

_____

7. Found beside a dumpster. The coffee table looks good with a coat of paint.

_____

8. Harriet went over to the candy dish. And picked out all the licorice drops.

_____

9. The child tried to stay awake all night. To see if the tooth fairy was real.

_____

10. We left the house forty-five minutes early. To take the car to the dealership.

_____

exercise 26.2   Underline and correct each fragment in the following exercise. Write your correction on the line provided.

1. Except for the shower, which produced just a small dribble of water. The hotel room was comfortable and inviting.

    _____

2. Although Mu Lan is happy to be attending college in the United States. She misses her family in Beijing.

    _____

3. When they went on vacation, the Colesons packed everything they thought they would need. But did not consider the possibility of snow.

    _____

4. The young man wore a green shirt. That said, "My parents were kidnapped by aliens and all I got was this lousy T-shirt."

    _____

5. Worn through at the toe and battered from use. Jennifer's sneakers need to be replaced.

    _____

6. With the top down and the music turned up loud. Anita sailed down the moonlit highway.

    _____

7. Cheering loudly and clapping rhythmically. The audience demanded an encore.

    _____

8. Interrupted by dozens of long commercials. The TV show ground slowly toward its conclusion.

    _____

9. Ayesha went to the library to return a book. That was three weeks overdue.

    _____

10. At the garage sale, Mark looked at the worn wooden desk. And wondered if it would fit into the back of his vehicle.

    _____

27 Pronoun Case

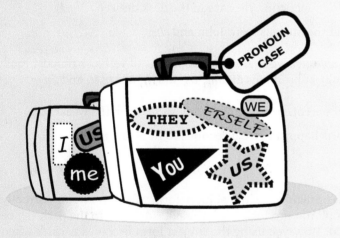

I travel with a pronoun case;
I bring myself and I.
As you and he hop in my case,
Whoever waves goodbye.

We, them, himself, herself, and who
Pile in with she and him.
Someday I'd like to travel light;
The chances seem quite slim.

But when we reach the station,
All getting on the bus,
I look for fellow travelers,
And no one's here but us.

Pronouns are words that stand in for nouns or for other pronouns. They are useful words that keep writers and speakers from tedious repetition of words.

However, the rules that govern pronoun use are complex, and confusion over pronoun use is common. If you have ever hesitated between "Stacy and me" or "Stacy and I," or wondered whether to say "between you and I" or "between you and me," this chapter will help you find the answers.

Subject and Object Pronouns

Personal pronouns (*I, we, you, he, she it, they*) refer to specific people or things. These pronouns take different forms, called **cases,** as they perform different jobs in a sentence. Look at the example that follows to see how the first person pronoun *I* changes form as its role in a sentence changes.

✔ *I* borrowed a book from the library and forgot about it. Early this week, the library sent *me* a notice saying the book was overdue.

Subject pronouns (*the subjective case*) are used as subjects or subject complements. Some commonly used subject pronouns are *I, we, you, he, she, it,* and *they.*

✔ *I* know James well; *we* have been friends for years.

✔ If *you* are looking for paper clips, *they* are in the desk drawer.

✔ Allison was told that the finalists were John and *she.*

Object pronouns (*the objective case*) are used as objects of verbs or prepositions. Some commonly used object pronouns are *me, us, you, him, her, it,* and *them.*

✔ Rachel spoke to her parents and promised to visit *them* on the weekend.

✔ The police officer was happy to give directions to Raul and *me.*

Subject Pronouns

In most instances, you probably use the subject form of the pronoun correctly without thinking about it. You probably haven't said, "Me went to the park" since you were three years old. However, using the subject form becomes trickier when a *compound subject* is used. Is it "Tiffany and her went to the concert" or "Tiffany and she went to the concert"? Usually, trying the sentence with the pronoun alone will help you hear the correct answer. Without *Tiffany and,* the sentence becomes clear. "*She* went to the concert" is correct, not "*Her* went to the concert."

EXAMPLE   ? *Him and his brother* went hunting this morning.

Step 1: To determine if the sentence is correct, try the pronoun alone.

✗ *Him* ~~and his brother~~ went hunting this morning.

✗ *Him* went hunting this morning.

Step 2: If the pronoun sounds incorrect, try changing the form.

✔ *He* went hunting this morning.

✔ *He and his brother* went hunting this morning. (corrected sentence)

practice 27.1   ## Using Subject Pronouns

Underline the correct pronoun in each of the following sentences. To determine the correct pronoun form, try the pronoun alone without the compound element.

1. Cynthia and (I, me) played two games of tennis yesterday afternoon.

2. Cecil and (they, them) are meeting us over at the new ice-skating rink.

3. I heard that Wally and (she, her) had made the highest grades in class.

4. (He and I, Him and me) have been friends since grade school.

5. Do you think that you and (I, me) could study our grammar together tomorrow?

Subject Pronouns with Linking Verbs
"Hello?"
"May I speak to Tanisha Jones, please?"
"This is she."
"Hello, Tanisha, this is Randall Groover from your biology class. I was wondering . . ."

This polite exchange is typical of the way many telephone conversations begin, and it illustrates a rule that many people use in telephone conversations but ignore otherwise: When a pronoun renames the subject (that is, when it is a *subject complement*) and follows the verb *to be* or any *linking verb,* that pronoun takes the subject form.

EXAMPLE   ✔ The keynote   *subject* speaker   *linking verb* will be   *subject complement* she. (not *her*)

✔ It is *I*. (not *me*)

✔ If you are looking for Mr. Smith, that is *he* in the blue jacket. (not *him*)

✔ Ms. Smith, you say it was the defendant who robbed you. Look at him carefully. Can you be absolutely sure it was *he*? (not *him*)

practice 27.2   ## Using Subject Pronouns after Linking Verbs

In each sentence, underline the correct pronoun.

1. I would have spoken to Randy, but I wasn't sure that it was (he, him).

2. If you need to speak with the manager, that is (she, her) at the desk by the window.

    3. You said you were looking for your gloves. Are these (they, them)?

    4. "Who is it?" said Sandra. "It is (I, me)," said Ken.

    5. I have talked to Professor Smalls before, but I did not know at the time that it was (she, her).

Object Pronouns

Object pronouns are used as objects of verbs and prepositions. Again, problems with object pronouns commonly occur in compound constructions. These problems can usually be resolved by isolating the pronoun.

EXAMPLE

  ?   The supervisor asked *Lou and I* to work overtime.

  ✗   The supervisor asked Lou and *I* to work overtime.

  ✗   The supervisor asked *I* to work overtime.

  ✔   The supervisor asked *Lou and me* to work overtime.

Object Pronouns with between Object pronouns always follow the preposition *between*. Thus, it is always *between you and me, between us and them, between him and her, between Larry and him.*

  ✗   Just between you and *I*, I heard that Alan has found a new job in Phoenix.

  ✔   Just between you and *me*, I heard that Alan has found a new job in Phoenix.

  ✗   The argument was between Leo and *she;* I tried to stay out of it.

  ✔   The argument was between Leo and *her;* I tried to stay out of it.

Reader's *Tip*   Grammar Alert

Pronouns are often misused with *between*. Remember to use the object form: between you and *me, him, her,* or *them.*

practice 27.3   **Using Object Pronouns**

Underline the correct pronoun in each of the following sentences.

1. Renata told Sandra and (I, me) where to recycle our glass bottles and aluminum cans.

2. When we went to see the performance at the Grand Opera House, Fran sat between Gerard and (I, me).

3. Anna gave Clay and (she, her) an extra pair of tickets to Tuesday's performance of *Big River.*

4. Someone told Catherine and (I, me) that the wildlife park was worth visiting.

5. It is a small apartment, but it is perfect for Connie and (he, him).

28 Pronoun Agreement, Reference, and Point of View

Abbott:	I'm telling you Who is on first.
Costello:	Well, I'm asking YOU who's on first!
Abbott:	That's the man's name.
Costello:	That's who's name?
Abbott:	Yes.
Costello:	Well, go ahead and tell me.
Abbott:	Who.
Costello:	The guy on first.
Abbott:	Who!

From Abbott and Costello's "Who's on First?"

Abbott and Costello's classic comedy routine deliberately causes confusion through use of pronouns. Sometimes, writers unintentionally cause confusion through errors in pronoun reference, agreement, and point of view. Each sentence following contains a pronoun error. Can you figure out why the pronouns in bold type are incorrect?

✘ The coffee shop usually closes at midnight, but on Sundays, **they** close at 6:00 P.M.

✘ Josh told Marquez that **he** needed to work on his social skills.

✘ Clara did not get the job she wanted, but what can **you** expect if you go to an interview in jeans and a ripped T-shirt?

Each of the sentences above contains a pronoun error that could cause confusion for the reader. The first sentence contains an error in pronoun agreement. The pronoun *they* is plural, but the word it refers to is singular. Here is the corrected sentence:

✔ The coffee shop usually closes at midnight, but on Sundays, it closes at 6:00 P.M.

The second sentence contains an error in pronoun reference. The reader cannot be sure whether *he* refers to Josh or Marquez. The corrected sentence clears up the confusion:

✔ Josh told Marquez, "I need to work on my social skills."

The third sentence contains an error in pronoun point of view. The writer switches from the third person (the job *she* wanted) to the second person (what can *you* expect).

✔ Clara did not get the job she wanted, but what can she expect if she goes to an interview in jeans and a ripped T-shirt?

Keeping your writing free of errors in pronoun agreement, reference, and point of view ensures that your reader will move through your work smoothly and without confusion.

Pronoun Agreement

Pronoun agreement means that a pronoun must agree in number with the word it refers to. In other words, a singular pronoun can refer only to a singular noun or pronoun, and a plural pronoun can refer only to a plural noun or pronoun.

The word that a pronoun refers to is called its **antecedent.** An antecedent may be a noun or pronoun, or even a compound construction, such as *pens and pencils* or *Sam or Lilah.*

EXAMPLE

                       antecedent   pronoun

✔ Julian picked up the <u>hammer</u> and put <u>it</u> in the toolbox.

In the sentence above, the singular pronoun *it* refers to one word in the sentence, the singular word *hammer.*

                        antecedent   pronoun
✔ Julian picked up the <u>upholstery tacks</u> and put <u>them</u> in the toolbox.

In the above sentence, the plural pronoun *them* refers to the plural antecedent *tacks*.

                                    antecedent   pronoun
✔ Julian picked up <u>the measuring tape and the staple gun</u> and put <u>them</u> in the toolbox.

Above, the plural pronoun *them* refers to the compound antecedent *measuring tape and staple gun*.

Problems in Pronoun Agreement

Errors in pronoun agreement occur when a singular pronoun is used to refer to a plural word or when a plural pronoun is used to refer to a singular word.

EXAMPLE   **Error in Pronoun Agreement:**
                          singular   plural
✘ Sarita went to the <u>post office</u>, but <u>they</u> were already closed.

Corrected:
                          singular   singular
✔ Sarita went to the <u>post office</u>, but <u>it</u> was already closed.

Error in Pronoun Agreement:
                    plural   singular
✘ Rick ate the <u>cookies</u> even though he knew <u>it wasn't</u> good for him.

Corrected:
                    plural   plural
✔ Rick ate the <u>cookies</u> even though he knew <u>they weren't</u> good for him.

                    plural   reworded to eliminate pronoun
✔ Rick ate the <u>cookies</u> even though he knew <u>eating sweets</u> wasn't good for him.

practice 28.1   **Making Pronouns Agree**

Underline the correct pronoun in each sentence below.

1. The tenor had a rich, strong voice. (It, They) filled the small auditorium without the aid of a microphone.

2. Sharon is prone to migraines, but she has found that avoiding caffeine and chocolate keeps (it, them) to a minimum.

3. My mother likes to shop at Barton's because (it is, they are) locally owned.

4. Sanjay lost his driver's license last week; today he is going to the Division of Motor Vehicles to have (it, them) replaced.

5. The leaves on the peace lily have lost (its, their) shine.

Pronoun Agreement with Indefinite Pronouns

The following indefinite pronouns are always plural.

both   few   many   several

EXAMPLE

✔ <u>Both</u> of the children had chocolate on <u>their</u> faces.
   plural (Both), plural (their)

✔ <u>Many</u> of the courses in the catalog should be removed because <u>they</u> are seldom offered.
   plural (Many), plural (they)

The following indefinite pronouns are singular or plural, depending on their antecedents.

  all   any   most   none   some

EXAMPLE

✔ <u>All</u> of the <u>pines</u> were cut down because <u>they</u> were diseased.
   plural (All), plural (pines), plural (they)

✔ We ate <u>all</u> of the noodle <u>soup</u> in one sitting. <u>It</u> was delicious.
   singular (all), singular (soup), singular (It)

✔ <u>None</u> of the <u>children</u> seemed afraid as <u>they</u> came forward to pet the boa constrictor.
   plural (None), plural (children), plural (they)

✔ <u>None</u> of the <u>coffee</u> had been drunk, but Karen threw <u>it</u> away because <u>it</u> was starting to look like sludge.
   singular (None), singular (coffee), singular (it), singular (it)

Reader's *Tip* ── Memory Jogger

Remember the singular indefinite pronouns more easily by grouping them:

    each   all the *bodies*

    either   all the *ones*

    neither   all the *things*

The following indefinite pronouns are always singular.

anybody	either	neither	one
anyone	everybody	nobody	somebody
anything	everyone	no one	someone
each	everything	nothing	something

EXAMPLE

✘ <u>Somebody</u> called you, but <u>they</u> didn't leave a message.
   singular (Somebody), plural (they)

✔ <u>Somebody</u> called you, but <u>he</u> didn't leave a message.
   singular (Somebody), singular (he)

✘ <u>Each</u> of the team members has <u>their</u> own particular strength.
   singular (Each), plural (their)

✔ <u>Each</u> of the team members has <u>her</u> own particular strength.
   singular (Each), singular (her)

Pronouns and Gender Fairness

Gender fairness means using gender-neutral terms such as *server, police officer,* and *firefighter.* It means not stereotyping professions: Gary Kubach is a *nurse,* not a *male nurse;* Sarita Gray is a *doctor,* not a *woman doctor.* Naturally, gender fairness also includes avoiding descriptions of women solely in terms of their looks or of men solely in terms of their bank accounts. Those things are fairly simple. The area of gender fairness and pronouns, however, requires more thought. Using *he or she* or *his or her* is often awkward, and constructions such as *he/she* or *(s)he* are downright ungraceful. How, then, can a writer's language be unbiased, graceful, and grammatically correct, all at the same time? There are several possible solutions.

EXAMPLE

          singular   plural
✗ <u>Nobody</u> has received <u>their</u> grades from the last term yet.

This sentence contains an error in pronoun agreement. The singular indefinite pronoun *nobody* does not agree with the plural pronoun *their.* The following section shows several ways to correct pronoun agreement errors such as this one while remaining gender-fair.

    Solution 1: Choose a gender and stay with it throughout a single example or paragraph. Then, in your next example or paragraph, switch to the other gender.

          singular   plural
✗ <u>Nobody</u> has received <u>their</u> grades from the last term yet.
          singular   singular
✔ <u>Nobody</u> has received <u>his</u> grades from the last term yet.
          singular   singular
✔ <u>Nobody</u> has received <u>her</u> grades from the last term yet.

    Solution 2: Use a "his or her" construction. Because this solution is grammatically correct but stylistically awkward, use it in situations where you will not have to repeat the construction.

          singular   plural
✗ <u>Nobody</u> has received <u>their</u> grades from the last term yet.
          singular   singular
✔ <u>Nobody</u> has received <u>his or her</u> grades from the last term yet.

    Solution 3: Use plural rather than singular constructions.

          singular   plural
✗ <u>Nobody</u> has received <u>their</u> grades from the last term yet.

          plural   plural
✔ The <u>students</u> have not received <u>their</u> grades from the last term yet.

    Solution 4: Remove the pronoun agreement problem by removing the pronoun.

          singular   plural
✗ <u>Nobody</u> has received <u>their</u> grades from the last term yet.

✔ Nobody has received grades from the last term yet.

   singular   singular   plural
✗ <u>Each</u> manager has the same job description, yet <u>each</u> has developed <u>their</u> own style.

✔ Each manager has the same job description, yet each has developed an individual style.

practice 28.2   **Making Pronouns Agree**

Correct the pronoun agreement errors in each sentence below. Use all four of the solutions previously listed.

1. Both of the restaurant patrons had finished his coffee.

   _____

2. I do not agree with you, but everybody is entitled to their own opinion.

   _____

3. Does everybody know what their schedule will be for next month?

   _____

4. Nobody on the *Titanic* realized that the trip might be their last.

   _____

5. Neither of the prisoners had seen their children for months.

   _____

6. Each member of the audience took away their own special memory of the singer's performance.

   _____

7. If one of the librarians is not busy, maybe they can help you.

   _____

8. Everyone ate as if they were starving.

   _____

9. If someone finds my wallet, maybe they will turn it in.

   _____

10. Few of the students finished his or her test.

    _____

Pronoun Reference

If a sentence has problems with **pronoun reference,** then either a pronoun has no antecedent or it has more than one possible antecedent.

Pronoun Reference Problem: No Antecedent

A pronoun that does not logically refer to any noun or pronoun has no antecedent.

EXAMPLE   ✘   When I went to the bank to cash my check, *she* asked for two forms of identi-fication.

        ✘   Mary applied for a scholarship, but *they* said she didn't meet the requirements.

To correct the problem, replace the pronoun with a more specific word.

        ✔   When I went to the bank to cash my check, *the teller* asked for two forms of identification.

        ✔   Mary applied for a scholarship, but *the committee* said she didn't meet the requirements.

practice 28.3   **Correcting Problems in Pronoun Reference**

Correct the pronoun reference problems in each of the following sentences.

1. Carrie tried to avoid taking college algebra, but they said she had to have it.

   _____

2. We had looked forward to the concert, but they were so loud we could not enjoy the music.

   _____

3. When Tomas went to the FotoMart to pick up his vacation photographs, they gave him pictures of a baby's christening by mistake.

   _____

4. April stopped by the dry cleaners on her way home from work, but her husband had already picked it up.

   _____

5. James called the computer repair shop after he turned it on and could not get his mouse or his keyboard to work.

   _____

Editing Exercises: Basic Grammar

The following exercises allow you to test the grammar skills you have learned in Chapters 22 through 28. The exercises focus on verbs, pronouns, run-on sentences, and sentence fragments.

Basic Grammar: Five Editing Exercises

editing
exercise 28.1 **Subject-Verb Agreement and Run-ons**

In the following paragraph, correct the subject-verb agreement errors and run-ons.

6 subject-verb agreement errors

2 run-on sentences

2 comma splices

¹Why does men find the entire question of clothing so much simpler than women do? ²The answer lie in the differing approach of each sex toward clothing. ³Most women uses the "outfit" concept of dressing. ⁴In this system, each of a woman's dresses, sweaters, and skirts have to be accessorized with the proper shoes, belt, undergarments, jewelry, and hosiery. ⁵A woman may own a mid-calf black skirt, a knee-length blue dress, and tan slacks, however, only her long slip, silver-buckled belt, and black shoes go with the mid-calf black skirt. ⁶If she chooses to wear the blue dress or tan slacks, she must choose a different slip, belt, and shoes the system is complicated, so women spend a lot of time choosing their clothing. ⁷Men, on the other hand, follows the "uniform" concept of dressing. ⁸If the dress code in his office require a man to wear a shirt and tie, he will wear a shirt, a tie, and a pair of pants every day. ⁹His underwear will go with any shirt or pair of pants he has in his wardrobe except for coordinating the color of his tie with the color of his shirt, he has little to worry about. ¹⁰Men spend less time thinking about what they wear, their system of choosing clothes is a simpler one.

_____ _____
_____ _____
_____ _____
_____ _____
_____ _____

editing
exercise 28.2 **Run-ons and Fragments**

In the following paragraph, correct the fragments, run-ons, and comma splices.

5 fragments

2 run-ons

3 comma splices

¹Last spring, when I decided to plant a vegetable garden. ²I discovered that gardening has its unpleasant aspects. ³Two hours in the garden convinced me of one fact gardening is a dirty job. ⁴Even though I wore gardening gloves, dirt found its way under my fingernails, my shoes and jeans were caked with mud. ⁵After half an hour of gardening. ⁶I discovered a second unpleasant aspect of gardening—heat. ⁷The sun

beat down on me as I worked. [8]Causing beads of sweat to pop out on my forehead and run into my eyes. [9]Sweat stung my eyes and soaked my T-shirt I was extremely uncomfortable. [10]The dirt and the heat were bad enough, pesky bugs and slimy worms were even worse. [11]The sweat attracted flies, they hovered and buzzed around my head. [12]When I turned over the soil with my trowel, I unearthed slimy worms and grubs that squirmed palely in the sunlight. [13]Then burrowed back into the dark earth. [14]A ripe tomato from the garden may taste better than one from the grocery store. [15]But is not worth the trouble it takes to grow it.

_____

_____

_____

_____

_____

_____

_____

_____

_____

_____

_____

editing
exercise 28.3   ## Verbs, Run-ons, and Fragments

In the following paragraph, correct the verb errors, run-ons, and fragments.

3 subject-verb agreement errors

2 comma splices

2 fragments

2 irregular verb errors

1 run-on

[1]I can't recall the exact moment when my cat Molly become the true head of the household. [2]Molly came to me as a tiny, defenseless kitten, the neighbor who convinced me to take Molly said that she was the runt of the litter, the kitten that no one wanted. [3]She stood trembling in a cardboard box. [4]Looking up through moist, blue-green eyes and mouthing the first of many silent meows that soon reduced me to a lowly member of her entourage. [5]Over the past few months, the trembling kitten has growed strong and sure, quickly gaining control of the family. [6]She meow loudly if left alone for long without attention. [7]Molly will not be ignored; she hops into my lap and looks offended. [8]If I don't drop everything and pay attention to her. [9]In the morning, she slides a paw under the bedroom door and rattle it loudly to awaken her human servants if breakfast is late. [10]She refuses to eat inexpensive store-brand cat food; instead, she insist on small, expensive cans of name-brand food. [11]If she wants to come in or go out, her meow takes on a demanding tone it almost sounds as if she is

saying, "Now!" ¹²Molly commands naturally and without a second thought, the timid, trembling kitten is gone forever.

_____ _____

_____ _____

_____ _____

_____ _____

_____ _____

editing
exercise 28.4 **Fragments and Pronouns**

In the following paragraph, correct the sentence fragments and pronoun errors.

6 fragments

4 pronoun errors

¹Smoking may be a vile and harmful habit, but workplaces can go too far. ²In penalizing employees who smoke. ³While few would want to work in an office thick with smoke. ⁴Employers could provide smoking lounges for employees who smoke. ⁵Instead, sending workers outside in twenty-degree weather to shiver and smoke. ⁶Some workplaces won't allow you to smoke anywhere on company property. ⁷Smokers must wait a jittery eight hours before lighting up. ⁸Or use their lunch hour to drive off company property to smoke. ⁹To keep insurance costs down. ¹⁰Other companies forbid smoking entirely. ¹¹An employee who is caught smoking, even at home, faces dismissal from their job. ¹²Employees who smoke may be more likely to become ill and to use his or her insurance benefits, but the same can be said of people who eat cholesterol-rich diets and even those who are depressed. ¹³What's next, a company representative knocking on your door for a refrigerator inspection or a mood check? ¹⁴Companies should back off and show a little more tolerance. ¹⁵Toward employees who smoke.

_____ _____

_____ _____

_____ _____

_____ _____

_____ _____

editing
exercise 28.5

Subject-Verb Agreement, Fragments, Run-ons, and Pronouns

In the following paragraph, correct the fragments, run-ons, and errors in pronoun use and subject-verb agreement.

3 subject-verb agreement errors

2 fragments

2 comma splices

3 pronoun errors

¹The gym where I work out have both advantages and disadvantages. ²One of the biggest advantages are that Rocky's is just a five-minute drive from my home and my work. ³It is easy to stop by on your way home from work or to drive over for a quick workout on weekends. ⁴In addition, the gym is open 24 hours a day for people like myself who have busy schedules. ⁵Though no staff members are on duty at night. ⁶Security is adequately provided by cameras, a key card entry system, and a huge plate glass window that make the interior of the gym visible from the street. ⁷In addition, unlike many gyms, Rocky's does not require a lengthy contract, a member can choose a month-to-month contract instead of a long-term commitment. ⁸The disadvantages of Rocky's includes a lack of locker room space. ⁹If a member comes straight from work, they have to change into workout gear in the tiny restroom and stow work clothing on one of the open shelves. ¹⁰Since a staff member is on duty only a few hours a day, from ten a.m. until five p.m. ¹¹Members who work out in the mornings or evenings have no one to answer questions or help them with unfamiliar equipment. ¹²However, the advantages of the gym far outweigh the disadvantages, I enjoy my membership at Rocky's.

_____   _____

_____   _____

_____   _____

_____   _____

_____   _____

29 Misplaced and Dangling Modifiers

The Brush-off
The English major caught his eye,
He smelled her sweet perfume.
He said, "While dancing cheek
to cheek,
Romance is sure to bloom."

She said, "To say romance
can dance
Is silly from all angles,
And I could never love a man
Whose modifier dangles."

While dangling and misplaced modifiers probably won't ruin your next romance, they may confuse your readers. That's reason enough to learn what they are and how to avoid them.

Look at the two versions of the sentence below:

✘ *Perched at the top of the flagpole,* Orville saw a red-tailed hawk.

✔ Orville saw a red-tailed hawk *perched at the top of the flagpole.*

The words in italic type are modifiers. A **modifier** is a word, phrase, or clause that gives information about another word. In the preceding sentences, the placement of the words *perched at the top of the flagpole* makes a great deal of difference. It is easy to imagine a bird sitting on top of the flagpole, but the idea of Orville perched there does not seem logical.

Although they are not always as obvious as the problem in the example, problems with modifiers are always problems in logic. If you approach this chapter—and your writing in general—with the idea that good writing should above all make sense, you will have an easier time spotting and correcting misplaced and dangling modifiers.

Misplaced Modifiers

✘ Hot off the griddle, the family enjoyed pancakes.

Do you see what is not logical about the sentence above? Of course. The family is not hot off the griddle, the pancakes are. This type of modifier problem is called a **misplaced modifier.** The modifier *hot off the griddle* is misplaced to modify *family* instead of *pancakes.* To fix a misplaced modifier, remember this principle: **A modifier should be placed as close as possible to the word it modifies.**

✔ The family enjoyed pancakes hot off the griddle.

 ✘ The dog was examined by a veterinarian that had just had a litter of puppies.

The sentence seems to suggest that the veterinarian had given birth to puppies. Putting the modifier *that had just had a litter of puppies* closer to the word it modifies makes the meaning clear.

✔ The dog that had just had a litter of puppies was examined by the veterinarian.

Reconstructing the sentence is also a possibility.

✔ The veterinarian examined the dog that had just had a litter of puppies.

✘ Hisako watched the movie eating popcorn.

The sentence is worded as though *the movie* ate the popcorn.

✔ Eating popcorn, Hisako watched the movie.

✘ Pregnant and tired-looking, the old man gave his seat to the young woman.

It sounds as though the old man has defied the laws of nature.

✔ The old man gave his seat to the pregnant and tired-looking young woman.

practice 29.1 **Correcting Misplaced Modifiers**

Correct the misplaced modifiers in the following sentences.

1. Antoinette walked the dog wearing high heels.

   _____

2. Sam placed the suitcase on the bed that he was going to carry on the trip.

   _____

3. The man kept a close eye on the toddler sitting on a bench and smoking a cigar.

   _____

4. Snapping and growling, the letter carrier was afraid to approach the dog.

   _____

5. The student visited the office of the English professor who needed tutoring in grammar.

   _____

   _____

Single-Word Modifiers

A misplaced modifier that is a single word may be more difficult to spot, but the idea is still the same: An error in logic needs to be corrected.

The words *almost, just, nearly,* and *only* are often carelessly misplaced in sentences. Look at the following example to see the difference that word placement can make:

✔ *Only* James tasted the melon. (*no one but James*)

✔ James *only* tasted the melon. (*only sampled the melon,* or possibly, *no one but James*)

✔ James tasted *only* the melon. (*nothing but the melon*)

✔ James tasted the *only* melon. (*the only melon available*)

✔ James tasted the melon *only.* (*nothing but the melon*)

Next, look at the following examples of illogical modifier placements and corrections:

✗ While watching the football game, Kyle *almost* ate a whole pizza.

If he *almost* ate it, he thought about eating but never actually took a bite. The writer more likely means something like "he ate eight of the ten pieces."

✔ While watching the football game, Kyle ate *almost* a whole pizza.

✗ Cara *nearly* spent a hundred dollars at the mall.

If she *nearly* spent a hundred dollars, she thought about it but decided to keep her money. A more probable meaning is shown below.

✔ Cara spent *nearly* a hundred dollars at the mall.

✗ Because she felt ill, Miriam *just* ate a few bites of chili.

Because *just* can mean "just now" or "only," placement is important. *Just ate* suggests the meaning *just now ate*, but the writer more likely means *ate only a few bites.*

✔ Because she felt ill, Miriam ate *just* a few bites of chili.

✗ Though she received many toys for Christmas, Amber *only* played with her teddy bear.

If she played with the bear and nothing else, then she played with *only* her teddy bear.

✔ Though she received many toys for Christmas, Amber played with *only* her teddy bear.

practice 29.2 **Using Single-Word Modifiers**

Place the listed modifier in the sentence to make each sentence match its intended meaning. The first one is done for you.

1. The distraught mother believed her child was gravely ill.

   Modifier to insert: only

   Intended meaning: No one but the mother believed it.

   New sentence: Only the distraught mother believed her child was gravely ill.

2. The distraught mother believed her child was gravely ill.

   Modifier to insert: only

   Intended meaning: The mother had no other children.

   New sentence: _____

   _____

3. Kim ate a whole bucket of popcorn at the movies.

   Modifier to insert: nearly

   Intended meaning: She ate all but a handful or two.

   New sentence: _____

   _____

4. After buying lunch, Mollie had enough for bus fare home.

   Modifier to insert: just

   Intended meaning: She would have no money left after paying her fare.

   New sentence: _____

   _____

5. Leo said, "Mandy, I agreed to watch your poodle for one hour."

   Modifier to insert: just

   Intended meaning: He agreed to one hour only; Mandy has been gone two hours.

   New sentence: _____

   _____

6. Simon's reading speed test shows he reads 400 words per minute.

   Modifier to insert: almost

   Intended meaning: He reads 394 words per minute.

   New sentence: _____

   _____

7. Dion bypassed the appetizers because he was watching his weight.

   Modifier to insert: only

   Intended meaning: His diet was the sole reason.

   New sentence: _____

   _____

8. Deborah took a job in Seattle for $30,000 per year.

   Modifier to insert: almost

   Intended meaning: She thought about it but did not take the job.

   New sentence: _____

   _____

9. Jarvis took a job in Louisville for $25,000 per year.

Modifier to insert: almost

Intended meaning: The job pays a bit less than the figure mentioned.

New sentence: _____

_____

10. Marisa says her math professor is grumpy on days that end in *y*.

Modifier to insert: only

Intended meaning: The professor is grumpy just on the days mentioned.

New sentence: _____

_____

practice 29.3 **Correcting Misplaced Modifiers**

Correct the misplaced one-word modifiers in the following sentences.

1. We almost saw ten of our friends at the concert.

_____

2. Chad nearly got two weeks' vacation last month.

_____

3. Alice only waited on four tables of customers all evening.

_____

4. Though Benjamin was speeding, the police officer just let him off with a warning.

_____

5. Sandra almost sent out resumés to twenty different companies.

_____

6. Giorgio nearly wrote a paper of five hundred words.

_____

7. After his surgery, Karl said, "It only hurts when I laugh."

_____

8. The candidate said he only wanted one thing—our vote.

_____

9. The list of people Ben wanted to invite almost included all his friends.

_____

10. Grover only gave his love to one woman.

_____

Dangling Modifiers

Unlike a misplaced modifier, which needs to be moved closer to the word it modifies, a dangling modifier has no word to modify.

✘ With a wave of his wand, the rabbit was pulled from the magician's hat.

The phrase *with a wave of his wand* has no word in the sentence to modify. The only two possibilities are *rabbit* and *magician's hat,* neither of which is likely to wave a wand. To fix the misplaced modifier, you have to put a magician in the sentence. The easiest way to fix a dangling modifier is to give it a word to modify. Place the word immediately after the dangling modifier.

✔ With a wave of his wand, **the magician** pulled a rabbit from his hat.

The sentence may also be reconstructed.

✔ As the magician waved his wand, he pulled a rabbit from his hat.

✘ Waking from a nightmare, Makeisha's alarm buzzed loudly.

Obviously, it is Makeisha who has had a nightmare, not her alarm. The easiest way to fix the sentence is to put the word *Makeisha* (not the possessive form *Makeisha's*) immediately after the modifier.

✔ Waking from a nightmare, **Makeisha** heard her alarm buzz loudly.

But it is also permissible to reconstruct the sentence entirely.

✔ The alarm buzzed loudly as Makeisha awoke from a nightmare.

✔ Makeisha's alarm buzzed loudly as she awoke from a nightmare.

✘ By carefully constructing a resumé, the potential employer is impressed.

It is not the employer who constructs the resumé, but the applicant. The sentence can be fixed by indicating, immediately after the modifier, who constructed the resumé.

✔ By carefully constructing a resumé, an applicant can impress a potential employer.

The sentence can also be reworked entirely.

✔ A carefully constructed resumé can impress a potential employer.

✘ Bored and restless, the minutes seemed to crawl.

Who was bored and restless? (If the sentence does not say, the decision is yours.)

✔ Bored and restless, **I** felt the minutes crawl.

✔ Because **Sherman** was bored and restless, the minutes seemed to crawl.

✘ Listless and feverish, the pediatrician suspected the flu.

Sometimes, the only solution is to reconstruct the sentence. If you try putting the child after *listless and feverish,* you will probably change the meaning of the sentence.

✔ The pediatrician suspected that the listless and feverish child had the flu.

✔ Because the child was listless and feverish, the pediatrician suspected the flu.

practice 29.4

Correcting Dangling Modifiers

Correct the dangling modifiers in the following sentences.

1. Walking across the tile floor, the coffee cup slipped from my hand.

   _____

2. Unhappy with his current job, Malcolm's resumé was updated and employment ads scanned.

   _____

   _____

3. Blinded by the setting sun, Janna's car nearly ran off the road.

   _____

4. By spending hours in the library, careful research for a term paper can be done.

   _____

5. Whistling cheerfully, the luggage was loaded into Quinton's trunk.

   _____

Review Exercises

Complete the Review Exercises to see how well you have learned the skills addressed in this chapter. As you work through the exercises, go back through the chapter to review any of the rules you do not understand completely.

exercise 29.1

Rewrite the sentences to correct the italicized misplaced or dangling modifiers.

1. *After sitting in a jar of brandy for a month,* Mrs. Smith decided that her "drunken peaches" were ready to serve.

   _____

   _____

2. *Speaking in a stern voice,* the children soon became quiet.

   _____

3. The bride walked down the aisle with her father *dressed in a white satin gown.*

   _____

4. *Working with full concentration,* the hours passed quickly.

   _____

5. *Hanging on a chain,* Melinda wears her child's picture around her neck.

   _____

6. *Sitting on the deck,* the light became too dim for reading.

   _____

7. *By shopping early for Christmas,* a last-minute rush will be avoided.

   _____

8. Jared *almost* saved 15 percent of his income last year.

   _____

9. *With a huge yawn,* Al's TV was turned off and the door was locked.

   _____

10. *Paying for my groceries,* the clerk said that the store was going out of business.

    _____

30 Parallel Structure

Choose the best answer to complete each sequence.

1. **a, b, c,**_____   a. **t**   b. **z**   c. **d**
2. ↘, ↗↗, ↘, ↗↗,_____   a. ↗   b. ↗↗   c. ↘
3. 20, 40, 60,_____   a. 10   b. 120   c. 80
4. ▣, ■,_____   a. •   b. □   c. ▣

If you chose *c* each time, you are correct. Your mind was responding to the patterns you saw developing in each sequence. Patterns are pleasing to the human mind, and that is why parallel structure works.

In any famous speech, such as Abraham Lincoln's Gettysburg Address or Martin Luther King, Jr.'s "I Have a Dream," you hear the regular, memorable rhythm of **parallel structure**—parallel words, parallel phrases, and parallel clauses. You see it in good writing, too, lending elegance to ordinary sentences. Once you are used to seeing parallel structure, anything else seems awkward. Look at the following lists to see examples of nonparallel and parallel structure.

EXAMPLE

✗ **Nonparallel:**

eating at fast-food places

to snack on sweets and chips

avoiding exercise

The phrase *to snack on sweets and chips* is not parallel with the *-ing* constructions of the other two phrases.

✔ **Parallel:**

eating at fast-food places

snacking on sweets and chips

avoiding exercise

All phrases in the revised list above have the same structure; that is, they are parallel.

✗ **Nonparallel:**

medium blue

light gray

with a bright orange hue

✔ **Parallel:**

medium blue

light gray

bright orange

✗ **Nonparallel:**

studied for her midterm exam

worked on her term paper

researching at the library was also done

✔ **Parallel:**

> studied for her midterm exam
>
> worked on her term paper
>
> researched at the library

practice 30.1   **Using Parallel Structure**

Each of the following lists contains one item that is not parallel. Cross out the nonparallel item and reword it to make it parallel with the other items. Then write the reworded version on the line provided.

1. sitting on the deck

   reading a book

   to swat at mosquitoes

   _____

2. calm

   had an easygoing personality

   friendly

   _____

3. frustrated by deadlines

   under pressure from her boss

   hassled by customers

   _____

4. a beautiful campus

   excellent food service

   dorm rooms that are large

   _____

5. the fact that it was unheated

   it had no television

   it had no lights

   _____

In sentences, items given equal emphasis should be parallel in structure whenever possible. These items include words, phrases, and clauses in pairs or lists. Look at the following examples of nonparallel and parallel structure within sentences.

✔ The chef *chopped* the garlic and then *was sprinkling* it on the pizza.

✔ The chef *chopped* the garlic and then *sprinkled* it on the pizza.

✘ Alberto is sometimes late for class because he has to *wait* for elevators, *looking* for access ramps, and *navigate* his wheelchair through crowded hallways.

✔ Alberto is sometimes late for class because he has to *wait* for elevators, *look* for access ramps, and *navigate* his wheelchair through crowded hallways.

✘ Kristi hoped for a roommate who was *quiet, studious, and who was also friendly.*

✔ Kristi hoped for a roommate who was *quiet, studious, and friendly.*

✘ James feared *he would fail* but knew *quitting was not an option.*

✔ James feared *he would fail* but knew *he could not quit.*

practice 30.2   **Using Parallel Structure**

Each of the following sentences contains one item that is not parallel. Cross out the nonparallel item and reword it to make it parallel with the other items. Then write the reworded version on the line provided.

1. Swimming, jogging, and to waterski are my athletic sister's favorite pastimes.

_____

2. The squirrel leaped from the roof, had scampered up a tree, and watched us from the safety of a high branch.

_____

3. For dinner, Lisa had iced tea, a tomato sandwich, and she also ate a salad.

_____

4. Mandy could not concentrate because the dogs were barking, the children were whining, and because the television also blared.

_____

5. Ed's yard sale table looked good once he stripped the old paint, the rough spots had been sanded, and painted the table white.

_____

Review Exercises

Complete the Review Exercises to see how well you have learned the skills addressed in this chapter. As you work through the exercises, go back through the chapter to review any of the rules you do not understand completely.

exercise 30.1   Each of the following lists contains one item that is not parallel. Cross out the nonparallel item and reword it to make it parallel with the other items. Then write the reworded version on the line provided.

1. to have a rewarding career
   buying a comfortable home
   to have healthy children

   _____

2. dirty
   old
   having many dents

   _____

3. supported by his family with
   encouragement from his teachers
   admired by his friends

   _____

4. covers that were warm
   soft pillows
   freshly laundered sheets

   _____

5. that the test was fair
   if it covered assigned chapters
   that students had time to finish

   _____

6. barking loudly
   a fierce growl
   jumping at the fence

   _____

7. pressed trousers
   starched shirt
   shoes that had been shined

   _____

8. on street corners
   in bowling alleys
   grocery stores

   _____

9. without a cent to his name
   lonely
   homeless

   _____

10. go down two blocks
    turn left
    at the light you will turn right

    _____

exercise 30.2 In each of the following sentences, one italicized item is not parallel. Cross out the nonparallel item and reword it to make it parallel with the other items. Then write the reworded version on the line provided.

1. When it's time to study, Carl always remembers that he has to *do his laundry, shop for groceries,* or *his car needs washing.*

   _____

2. Today the children want *to go to the movies* and *visiting the museum.*

   _____

3. Kevin's project failed because he ran *out of time, out of money,* and *he also had bad luck.*

   _____

4. The tail of a comet always *points* toward the sun, while the nose *is pointed* away from the sun.

   _____

5. Grandma says she remembers when gas stations *filled the tank, they would check the oil,* and *washed the windshield.*

   _____

6. Before going to bed, Kay checked to make sure *her children were in bed* and *that she had locked the door.*

   _____

7. Real estate agents say that there are three important considerations when buying property: *location, where it is located,* and *location.*

   _____

8. The lion's *scratched nose* and *ear that was torn* bore testimony to the many battles he had fought.

   _____

9. Sam said he was having *problems at work, problems with his math class,* and *health problems.*

   _____

10. "My neighbors are a pain," said Michelle. *"Their music is loud, their yard is messy,* and *they have children who are rude".*

    _____

31 Verb Shifts

A Shifty Excuse
*"I brought my term paper with me,
Professor Lipton, but when I opened
my notebook, it's gone. I can't print
out another copy because the file
was eaten by the computer."*

The excuse above is shifty—but not just because it is unconvincing. It contains two common types of **verb shifts.** The first sentence contains an unnecessary shift from past tense to present tense, and the second contains an unnecessary shift from active voice to passive voice. In this chapter, you will learn to correct unnecessary shifts from past to present tense and to make necessary shifts into the past perfect tense. You will also learn to recognize active voice and passive voice and to correct unnecessary shifts between the two.

Shifts in Tense

Verb tenses give the English language its sense of time, its sense of *when* events occur. The following timeline shows six verb tenses, and the chart below the timeline briefly explains how each tense is used.

Verb Tense Timeline

	past I walked	present I walk	future I will walk
past ◁← - - - * - - - - - - * - - - - - * - - - - * - - - - - - - - - - * - - - * - - - - - →◊ future
	I had walked past perfect	I have walked present perfect	I will have walked future perfect

Verb Tense Chart

◊◊◊	Furthest in the past; happened before another past action	past perfect *had* + *-ed* verb form	I *had walked* up the stairs, and I was out of breath.
◊◊	In the past; happened before now.	past *-ed* verb form	I *walked* all the way around the nature trail.
◊ •	In the past but extending to the present	present perfect *have* or *has* + *-ed* verb form	I *have walked* every day for the last month. He *has walked* a mile already.
•	Happens regularly or often, or is happening now.	present base verb form or base verb + *-s*	I *walk* at least five miles a week. She *walks* quickly.
◊	Happens in the future but before another future event	future perfect *will have* + *-ed* verb form	By the time you join me on the track, I *will have walked* at least two miles.
◊◊	Happens at some time in the future	future *will* + base verb	I *will walk* with you tomorrow if we both have time.

Avoiding Unnecessary Tense Shifts

With so many ways of designating time, it is easy to make mistakes. The most common error in verb tense is an unnecessary shift from past tense to present tense. A writer may become so caught up in describing a past event that it becomes, at least temporarily, a part of "the now." Look at the following examples to see the difference between a necessary shift and an unnecessary shift in verb tense.

Necessary Shift:

          past   present

✔ Coral was a poor student in high school, but she is doing well in college.

Because the sentence above refers to both the *past* (high school) and the *present* (college), the verb tense shift is necessary.

Unnecessary Shift:

           past   present   present

✗ When Joe came into the room, he breaks into a big smile and says, "Guess what?"

Since the action in this sentence is a single, continuous event, there is no need for a shift to present tense. To correct an unnecessary tense shift, decide which tense is appropriate and use that tense for all verbs in the sentence.

Corrected:

           past   past   past

✔ When Joe came into the room, he broke into a big smile and said, "Guess what?"

Unnecessary Shift:

           past   present

✗ Annie boarded the bus, and she sees her friend Chloe sitting in a window seat.

Corrected:

           past   past

✔ Annie boarded the bus, and she saw her friend Chloe sitting in a window seat.

practice 31.1   **Maintaining Consistent Tense**

Underline the correct verb in each sentence.

1. When Amanda finally arrived at the restaurant, her friends (have, had) already ordered.

2. The plumber knocked on the door, checking his watch impatiently, but no one (is, was) home.

3. The car rounded the corner too quickly, skidded on the wet pavement, and (slams, slammed) into a telephone pole.

4. Every day, Horace works in his garden until the sun (falls, fell) below the horizon.

5. The trees in the front yard look beautiful all year long; however, they (bloom, bloomed) only in spring.

practice 31.2   **Correcting Unnecessary Tense Shifts**

In each of the following sentences, correct the unnecessary shift from past to present.

1. Yoshi had just settled down to watch the ball game when suddenly his cable goes out.

   _____

   _____

2. The plane gained speed as it moved down the runway, and then it is airborne.

   _____

   _____

3. Edward accidentally left his headlights on, so his car battery dies before he gets out of class.

   _____

   _____

4. After I had put my heart and soul into studying the first six chapters, the professor moves the test to next Friday.

   _____

   _____

5. The troops moved quietly, knowing enemy soldiers are nearby.

   _____

   _____

Providing Necessary Tense Shifts

Another common type of verb tense error is likely to occur when a writer needs to shift from the past tense into the more distant past, using the past perfect tense. Often, writers omit this needed shift and stay in the simple past tense, thus taking the risk of confusing the reader.

EXAMPLE

✗ By the time Jill woke up [past], her husband made [past] coffee.

Made coffee is further in the past than *woke up*. *Had* needs to be used to push *made* to a time before that indicated by the simple past tense verb *woke*.

✗ The minister said a prayer at the grave of Florence Jones, who attended his church.

Without *had*, the two verbs in the sentence are, as far as the reader can tell, occupying the same space in the past. Look at the corrected versions of the sentences:

✔ By the time Jill woke up [past], her husband had made [past perfect] the coffee.

✔ The minister said [past] a prayer at the grave of Florence Jones, who had attended [past perfect] his church.

Notice in the following example that if the sequence of events is clearly shown in other ways, the past perfect tense is not needed:

✔ Carl made coffee *before* Jill woke up.

practice 31.3

Making Necessary Tense Shifts

In the following sentences, provide the necessary shift to the past perfect tense by using *had* + the past participle (the *-ed* or *-en* form of the verb). Some of the verbs in the sentences below are irregular and do not form their past participle by adding *-ed*.

1. I was stranded on a lonely road, and I left my cell phone at home.

   _____

   _____

2. When the landlady called about the rent, I told her I mailed it.

   _____

   _____

3. When Vijay asked his daughter if she had homework, she told him she finished it.

   _____

   _____

4. When someone asked Michael for a cigarette, he said he quit smoking.

_____

_____

5. The dog ate as if no one fed him for days.

_____

_____

32 Commas

Unreliable Rules
"When in doubt, leave it out."
"Put a comma where there is a natural pause."
"Sprinkle them sparingly, like salt."

There are so many comma rules that, in desperation, people often resort to makeshift rules like the ones above. Unfortunately, these blanket statements don't always work. When it comes to commas, rules—and exceptions—abound. The rules presented in this chapter will give you a head start in coping with the complexities of comma usage.

Commas to Set Off Introductory Words, Phrases, and Clauses

Use commas after an introductory word, phrase, or clause.

EXAMPLE   Instead, Van decided to take the summer off.

The next morning, the newspaper reported the election results.

Since the class did not meet yesterday, Mitzi spent the day in the library.

practice 32.1   **Using Commas with Introductory Elements**

Insert commas after introductory words, phrases, and clauses.

1. Reluctantly the instructor agreed to postpone the test.

   _____

2. When Kim plays video games she shuts out the world.

   _____

3. During the seventh-inning stretch Harry Caray led the fans in "Take Me Out to the Ball Game."

   _____

4. In fact the car has had very few problems.

   _____

5. Yawning loudly Eric said, "Is it morning already?"

   _____

Commas to Join Items in a Series

When a series of three or more words, phrases, or clauses is connected with *and* or *or,* place a comma after each item except the last one. The final comma goes before *and* or *or.*

EXAMPLE Iguanas, chameleons, and salamanders were Ted's passion when he was seven.

Motorcycles, off-road vehicles, and cars are his passion at seventeen.

The dog had tracked mud across the porch, into the kitchen, and up the stairs.

The doctor asked Neville if the pain occurred before he ate, after he ate, or while he ate.

If only two items appear in the series, no comma is used.

Stacy said her two worst vices were soap operas and talk shows.

Arnold was slowed by a traffic tie-up in the tunnel and a wreck near the downtown connector.

Jason takes care of his parents because they are old and because they once took care of him.

practice 32.2 **Using Commas to Join Items in a Series**

Insert commas to join words, phrases, and clauses in a series of three or more. Write *correct* below the sentence that does not need a comma.

1. Mycology is the study of yeasts molds mushrooms and other fungi.

   _____

2. The ancient Maya restricted the consumption of cocoa to the aristocracy because of the cost of growing the beans and the labor involved in processing them.

   _____

3. The dog looked as if he had been dipped in water coated with dirt and set out to dry.

   _____

4. The children watched in fascination as the magician reached into his hat pulled out a dove and released it into the air.

   _____

5. Students screamed as the lights flickered the alarm sounded and the elevator jerked to a halt.

_____

Commas to Join Independent Clauses

Use a comma with a **FANBOYS** conjunction (*for, and, nor, but, or, yet, so*) to join independent clauses.

EXAMPLE Harrison thought that researching would be the easy part of his project, but it turned out to be the hardest.

I feel exhausted already, and tomorrow is just Tuesday.

Karen's sinus medication makes her sleepy, so she avoids taking it during the day.

Do not use a comma if the **FANBOYS** connects verb to verb rather than clause to clause. In other words, do not use a comma unless there is a complete sentence on both sides of the **FANBOYS**.

Ernestine lay in a hammock and read a book.

Nick looked for his glasses but couldn't find them.

Alberto couldn't decide whether to sign up for biology in the fall or wait until spring.

practice 32.3 **Using Commas to Join Independent Clauses**

Place commas before **FANBOYS** conjunctions that join two independent clauses. One of the sentences does not need a comma.

1. The weeds were tall and the mower died whenever Helen tried to cut through them.

_____

2. The upholstery was worn and faded but the couch was still comfortable.

_____

3. Leo received a credit card in the mail but did not remember requesting it.

_____

4. Lorenzo was studying so he let the answering machine pick up his calls.

_____

5. "You can pay now or you can take up to ninety days to pay on our easy credit plan," said the salesclerk.

_____

Commas Around Interrupters

An **interrupter** is a word, phrase, or clause inserted into a sentence to give more information about some element within the sentence. An interrupter is never essential to the structure of the sentence. If you took it out, the sentence would still make perfect sense.

EXAMPLE   The dog, tail wagging, bounded toward its owner.

The student, disappointed by her grades, withdrew from the course at midterm.

practice 32.4   **Using Commas Around Interrupters**

Insert commas around interrupters in the following sentences.

1. The interruption brief as it was distracted Heather and made it hard for her to focus on her work again.

_____

2. Mr. Angelo a friend of my family runs the delicatessen on Third Street.

_____

3. Breanna sighing heavily opened her book to study.

_____

4. The banana apparently left by one of the children lay forgotten in the back seat until it was brown and shriveled.

_____

5. Lava lamps which first appeared in the 1970s became popular again in the 1990s.

_____

Commas with Direct Quotations

A **direct quotation** is an exact repetition of the words that someone speaks or thinks. When a comma is used with a direct quotation, it is always placed in front of the quotation mark.

1. When a direct quotation is followed by a tag (such as *he said*), a comma goes after the quoted words and *in front of the quotation mark:*

   "I think I can find the information I need on the Internet," Javier said.

2. When a tag leads into a direct quotation, a comma goes after the tag and *in front of the quotation mark:*

   Sophie said, "If I had the time, I would audit a world history class."

3. When a sentence is written as a split quotation, commas are placed *in front of the quotation marks:*

> "If it had not been for Hal," said the supervisor, "I don't know what we would have done."

practice 32.5 **Using Commas with Direct Quotations**

Insert commas to set off direct quotations in the following sentences.

1. Karin asked "Would you mind helping me move this ladder?"
   _____

2. "If you are not going to watch television" said Patrick "let me have the remote control."
   _____

3. "I can never remember where I put my keys" said Mike.
   _____

4. "You may like that herbal tea" said Gerry "but it tastes like dishwater to me."
   _____

5. Ben Franklin said "Lost time is never found again."
   _____

Commas in Names and Dates

When a professional title or family designation follows a name, it is set off with commas.

> The woman's name tag read, "Judy Smith, L.P.N."
>
> Raymond J. Johnson, C.P.A., rented an office on Second Street.

When you write the month, day, and year, a comma goes between the day and year.

> The Declaration of Independence was signed on July 4, 1776.

When you write just the month and year, no comma is used.

> The Declaration of Independence was signed in July 1776.

practice 32.6 **Using Commas in Names and Dates**

Insert commas as needed in the following sentences. One sentence needs no comma.

1. Dave says he quit smoking on January 1 1999.

   _____

2. The letter was addressed to Jeana S. Reynolds D.D.S., but there was no return address.

   _____

3. Avery says he will graduate in June 2010.

   _____

4. Carla Anderson C.P.A. will hold a seminar on the new tax laws.

   _____

5. Jonathan Burns M.D. has been our family doctor for five years.

   _____

Review Exercises

Complete the Review Exercises to see how well you have learned the skills addressed in this chapter. As you work through the exercises, go back through the chapter to review any of the rules you do not understand completely.

exercise 32.1 Insert commas where they are needed in the following sentences.

1. Infotainment is a store that sells books compact discs and videos.

   _____

2. In fact only 12 percent of the students surveyed said they had seriously considered dropping out during their first year of college.

   _____

3. Kudzu a vine native to Japan now flourishes throughout the South.

   _____

4. At the end of June 2006 Felicia graduated from the university.

   _____

5. As the plane disappeared into the clouds Andrea turned away from the window and walked slowly toward the parking lot.

   _____

6. Broken shells dead jellyfish and tangled seaweed were left behind by the receding tide.

_____

7. Darlene knew she was too ill to work but she still felt guilty about calling in sick.

_____

8. The computer disk had a gummy substance on it and Raoul was afraid to put it into the disk drive.

_____

9. A graduation tassel a pair of fuzzy dice and a pine air freshener hung from the car's rearview mirror.

_____

10. Renaldo the dispatcher on duty said that it had been a quiet night.

_____

exercise 32.2   Insert commas where they are needed in the following sentences.

1. Yolanda found a cat toy a dusty sock and a fuzzy piece of Halloween candy under the couch.

_____

2. Janis Monroe R.N. was staffing the phone lines at Ask-a-Nurse.

_____

3. When Rakesh picked up the telephone he heard no dial tone.

_____

4. The driver of the red sports car unaware of the state trooper's presence whipped past at 85 miles per hour.

_____

5. In the garage piles of _National Geographics_ were stacked against one wall as high as Nell's shoulders.

_____

6. With only one day left before finals students flocked to the library's study rooms.

_____

7. The courtyard was filled with students chatting studying or just enjoying the spring weather.

_____

8. The phone book listed the accountant as Harold Smith C.P.A.

_____

9. Driving down the lonely stretch of highway, Paul saw asphalt pastureland and cattle bunched under the occasional shade tree.

_____

10. When Kendrick saw the puddle on the kitchen floor he realized his attempts to fix the dishwasher had been unsuccessful.

_____

exercise 32.3   Insert commas where they are needed in the following sentences. Each question contains two types of problems that require the addition of a comma or commas.

1. "I can be a full-time student" said Kasey "or I can be a full-time worker. However I can't do both."

_____

_____

2. Because Ashley won the coin toss she was the one who chose the toppings for the pizza. She ordered mushrooms black olives onions and pepperoni.

_____

_____

3. Putting toe tags on the preserved frogs planting clues to point to the "murderer" and letting the students serve as coroners were ways to get students interested in dissection. "Science can be fun as well as educational" said the teacher.

_____

_____

_____

4. The apartment was small cramped and dark. "I can't believe the landlord wants $500 a month for this place" said Felice.

_____

_____

5. "The label on this freezer bag says June 6 2003," Harold told his wife. "Should I throw the bag away or should we keep it as a souvenir?

_____

_____

exercise 32.4   Insert commas where they are needed in the following sentences.

1. Even as an adult Jamie remembers a particular Christmas from his childhood. On the evening of December 24 1989, Santa Claus did not visit the Thaxton household.

_____

_____

2. Sounding cranky Melissa sleepily answered the phone. "This had better be important" she told the caller.

_____

_____

3. As he came in from his morning run Andre kissed his daughter. "You smell like an old, sweaty shoe" she told him.

_____

_____

4. Clouds slid in from the west and the wind began to pick up. "At least the rain will cool things off" said Calvin.

_____

_____

5. A golf ball had smashed through the window striking the television. Glass lay on the windowsill on the floor and on the arm of the sofa.

_____

_____

exercise 32.5   Insert commas where they are needed in the paragraph below. Each sentence contains one type of comma problem, which may require more than one comma to correct.

[1]For many people waiting is a fact of life. [2]People wait in train stations doctor's offices and employment offices. [3]However people's attitudes about waiting are even more interesting and varied than the places where they wait. [4]My dentist Jack Davis values his time and his patients' time. [5]"I hate to wait" he says "so I don't keep my patients waiting, either." [6]Some people become angry and they make sure that those who keep them waiting get the message. [7]One of my neighbors once told me "If I'm kept waiting more than an hour, I send a bill for my time." [8]Other people endowed with more philosophical natures try to make waiting productive. [9]These are the people who are seen in airport terminals and doctors' offices reading books knitting or catching up on their correspondence. [10]Though some endure it more patiently than others waiting is a fact of life for everyone.

1. _____
2. _____
3. _____
4. _____
5. _____
6. _____
7. _____
8. _____
9. _____
10. _____

Index